Fundamentals of Income Taxation

THE AMERICAN COLLEGE
OF FINANCIAL SERVICES
PRESS

Huebner School Series

Fundamentals of Income Taxation

13th Edition

Christopher P. Woehrle

HS321-13

This publication is designed to provide accurate and authoritative information about the subject covered. While every precaution has been taken in the preparation of this material, the authors, and The American College assume no liability for damages resulting from the use of the information contained in this publication. The American College is not engaged in rendering legal, accounting, or other professional advice. If legal or other expert advice is required, the services of an appropriate professional should be sought.

© 2017 The American College Press
270 S. Bryn Mawr Avenue
Bryn Mawr, PA 19010
(888) AMERCOL (263-7265)
theamericancollege.edu
All rights reserved
Library of Congress Control Number: 2017942070
ISBN-10: 1-58293-261-1
ISBN-13: 978-1-58293-261-3
Printed in the United States of America

TABLE OF CONTENTS

ACKNOWLEDGMENTS

The editor wishes to express his appreciation and gratitude to all the individuals who were involved in the development and production of this book, including (but certainly not limited to) the following individuals:

Each of the contributors to chapters in this text:

- Burton T. Beam, Jr., former associate professor of insurance at The American College
- Ryan Bornstein, adjunct professor of law in the graduate tax program at Villanova Law School
- Thomas M. Brinker, professor of accounting at Arcadia University in Glenside, PA
- Fred J. Dopheide, former vice president of Educational Resources at the Society of Financial Service Professionals
- Edward E. Graves, former associate professor of insurance and Charles J. Zimmerman Chair in Life Insurance Education at The American College
- Michael R. Harris, attorney at law
- James F. Ivers III, former professor of taxation at The American College and guiding force in the creation and many successful revisions of this book
- Deborah A. Jenkins, former librarian at The American College
- Stephen N. Kandell of Consolidated Brokerage Services, Inc.
- Ted Kurlowicz, professor of taxation and holder of the Charles E. Drimal Professorship in Estate Planning at The American College
- Stephan R. Leimberg, former professor of taxation at The American College
- Craig W. Lemoine, associate professor of financial planning at The American College and holder of the Jarrett L. Davis Distinguished Professorship in Financial Planning and Technology
- John J. McFadden, former professor of taxation and pensions at The American College
- Alban Salaman, attorney at law
- Virginia E. Webb, former librarian/manager at The American College's Knowledge Center

Sophia Duffy, associate dean at The American College, for her support and encouragement.

C. Bruce Worsham, former associate professor of taxation and insurance at The American College, for the development and writing of the answers to the questions in this textbook and its supplement, and for his support and assistance with various elements and passages in the text.

Ronald F. Duska, former professor of ethics and Charles Lamont Post Chair of Ethics and the Professions at The American College, for assistance with ethics-related material in the text.

All the capable students, American College instructors, and other colleagues, friends, and family members whose constructive suggestions have been incorporated in this book.

It should also be noted that chapter 16 of this text, "Income Taxation of Life Insurance," is an updated revision of a reading copyrighted in 1973 by Richard D. Irwin, Inc., as a chapter in the third edition of *The Life and Health Insurance Handbook*, edited by Davis W. Gregg and Vane B. Lucas, portions of which are used herein by permission and with all rights reserved.

— Christopher P. Woehrle, J.D., LL.M (Tax)
The Guardian/Deppe Chair in Pensions and Retirement Planning

ABOUT THE EDITOR

Christopher P. Woehrle, J.D., LL.M (Tax)

Chris is an associate professor of taxation at The American College and serves as The Guardian/Deppe Chair in Pensions and Retirement Planning. A member of the Pennsylvania Bar, Chris has course responsibility for Huebner School 321 *Income Taxation*, Irwin Graduate School 817 *Personal Tax Planning*, GS 814 *Qualified Retirement Plans*, and GS 842 *Executive Compensation*. Chris also teaches the online editions of GS 839 *Planning for Philanthropic Impact*, GS 849 *Charitable Giving Applications and Planning*, and GS 859 *Gift Planning in a Nonprofit Context*.

Prior to his arrival at The American College, Chris enjoyed a 17-year career as a senior development professional and executive. During his tenure as Senior Associate Vice President and Acting Senior Vice President of Institutional Advancement, Drexel University was a five-time achiever of *Philanthropy 400* status awarded to the most productive development programs in the United States. As Vice President of Development for The Kimmel Center for the Performing Arts, Chris led the completion of its highly successful endowment campaign creating one of the largest endowed funds for a performing arts organization. Most recently, Chris served as Director of Planned Giving for the Princeton HealthCare System Foundation during its *Design for Healing* campaign, one of the largest ever for a community hospital system.

A *magna cum laude* graduate of Cornell University, Chris earned his JD and LLM (Taxation) from Villanova Law School. Chris holds an appointment at Villanova Law as an adjunct professor of tax law where he teaches the course in charitable gift planning in its Master of Laws in Taxation program.

Chris is married to Lann Salyard Woehrle, MD, a retired member of the medical staff at Pennsylvania Hospital. In addition to supporting his wife's philanthropy in pancreatic cancer research, Chris has endowed a named scholarship at his prep school and supported a bricks and mortar campaign each at the major gift level.

THE AMERICAN COLLEGE

The American College® is an independent, nonprofit, accredited institution founded in 1927 that offers professional certification and graduate-degree distance education to men and women seeking career growth in financial services.

The Solomon S. Huebner School® of The American College administers the Chartered Life Underwriter® (CLU®); the Chartered Financial Consultant ®(ChFC®); the Chartered Special Needs Consultant® (ChSNC®); the Chartered Leadership Fellow® (CLF®); the Retirement Income Certified Professional® (RICP®); and the Financial Services Certified Professional® (FSCP®); professional designation programs. In addition, The College offers a prep program for the CFP® certification.[1]

The Richard D. Irwin Graduate School® of The American College offers a Master of Science in Financial Services (MSFS) degree, a Master of Science in Management (MSM), a one-year program with an emphasis in leadership, and a PhD in Financial and Retirement Planning. Additionally, it offers the Chartered Advisor in Philanthropy® (CAP®) and several graduate-level certificates that concentrate on specific subject areas.

The American College is accredited by **The Middle States Commission on Higher Education**, 3624 Market Street, Philadelphia, PA 19104 at telephone number 267.284.5000.

The Middle States Commission on Higher Education is a regional accrediting agency recognized by the U.S. Department of Education and the Commission on Recognition of Postsecondary Accreditation. Middle States accreditation is an expression of confidence in an institution's mission and goals, performance, and resources. It attests that in the judgment of the Commission on Higher Education, based on the results of an internal institutional self-study and an evaluation by a team of outside peer observers assigned by the Commission, an institution is guided by well-defined and appropriate goals; that it has established conditions and procedures under which its goals can be realized; that it is accomplishing them substantially; that it is so organized, staffed, and supported that it can be expected to continue to do so; and that it meets the standards of the Middle States Association. The American College has been accredited since 1978.

The American College does not discriminate on the basis of race, religion, sex, handicap, or national and ethnic origin in its admissions policies, educational programs and activities, or employment policies.

The American College is located at 270 S. Bryn Mawr Avenue, Bryn Mawr, PA 19010. The toll-free number of the Office of Professional Education is (888) 263-7265; the fax number is (610) 526-1465; and the home page address is theamericancollege.edu.

---

1. Certified Financial Planner Board of Standards, Inc., owns the certification marks CFP®, CERTIFIED FINANCIAL PLANNER®, and CFP® (with flame logo), which it awards to individuals who successfully complete initial and ongoing certification requirements.

Chapter 1

Access to Sources of Tax Law and New Legislation

Learning Objectives

An understanding of the material in this chapter should enable you to

LO 1.1   **Describe the major income tax services, and explain how each one is organized.**

LO 1.2   **Identify several periodicals that publish tax articles.**

LO 1.3   **Identify several sources where new tax legislation is published and analyzed.**

> Our tax code is so long it makes *War and Peace* seem breezy.
>
> —Steven LaTourette

LO 1.1   **Describe the major income tax services, and explain how each one is organized.**

MAJOR TAX SERVICES AND RESEARCH TOOLS

Students of federal income taxation and financial services professionals frequently need information regarding a particular issue or new piece of legislation and must know how to acquire it. A few trips to the tax section of a law library will make the student familiar with the ways in which tax law is developed and reported. Researchers who prefer working by computer can also develop effective researching skills that way. In view of the importance of tax matters in virtually every aspect of the financial planning process, basic research techniques should be of interest to the student.

There are two types of tax services currently available in the area of federal income tax: "annotated" and "topical." Some of the major federal income tax services are as follows:

- *Topical services: Federal Tax Coordinator 2d*, published by RIA (Research Institute of America), *Tax Management Portfolios*, published by BNA (Bureau of National Affairs), and *CCH Federal Tax Service*, which is currently published by CCH (a Wolters Kluwer business).

- *Annotated Services: Standard Federal Tax Reporter*, published by CCH, and *United States Tax Reporter*, published by RIA.

Each of these services consists of multi-volume sets with updates provided regularly in the form of replacement sheets or add-ons for the loose-leaf printed format each service uses, or online with multiple-user access. Online users can search by topic, keyword, or citation.

Each includes the Internal Revenue Code sections and the current regulations promulgated thereunder. In addition, each includes explanatory material and case citations or annotations that summarize court decisions and provide references to the full text of opinions related to a particular subject or issue.

The topical services are organized by topic and chapter, and are likely to encompass several Internal Revenue Code (IRC) sections. Editorial commentary is also provided. For example, RIA's *Federal Tax Coordinator 2d* is organized by topic and chapter, and volumes run alphabetically in sequence.

The annotated services are organized by Internal Revenue Code sections and are likely to encompass several topics. For example, CCH's *Standard Federal Tax Reporter* contains a thorough subject index volume.

In general, it may be easier for the fledgling researcher to use a topical service, such as RIA's *Federal Tax Coordinator 2d*, since it is organized by subject and contains lengthy explanatory text. This RIA service offers a *Practice Aids* volume, which contains tax ideas along with reprints of IRS audit manuals. It also provides proposed regulations, reprints of recent revenue rulings, revenue procedures, and revenue bulletins.

The *CCH Standard Federal Tax Reporter*, on the other hand, offers more verbatim reprints of various elements of primary-source tax law. It also offers more extensive annotations of court decisions. In addition, this CCH service offers a two-volume *Citator* that shows where each listed decision has been cited and discussed in later court decisions. A key feature of this service and RIA's *United States Tax Reporter* is the annotations accompanying the editorial commentaries.

Each service has its own advantages and character. The researcher will likely become more familiar with one and will develop a preference based on that familiarity whether using a printed or online version. Although the distinction between topical and annotated methods is important in the paper services, it is of less significance in the online environment when utilizing key word searches. Several research providers, including CCH and RIA, include annotated services in which editorial analysis and commentary are arranged by IRC section on their online versions. Both topical and annotated services (and others, such as Lexis/Nexis) can be found in most law libraries as well as in other selected libraries, including The American College's Knowledge Center. There is a trend toward the use of the online versions of both the CCH and RIA services.

The researcher should note that these services are referenced by paragraph number, not page number. The upper corner of each page contains the paragraph numbers, while the page number appears in the bottom corner of the page.

A major encyclopedia-type multi-volume tax treatise is Rabkin and Johnson's, *Federal Income, Gift, and Estate Taxation*, published by LexisNexis/Matthew Bender. This treatise is organized by subject and is characterized by its economy of language and its clear explanatory material. It is supplemented several times per year. The treatise includes congressional committee reports to inform the researcher of legislative history with respect to various Code sections.

LO 1.2   Identify several periodicals that publish tax articles.

PERIODICALS

There is a host of periodicals that publish tax articles, and this chapter is not intended to recommend a selective list over any others.

CCH publishes *Federal Tax Articles*, a comprehensive list of tax-related articles published in all types of professional journals, complete with synopses.

Among the periodicals devoted exclusively to taxation are the *Journal of Taxation*, *Taxes—The Tax Magazine*, and *Tax Notes*.

The *Journal of Financial Service Professionals* also publishes many tax-related articles in addition to other articles of interest. Numerous other periodicals include tax articles of interest to the financial services professional.

NEW LEGISLATION AND RELATED MATERIAL

LO 1.3   Identify several sources where new tax legislation is published and analyzed.

Each of the major tax services publishes verbatim versions of new tax legislation and accompanying legislative history, explanatory material, and analysis. These are available in both print form and online.

Within the basic tax services are sections covering current developments. A printed volume of CCH, entitled *New Matters or New Developments*, contains new legislation, recent cases, and rulings that have not yet been incorporated into the main body of the printed version of the service. It also includes a cumulative index to new developments. Additional volumes of CCH provide advance sheets on court decisions in tax cases in the federal courts.

In addition to materials published by the major tax services, major accounting firms also publish summaries of each new piece of federal tax legislation both in printed form and online.

These are generally easy to read, although depth of coverage may not be the same as the publications of the major services. However, these summaries can be quite satisfactory for an overview of the highlights of new tax legislation. They are generally available by contacting the local office or web site of major accounting firms shortly after new tax legislation is signed by the president.

Various government web sites online, such as the "Thomas" site, also provide texts of new legislation, committee reports, and related material.

One leading report for the latest tax developments is the *Daily Tax Report* published by the Bureau of National Affairs (BNA). The *Daily* is thorough, well written, and appropriate not only for the tax specialist but also for the financial planner. It is available as a printed and/or online service. Another good daily service is the CCH *Tax Tracker News*.

CCH has many features online that provide quick access to the latest developments in all areas of tax law. For information regarding features, cost, and computer compatibility, contact the publisher. RIA also has an internet product available by subscription called "Checkpoint" that provides information comparable to *Federal Tax Coordinator 2d*.

CHAPTER REVIEW

Review Questions

Review questions are based on the learning objectives in this chapter. Thus a [1.3] at the end of a question means that the question is based on Learning Objective 3. If there are multiple objectives, they are all listed.

1. Name a tax-reporting service published by Research Institute of America (RIA) and CCH. [1.1]

2. Describe the tax information available in both the RIA (topical) and CCH (annotated) services. [1.1]

3. Explain how a researcher can obtain information regarding new tax legislation. [1.3]

Review Answers

1. A primary RIA service is the "Federal Tax Coordinator," and for CCH, the "Standard Federal Tax Reporter."

2.   Printed versions of each consist of multi-volume loose-leaf sets with updates provided regularly in the form of replacement sheets or add-ons. Each also includes Code sections and the current regulations promulgated thereunder. In addition, each includes explanatory material and case citations or annotations that summarize court decisions and provide reference to the full text of opinions related to a particular subject or issue. Online versions of both services are also available.

     RIA's "Federal Tax Coordinator" offers a "Practice Aids" volume, which contains tax ideas along with reprints of IRS audit manuals. It also provides proposed regulations, reprints of recent revenue rulings, revenue procedures, and revenue bulletins.

     The "CCH Standard Federal Tax Reporter" service, on the other hand, offers more verbatim reprints of various elements of primary-source tax law and more extensive annotations of court decisions. In addition, it offers a two-volume "Citator" that shows where each listed decision has been cited and discussed in later court decisions.

3.   Each of the major tax services publishes verbatim versions of new tax legislation and accompanying legislative history, explanatory material, and analysis. Major accounting firms also publish summaries of each new piece of federal tax legislation both in printed form and online. In addition, various government web sites, such as the "Thomas" site, also provide text of new legislation, committee reports, and related material.

     One leading report for the latest tax developments is the "Daily Tax Report" published by the Bureau of National Affairs (BNA). Another is the "CCH Tax Tracker News." Both CCH and RIA have online products that provide quick access to the latest developments in all areas of tax law.

Chapter 2

A History of the Income Tax Law and a Glance at the Sources of Current Law

Learning Objectives

An understanding of the material in this chapter should enable you to

LO 2.1   **Describe the pressure for revenues that led to the adoption of the 16ᵗʰ Amendment by Congress, and explain the Amendment's significance for modern tax law.**

LO 2.2   **Describe the functions of the income tax system.**

LO 2.3   **Describe the three basic sources of income tax law today, and explain the role played by each source.**

> What at first was plunder assumed the softer name of revenue.
>
> —Thomas Paine

> That most delicious of all privileges—spending other people's money.
>
> —John Randolph

The history of the income tax parallels the history of the financial needs of the United States. The strain of a modern government attempting to meet the costs of both wartime expenditures and peacetime services created a demand for additional revenues. Once established, the overriding importance of the individual and corporate income taxes in the federal revenue structure has never diminished.

Aside from revenue purposes, the income tax has been used with varying degrees of success to perform social, economic, and regulatory functions.

The source of the federal income tax law is ultimately the people. The intent of the people was expressed through the Constitution, which in turn gives legislative power to Congress. Congress exercises this power in the form of the Internal Revenue Code, which is further modified and expanded by the Internal Revenue Service's regulations and rulings. Court decisions on particular issues further interpret and expound on statutory law as well as IRS regulations and rulings. The importance and effect of these court cases is in turn determined by the status of the court. The hierarchy of the court system (and hence the weight given to a decision of that particular court) at the highest level starts with the Supreme Court and works its way down to courts of original jurisdiction known as the United States Court of Federal Claims, the United States District Court, and the United States Tax Court.

EARLY TAX LAW

The tax history of the United States mirrors the general history of this country. Under the Articles of Confederation, the first governing instrument adopted by the Continental Congress in 1777, the federal government had no taxing power or right to collect custom duties. Several attempts to amend the Articles and give Congress a power to tax failed.

Because the Articles of Confederation proved to be too weak, the Constitution, written in 1787 and ratified in 1789, enlarged the powers of the federal government. However, the framers of the Constitution feared that the accumulation of power by the federal government would result in tyranny similar to the absolute monarchy of King George III of England. Therefore the government was divided into three coequal branches of government (legislative, executive, and judicial) with a system of checks and balances. The original taxing power of the federal government under the Constitution was sharply limited by the uniformity and apportionment clauses—Article I, Sections 8 and 9, of the Constitution. A detailed explanation is beyond the scope of this chapter, but it is sufficient to say that, in retrospect, these clauses precluded the federal government from imposing an income tax.

LO 2.1   **Describe the pressure for revenues that led to the adoption of the 16th Amendment by Congress, and explain the Amendment's significance for modern tax law.**

INCREASED PRESSURE FOR REVENUES

The high cost of the Civil War brought about the first governmental attempt to collect a tax on income. The tax soon expired, but by 1894 governmental needs for revenue led to the adoption of another income tax. Within a year, the constitutional validity of this tax was tested. In the famous case of *Pollock v. Farmers' Loan and Trust Company*, the U.S. Supreme Court held that the tax was neither apportioned among the states nor uniform and was therefore unconstitutional, as Pollock had claimed.

Congressional reaction to the Pollock decision was shaped by the increasing pressures as well as the demands for a steady and sufficient source of revenue. The result was a political compromise in 1909 that levied a tax on corporations. However, even while the constitutionality of the Revenue Act of 1909 was being considered, Congress realized the need for a broader tax base.

THE 16TH AMENDMENT

16th Amendment

In 1909, the **16th Amendment** to the Constitution, which nullified the Pollock decision, was adopted by Congress. After appropriate action by the states, it was declared ratified on February 25, 1913. The 16th Amendment says the following:

> The Congress shall have the power to lay and collect taxes on income, from whatever source derived, without apportionment among the several States, and without regard to any census or enumeration.

It is this amendment that dispensed with the apportionment requirement and therefore became the foundation for the basic framework of our modern tax law. The broad and sweeping language that permitted "income, from whatever source derived" to be taxed pervades the entire income tax law and has far-reaching implications.

Congress quickly utilized the newly sanctioned revenue source. The corporate income tax created by the Revenue Act of 1909 was discontinued. Individuals, as well as corporations, then became subject to the broad new income tax introduced by Congress in 1913.

THE CODE

The Revenue Act of 1913 was quickly followed by a series of additional revenue acts. In 1939 the entire federal tax law was codified and entitled the Internal Revenue Code of 1939. The crucial need to raise revenue to finance World War II turned the income tax from a tax on wealthy taxpayers to a tax on the majority of the population. This period also saw the introduction of the withholding provisions for employees. After the war the Code provisions were rearranged and revised. The result was the Internal Revenue Code of 1954. The Code is now called the Internal Revenue Code of 1986, however, as a result of the voluminous changes wrought by the Tax Reform Act of 1986. Numerous additional changes have been made since 1986.

LO 2.2   Describe the functions of the income tax system.

FUNCTIONS OF THE INCOME TAX SYSTEM

Revenue-Producing Function

The income tax law originated as a revenue-producing mechanism to supply money for the administration and operation of the federal government. The bulk of the government's net receipts are still produced by the federal income tax. Congress, however, does not enact tax laws solely to raise revenue. The tax law also serves economic, social, and regulatory functions.

Economic Function

The Internal Revenue Code plays an important role in the management of the nation's economy. According to current economic thinking, greater taxes result in lower spending by consumers. The reasoning concludes that by reducing consumer spending (without increasing governmental expenditures) the income tax system can be used to reduce inflationary trends. Conversely, the use of tax incentives or lower tax rates leaves consumers with more cash that, in turn, translates into increased spending, saving, and investment. The hoped-for result is an increase in the national product that will increase the demand for new workers and thus reduce unemployment. Thus the tax system can prevent or reduce the impact of recessions.

Some economic experts feel that the very nature of a progressive income tax will automatically perform both anti-inflationary and anti-recessionary functions without Congress actually changing the rates. The theory is that when more dollars (through increased salaries) are available to consumers, their income taxes will increase more than proportionately, resulting in a dampening of their ability to make inflationary expenditures with their increased incomes. During a recession the amount of money collected through the federal income tax decreases more than proportionately as the amount of a taxpayer's income decreases. Thus the relative reduction in income available to taxpayers is less than the reduction in their wages and salaries. Consequently, recessionary forces should be smaller than they otherwise would be. However, it is not always true that recessionary signs are coupled with a reduction in salaries. The value of the dollar is continually being eroded. Salary increases push the taxpayer into increasingly higher tax brackets, leaving less spendable income than before. As a result, our progressive tax structure does not automatically provide an anti-inflationary function during the type of combined recession-inflation that the United States has sometimes experienced.

Further, the Code has used incentives to encourage economic activity at the taxpayer level. For example, liberal depreciation rules encourage taxpayers to invest capital in their businesses that, in turn, may create more jobs for the nation. Such incentives have been enacted from time to time.

Social Function

As the tax base grew wider and rates became higher, Congress found that in addition to producing revenue, the tax structure could be used as a method of effectuating governmental policy. For example, the income tax, as a progressive tax, could be used to redistribute the national wealth. A progressive tax is one in which the amount of tax increases more than proportionately as the amount of the taxpayer's taxable income increases. Therefore in theory, if not in practice, by taking a higher proportion of tax dollars from higher incomes rather than from lower incomes (and using those dollars for governmental expenditures that benefit lower income taxpayers), the distribution of national wealth can be changed significantly. The social function of the income tax, as well as the progressiveness of the rate structure, is a subject of continuing debate.

Regulatory Function

The income tax system performs a limited regulatory function as well as the revenue and social functions mentioned above. Two examples of this use of the tax system to discourage socially undesirable activities are the punitive taxes on certain controlled substances and the tax on automatic weapons.

Counterbalancing Factors

There are, of course, factors that shape the methods used to achieve these ends. Balancing the need of the federal government for revenues is the desire of Congress to be fair to the parties affected. Generally, fairness is recognized as being "equal treatment of equals" and reasonable differences in the treatment of unequals. The test of this fairness is how well the tax imposed matches a taxpayer's ability to pay. Counterbalancing a desire to be fair, Congress is keenly aware of the political consequences of its actions. For example, it is generally politically more expedient to tax a small and unorganized group of voters than to tax a large, organized group with an effective and well-financed lobby.

Thus a tax law is a compromise between purposes and people—with great pressures exerted by the economic, political, and social groups who are affected by particular laws, and who constantly lobby in Congress in an attempt to have tax laws changed to their advantage.

LO 2.3   **Describe the three basic sources of income tax law today, and explain the role played by each source.**

SOURCES OF TAX LAW TODAY

Each of the three coequal branches of the federal government has a major role in the federal income tax system. These roles can be shown graphically by the following illustration.

Figure 2-1: Sources Of Tax Law

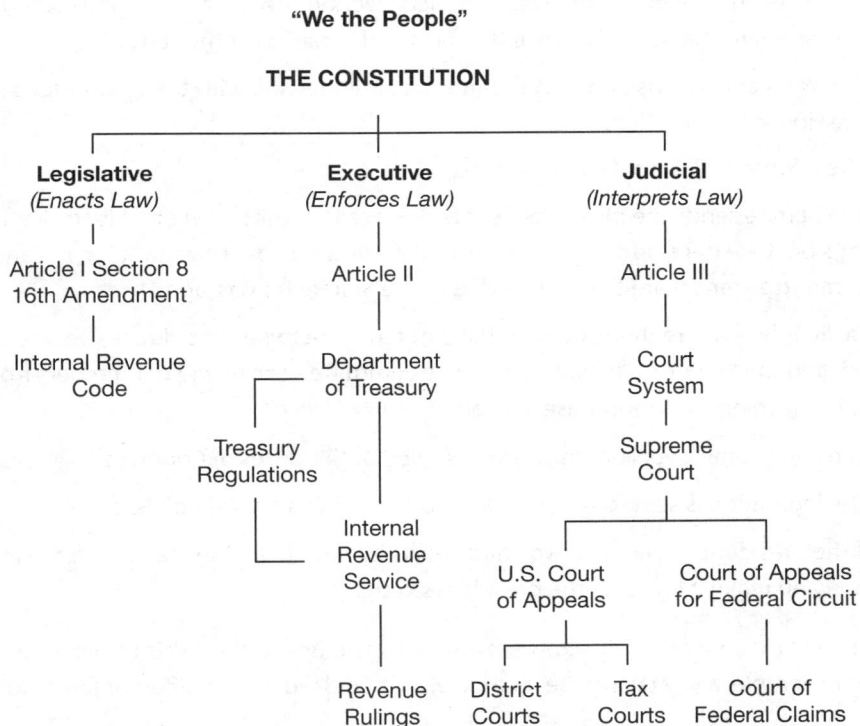

Legislative

The 16th Amendment to the U.S. Constitution empowered Congress to enact an income tax law now compiled in the Internal Revenue Code. The importance of the Code is that federal taxation must proceed from a statutory origin. The present Code came into effect in 1986. It is revised and updated almost annually by Congress. Specific Code sections or parts of sections can be amended or repealed through the passage of revenue bills, which then supersede the older law as to those provisions. The House of Representatives has the constitutional responsibility for initiating revenue bills. A revenue bill becomes law, in most cases, through the following process:

- Revenue bills are written by the Ways and Means Committee of the House of Representatives, or bills are received by the Ways and Means Committee through referral by the House of Representatives (1) from a member of the House or (2) by suggestion of the Joint Committee on Internal Revenue and Taxation (this is a committee of 10 members—five from the House Ways and Means Committee and five from the Senate Finance Committee).

- The Ways and Means Committee conducts hearings on the revenue bill. Expert opinion will be heard that may influence the form and meaning of the statute.

- The Ways and Means Committee sends an amended bill with the committee's report to the House for adoption.

- The adopted bill is sent to the Senate.

- The Senate sends the bill to the Senate Finance Committee where it is studied, hearings on it are held, and amendments to the bill are made. The amended bill and the committee report are then forwarded to the Senate for passage.

- Ordinarily—where there are material differences between the House's version of the bill and the Senate's—a joint conference committee consisting of members from both sides develops a compromise version.

- The compromise version must be passed by both houses of Congress.

- The legislation is sent to the president for his or her signature or veto.

- If the president vetoes it, a two-thirds majority of both houses can revise the legislation and make it law over the president's veto.

Once a law becomes effective, all taxpayers must follow it unless the law is declared unconstitutional. For example, a law taxing the income of men and women at different rates would be unconstitutional.

Once effective, the law is subject to a great deal of interpretation. The House Ways and Means Committee and the Senate Finance Committee reports become extremely important. Both the courts and the Department of Treasury Regulations (discussed below) rely heavily on these reports to determine the intent of the creators before an interpretation is made.

The Code itself contains seven subtitles. Subtitle A is concerned with income taxes; Subtitle B is concerned with estate and gift taxes; and the rest are concerned with other areas of taxation. The Code is then further subdivided. Each subtitle consists of chapters, subchapters, parts, subparts, sections, subsections, paragraphs, subparagraphs, and subparagraph subdivisions known as clauses.

Executive

The president, as the chief enforcer of the law under Article II of the Constitution, has the duty to enforce the collection of tax. He or she has delegated his or her responsibility to the Department of the Treasury that, in turn, has delegated the responsibility to its subdivision, the Internal Revenue Service.

The Department of the Treasury has also been granted the power by Congress to enact regulations under the Code. Congress, recognizing that the Code must be written in legal language but that it would not be the proper place to explain how the law will be applied to specific taxpayers, empowered the secretary of the Treasury or his or her delegate to promulgate the rules and regulations that are necessary to enforce the law. Thus the Code itself provides for the Treasury Department to prescribe the rules and regulations needed for the enforcement of the Code. Actually, the Internal Revenue Service writes these regulations, and the secretary of the Treasury approves them. Regulations are issued first in proposed form so that interested taxpayers may file objections or participate in public hearings before the proposed regulations are finalized.

regulations

The **regulations**, or "regs" as they are often called, constitute the official Treasury interpretation of the Code. Regulations may particularize, define, clarify, illustrate, or even amplify the Code. To the extent that these regs are not inconsistent with the Code, they are said to have the force and effect of law. Generally they are presumed to be correct, are followed by Treasury personnel, and are seldom invalidated by the courts. Because they are carefully prepared and unlikely to be quickly changed, taxpayers can ordinarily rely on them in everyday transactions.

Regulations can be held invalid by the courts for a number of reasons. The two principal ones are (1) the regulation is ambiguous and without persuasive force in determining the true construction of a statute, and (2) the regulation goes beyond the statute (the Code) and thus has no effect. Even if a regulation is held invalid by a lower court, the Treasury can still continue to enforce it unless the Supreme Court itself holds the regulation invalid.

Thus the IRS does not consider itself bound (beyond that particular case) where a regulation is held invalid by any court lower than the Supreme Court, although it now conforms to circuit court decisions for the taxpayer's circuit. At times, therefore, the Service will continue to enforce a regulation (held invalid in a given case) against other taxpayers (even in almost identical circumstances) until the issue is decided by the Supreme Court itself.

The regulations can be accessed in a manner similar to the Code. For example, the regulations pertaining to Section 303 of the Code would use the number 303. Income tax regulations are preceded by the number one (1). Therefore the regulations pertaining to Code Section 303, "Distributions in Redemption of Stock to Pay Death Taxes," could be found under the number 1.303 of the regulations.

Treasury Regulations
- written by IRS personnel and approved by Treasury
- can be challenged by taxpayers
- seldom overturned by courts
- may be overturned if ambiguous or beyond the scope of statute

Revenue Rulings and Private Rulings

It would be impossible for the Code and regulations to cover the tax consequences of every possible factual situation that can arise. Frequently taxpayers request the Internal Revenue Service's view on the interpretation of a doubtful point of law. In response to these requests, the Service issues various types of administrative rulings.

revenue rulings

Revenue rulings are based on a stated set of facts that usually involve a problem common to a number of taxpayers. These pronouncements are binding on officials of the IRS, and they follow them in their handling of issues arising in particular cases. For example, suppose the law is unclear as to whether a taxpayer can deduct the cost of moving a pet under the moving-expense deduction. If the Internal Revenue Service issues a revenue ruling to the effect that the cost of moving a pet is not deductible, all revenue agents will adhere to the ruling. The taxpayer has the choice of (1) relying upon rulings if the facts and circumstances are substantially the same or (2) challenging rulings in the courts. Unlike Treasury regulations, the courts need not give rulings any weight.

Revenue rulings are published in the IRS Cumulative Bulletin. They can be found in the following manner. The first number following the abbreviation "Rev. Rul." gives the year the ruling was issued. This is followed by a dash. The second number is in numerical sequence, denoting the order in which the ruling was issued. Rev. Rul. 61-201 would be a ruling issued in 1961 and the 201st revenue ruling issued in that year. The citation in the Cumulative Bulletin would also include (1) the year, (2) the volume of the Cumulative Bulletin for that year, and (3) the page under which the ruling could be found. For example, Rev. Rul. 61-201, 1961-2 C.B. 46 means that the particular ruling in 1961 was the 201st of that year. It would be found in the second volume of the Cumulative Bulletin for 1961 on page 46. Generally, online research services will retrieve a ruling if the user provides the year and the ruling number.

private rulings

Private rulings arise when a taxpayer requests an administrative interpretation on a prospective transaction or on completed transactions that are not involved in returns already filed. Although private rulings are personal to the taxpayer, they have been made available to the public in recent years and are now published after the deletion of certain information. Deleted materials include names and addresses of taxpayers, trade secrets, classified matter, and so forth. Even though published, they still have the same effect—they may not be claimed by another taxpayer as a precedent.

Revenue Procedures

revenue procedures

Revenue procedures describe internal practices and procedures within the IRS. Like revenue rulings, they are published in the Internal Revenue Bulletin. Generally revenue procedures state changes in techniques and administrative procedures used by the Internal Revenue Service. Revenue procedures are generally designated by the abbreviation "Rev. Proc."

Determination Letters

The National Office of the Internal Revenue Service issues revenue rulings. IRS officials within specific operating divisions have the power to write determination letters regarding various transactions to be reflected on returns that will be filed by various types of taxpayers and organizations. Determination letters are issued only if the answer to the question presented is covered specifically by statute, Treasury decision, or regulation, or specifically by a court decision or ruling opinion published in the Internal Revenue Bulletin. Determination letters contrast with revenue rulings in that such letters are never issued about unclear points of law.

Conflict between Taxpayers and the IRS

Individual taxpayers must generally file returns by April 15 for the previous calendar year or, if they are fiscal taxpayers, by the 15th day of the fourth month after their fiscal year ends. C Corporations must file tax returns by April 15, or the 15th day of the fourth month after their fiscal year ends.

Once a return is filed, the Internal Revenue Service processes the form for mathematical accuracy and audit selection at its service center. The IRS has 3 years from the time the return is filed within which to assess additional taxes. Early returns are deemed to be filed on their due date. One important exception to the 3-year statute of limitations applies when fraud is involved. In such situations, there is unlimited time to audit.

Taxpayers who file incorrect returns may be subject to an accuracy-related penalty that is equal to 20 percent of the amount of the underpayment of tax actually due. The penalty applies to situations involving negligence or disregard of tax laws, substantial understatement of income tax, and substantial valuation misstatements. If fraud is involved, additional civil and criminal penalties can be imposed.

Tax return preparers may also be subject to one or more of several different penalties. These include a penalty for each return equal to the greater of $5,000 or 75% of the income derived or to be derived from each return for a willful or reckless understatement of a taxpayer's tax liability. There also is a penalty equal to the greater of $1,000 or 50% of the income derived or to be derived from the return due to the unreasonable position.

An initial income tax audit by an IRS examiner may take place at an IRS office or at the taxpayer's home or business. A preliminary letter advising the taxpayer of the agent's recommendation and a 30-day right to appeal from that determination will then be sent. If the taxpayer disagrees with the conclusion, he or she may write to the IRS to request a hearing before its Appeals organization.

When a dispute with the IRS is being considered in Appeals, the appeals officers are not permitted to engage in substantive discussions regarding a specific case with other IRS officials in the absence of the taxpayer or his or her representative.

FOCUS ON ETHICS: Tax "Avoidance" vs. Tax "Evasion"

Taxpayers and their advisors should draw a clear distinction between the terms "tax avoidance" and "tax evasion" when striving to maximize benefits provided by law. Distinguishing these terms can help to provide an understanding of what is and is not ethical when dealing with the income tax law.

Tax "avoidance" is generally thought of as the utilization of legitimate strategies and techniques in order to minimize the amount of money a taxpayer will owe to the government. Avoidance techniques do not violate tax laws, but rather use them to the taxpayer's advantage. Timing strategies, permissible income-shifting techniques, and maximizing allowable deductions and credits are general examples of such techniques.

Tax "evasion," on the other hand, refers to the violation of tax laws as a strategy to reduce income tax liability. Examples of tax evasion techniques include underreporting of income, overstatement of deductions (claiming amounts in excess of those actually paid or incurred), claiming tax deductions or other benefits for which the taxpayer does not qualify under applicable law, and other, more sophisticated illegal manipulations of the tax system. Taxpayers should also remember that our income tax system is not illegal or unconstitutional, and that its rules are ignored at the taxpayer's peril. Both civil and criminal penalties can be imposed by the Internal Revenue Service and the U.S. Department of Justice for tax-related violations of the law.

There are, of course, gray areas that fall somewhere between the clear lines of demarcation between tax avoidance and tax evasion. Such gray areas include tax issues that are uncertain due to ambiguous or insufficiently specific tax laws, or issues involving fact patterns not clearly contemplated by applicable law. If a taxpayer is confronted with such an issue, there are a number of different avenues to choose from. Such decisions should be thoughtfully and responsibly made by taxpayers and their advisors. However, taking an overly aggressive position with respect to an unresolved issue of tax law can result in penalties or, in extreme and unreasonable cases, even criminal prosecution.

While a case is pending with the Appeals officers, the taxpayer also has the right to request that the issue be referred to the National Office staff for technical advice. Grounds for referral include a lack of uniformity in the disposition of the issue or significant complexity or uniqueness of the issue. Dispute resolution methods in Appeals now also include mediation and arbitration.

statutory notice of deficiency

If no agreement is reached with Appeals, **statutory notice of deficiency** is issued by the commissioner of Internal Revenue. Following this notice, taxpayers have 90 days to file a petition with the U.S. Tax Court to have their cases heard. If taxpayers allow the 90 days to pass without either paying the tax and/or instituting suit, the IRS can assess a tax deficiency, enter judgment, and seize the taxpayers' property to collect the deficiency.

No tax need be paid in advance for cases to be litigated in the U.S. Tax Court. Once a case has been docketed there, an appeals officer is assigned to the case and given exclusive authority to settle within a 4-month period. If no settlement is reached in that time, the case is scheduled for trial.

Alternatively, the taxpayer may choose to pay the tax deficiency and then file a claim for a refund with the IRS. Taxpayers can file suit for a refund in either the U.S. District Court or the U.S. Court of Federal Claims if the claim for a refund is disallowed. Various factors discussed below will affect the taxpayer's choice of the best tribunal before which to try the case. By statute, the taxpayer has 2 years from the date the IRS notice of disallowance of the taxpayer's claim was mailed in which to sue the government for a refund. This 2-year period may be extended only by a written agreement between the taxpayer and the secretary of the Treasury.

A privilege of confidentiality generally applies to communications between a taxpayer and a tax adviser authorized to practice before the IRS, including an attorney, CPA, or enrolled agent. The privilege may be asserted in noncriminal tax disputes. It does not apply to disputes involving tax shelter promotions.

Judicial

Article III of the U.S. Constitution states that judicial power shall be vested in one Supreme Court and in such lower courts as Congress shall establish. The jurisdiction of the federal courts includes all cases arising under the laws of the United States, including revenue laws.

The court system that Congress has established comprises trial courts that decide issues of fact and law, appellate courts for a review of issues of law, and the Supreme Court, which is the ultimate reviewer of questions of law.

U.S. Tax Court

U.S. Tax Court

The **U.S. Tax Court** was established for taxpayers who seek a redetermination of a deficiency asserted against them but do not wish first to pay the deficiency. A large majority of tax cases are heard by the Tax Court for this reason. Trial by jury is not available in the Tax Court. Questions of law and fact are decided by Tax Court judges.

The Tax Court has its main offices and trial rooms in Washington, D.C., but trials are conducted also in principal cities throughout the United States. The Tax Court is a special court designed principally for taxpayers who appeal tax deficiencies imposed by the Treasury Department.

To expedite hearings on deficiencies of $50,000 and under, the Tax Court has a small tax case division. These cases are handled much less formally and much more quickly than other Tax Court cases. Decisions of this division may not be appealed or treated as authority in other cases. The small case procedure is optional at the taxpayer's request.

The IRS does not consider itself bound by a Tax Court decision any more than it does by a Court of Federal Claims or district court decision (except for the particular case in which an adverse decision has been rendered). Thus the IRS often will continue to litigate the same issue in other cases before the same court or in other courts. However, rather than have the Tax Court rule against it in a number of cases (which establishes precedent), the IRS will often negotiate a settlement. When the Service loses a Tax Court case, it will indicate its willingness or unwillingness to follow the case in the future by reporting in the Internal Revenue Bulletin its acquiescence ("acq.") or nonacquiescence ("non-acq.") to the principle of tax law established in that case.

Appeals from the Tax Court by either an unsuccessful taxpayer or the IRS are heard by the U.S. Court of Appeals in the region of the country in which the taxpayer resides. If there is a difference of opinion in the various courts of appeal as to the interpretation of the tax law, the Tax Court follows the decisions of that court of appeals to which the taxpayer may appeal.

> **Tax Court**
> - does not require prepayment of assessed deficiency
> - no trial by jury available
> - appeals taken to U.S. Court of Appeals for taxpayer's circuit
> - IRS need not "acquiesce"

U.S. Court of Federal Claims

U.S. Court of Federal Claims

The **U.S. Court of Federal Claims** (called the U.S. Claims Court until its name was changed in December 1992) is a trial court that became operative on October 1, 1982, when the U.S. Court of Claims ceased to exist as such. It continues to hear cases that would have been heard by the old Court of Claims, whose jurisdiction was limited to refund cases (the tax must be paid before jurisdiction can be invoked). Appeals from the Court of Federal Claims are heard by another court simultaneously created under the Federal Courts Improvement Act of 1982. This appellate court is called the Court of Appeals for the Federal Circuit and is, in fact, a merger of the old U.S. Court of Claims and the Court of Customs and Patents Appeals. Both of these courts generally follow the tax precedents of the Court of Claims as opposed to following the tax precedents established by the taxpayer's home district court. Since the abolishment of the U.S. Court of Claims, there is no longer any tax forum where appeal is taken directly to the U.S. Supreme Court.

U.S. District Court

U.S. District Court

The **U.S. District Court** (of which there is at least one for each state), like the U.S. Court of Federal Claims, can only hear tax cases in which the taxpayer has first paid the deficiency and has been denied a refund by the Internal Revenue Service.

The U.S. District Court is unique in that it is the only court in which a taxpayer may request a jury trial. In a case where there is a jury, the jury decides questions of fact; the judge decides questions of law. For example, sometimes taxpayers will choose to institute suit in a district court because their battles with the IRS are essentially factual, and they believe they will obtain a sympathetic jury. As to questions of law, a district court in a certain location must follow decisions of that particular court's corresponding court of appeals as precedent. Appeals from a district court can be made to the U.S. Court of Appeals and then further to the Supreme Court.

U.S. Court of Appeals

U.S. Court of Appeals

The **U.S. Court of Appeals** consists of 12 circuit courts located throughout the country. These courts hear appeals that are taken by either taxpayers or the Treasury from decisions rendered by the Tax Court or a district court. The U.S. Court of Appeals is the second highest level in the court system. Its importance is underscored by the fact that the only appeal from one of its decisions is to the Supreme Court itself. Both district courts and the Tax Court must follow decisions of the Court of Appeals to which the taxpayer may appeal. The Court of Appeals of one region is not bound to follow decisions by the Court of Appeals in another region. Although a favorable decision in a sister court may be persuasive, it is not controlling. Taxpayers who must use the Court of Appeals in a region other than where the favorable decision was rendered cannot be sure of the outcome of their cases, even if the facts of their cases are almost identical to the facts of a case previously decided elsewhere. Of course, a favorable decision in one circuit may be relied upon by other taxpayers in that same circuit.

U.S. Supreme Court

U.S. Supreme Court

The **U.S. Supreme Court** is the highest court in the land. Supreme Court decisions are required to be followed by taxpayers as well as by the Internal Revenue Service. However, there are few tax cases that the high court decides. This is because Supreme Court review of tax cases is generally available only if the Court itself grants petitions for appeal. Supreme Court review, therefore, is a matter of discretion with the Supreme Court and not a matter of right. The Supreme Court will most probably review a tax case if (1) there is a conflict between the courts of appeal for different circuits, or (2) an important and recurring problem in tax law administration is involved, or (3) many taxpayers are involved, or (4) the decision of a lower court conflicts with long-standing practice or existing legal authority.

A Supreme Court interpretation of tax law is the law of the land until (1) Congress enacts a new statute, tantamount to overturning a decision interpreting the Internal Revenue Code, or (2) the Court overrides its own prior decision in rare situations.

CHAPTER REVIEW

Key Terms and Concepts

16th Amendment
regulations
revenue rulings
private rulings
revenue procedures
statutory notice of deficiency

U.S. Tax Court
U.S. Court of Federal Claims
U.S. District Court
U.S. Court of Appeals
U.S. Supreme Court

Review Questions

Review questions are based on the learning objectives in this chapter. Thus a [2.3] at the end of a question means that the question is based on learning objective 3. If there are multiple objectives, they are all listed.

1. What powers does the 16th Amendment give Congress with regard to the collection of taxes? [2.1]

2. a. Describe the historical evolution of the codified tax system that culminated in the current Internal Revenue Code.

    b. What is the legal effect of the Code? [2.1]

3. Identify the functions of the income tax system, and describe generally the purposes that each function is designed to accomplish. [2.2]

4. Explain how the income tax system can be used to help curb inflation or lessen the adverse effects of a recession. [2.2]

5. Describe the procedure for the passage and adoption of tax bills. [2.3]

6. Describe the executive powers regarding tax law as well as the delegation of authority for enforcing the law and collecting taxes. [2.3]

7. Explain the function of a Treasury regulation. [2.3]

8. Describe the effect of a particular regulation when it has been held invalid by

    a. trial or appeals court

    b. the Supreme Court [2.3]

9. a. What is a revenue ruling and why is it important?

    b. By whom are revenue rulings issued and where can the rulings be found? [2.3]

10. How does a private ruling differ from a revenue ruling? [2.3]

11. Describe the purpose of revenue procedures. [2.3]

12. Explain what is meant by a determination letter. [2.3]

13. a. When there is a conflict between a taxpayer and the IRS with regard to the amount of tax owed, explain the statutory procedure for resolution of the conflict.

    b. If the conflict is not resolved, how may an appeal be taken to the courts? [2.3]

14. Distinguish among the three courts that have original jurisdiction to hear tax matters. [2.3]

15. Assume a tax question is at issue in completing the following sentences:

    a. The only trial court that allows jury trials is the _____.

    b. Cases heard by the U.S. Court of Federal Claims may be appealed to the _____.

    c. The trial court in which a taxpayer can litigate without first paying an assessed deficiency is the _____. [2.3]

16. When is the IRS bound to follow a court decision? [2.3]

17. What avenues of appeal exist if a taxpayer loses a tax case in a trial court? [2.3]

18. Under what circumstances would the Supreme Court review an appeal in a tax case? [2.3]

19. Joe Smith runs an independent trucking company out of Wilmington, Delaware. He travels the Wilmington-New Jersey-New York route. The New Jersey state legislature enacted tough new safety measures for trucks including lower weight limits than those of the surrounding states. Joe decided that it was cheaper for him to continue to use the same heavier trucks and pay a fine in New Jersey for the weight violation,

rather than to use numerous smaller trucks to carry his loads. Joe deducted the fines paid on his federal income tax return as an ordinary and necessary business expense. Joe was audited by the IRS and the agent denied the deduction for the fines. The agent denied the deduction on the grounds that the Internal Revenue Code prohibits such a deduction. (Focus on the tax procedure and not on the issue of whether the fines are actually deductible.)

a. What alternatives are now open to Joe (1) administratively, within the Internal Revenue Service, and (2) through the courts?

b. Suppose Joe selects the Tax Court, and the Tax Court allows his deduction. What effect does this have on (1) the Internal Revenue Service, and (2) Bill Zilch, whose company is based in San Francisco and who has a problem similar to Joe's on the San Francisco-Oregon route?

c. Assume Joe lost his case in the Tax Court and he appeals to the Third Circuit Court of Appeals, which allows the deduction. What is the effect on (1) the Internal Revenue Service, (2) Roy Jones, a competitor of Joe's in Wilmington, who runs the same route as Joe and also deducted the fines, and (3) Bill Zilch?

d. Assume Joe's original case reaches the Supreme Court of the United States, which allows the deduction. What is the effect on (1) the Internal Revenue Service, (2) Roy Jones, and (3) Bill Zilch? [2.3]

Review Answers

1. The 16th Amendment, ratified in 1913, gives Congress the power to impose and collect taxes on all forms of income without apportionment among the states and without regard to census or enumeration. The all-encompassing language, "income, from whatever source derived," gave Congress authority to pass the first broad income tax law known as the Revenue Act of 1913.

2. a. The entire federal tax law was codified in 1939 as the Internal Revenue Code of 1939. The present statutory source of our income tax law is the Internal Revenue Code of 1986, as amended.

   b. The Internal Revenue Code contains our income tax statutes. It must be followed by all taxpayers unless a provision is declared unconstitutional. The Code is subject to much interpretation but can be amended only by an act of Congress. The present Code is revised and updated almost annually. Parts of it can be amended or repealed through the passage of tax bills.

3. The four functions of the income tax system are the revenue-producing function, the economic function, the social function, and the regulatory function. The purpose of the revenue-producing function is to supply money for the administration and operation of the federal government. The economic function plays an important role in the management of the nation's economy. The social function's purpose is to effectuate government policy. And the purpose of the regulatory function is to discourage socially undesirable activities by taxing them.

4. Greater taxes result in lower spending by consumers. By reducing consumer spending without increasing governmental expenditures, the income tax system helps curb inflationary pressures. Conversely, the use of tax incentives or lower tax rates leaves consumers with more cash that, in turn, translates into increased spending, saving, and investment. The hoped-for result is an increase in the national product that will increase the demand for new workers and hence reduce unemployment. Thus the tax system can prevent or reduce the impact of recessions.

5. A revenue bill becomes law, in most cases, through the following process:

    *   The bill is written by or referred to the House Ways and Means Committee.

    *   The committee conducts hearings on the bill and then sends the amended bill with the committee's report to the House for adoption.

    *   The adopted bill is then sent to the Senate Finance Committee for study and amendments.

    *   The amended bill is then forwarded to the Senate for passage.

    *   A joint conference committee consisting of members from both the House and Senate develops a compromise version of the bill if material differences exist between the two versions.

    *   If the compromise version passes both the House and Senate, the bill is then sent to the President for his or her signature or veto.

    *   If the bill is vetoed, a two-thirds majority of both the House and Senate can revive the bill and make it law over the President's veto.

6. The president is the chief of the executive branch of the federal government. The Constitution gives him or her the duty to enforce the collection of taxes. The president has delegated this duty to the Department of the Treasury, which in turn has delegated this 37 responsibility to the Internal Revenue Service, one of its subdivisions. The Department of the Treasury also has the power, granted by Congress, to enact regulations to interpret the Code.

7. The function of a regulation is to give a fuller explanation and interpretation of an Internal Revenue Code section. The Code specifically provides that the Secretary of the Treasury or his or her delegate will prescribe these regulations.

8. a. The IRS does not consider itself bound (beyond the particular case) where a regulation is held invalid by any court lower than the Supreme Court, although it now conforms to circuit (appeals) court decisions for the taxpayer's circuit. Therefore, if a regulation is held invalid by a lower (trial) court, the IRS can and will continue to enforce it against other taxpayers.

   b. If a regulation is held invalid by the Supreme Court, the IRS is bound by the decision for all cases and must cease enforcement of the regulation.

9. a. Revenue rulings are based on a stated set of facts that usually involve a problem common to a number of taxpayers. They are binding on the IRS, which follows them in the handling of issues arising in particular cases.

   b. Revenue rulings are issued by the IRS and are published in a weekly bulletin called the Internal Revenue Bulletin. The first number following "Rev. Rul." is the year it was issued. The second number is in numerical sequence, denoting the order in which it was issued.

10. Private rulings arise when a taxpayer requests an administrative interpretation on a prospective transaction or on completed transactions that are not involved in returns already filed. Private rulings are personal to the taxpayer but, nonetheless, have been made available to the public in recent years and are now published. Even though published, however, they still may not be claimed by another taxpayer as a precedent.

    Revenue rulings, on the other hand, usually involve a problem common to a number of taxpayers instead of just one. They are binding on officials of the IRS and may be relied upon by taxpayers who have cases with facts and circumstances substantially the same as those in the rulings.

11. Revenue procedures describe internal practices and procedures within the IRS and are published in the Internal Revenue Bulletin. New revenue procedures are usually prompted by changes in techniques and administrative procedures used by the IRS.

12. Determination letters are written by IRS officials within specific operating divisions. They are written in regard to various transactions to be reflected on returns that will be filed by various types of taxpayers and organizations. They are issued only if the answer to the question presented is covered specifically by statute, Treasury decision, or regulation, or specifically by a court decision or ruling opinion published in the

Internal Revenue Bulletin. Determination letters contrast with revenue rulings in that such letters are never issued about unclear points of law.

13. a. If a taxpayer disagrees with the IRS concerning the amount of tax owed, he or she may request a hearing before the IRS Appeals organization. While the dispute with IRS is being considered, the appeals officers are not permitted to engage in substantive discussions regarding the specific case with other IRS officials in the absence of the taxpayer or his or her representative. In addition, the taxpayer may request that the issue be referred to the National Office staff for technical advice if there is a lack of uniformity in the disposition of the issue or if the issue is significantly complex or unique. Dispute resolution methods in Appeals now also include mediation and arbitration.

   b. If the taxpayer and the IRS are not able to resolve their conflict in Appeals, statutory notice of deficiency is issued by the IRS Commissioner. Following this notice, taxpayers have 90 days to file a petition with the U.S. Tax Court to have their cases heard. If the 90 days pass without either the tax being paid or suit being filed, the IRS can assess a tax deficiency, enter judgment, and seize the taxpayer's property to collect the deficiency. However, no tax need be paid in advance for cases to be litigated in the Tax Court. Once a case has been docketed there, an appeals officer is assigned to the case and given exclusive authority to settle within a 4-month period. If no settlement is reached in that time, the case is scheduled for trial.

   Alternatively, the taxpayer may choose to pay the tax deficiency and then file a claim for a refund with the IRS. Unless a notice of claim disallowance is sent before 6 months expire, the taxpayer must wait that time period before he or she can file suit for a refund in either the U.S. District Court or the U.S. Court of Federal Claims.

14. The U.S. Tax Court was established for taxpayers who seek a redetermination of a deficiency asserted against them but do not wish first to pay the deficiency. Trial by jury is not available in the Tax Court. Questions of law and fact are decided by Tax Court judges.

   The U.S. District Court can only hear tax cases in which the taxpayer has first paid the deficiency and has been denied a refund by the IRS. The District Court is the only court in which a taxpayer may request a jury trial. In a case where there is a jury, the jury decides questions of fact; the judge decides questions of law.

   The U.S. Court of Federal Claims, like the U.S. District Court, can only hear tax cases in which the taxpayer has first paid the deficiency and has been denied a refund by the

IRS. The Court of Federal Claims is a trial court that became operative on October 1, 1982, when the U.S. Court of Claims ceased to exist as such.

15. a. U.S. District Court

b. Court of Appeals for the Federal Circuit

c. U.S. Tax Court

16. The IRS does not consider itself bound by a Tax Court decision, a Court of Federal Claims decision, or a District Court decision (except for the particular case in which an adverse decision has been rendered). The U.S. Supreme Court is the highest court in the land and its decisions are required to be followed by the IRS as well as by taxpayers.

17. Appeals from the Tax Court by an unsuccessful taxpayer are heard by the U.S. Court of Appeals in the region of the country in which the taxpayer resides. If there is a difference of opinion in the various courts of appeal, the Tax Court follows the decisions of that Court of Appeals to which the taxpayer may appeal.

Appeals from the Court of Federal Claims are heard by the Court of Appeals for the Federal Circuit, while appeals from a U.S. District Court are heard by that particular court's corresponding U.S. Court of Appeals. Appeals from a U.S. Court of Appeals or the Court of Appeals for the Federal Circuit are taken to the highest court in the land, the U.S. Supreme Court.

18. Supreme Court review of tax cases is generally available only if the Court itself grants petitions for appeal. Reasons for review typically are that (1) there is a conflict between the courts of appeal for different circuits, or (2) an important and recurring problem in tax law administration is involved, or (3) many taxpayers are involved, or (4) the decision of a lower court conflicts with longstanding practice or existing legal authority.

19. a. (1) Joe will probably request an appeals conference. Assuming no agreement is reached, the IRS will send a statutory notice of deficiency for tax due. Joe now has 90 days to decide whether to pay or file suit. If he does not make a decision, the IRS may assess, obtain a judgment, and seize his property.

(2) Joe could file suit in the U.S. Tax Court. He pays no tax before the court (non-jury) decides the case. If Joe loses in the Tax Court, he can appeal to the court of appeals in his circuit (12 circuit courts), and finally, he can request the U.S. Supreme Court to hear the case. On the other hand, Joe could pay the tax due and sue for a refund in a U.S. district court. The district court judge decides the issue of law as to whether fines may be deductible as a business expense. If

Joe loses on the legal issue, he may appeal to the Court of Appeals, and if he loses again, he may request the U.S. Supreme Court to hear the case. Appellate courts review only questions of law, not of fact. Or, Joe could pay the tax due and sue the government for a refund in the U.S. Court of Federal Claims. The Court of Federal Claims hears suits for tax refunds only. An adverse decision may be appealed to the Court of Appeals for the Federal Circuit and then on to the U.S. Supreme Court. Since the Supreme Court has discretion over cases it takes, it is unlikely the average case will be reviewed.

Joe will decide which court to sue in depending on the following considerations:

- precedent decisions of that particular court
- payment of tax before or after suit
- need for jury on sympathetic factual issue

b. (1) The Internal Revenue Service is not bound by this decision in other similar cases even though Joe Smith is entitled to the deduction. The IRS may appeal a decision to the Third Circuit Court of Appeals. The IRS publishes lists of Tax Court cases to which it acquiesces or nonacquiesces.

   (2) If Bill Zilch takes a deduction, the IRS will probably deny it. Bill must pay the tax or institute suit in one of three courts. Bill would probably choose the Tax Court because of the favorable precedent. The U.S. Supreme Court, as its name implies, is the final authority as to any question of federal law.

c. (1) The Internal Revenue Service is not bound by this decision in other similar cases outside the Third Circuit, even though Joe's deduction was allowed in that circuit.

   (2) The IRS will follow this decision in all Third Circuit cases. Roy Jones, who has the same truck route, could take the deductions knowing the IRS would not litigate.

   (3) If Bill Zilch takes the deduction, the IRS will probably deny it. He must pay the tax or institute suit. If the IRS is upheld by the Ninth Circuit Court of Appeals (which covers Bill's area), then there is a conflict in the circuit courts. When this situation arises, it is more likely that the Supreme Court will grant a review.

d. When the Supreme Court decides the case, all parties—Joe, Bill, Roy, and the IRS—are bound to follow the decision. The Supreme Court will hear appeals, in most cases, only where there is a conflict between decisions of lower courts, where the decision is probably in conflict with significant existing precedent, or where the issue is considered of major importance. The Supreme Court can choose (with few exceptions) which cases it will or will not hear. In other words, it can decline to hear the appeal by denying the petition for review. The U.S. Supreme Court, as its name implies, is the final authority as to any question of federal law.

Chapter 3

An Introduction to Four Basic Income Tax Concepts

Learning Objectives

An understanding of the material in this chapter should enable you to

LO 3.1   **Explain the meaning of the term "gross income."**

LO 3.2   **Explain the doctrine of constructive receipt.**

LO 3.3   **Explain the economic-benefit theory.**

LO 3.4   **Explain the principle of assignment of income.**

> The hardest thing in the world to understand is the Income Tax. This [preparing my tax return] is too difficult for a mathematician. It takes a philosopher.
>
> —Albert Einstein

Four concepts are essential in gaining a fundamental understanding of how the income tax laws work. The first is the concept of gross income. This concept is a guide to items and transactions that are subject to taxation. The second concept is the doctrine of constructive receipt, which applies in determining when an item of income will be taxed to a particular taxpayer. The third concept is the economic benefit theory. This theory helps to ascertain under what circumstances a taxpayer has realized income subject to taxation, even though no cash has been directly received by the taxpayer. The fourth concept is the principle of assignment of income. This principle deals with the question of to whom income is taxed in situations where the income is received by a taxpayer other than the taxpayer whose efforts generated the income.

The four concepts are fundamental to understanding income tax law. Each of them is represented in various ways by portions of the Internal Revenue Code, by judicial decisions, by IRS practices, and by other elements of tax law authority. These concepts help students of the tax law to know the specific tax result of a given transaction or situation and also to understand why the result occurs.

LO 3.1   **Explain the meaning of the term "gross income."**

GROSS INCOME UNDER THE INTERNAL REVENUE CODE

Question: What is the meaning of the term "gross income"?

gross income

Answer: **Gross income** is income that must be included on a taxpayer's income tax return. The Internal Revenue Code defines gross income as "all income from whatever source derived," including (but not limited to) the following items:

- compensation for services, including fees, commissions, fringe benefits, and similar items
- gross income derived from business
- gains derived from dealings in property
- interest
- rents
- royalties
- dividends
- alimony and separate maintenance payments
- annuities
- income from life insurance and endowment contracts
- pensions
- income from discharge of indebtedness
- distributive share of partnership gross income
- income in respect of a decedent
- income from an interest in an estate or trust

Under this definition, the 15 items listed are examples of items includible in a taxpayer's gross income. They are by no means an exclusive list. In fact, the general rule for inclusion is that any item of income received by a taxpayer is includible in gross income unless a specific provision in the Internal Revenue Code specifically states that the item may be excluded. The rule that all items of income are includible in gross income unless the Code explicitly provides otherwise is an important fundamental income tax concept.

Question: What is the difference between "income" and "capital" for income tax purposes?

Answer: To begin with, "income" is subject to income taxation, while "capital" (including transactions in which a taxpayer receives a return of capital) is not. The trick is how to differentiate the receipt of income from the receipt, return, or replacement of a capital item. An example of a return of capital is where a taxpayer purchases 100 shares of corporate stock for $50 a share and later sells the stock for the same amount per share. The sales proceeds of $50 per share do not constitute gross income to the taxpayer, because the taxpayer already had that much money invested in the property. To the extent the taxpayer is receiving back only what was paid for the property, he or she does not have "gains derived from dealings in property."

On the other hand, if the stock had been sold for $70 a share, the difference of $20 per share between the amount the taxpayer invested in the property and the amount he or she received for it would be includible in gross income.

Another example of an item that is not considered "income" is where a creditor receives repayment of the principal amount of a debt. The repayment of the principal by the debtor is not gross income to the creditor. The creditor is simply receiving back the amount of money that was, in a sense, "invested" in the debtor. However, any interest payments on the debt received by the creditor would generally be includible in gross income.

Question: What is the significance of the term "realization of income" for tax purposes?

Answer: In order for income to be taxable, the income must be "realized" or obtained by the taxpayer. For example, gain is generally not realized from dealings in property until there is a disposition of the property. The disposition is the event that causes the gain in the property to be realized by the taxpayer and therefore taxed. An increase in value without an event such as a disposition of the property does not result in taxation of gain. An individual taxpayer who uses the cash-basis method of tax accounting is not taxed on income unless and until the income is actually or constructively received. As a general rule, there must be a "taxable event" (such as a sale of property, payment of a salary, or receipt of an economic benefit) that brings the income into the taxpayer's possession.

In certain situations, there can be a dispute as to whether a taxpayer has realized an item of income. The tax concept of realization has been fairly well developed both in court decisions and in the Internal Revenue Code, and it will be touched upon in certain other portions of this text. In general, income is taxable when it is realized by the taxpayer, although the Code does contain certain rules that defer or even eliminate the taxation of certain types of realized income.

Question: What are some examples of situations in which a taxpayer may unexpectedly be subject to income tax?

Answer: Certain items of gross income may result from situations in which the taxpayer does not expect to be taxed. A good example is the rule that imposes taxation on a debtor when that debtor is discharged or relieved of the obligation to pay a debt. As a general rule, the release of an obligation to pay a debt results in "income from discharge of indebtedness" to the debtor. The extent to which such income is taxed may be limited by specific rules regarding the financial position of the debtor. The underlying concept is that the debtor has received a monetary benefit from no longer having to repay money that was borrowed under a legal obligation to repay. Therefore the discharge of indebtedness is a taxable event that results in gross income, unless the discharge of the debt can be treated as a nontaxable gift.

A gift is specifically excludible from the gross income of the donee under the Internal Revenue Code. However, there is frequently an issue of fact as to whether a given transaction is really a gift. The taxation of income from discharge of indebtedness is one area where the issue can arise. It may also arise in determining whether a given transaction is a taxable payment for the taxpayer's personal services or merely a gift. In order for a payment to be treated as a gift, the donor must intend for the payment to be a gift and not a payment for services. Donative intent is a must in order to properly characterize a transaction as a gift. In an employer-employee relationship, it will generally be presumed that payments are for services rendered and not a result of the employer's generosity or concern for the employee's personal welfare even if the employer was not legally obligated to make the payment. However, in certain cases, courts have decided that payments received by employees were nontaxable gifts from the employer. In any event, this is not a fertile ground for income tax planning because the IRS will generally treat such payments as taxable, unless the gift is a "de minimis" (minimal) payment, such as a holiday turkey or a similar item. The Code also specifically excludes certain (but not all) employee fringe benefits from the gross income of employees. A detailed discussion of fringe benefits is beyond the scope of this text.

Income does not have to be received in cash in order to be taxable. If income is received in a form other than cash, the general rule is that the fair market value of the property received is the amount includible in gross income. An example of non-cash income subject to taxation is a barter transaction. If two taxpayers agree to exchange the performance of valuable services for each other, the exchange is taxable to each. For example, if an attorney performs legal services for a dentist in exchange for receiving root canal work, both the attorney and the dentist have realized gross income equal to the value of the services received. Although many transactions in the so-called "barter" economy are not actually reported on tax returns, they are still taxable as a matter of law.

Other common examples of non-cash income will be discussed below in the context of the economic benefit theory.

LO 3.2   Explain the doctrine of constructive receipt.

DOCTRINE OF CONSTRUCTIVE RECEIPT

Question: What is the doctrine of constructive receipt?

Answer: Before answering that question directly, it is necessary to review what is meant by the cash-receipts-and-disbursements or cash-basis method of accounting. Most financial services professionals and their clients are cash-basis taxpayers, which means that they report income and pay taxes on that income only if it is received during the taxable year. Almost all individual taxpayers who do not own a trade or business (and many who do) use this method of accounting.

For example, suppose your client—a doctor using the cash-basis method of accounting—renders services but is not paid for them until January of next year. The income will not be includible in the doctor's income for this year (even though the services were performed this year) but it will be reportable next year.

In a nutshell, the cash-basis method of accounting means that an individual reports income in the year it is received. More formally stated, the amount of any item of gross income is included in the taxpayer's gross income for the taxable year in which it is received, unless an accounting method is used in which such income is to be properly accounted for in a different taxable year.

Question: Generally, then, a cash-basis taxpayer does not have to report income until and unless this person actually receives it. How does the doctrine of constructive receipt apply to this general rule?

doctrine of constructive receipt

Answer: There is an exception to the general rule that income is reported by a cash-basis taxpayer only when it is actually received. The exception is known as the theory or **doctrine of constructive receipt**. This doctrine might best be illustrated by restating two questions often asked of financial services professionals:

1. Is the interest earned on accumulated policy dividends paid from traditional types of cash-value life insurance currently taxable to the policyholder at the time it is credited to the policyholder's account, even though the interest is not actually received by the policyholder at that time?

2. If a policyholder takes the maturity proceeds or cash surrender value of the life, endowment, or annuity contract in the form of a life income or in installments (rather

than as a lump sum), is the entire gain on the policy taxable to him or her in the year of maturity or surrender?

Question: What is the problem? It is evident that in either case the policyholder does not have actual receipt of income.

Answer: In both situations above, the policyholder might have received income constructively, even though he or she has not actually reduced income to his or her possession. The problem is caused by a section of the income tax regulations that provides that income must be included in the taxpayer's gross income for the taxable year in which it is "actually or constructively received." This means that a taxpayer does not have to reduce income to actual possession before it has to be reported. An individual must report it as soon as it is either actually received or constructively received.

Regulations elaborate by stating that even though income is not actually reduced to a taxpayer's possession, the taxpayer is deemed to have constructively received it in the taxable year during which (1) it is credited to the taxpayer's account, (2) set apart for the taxpayer, or (3) otherwise made available to be drawn from at any time.

Question: These rules seem very strict. Are there exceptions?

Answer: The regulations qualify the constructive-receipt rules by stating that income is not constructively received if the taxpayer's control of its receipt is subject to substantial limitations or restrictions. In essence, therefore, the implications of these regulations to cash-basis life underwriters and their cash-basis policyholders is that they must currently report any income that has become unconditionally subject to their demand, although in fact they have not chosen to actually receive or reduce that income to their possession.

The doctrine of constructive receipt might be considered the "Can I get it when I want it?" doctrine. When taxpayers decide to actually obtain items of income and only their volition stands between them and the income, they have constructively received the income at that time (and are therefore taxed on it).

Question: What is the reason for the doctrine?

Answer: The purpose of the constructive-receipt rules is to prevent taxpayers from unilaterally determining the tax year when an item of income is "received by" them for federal income tax purposes. Were it not for this doctrine, cash-basis taxpayers could shift, at will, the year in which they will report an item of income merely by not taking any steps to reduce that income to their possession. The rule prevents cash-basis taxpayers from avoiding taxes by putting off actual receipt of income until their tax circumstances are more favorable, tax rates are lower, or they have a lower amount of other includible income.

The thrust of the doctrine of constructive receipt may therefore be capsulized by the statement that a cash-basis taxpayer "may not deliberately turn his back upon income and thus select the year for which he will report it." If income is payable on the demand of a taxpayer in a given taxable year, he or she must include such amounts in his or her taxable income for that year. To hold otherwise would permit a taxpayer to defer taxable income by merely choosing not to exercise the right to receive it. Therefore the owner of a savings account cannot defer the year in which interest earnings must be reported by deciding in December not to walk into a bank but instead to wait until the following January to have that interest credited on his or her passbook.

Question: What is the effect when there are substantial limitations or restrictions placed on a taxpayer's right to receive income?

Answer: The regulations qualify the rules on inclusion of constructively received income by stating that income will not be constructively received if the taxpayer's control of its receipt is subject to substantial limitations or substantial restrictions. For example, suppose Lee, a pension consultant, signs a contract to perform actuarial services during this year. Lee actually performs those services during this year. However, the contract specifies that payment will not be made until 5 years from now. Lee has no right to require earlier payment. Because payment to Lee (a cash-basis taxpayer) was subject to a substantial restriction (that is, it was not payable until 5 years later), it should not be considered constructively received this year. Thus where a taxpayer is not legally entitled to receive payment in a year prior to actual receipt, this individual will not be held to have constructively received that income in the prior year.

This raises the central question of whether the taxpayer merely refrained from exercising a legal right to receive current payment or whether there was actually never a legal right to receive payment in the prior year. The answer is a question of fact that will be determined by examining the agreement between the parties in each situation. Court cases indicate that if there is any substantial limitation or restriction on either the time or the manner of payment of income, there can be no constructive receipt until the limitation or restriction is removed. There would be no constructive receipt, for example, if the Tyler Corporation raises Robert's salary but does not pay that salary increase until a later year when wage freeze rules are changed to permit payment. Robert will not be deemed to be in constructive receipt in the earlier year.

Question: How does the effect of substantial limitations or restrictions apply to life insurance?

Answer: The cash value of a life insurance policy earns interest, which is reflected in the increase in the policy cash value from year to year. Although a policyholder could easily reduce any gain reflected by the excess of the cash value over the cost of the contract, the policyholder is not required to include such gain in his or her gross income each year. This is because the right to receive that income is subject to substantial limitations or restrictions. In other words, to receive the gain the policyholder must complete a transaction that will affect the nature and extent of his or her valuable insurance coverage and contractual rights.

Question: Suppose amounts are credited or set apart for a taxpayer, but there are no funds to pay the promised amounts. What is the effect on an inability to pay amounts credited?

Answer: If the financial condition of the debtor makes payment of the income in question impossible, there will be no constructive receipt by the creditor. For example, suppose Pam loaned the Esposito Corporation $10,000. In return Pam received an interest-bearing note. If the Esposito Corporation had insufficient funds to pay the interest, Pam would have no constructive receipt even if her account was credited with the interest on the corporation's books. Likewise, if the Martin Corporation issued a salary check to Oliver, an officer, but the corporation lacked the funds to pay the check, Oliver would not be taxed. This result would hold even if the Martin Corporation could have borrowed money or sold assets to pay the check.

Question: Specifically, how does the doctrine of constructive receipt affect life insurance?

Answer: At this point it is appropriate to answer the two questions asked earlier:

1. Is the interest earned on accumulated policy dividends paid from traditional types of cash-value life insurance currently taxable to the policyholder as soon as it is credited to the policyholder's account, even if the policyholder has not actually received the interest?

2. If a policyholder takes the maturity proceeds or cash surrender value of the life, endowment, or annuity contract in the form of a life income or in installments (rather than in a lump sum), is the gain on the policy taxable to him or her in the year of maturity or surrender?

The first question pertains to the time at which interest earned on policy dividends becomes taxable. The general rule is that the interest earned on policy dividends must be included in the policyholder's gross income for the first taxable year during which the policyholder has the right to withdraw the interest. This result applies even if the taxpayer, in fact, does not withdraw the interest. The key issue is as follows: When can the policyholder withdraw the interest on the policy dividends? If the policy provides that interest can be withdrawn only on the policy's anniversary date, the interest income is not constructively received in the year prior to the anniversary date.

The second question pertains to the result that occurs when the maturity proceeds or cash surrender value of a policy are taken in the form of installments of lifetime payments rather than in the form of a lump sum. When an endowment contract matures (or an ordinary life contract is surrendered), gain on the lump sum available to the policyholder will be immediately taxable. However, if a policyholder decides to select an installment payment or annuity settlement option rather than taking the lump sum that could be chosen at will, is the policyholder in constructive receipt of the lump sum? If there is a gain on the contract and if proceeds are constructively received, the full gain would be taxable—just as if the policyholder had actually received a lump-sum payment.

A constructive-receipt problem can occur in three typical situations. The first situation is when the policyholder elects before the maturity or surrender date to postpone receipt of the proceeds and take income in the form of an annuity or installments. In this case, however, the policyholder avoids constructive receipt since there is no point in time when he or she had an unqualified right to take the lump sum. The policyholder will be taxed on the gain reflected in each installment when he or she actually receives it.

The second situation is when a policyholder does not make an election before the maturity or surrender date. Were it not for Sec. 72(h) in the Internal Revenue Code, the policyholder would be considered to be in constructive receipt of the lump sum when it became available. However, because of this special provision, a policyholder will not be deemed to be in constructive receipt of the lump sum (1) within 60 days after the lump sum becomes payable and (2) if before receiving any payment in cash, the policyholder exercises an option or agrees with the insurer to take the proceeds in the form of a life income annuity or other installment-type settlement.

The third situation occurs when a policyholder decides to give up the right to withdraw principal, leaves proceeds on deposit, and receives only the interest that those proceeds generate. Constructive receipt in this case can be avoided only if an election to receive interest is made before the maturity or surrender date. Thus the 60-day extension is allowed only for the election of a life income or other installment-type settlement and not for an election to leave proceeds on deposit at interest.

Question: Does the doctrine of constructive receipt affect agreements to defer compensation?

Answer: It is in the area of deferred compensation that the doctrine of constructive receipt proves to be most complex and troublesome. The reason for deferring compensation is quite simple: If all or a part of an individual's current earnings are not payable by an employer until a specified date, or if those earnings are spread out over a number of years in the future when the individual is in a lower income tax bracket, the net after-tax compensation will be increased.

Therefore it is possible to defer the tax of a cash-basis employee or independent contractor, but this deferral requires careful planning.

Basically there are two types of deferred-compensation methods: funded and unfunded. A funded deferred-compensation agreement entails the actual deposit of funds by the employer into a trust, escrow, or custodial account. Unfunded deferred compensation implies that no funds are irrevocably set aside (that is, outside the corporation's control and beyond the reach of its creditors) by an employer. In this case, the employee must rely solely on the employer's unsecured promise and ability to pay the deferred amount (plus any interest that is applicable) in the future. Taxation generally depends not only on whether the agreement is funded or unfunded but also on whether the rights of the employee whose income is deferred are forfeitable or nonforfeitable.

Where the agreement can be classified as funded (according to the definition above), the deferred compensation will be taxable to the employee in (1) the first year the employee's rights are not subject to a substantial risk of forfeiture, or (2) the first year the employee's rights can be transferred to another party (that is, assigned free of the substantial risk of forfeiture).

If the agreement can be classified as unfunded (according to the definition above), such compensation will not be taxable until it is actually paid to the employee provided (1) the agreement to defer the compensation is made prior to the time the compensation is earned, and (2) the employer's promise is not secured by specific assets. In other words, the obligation may not be evidenced by specified financial instruments, such as a negotiable note. If these two requirements are met, constructive receipt will be avoided until the deferred compensation is actually received. This is because receipt of the compensation is not within the employee's control. This result will apply regardless of whether such compensation was or was not forfeitable by the employee. Therefore even if the employee had a nonforfeitable right to such compensation, no tax would be imposed until actual receipt since the agreement was unfunded.

For example, suppose the Rawlins Corporation offered Elaine a 5-year employment contract to entice her to join. The agreement provides that Elaine will be paid $50,000 a year currently, plus an additional $10,000 of nonforfeitable deferred compensation credited to a reserve account each year. However, Elaine will receive the money only upon her retirement, death, or disability. Elaine receives neither notes from the corporation nor evidence of its debt other than the agreement signed by the corporation and Elaine. She is to receive the deferred salary in 10 equal annual installments.

Even though the compensation that has been deferred is nonforfeitable, Elaine does not have constructive receipt. The agreement to defer the compensation was made before Elaine earned it. The Rawlins Corporation did not put aside funds in an escrow account for her benefit.

In no way did the Rawlins Corporation secure its promise to Elaine other than through an employment agreement, and thus she has no right to the funds. They have not been credited or set apart so that she may draw from them at will. All Elaine has is a promise by the Rawlins Corporation to be paid income upon her retirement, death, or disability. Nothing has been placed beyond the access of the corporation's creditors, and no control over the funds has been given to Elaine. Likewise, upon retirement, death, or disability, when the Rawlins Corporation's promise matures and Elaine becomes entitled to receive installment payments, there is still no constructive receipt. The only income subject to her unqualified control is the installment payment she actually receives each year. These payments, of course, will be taxable income when actually paid to Elaine.

The Internal Revenue Service has allowed the use of so-called rabbi trusts in connection with deferred-compensation agreements without imposing current taxation on the funds placed in the trust to be paid later to the employee. The employee avoids current taxation only if the funds in the trust can be reached by the creditors of the employer. The rabbi trust was a significant development in terms of how the IRS regards the doctrine of constructive receipt, since it involved setting aside funds for the payment of deferred compensation without the arrangement being treated as a "funded" agreement.

Question: How is the use of life insurance in deferred-compensation agreements affected by the doctrine of constructive receipt?

Answer: Life insurance or annuity policies are often used by an employer to finance its obligation under the deferred-compensation agreement. For example, suppose the Mitchell Corporation executed a deferred-compensation contract with Sam, a key employee. The agreement stated that Mitchell would credit a specific sum on behalf of Sam to a bookkeeping account each month for the entire term of the contract. (This agreement is unfunded, since no amounts are set aside in trust or in an escrow account beyond the reach of the corporation's creditors.)

The Mitchell Corporation could invest all or any portion of the amount credited to Sam. Payout would not commence until the earlier of (1) Sam's 65th birthday, (2) his death prior to retirement, or (3) his disability. At that time the value of the account would be paid out in equal installments over a period of 10 years to Sam or to his named beneficiary. To finance this liability under the agreement, Mitchell purchased a life insurance contract. Mitchell applied for, owned, and was beneficiary of the contract. The policy was carried as a corporate asset on the Mitchell Corporation's books and was subject at all times to the claims of its general creditors.

The employee under this type of deferred-compensation contract will be successful in avoiding constructive receipt of the money set aside. The employee will recognize no income until the taxable year in which the income is actually received (or it is made available to the employee in some other way). The rationale is that the employee has no present interest in either the account or the policy, both of which are general assets of the employer. Note that the agreement gave the employee or his or her beneficiary no direct interest in any specific account, insurance or annuity policy, or in any other employer assets. The account merely served as a measure of the employer's liability for bookkeeping purposes.

LO 3.3   Explain the economic-benefit theory.

ECONOMIC-BENEFIT THEORY

Question: What is the economic-benefit theory?

economic-benefit theory

Answer: Sec. 61 of the Internal Revenue Code defines gross income as including "income from whatever source derived. . . ." In cases dealing with this section of the Code, courts have held that the language of the section is "broad enough to include as taxable income any economic or financial benefit conferred on the employee as compensation, whatever the form or mode by which it is effected." This concept has appropriately been entitled the **economic-benefit theory** or doctrine. Its purpose is to force an employee to include in income any compensation regardless of its form. It has been applied to situations involving a payment in kind or where an employer has made available to an employee the equivalent of cash.

Question: How does this principle differ from the doctrine of constructive receipt?

Answer: The constructive-receipt doctrine forces the inclusion of income when the employee has an unqualified choice—to take or not to take income set apart or credited to his or her account. The economic-benefit theory or doctrine, on the other hand, forces the inclusion of income, even if the employee cannot take the income. All that is necessary under the economic-benefit theory is that the employee receive from an employer the equivalent of cash, something with a (1) current, (2) real, and (3) measurable value.

For example, if Pete is given the right to receive his bonus in cash or in the form of a nontransferable annuity with no currently accessible cash values, he has constructive receipt of the bonus regardless of the choice he makes. The reason is that he has the unrestricted right to take the cash. Alternatively, if Pete was given no choice as to the form of his bonus—if it was only available to him in the form of a nontransferable, single-premium deferred annuity with no currently accessible cash value—he would not have constructively received his bonus. This is because he can neither take cash nor draw down cash values from the annuity. Still, he would realize current income. He has received a promise from an insurance company, a financial institution in the business of making such promises, that he will receive benefits (his bonus) in the future.

The second situation illustrates the economic-benefit theory. The secured promise of an insurance company or banking company to pay income in the future can be currently and adequately valued and is therefore immediately taxable. This is unlike the naked promise of an employer that is, in effect, a nonnegotiable, nonassignable agreement generally incapable of valuation. This is so because the employer's promise is subject, according to the courts, to the hazards of economic and business conditions regardless of the size or financial state of the employer.

The following case may further illustrate the distinction between the doctrine of constructive receipt and the economic-benefit theory. An employer established a trust for the benefit of one of its key employees. The employer placed $10,500 in the trust that year. The trustee was directed to pay that employee $5,000 the next year and the balance in 2 years. In other words, the deferred compensation was irrevocably set aside in a trust and payable over a 2-year period. The court held that in the first year the amount of $10,500 was fixed and irrevocably paid out by the employer for the sole benefit of the taxpayer. The court recognized that the employee technically had neither actual nor constructive receipt of the trust money. During that year he had no right whatsoever to draw from those funds. Therefore the court reasoned that there was a substantial limitation on the employee's control that prevented constructive receipt. However, the court concluded that the employee did have an actual receipt of the economic or financial benefit conferred on him in that first year. This was the year in which the employer established the irrevocable trust for the employee's benefit in which the employee's rights were nonforfeitable. In such a case, the employee would pay tax on the present value of the right to receive $5,000 one year later and an additional $5,500 2 years later.

Even though the funds were not immediately subject to his actual expenditure, they were there solely for his benefit. Therefore the amount of income he is to realize in the year in which the funds were set apart for his benefit must be measured by the amount of money paid, appropriately discounted to reflect the postponement of possession or enjoyment. Even this discount would not be allowed if the funds were placed in an interest-bearing account on which the employee would ultimately receive the interest.

Question: How might the economic-benefit theory be applied in a life insurance situation?

Answer: There are several life insurance related situations in which the economic-benefit theory is applied. One such situation is the taxation of employees covered under a qualified pension or profit-sharing plan that contains life insurance on their lives. Another situation is where an employee receives group life insurance in excess of the $50,000 excludible limit.

Alternatively, an employee may own an individual policy insuring his or her own life and designate a chosen beneficiary for the death proceeds, and the employer may pay the premiums on the policy. The payment of such premiums is taxed as compensation to the employee. Although the employee owning the policy receives no outright cash payment, the funding of the life insurance policy provides a clear economic benefit to the employee and results in taxation of that benefit. An employee's coverage under a split-dollar life insurance arrangement with the employer can also result in taxation to the employee under the economic benefit theory. The IRS has issued regulations that specify the income tax treatment of split-dollar plans. Their tax treatment depends on the type of plan being used, the ownership configuration of the policy, how the policy's cash value is allocated between the employer and the employee, and other factors. The arrangement can be taxed under either an economic benefit theory or a loan theory using imputed interest rules. Taxation of split-dollar plans can become quite complicated.

LO 3.4   Explain the principle of assignment of income.

THE PRINCIPLE OF ASSIGNMENT OF INCOME

Question: What is the principle of assignment of income?

assignment of income

Answer: The principle of **assignment of income** requires the taxpayer whose personal efforts generate income or who is the owner of property that generates income to report or declare the income on his or her own tax return. It provides that the taxation of income cannot be shifted from one taxpayer to another merely by transferring or assigning to another taxpayer the right to receive the income. This principle was developed in the tax law mostly through judicial decisions. Litigation with the IRS arose as a result of the efforts of crafty taxpayers to shift the taxation of income to other taxpayers (such as family members) whose marginal rate of taxation was lower than their own. Such techniques would result in lower overall taxes for the parties concerned. The issue here is not what income is taxable or when it is taxable, but rather to whom it is taxable.

Question: How does the principle of assignment of income operate?

Answer: The principle operates in two basic ways: first, by requiring that income that is generated by the performance of personal services be taxed to the person who performed the services; and second, by requiring that income generated by property be taxed to the taxpayer who owns the property. For example, suppose an executive of a large corporation enters into a written contract with her son, providing that her salary from the corporation be paid directly to her son. Even though the son actually receives the income under this arrangement, it will still be taxable to the executive because it was her personal services rendered for the company that produced the income. The income would also be treated as a gift to the son. Another example would be where a father arranges for the income from his portfolio of corporate securities to be paid directly to his daughter. Again, even though the daughter receives the income, the father is still taxed on the income because he is the owner of the underlying property.

Question: How can a taxpayer successfully shift the burden of taxation of income to another taxpayer who is in a lower tax bracket?

Answer: In the case of income generated by most types of personal services, there is no reliable planning technique that can legally shift taxation to another taxpayer. In addition to the general assignment of income principle, there are various statutory roadblocks set up in the tax law to defeat or discourage such efforts. The best example of a legitimate shift in the taxation of personal service income is not useful for planning purposes: where a taxpayer dies before receiving income for services rendered and the income becomes "income in respect of a decedent" that is taxable to the beneficiary who receives it.

In the case of income generated by the ownership of property, a bona fide transfer of the ownership of the property will result in the income from the property being shifted for tax purposes to the transferee. Suppose that in the example discussed above, the father transferred outright ownership of his portfolio of securities to his daughter rather than merely assigning the income to her. The income earned on the securities after the transfer would then be taxable to the daughter because she would be the owner of the property.

This requirement of transfer of property ownership is often referred to as the doctrine of "the fruit and the tree." This metaphor indicates that in order to shift the burden of taxation, the entire "tree" or underlying asset—and not merely the "fruit" or income generated by it—must be transferred to another taxpayer. The economic reality of such situations is that the property owner must relinquish control of property in order to avoid taxation on its income. This is a more difficult decision than simply assigning the income from the property to another person or entity.

Question: Must there be an outright transfer of property to another person to shift the burden of taxation of income from the property?

Answer: There need not always be an outright transfer. For example, minor children are limited by law in how they are able to control and manage property. In situations where parents wish to shift the taxation of income to children, certain types of trusts can be used to hold ownership of property while effectively shifting taxation. However, the principle that the donor must relinquish ownership and control over the property still holds. The trust must be drafted in a way that complies with applicable federal, state, and local tax and property laws. Trusts used for income-shifting purposes include so-called "Sec. 2503(b) income trusts" and "Sec. 2503(c) accumulation trusts," which are named for the Internal Revenue Code provisions that govern them. The specific provisions and techniques used in such trusts are not covered in detail in this text but are covered in *Fundamentals of Estate Planning* (16th edition) published by The American College Press.

CHAPTER REVIEW

Key Terms and Concepts

gross income

doctrine of constructive receipt

economic-benefit theory

assignment of income

Review Questions

Review questions are based on the learning objectives in this chapter. Thus a [3.3] at the end of a question means that the question is based on learning objective 3. If there are multiple objectives, they are all listed.

1. What are 15 items that are specifically included in gross income under the Internal Revenue Code? [3.1]

2. How is the tax concept of income differentiated from the tax concept of capital? [3.1]

3. Don purchases stock at $30 a share. The price per share goes up to $50 in one week. Has he realized income? Explain. [3.1]

4. Does your client, Mrs. Eidson, have income when interest earned on her life insurance policy dividends is credited to her policy account? Explain. [3.2]

5. Under what circumstances will an employee be taxed on compensation under the economic-benefit theory? [3.3]

6. Paul is the sales manager for the Freeman Corporation. The company pays premiums on a $100,000 whole life policy owned by Paul insuring his life. Paul has named his wife as beneficiary. What is the relevant income tax concept and its implications to Paul? [3.3]

7. Describe the principle of assignment of income. [3.4]

8. John Jones, an agent for Podunk Mutual, assigns his renewal commissions to his 25-year-old daughter, Jane. In this situation, explain who the taxpayer is for income tax purposes as well as the principle of tax law that applies here. [3.4]

Review Answers

1. The Internal Revenue Code defines gross income as "all income from whatever source derived," including (but not limited to) the following 15 items:

    *   compensation for services, including fees, commissions, fringe benefits, and similar items

    *   gross income derived from business

    *   gains derived from dealings in property

    *   interest

    *   rents

    *   royalties

    *   dividends

    *   alimony and separate maintenance payments

    *   annuities

    *   income from life insurance and endowment contracts

    *   pensions

    *   income from discharge of indebtedness

    *   distributive share of partnership gross income

    *   income in respect of a decedent

    *   income from an interest in an estate or trust

2. Income is subject to income taxation, while capital is not. Therefore the receipt of an item of income (in whatever form) is an event subject to income taxation, while the receipt, return, or replacement of a capital item is not a taxable event.

3. Don has not realized income because there has been no disposition of the property.

4. Mrs. Eidson has received income when interest earned on her life insurance policy dividends is credited to her policy account. Even though she has not actually reduced the income to her possession, she has received it constructively. The income tax regulations state that income must be included in a taxpayer's gross income for the taxable

year in which it is "actually or constructively received." The regulations elaborate by stating that even though income is not actually reduced to a taxpayer's possession, the taxpayer is deemed to have constructively received it in the taxable year during which (1) it is credited to the taxpayer's account, as in the case of Mrs. Eidson, (2) set apart for the taxpayer, or (3) otherwise made available to be drawn from at any time.

5. Courts have held that Sec. 61 of the Code is broad enough to include as taxable income any economic or financial benefit conferred on an employee as compensation, regardless of its form. This concept is known as the economic-benefit theory or doctrine, and it has been applied to situations involving a payment in kind or where the employer has made available to the employee the equivalent of cash—in other words, when the employee receives from the employer something with a current, real, and measurable value.

6. Paul receives an economic benefit from his employer intended as compensation in the form of life insurance premium payments. Therefore the amount of the premium is ordinary income to Paul.

7. The principle of assignment of income provides that the taxation of income cannot be shifted from one taxpayer to another merely by transferring or assigning to another taxpayer the right to receive the income. Consequently, the taxpayer whose personal efforts generated the income or who is the owner of the property that generated the income must report or declare the income on his or her own tax return. Assigning the income to another taxpayer (such as a family member whose marginal rate of taxation is lower) will not shift the burden of taxation for the income to that taxpayer.

8. Jones, not his daughter, would be taxed on commissions based on the assignment-of-income doctrine. Jones cannot assign income that he has earned to another party.

Chapter 4

Determination of Income Tax Liability

Learning Objectives

An understanding of the material in this chapter should enable you to

LO 4.1   **Explain the concept of adjusted gross income.**

LO 4.2   **Explain the determination of taxable income.**

LO 4.3   **Explain how tax liability is determined.**

LO 4.4   **Explain what is meant by the kiddie tax.**

LO 4.5   **Explain the due dates for filing income tax returns.**

> The Higher the Tax Bracket, the Better the View.
>
> —Advertisement for luxury Florida real estate development

The basic steps in determining an individual's income tax liability begin with a discussion of how an individual's adjusted gross income is determined using gross income as a starting point. Then the determination of taxable income is examined, followed by the calculation of actual tax payable.

In the course of following this process, several fundamental tax rules applicable to individuals include exclusions and deductions, the standard deduction, personal and dependency exemptions, filing status, tax rates, and the "kiddie tax."

THE DETERMINATION OF ADJUSTED GROSS INCOME

The Nature of Exclusions

Gross income is essentially all income that a taxpayer realizes during the tax year minus any available exclusions from gross income. An exclusion may be defined as an item of income that is not required to be included in gross income pursuant to a specific provision of the income tax law. It is something quite different from a deduction. A deduction is an expense paid or incurred by a taxpayer that the tax law specifically allows to be subtracted from the amount of income that is otherwise subject to tax. It is an item of expense. An exclusion, on the other hand, is an item of income that may be received by a taxpayer without being included in gross income. As previously stated, a taxpayer's gross income equals all items of income received by the taxpayer during the year minus all available exclusions from gross income. Once gross income has been determined, the next step is to reduce gross income by all deductions that are allowable in determining adjusted gross income.

LO 4.1   Explain the concept of adjusted gross income.

What Is Adjusted Gross Income?

adjusted gross income (AGI)

The calculation of an individual taxpayer's **adjusted gross income (AGI)** is an intermediate step in the process of calculating taxable income. To calculate adjusted gross income, certain deductions are subtracted from the individual's gross income.

above-the-line deductions

below-the-line deductions

There are two fundamental categories of deductions for individual taxpayers: deductions allowable in determining adjusted gross income and deductions allowable in determining taxable income. Deductions subtracted from gross income in determining adjusted gross income are referred to as **above-the-line deductions**. Deductions subtracted from adjusted gross income in determining taxable income are referred to as **below-the-line deductions**.

Although the calculation of AGI is an intermediate step, it is an important one. Two of the most significant reasons why are as follows:

- Above-the-line deductions allowable in determining adjusted gross income are available regardless of whether the taxpayer claims "itemized" deductions. As explained below, the taxpayer claims itemized or below-the-line deductions only if the total of such deductions exceeds the available standard deduction. For this reason, above-the-line deductions are often more valuable to the taxpayer.

- Many tax benefits are currently reduced if the taxpayer's AGI exceeds certain specified amounts. Certain other deductions are available only to the extent that the amount of such deductions exceeds a specified percentage of AGI (a deduction "floor"). Also, the deduction for charitable contributions is allowed only to the extent that contributions do not exceed a specified percentage of AGI (a deduction "ceiling").

The reduction of an individual's AGI results in the increased availability of other tax benefits. In fact, the maximum allowable reduction of an individual's AGI is one of the most important individual tax planning objectives. Above-the-line deductions reduce AGI, while below-the-line deductions do not.

With a few exceptions, above-the-line deductions generally relate to business or income-pro-ducing activities of the taxpayer. On the other hand, the majority of the taxpayer's itemized or below-the-line deductions are expenses or losses of a personal nature for which Congress has provided income tax deductions for social and economic policy reasons.

Deductions Allowable in Determining Adjusted Gross Income

The following expenses are some, though not all, of the more important deductions that are claimed above-the-line by individual taxpayers. They are as follows:

- all deductions attributable to a trade or business carried on by the taxpayer, if such trade or business does not consist of the performance of services by the taxpayer as an employee

- certain business expenses of employees, including expenses reimbursed by the tax-payer's employer, business expenses of performing artists, and business expenses of certain public officials

- losses from the sale or exchange of property subject to limitations described in the taxation of gains from capital and business assets

- deductions attributable to rents and royalties

- deductible contributions to pension and profit-sharing plans of self-employed individuals

- deductible contributions to IRAs

- penalties or other forfeitures resulting from premature withdrawals from time savings accounts or deposits (including certificates of deposit)

- deductible alimony payments

- the portion of jury duty pay remitted to the taxpayer's employer

- deductible moving expenses

- contributions to medical savings accounts or health savings accounts

- deductible interest payments made on qualified education loans

- qualified tuition and related expenses through 2016

- the deduction for legal costs paid in connection with certain civil rights actions

LO 4.2   **Explain the determination of taxable income.**

THE DETERMINATION OF TAXABLE INCOME

Introduction

taxable income

An individual's **taxable income** is determined by subtracting the following items from adjusted gross income:

- either the total of the taxpayer's allowable itemized deductions or the taxpayer's applicable standard deduction amount, whichever is greater, and

- the total allowable amount of the taxpayer's personal and dependency exemptions

The amount of the taxpayer's standard deduction is based on filing status. Increased amounts are available for blind taxpayers and taxpayers aged 65 and over. Under current law, personal and dependency exemptions are "phased out" for upper income taxpayers as described below.

The Standard Deduction

The standard deduction is a specified amount, indexed annually for inflation, that may be claimed in calculating taxable income by taxpayers who do not itemize their deductions. As stated above, taxpayers claim itemized deductions if the total amount of such deductions exceeds the available standard deduction. For tax years beginning in 2017 the standard deduction amounts are

Table 4-1: Standard Deduction Amounts	
Filing Status	Amount
Married filing jointly	$12,700
Unmarried head of household	$9,350
Single	$6,350
Married filing separately	$6,350

Standard Deduction for Dependents

A special rule applies to taxpayers who are dependents. A dependent is an individual for whom another taxpayer claims a dependency exemption. Dependents are not eligible to claim the regular standard deduction amounts on their own returns. As indexed for inflation for the 2017 tax year, the special standard deduction amount allowable on a dependent's tax return is the greater of

- a sum equal to the amount of the dependent's earned income for the year plus $350 (but not more than the regular standard deduction amount), OR

- $1,050 (for 2017)

For example, a dependent with earned income of $1,050 would be entitled to a standard deduction of $1,400 ($1,050 plus $350). A dependent with earned income of $400 in 2017 would be entitled to a standard deduction of $1,050 because that amount is greater than his or her earned income of $400 plus $350 ($750).

Aged or Blind Taxpayers

Another special rule applies to taxpayers who are 65 years of age or older and/or are legally blind. Such taxpayers (including dependents) are entitled to increase their standard deduction by specified amounts. For married taxpayers filing jointly, each spouse who qualifies may add the additional amount or amounts to the standard deduction claimed on the joint return. As indexed for inflation for the 2017 tax year, these "additional amounts" are as follows:

- $1,550 for taxpayers who are unmarried filing as either head of household or single.

- $1,250 for married taxpayers filing jointly, separately or as a surviving spouse.

Example

Mr. and Mrs. Volare file a joint return for 2017. Mr. Volare is 64 years old, and Mrs. Volare is 67. Their standard deduction amount is $13,950, the sum of the regular amount of $12,700 plus the applicable additional amount of $1,250. Mr. and Mrs. Volare will claim the standard deduction in calculating their taxable income unless the total of their itemized deductions exceeds $13,950. If so, they will itemize their deductions and not claim the standard deduction.

The Overall Limitation on Itemized Deductions

In discussing the process of calculating individual income tax liability, it has been important to consider the "overall limitation" on itemized deductions. Like the many "phaseout" provisions in the Internal Revenue Code, this rule aims to reduce or eliminate tax benefits for taxpayers with income above certain levels in a given year.

If an individual taxpayer's adjusted gross income exceeds a specified threshold amount that is indexed annually for inflation, the taxpayer's itemized deductions are reduced by 3 percent of the amount by which AGI exceeds the threshold amount. For 2017, that specified amount for joint filers and surviving spouses is $313,800 ($287,650 for head of household and $261,500 for individual filers.) If itemized deductions were reduced by the overall limitation, the reduction could not exceed 80 percent of the total itemized deductions that are subject to the reduction. However, the overall limitation did not apply to deductions for medical expenses, investment interest expenses, casualty and theft losses, or allowable gambling losses. These are the so called "MaGIC" deductions.

Example

Mark and Terry Sellers are married taxpayers filing jointly. For 2017, their adjusted gross income is $378,800. Mark and Terry have the following itemized deductions: $25,000 for state and local taxes, $18,000 of deductible interest on a home mortgage, and a deductible casualty loss from uninsured flood damage of $40,000 (after all the specific restrictions on the deduction for personal casualty losses have been applied). Their AGI exceeds the threshold amount of $313,800 by $65,000 ($378,800 − $313,800). Three percent of that amount is $1,950 ($65,000 × .03). The couple's state and local taxes and their home mortgage interest are subject to the overall limitation, but their deductible casualty loss is not. Therefore the total amount subject to the limit is $43,000 ($25,000 + $18,000). Of that $43,000, Mark and Terry will lose $1,950.

The overall limitation on itemized deductions is applied after the rules and limits for each specific itemized deduction have been applied. These specific rules include the 50 percent of AGI "ceiling" on charitable contributions, the dollar amount loan limits for qualified residence interest, and the 2 percent of AGI "floor" on most miscellaneous itemized deductions. All of these topics are covered in detail in later chapters of this text.

Personal and Dependency Exemptions

Introduction

In the computation of taxable income, taxpayers are permitted to subtract from AGI the total amount of their allowable personal and dependency exemptions. Each exemption is the equivalent of a deduction for a specified amount that is indexed annually for inflation. This amount is referred to as an "exemption" rather than as a "deduction" because it is not attributable to any actual or determinable expense made by the taxpayer. Rather, it is an arbitrary amount that is granted to taxpayers under the tax law to help reduce the net cost of their personal expenses.

Personal and dependency exemptions are allowable regardless of whether the taxpayer claims the standard deduction or itemizes deductions.

These exemptions are available in two forms: personal exemptions and dependency exemptions. The amount is the same for each type of exemption. For the year 2017, the exemption amount is $4,050. For each individual with respect to whom either a personal or dependency exemption is claimed on a tax return, a taxpayer identification number (Social Security number) must be included on the return.

Personal Exemptions

Each taxpayer is generally permitted to claim one personal exemption for himself or herself on the individual tax return. Married taxpayers filing jointly are allowed one personal exemption for each spouse. If married taxpayers file a separate return, generally only one exemption is allowed. However, if the spouse of the taxpayer filing the separate return has no gross income and is not the dependent of another taxpayer, an exemption for that spouse is allowed.

A special rule applies to individuals with respect to whom a dependency exemption is claimed by another taxpayer. Taxpayers who are "dependents" in this sense are not permitted to claim their own personal exemption on their individual returns. In this way, a total of only one exemption is claimed for each person. The rules for dependency exemptions are discussed below.

Dependency Exemptions

Taxpayers are entitled to claim one additional exemption for each individual who is a dependent of the taxpayer.

Currently, an individual is eligible to be claimed as a dependent of a taxpayer if that individual is either a "qualifying child" or a "qualifying relative" of the taxpayer. Following are definitions for those terms.

"Qualifying Child" Definition

The definition of a "qualifying child" has four basic elements.

First, the individual must bear a relationship to the taxpayer that meets ONE of the following three descriptions:

- a child of the taxpayer or descendant of such child. A "child" for this purpose includes a son, daughter, stepson, or stepdaughter of the taxpayer, or an eligible foster child of the taxpayer. Relationship by adoption is treated the same as relationship by blood.

- a descendant of any individual who meets the definition of a "child," or

- a brother, sister, stepbrother, or stepsister of the taxpayer, or a descendant of any such person

Second, the individual must have the same principal place of abode as the taxpayer for more than half of the taxable year. Temporary absences due to special circumstances (such as illness, education, vacation, or military service) will not be treated as absences for purposes of this rule.

Third, the individual must meet ONE of the following three requirements:

- The individual must be under the age of 19 at the end of the year.

- The individual must be a student under the age of 24 at the end of the year (a "student" for this purpose is an individual who is a full-time student during each of five calendar months during the year), OR

- The individual must be totally and permanently disabled at any time during the year.

Fourth, the individual must NOT have provided more than half of his or her own support during the year.

"Qualifying Relative" Definition

There are four basic requirements that an individual must meet to be treated as a "qualifying relative." These are as follows:

First, the individual must NOT be a "qualifying child" of any taxpayer for the year. This, in effect, makes the definitions of "qualifying child" and "qualifying relative" mutually exclusive. However, under certain circumstances a son or daughter of the taxpayer who is not a "qualifying child" may meet the tests for a "qualifying relative."

Second, the individual must meet ONE of the following two requirements:

- He or she must bear a specified relationship to the taxpayer. Specified relationships include a child of the taxpayer; a descendant of such a child; a brother, sister, step-brother, stepsister, father, or mother; an ancestor of a father or mother; a stepfather or stepmother; a nephew or niece; an uncle or aunt; and a son-in-law, daughter-in-law, father-in-law, mother-in-law, brother-in-law, or sister-in-law.

- He or she must be an individual (other than the taxpayer's spouse) whose principal place of abode during the tax year was the home of the taxpayer and who is a member of the taxpayer's household. This rule does not require that the individual be related to the taxpayer, and may include a domestic partner of the taxpayer, so long as the relationship between the taxpayer and the individual does not violate local law. Note that the taxpayer's spouse cannot be a qualifying relative.

Third, the individual's gross income for the year must be less than the "exemption amount" ($4,050 for 2017 as indexed for inflation).

Fourth, the taxpayer must provide over one-half of the individual's support for the year. The term "support" for purposes of the dependency exemption rules generally means expenses for the necessities of life and other important expenses, such as those for education and activities of the individual. However, certain scholarships granted to full-time students are not included in the calculation of support.

Additional Requirements

For an individual who meets either the definition of a "qualifying child" or a "qualifying relative," there are three more rules that must be met in order for him or her to be claimed as a dependent. These are as follows:

First, the individual being claimed as a dependent may not claim any other individual as his or her own dependent for income tax purposes.

Second, the individual being claimed as a dependent may not file a joint return with his or her spouse for the year (unless the individual and his or her spouse are not required to file a return and the only purpose for filing is to obtain a refund of tax withheld).

Third, an individual who is not a U.S. citizen or national cannot be claimed as a dependent unless that individual is a resident of either the United States or a country contiguous to the United States (i.e., Mexico or Canada). However, a legally adopted child of the taxpayer (or one legally placed for adoption) can be claimed as a dependent of the taxpayer if the child has the same principal place of abode as the taxpayer for the year and is a member of the taxpayer's household (provided that the taxpayer is a U.S. citizen or national).

"Tie-Breakers" to Determine Who Gets the Exemption

The rules can result in situations where more than one taxpayer is able to claim an individual as a dependent. So, the law provides tie-breaking rules. First, if only one of the taxpayers eligible to claim an individual as a dependent is a parent of that individual, the parent is entitled to the exemption. This can occur, for example, where both a grandparent and a parent are eligible. Second, if a child's parents don't file a joint return, and each of them is eligible to claim the child as a dependent, the parent with whom the child resided for the longer period of time during the year gets the exemption. If that amount of time is equal, then the parent with the greater amount of AGI for the year gets the exemption. Third, if the child or other individual is not claimed as a dependent by either of his or her parents, and other taxpayers are able to claim the individual as a dependent, then the taxpayer with the highest AGI for the year gets the exemption. Note that these rules will apply where more than one taxpayer attempts to claim an exemption for the same person. Eligible taxpayers are generally free to agree among themselves who will claim a dependency exemption for an individual who can be claimed by more than one taxpayer.

"Phaseout" Rule for Personal and Dependency Exemptions

Another "phaseout" provision applies to the personal and dependency exemptions of upper-income taxpayers.

For 2017, the dollar amount of each available exemption is phased out in increments of 2 percent of the exemption amount for taxpayers with income above specified threshold levels. All the taxpayer's personal and dependency exemptions are phased out simultaneously, rather than sequentially or "one by one." The threshold income levels for the phaseout are based on adjusted gross income, are indexed annually for inflation, and vary according to the filing status of the taxpayer.

The AGI amounts at which the phaseout begins and at which the phaseout is maximized are as follows for 2017:

Table 4-2: AGI Phaseout Amounts		
Filing Status	**AGI Threshold Phaseout Amount**	**AGI Amount at Which Phaseout is Maximized**
Married filing jointly	$313,800	$436,300
Head of household	$287,650	$410,150
Single	$261,500	$384,000
Married filing separately	$156,900	$218,150

Each personal and dependency exemption otherwise allowable to a taxpayer is phased out by 2 percent of each $2,500 or any fraction of $2,500 by which AGI is in excess of the threshold phaseout amount. The term "any fraction of $2,500" essentially means that the first dollar of each $2,500 increment of AGI above the threshold phaseout amount results in the loss of 2 percent of the exemption amount. For example, a taxpayer with AGI of $2,501 above the threshold amount would lose 4 percent of the exemption amount for all personal and dependency exemptions. For married persons filing separately, the exemption deduction is reduced by 2 percent for each $1,250 or any fraction of $1,250 by which AGI exceeds the beginning of the phaseout amount.

Example

Louise and Don McGill are married and file a joint return for 2017. This year, their adjusted gross income is $436,302. Except for their income level, they would be entitled to two personal exemptions on their return. Because of their income level, their exemption amount is phased out by 2 percent for each $2,500 or fraction thereof by which their AGI exceeds $313,800. The range of income over which their exemption amount is reduced is $122,502 ($436,302 − $313,800). This amount is equal to $2,500 × 49, plus $1 under the fractional rule. The first 49 increments of $2,500 of AGI over the threshold amount reduce their exemption by 98 percent. The next dollar of income increases the phaseout percentage to 100 percent. Since the McGills' AGI of $436,302 is in excess of the phaseout completion amount of $436,300, they have reached the 100 percent phaseout percentage.

Other Phaseout Rules

Phaseout rules essentially increase the effective rate of income tax on upper-income taxpayers. Many taxpayers are subject to more than one phaseout. The loss of these tax benefits results in additional increments of the taxpayer's income being taxed at effective rates higher than the marginal rate of tax imposed by the Internal Revenue Code, so long as the taxpayer's income is still within the ranges of income at which tax benefits are being phased out.

In addition to the marginal rate of tax imposed by the rate system as discussed below, taxpayers are also losing deductions (and/or credits) with each additional increment of income that results in phaseouts. Therefore the actual effective tax rate on the increments of income that result in the phaseout of tax benefits may be significantly higher than the statutory marginal rate.

Phaseouts have become widespread in the tax law. Many of them will be covered in later chapters of this text. Some of the other tax benefits that are subject to variations of the phaseout concept are as follows:

- tax credit for children

- tax credits for higher education
- deductible IRA contributions
- tax credit for adoption expenses
- "active participation" exception to the passive loss rules
- exclusion for certain income from U.S. savings bonds used for higher education
- deduction for interest on qualified higher education loans
- tax credit for child-care expenses
- earned income credit

The above list, although not all inclusive, is indicative of how Congress has become enamored with the phaseout concept in the income tax law.

Divorced or Separated Parents

The general rule for claiming a dependency exemption for a child of divorced or separated parents is that the custodial parent is entitled to the dependency exemption. However, if the custodial parent signs a written declaration that he or she will not claim the child as a dependent for tax purposes (that is, "releases" the exemption), the noncustodial parent may claim the exemption if the written declaration is attached to his or her tax return. A "custodial parent" for this purpose is the parent who has custody of the child for the greater portion of the calendar year. This rule applies regardless of the general requirement that a "qualifying child" have the same principal place of abode as the taxpayer.

Multiple Support Agreements

There is a special rule for certain situations in which no one individual provides over half of a qualifying relative's support. The most common example of such a situation is probably where siblings provide combined support to an elderly parent. Normally, each individual providing support would be entitled to claim the dependent for tax purposes, except that the "more than half" support test is not met by any one individual providing support. The rule for such cases is that an individual who contributed more than 10 percent of the dependent's support for the year and who is entitled to claim the exemption except for the support test may claim the dependency exemption. However, every other individual who provided more than 10 percent of the dependent's support (and is also eligible to claim the exemption except for the support test) must file a written declaration with the IRS stating that he or she will not claim the dependency exemption.

TAX RATES AND FILING STATUS

LO 4.3   Explain how tax liability is determined.

Tax Rates and Brackets

Once taxable income has been determined, tax rates are applied to determine the individual's tentative income tax liability. That liability may then be reduced by any tax credits for which the taxpayer is eligible. For taxpayers other than corporations, there are seven sets of tax rates that differ according to the taxpayer's filing status. For individuals, each filing status or set of rates includes different amounts of taxable income that are subject to each of the seven basic federal income tax rates under current law. The lowest tax rates are 10 and 15 percent. Under current law, the five other rates are 25, 28, 33, 35 and 39.6 percent.

The filing status for taxpayers other than corporations includes the following five groups:

- married taxpayers filing jointly
- unmarried heads of households
- unmarried or "single" taxpayers
- married taxpayers filing separately
- estates and trusts

The amount of taxable income subject to each tax rate for each filing status can be referred to as a tax "bracket." These brackets are indexed annually for inflation. For 2017, the tax brackets (also referred to as "tax rate schedules") for each filing status are shown in the Table 4-3.

Example

Garry and Karen are married taxpayers filing jointly. Their taxable income in 2017 is $500,700.

Their tax due is $143,508 computed as follows:

Since their taxable income of $500,700 places them in the "over $470,700 bracket," their marginal rate of tax is 39.6%. Their tax is the sum of $131,628 and 39.6% of $30,000 or $131,628 plus $11,880. Their average rate of taxation of $143,508 divided by their taxable income of $500,700 or 28.7% which is less than their marginal rate of 39.6%.

Table 4-3: Individual Tax Rate Schedules for 2017

Married filing joint returns and surviving spouses.

Married taxpayers filing joint returns and surviving spouses who can't use the tax tables compute their tax on the basis of the rates indicated below.

If taxable income is	The tax is
not over $18,650	10% of taxable income
over $18,650 but not over $75,900	$1,865.00 plus 15% of the excess over $18,650
over $75,900 but not over $153,100	$10,452.50 plus 25% of the excess over $75,900
over $153,100 but not over $233,350	$29,752.50 plus 28% of the excess over $153,100
over $233,350 but not over $416,700	$52,222.50 plus 33% of the excess over $233,350
over $416,700 but not over $470,700	$112,728.00 plus 35% of the excess over $416,700
over $470,700	$131,628 plus 39.6% of the excess over $470,700

Head of household.

Unmarried persons maintaining households who can't use the tax tables compute their tax on the basis of the rates indicated below.

If taxable income is	The tax is
not over $13,350	10% of taxable income
over $13,350 but not over $50,800	$1,335.00 plus 15% of the excess over $13,350
over $50,800 but not over $131,200	$6,952.50 plus 25% of the excess over $50,800
over $131,200 but not over $212,500	$27,052.50 plus 28% of the excess over $131,200
over $212,500 but not over $416,700	$49,816.50 plus 33% of the excess over $212,500
over $416,700 but not over $444,550	$117,202.50 plus 35% of the excess over $416,700
over $444,550	$126,950.00 plus 39.6% of the excess over $444,550

Single individuals.

Taxpayers who aren't married *at year's end* and who don't qualify as surviving spouses or heads of household, and certain married taxpayers living apart compute their tax under the following tax rates for single persons if they can't use the tax tables.

If taxable income is	The tax is
not over $9,325	10% of taxable income
over $9,325 but not over $37,950	$932.50 plus 15% of the excess over $9,325
over $37,950 but not over $91,900	$5,226.25 plus 25% of the excess over $37,950
over $91,900 but not over $191,650	$18,713.75 plus 28% of the excess over $91,900
over $191,650 but not over $416,700	$46,643.75 plus 33% of the excess over $191,650
over $416,700 but not over $418,400	$120,910.25 plus 35% of the excess over $416,700
over $418,400	$121,505.25 plus 39.6% of the excess over $418,400

Married filing separate returns.

Married taxpayers filing separate returns who can't use the tax tables compute their tax on the basis of the rates indicated below.

If taxable income is	The tax is

Table 4-3: Individual Tax Rate Schedules for 2017	
not over $9,325	10% of the taxable income
over $9,325 but not over $37,950	$932.50 plus 15% of the excess over $9,325
over $37,950 but not over $76,550	$5,226.25 plus 25% of the excess over $37,950
over $76,550 but not over $116,675	$14,876.25 plus 28% of the excess over $76,550
over $116,675 but not over $208,350	$26,111.25 plus 33% of the excess over $116,675
over $208,350 not over $235,350	$56,364 plus 35% of the excess over $208,350
over $235,350	$65,814 plus 39.6% of the excess over $235,350

Estates and trusts

If taxable income is	The tax is
not over $2,550	15% of taxable income
over $2,550 but not over $6,000	$382.50 plus 25% of the excess over $2,550
over $6,000 but not over $9,150	$1,245 plus 28% of the excess over $6,000
over $9,150 but not over $12,500	$2,127 plus 33% of the excess over $9,150
over $12,500	$3,232.50 plus 39.6% of the excess over $12,500

Note that these tax rate schedules are those which apply to ordinary income and not to capital gains of individual taxpayers. Qualified dividends are also subject to special tax rates.

Filing Status for Individual Taxpayers

Married Taxpayers Filing Jointly

Taxpayers who are married at the end of the tax year are generally permitted to file a joint return. A joint return may also be filed if one of the spouses dies during the tax year. A taxpayer who qualifies as a "surviving spouse" as discussed below is also eligible to file as a married taxpayer filing jointly. Since the Supreme Court decision in *Windsor*, the term spouse now includes same-sex partners so long as the marriage was performed in a "state of celebration." Should the couple then move to a state not recognizing same-sex marriage, their Federal tax status remains married. If a couple has obtained a decree of divorce or of separate maintenance, neither partner is eligible to file jointly.

Married couples who file jointly are, as a general rule, jointly and severally liable for the tax due. However, if one of the spouses qualifies as an "innocent spouse" under a special set of rules, that spouse may be relieved of all or a portion of the liability to pay tax arising from the joint return.

Surviving Spouses

A surviving spouse is permitted to file and use the tax brackets applicable to joint returns for a period of 2 years beginning with the year following the year of the spouse's death. In order to qualify, the surviving spouse must maintain as his or her home a household that includes as a member of the household a son, stepson, daughter, or stepdaughter of the surviving spouse who is eligible to be claimed as the surviving spouse's dependent under the dependency exemption rules. The surviving spouse must furnish over half the cost of maintaining such a household.

Why would a surviving spouse wish to file as a married taxpayer filing jointly? The answer lies in the structure of the tax rate schedules. The tax rate schedules for joint returns produce the lowest tax payable for any one amount of income as compared with any other filing status. This is so because the brackets to which the lower income tax rates apply are larger for joint filers.

Head of Household Filing Status

The rate schedules applicable to an unmarried head of household are more beneficial than those for single taxpayers but not as beneficial as joint return rate schedules. The rules for qualifying as an unmarried head of household are somewhat complicated. These rules can be summarized using four basic components:

- the marital status requirement. The taxpayer must be unmarried at the close of the taxable year, unless the taxpayer's spouse was not a member of the household for the last 6 months of the tax year and the household includes a child for whom the taxpayer is eligible to claim a dependency exemption (a so-called "abandoned spouse"). Taxpayers who are legally separated under a decree of divorce or separate maintenance (other than an interlocutory decree) are not considered to be married. Taxpayers who qualify as surviving spouses under the rules discussed above will use joint return rate schedules and are not treated as heads of households.

- the household requirement. The taxpayer must maintain a household as his or her home and furnish over half the cost of maintaining that household during the taxable year. At least one "qualifying person" must be a member of this household.

- the "qualifying person" requirement. A person who qualifies an unmarried taxpayer (who pays more than half the cost of maintaining a household) for head of household filing status may be any ONE of the following examples:

  - a "qualifying child" of the taxpayer under the dependency exemption rules

  - a "qualifying relative" under the dependency exemption rules, provided that the relative lives in the taxpayer's household for more than half the year (not always required for dependency exemption purposes) AND provided that the "qualifying relative" is actually related to the taxpayer (i.e., a domestic partner or other unrelated dependent would not suffice), OR

-   a dependent parent not living with the taxpayer, for whom the taxpayer provides more than half the cost of providing a household

A release of the dependency exemption from the custodial parent to the noncustodial parent is ignored for purposes of determining head of household filing status. Adopted children are, of course, treated the same way as biological children.

-   the rule for parents. A parent may be a "qualifying person," even if the parent does not live in the taxpayer's household, if the taxpayer is eligible to claim a dependency exemption for the parent, and the taxpayer furnishes over half the cost of maintaining the parent's household. This makes it possible for unmarried taxpayers who pay for a parent's residence in a long-term care facility to be treated as heads of households.

Other Filers

The remaining types of filing status include single taxpayers, married taxpayers filing separately, and estates and trusts. The tax rate schedules applicable to estates and trusts are the most "compressed"; that is, the highest tax rates take effect at the lowest levels of taxable income for these taxpayers. Single taxpayers use rate schedules that are less compressed than those applicable to both marrieds filing separately and estates and trusts. Subchapter C corporations are subject to their own rate structure detailed in Chapter 18.

TAX CREDITS

After the tax has been computed on taxable income using the applicable filing status, the actual tax liability shown on the return may be reduced if the taxpayer qualifies for credits. Tax credits are dollar-for-dollar reductions in the actual tax owed; deductions, on the other hand, only reduce the amount of income subject to tax. Therefore credits are quite beneficial to taxpayers. Several significant tax credits may be available to individual taxpayers.

LO 4.4   **Explain what is meant by the kiddie tax.**

THE KIDDIE TAX

One popular tax planning strategy is the shifting of income to a taxpayer who is subject to a lower marginal rate. Since parents generally have more income than young children, investment assets are often transferred to children by parents in order to gain the benefit of lower marginal tax rates. Custodial accounts or certain trusts can be used for this purpose.

kiddie tax

Under current tax law, however, this planning strategy is significantly curtailed. Families are prevented from shifting large amounts of unearned income to children and making the shift effective for income tax purposes. The provision that limits such income shifting is referred to as the **kiddie tax**.

The mechanics of the kiddie tax are essentially as follows:

- If a child who is under the age of 18 at the end of the tax year, or 18 or 19 but under the age of 24, and a full time student with unearned income above a specified amount, the excess is taxed at the highest marginal rate applicable to the child's parents for the year rather than at the child's marginal rate. The child's excess unearned income above the specified amount is called "net unearned income." The specified amount is the amount of a dependent child's regular standard deduction ($1,050 as adjusted for inflation in 2017) plus another $1,050, or $2,100 for 2017. Therefore unearned income in excess of $2,100 is "net unearned income" and is taxed at the parents' rates in 2017.

- This prevention of the income-shifting technique generally applies to income generated by any asset the child owns, regardless of whether the asset was received from the child's parents or from another source. It also applies regardless of when any income-producing assets were transferred to the child. If the income is unearned and is included in the child's taxable income, it is subject to these rules. However, an important exception applies to income from certain disability trusts that are qualified under Social Security laws. Income from such trusts is treated as earned income under the kiddie tax rules, so the kiddie tax does not apply to such income.

- The additional tax paid with the child's return is equal to the difference between the tax payable at the child's rates and the amount of tax the parents would have paid on the net unearned income if it had been included on the parents' return. If more than one child in the same family has net unearned income, the total net unearned income is added together to determine the total tax on the income. Then the additional tax payable is allocated to the children's returns on a pro-rata basis. Instead of paying the kiddie tax on the child's return, the parents may elect to include the income of the child on their own return. This election can be made if the child has no income other than dividends and interest, and if such income is more than $1,050 and less than $10,500 (as adjusted for inflation for 2017). In addition, there can be no withholding or estimated tax payments using the child's Social Security number for the parents to be eligible for this election.

- The kiddie tax rules apply only if the child's earned income for the year does not exceed 50 percent of his or her support.

- The kiddie tax applies only if the child has at least one parent living at the end of the taxable year.

- The kiddie tax does not apply if the child is married and files a joint return with his or her spouse.

- The rules become a bit more complicated if a child has both earned and unearned income. Dependent children are entitled to a standard deduction equal to the greater of $1,050 in 2017 or the amount of the child's earned income plus $350, up to the regular standard deduction amount. If a child has both earned and unearned income, up to $1,050 of the child's standard deduction is allocated to unearned income first. The next $1,050 of unearned income is taxed at the child's marginal rate. Any remaining standard deduction allowable to the child is allocated to the child's earned income.

- If the child's unearned income includes qualified dividends subject to a maximum tax rate of 20 percent, the child will be taxed at the maximum 20 percent rate rather than the otherwise available lower rates if the parents' highest marginal rate on ordinary income exceeds 20 percent.

Example 1

Kyle Bradford is 10 years old. He lives with his mother, Melody, who is unmarried. This year, he has $5,700 in earned income from doing work for neighbors, and $3,200 in interest income from a custodial bank account. Kyle's standard deduction is $6,050 which is the greater of $1,050 or the sum of earned income of $5,700 and $350. Kyle's taxable income is $2,850 the difference between his total income of $8,900 and his standard deduction of $6,050. The amount of this taxable income taxed at his parent's rate is $1,100 yielding at tax of $385. The remaining $1,750 of taxable income is taxed at Kyle's marginal rate of 10 percent yielding a tax of $175. Kyle's total income tax owed is $560 ($385 + $175).

Example 2

Jimmy Smith is 17 years old and is claimed as a dependent by his parents. Jimmy's sole source of income for the current year is $3,200 of interest income. His parents are in the 35 percent income tax bracket. His taxable income is $2,150 ($3,200 interest income – $1,050 standard deduction) and his net unearned income is $1,100 ($3,200-$2,100 [$1,050 + $1,050]). His tax is $490 ($105 [$1,050 × 10 percent] plus $385 [$1,100 × 35% percent]). The first $1,050 is taxed at Jimmy's tax rate of 10 percent, with the balance of his $1,100 in taxable income taxed at the parental rate of 35 percent.

LO 4.5   Explain the due dates for filing income tax returns.

DUE DATES FOR FILING INCOME TAX RETURNS

Tax returns other than returns of a corporation are generally due on or before the fifteenth day of the fourth month following the close of the taxable year. Taxpayers whose tax year is the calendar year (including almost all individual taxpayers) are therefore required to file tax returns by April 15. Individuals can receive an automatic 6-month extension by filing Form 4868 on or before the due date. However, this is an extension of the due date for filing a return and not an extension of the time for payment of tax. Therefore any tax due with the return should be paid with Form 4868 to avoid interest and penalty charges.

Effective 2015, C corporations are generally required to file returns on or before the fifteenth day of the fourth month following the close of the taxable year. C corporations file Form 1120. Therefore a corporation using the calendar year as its tax year would be required to file its return by April 15. However, some C corporations may have a tax year that operates on a 12-month period other than the calendar year. For example, the tax year might begin on April 1 and end on March 31. If so, the C corporation's return would be due on July 15. In addition, similar to individuals, corporations can receive an automatic 6-month extension by filing Form 7004 on or before the original due date of the return. Like individuals, this is an extension to file the return, and not an extension to remit any tax due.

S corporations, though not owing income tax, must file a Form 1120S which is due the 15th day of the third month after the close of the tax year.

CHAPTER REVIEW

Key Terms and Concepts

adjusted gross income (AGI)   taxable income
above-the-line deductions   kiddie tax
below-the-line deductions

Review Questions

Review questions are based on the learning objectives in this chapter. Thus a [4.3] at the end of a question means that the question is based on learning objective 3. If there are multiple objectives, they are all listed.

1. a. What is "adjusted gross income"?

    b. List several items that are deductible from gross income in determining adjusted gross income. [4.1]

2. What is the standard deduction and how is it used? [4.2]

3. Explain how the standard deduction available to a taxpayer who is the dependent of another taxpayer is limited. [4.2]

4. Explain the additional amounts that increase the standard deduction for aged and blind taxpayers. [4.2]

5. a. Explain when and how a taxpayer's itemized deductions are limited or phased out when the taxpayer's adjusted gross income exceeded a certain level.

    b. What itemized deductions are not subject to the phaseout rule? [4.2]

6. a. How is the personal exemption amount determined each year?

    b. Does the fact that a taxpayer is the dependent of another for tax purposes affect the availability of a personal exemption? Explain. [4.2]

7. a. Explain how a dependency exemption is treated on a tax return.

    b. Who may a taxpayer claim as a dependent for tax purposes? [4.2]

8. Describe the "tie-breakers" that determine what taxpayer is entitled to claim a dependency exemption for an individual. [4.2]

9. Explain how a taxpayer's personal and dependency exemptions are phased out when the taxpayer's adjusted gross income exceeds a certain level. [4.2]

10. Explain how the phasing out of a deduction or tax credit can combine to change the effective marginal tax rates of individual taxpayers. [4.2]

11. Explain the rules for divorced and separated parents with regard to the dependency exemption. [4.2]

12. How many basic federal income tax rates are there? [4.3]

13. What are the five different filing statuses for taxpayers other than corporations? [4.3]

14. What is the general rule regarding the liability of spouses for payment of tax due with respect to a joint return? [4.3]

15. a. Explain the rules for filing a tax return as a "surviving spouse."

    b. For how many years may this category be claimed? [4.3]

16. How may a taxpayer qualify under the category of "head of household"? [4.3]

17. What tax-avoidance technique is the kiddie tax designed to prevent? [4.4]

18. Explain the mechanics of the kiddie tax. [4.4]

19. Does the kiddie tax generally apply to income generated by assets gifted to a child by his or her grandparents? Explain. [4.4]

20. What is the due date for filing individual income tax returns? [4.5]

Review Answers

1. a. The calculation of an individual taxpayer's adjusted gross income (AGI) is an intermediate step in the process of determining taxable income. To ascertain AGI, certain deductions are subtracted from the taxpayer's gross income. These deductions are referred to as "above-the-line" deductions and are available regardless of whether the taxpayer claims "itemized" deductions. Above-the-line deductions reduce AGI, which is one of the most important tax planning objectives for individual taxpayers because if AGI exceeds certain specified amounts, many tax benefits are either reduced or "phased out."

    b. Above-the-line deductions generally relate to business or income-producing activities of the taxpayer. Although not an all-inclusive list, the following are several of the more important above-the-line deductions claimed by individual taxpayers:

- deductible contributions to pension and profit-sharing plans of self-employed individuals
- deductible alimony payments
- deductible moving expenses
- contributions to medical savings accounts or health savings accounts
- deductible contributions to IRAs
- deductible interest payments made on qualified education loans
- penalties or other forfeitures resulting from premature withdrawals from time savings accounts or deposits

The textbook also lists additional items.

2.   The standard deduction is a specified amount, indexed annually for inflation, that may be claimed in calculating taxable income by taxpayers who do not itemize their deductions. The amount of the taxpayer's standard deduction is based on filing status. Increased amounts are available for blind taxpayers and taxpayers aged 65 and over. In choosing between itemizing deductions and taking the standard deduction, the typical taxpayer would opt to itemize if the total amount of such deductions exceeds the applicable standard deduction.

3.   Dependents are not eligible to claim the regular standard deduction amounts on their own tax returns. The special standard deduction amount allowable on a dependent's tax return is the greater of a specified dollar amount, or a smaller dollar amount plus the dependent's earned income for the year (but not more than the regular standard deduction amount). The dollar amounts are indexed annually for inflation.

4.   A special rule applies to taxpayers who are 65 years of age or older and/or are legally blind. Such taxpayers (including dependents) are entitled to increase their standard deduction by specified amounts. For married taxpayers filing jointly, each spouse who qualifies may add the additional amount or amounts to the standard deduction claimed on the joint return.

5.   a.   If an individual taxpayer's AGI exceeds a specified threshold amount (that is indexed annually for inflation), his or her itemized deductions are reduced by 3 percent of the amount by which AGI exceeds the threshold amount. If itemized

deductions are reduced by the overall limitation, the reduction cannot exceed 80 percent of the total itemized deductions that are subject to the reduction.

b. The overall limitation on itemized deductions does not apply to deductions for medical expenses, investment interest expenses, casualty and theft losses, or allowable gambling losses. Moreover, the overall limitation on itemized deductions is applied only after the rules and limits for each specific itemized deduction have been applied. These specific rules include the 50 percent of AGI "ceiling" on charitable contributions, the dollar amount loan limits for qualified residence interest, and the 2 percent of AGI "floor" on most miscellaneous itemized deductions.

6. a. The personal exemption amount is indexed annually for inflation by applying an indexing factor to each year's exemption amount.

b. A taxpayer who may be claimed as a dependent of another taxpayer is not entitled to a personal exemption for himself or herself.

7. a. A taxpayer is entitled to claim one additional exemption for each individual who is a dependent of the taxpayer. This dependency exemption is allowable regardless of whether the taxpayer claims the standard deduction or itemizes deductions. Each exemption is the equivalent of a deduction from AGI for a specified amount (that is indexed annually for inflation). The amount is the same as the personal exemption amount.

b. A taxpayer may claim any individual as a dependent who meets the definition of either a "qualifying child" or a "qualifying relative." Such individuals must also meet the following additional requirements:

- First, the individual being claimed as a dependent may not claim any other individual as his or her own dependent for income tax purposes.

- Second, the individual being claimed as a dependent may generally not file a joint return with his or her spouse for the year.

- Third, an individual who is not a U.S. citizen or national generally cannot be claimed as a dependent unless that individual is a resident of either the United States or a country contiguous to the United States. However, a legally adopted child of the taxpayer (or one legally placed for adoption) can be claimed as a dependent of the taxpayer if the child has the same principal place of abode as the taxpayer for the year and is a member of the taxpayer's household (provided that the taxpayer is a U.S. citizen or national).

8. First, if only one of the taxpayers eligible to claim an individual is a parent of that individual, the parent is entitled to the exemption. This can occur, for example, where both a grandparent and a parent are eligible. Second, if a child's parents don't file a joint return, and each of them is eligible to claim the child as a dependent, the parent with whom the child resided for the longer period of time during the year gets the exemption. If that amount of time is equal, then the parent with the greater amount of adjusted gross income (AGI) for the year gets the exemption. Third, if the child or other individual is not claimed as a dependent by either of his or her parents, and other taxpayers are able to claim the individual as a dependent, then the taxpayer with the highest AGI for the year gets the exemption. Note that these rules will apply where more than one taxpayer attempts to claim an exemption for the same person.

9. Each personal and dependency exemption otherwise allowable to a taxpayer is phased out by 2 percent of each $2,500 or any fraction of $2,500 by which AGI is in excess of the threshold amount (the amount is $1,250 for married taxpayers filing separately). The threshold income levels for the phaseout are based on AGI, are indexed annually for inflation, and vary according to the filing status of the taxpayer.

10. In addition to the marginal rate of tax imposed by the Code, taxpayers lose deductions (and/or credits) with each additional increment of income that results in phaseouts. Therefore the actual effective tax rate on the increments of income that result in the phaseout of tax benefits may be significantly higher than the statutory marginal rate.

11. The general rule for claiming a dependency exemption for a child of divorced or separated parents is that the custodial parent is entitled to the dependency exemption. However, if the custodial parent signs a written declaration that he or she will not claim the child as a dependent for tax purposes (that is, "releases" the exemption), the noncustodial parent may claim the exemption if the written declaration is attached to his or her tax return. A "custodial parent" for this purpose is the parent who has custody of the child for the greater portion of the calendar year. This rule applies regardless of the general requirement that a "qualifying child" have the same principal place of abode as the taxpayer.

12. There are seven basic federal income tax rates under current law. The lowest marginal tax rates are 10 and 15 percent. The highest marginal rate is currently 39.6 percent.

13. The filing status for taxpayers other than corporations includes the following five groups:

    • married taxpayers filing jointly
    • unmarried heads of households

- unmarried or single taxpayers
- married taxpayers filing separately
- estates and trusts

14. The general rule is that each spouse is jointly and severally liable for the tax payable with respect to a joint return. However, the "innocent spouse" rules may provide an exception to this treatment for a spouse who qualifies under those rules.

15. a. A "surviving spouse" is permitted to file and use the tax brackets applicable to joint returns. To qualify for joint return status, the surviving spouse must maintain a household that includes a son, stepson, daughter, or stepdaughter who is eligible to be claimed as a dependent under the dependency exemption rules. The surviving spouse must furnish over half the cost of maintaining the household.

    b. The surviving spouse may file under the joint return status for a period of 2 years, beginning with the year following the year of the spouse's death.

16. The rules for qualifying as an unmarried head of household can be briefly summarized as follows:

- the marital status requirement. The taxpayer must be unmarried at the close of the taxable year except when he or she is considered an abandoned spouse.
- the household requirement. The taxpayer must maintain a household and furnish over half the cost of doing so during the taxable year.
- the qualifying person requirement. A qualifying person must generally be a member of the taxpayer's household for more than one-half of the taxable year. That person must be either a "qualifying child" of the taxpayer under the dependency exemption rules, or a "qualifying relative" under those rules who is actually related to the taxpayer.
- the rule for parents. A parent may be a qualifying person, even if the parent does not live in the taxpayer's household but can still be claimed by the taxpayer as a dependent while living in a long-term care facility.

17. Since parents generally have more income than their young children, they desire to transfer investment assets to the children to gain the benefit of lower marginal tax rates. The "kiddie tax" is designed to prevent the parents from shifting large amounts of unearned income to their children and making the shift effective for income tax purposes.

18. The mechanics of the kiddie tax can be summarized as follows:

- If a child under a specified age has unearned income above a specified amount, the excess is taxed at the highest marginal rate applicable to the child's parents for the year rather than at the child's marginal rate.

- It applies to unearned income generated by any asset the child owns, regardless of when or by whom the asset was transferred to the child (except for income from certain qualified disability trusts).

- The additional tax paid with the child's return is equal to the difference between the tax payable at the child's rates and the amount of tax the parents would have paid on the net unearned income if it had been included on the parent's return.

- It applies only if a child has at least one parent living at the end of the taxable year.

- It does not apply if the child is married and files a joint return with his or her spouse.

- The rules become more complicated if a child has both earned and unearned income.

19. Yes, the kiddie tax rules call for net unearned income of children under a specified age to be taxed at the marginal rate of the parents, not just unearned income generated by assets received from the child's parents. Therefore income generated by assets gifted by grandparents is generally subject to the kiddie tax.

20. Individuals are generally required to file income tax returns by April 15, unless an extension is obtained.

Chapter 5

Items of Gross Income

Learning Objectives

An understanding of the material in this chapter should enable you to

LO 5.1   **Explain the tax treatment of payments in connection with separation or divorce.**

LO 5.2   **Explain the tax treatment of annuities.**

LO 5.3   **Explain the tax treatment of employee group life insurance.**

LO 5.4   **Explain the tax treatment of property transferred in connection with the performance of services.**

> [A] tax lawyer is a person who is good with numbers but does not have enough personality to be an accountant.
>
> —James D. Gordon III

The Internal Revenue Code contains many provisions that exclude specific items from the calculation of a taxpayer's gross income. These provisions are called exclusions. Many items of income may be partially includible in gross income and partially excludible from gross income. Alternatively, some items are either includible in or excludible from the taxpayer's gross income, depending on whether the circumstances under which the item was received meet the requirements of a specific exclusion rule. Many items are either partially includible in gross income or excludible only if they meet certain rules and definitions. For example, annuity payments are generally partially includible in gross income. Also, the value of employer-provided group life insurance coverage may be includible if certain requirements are not met or if the amount of the coverage exceeds a specified limit. As a result, this and the next chapter should be viewed together in developing a familiarity with the ways in which the Internal Revenue Code provides definitions and limitations for the taxation of certain items of income that are treated in special ways.

LO 5.1   **Explain the tax treatment of payments in connection with separation or divorce.**

PAYMENTS IN CONNECTION WITH SEPARATION OR DIVORCE

Alimony or Separate Maintenance Payments

alimony

The basic rule for **alimony** or separate maintenance payments is that they are includible in the gross income of the payee. Correspondingly, alimony payments includible in the gross income of the payee are deductible for income tax purposes from the gross income of the payer. The term "alimony or separate maintenance payments" means payments that are

- received by or on behalf of a spouse under a divorce or separation agreement

- not designated under the divorce or separation agreement as payments for the support of minor children, which are not includible in the gross income of the payee spouse and not deductible by the payer spouse

- not required under the divorce or separation agreement to be made for any period or in any other form after the death of the payee spouse and are not in fact so paid, and

- are made in cash or cash equivalent

In the case of spouses who are legally separated under a legal decree of divorce or of separate maintenance, in order for payments to qualify as alimony the payee spouse and the payer spouse must not be members of the same household at the time the payment is made.

Because of the requirement that alimony payments be made in cash, such benefits as rent-free occupancy of a home by one spouse and the couple's children will not be treated as alimony payments for tax purposes.

Excess "Front-Loading" of Alimony Payments

If a payer makes "excess" alimony payments, a special rule applies to include the excess payment in the gross income of the payer beginning in the third post separation year. At first glance, it seems illogical to include a payment in the income of the taxpayer who made the payment. However, the inclusion of an excess payment in the payer's income eliminates the prior tax benefit of the deduction that was claimed for the payment before it was characterized as an excess payment since payments made as part of divorce property settlements are not deductible. Correspondingly, if there is an "excess" alimony payment includible in the payer's income, the payee spouse receives a deduction for such amount that was previously included in his or her gross income to balance the tax treatment of the excess payment. The purpose of these rules is to prevent taxpayers from characterizing property settlements as alimony for tax purposes.

The calculation of an "excess" alimony payment is based on the relative amounts of the payments made during the first three post separation years. In computing the "excess" alimony payment, one starts with the second-year payment. To the extent that the second year's payment exceeds the combination of the third post-separation year's payment plus $15,000, the excess is classified as an "excess alimony payment" and added to the income of the payer. In addition, for the first post-separation tax year, the "excess" payment is computed by taking the average of the alimony payments in the second and third post-separation years (as adjusted for any recapture from the second year's payment) and adding $15,000 to that figure. Any alimony payment for the first post separation year that is in excess of that amount is the "excess alimony payment." The combination of the second- and first-year payment calculations represent the total "excess alimony payment" included in the income of the payer and deductible by the payee in the third post-separation year.

Example

Roberta has paid her former husband, Bobby, alimony in each of the 3 years since their divorce settlement. In the first year Roberta paid Bobby $100,000 and deducted that amount on her tax return. Bobby included the $100,000 in his gross income for that year. In the second post separation year, the payment was $60,000. In the third year, it was $25,000. The second-year payment exceeds the third-year payment plus $15,000 by $20,000. The average of the payments for the second and third post separation years is $32,500 ([$60,000 + $25,000 – $20,000] ÷ 2). To this amount is added $15,000 for a total of $47,500. Any alimony payment in excess of $47,500 for the first year is an excess payment. Therefore Roberta's excess alimony payment for the first post separation year is $52,500 ($100,000 – $47,500). Roberta will have to include $72,500 in her income in the third post separation year. Bobby will receive a corresponding deduction in that year to equalize the tax treatment of the excess alimony payment.

If either spouse dies before the end of the third post separation year, or if either spouse remarries before the end of that year and payments cease as a result of such event, then the front-loading rules for excess alimony payments do not apply.

Treatment of Child Support Payments

child support

As stated above, payments for support of minor children are not treated as alimony for tax purposes. Such payments are not deductible by the payer spouse and not includible in the gross income of the payee spouse. Payments are treated as **child support** to the extent that the terms of the applicable divorce or separation agreement fix or designate them as such. For purposes of this rule, a provision in the agreement calling for a reduction in total payments based on certain specified contingencies relating to a child is considered to be designating such payments as child support. These contingencies include a reduction in payments happening at the time or associated with the time when a child attains a specified age, marries, leaves school, or dies. The amount of the reduction in the payment that would result from the occurrence of one of these contingencies under the agreement is the amount treated as child support for tax purposes. The remainder is considered alimony.

The application of the terms of the divorce agreement to fix certain payments as child support provides certainty for planning for the tax consequences of periodic payments. Under these rules, both parties can be confident of the applicable tax treatment. In fact, the divorce or separation agreement may also provide that payments that are not child support under the contingency rules will not be treated as alimony for tax purposes. The tax law respects such a characterization according to the intent of the parties. Therefore spouses can basically choose whether or not they wish to have payments deductible by the payer and taxable to the payee.

Use of Life Insurance Arrangements in Property Settlements

life insurance and divorce

Life insurance contracts will often be involved in property settlement agreements incident to a divorce. The protection afforded by life insurance coverage may be an important component of the settlement. Perhaps the most common arrangement is to transfer the ownership of an existing life policy that insures the life of one spouse to the other spouse. The transfer of the policy itself does not have income tax consequences for either spouse regardless of the policy's cash value. Such a transfer is neither alimony nor child support but a nontaxable transfer of property incident to a divorce. However, if the spouse who transferred the policy is obligated to continue to pay premiums on the transferred policy, the payment of such premiums is generally treated as an alimony payment. The same is true for premiums paid on other insurance coverages that benefit the other spouse.

The transfer of a life insurance policy will not cause the subsequent payment of death benefits to be subject to income tax under the "transfer-for-value" rule. Transfers incident to divorce are not subject to the transfer for value rule. Therefore such death benefits retain their income-tax-free character.

Alternatively, the ownership of an existing policy might be retained by the insured spouse, while premium payments continue to be made by the policyowner spouse with the other spouse named as policy beneficiary. In such a case, the payments of the premiums by the policyowner spouse are not alimony payments and are not deductible. Clearly, the ownership rights of the insured spouse may be compromised by a provision in the divorce agreement requiring him or her to pay premiums and/or to maintain the other spouse as the death beneficiary under the policy. Even so, the payment of premiums in such a situation does not constitute alimony payments. As in the case of a transferred policy, a subsequent payment of death benefits from a policy under such an arrangement will not be subject to income tax under the transfer-for-value rule.

A third possible arrangement is to set up a new life insurance policy that insures the life of one spouse and is owned by the other spouse. The policyowner spouse can pay premiums on the new policy and have death benefit protection in the event of the former spouse's death. A portion of alimony payments received from the former spouse could be used to fund the premium obligation.

LO 5.2   Explain the tax treatment of annuities.

INCOME TAXATION OF ANNUITIES

Introduction

Annuities may be a significant part of an individual's comprehensive financial plan. There are special income tax rules that apply to annuity contracts. These rules are derived from the unique nature of these contracts and the ways that they are used to enhance wealth accumulation. In this text, the discussion will focus on nonqualified commercial annuities, that is, annuity contracts issued by commercial insurers that are not used in connection with a qualified plan of deferred compensation.

annuity

An **annuity** may be defined as a systematic liquidation of a sum of money, including a principal amount and an interest element, over either a period of time determined by reference to the life expectancy of one or more individuals or a fixed period of time. A commercial annuity involves the payment of one or more premiums by the contract owner to an insurance company in return for the company's obligation to make annuity payments to one or more contract beneficiaries or "annuitants" at either a specified or an unspecified time in the future.

The taxation of the actual annuity payments under the contract is subject to specific tax rules. In addition, such payments are typically deferred for some period of time after the inception of the contract, either until the annuitant reaches a specified age or for some period thereafter at the discretion of the contract owner. During this period of "deferral," the funds in the contract are generally permitted to accumulate on a tax-deferred basis. However, if a withdrawal, loan, or other financial transaction involving the contract is done before the commencement of the stream of annuitized payments, additional tax rules apply to the transaction.

The general theory of annuity taxation involves the concept that the contract owner's capital investment in the contract may be recovered tax free when distributions are made. But the interest or other earnings on the contract funds must be subject to taxation at some point in time. When and how the earnings on the contract are taxed will be explained below.

The "Exclusion Ratio" for Annuitized Payments

The income taxation of a payment in the form of an annuity is determined by using a fraction called the "exclusion ratio." The numerator of the fraction is the amount of the "investment in the contract." The denominator of the fraction is the total "expected return" under the contract. The periodic annuity payment is multiplied by this fraction to calculate the portion of the payment that is received tax free by the annuitant as a return of the investment in the contract. The balance of the payment is taxable to the annuitant.

investment in the contract

The **investment in the contract** may be defined as the aggregate amount of premiums or other consideration paid for the contract minus any distributions already made from the contract that were excludible from the recipient's gross income as a return of capital.

expected return

The **expected return** under the contract may be defined as the total of the amounts that are expected to be received in the form of an annuity under the contract. If the annuity payment is calculated using the life expectancy of one or more annuitants, the expected return is calculated by reference to actuarial tables found in the Treasury regulations promulgated pursuant to IRC Sec. 72.

Under the regulations, there are tables used to determine life expectancy for annuity taxation purposes. One set of tables applies to annuity contracts that were fully funded before July 1986, and a second set of tables applies to contracts that are fully or partially paid for after June 1986. The tables provide "expected return multiples" expressed as the number of years that the annuitant is expected to live beginning as of the annuity starting date. The older tables differ depending on the gender of the annuitant, while the newer tables are unisex. Taxpayers who funded contracts before July 1986 may generally elect to compute their exclusion ratio under the newer unisex tables.

Example

Jay is 60 years old and is the owner and annuitant under a contract that begins annuitized payments this year. Jay will receive annuity payments for as long as he lives. His investment in the contract is $100,000. His life expectancy under the regulations is 24.2 years. His annuity payment will be $10,000 per year for life. The expected return under the contract is $242,000 ($10,000 × 24.2). Jay's exclusion ratio for the annuity payments is 41.32 percent ($100,000/$242,000). Therefore Jay may exclude from his gross income $4,132 of his $10,000 annuity payment each year. The $5,868 balance of the payment ($10,000 – $4,132) will be taxable to Jay.

Sometimes an annuity payment is made over a fixed period of time rather than for the annuitant's lifetime. If the payment of the annuity is to be made over a fixed period (such as a number of years), and assuming the number of years is less than the annuitant's life expectancy, the expected return under the contract is calculated by multiplying the amount of the annuity payment by the number of payments that are to be made.

Example

Suppose that in the example above Jay will receive the same annuity payments except that he will be paid over a fixed 20-year period rather than over his lifetime. Jay's expected return will be $200,000 ($10,000 annual payment × 20 years). Therefore his exclusion ratio will be 50 percent: $100,000 investment in the contract/$200,000 expected return.

The Small Business Jobs Act of 2010 amended Section 72 to authorize the partial annuitization of a nonqualified annuity (as well as an insurance or endowment contract). Effective for tax years beginning after December 31, 2010, a taxpayer will not be required to annuitize fully an annuity to avail himself or herself of an exclusion ratio.

Section 72(a) requires that the partial annuity be received for a period of "ten years or more or during one or more lives" of "any portion of an annuity, endowment or life insurance contract".

The investment in the annuity contract shall be allocated "pro rata" between the portion of the contract from which the annuity is paid and the portion of the contract "from which amounts are not received as an annuity." Partial annuitization could be an option for a taxpayer needing some income from an annuity, but still desiring continued tax-free growth on the remainder of the annuity.

Deduction for Unrecovered Investment in the Contract

If the annuitant lives beyond his or her period of life expectancy as determined under the regulations, no exclusion ratio is applied to payments received after the end of the life expectancy period. Therefore the full amount of payments received after the life expectancy period will be taxable. Correspondingly, if the annuitant dies after the stream of annuity payments begins but before the end of the life expectancy period, an income tax deduction may be claimed for the unrecovered amount of the investment in the contract. This deduction may be claimed on the annuitant's final income tax return. The "unrecovered investment" would be the total investment in the contract reduced by the total of all payments previously received under the contract that were excluded from gross income.

However, different rules apply to contracts with respect to which annuity payments commenced before January 1, 1987. For such contracts, there is no deduction available for an unrecovered investment at the annuitant's death. Therefore the tax benefit of the unrecovered investment is lost. However, a corresponding rule is more favorable: if the annuitant under such contracts lives beyond his or her life expectancy, the exclusion ratio is applied to payments for as long as the annuitant lives, making it possible for the annuitant to recover a total amount tax free that is more than the actual investment in the contract.

Refund or "Period Certain" Features

refund feature

10-year certain annuity

Some annuity contracts contain a **refund feature** providing that, in the event the annuitant dies after the stream of annuity payments has begun but before a specified number of annuity payments have been received, the annuitant's estate or designated beneficiary will receive the remainder of the specified number of payments. An example of this feature would be a so-called **10-year certain annuity** under which the annuitized payments, once begun, are guaranteed to be paid for at least 10 years.

Contracts that contain such refund features are subject to a special tax rule regarding the calculation of the investment in the contract for exclusion ratio purposes. In calculating the exclusion ratio, the actuarial value of the guarantee or "refund" feature must be subtracted from the amount paid for the contract to determine the "investment in the contract." This actuarial value is also calculated using the tables in the regulations. The investment in the contract, as adjusted, is then used to calculate the excludible portion of the annuity payment.

Example

Suppose that in the previous example, Jay's annuity is to be paid over his lifetime but also has a feature that guarantees that Jay or his designated beneficiary will receive a total of at least 10 annual annuity payments even if Jay dies during that time. Assume that the actuarial value of that guarantee, based on Jay's life expectancy, is $4,000. In calculating Jay's exclusion ratio for his annuity payments, his $100,000 investment in the contract must be reduced to $96,000 ($100,000 – $4,000). Therefore his exclusion ratio for a contract with this guarantee will be 39.67 percent ($96,000/$242,000).

Treasury Regulations 1.72-11(a) and 1.72-11(c) address the taxation of payments under a refund feature to a beneficiary after the primary annuitant has died on or before the annuity starting date. Distributions will not be taxed to the beneficiary so long as there remains an investment in the contract to be recovered. Once distributions exceed the investment in the contract, they will be taxed as ordinary income.

Certain guarantees provided by modern annuity contracts should be distinguished from the traditional refund feature or period-certain guarantee. For example, many annuity contracts provide for a repayment of premium paid (or premium plus interest) in the event the contract owner dies before annuity payments begin under the contract. Such a guarantee does not appear to be a "refund" feature for income tax purposes because it applies to the contract owner's death before annuitization of the contract rather than to the annuitant's death after the stream of annuity payments has begun. As a result, a guarantee that applies only in the event of the owner's death while the annuity is still in the deferral or accumulation stage would not reduce the investment in the contract for exclusion ratio purposes.

Annuity "Refund Features"
- Preannuitization guarantees are NOT treated as refund features.
- Rules apply to "period-certain" and similar traditional types of guaranteed payments.
- The actuarial value of refund feature reduces "investment in the contract," thereby increasing taxable portion of annuity payment.

Contracts with More than One Annuitant

joint and survivor annuity

Annuity payment arrangements may involve more than one annuitant. An annuity may be payable in a fixed amount over the life of an annuitant, then payable in the same amount after the first annuitant's death over the life of a second annuitant. For example, a married couple might receive a fixed payment for as long as either one of the spouses is still alive. This would be one type of **joint and survivor annuity** arrangement.

Another annuity arrangement could be the payment of a fixed amount to one annuitant followed by the payment of a lesser amount to a second annuitant for life after the first annuitant's death. A different type of arrangement would be where the annuity payments cease after the death of one of the annuitants. In each of these variations, the expected return under the contract can be calculated by using various tables contained in Treasury regulations.

In the case of an annuity under which an annuity payment is made to two annuitants while both are alive, then to the survivor in the same amount, the multiple for calculating expected return under the contract is found in table VI in the regulations pursuant to IRC Sec. 72.

> ### Example
>
> Howard and Janet, a married couple, will receive annual payments under an annuity contract beginning this year. They paid $40,000 for the contract and have taken no prior distributions from it. The annuity payment will be $2,200 per year for as long as either Howard or Janet is alive. Howard is 48 years old, and Janet is 50. Under table VI, their joint life expectancy is 40.2 years. Therefore their expected return under the contract is $88,440 ($2,200 × 40.2). Their applicable exclusion ratio is 45.23 percent ($40,000/$88,440). The excludible amount of their annual annuity payment will be $995 ($2,200 × .4523).

Special Rules for Variable Annuity Contracts

variable annuity

Variable annuities have become more popular in recent years. In a **variable annuity**, all or a substantial portion of the funds in the contract are placed in equity-based investments, such as publicly traded stocks and stock mutual funds. If the contract is annuitized and payments begin, the amount of the payments may vary according to the specific design of the contract, using a calculation based on the investment performance of the contract funds. As a result, the "expected return" under such a contract cannot be accurately calculated for purposes of determining an exclusion ratio for the annuity payments. Therefore the exclusion ratio calculation is not used to determine the taxation of the annuity payments under a variable contract. Rather, the investment in the contract is divided by the number of years of the annuitant's life expectancy to determine the dollar amount of each payment that is excludible from the annuitant's gross income.

Example

Tyler is the owner and annuitant under a variable annuity contract. Tyler's investment in the contract is $250,000. At the time that annual annuity payments commence, Tyler's life expectancy is 30 years. Therefore Tyler may exclude $8,333 of each annual payment from his gross income ($250,000/30).

Because the payments may be subject to fluctuations, it is possible that the amount of an annuity payment under a variable contract will be less than the amount of each payment that was determined to be excludible. In such cases, the entire payment will be excludible from gross income, and the "unused" portion of the excludible amount can be recovered later for income tax purposes by recomputing the annual dollar amount of the annuity payment that is excludible from gross income. The recomputation of the excludible amount can be made at the election of the annuitant and is accomplished by the following steps:

- The dollar amount of the exclusion that was not utilized is determined.

- The annuitant's life expectancy at the time of the recomputation is found by consulting the appropriate table in the regulations.

- An additional excludible amount is determined by dividing the amount of the unused exclusion by the life expectancy of the annuitant at the time of the election to recompute.

- The additional amount is then added to the original excludible amount to determine the adjusted excludible amount.

Example

Assume that in the previous example Tyler receives an annual annuity payment of $5,000. His excludible amount is $8,333, so the amount of his unused exclusion is $3,333 ($8,333 – $5,000). Tyler elects to recompute his excludible amount. At that time, he is 70 years old, and his life expectancy is 16 years. The additional excludible amount is $208 ($3,333/16). This additional amount is added to Tyler's original excludible amount ($8,333) to arrive at the adjusted excludible amount of $8,541.

Remember that unless the annuity starting date was on or before December 31, 1986, the annuitant cannot exclude a cumulative total of more than his or her total investment in the contract. Therefore, if the annuitant lives beyond his or her life expectancy, payments will be fully taxable once the annuitant has excluded a cumulative amount equal to the investment in the contract.

Withdrawals and Other Transactions during the "Accumulation" Period

Introduction

immediate annuities

deferred annuities

Some annuity contracts are so-called **immediate annuities**, that is, contracts in which annuity payments begin no later than one year from the date the annuity is purchased. However, the majority of contracts sold in the nonqualified market are **deferred annuities**, that is, contracts in which the annuity payments do not commence within one year. In many contracts, it is possible that actual annuitized payments will never be made. The contract owner may be purchasing the annuity primarily for the purpose of obtaining tax deferral of the funds accumulating within the contract. Of course, at some point in time the income earned on the contract funds will be taxed. If the owner never annuitizes the contract, rules apply upon the death of the contract owner that provide for the taxation of interest or other investment gains that have been realized within the annuity contract. In the meantime, it is possible for the contract owner to make partial withdrawals from the contract, borrow funds from the contract, or even surrender the contract and obtain its cash surrender value.

Amounts "Not Received As an Annuity"

LIFO (last-in, first-out) taxation

The funds in a deferred annuity contract accumulate free of income taxation until one of the following occurs: a loan, collateralization, or withdrawal from the contract; an annuitization of the contract; or the death of the contract owner. Partial withdrawals or loans from an annuity contract during the deferral or accumulation period are subject to different income tax rules than actual annuitized payments. Withdrawals and loans are treated as taxable events for income tax purposes. No exclusion ratio applies. The general rule is that the loan or withdrawal will be taxed to the extent of "income on the contract." "Income on the contract" is the amount by which the cash value of the contract (without regard to surrender charges) exceeds the owner's investment in the contract. This is, in effect, a form of **LIFO (last-in, first-out)** taxation in which the earnings on the contract are taxed before the investment in the contract can be recovered tax free as a return of capital.

Example

Anna owns a deferred annuity under which annuity payments have not commenced. Her investment in the contract is $125,000. The cash value of the contract is currently $160,000. Anna withdraws $25,000 from the contract. The income on the contract is $35,000 ($160,000 – $125,000). Therefore all of Anna's $25,000 withdrawal will be taxed because her withdrawal is less than the existing income on the contract.

This "income first" or "LIFO" rule of income taxation applies to annuity contracts that were funded after August 13, 1982. If a taxpayer owns a contract that was funded on or before August 13, 1982, "FIFO" (first-in, first-out) rather than LIFO taxation will apply to a withdrawal from the contract that is not in the form of an annuity payment. This means that the taxpayer will be able to treat the distribution as a nontaxable return of capital until the taxpayer's investment in the contract has been fully recovered.

Example

Assume the same facts as in the example above, except that Anna's annuity was fully funded before August 14, 1982. Her $25,000 withdrawal will be nontaxable as a partial return of her investment in the contract. However, her investment in the contract for purposes of determining an exclusion ratio when the contract is annuitized or for purposes of determining the tax treatment of future withdrawals will be reduced from $125,000 to $100,000 by the $25,000 nontaxable withdrawal.

Complete surrenders of annuity contracts are taxable to the extent that the cash value of the annuity exceeds the investment in the contract. However, in the case of a complete surrender of the contract, the taxpayer is permitted to reduce the cash value by any surrender charges in order to determine the taxable amount.

The 10 Percent Penalty for Premature Distributions

There is a 10 percent penalty tax that generally applies to amounts received from annuity contracts that

- are not received in the form of annuity payments and
- are received by a taxpayer who has not attained the age of 59½

This 10 percent penalty tax applies only to the portion of any withdrawal, loan, or collateral-ization of the contract that is taxable under the rules described above. It applies in addition to the regular income tax. It does not apply to any portion of the transaction that is treated as a nontaxable return of capital. In addition, the penalty tax does not apply to distributions that are part of a series of substantially equal periodic payments based on the taxpayer's life expectancy (that is, payments in the form of a life or joint life annuity). In addition to the life expectancy exception, the following types of distributions are also not subject to the 10 percent penalty tax:

- distributions allocable to an investment in the contract made before August 14, 1982
- distributions attributable to the disability of the recipient
- distributions under an immediate annuity contract
- distributions made on or after the death of the contract owner

These rules are similar but not identical to the 10 percent penalty rules applicable to certain distributions from qualified plans of deferred compensation and IRAs. Those rules are beyond the scope of this text.

Gifts of Annuity Contracts

Generally, a gift of an asset from one taxpayer to another involves transfer tax, but not income tax, consequences. The general rule for gifts is that the gift is not includible in the donee's gross income. However, when an annuity contract is transferred by gift, the donor of the annuity (not the donee) is subject to special income tax rules.

The first rule applies to contracts that were issued after April 22, 1987. If such contracts are gifted, the owner has a taxable event at the time of the gift. The amount taxable to the donor is the cash surrender value of the contract minus the investment in the contract. In essence, the gift is treated as a complete surrender followed by a gift of cash.

Example

Maxie owns an annuity contract with a cash surrender value of $100,000. His investment in the contract is $70,000. The contract was issued 5 years ago. Maxie gives the annuity to his brother, Jake. As a result of the gift, Maxie must include $30,000 ($100,000 – $70,000) in his gross income for the year in which the gift is made.

A second rule applies to gifts of annuity contracts that were issued on or before April 22, 1987. For such contracts, the donor does not have a taxable event at the time of the gift. However, if the donee later surrenders the contract, the donor will be taxed on an amount equal to the difference between the cash surrender value and the investment in the contract as of the time of the prior gift (not as of the time of surrender). The balance of the gain upon surrender of the contract will be taxable to the donee.

Although other exceptions apply (i.e., transfers between spouses), these rules make it important to remember that transfers of annuity contracts for less than adequate consideration can result in income tax problems as well as gift tax problems.

The "Non-Natural Person" Rule

There is another special income tax rule that prospective purchasers of annuity contracts should be aware of. It is referred to as the "non-natural person" rule. This rule provides that a deferred annuity contract held by an owner other than a human being (such as a trust or business entity) will generally not be treated as an annuity for income tax purposes. If the rule applies, the tax deferral feature of the annuity will be lost, and the income earned on the contract will be taxed each year to the contract owner, regardless of whether any distributions from the contract are made. This is clearly an undesirable result. In almost all cases a deferred annuity contract should not be placed with an owner that would violate the non-natural person rule.

Fortunately, the rule does have some exceptions. It does not apply in the following situations:

- where the contract is owned by the estate of a deceased annuity owner
- where the annuity contract is an immediate annuity
- where the annuity contract is owned by an IRA or a qualified plan of deferred compensation
- where the entity owns the annuity as an "agent for a natural person." The "agent for a natural person" exception has been approved by the IRS in the case of annuity ownership by various types of trusts, including, but not limited to, single beneficiary trusts and certain trusts that are "grantor" trusts for income tax purposes. Any situation in which trust ownership is proposed for an annuity should be reviewed by a competent tax professional to evaluate the application of the non-natural person rule.

LO 5.3   Explain the tax treatment of employee group life insurance.

GROUP TERM LIFE INSURANCE

Introduction

The growth of group life insurance has been greatly influenced by the favorable income tax treatment afforded it under federal tax laws. This chapter discusses the effects of these tax laws on basic group term insurance, coverages that may be added to a basic group term insurance contract, and group life insurance with permanent benefits. A complete explanation of the federal income tax laws pertaining to group life insurance, as well as their interpretation by the Internal Revenue Service, would be lengthy and is beyond the scope of this chapter. Consequently, this discussion only highlights these laws.

Deductibility of Premiums

In general, employer contributions for an employee's group term insurance coverage are fully deductible to the employer under Sec. 162 of the Internal Revenue Code as an ordinary and necessary business expense as long as the overall compensation of the employee is reasonable. The reasonableness of compensation (which includes wages, salary, and other fringe benefits) is usually only a potential issue for the owners of small businesses or the stockholder-employees of closely held corporations. Any compensation that is determined by the Internal Revenue Service to be unreasonable may not be deducted by a firm for income tax purposes. In addition, the Internal Revenue Code does not allow a firm to take an income tax deduction for contributions (1) that are made on behalf of sole proprietors or partners under any circumstances or (2) that are made on behalf of stockholders, unless they are providing substantial services to the corporation. Finally, no deduction is allowed under Sec. 264 of the Internal Revenue Code if the employer is named as beneficiary.

Contributions by any individual employee are considered payments for personal life insurance and are not deductible for income tax purposes by that employee. Thus the amount of any payroll deductions authorized by an employee for group term insurance purposes are included in the employee's taxable income.

Income Tax Liability of Employees

In the absence of tax laws to the contrary, the amount of any compensation for which an employer receives an income tax deduction (including the payment of group insurance premiums) represents taxable income to the employee. However, Sec. 79 of the Internal Revenue

Code provides favorable tax treatment to employer contributions for life insurance that qualifies as group term insurance.

Sec. 79 Requirements

In order to qualify as group term insurance under Sec. 79, life insurance must meet the following conditions:

- It must provide a death benefit excludible from federal income tax.

- It must be provided to a group of employees. A group of employees is defined to include all employees of an employer. If all employees are not covered, membership must be determined on the basis of age, marital status, or factors relating to employment.

- It must be provided under a policy carried directly or indirectly by the employer. This includes (1) any policy for which the employer pays any part of the cost or (2) if the employer pays no part of the cost, any policy arranged by the employer if at least one employee is charged less than his or her cost (under Table I, discussed below) and at least one other employee is charged more than his or her cost. If no employee is charged more than the Table I cost, a policy is not group term insurance for purposes of Sec. 79. A policy is defined to include a master contract of a group of individual policies. The term "carried indirectly" refers to those situations where the employer is not the policyowner, but rather provides coverage to employees through master contracts issued to organizations such as negotiated trusteeships or multiple-employer trusts.

- The plan must be arranged in such a manner as to preclude individual selection of coverage amounts. However, it is acceptable to have alternative benefit schedules based on the amount an employee elects to contribute. Supplemental plans where an employee is given a choice, such as either 1, 1½, or 2 times salary, are considered to fall within this category.

All life insurance that qualifies under Sec. 79 as group term insurance is considered a single plan of insurance, regardless of the number of insurance contracts used. For example, an employer might provide coverage for union employees under a negotiated trusteeship, for other employees under an individual employer group insurance contract, and additional coverage for top executives under a group of individual life insurance policies. Under Sec. 79 these constitute a single plan. This plan must be provided for at least 10 full-time employees at some time during the calendar year. For purposes of meeting the 10-life requirement, employees who have not satisfied any required waiting periods may be counted as participants. In addition, employees who have elected not to participate are also counted as participants—but only if they would not have been required to contribute to the cost of other benefits besides group term insurance if they had participated. As described later, a plan with fewer than 10 full-time employees may still qualify for favorable tax treatment under Sec. 79 if more restrictive requirements are met.

Exceptions to Sec. 79

Even when all the previous requirements are met, there are some situations in which Sec. 79 does not apply. In some cases different sections of the Internal Revenue Code provide alternative tax treatment. For example, when group term insurance is issued to the trustees of a qualified pension plan and is used to provide a death benefit under the plan, the full amount of any life insurance paid for by employer contributions results in taxable income to the employee.

There are three situations in which employer contributions for group term insurance do not result in taxable income to an employee, regardless of the amount of insurance: (1) if an employee has terminated employment because of disability; (2) if a qualified charity (as determined by the Internal Revenue Code) has been named as beneficiary for the entire period during the tax year for which the employee receives insurance; or (3) if the employer has been named as beneficiary for the entire year.

Coverage on retired employees is subject to Sec. 79, and these persons are treated in the same manner as active employees. Thus they will have taxable income in any year in which the amount of coverage received exceeds $50,000. However, a grandfather clause to this rule stipulates that it does not apply to group term life insurance plans (or to comparable successor plans or to plans of successor employers) in existence on January 1, 1984, for covered employees who (1) retired before 1984 or (2) were at least 55 years of age before 1984 and were employed by the employer any time during 1983. In such situations, the value of coverage is not taxed at all. This grandfather clause does not apply to persons retiring after 1986 if a plan is discriminatory.

General Tax Rules

Under Sec. 79 the cost of the first $50,000 of coverage is not taxed to the employee. Since all group term insurance that qualifies under Sec. 79 is considered one plan, this exclusion applies only once to each employee. For example, an employee who has $10,000 of coverage under a policy for all employees and $75,000 of coverage under a separate insurance policy for executives would have a single $50,000 exclusion. The cost of coverage in excess of $50,000, minus any employee contributions for the entire amount of coverage, represents taxable income to the employee. For purposes of Sec. 79, the cost of this excess coverage is determined by a government table called the Uniform Premium Table I. This table will often result in a lower cost than would be calculated by using the actual premium paid by the employer for the coverage.

To calculate the cost of an employee's coverage for one month of protection under a group term insurance plan, the Uniform Premium Table I cost shown for the employee's age bracket (based on the employee's attained age at the end of the tax year) is multiplied by the number of thousands in excess of 50 of group term insurance on the employee.

Table 5-1: Uniform Premium Table	
Age	**Cost per Month per $1,000 of Coverage**
Under 25	$0.05
25–29	0.06
30–34	0.08
35–39	0.09
40–44	0.1
45–49	0.15
50–54	0.23
55–59	0.43
60–64	0.66
65–69	1.27
70 and over	2.06

Example

An employee, aged 57, is provided with $150,000 of group term insurance. The employee's monthly cost (assuming no employee contributions) would be calculated as follows:

Coverage provided	$150,000
Minus Sec. 79 exclusion	– 50,000
Amount subject to taxation	$100,000
Uniform Premium Table I monthly cost per $1,000 of coverage at age 57	$0.43
Monthly cost ($0.43 × 100)	$43.00

The monthly costs are then totaled to obtain an annual cost. Assuming no change in the amount of coverage during the year, the annual cost is $516. Any employee contributions for the entire amount of coverage are subtracted from the annual cost to determine the taxable income that must be reported by an employee. If the employee contributed $.15 per month ($1.80 per year) per $1,000 of coverage, the employee's total annual contribution for $150,000 of coverage is $270. This reduces the amount reportable as taxable income from $516 to $246.

It is important to note that group term insurance coverage can often be purchased at a lower cost than Table I rates. There are some who argue that, in these instances, the actual cost of coverage can be used in place of the Table I cost for determining an employee's taxable income. From the standpoint of logic and consistency with the tax laws, this view makes sense. However, the law clearly provides that Table I costs must be used.

> **Operation of Table I**
> - describes MONTHLY cost per $1,000 of coverage
> - table is used for purposes of Sec. 79 taxation regardless of actual cost
> - applies to employer-paid group coverage in excess of $50,000 for one insured
> - any contributions by employee directly reduce taxable amount under Table I

Nondiscrimination Rules

Any plan that qualifies as group term insurance under Sec. 79 is subject to nondiscrimination rules, and the $50,000 exclusion will not be available to key employees if a plan is discriminatory. Such a plan might favor key employees in either eligibility or benefits. If the plan is discriminatory, the value of the full amount of coverage for key employees, minus their own contributions, will be considered taxable income, based on the greater of actual or Table I costs. A key employee of a firm is defined as any person (either active or retired) who at any time during the current plan year is any of the following:

- an officer of the firm who earns more than $175,000 (in 2017) in annual compensation from the firm. This amount is subject to periodic indexing. For purposes of this rule the number of employees treated as officers is the greater of 3 or 10 percent of the firm's employees, subject to a maximum of 50. In applying the rule certain employees can be excluded. These include persons who are part-time, under 21, or have less than 6 months of service with the firm.

- a more-than-5-percent owner of the firm

- a more-than-1-percent owner of the firm who earns over $150,000 in annual compensation from the firm

Eligibility requirements are not discriminatory if (1) at least 70 percent of all employees are eligible, (2) at least 85 percent of all employees who are participants are not key employees, or (3) participants comprise a classification that the IRS determines is nondiscriminatory. For purposes of the 70 percent test, employees with less than 3 years' service, part-time employees, and seasonal employees may be excluded. Employees covered by collective-bargaining agreements may also be excluded if plan benefits were the subject of good-faith bargaining.

Benefits are not discriminatory if neither the type nor amount of benefits discriminates in favor of key employees. The statute specifies that it is permissible to base benefits on a uniform percentage of salary. In addition, Sec. 79 applies separately with respect to former employees as provided in the regulations.

Groups with Fewer than 10 Full-Time Employees

A group insurance plan that covers fewer than 10 employees must also satisfy another set of nondiscrimination requirements before it is eligible for favorable tax treatment under Sec. 79. These requirements, which are set forth in Treasury regulations, make smaller groups subject to two separate and somewhat overlapping sets of rules.

Again note that Sec. 79 applies to an employer's overall plan of group insurance, not to separate group insurance contracts. For example, an employer providing group insurance coverage for its 50 hourly employees under one group insurance contract and for its 6 executives under a separate contract is considered to have a single plan covering 56 employees, and thus is exempt from the under-10 requirements. Although the stated purpose of the under-10 requirements is to preclude individual selection, their effect is to prevent the group insurance plan from discriminating in favor of the owners or stockholder-employees of small businesses.

With some exceptions, plans covering fewer than 10 employees must provide coverage for all full-time employees. For purposes of this requirement, employees who are not customarily employed for more than 20 hours in any one week or 5 months in any calendar year are considered part-time employees. It is permissible to exclude full-time employees from coverage under the following circumstances:

- The employee has reached age 65.

- The employee has not satisfied the waiting period under the plan. However, the waiting period may not exceed 6 months.

- The employee has elected not to participate in the plan but only if the employee would not have been required to contribute to the cost of other benefits besides group term life insurance if he or she had participated.

- The employee has not satisfied the evidence of insurability required under the plan. However, this evidence of insurability must be determined solely on the basis of a medical questionnaire completed by the employee and not by a medical examination.

The amount of coverage must be either a flat amount, a uniform percentage of salary, or an amount based on different employee classifications. These employee classifications, which are referred to as coverage brackets in Sec. 79, may be determined in the manner described earlier.

The amount of coverage provided each employee in any classification may be no greater than 2½ times the amount of coverage provided each employee in the next lower classification. In addition, each employee in the lowest classification must be provided with an amount of coverage that is equal to at least 10 percent of the amount provided each employee in the highest classification. There must also be a reasonable expectation that there will be at least one employee in each classification. The following benefit schedule would be unacceptable for two reasons. First, the amount of coverage provided for the hourly employees is only 5 percent of the amount of coverage provided for the president. Second, the amount of coverage on the supervisor is more than 2½ times the amount of coverage provided for the hourly employees.

Classification	Amount of Coverage
President	$100,000
Supervisor	40,000
Hourly employees	5,000

The following benefit schedule, however, would be acceptable:

Classification	Amount of Coverage
President	$100,000
Supervisor	40,000
Hourly employees	20,000

If a group insurance plan that covers fewer than 10 employees does not qualify for favorable tax treatment under Sec. 79, any premiums paid by the employer for such coverage represent taxable income to the employees. The employer, however, still receives an income tax deduction for any premiums paid on behalf of the employees, as long as overall compensation is reasonable.

Income Taxation of Proceeds

In most instances the death proceeds under a group term insurance contract do not result in any taxable income to the beneficiary if they are paid in a lump sum. If the proceeds are payable in installments over more than one taxable year of the beneficiary, only the interest earnings attributable to the proceeds are included in the beneficiary's income for tax purposes. The tax treatment of so-called "accelerated death benefits" paid to or on behalf of insureds who are terminally or chronically ill can be excluded from gross income if certain requirements are met. The law provides specific definitions of what constitutes a terminally ill or chronically ill individual for purposes of the exclusion for such benefits.

Under certain circumstances the exemption of the proceeds from income taxation does not apply if the coverage was transferred (either in whole or in part) for a valuable consideration. Such a situation will arise when the stockholder-employees of a corporation name each other as beneficiaries under their group term insurance coverage as a method of funding a buy-sell agreement. The mutual agreement to name each other as beneficiaries is the valuable consideration. Under these circumstances any proceeds paid to a beneficiary constitute ordinary income to the extent that the proceeds exceed the beneficiary's tax basis, as determined by the Internal Revenue Code.

In many cases benefits paid by an employer to employees or their beneficiaries from the firm's assets receive the same tax treatment as benefits provided under an insurance contract. This is not true for death benefits. If they are provided other than through an insurance contract, the amount of the proceeds represents taxable income to the beneficiary. For this reason employers are less likely to use alternative funding arrangements for death benefits than for disability and medical expense benefits.

Treatment of Added Coverages

Supplemental life insurance can be written as either a separate contract or as part of the contract providing basic group term life insurance coverage. If it is a separate contract and if the supplemental group life insurance meets the conditions of qualifying as group term insurance under Sec. 79, the amount of coverage provided is added to all other group term insurance for purposes of calculating the Uniform Premium Table I cost. Any premiums paid by the employee for the supplemental coverage reduce the taxable income resulting from the coverage. In all other ways, supplemental life insurance is treated the same as group term insurance.

When supplemental life insurance coverage is written in conjunction with a basic group life insurance plan, employers have the option of treating the supplemental coverage as a separate policy of insurance as long as the premiums are properly allocated between the two portions of the coverage. There is no advantage in treating the supplemental coverage as a separate policy if, by itself, it would still qualify as group term insurance under Sec. 79. However, this election will minimize taxable income to employees if the cost of the supplemental coverage is paid entirely by the employees and all employees are charged rates that are at or below Table I rates. There is no taxable income if the employee pays the entire cost of the coverage.

Premiums paid for accidental death and dismemberment insurance are considered to be health insurance premiums rather than group term insurance premiums. However, these are also deductible to the employer as an ordinary and necessary business expense the same as they are for group term insurance. Benefits paid to an employee under the dismemberment portion of the coverage are treated like benefits received under a health insurance contract and are received income tax free. Death benefits received under the coverage are treated like death benefits received under group term life insurance.

For federal tax purposes, survivor income benefit insurance is considered to be a group term insurance coverage. Under Sec. 79, the amount of benefit is equal to the commuted value of benefit payments that would have been received by eligible survivors if the employee had died during the year. This amount normally is provided annually by the insurance company. A commuted value is also used for estate tax purposes. In all other respects survivor income benefit insurance is treated the same as group term insurance.

Employer contributions for dependent life insurance coverage are fully deductible by the employer as an ordinary and necessary business expense if overall compensation of the employee is reasonable. Employer contributions do not result in taxable income to an employee as long as the value of the benefit is de minimis. This means that the value is so small that it is administratively impractical for the employer to account for the cost on a per-person basis. Dependent coverage of $2,000 or less on any person falls into this category. The Internal Revenue Service considers amounts of coverage in excess of $2,000 on any dependent to be more than de minimis. If more than $2,000 of coverage is provided for any dependent from employer contributions, the cost of the entire amount of coverage for that dependent (as determined by Uniform Premium Table I rates) will be considered taxable income to the employee.

Death benefits are free of income taxation and will not be included in the taxable estate of the dependent for estate tax purposes.

State Taxation

In most instances state tax laws affecting group term insurance are similar to the federal laws. However, two major differences do exist. In most states the payment of group term insurance premiums by the employer does not result in any taxable income to the employee, even if the amount of insurance exceeds $50,000. In addition, death proceeds receive favorable tax treatment under the estate and inheritance tax laws of most states. Generally the death proceeds are partially, if not totally, exempt from such taxation.

Group Universal Life Insurance

It is increasingly common for employers to make group universal life insurance plans available to employees—either to replace existing supplemental life insurance or as additional supplemental plans. Group universal life insurance products are not designed to be policies of insurance under Sec. 79. In addition, each employee pays the full cost of his or her coverage.

Therefore the tax treatment is the same to employees as if they had purchased a universal life insurance policy in the individual insurance marketplace.

LO 5.4   **Explain the tax treatment of property transferred in connection with the performance of services.**

PROPERTY TRANSFERRED IN CONNECTION WITH THE PERFORMANCE OF SERVICES

Introduction

In the early days of the tax law employers frequently tried to reduce their employees' tax liability by paying them with noncash items—cars, houses, clothing, and so forth—on the theory that such items were not taxable income. The courts quickly held otherwise; taxable income includes noncash as well as cash receipts. Moreover, if the property transferred to the employee has restrictions that temporarily eliminate or reduce its value to the employee, taxable income must ultimately be reported. The courts have held that the recipient of the property must include its value in income in the year in which the recipient becomes vested in the value of the property.[1] The court-made rules in this area are sometimes summarized as the "economic benefit doctrine." The doctrine focuses on the vested benefits provided to the employee rather than on the type of property or its form of ownership.

Currently this issue affects "restricted stock" plans, under which an employer compensates an employee for services with stock of the employer corporation, subject to provisions under which the stock must be paid back to the employer if the employee fails to complete specified services. The issue also arises in plans providing life insurance for employees, affecting both the pure death benefit (term insurance) amount and also the year of inclusion of any policy cash values owned by or benefiting the employee.

The economic benefit doctrine as it applies to property transferred for services is codified in IRC Sec. 83, which provides specific rules for (1) the year in which the value of the property is included, and (2) the amount to be included in that year.

---

1.   *Sproull v. Commissioner*, 16 TC 244 (1951), aff'd per curiam, 194 F.2d 541 (6th Cir. 1952).

Year of Inclusion

Sec. 83 provides that the value of property (the excess over the amount paid by the recipient for the property) that is transferred for services is included in income "at the first time the rights of the person having the beneficial interest in such property are transferable or are not subject to a substantial risk of forfeiture. . ." Sec. 83(c)(1) provides that "the rights of a person in property are subject to a substantial risk of forfeiture if such person's rights to full enjoyment of such property are conditioned upon the future performance of substantial services by any individual."

Example

Fothrex Corporation transfers 1,000 shares of Fothrex stock to employee Hanson under the condition that Hanson may not sell the stock during a 5-year period. If Hanson leaves employment with Fothrex during the 5-year period, he must return the stock to the company. Hanson pays nothing for the stock. He must include the value of the stock in his income in the year in which the 5-year period expires.

Employers may wish to adopt restricted property plans that are more complex and custom-designed than the simple illustration above. Understanding the term "substantial risk of forfeiture" is the key to designing appropriate forfeiture provisions in restricted property plans. As discussed below, the regulations under Sec. 83 provide some specific rules and illustrations that are helpful.

Discharges for Cause

The regulations state that requiring that property be returned to the employer if the employee is discharged for cause or for committing a crime will not be considered to result in a substantial risk of forfeiture.[2]

Noncompetition and Consulting Provisions

The Sec. 83 regulations in effect create a presumption against the existence of a substantial risk of forfeiture where the forfeiture will occur only if the employee accepts a job with a competing firm. In that case, a "facts and circumstances" test will apply. Factors taken into account in determining whether the noncompetition provision constitutes a substantial risk of forfeiture include

---

2.   Treas. Reg. Sec. 1.83-3(c)(2).

- the age of the employee

- the availability of alternative employment opportunities

- the likelihood of the employee's obtaining such other employment and the employee's degree of skill

- the employee's health

- the practice (if any) of the employer to enforce such covenants

For example, a consulting provision applicable to a majority shareholder of the employer would not generally be given much weight because there would be little likelihood of his or her competing with his/her own business. The enforcement of such a provision would be entirely at his or her discretion as majority owner of the company.

The regulations also state that property transferred to a retiring employee subject to the sole requirement that the property will be returned unless he or she renders consulting services upon the request of his former employer will not be considered subject to a substantial risk of forfeiture unless he is in fact expected to perform substantial services.[3]

Organizational Performance and Other Forfeiture Provisions

The regulations state that where an employee receives property from an employer subject to a requirement that it be returned if the total earnings of the employer do not increase, such property is subject to a substantial risk of forfeiture.[4] Note that this "performance" standard does not actually involve a requirement that services be performed; it appears from this provision in the regulations that the IRS finds this acceptable although it does not strictly fit the language of Sec. 83.

The regulations state that a forfeiture provision can be valid if it is "related to the purpose of the transfer." The performance standard discussed in the preceding paragraph may be an example of this type of provision. One case dealt with a provision under which stock was transferred to an employee under a condition that if he wished to dispose of it within one year he had to sell it back to the employer at the original cost. The court viewed this as a substantial risk of forfeiture and noted that this provision served a substantial corporate purpose of avoiding insider trading.[5] This is arguably also a purpose related to the transfer, though it is not specifically related.

---

3. Treas. Reg. Sec. 1.83-3(c)(2).
4. Treas. Reg. Sec. 1.83-3(c)(2).
5. *Robinson v. Comm'r*, 805 F.2d 38 (1st Cir. 1986), rev'g 82 TC 444.

The Committee Reports for Sec. 83 state that "In other cases [besides those involving service conditions] the question of whether there is a substantial risk of forfeiture depends upon the facts and circumstances."[6]

Employee Election to Include in Current Income

If an employee receives restricted property and wants to include it in income currently (perhaps because he/she expects it to increase considerably in value) he or she can elect under Sec. 83(b) to include the current value (the fair market value at the time of transfer) in income currently. The fair market value of the property is determined without regard to restrictions (except a restriction that by its terms will not lapse).

Example

Hott Software transfers stock this year to employee Geeke, with the provision that if Geeke leaves employment during the next 10 years, her stock is forfeited. The fair market value of the stock at the time of transfer is $20,000. Geeke expects it to more than quadruple in value in 10 years, so she elects to pay taxes at that time on the $20,000 current value.

An employee making a Sec. 83(b) election like that in the example is betting on the company to succeed, since if the value of the stock drops below its value at the time of transfer, no loss deduction is allowed.

Amount to Be Included under Sec. 83

The general rule under Sec. 83 is that property is included in income at its fair market value (determined without regard to any restriction other than a restriction that by its terms will never lapse) at the first time when the rights to the property are transferable or no longer subject to a substantial risk of forfeiture, as discussed above. If the employee paid any consideration for the property, the taxable amount is reduced by the amount paid.

The amount included is the value at the time of vesting, not at the time of transfer.

Example

This year, Fothrex corporation transfers 1,000 shares of Fothrex stock to employee Hanson, subject to a provision that Hanson must continue in employment for 5 years. The stock is worth $30,000 at the time of transfer. Hanson sticks it out and is still

---

6.   H.R. Rep. No. 413 (Part 1), 91st Cong., 1st Sess 88 (1969) and S. Rep. No. 552, 91st Cong., 1st Sess. 121 (1969).

> working for Fothrex on the fifth anniversary of the transfer, at which time the stock is
> worth $50,000. Hanson must report the $50,000 as compensation income at that time.
> There is no discount to reflect the fact that the stock was restricted during the preceding
> 5 years.

As the example notes, the existence of a restriction that eventually lapses does not affect the valuation of the stock. However, if the stock was subject to a nonlapsing restriction it would affect valuation. Suppose that in the example the Fothrex stock that Hanson received continued after 5 years to be subject to a provision that any shares that Hanson wanted to dispose of would have to be first offered to the company for $40 per share. (This is not considered to be a forfeiture provision.) This provision would affect the value of the stock at that time and would reduce the amount that Hanson would have to report in that year. The actual reduction in value is an issue of facts and circumstances, and some kind of independent valuation would probably have to be made for tax purposes.

Employer's Deduction

Under Sec. 83(h), the employer's deduction is equal to the amount included in income by the employee. The deduction is taken in the year in which the employee includes the amount in gross income. (The exact Code provision is that the deduction is allowed in the employer's taxable year in which or with which ends the taxable year in which the amount is included in the gross income of the person who performed the services.) Restricted property is a form of compensation that does not provide the employer with an "upfront" deduction—a deduction in the year the services are performed—as is the case with a qualified pension or profit-sharing plan. For compensation governed by Sec. 83, the year of deduction is tied to the year of the employee's inclusion of income.

CHAPTER REVIEW

Key Terms and Concepts

alimony	joint and survivor annuity
child support	variable annuity
life insurance and divorce	immediate annuities
annuity	deferred annuities
investment in the contract	LIFO (last-in, first-out) taxation
expected return	
refund feature	
10-year certain annuity	

Review Questions

Review questions are based on the learning objectives in this chapter. Thus a [5.3] at the end of a question means that the question is based on learning objective 3. If there are multiple objectives, they are all listed.

1. What is the basic income tax rule regarding alimony payments? [5.1]

2. Can rent-free occupancy of a home by a former spouse and children be treated as alimony? [5.1]

3. a. In what post separation year will the payer of an "excess alimony payment" be required to include the excess in income?

    b. How is the excess alimony payment determined? [5.1]

4. Explain whether child support qualifies as alimony. [5.1]

5. Explain the federal tax consequences of transferring a life insurance policy pursuant to a separation agreement or divorce decree. [5.1]

6. Bob and Helen Hession's divorce decree became final this year. The provisions of the decree are as follows:

    a. Bob will pay Helen $150 per week for 5 years for herself. The decree does not specifically state that payments will cease in the event of Helen's death. Bob will also pay $100 per week as child support for their 13-year-old son, Timmy. Will Bob be entitled to a deduction for payments to Helen and Timmy?

    b. Helen and Timmy may continue to live in the family home rent free. The title to the home is in the name of Bob Hession. Can Bob take a deduction for the value of the rent?

    c. To secure these payments, Bob will transfer ownership of his whole life insurance policy to Helen. He will continue to pay the $500 annual premium for the whole life policy. He will obtain an additional whole life policy and Helen will be named revocable beneficiary of this policy.

        (1) What are the tax consequences to Bob and Helen with respect to the annual premium payments?

        (2) If Bob dies, will the life insurance proceeds be taxable to Helen? [5.1]

7. a. Describe the general theory of annuity taxation.

   b.   How is the excludible portion of either an annuity or a "partial annuity" payment determined? [5.2]

8.   Mrs. McGinniss recently purchased a single-premium immediate annuity. The premium was $13,000. She will receive payments of $100 a month for life. Assume that government tables show her life expectancy multiple to be 13.2 years.

   a.   What is her investment in the annuity contract?

   b.   Calculate her expected return.

   c.   Calculate the amount she may exclude annually from income until her investment in the contract is recovered.

   d.   Calculate the amount she must include in her income each year. [5.2]

9.   How would your answer to question 8 be affected if there was a refund feature included in Mrs. McGinniss's annuity? Assume for the purposes of this question that the premium is still $13,000, the monthly payment is still $100, and the actuarial present value of the refund feature is $2,000. [5.2]

10. a.   Explain how the taxation of an annuity payment changes if the annuitant lives beyond life expectancy.

   b.   Is this tax treatment different for individuals whose annuity starting dates were before January 1, 1987? Explain. [5.2]

11. a.   What is meant by a joint and survivor annuity?

   b.   Explain how the expected return is calculated. [5.2]

12. Mr. and Mrs. Gillen purchased a single-premium immediate joint and survivor annuity for $22,000. The couple will receive a monthly payment totaling $100 as long as both Mr. and Mrs. Gillen are alive. The $100-per-month payment will continue until the death of the survivor of Mr. and Mrs. Gillen. Assume that the joint and survivor life expectancy multiple for the couple is 23 years.

   a.   What is the investment in the annuity contract?

   b.   Calculate the expected return.

   c.   Calculate the amount excludible from income each year until the investment in the contract is recovered.

   d.   Calculate the amount that must be included in income each year until the investment in the contract is recovered. [5.2]

13. Describe the tax treatment of variable annuities. [5.2]

14. Explain the adjustment procedure where the annuitant receives less than the amount originally determined to be excludible in a variable annuity. [5.2]

15. Mr. Glikes purchased a variable annuity. The premium was $25,000. He will receive monthly income for life under the contract. Assume that his life expectancy multiple is 14.4 years.

    a.   What is his investment in the contract?

    b.   Compute the amount that Mr. Glikes can exclude annually.

    c.   Assume Mr. Glikes only receives $1,500 in the 10th year of the contract. Assume his life expectancy multiple is 9.1 years at that time. Redetermine the amount he may exclude until his investment is recovered tax free. [5.2]

16. How will a partial withdrawal of cash from an annuity contract prior to the annuity starting date be treated for income tax purposes? [5.2]

17. What is the penalty tax on a premature distribution from a deferred annuity? [5.2]

18. What are the basic requirements for treatment of a group life insurance plan under Sec. 79? [5.3]

19. Explain the tax treatment of group term insurance protection that provides benefits in excess of $50,000. [5.3]

20. a.   Last year Sarah Johnson, aged 32, was provided with $75,000 of group term life insurance by her employer for the entire year. The employer paid the entire premium. The plan meets the nondiscrimination requirements. Calculate the amount of taxable income Sarah had because of this coverage.

    b.   How would the answer change if Sarah had contributed $3 per month for her coverage? [5.3]

21. Explain the nondiscrimination requirements with regard to key employees that apply to the exclusion for group life insurance coverage. [5.3]

22. How are the death proceeds paid under a group term insurance contract treated for income tax purposes? [5.3]

23. When is property that is transferred in connection with the performance of services taxable to an employee? [5.4]

24. Explain what is meant by a substantial risk of forfeiture with respect to restricted property. [5.4]

25. What is meant by an employee's election with respect to restricted property? [5.4]

26. When is the employer entitled to a deduction for restricted property transferred to an employee? [5.4]

Review Answers

1. The basic rule for alimony or separate maintenance payments is that they are includible in the gross income of the payee. Correspondingly, alimony payments includible in the gross income of the payee are deductible for income tax purposes from the gross income of the payer.

2. Alimony payments are required to be in cash or a cash equivalent. Because of this requirement, such benefits as the rent-free occupancy of a home by a former spouse and the couple's children cannot be treated as alimony payments for tax purposes.

3. a. The payer of an "excess alimony payment" is required to include the excess payment in his or her gross income in the third postseparation year.

   b. The calculation of an "excess" alimony payment is based on the relative amounts of the payments made during the first 3 postseparation years. In computing the "excess" alimony payment, compare the second postseparation year to the third postseparation year payment. The second year's "excess" payment is the amount by which the second year payment exceeds the payment in the third postseparation year plus $15,000. In the payer's first postseparation tax year, the "excess" payment is computed by taking the average of the alimony payments in the second and third postseparation years as adjusted by the initial calculation and adding $15,000 to that figure. Any alimony payment for the first postseparation year that is in excess of that amount is the "excess" alimony payment for the first year payment. The total "excess" alimony payment that needs to be recaptured is the combination of both calculations.

   If either spouse dies before the end of the third postseparation year, or if either spouse remarries before the end of that year and payments cease as a result of such event, then the front-loading rules for excess alimony payments do not apply.

4. Payments for support of minor children are not treated as alimony for tax purposes. Such payments are not deductible by the payer spouse and not includible in the gross

income of the payee spouse. Payments are treated as child support to the extent that the terms of the applicable divorce or separation agreement fix or designate them as such. For purposes of this rule, a provision in the agreement calling for a reduction in payments based on certain specified contingencies relating to a child is considered to be designating such payments as child support. These contingencies include a reduction in payments happening at the time or associated with the time when a child attains a specified age, marries, leaves school, or dies. The amount of the reduction in the payment that would result from the occurrence of one of these contingencies under the agreement is the amount treated as child support for tax purposes.

5. Perhaps the most common arrangement is to transfer the ownership of an existing life policy that insures the life of one spouse to the other spouse. The transfer of the policy itself does not have income tax consequences for either spouse regardless of the policy's cash value. Such a transfer is neither alimony nor child support, but a nontaxable transfer of property incident to a divorce. However, if the spouse who transferred the policy is obligated to continue to pay premiums on the transferred policy, the payment of such premiums is generally treated as an alimony payment.

    The transfer of a life insurance policy will not cause the subsequent payment of death benefits to be subject to income tax under the "transfer-for-value" rule. Transfers incident to divorce are not subject to the transfer-for-value rule. Therefore such death benefits retain their income-tax-free character.

6. a. Each $150 payment is income to Helen and a deduction for Bob because the payments are pursuant to a divorce decree and no part of the payments is an excess alimony payment. Also, there is no requirement that the decree must specifically state that payments will cease at Helen's death in order to claim a deduction. There is no deduction for child support payments, so the $100 child support for Timmy will neither be deductible by Bob nor includible in Helen's income.

    b. Although Helen possibly has an economic benefit here, the Internal Revenue Service does not consider rent-free occupancy to be taxable alimony.

    c. (1) Helen, as absolute owner of the transferred life insurance policy, has income upon payment of the whole life policy premium. Likewise, Bob may deduct his whole life premium. The payment of premiums for the new whole life policy does not give rise to either income or a deduction, since Helen is not the absolute owner of the policy. (2) Such life insurance proceeds will be exempt from income tax.

7. a. The general theory of annuity taxation involves the concept that the contract owner's capital investment in the contract may be recovered tax free when distributions are made. However, the interest or other earnings on the contract funds must be subject to taxation at some point in time.

   b. The income taxation of a payment in the form of a full or immediate payment annuity is determined by using a fraction called the "exclusion ratio." The numerator of the fraction is the amount of the "investment in the contract." The denominator of the fraction is the total "expected return" under the contract. The periodic annuity payment is multiplied by this fraction to calculate the portion of the payment that is received tax free by the annuitant as a return of the investment in the contract. The balance of the payment is taxable to the annuitant.

      The "investment in the contract" may be defined as the aggregate amount of premiums or other consideration paid for the contract minus any distributions already made from the contract that were excludible from the recipient's gross income as a return of capital.

      The "expected return" under the contract may be defined as the total of the amounts that are expected to be received in the form of an annuity under the contract. If the annuity payment is calculated using the life expectancy of one or more annuitants, the expected return is calculated by reference to actuarial tables found in the Treasury regulations promulgated pursuant to IRC Sec. 72. An exclusion ratio can be calculated for a partial annuitization meeting the requirements of section 72 (a) (2) under similar principles. If any amount is received as an annuity for at least 10 years or during the lives of one or more individuals, then that portion of the annuity contract is treated as a separate contract for calculation of the exclusion ratio. The investment in the contract is allocated pro rata between each portion of the annuity contract from which amounts (a) are received as annuity and (b) the portion of the contract from which amounts are not received as an annuity.

8. a. $13,000

   b. $100 × 12 × 13.2 = $15,840

   c. $13,000 ÷ $15,840 = .8207 × $1,200 = $984.84

   d. $1,200 − $984.84 = $215.16

9. The refund feature would be subtracted from the investment in the contract before the exclusion ratio is determined. Therefore the investment in the contract would be $11,000 ($13,000 − $2,000), and the exclusion ratio would be .694 ($11,000 ÷ $15,840).

The amount excluded from income annually is $832.80 (.694 × $1,200). Taxable income is $367.20 ($1,200 − $832.80).

10. a. If the annuitant lives beyond his or her period of life expectancy as determined under the regulations, no exclusion ratio is applied to payments received after the end of the life expectancy period. Therefore the full amount of payments received after the life expectancy period will be taxable.

   b. Yes, the tax treatment is different for individuals whose annuity starting dates commenced before January 1, 1987. If the annuitant under such contracts lives beyond his or her life expectancy, the exclusion ratio is applied to payments for as long as the annuitant lives, making it possible for the annuitant to recover a total amount tax free that is more than the actual investment in the contract.

11. a. An annuity that provides for income payments to be made as long as either of two persons live is known as a joint and survivor annuity. In its most common form, it continues the same fixed amount of income to the survivor as is payable while both annuitants are alive. A common modification provides that the income to the survivor will be reduced to either two-thirds or one-half of the original amount. In other words, a joint and survivor annuity provides for the payment of a fixed amount of income while two annuitants live, then upon the death of one, it continues to pay the same or a lesser amount of income to the survivor for the duration of his or her life.

   b. The expected return under a joint and survivor annuity can be calculated by using the tables contained in the Treasury regulations pursuant to Code Sec. 72. These tables provide the joint life expectancy for two annuitants depending on their individual ages.

12. a. $22,000

   b. $27,600 ($1,200 × 23 years = $27,600)

   c. $956.52

   d. $243.48

13. In the case of a variable annuity, the "expected return" under the contract cannot be accurately calculated for purposes of determining an exclusion ratio for the annuity payments. Therefore the exclusion ratio calculation is not used to determine the taxation of the annuity payments under a variable contract. Consequently, the investment in a variable contract is divided by the number of years of the annuitant's life

expectancy to determine the dollar amount of each payment that is excludible from the annuitant's gross income.

14. Because the variable annuity payments are subject to fluctuations, it is possible that the amount of an annuity payment under a variable contract will be less than the amount of each payment that was determined to be excludible. In such cases, the entire payment will be excludible from gross income, and the "unused" portion of the excludible amount can be recovered later for income tax purposes by recomputing the annual dollar amount of the annuity payment that is excludible from gross income. The recomputation of the excludible amount can be made at the election of the annuitant and is accomplished by the following steps:

   • The dollar amount of the exclusion that was not utilized is determined.

   • The annuitant's life expectancy at the time of the recomputation is found by consulting the appropriate table in the regulations.

   • An additional excludible amount is determined by dividing the amount of the unused exclusion by the life expectancy of the annuitant at the time of the election to recompute.

   • The additional amount is then added to the original excludible amount to determine the adjusted excludible amount.

15. a. $25,000

    b. $25,000 ÷ 14.4 years = $1,736.11

    c. Mr. Glikes has a $236.11 unused exclusion that he may add proportionately over his remaining life expectancy to the original amount excludible annually. His new excludible amount is $1,762.06 ([$236.11 ÷ 9.1 years] + $1,736.11).

16. A partial withdrawal of funds from a deferred annuity contract is treated as a taxable event for income tax purposes. The general rule is that the withdrawn amount will be taxed to the extent of "income on the contract." "Income on the contract" is the amount by which the cash value of the contract (without regard to surrender charges) exceeds the owner's investment in the contract. This is a form of "LIFO" (last-in, first-out) taxation in which the earnings on the contract are taxed before the investment in the contract can be recovered tax free as a return of capital.

This "LIFO" rule of income taxation applies to annuity contracts that were funded after August 13, 1982. Contracts funded on or before this date follow a FIFO rule of taxation for withdrawals.

17. There is a 10 percent penalty tax that generally applies to amounts received from annuity contracts that

    • are not received in the form of annuity payments and

    • are received by a taxpayer who has not attained the age of 59½

    It applies only to the portion of any withdrawal, loan, or collateralization of the contract that is taxable under the rules pertaining to "amounts not received as an annuity." Moreover, the penalty is in addition to the regular income tax, but it does not apply to any portion of the transaction that is treated as a nontaxable return of capital.

18. To qualify as group term insurance under Sec. 79, the insurance must meet the following conditions:

    a. It must provide a death benefit excludible from federal income tax.

    b. It must be provided to a group of employees.

    c. It must be provided under a policy carried directly or indirectly by the employer.

    d. The plan must be arranged in such a manner as to preclude individual selection of coverage amounts.

19. Under Sec. 79 the cost of the first $50,000 of coverage is not taxed to the employee. The cost of coverage in excess of $50,000, less any employee contributions for the entire amount of coverage, represents taxable income to the employee. For purposes of Sec. 79, the cost of this excess coverage is determined by a government table called the Uniform Premium Table I.

20. a. The amount of taxable income is determined by using the Uniform Premium Table I cost for the amount of coverage in excess of $50,000.

Coverage provided:	$75,000
Less Sec. 79 exclusion:	$50,000
Amount subject to taxation:	$25,000
Uniform Premium Table I monthly cost per $1,000 of coverage at age 32:	$0.08
Monthly cost ($0.08 x 25):	$2.00
Annual cost ($2 x 12):	$24.00 of taxable income

    b. The full $36 annual contribution could have been deducted from the Table I annual cost of $24. Therefore no income would have resulted from the group insurance coverage.

21. Any plan that qualifies as group term insurance under Sec. 79 is subject to nondiscrimination rules, and the $50,000 exclusion will not be available to key employees if a plan is discriminatory. Such a plan might favor key employees in either eligibility or benefits. If the plan is discriminatory, the value of the full amount of coverage for key employees, minus their own contributions, will be considered taxable income, based on the greater of actual or Table I costs.

22. Generally, death proceeds under a group term insurance contract do not result in taxable income to the beneficiary if paid in a lump sum.

23. The courts have held that an employee who receives property as payment for the performance of services must include its value in income in the year in which he or she becomes vested in the value of the property. The court-made rules in this area are sometimes summarized as the "economic benefit doctrine." This doctrine as it applies to property transferred for services is codified in Code Sec. 83, which provides that the value of property that is transferred for services is included in income "at the first time the rights of the person having the beneficial interest in such property are transferable or are not subject to a substantial risk of forfeiture."

24. Sec. 83(c)(1) provides that "the rights of a person in property are subject to a substantial risk of forfeiture if such person's rights to full enjoyment of such property are conditioned upon the future performance of substantial services by any individual."

    The Committee Reports for Sec. 83 state that "In other cases (besides those involving service conditions) the question of whether there is a substantial risk of forfeiture depends upon the facts and circumstances." For example, the regulations state that where an employee receives property from an employer subject to a requirement that it be returned if the total earnings of the employer do not increase, such property is subject to a substantial risk of forfeiture. Note that this performance standard does not actually involve a requirement that services be performed. Moreover, the regulations also state that a forfeiture provision can be valid if it is related to the purpose of the transfer. A performance standard is an example of this type of provision.

25. If an employee receives restricted property and wants to include it in income currently, he or she can elect under Sec. 83(b) to include the current (fair market) value in income currently. The current value of the property is determined without regard to restrictions (except for one that will not lapse).

26. Under Sec. 83(h) the employer's deduction is equal to the amount included in income by the employee and is deducted in the year in which the employee includes the amount.

Chapter 6

Exclusions from Gross Income

Learning Objectives

An understanding of the material in this chapter should enable you to

LO 6.1   **Explain the general rule regarding the income taxation of amounts received by gift or inheritance.**

LO 6.2   **Describe the rules regarding the taxation of interest on state and municipal bonds, U.S. Treasury obligations, and educational savings bonds, and explain how the gain on the sale of tax-exempt securities is treated for tax purposes.**

LO 6.3   **Explain the rules regarding the income taxation of Social Security benefits.**

LO 6.4   **Explain the rules regarding the income taxation of accident and health benefits.**

LO 6.5   **Explain the rules for qualifying for an "Achieving a Better Life Experience" (ABLE) account as well as the tax consequences of contributions to and distributions from such account.**

LO 6.6   **Explain the extent to which dependent-care assistance benefits are taxed.**

> The income tax has made more liars out of the American people than golf has. Even when you make a tax form out on the level, you don't know when it's through if you are a crook or a martyr.
>
> —Will Rogers

Although the majority of items a taxpayer receives are includible in gross income, there are exceptions. That which is excludible from gross income is commonly referred to as an exclusion. Obviously, an item of income that can be excluded from tax is worth more than an item of income that is subject to taxation. The Internal Revenue Code identifies which items—in the form of money, property, or benefits—are includible or excludible from gross income.

Items specifically included in gross income are fairly comprehensive. However, income may be defined in a much broader sense. Income, in the broadest of terms, represents all wealth that flows to the taxpayer other than as a mere return of capital. Income includes gains and profits from any source. For example, it includes any gain realized from the sale, exchange, or other disposition of a capital asset. However, income does not include a mere increase in capital, but a gain or a profit derived from the capital. It is normally evidenced by a closed and completed transaction fixed by identifiable events. Income is not a "return of capital," nor is it a "growth" or "increase" in the investment's value.

Example

John owns AG&Z stock that he acquired 15 years ago for $20,000. This year the stock's value is $45,000. This growth in value is not taxable to John until the stock is sold or exchanged. When the stock is sold or exchanged, John will have a gain representing the difference between the selling price and his basis in the stock. If the stock's fair market value is $45,000 when John sells the stock, he will have a taxable gain of $25,000. His $20,000 investment represents a return of capital and therefore is not taxable.

As previously discussed, gross income represents all income minus exclusions. Gross income is the starting point in preparing an individual income tax return. Items included in gross income are often termed inclusions. An exclusion is an item that is exempt from taxation. Exclusions should not be confused with deductions. Deductions are expense items that reduce gross income in arriving at adjusted gross income or taxable income.

WHAT ARE EXCLUSIONS?

exclusion

An **exclusion** represents an item that is not included in gross income, which is the starting point in calculating the income tax. Items may be excluded for any one of the following reasons:

1. An item is not defined as "income."

2. An item is not taxable under the U.S. Constitution.

3. An item is expressly excluded under a provision in the Internal Revenue Code.

Items falling under (1) or (2) are entirely exempt from federal taxation. However, items falling under (3) may be either partially or wholly exempt, depending on the Internal Revenue Code statute.

In addition to the specific areas of exclusions covered in this chapter, other types of exclusions are addressed in later chapters of this text.

LO 6.1   **Explain the general rule regarding the income taxation of amounts received by gift or inheritance.**

GIFTS AND INHERITANCES

General Rule

The value of money or property received as a gift, bequest, devise, or inheritance is generally excluded from gross income under IRC Sec. 102. However, the income from the property received is taxable. If income from property is assigned, the donor of the income is taxable, because income is taxed to the property owner. However, if the donor permanently disposes of the income-producing property, the income generated from the property is taxed to the recipient.

A gift can be defined as any voluntary transfer of property by one person to another that is not made as compensation and in return for which no consideration is given. If there is valuable consideration in money or money's worth for the transfer of the property, the transaction is not treated as a gift—it is a sale. A gift is defined as a gratuitous transfer of property. To be considered a gift, the following elements are essential:

- a donor competent to make the gift
- a clear and unmistakable intention on the donor's behalf to make the gift
- a donee capable of receiving the gift
- an irrevocable conveyance, assignment, or transfer sufficient to vest legal title to the property in the donee
- a donor's relinquishment of dominion and control of the property by delivery to the donee

In order to have a valid gift for federal income tax purposes, the donor must have acted out of a "detached and disinterested" generosity in transferring the property. Gifts are normally made out of "affection, respect, admiration, charity, or like impulses."[1] Valid gifts have no strings attached.

Questions regarding gift or compensation normally arise as to payments where there is a past or present employment relationship. For federal income tax law purposes, a voluntary transfer without compensation is not necessarily a gift. It is not a gift if there is a legal or moral

---

1.   *Placko v. Comm'r.*, 74 T.C. 452 (1980).

obligation for the transfer or if the donor expects to receive a benefit from the "gift." However, the mere absence of a legal or moral obligation for the transfer does not necessarily qualify the transfer as a gift. As previously stated, a transfer is a gift if it is made from detached or disinterested generosity. Ultimately, the question of gift or compensation is resolved by reviewing the donor's dominant reason for making the transfer.

Example 1

Mrs. Adams hires Julie to baby-sit her two young children while she goes shopping. Upon returning, Mrs. Adams gives Julie $20 for minding the children. Julie has $20 of taxable income. She has given consideration (rendered services) in return for the amount received.

Example 2

Michael is a tax accountant for a CPA firm. During tax season, he works 300 hours of overtime. The firm's policy is to compensate all employees at time and one-half for all overtime hours up to a maximum of 250 hours of overtime. During his post-tax season review, the firm announces to Michael that in recognition of his outstanding work ethic and overtime contributions, the firm will make a gift to him of $2,500.

Because of the employer-employee relationship, Michael has taxable income. The "gift" has been made to Michael in recognition of his work ethic and overtime hours. The IRS will treat the $2,500 payment as compensation for past services rendered and not as a gift.

As illustrated, amounts transferred from an employer to an employee will not generally be treated as gifts.

Income from Gifts

Sec. 102 of the Code does not apply to the income generated from excludible property or to a gift of income. For example, if a father gifts a mutual fund investment to his daughter, the value of the mutual fund is not taxable to her. However, any dividends or capital gains earned on that fund subsequent to the gift would be taxable to her.

Gifts of Income

Similar to the concept of income from gifts is that of gifts of income. Neither income from gifts nor gifts of income is excludible from gross income. If payments under the terms of a gift are to be made at intervals, the payments are taxable to the donee to the extent they are made out of income.

Example

A father establishes a trust for his daughter. The daughter is given a life interest in the trust. She is not permitted to invade the principal of the trust. On an annual basis, she receives the income from the trust. The annual income from the trust is not a gift and is taxable to the daughter upon receipt.

However, a bequest of a specific sum of money or property is excluded, even if it is paid out of income. This treatment applies only if the bequest is paid or credited all at once or in not more than three installments. If the bequest is paid in more than three installments, it is taxable to the recipient to the extent it is actually paid from the income generated.

Example

A decedent's will directs that a trustee will pay her husband $40,000 a year for 5 years. The husband is scheduled to receive the $40,000 regardless of how much income is earned on the trust's assets. Since payments extend for more than 3 years, the husband will be taxed annually on the amount he receives to the extent of income earned on the trust's assets. If trust earnings are $50,000 and $45,000 during the first 2 years, the husband will be taxed on the full $40,000 he receives each year. However, if in years 3 through 5, the trust's earnings dip to $35,000, $31,000, and $28,500, respectively, the outcome is different. Since the trustee is required to distribute $40,000 annually to the husband, he or she will be forced to invade principal to make the payments. As a result, the husband will only be taxed to the extent of the trust's income—$35,000, $31,000, and $28,500 in years 3, 4, and 5, respectively.

Inheritances

The rules pertaining to gifts also extend to inheritances. The value of property acquired by inheritance is tax-free to the recipient. However, income earned on that property subsequent to the transfer is taxable to the recipient.

Although the exclusion rules are similar for gifts and inheritances, the basis rules are significantly different. The recipient's basis in inherited property is generally the fair market value of the property at the decedent's death. As a result, appreciation of the property prior to the decedent's death escapes federal income taxation. In contrast, a donee's basis in property acquired by gift is generally the donor's basis in the property at the time of the gift.

Gifts and Inheritances
- Elements of gift must be evident.
- Receipt of gift is generally not taxable to donee.

- Receipt of bequest or inheritance is also generally not taxable to beneficiary.
- Income FROM gifts and inheritances is generally taxable.
- There is a special rule for bequests paid in more than three installments.

LO 6.2   **Describe the rules regarding the taxation of interest on state and municipal bonds, U.S. Treasury obligations, and educational savings bonds, and explain how the gain on the sale of tax-exempt securities is treated for tax purposes.**

INTEREST ON CERTAIN GOVERNMENTAL OBLIGATIONS

State and Local Bonds

Sec. 103 of the Internal Revenue Code provides that interest paid on certain state and local bonds is tax exempt and therefore excluded from gross income. This exemption applies specifically to the interest earned on these obligations. Interest earned on qualified bonds of any political subdivision (that is, county, city, town, or other municipality) is exempt from federal income taxation under this provision. The provision also covers bonds issued by the District of Columbia or by any possession of the United States. Such "tax-exempt" state and municipal bonds are generally "public purpose" bonds; that is, bonds used to finance essential governmental activities.

The exclusion exists to encourage taxpayers to invest in state and municipal bonds. Because of their tax-exempt status, the states and municipalities are able to borrow at relatively low interest rates when compared with taxable investments. To an investor, 100 percent of the interest income received is generally free from federal taxation. Prior to acquiring a tax-exempt obligation, investors need to compare the after-tax return of both tax-exempt and taxable obligations. A taxable obligation yields a before-tax interest rate. This interest rate can also be expressed as an after-tax rate of return. An overall comparison requires knowledge of the investor's federal, state, and local marginal tax brackets. The following examples illustrate comparisons using federal income tax brackets only.

Example 1

Mr. and Mrs. Joe Investor are married and file a joint tax return. Their projected current taxable income is $412,000 (a 35 percent marginal federal income tax bracket this year). The Investors have the option of acquiring a tax-free bond fund yielding 4 percent or a corporate bond earning a 6 percent interest rate. The key for the Investors is to determine the after-tax return. The after-tax return on the tax-free bond fund is 4 percent. This represents a 6.15 percent equivalent to a taxable alternative (4% ÷ [1 − .35 tax rate]). The after-tax return on the corporate bond is only 3.9 percent (6% × [1 − .35 tax rate]).

Example 2

If Mr. and Mrs. Joe Investor are in the 15 percent federal tax bracket, the investment choice is not as clear. Similar to the above example, the Investors have the option of acquiring a 4 percent tax-free bond fund or a corporate bond earning a 6 percent interest rate. The after-tax return on the tax-free bond fund is 4 percent (or a 4.71 percent equivalent to a taxable alternative). The after-tax return on the corporate bond is 5.1 percent.

As illustrated, the exclusion is beneficial to both governments and investors. State and local governments benefit by paying a "below-market" interest rate to investors. Wealthier investors also benefit because of their higher marginal federal and state income tax brackets. Also, the majority of states exempt the interest income earned on their own state's obligations. As income tax rates increase, a tax-free investment's taxable equivalent also increases.

However, the exclusion for municipal bond interest does not extend to

- private activity bonds that are not "qualified bonds"
- arbitrage bonds
- certain bonds not in registered form

The interest income of arbitrage bonds, industrial development bonds, and most other private activity bonds is subject to the regular federal income tax. Obligations issued under this category may include obligations to finance sports facilities, convention or trade show facilities, parking facilities, and air and water pollution control facilities. These bonds are considered taxable municipal bonds and offer security comparable to their tax-exempt counterparts.

The interest income from "nongovernmental purpose" bonds, including bonds used to finance subsidized housing and student loans and redevelopment bonds, is not subject to the regular federal income tax. However, the income from these bonds is subject to the alternative minimum tax. The activities financed by such bonds are of a quasi-governmental nature.

Generally, the more essential the bond is to the issuing authority, the better the tax treatment. Tax-free public purpose municipal bonds typically include obligations issued to finance highway construction or school financing, airports, docks, wharves, mass commuting facilities, sewage, and solid waste disposal facilities.

In addition, municipal bonds issued before August 7, 1986, generate tax-exempt interest to the extent they were exempt under prior law.

U.S. Treasury Obligations

As a general rule, interest on U.S. obligations and obligations issued by U.S. agencies or instrumentalities are included in gross income. For example, interest income earned on U.S. Treasury Bills and Notes is included in gross income. In addition, interest income earned on U.S. savings bonds is also taxable. Although taxpayers have a choice of including the incremental interest income annually, most taxpayers report the entire amount of interest income over the life of the bond upon redemption. Note that interest on U.S. obligations may be exempt from state and local taxation.

Educational Savings Bonds

Despite the general rule stated above, an exception exists for U.S. savings bonds redeemed to finance certain educational expenses. Accrued interest income on certain Series EE savings bonds may be excluded from gross income if the bonds are redeemed to pay for qualified higher educational expenses of the taxpayer, the taxpayer's spouse, or the taxpayer's dependents. IRC Sec. 135 defines "qualified higher education expenses" as tuition and required fees (net of scholarships, fellowships, employer-provided educational assistance, and other tuition-reduction amounts) for enrolling in or attending a college or eligible vocational school. The qualified expenses must also be exclusive of expenses used in computing the Lifetime, Hope, or American Opportunity Tax credits. The Code also stipulates that the taxpayer must be at least 24 years of age when the bonds are purchased. The exclusion is available only to the original purchaser of the bond or his or her spouse. The exclusion therefore precludes a gift of qualified Series EE savings bonds.

To qualify for the interest exclusion, the total of the interest and principal on the U.S. savings bonds redeemed may not exceed the qualified higher education expenses for the year. If the interest and principal exceed the educational expenses, the amount of the interest exclusion must be reduced.

Example

This year, Kathy Jones, aged 58, redeems Series EE savings bonds for $10,000, $2,500 of which is accrued interest. Kathy's son Joe attends a local university and has qualified educational expenses of $12,000. Kathy may exclude the entire $2,500 from her gross income. However, if Joe's qualified expenses were only $8,500, Kathy could exclude from her gross income only $2,125 determined as follows:

$$(\text{qualified expenses} \div \text{Series EE proceeds}) \times \text{interest} =$$
$$(\$8,500 \div \$10,000) \times \$2,500 = \$2,125$$

This special exclusion is designed to benefit only those taxpayers with moderate incomes. The exclusion for 2017 is phased out between the following modified adjusted gross income levels: $78,150 to $93,150 for taxpayers filing as single or head of household and $117,250 to $147,750 for married taxpayers filing jointly. Above these ranges, no exclusion is allowed. This phaseout range is adjusted annually for inflation. Married taxpayers who file separate tax returns are not eligible for the exclusion.

Sales of Nontaxable Municipal Bonds

Although the interest earned on certain bonds and other obligations of state and local municipalities is excluded from gross income, Sec. 103 does not extend the exemption to any gain or loss upon their sale. If a tax-exempt security is sold at a gain, the gain is taxable in computing gross income. However, if a sale results in a loss, the loss may prove deductible in computing taxable income.

Example

On July 1 of last year, Mary purchased a $25,000, 10-year tax-exempt municipal bond at par value. The bond's yield was 5 percent. On May 30 of this year, Mary sells the municipal bond for $25,875. During the period Mary owned the bond, she also received $625 of interest. Although the tax-exempt interest of $625 is excludible, the capital gain of $875 ($25,875 – $25,000) is taxable (short-term capital gain) in this year.

LO 6.3   **Explain the rules regarding the income taxation of Social Security benefits.**

SOCIAL SECURITY BENEFITS AND SIMILAR BENEFITS

Prior to 1984, Social Security and railroad retirement benefits were excluded from gross income. During the period from 1984 through 1993, a maximum of 50 percent of these benefits was exposed to federal taxation. Starting in 1994, an additional amount of these benefits became exposed to federal taxation. Currently, recipients of Social Security and railroad retirement benefits may have up to 85 percent of their benefits subjected to tax. Sec. 86 of the Internal Revenue Code outlines the procedures for determining if a benefit is taxable.

Social Security and railroad retirement benefits are included in gross income when the individual's "provisional income" exceeds certain threshold amounts. Provisional income is defined as "modified adjusted gross income" plus one-half of the Social Security or tier 1 railroad retirement benefits. Modified adjusted gross income is adjusted gross income with certain modifications. These modifications include the adding back of both tax-exempt interest received (including the interest excluded on Series EE savings bonds used to finance higher education) and the amount of deductible higher education expenses (including the interest expense deducted on educational loans) claimed by the taxpayer in determining AGI. Social Security recipients should be aware that tax-exempt interest from municipal bonds and bond funds could indirectly increase the amount of Social Security benefits subject to tax. (Note: If Social Security benefits are subject to taxation, recipients should consider shifting money from their tax-free municipal bond portfolio to tax-deferred investments—growth stocks, Series EE savings bonds, annuities, and so forth.)

The calculation used to determine the taxable portion of the benefits involves two tiers. Figure 6-1 illustrates the taxation of Social Security benefits at various income levels. If the taxpayer's provisional income is less than the first-tier base amount, there is no taxable benefit to report. However, if the provisional income exceeds the first-tier base amount but does not exceed the second-tier base amount, the taxable portion of the Social Security or railroad retirement benefit is limited to the lesser of

- one-half (50 percent) of the benefits received or
- one-half (50 percent) of the excess of the provisional income over the first-tier base amount

The base amounts (thresholds) are

	First-Tier	Second-Tier
Married filing jointly	$32,000	44,000
Single	25,000	34,000
Married filing separately	0	0

If the taxpayer's provisional income exceeds the applicable second-tier base amount, the amount of Social Security or railroad retirement benefits exposed to taxation increases to 85 percent. In this case, the taxpayer must then include in gross income the lesser of

- 85 percent of the Social Security or railroad retirement benefits received or the total of

- 85 percent of the amount of provisional income in excess of the second-tier base amount plus the lesser of 50 percent of the Social Security benefits received (the amount of the first-tier income calculation) or the statutory amount ($6,000 if married filing jointly; $4,500 if filing as a single person; or zero if married filing separately)

Figure 6-1: Calculation of Taxable Portion of Social Security Benefits

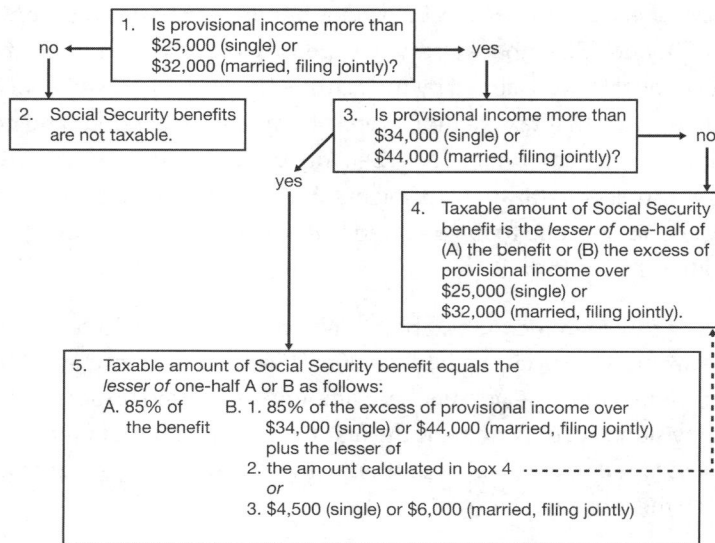

Example 1

Bob, a single taxpayer, has an adjusted gross income for the year of $26,000. He has no tax-exempt interest and has received $6,000 of Social Security benefits this year. Therefore his provisional income is $29,000 ($26,000 plus $3,000). According to figure 6-1, the taxable portion of his benefits is calculated as follows:

1. one-half of the benefits received = $6,000/2 or $3,000, or
2. one-half of the excess of the provisional income over the first-tier base amount ($25,000) = $4,000/2 or $2,000

The lesser of A or B is B, or $2,000. Therefore $2,000 of Bob's benefits are taxable.

Example 2

Jack and Ruby are married taxpayers filing a joint tax return. Their adjusted gross income is $60,000 this year. They also received $10,000 in tax-exempt interest and $15,000 in Social Security benefits. Consequently, their provisional income is $77,500

($60,000 + $10,000 + [$15,000/2]). Using figure 6-1, the taxable portion of their benefits is calculated as follows:

1.   85 percent of the benefits received = $12,750 ($15,000 × .85) or
2.   85 percent of the amount of provisional income in excess of the second-tier base amount ($44,000) equals $28,475 ($77,500 − $44,000 = $33,500 × .85 or $28,475) plus the lesser of
      a.   the amount of the first-tier income of $7,500 (one-half of the Social Security benefits received: $15,000/2) or
      b.   the statutory amount of $6,000 (married filing jointly)

Since the $6,000 amount in (b) is less than the $7,500 amount in (a), $6,000 is added to $28,475 for a total potential taxable benefit of $34,475.

According to figure 6-1, Jack and Ruby are required to include $12,750 of their Social Security benefits in gross income (the lesser of A or B).

These complex formulas for the taxation of Social Security benefits are an example of the convoluted calculations that can result in the tax law from what once was a simple concept in a human mind that a portion of the benefits should be taxable.

LO 6.4   Explain the rules regarding the income taxation of accident and health benefits.

ACCIDENT AND HEALTH BENEFITS

Medical and Disability Benefits

Internal Revenue Secs. 104 through 106 deal with a variety of benefits that may be received tax free by individuals on account of injuries or sickness. Such benefits include

- medical expense reimbursement plans
- disability policies
- workers' compensation acts
- certain damages
- government disability programs

Medical expense reimbursements from accident and health insurance plans are excluded from gross income to the extent the taxpayer has not claimed a medical expense deduction for the underlying medical costs as an itemized deduction (Schedule A of Form 1040).

Example

Mr. Apple, age 50, had $10,000 of deductible medical expenses last year. In itemizing his deductions, he deducted a net medical expense of $2,000 (after subtracting 10 percent of adjusted gross income). This year, he received a medical reimbursement check for $7,500 covering some of the costs incurred last year. Mr. Apple must include $2,000 of the reimbursement as income this year (representing the tax benefit he derived on last year's return). The balance of the reimbursement, $5,500, is excluded from gross income.

A disability policy or income replacement policy protects the insured against a financial loss that may occur if the individual is incapacitated and unable to work. If the taxpayer purchases the policy with after-tax dollars, the entire proceeds from the policy are excluded from gross income.

Example

Tom Hanes missed 12 weeks of work after falling two stories from a building in June. Because of the multiple fractures he suffered, he was unable to work in any capacity until September. As a result, Tom received $8,000 from a disability policy he had purchased several years ago. The entire amount of the proceeds are tax free because Tom had personally purchased the policy.

Amounts received by an employee under Social Security or workers' compensation as compensation for physical injury or physical sickness are excluded from gross income. In addition, workers' compensation acts extend to the survivors of a deceased employee and allow the recipients to exclude any benefits received on behalf of the deceased employee.

Government disability payments are also excluded from gross income if the payments (pension, annuity, or similar allowance) are received for the personal physical injuries or physical sickness of the taxpayer. These awards are tax exempt if attributable to active service in the armed forces of any country, or in the Coast Guard and Geodetic Survey or Public Health Service, or as a disability annuity payable under the Foreign Service Act of 1980.

In addition, the law provides an exclusion for amounts received by an individual as disability income attributable to injuries incurred as a direct result of a terrorist attack. The attack must have occurred while the individual was an employee of the United States and engaged in performing official duties outside of the United States.

Damages

Certain damages may also be excluded from gross income. The exclusion applies to financial awards for damages received because of personal physical injury or physical sickness. The exclusion is limited to nonpunitive damages. Sec. 104 prohibits the exclusion of punitive damages. However, an exception to this rule exists for wrongful death cases. If under a state law in effect on September 13, 1995, the only damages awarded in a wrongful death action are punitive damages, then the wrongful death award is excluded from gross income.

Nonpunitive damages for personal injury are currently excludible from gross income only if they are paid on account of a physical injury or physical sickness. Financial awards related to emotional distress are generally not excludible under current law. The exclusion would apply only if the emotional distress award is attributed to a physical injury or physical sickness or represents reimbursement for medical expenses arising from the emotional distress. This same logic now applies to the taxation of financial awards for loss of employment, age and gender discrimination, and civil rights violations. The key test for excludibility is physical injury or physical sickness. Without this requirement, these awards are included in gross income. The exclusion extends to both court awards and settlement agreements received outside of litigation.

Employer-Provided Accident and Health Plans

Employers often contribute to the cost of an employee's accident and health care insurance. The plan will often make payments directly to the employee or health care provider. Under certain conditions, benefits received from the employer-sponsored plan may be excluded from the employee's gross income. IRC Sec. 105 addresses amounts received under accident and health plans. Employer contributions to accident and health plans are covered under Sec. 106.

In general, the tax treatment of amounts received under accident and health plans depends on why benefits are paid, who pays the premiums, and how the benefits are computed.

Although Sec. 104 permits the tax-free receipt of a disability or income replacement policy's proceeds, there is one catch. The exclusion from gross income results from the taxpayer's purchasing of the policy with after-tax dollars. Sec. 104 is therefore generally addressing self-purchased disability and income replacement policies. However, if the taxpayer's employer pays the premiums on a disability or income replacement policy as a tax-free fringe benefit to the employee, the tax issue regarding policy proceeds is somewhat different. Sec. 105 requires the employee to include in gross income the proceeds received from employer-purchased disability and income replacement policies, unless the employer allows the employee to elect to pay tax currently on the policy premiums paid by the employer.

If the employer and employee share the premium costs of a disability or income replacement policy, only part of the policy's proceeds are excluded from gross income.

The exclusion from gross income is proportional to the employee's after-tax contribution of the policy's premium.

Example

The ABC Corporation maintains a disability plan. The plan provides for regular wages to employees missing work because of personal injury or sickness. The corporation requires that all employees participate in the premium cost of the policy. Employees are required to contribute 35 percent of the policy's premium cost through after-tax payroll deductions. The balance is paid by the employer and is not taxable to the employees.

Johnson, an employee, suffered a personal injury during the year. As a result, Johnson missed 6 weeks of work. During his absence, Johnson received $3,000 in disability proceeds under the corporation's plan. Johnson must include $1,950 of the proceeds in gross income. The balance, $1,050, is excluded from gross income. The exclusion (35 percent of $3,000) is proportional to Johnson's premium payments.

As illustrated, the general rule is to tax amounts received for personal injuries or sickness under accident and health plans to employees where the employer pays for the cost of the plan. However, there are two significant exceptions to this general rule:

- amounts expended for medical care
- payments unrelated to absence from work

The first exception excludes from gross income amounts received as reimbursements from an accident or health plan for the medical care of the taxpayer, his or her spouse, or dependents. These benefits are excludible if an insurance company provides the accident and health insurance benefits. With the passage of the Patient Protection and Affordable Care Act and the Health Care and Education Reconciliation Act of 2010 , insured plans will be prohibited from discriminating in favor of highly compensated executives similar to the nondiscrimination rules for self-insured plans described below. Public comment on the implementing of the Section 105 nondiscrimination rules however, has resulted in the delay of the enforcement of this provision until the IRS issues clarifying regulations. IRS Notice 2011–1 acknowledges some of the difficulty in applying Section 105 to insured health plans.

Example

Sicck Corporation provides all employees with health care insurance. Amy, a Sicck Corporation employee, receives a $500 reimbursement for medical bills incurred during the

year. The reimbursement is excluded from gross income even though Sicck Corporation paid the health care insurance premiums.

The second exception excludes payments unrelated to absence from work. If a taxpayer, a spouse, or a dependent incurs an injury that results in permanent disfigurement, loss or loss of using a body part, or loss of a bodily function, then the amounts received under the employer's accident or health care plan are excluded from gross income. For example, benefits paid for the loss of an arm, leg, or other bodily function are tax exempt. In addition, amounts received under an accident policy based on the nature of the injury are tax free. However, as previously stated, no exclusion is permitted if the length of time an employee is absent is a factor in determining the amount of the payment (that is, disability income proceeds).

Example

The Reading Railroad Corporation maintains an accident plan that provides payments for certain injuries. The plan provides for a $15,000 payment in the event an employee loses a limb. John, an employee who lost a leg, receives $15,000 from the corporation's plan. The $15,000 payment is excludible from John's gross income.

The Reading Railroad Corporation's plan also provides for payments of $400 weekly to each employee missing work on account of an injury. The corporation's plan covers employees for a maximum period of 26 weeks, regardless of the employee's injury. John received the maximum benefit ($10,400) under the plan. The entire amount received by John is included in gross income (disability income).

Qualified long-term care insurance is treated as accident or health insurance under Secs. 104 through 106 (the related deduction rules appear under Sec. 213). As a medical expense reimbursement, long-term care reimbursements are excluded from gross income, subject to certain restrictions. For 2017, the exclusion for benefits paid from qualified long-term care insurance contracts is $360 a day per covered individual, as adjusted for inflation. Amounts in excess of the daily exclusion are also excluded from gross income to the extent that actual long-term care expenses exceed the daily benefit and are not otherwise reimbursed. In an employer-provided long-term care insurance plan, amounts received are treated in generally the same way as amounts received for medical care.

An employee's gross income does not include premiums paid by an employer for accident or health care insurance coverage for the employee, the employee's spouse, and the employee's dependents. Sec. 106 addresses contributions by employers to accident and health plans. This section specifically excludes contributions made by an employer to an accident or health plan to provide compensation, through insurance or otherwise, directly to an employee for personal injuries or sickness. This exclusion applies to both insured and self-funded (uninsured) plans regardless of the number of employees. However, if an employee is indemnified beyond the medical costs incurred under the accident and health insurance plan, the excess reimbursement represents taxable income to the employee.

Contributions continuing after an employee's death or retirement are also excluded under the statute.

In general, the employer may claim a tax deduction for premiums paid for accident and health care coverage for employees.

Self-Funded Medical Reimbursement Plans

self-funded

The tax situation may be different than the above if an employer provides medical expense benefits through a self-funded plan (referred to in Sec. 105 of the Internal Revenue Code as a self-insured medical reimbursement plan) under which employers either (1) pay the providers of medical care directly or (2) reimburse employees for their medical expenses. If a **self-funded** plan meets certain nondiscrimination requirements for highly compensated employees, the employer can deduct benefit payments as they are made, and the employee will have no taxable income. If a plan is discriminatory, the employer will still receive an income tax deduction. However, all or a portion of the benefits received by "highly compensated individuals," but not by other employees, will be treated as taxable income. A highly compensated individual is (1) one of the five highest-paid officers of the firm, (2) a shareholder who owns more than 10 percent of the firm's stock, or (3) one of the highest-paid 25 percent of all the firm's employees. There are no nondiscrimination rules if a plan is not self-funded and provides benefits through an insurance contract, Blue Cross-Blue Shield plan, HMO, or PPO.

Nondiscriminatory Plans

To be considered nondiscriminatory, a self-funded plan must meet certain requirements regarding eligibility and benefits. The plan must provide benefits for 70 percent or more of "all employees" or for 80 percent or more of all eligible employees if 70 percent or more of all employees are eligible. Certain employees can be excluded from the all-employees category without affecting the plan's nondiscriminatory status. These include

- employees who have not completed 3 years of service
- employees who have not attained age 25
- part-time employees. Anyone who works less than 25 hours per week is automatically considered a part-time employee. Persons who work 25 or more hours but less than 35

hours per week may also be counted as part-time as long as other employees in similar work for the employer have substantially more hours.

- seasonal employees. Anyone who works less than 7 months of the year is automatically considered a seasonal employee. Persons who work between 7 and 9 months of the year may also be considered seasonal as long as other employees have substantially more months of employment.

- employees who are covered by a collective-bargaining agreement if accident and health benefits were a subject of collective bargaining

Even if the plan fails to meet the percentage requirements regarding eligibility, it can still qualify as nondiscriminatory as long as the IRS is satisfied that the plan benefits a classification of employees in a manner that does not discriminate in favor of highly compensated individuals. This determination is made on a case-by-case basis.

To satisfy the nondiscrimination requirements for benefits, the same type and amount of benefits must be provided for all employees covered under the plan regardless of their compensation. In addition, the dependents of other employees cannot be treated less favorably than the dependents of highly compensated individuals. However, because diagnostic procedures are not considered part of a self-funded plan for purposes of the nondiscrimination rule, a higher level of this type of benefit is permissible for highly compensated employees.

Discriminatory Plans

If a plan is discriminatory in either benefits or eligibility, highly compensated individuals must include the amount of any "excess reimbursement" in their gross income for income tax purposes. If highly compensated individuals receive any benefits that are not available to all employees covered under the plan, then these benefits are considered an excess reimbursement. For example, if a plan pays 80 percent of covered expenses for employees in general, but 100 percent for highly compensated individuals, the extra 20 percent of benefits constitutes taxable income for the highly compensated.

If a self-funded plan discriminates in the way it determines eligibility, then highly compensated individuals will have excess reimbursements for any amounts they receive. The amount of this excess reimbursement is determined by a percentage that is calculated by dividing the total amount of benefits received by highly compensated individuals (exclusive of any other excess reimbursements) by the total amount of benefits paid to all employees (exclusive of any other excess reimbursements).

A plan might discriminate with respect to both eligibility and benefits. Using the example above, assume a highly compensated individual receives $2,000 in benefits during a certain year. If other employees received only 80 percent of this amount (or $1,600), then the highly compensated individual would have received an excess reimbursement of $400. If the plan also discriminates in the area of eligibility, the highly compensated individual will incur additional excess reimbursement. For example, if 60 percent of the benefits (ignoring any benefits already considered excess reimbursement) were given to highly compensated individuals, then 60 percent of the remaining $1,600 ($2,000 – $400), or $960, would be added to the $400, for a total excess reimbursement of $1,360.

If a plan provides benefits only for highly compensated individuals, then all benefits received will be considered an excess reimbursement, as the percentage of total benefits received by the highly compensated group would be 100 percent.[2]

LO 6.5   **Explain the rules for qualifying for an "Achieving a Better Life Experience" (ABLE) account as well as the tax consequences of contributions to and distributions from such account.**

ABLE ACCOUNTS

The Tax Increase Prevention Act of 2014 permits any state to create an ABLE ("Achieving a Better Life Experience") program to assist the blind or disabled with expenses including education, housing and transportation among others.

The ABLE account is income tax-exempt though it is subject to the unrelated business income tax which applies to tax-exempt organization.

Cash contributions to the account may not exceed the gift tax annual exclusion which was $14,000 in 2017. None of the contributions to the account will be deductible.

While the earnings on the fund grow tax-free, the distributions from an ABLE account may or may not be subject to federal income tax. If the amount of the distributions is less than or equal to qualifying expenses, then the distribution is tax-free. To the extent the distribution(s) exceed qualified expenses, then Code Sec. 72 determines the exclusion ratio of the distributions. Any amount includible in gross income is also subject to an additional 10% tax.

---

2.   This portion of the text (Self-Funded Medical Reimbursement Plans) was excerpted from *Group Benefits: Basic Concepts and Alternatives*, 11th ed., by Burton T. Beam, Jr. (Bryn Mawr, PA: The American College Press, 2006).

Example

Frank establishes an ABLE account for his daughter Sarah who was disabled by injuries incurred during her service in Iraq. The account has grown to $100,000 with $64,000 representing contributions made over the years. During the current year, the account pays $25,000 on behalf of Sarah who is enrolled in a graduate program in education. Her qualified expenses for that year are $15,000 for education and $5,000 for assistive technology. $20,000 is not taxed since it is used for a qualified purpose of the ABLE account. Since $5,000 is not qualified, a portion is not taxed and the balance is according to the exclusion ratio ($64,000/$100,000). Therefore 64 percent of the $5,000 or $3,200 is not taxed. The remaining 34 percent of the $5,000 or $1,800 is included in Sarah's gross income. The $1,800 is also subject to an additional tax of 10 percent or $180.

LO 6.6   **Explain the extent to which dependent-care assistance benefits are taxed.**

DEPENDENT-CARE ASSISTANCE PROGRAMS

Under IRC Sec. 129, an employee may exclude from gross income the value of child- and dependent-care costs provided by an employer under a written nondiscriminatory plan. The dollar amount of the exclusion cannot exceed $5,000 for single parents and married couples filing jointly. The exclusion is reduced to $2,500 if the filing status is married filing separately. However, the amount excludible from income cannot exceed the employee's earned income for the year. In the event the employee is married, the earned income limitation applies to the lower earner's wages.

In addition to dependent-care assistance programs, the tax law allows a child-care credit under Sec. 21. This section allows employed individuals a limited credit for their child-care expenses depending on the employee's income and number of children. Although the law allows these two tax benefits related to child care, they are mutually exclusive. Sec. 129 prohibits utilizing both provisions by reducing any benefits qualifying for the credit by the amount of any excluded benefits under this section. Therefore reimbursements under dependent-care assistance programs reduce the dollar limit on expenses qualifying for the child-care credit.

Example

Mrs. Thomson , a returning veteran from Iraq, works for R&H Corporation. The corporation provides a day-care facility for the children of its employees. Every working morning, Mrs. Thomson leaves her young daughter at her employer's day-care center prior to commencing work. The employer estimates the value of the day-care center to Mrs. Thomson at $5,000. Mrs. Thomson may exclude the $5,000 from her income to the extent that both she and her husband have earned income up to $5,000. Alternatively, if Mrs. Thomson personally pays for the day-care center and is reimbursed for $5,000, the reimbursement is excluded from gross income. The amount of her qualifying child-care expenses for purposes of the tax credit would be zero. However, if Mrs. Thomson paid for all or part of the cost of the day-care center and was not reimbursed by her employer, her payments (up to the applicable limit) would qualify for the child-care credit.

In order to claim the dependent-care assistance exclusion or child-care credit, a series of special rules must be followed. For example, an employer's payments for dependent-care services to an employee's child under the age of 19 (or to anyone for whom the employee can claim a dependency exemption) do not qualify for the exclusion.

CHAPTER REVIEW

Key Terms and Concepts

exclusion   self-funded

Review Questions

Review questions are based on the learning objectives in this chapter. Thus a [6.3] at the end of a question means that the question is based on learning objective 3. If there are multiple objectives, they are all listed.

1. What is the general rule for income tax treatment of property received by gift or inheritance? [6.1]

2. What are the essential elements of a gift? [6.1]

3. What factors distinguish a gift from payment for services? [6.1]

4. James gives all the apartment houses he owns to his nephew, Scoop.

    a. Is the gift of the apartment houses subject to inclusion in Scoop's gross income? Explain.

    b. How will rental income be treated when received by Scoop?

    c. Would your answer to 4a be different if James gives Scoop only the right to the income produced by the apartment houses? Explain. [6.1]

5. How is a bequest treated for income tax purposes when it is a specific lump-sum amount paid in one installment out of estate income? [6.1]

6. Under the terms of Ed Blair's will, Mrs. Blair is to receive $80,000 as a specific bequest. The executor pays the bequest out of the income of the estate.

    a. Ed's will directs that the payments be made in no more than 2 years. Are there any income tax consequences to Mrs. Blair as a result of this action?

    b. Assuming the will directs that payments are to be made in equal annual amounts over 5 years, will Mrs. Blair have any income tax to pay? [6.1]

7. What is the general rule for taxation of interest on state and municipal bonds? [6.2]

8. Frank Peters purchased nontaxable municipal bonds with a yield of 6 percent. What would be the equivalent yield for a taxable investment if Frank's marginal income tax rate was 35 percent? [6.2]

9. Explain how the following categories of municipal bonds are taxed:

    a. public purpose bonds

    b. nongovernmental purpose bonds

    c. taxable municipal bonds

    d. bonds issued prior to August 7, 1986 [6.2]

10. Which of the following types of bonds will be exempt from federal income tax?

    a. municipal bonds issued this year to finance the construction of a waste disposal facility

    b. municipal bonds issued this year to finance the construction of a convention facility

    c. municipal bonds issued this year to finance subsidized housing [6.2]

11. Is interest on U.S. savings bonds tax free for income tax purposes? [6.2]

12. If tax-exempt securities that were purchased for a discount are sold at a gain, how will the gain be treated for income tax purposes? [6.2]

13. Bob and Sharon Stevens, both aged 69, are married and file a joint tax return. During the year, Mr. and Mrs. Stevens received $17,000 in Social Security benefits. In addition to the Social Security benefits, the Stevens's received $3,000 of interest income on their tax-exempt municipal bond fund, $5,000 of interest on their savings accounts,

and $12,000 in fully taxable pension benefits. Do Bob and Sharon have to include any of their Social Security benefits in gross income? Explain. [6.3]

14. What is the general rule for exclusion from gross income of medical expense reimbursements from accident and health insurance plans? [6.4]

15. Describe the income tax treatment of punitive damages paid pursuant to an action for personal injury. [6.4]

16. Describe the income tax treatment of damage awards for emotional distress. [6.4]

17. a.   What is the general rule for taxation of amounts received under an employer-provided accident and health plan?

    b.   Explain the exception to the general rule with regard to amounts expended for medical care.

    c.   Explain the exception to the general rule with regard to payments unrelated to absence from work. [6.4]

18. Explain the exclusion for benefits paid from qualified long-term care insurance contracts. [6.4]

19. a.   How are premiums contributed by an employer to an accident and health plan treated by the employee for income tax purposes?

    b.   How are these payments treated by the employer? [6.4]

20. a.   What is a self-funded medical-reimbursement plan?

    b.   Explain the nondiscrimination rules that are applicable to self-funded medical-reimbursement plans.

    c.   How will excess reimbursements be taxed to a highly paid employee covered in a self-funded medical-reimbursement plan? [6.4]

21. A shareholder-employee who is the highest-paid employee of a company received $4,000 as medical reimbursements for himself and his family this year from a self-funded medical-reimbursement plan. The only other medical reimbursement made by the company that year was to a secretary, who is not highly compensated. She was reimbursed $1,000 for noninsured medical expenses.

    a.   Would the payments to the shareholder-employee be discriminatory in favor of the highly compensated employee?

    b.   What would the tax result be if the answer was yes? [6.4]

22. Frank establishes an ABLE account for his daughter Sarah who was disabled by injuries incurred during her service in Iraq. The account has grown to $125,000 with $80,000 representing contributions made over the years. During the current year, the account pays $25,000 on behalf of Sarah who is enrolled in a graduate program in education. Her qualified expenses for that year are $15,000 for education and $5,000 for assistive technology. Describe the tax consequences of the distribution. [6.5]

23. Bob and Frieda McDaniels receive benefits under a qualified dependent-care assistance program provided by Frieda's employer. They file a joint return every year. Bob, the lower-earning spouse, earns $17,000 annually. They receive $7,000 under the program this year. How much, if any, of this benefit will be taxed to Bob and Frieda? [6.6]

Review Answers

1. The value of money or property received as a gift, bequest, devise, or inheritance is generally excluded from gross income under Code Sec. 102.

2. A gift is defined as a gratuitous transfer of property. To be considered a gift, the following elements are essential:

    • a donor competent to make the gift

    • a clear and unmistakable intention on the donor's behalf to make the gift

    • a donee capable of receiving the gift

    • an irrevocable conveyance, assignment, or transfer sufficient to vest legal title to the property in the donee

    • a donor's relinquishment of dominion and control of the property by delivery to the donee.

    In order to have a valid gift for federal income tax purposes, the donor must have acted out of a "detached and disinterested" generosity in transferring the property. Gifts are normally made out of "affection, respect, admiration, charity, or like impulses." Valid gifts have no strings attached.

3. Questions regarding gift or compensation normally arise as to payments where there is a past or present employment relationship. For federal income tax law purposes, a voluntary transfer without compensation is not necessarily a gift. It is not a gift if there is a legal or moral obligation for the transfer or if the donor expects to receive a benefit from the "gift." However, the mere absence of a legal or moral obligation for the transfer does not necessarily qualify the transfer as a gift. A transfer is a gift if it is made

from detached or disinterested generosity. Ultimately, the question of gift or compensation is resolved by reviewing the donor's dominant reason for making the transfer. Amounts transferred from an employer to an employee will not generally be treated as gifts.

4.   a.   The general rule is that gross income does not include the value of property acquired by gift.

      b.   Rental income from the property will be taxed to Scoop.

      c.   If James gives Scoop the right to income only, the income will be taxed to James under the assignment-of-income doctrine discussed in Chapter 3.

5.   A bequest of a specific sum of money or property is generally excluded from income for tax purposes even when it is paid out of income. This treatment applies only if the bequest is paid or credited all at once or in not more than three installments. If the bequest is paid in more than three installments, it is taxable to the recipient to the extent it is actually paid from the income generated.

6.   a.   The specific bequest of $80,000 to Mrs. Blair will be excluded from income taxation even though the executor pays the bequest out of the estate's income. This exemption will apply provided the bequest is paid to Mrs. Blair in no more than three installments. Therefore, if payment is made in two annual installments, the $80,000 bequest will be exempt from income taxation.

      b.   If the will directs that the specific bequest of $80,000 is to be paid in equal annual amounts over 5 years, Mrs. Blair must pay income tax annually on each $16,000 installment to the extent it is paid out of the estate's income.

7.   Sec. 103 of the Code provides that interest earned on certain obligations of a state are tax exempt and therefore excluded from gross income. In addition, interest earned on the obligations of a political subdivision of a state (that is, a county, city, and/or town) is also exempt from federal income taxation. Such tax-exempt state and municipal bonds are generally public purpose bonds; that is, bonds used to finance essential governmental activities.

8.   The equivalent yield is 9.23 percent at Frank's marginal tax rate of 35 percent, and is derived as follows: 6% ÷ .65 (1.00 − .35 marginal tax bracket).

9.   a.   State and municipal "public purpose" bonds are tax-exempt with respect to interest earned. This means that 100 percent of the interest income received by an investor is generally free from federal taxation.

b. The interest income from "nongovernmental purpose" bonds is not subject to the regular federal income tax. However, the income from these bonds is subject to the alternative minimum tax.

c. The interest income of arbitrage bonds, industrial development bonds, and most other private activity bonds is subject to the regular federal income tax. Obligations issued under this category may include sports facilities, convention or trade show facilities, parking facilities, and air and water pollution control facilities. These bonds are considered taxable municipal bonds.

d. Municipal bonds issued before August 7, 1986, generate tax-exempt interest to the extent they were exempt under prior law.

10. a. Obligations issued to finance the construction of a waste disposal facility are considered to be tax-free public purpose municipal bonds.

b. Obligations issued to finance the construction of a convention facility are considered to be taxable municipal bonds, which are subject to the regular federal income tax.

c. Obligations issued to finance subsidized housing are considered to be "nongovernmental purpose" bonds, which are not subject to the regular federal income tax but are subject to the alternative minimum tax.

11. No, interest income earned on U.S. savings bonds is taxable. Taxpayers have a choice of including the incremental interest income annually or reporting the entire amount of interest income over the life of the bond upon redemption.

12. If a tax-exempt security is sold at a gain, the gain is taxable in computing gross income.

13. The Stevens's provisional income is $28,500 ($3,000 tax-exempt interest plus $5,000 taxable interest plus $12,000 pension income plus one-half of their Social Security benefits of $17,000). This amount is less than the applicable first-tier base amount of $32,000. Therefore their benefits are fully excludible from gross income.

14. Medical expense reimbursements from accident and health insurance plans are excluded from gross income to the extent the taxpayer has not claimed a medical expense deduction for the underlying medical costs as an itemized deduction.

15. Code Sec. 104 prohibits the exclusion of punitive damages. Therefore punitive damages paid pursuant to an action for personal injury are fully taxable for federal income tax purposes.

16. Financial awards related to emotional distress are generally not excludible from gross income under current law. There would be an exclusion from gross income if the emotional distress award was attributed to a physical injury or sickness or represents reimbursement for medical expenses arising from the emotional distress.

17. a. The general rule is to tax amounts received for personal injuries or sickness under accident and health plans to employees where the employer pays for the cost of the plan.

    b. An exception to the general rule excludes from gross income amounts received as reimbursements from an accident or health plan for the medical care of the taxpayer, his or her spouse, or dependents. These benefits are excludible if an insurance company provides the accident and health insurance benefits.

    c. An exception to the general rule excludes payments unrelated to absence from work. If the taxpayer, his or her spouse, or a dependent incurs an injury that results in permanent disfigurement, loss or loss of using a body part, or loss of a bodily function, then the amounts received under the employer's accident or health care plan are excluded from gross income. However, no exclusion is permitted if the length of time an employee is absent from work is a factor in determining the amount of the payment (that is, disability income proceeds).

18. Qualified long-term care insurance is treated as accident or health insurance under Code Secs. 104 through 106. As a medical expense reimbursement, long-term care reimbursements up to a specified amount per day (as adjusted for inflation) per covered individual are excluded from gross income. Amounts in excess of the daily exclusion are also excluded from gross income to the extent that actual long-term care expenses exceed the daily benefit and are not otherwise reimbursed. In an employer-provided long-term care insurance plan, amounts received are treated in generally the same way as amounts received for medical care.

19. a. An employee's gross income does not include premiums paid by an employer for accident or health care insurance coverage for the employee, the employee's spouse, and the employee's dependents.

    b. In general, the employer may claim a tax deduction for premiums paid for accident and health care coverage for employees.

20. a. A self-funded medical reimbursement plan is one under which the employer will either pay the providers of medical care directly or reimburse employees for their medical expenses. If the plan meets certain nondiscrimination requirements, employees will have no taxable income. If the plan is discriminatory, all

or a portion of the benefits received by "highly compensated individuals" will be treated as taxable income. Whether the plan is discriminatory or not, the employer will receive an income tax deduction for benefit payments as they are made.

b. To be considered nondiscriminatory, a self-funded plan must meet certain requirements regarding eligibility and benefits. For eligibility purposes, the plan must provide benefits for 70 percent or more of all employees or for 80 percent or more of all eligible employees if 70 percent or more of all employees are eligible. Certain employees can be excluded from the all-employees category, including employees who have not completed 3 years of service, employees who have not attained age 25, part-time employees, seasonal employees, and employees who are covered by a collective-bargaining agreement if accident and health benefits were a subject of collective bargaining.

If the plan fails to meet the percentage test regarding eligibility, it can still qualify as nondiscriminatory if the IRS is satisfied that it does not discriminate. To satisfy the nondiscrimination requirements for benefits, the same type and amount of benefits must be provided for all employees under the plan regardless of their compensation. In addition, the dependents of other employees cannot be treated less favorably than the dependents of highly compensated individuals.

c. If highly compensated individuals covered under a self-funded plan receive any benefits not available to all employees in the plan, these benefits are considered an excess reimbursement and must be included in their gross income for income tax purposes. If the plan discriminates in the way it determines eligibility, then highly compensated individuals will have excess reimbursements for any amounts they receive. The amount of this excess reimbursement is determined by a percentage that is calculated by dividing the total amount of benefits received by highly compensated individuals (exclusive of any other excess reimbursements) by the total amount of benefits paid to all employees. It is possible that a plan might discriminate with respect to both eligibility and benefits.

21. a. If the secretary's actual medical expenses amounted to $1,000 but were not limited to that figure, then there would not be discrimination. However, if certain limitations were placed on her reimbursable amounts and not on the highly compensated employee, then there would be discrimination in benefits.

b. Assume that there is discrimination and the secretary's reimbursement is typical of other not highly compensated employees in that they received 25 percent of the highly compensated employee's benefit ($4,000 versus $1,000). The highly compensated employee would have received an excess reimbursement of $3,000 ($4,000 – $1,000) that would be includible in his gross income for this year.

22. The distribution of $25,000 is for a qualified disability expense in the amount of $20,000 so only a portion of the distribution will be includible into Sarah's gross income. The amount of the exclusion is calculated under the annuity exclusion ratio of Code Sec. 72.The exclusion ratio is $80,000/$125,000 or 64 percent. Therefore 36 percent of the distribution not used for a qualified disability expense ($25,000 less $20,000 =$5,000) or $1,800 is includible in Sarah's gross income. There also is an additional 10 percent tax on the $1,800 includible in income or $180.

23. Bob and Frieda may exclude $5,000 of the $7,000 benefit they receive, the maximum amount excludible. Therefore the remaining $2,000 will be taxed to Bob and Frieda.

Chapter 7

Business Expenses and Expenses for the Production of Income

Learning Objectives

An understanding of the material in this chapter should enable you to

LO 7.1   **Explain the requirements for deducting trade or business expenses.**

LO 7.2   **Explain the requirements for deducting business entertainment expenses.**

LO 7.3   **Explain the requirements for deducting nonbusiness expenses paid for the production of income.**

LO 7.4   **Explain the rules regarding the deductibility of expenses for home offices and vacation homes.**

LO 7.5   **Explain the 2 percent floor on miscellaneous itemized deductions.**

The income tax created more criminals than any other single act of government.

— Barry M. Goldwater

There are specific rules for deductibility of certain expenses paid or incurred for business or for the production of income, are as follows:

- specific types of business expenses

- business entertainment and related expenses

- expenses that are not business expenses but that are made in connection with the production of income

- home office expenses

- vacation home expenses

- the "2 percent floor" on individual miscellaneous itemized deductions

Deductible business expenses may generally be claimed by both individual taxpayers and business entities. However, the manner in which expenses are deductible can vary depending on both the type of taxpayer involved and the nature of the taxpayer's relationship to the business. For example, the business expenses of a regular or "C" corporation are deducted on the corporation's tax return to provide a benefit for the corporation as a taxpaying entity. In the case of so-called "pass-through" tax entities including partnerships and "S" corporations, the deductions are reported on the entity's tax return, but the individual business owners are the taxpayers who actually receive the benefit of the deductions because they are the actual taxpayers for the business. For individual owners of partnerships and "S" corporations, business deductions are, in effect, claimed on Schedule E of Form 1040. The tax treatment of business entities is discussed in more detail in later chapters of this text.

For individual taxpayers who are sole proprietors for income tax purposes, business expenses are claimed on Schedule C of Form 1040. Like partners and shareholders in "S" corporations, sole proprietors claim their business expenses "above the line," that is, such expenses are subtracted from gross income in determining adjusted gross income.

Individual taxpayers who are employees must generally claim their allowable business expenses as miscellaneous itemized deductions on Schedule A of Form 1040. A few employee business expenses (including deductions for reimbursed business expenses under nonaccountable plans, moving expenses, and certain expenses of performing artists) are deductible "above the line" in calculating adjusted gross income. The rest are treated as miscellaneous itemized deductions that are "below-the-line" deductions and are also generally subject to the limitations of the "2 percent floor" that will be covered in this chapter.

Expenses of individual taxpayers that are not business expenses but that are paid in connection with an activity engaged in for the production of income are also generally deductible. These deductions are often loosely referred to as "investor's expenses," although that terminology is not always appropriate. Expenses for the production of income are deductible in various ways depending on the nature of the income-producing activity. For example, expenses associated with a nonbusiness rental activity would be shown on Schedule E of Form 1040 and deducted above the line. On the other hand, expenses for financial planning or investment advisory fees would be deducted below the line as miscellaneous itemized deductions subject to the 2 percent floor.

There are specific limitations applicable to the deductibility of expenses attributable to the business use of a home. In addition, there are special restrictions on deducting expenses for the rental of a vacation home. Although these are two different topics, they are covered in the same section of the Internal Revenue Code.

LO 7.1   Explain the requirements for deducting trade or business expenses.

BUSINESS EXPENSES

Fundamental Rules

Internal Revenue Code Sec. 162 states that "there shall be allowed as a deduction all the ordinary and necessary expenses paid or incurred during the taxable year in carrying on any trade or business...." The Code then goes on to list special rules and requirements applicable to specific types of business expenses. However, the fundamental rules for deductibility are contained in the sentence quoted. The expense must be attributable to a business, be paid or incurred during the taxable year, and be both "ordinary" and "necessary" in the conduct of the business.

ordinary expense

The terms "ordinary" and "necessary" have been the subject of considerable interpretation by both the IRS and the courts. Essentially, an **ordinary expense** is a customary or usual expense made by many taxpayers involved in the same business activity. The expense does not necessarily have to be made at regular intervals in order to be considered ordinary. However, not all business expenses are considered to be ordinary. An example of an expense that is not ordinary is where a corporation pays the cost of a wedding reception for a majority stockholder's daughter. Even if most of the guests are customers of the corporation, such an expense is not customary and therefore not ordinary.

necessary expense

The **term necessary** expense has been accepted as including expenses that are appropriate and helpful to the taxpayer's business, even if the expense is not necessary in the strictest sense. In most situations, an expense that is ordinary will also be considered necessary.

The phrase "paid or incurred during the taxable year" means that the taxpayer cannot arbitrarily select the tax year in which to claim a deduction but must claim it in the year the deductible expense is paid or accrued. The term "accrued" refers to taxpayers on the accrual method of tax accounting. Such taxpayers deduct expenses in the tax year in which the liability to pay the expense becomes fixed, ascertainable, and certain. Taxpayers who use the cash method of tax accounting must deduct expenses in the year they are paid.

The phrase "in carrying on any trade or business" means that the expense must be business related. An activity must be engaged in with the intent and expectation of making a profit in order to be a business activity for tax purposes. There must also be an element of regularity and continuousness in the taxpayer's participation in the activity. Certain activities are engaged in with the primary intention of making money, but they are treated for tax purposes as nonbusiness activities engaged in for the production of income. This type of activity has its own income tax rules that will be discussed later in this chapter. If an activity is engaged in primarily for personal satisfaction or pleasure (such as a hobby), expenses associated with the activity will generally be nondeductible unless the activity actually becomes a profitable business.

capital expenditures

Another fundamental rule for deductibility of expenses is that the expense must not be a capital expenditure. Expenses of a capital nature generally cannot be fully deducted in the year they are made but must either be deducted over a period of years or not be deducted at all. **Capital expenditures** include the cost of acquiring or improving property with a useful life of more than one year. Other common examples include machinery and equipment, furniture and fixtures, and any expenditure on a similar asset having a useful life extending substantially beyond the current year.

Specifically Nondeductible Expenses

Although business expenses are generally deductible, the Code describes certain payments that are specifically nondeductible. Among these are payments that are illegal under federal or state law. Examples of illegal payments are bribes to government officials and kickbacks in consideration of the referral of a client, patient, or customer. Expenses paid in the conduct of an illegal business such as drug trafficking are nondeductible. Illegal payments include payments in violation of any federal law or of any state law that is generally enforced and subjects the payer to either a criminal penalty or the loss of a license or privilege to engage in a business. There is also a specific Code provision that disallows deductions for bribes and kickbacks made by any provider of services furnished under Medicare or Medicaid coverage.

A fine or penalty paid to a government for the violation of any law is also nondeductible. Such payments include penalties assessed with respect to a federal tax liability and fines for traffic violations or other criminal offenses. For example, payments for speeding or parking tickets received while traveling on business are nondeductible. Similarly, if a taxpayer pays treble damage in judgment or settlement of a lawsuit brought in connection with the taxpayer's criminal conviction or plea of "no-contest" under the antitrust laws, two-thirds of the damage payments (essentially the punitive portion) is nondeductible.

Certain expenses of a political nature are also nondeductible. These include the following examples:

- expenses in connection with influencing legislation

- expenses for participation in a political campaign on behalf of or in opposition to a candidate for public office

- expenses for influencing public opinion on a political issue

- expenses for communication with certain executive branch officials to influence their official positions

Note that expenses for influencing legislation at the local level are not subject to this rule and are therefore deductible. Also, if the taxpayer is a professional lobbyist who is paid to influence legislation, he or she may deduct expenses related to that activity as business expenses.

Payments in Compensation for Services

Reasonable Compensation

When a taxpayer engaged in a trade or business makes payment to an individual for services rendered, the general rule is that the payment is a deductible business expense. However, the amount of the payment must be reasonable to be deductible. In other words, the payment of any compensation in excess of a reasonable amount is nondeductible.

The tax issue of reasonable compensation has historically arisen mostly in cases involving compensation paid to employees of a corporation who are also its shareholders. The IRS has typically sought to recharacterize the excess portion of the compensation as a nondeductible dividend payment to the shareholder-employee. In such cases, the corporation had an incentive to characterize payments to the shareholder-employee as compensation rather than as dividends, because compensation payments are deductible by the corporation while dividend payments are not. As a result, the factual issue of reasonableness arose in many court cases.

The maximum tax rate on most corporate dividends received by individual taxpayers is 20 percent. This is considerably lower than the highest marginal rate applicable to compensation income which is 39.6 percent. As a result of our current tax environment, the IRS has less incentive to recharacterize a payment of compensation to a shareholder-employee as a dividend payment. The corporation would still lose the deduction for the payment at the corporate level, but the shareholder-employee would generally be taxed at a lower rate if the recharacterization occurred. In some cases the shareholder-employee may wish to have payments characterized as dividends rather than compensation, especially if the corporation's taxable income is low enough (i.e., the corporation's marginal tax rate is 15 percent) so that the loss of the deduction at the corporate level has no significant effect. Whether dividend characterization is now more favorable to the taxpayer or to the IRS depends upon the specific circumstances of each case. However, it is still important to examine the reasonable compensation issue from a legal standpoint.

reasonable compensation

Reasonable compensation may be loosely defined as that amount that would ordinarily be paid to an employee for similar services by similar companies operating in similar circumstances. Under the judicial decisions on this issue (of which there are many), several factors are taken into account in making the factual determination of reasonableness. These factors include (but are not limited to)

- the degree and nature of the employee's responsibility in his or her position (including responsibility for the production of profits)
- the amount the employee could have earned in similar employment for another company
- the salary paid in prior years for the same services
- the time the employee devotes to the performance of the services
- the nature of the services and any unique or peculiar abilities of the employee in rendering those services
- the amount of salaries paid to other employees providing similar services who are not shareholders
- general economic conditions in the region

The employee's total compensation is considered in determining reasonableness. Total compensation includes commissions, overrides, bonuses, and payments to pension, profit-sharing, or 401(k) plans.

One factor that may come into play in a dispute over this issue is that a court will consider a larger payment in a later year for the same services rendered in prior years to be reasonable if it can be shown that the total amount paid over the years is reasonable for the total services rendered. This means that a company can "make up" compensation in later years that an employee earned or deserved but the company was not previously able to pay.

If compensation is the desired characterization for tax purposes, a privately owned corporation might enter into an agreement with an officer-stockholder of the corporation that provides for a repayment of a portion of his or her compensation to the corporation in the event that it is determined by the IRS to be unreasonable and therefore partially nondeductible. The officer-stockholder may deduct such a repayment on his or her tax return if the agreement was made before the time of the payment and is otherwise enforceable. The problem with such agreements is that they may become a self-fulfilling prophecy: The IRS may use them as evidence that the parties themselves had an inkling that the compensation was unreasonable. The parties may be able to avoid this situation if the agreement is included in the general bylaws of the corporation rather than as a stand-alone contract with an individual officer-stockholder.

In certain situations, the IRS may assert that compensation paid to a shareholder-employee is unreasonably low rather than unreasonably high. This may occur where shareholder-employees are attempting to use the 20 percent dividend tax rate to reduce the tax paid on income which should be characterized as payment for services rendered to the company. The issue may also arise in partnerships and S corporations where low salaries are paid to owner-employees in order to allow more of the company's income to be allocated to lower-bracket owners (typically family members) of the so-called "pass-through" business entity, resulting in lower overall taxes. In this scenario, the IRS may reallocate income to high-bracket owner-employees whose efforts actually generated the income. Furthermore, the IRS may recharacterize "distributions" paid to S corporation shareholder-employees as salary where the salaries paid to such shareholder-employees are unreasonably low. This frequently occurs when the shareholder-employees are attempting to avoid or minimize the Social Security and Medicare taxes that apply to wages. Both S corporation distributions (and ordinary income) are currently not subject to Social Security and Medicare taxes. However, this exception does not apply to general partners in partnerships.

The Rule of "Excessive Employee Remuneration"

One special rule limiting deductions for compensation applies only to payments by publicly held corporations. The general definition of "excessive employee remuneration" is remuneration paid to a "covered employee" that is in excess of $1 million for the taxable year. A "covered employee" is either one of the following options:

- the chief executive officer of the corporation or an individual acting in such capacity at the close of the taxable year

- one of the four most highly paid officers of the corporation for the taxable year (other than the chief executive officer)

Under this definition, the rule applies to no more than five employees of a company for any taxable year.

There are also qualifying provisions that apply to the $1 million maximum amount. The following types of compensation or "remuneration" do not count toward the $1 million deductible limit:

- commissions generated by the taxpayer to whom the compensation is paid

- contributions to a qualified plan of deferred compensation
- the value of employee benefits that are excludible from the gross income of the employee (such as employer contributions to health plans)
- so-called "performance-based" compensation. In order to be treated as "performance-based," the compensation must be payable solely on account of the attainment of one or more performance goals, must be disclosed to and approved by a majority vote of the corporation's shareholders, and must be determined by a compensation committee of the corporation's board of directors comprised solely of two or more outside directors.

This provision has been criticized by commentators as not being strong enough to truly discourage the excessive compensation being paid to executives of public companies. However, it is at least a step in that direction by the income tax law.

Education Expenses

Expenses for Business-Related Education

Treasury regulations deal with the question of whether expenses incurred for education related to a business activity are deductible. Such expenses are deductible if they meet either of the two following criteria:

- The expenses are deductible if incurred primarily for the purpose of meeting the requirements of the taxpayer's employer or of local law as a condition for the taxpayer's retention of employment.
- The expenses are deductible if incurred primarily for the purpose of maintaining or improving skills needed by the taxpayer in his or her current employment or business activity.

On the other hand, expenses for education that qualifies a taxpayer for a new business or line of work are not deductible. Also, expenses for education leading to the minimum requirements necessary for obtaining employment (as distinguished from retaining employment) as determined by an employer or the standards of a profession or business are not deductible. For example, expenses for medical school would generally fall within this rule of disallowance.

Travel itself as a form of education is not a deductible expense. However, travel expenses incurred to and from an educational event are deductible if the education itself is deductible. Any meal expenses incurred in connection with deductible education may be deductible subject to the 50 percent limitation explained later in this chapter.

The availability of the deduction may be affected by interaction with other education tax incentives. For example, the same education expenses cannot be used to claim both the business expense deduction and the "Lifetime" learning credit. The taxpayer may have to choose between the two tax benefits. The choice will generally depend on the taxpayer's marginal tax bracket and perhaps also on whether the business deduction would be claimed above the line or below the line.

If the taxpayer is a sole proprietor, the deduction would be claimed above the line on Schedule C of Form 1040. If the taxpayer is an employee, the deduction is a miscellaneous itemized deduction claimed on Schedule A and subject to the "2 percent floor" discussed later in this chapter.

Certain education expenses that are deductible as business expenses may also be eligible for the deduction for "qualified higher education expenses" as explained below. Taxpayers who have expenses that qualify for either deduction will usually be better off claiming the expenses as business expenses, unless the taxpayer is an employee and the business expense is subject to the 2 percent floor. On the other hand, certain education expenses may qualify for one of these deductions but not the other.

Qualified Higher Education Expenses

Congress will need to reauthorize the deduction for qualified higher education expenses incurred in 2017 and subsequent years. Until it does, no such deduction is permitted.

For tax years beginning before 2017, individual taxpayers under current law can deduct certain expenses for higher education, subject to restrictions and limitations. Higher education expenses need not be business expenses to qualify for this special deduction. The deduction is claimed above the line, not as an itemized deduction, even though it represents an expense of a personal nature rather than a business expense.

Qualified expenses include tuition and fees paid for the attendance by the taxpayer, the taxpayer's spouse, or the taxpayer's dependents at a postsecondary educational institution offering credit toward a degree or other recognized postsecondary education credential. Room and board, transportation, and living expenses are not qualified expenses for purposes of the deduction.

There are limitations on the amount of higher education expenses that are deductible. The limits are based upon the taxpayer's adjusted gross income for the year, with certain modifications.

The maximum deductible amount is currently $4,000. Married taxpayers filing jointly with AGI in excess of $160,000 are not permitted to claim the deduction. Other eligible taxpayers with AGI in excess of $80,000 are not permitted to claim the deduction. A reduced deductible amount is available for married taxpayers filing jointly with AGI over $130,000 but not over $160,000, and for other eligible taxpayers with AGI over $65,000 but not over $80,000. The reduced deductible amount is $2,000.

Example

For 2016, Robert and Laurie Scott file a joint return showing AGI of $150,000. They pay $20,000 during that year in tuition for their son, Timmy, to attend Commonwealth University to pursue a bachelor's degree. Because their AGI falls between $130,000 and $160,000, they are eligible to claim the reduced deduction of $2,000 for Timmy's higher education expenses.

There are several coordinating provisions under Sec. 222 for this deduction that prevent the combined use of multiple tax benefits. For example, a taxpayer cannot claim a Hope scholarship, American opportunity, or Lifetime learning tax credit for the expenses of any student for whom the higher education expense deduction has been claimed for the same tax year. The American opportunity tax credit has expanded and replaced the Hope scholarship tax credit. Furthermore, any amounts taken into account for purposes of determining the exclusion from gross income of interest on U.S. savings bonds used for higher education may not also be used as qualified expenses under the deduction rules. There are also coordinating provisions that restrict the use of amounts distributed from Coverdell education savings accounts and qualified state tuition programs (QSTPs) as qualified expenses for deduction purposes.

A taxpayer may be fully eligible for both the American opportunity tax credit and the deduction for higher education expenses. However, as stated above, both of these tax benefits cannot be claimed with respect to expenses of the same student. Generally, it will be more beneficial for such taxpayers to claim the American opportunity tax credit for a student's expenses.

The deduction for higher education expenses may not be claimed by married taxpayers filing separately or by any individual who is eligible to be claimed as a dependent on another taxpayer's return.

Health Insurance Premiums Paid on Behalf of Self-Employed Individuals

If a sole proprietorship, partnership, or "S" corporation pays the health insurance premiums for a proprietor, partner, or more than 2 percent shareholder in the S corporation (including such person's spouse and/or dependents), this payment cannot be excluded from the gross income of such "self-employed" persons as it would be in the case of an employee. However, the covered person is entitled to an above-the-line deduction equal to 100 percent of the amount paid.

Medical expense deductions of individuals are generally claimed below the line as itemized deductions. However, this particular deduction is taken above the line in determining adjusted gross income. The deduction cannot exceed the individual's earned income from the business that provides the health plan. It is available only if the self-employed person is not eligible to participate in any subsidized health plan maintained by any employer of the self-employed person or the person's spouse. Premiums for qualified long-term care insurance as well as for health insurance coverage are eligible for this deduction. Applicable requirements and limits for the deduction are applied separately with respect to long-term care coverage.

Transportation and Travel Expenses

Business Transportation Costs

Expenses incurred for local transportation in the course of a business activity are generally deductible. Such expenses include taxi, railway, or bus fares, and expenses for the business use of a car.

Car expenses may be deducted in one of two different ways. The taxpayer may claim a standard mileage allowance for business transportation. This allowance is deemed to include depreciation, fuel, insurance, repairs, and other normal operating expenses. The only actual expenses that are deductible in addition to the mileage allowance are those for highway tolls, parking charges, and interest payments with respect to the car that are otherwise deductible under the tax law. Taxpayers who lease their cars may generally use the mileage allowance but it must be used for the entire lease period. The mileage allowance can be claimed only with respect to those miles actually driven for business purposes. For the year 2017, the standard allowance was 53.5 cents per mile. The basis of the car must be reduced by 25 cents per mile for the year 2017. This figure is subject to annual indexing for inflation. The standard mileage allowance cannot be used by taxpayers who

- use the car for livery or hire
- use two or more cars simultaneously for business purposes, or
- have previously claimed accelerated depreciation (i.e., MACRS and/or Sec. 179) for the same car

In lieu of claiming the standard mileage allowance, taxpayers may claim their actual expenses (including depreciation) in using a car for business. Any depreciation deductions will be limited by that percentage of the overall use of the car that represents business use. Cars used for business are also subject to special so-called "luxury auto" limits on depreciation. Repairs made to the car will also be deductible only to the extent of the percentage of business use. The "actual expense" method requires significant record keeping to substantiate deductions. Many taxpayers find it easier to simply keep a log of business miles, and claim deductions under the standard mileage allowance.

Taxpayers who lease a car used for business are not permitted to claim depreciation for the car, since the required ownership does not exist. However, such taxpayers are permitted to deduct their lease payments to the extent the car is used for business if the standard mileage allowance is not used. This deduction is, however, subject to an "add-back" rule. Depending on the car's fair market value, a specified amount of the lease payment must be included in the taxpayer's gross income to offset part of the lease payment deduction. This rule corresponds to the "luxury auto" limitations that apply to taxpayers who claim depreciation for the business use of a car. These add-back amounts are relatively low and are published annually by the IRS to reflect adjustments for inflation.

Commuting Expenses

Expenses for commuting do not qualify as business transportation expenses and are not deductible. Therefore the trip between a taxpayer's home and his or her place of business is generally nondeductible. However, if the taxpayer engages in business activities at more than one location during the day, the cost of transportation between one business location and another such location are deductible.

If a taxpayer has an office at home that qualifies as a home office because it is the taxpayer's principal place of business, transportation expenses between the home office and other business locations are treated as deductible transportation expenses rather than nondeductible commuting expenses. The income tax rules for home offices are discussed in more detail later in this chapter.

"Temporary" Work Locations

temporary business locations

Another situation in which transportation expenses from a taxpayer's home may be deductible involves so-called **temporary business locations**. Essentially, a temporary work location is one that is expected to last for no longer than one year, and actually lasts for no longer than one year.

For example, a work location will not be treated as temporary if it was expected to last more than one year, even if it actually does not last more than one year. In addition, the location is not temporary if it does in fact last longer than one year, even if it was not expected to.

If a taxpayer has a temporary work location that is outside the taxpayer's metropolitan area, a trip from the taxpayer's home to the temporary work location and back is deductible business transportation, rather than nondeductible commuting. However, if the temporary work location is within the taxpayer's metropolitan area, additional rules apply. In such cases, in order to deduct the trip from the residence to the temporary location, the taxpayer must either

- have a place of business in addition to the temporary work location, or
- have a home office that is the taxpayer's principal place of business for the business conducted at the temporary location

Business Travel Away from Home

Ordinary and necessary expenses incurred in the course of traveling away from home on business are deductible. A taxpayer is generally considered to be "away from home" on a trip in which the taxpayer stays overnight or longer at a temporary business location.

Expenses that would be deductible for such trips include travel to the business location, lodging costs, meals (to the extent of 50 percent of the cost of the meal), local business transportation expenses, and other business expenses incurred while at the destination. Expenses for meals and lodging are deductible only to the extent they are not lavish or extravagant. Expenses incurred for personal activities at the business location are not deductible.

If the taxpayer's trip away from home is partially for business and partially for pleasure, the availability of travel expense and related deductions is subject to additional rules that are based on

- the taxpayer's principal purpose for making the trip
- the number of days spent on business during the trip
- whether the trip is to a destination within or outside of the United States

LO 7.2 **Explain the requirements for deducting business entertainment expenses.**

DEDUCTIONS FOR ENTERTAINMENT EXPENSES

Entertainment of clients, customers, employees, and associates is an expense that practically every business person incurs. However, such expenses may be disallowed as deductible business expenses unless the strict requirements in the Internal Revenue Code are followed. This section is intended to highlight the requirements that must be met to obtain the proper deduction for entertainment expenses.

Entertainment Defined

entertainment

Entertainment is defined in the Treasury regulations as any activity that is considered "entertainment, amusement, or recreation." This includes entertaining at nightclubs, cocktail lounges, theaters, country clubs, or sporting events. It also includes activities satisfying the personal, living, or family needs of a business customer, such as providing food and beverages, a hotel room, or an automobile.[1] No deduction will be allowed for any entertainment or recreation that is lavish or extravagant.[2]

Special Requirements for Deduction

There are special requirements that apply specifically to entertainment expenses, in addition to the general requirement that the expense be "ordinary and necessary." Unless an entertainment activity is "directly related to" or "associated with" the active conduct of the trade or business,[3] a deduction will be disallowed. Furthermore, the taxpayer must be able to substantiate the entertainment expenditures with adequate records of the business-related event or with other sufficient corroborating evidence.

---

1.   Treas. Reg. Sec. 1.274-2(b)(1)(i).
2.   Treas. Reg. Sec. 1.274-1.
3.   IRC Sec. 274(a).

Directly Related Requirement

directly related requirement

The **directly related requirement** generally refers to entertainment provided during a period in which the taxpayer is actively engaged in a business negotiation or discussion.[4] Thus food and beverages served to sales prospects during a business discussion are deductible subject to limitations. Under this requirement the taxpayer must have more than a general expectation of deriving some business benefit at some future, indefinite time. The expenditure must relate to the person with whom the taxpayer engaged in the active conduct of business. Thus the entertainment expenses paid for nonbusiness persons, such as spouses, are excluded here but may qualify under the associated-with test discussed below.

The primary purpose of any combined business and entertainment activity must not be a social one, but one to further the taxpayer's business. For example, if incidental business discussions take place on hunting or fishing trips, it cannot be said that the principal aspect of the combined business and entertainment was the transaction of business.

The directly related test is also met when the expenditures are made in a clear business setting, such that the recipient knows that the taxpayer has no significant motive other than to further business (for example, the sponsorship of a hospitality room at a convention, or the entertainment of business representatives at the opening of a new hotel or theatrical production).[5] Large parties thrown by the taxpayer, such as a wedding where other than business associates are present, are not deductible under the directly related test as there is no clear business setting nor is the event related.

The expenses of entertainment are not directly related where there is little or no possibility of engaging in the active conduct of business, such as where the taxpayer is not present or when the distractions are substantial.[6] Discussions at nightclubs, cocktail parties, theaters, or sporting events are generally not considered directly related because of the substantial distractions.

Entertainment for goodwill purposes without business discussions is not deductible under the directly related requirement but may qualify under the associated-with test discussed below.

---

4.   Treas. Reg. Sec. 1.274-2(c)(2).
5.   Treas. Reg. Sec. 1.274-2(c)(4).
6.   Treas. Reg. Sec. 1.274-2(c)(7).

Associated-with Requirement

associated-with requirement

As previously stated, entertainment expenses to promote goodwill (for example, expenses incurred in an effort to obtain new business or to encourage the continuation of existing business relationships) are not deductible under the directly related requirements. However, such goodwill entertainment expenses are considered associated with the conduct of business; under the **associated-with requirement**, these expenses may be deductible if they "directly precede or follow" a bona fide business discussion.[7]

For example, Alan, a manufacturing representative, has complex business discussions during the day with Barbara. At night Barbara is Alan's guest at the theater. His entertainment expenses are deductible, because they are associated with the business as goodwill expenses and directly followed bona fide business discussions. However, if Alan merely invited Barbara, a long-time business associate, to the theater, Alan could not deduct expenses if there was no business discussion before or after the show. Similarly, cocktail parties for business associates and their spouses are not deductible under this test if there were no substantial business discussions preceding or following the party.

"Directly preceding or following" has been interpreted in the regulations to mean that the entertainment occurs on the same day as the business discussions. However, entertainment expenses incurred on a day other than the day of business discussion may still qualify depending on the facts and circumstances. To continue the previous example, assume Barbara lives in Los Angeles and travels to New York for the negotiations. If Barbara takes Alan to the theater the night before the negotiations, such entertainment expenses are still deductible.[8]

Unlike the directly related test, expenses allocable to the entertainment of spouses who are not business associates may be deductible under the associated-with test. Thus if Alan invites Barbara and her spouse to the theater after business negotiations, the entire cost of the spouse's ticket is deductible. If Alan's spouse comes also, the cost of this ticket is likewise deductible.[9] Stricter rules apply to travel expenses paid for spouses.

---

7.   S. Rep. no. 1881, 87th Cong. 2d Sess. 26 (1962).

8.   Treas. Reg. Sec. 1.274-2(d)(3)(ii).

9.   Treas. Reg. Sec. 1.274-2(d)(4).

Exceptions to the General Requirements

Exceptions to the directly related and associated-with requirements in the Code basically relate to employers' entertainment expenses for their employees. Food and beverages furnished on the business premises to employees, whether for recreational or social purposes (such as Christmas parties or summer picnics), and expenses incurred for business meetings of employees (and stockholders, agents, or directors) are deductible without regard to the directly related or associated-with tests. An employer may also deduct entertainment expenses regarded as compensation to the employee, such as a paid vacation trip.[10]

Although the exceptions to the general rules need not meet directly related or associated-with tests, they still must meet the substantiation requirement discussed below in order to be deductible.

The 50 Percent Limitation

Deductions for all business meal and business entertainment expenses are limited to 50 percent of the amount that is deductible after taking into account all other limitations and restrictions. This rule applies to both business entertainment meals and meals taken while the taxpayer is traveling on business. It does not, however, apply to business travel expenses other than meal expenses.

There are some minor exceptions to the 50 percent rule, including meals provided at meetings of business leagues and meals provided to employees on the employer's business premises. Items that are treated as de minimis fringe benefits are excluded from the limitation. Also if a meal is treated as compensation to the recipient for tax purposes, rather than as entertainment, the limitation does not apply. Certain individuals in the transportation industry are also subject to different limitations on business meals.

The 50 percent limitation increases the after-tax cost of business meals and entertainment.

Example

Jane entertains a business client just after a meeting in New York. The total cost of the entertainment is $500. Her deduction is limited to 50 percent. Therefore the deductible amount is $250. If Jane is in a 35 percent bracket, her after-tax cost of the entertainment has been increased by $88 because of the 50 percent limitation ($250 nondeductible portion × .35).

---

10.   IRC Sec. 274(e).

50 Percent Limit on Meals and Entertainment
- Applies to all business entertainment expenses
- Applies to business meals, whether entertainment-related or not
- Limited exceptions apply
- Does NOT apply to business travel expenses other than meal expenses

Entertainment Facilities and Tickets

Deductions for expenses paid or incurred in connection with the operation and maintenance of an entertainment facility are generally disallowed. No depreciation deductions may be taken even when a facility is primarily used for business entertainment. By eliminating the deductibility of these expenses, Congress has sought to curtail excessive and abusive use of these facilities under the guise of business entertainment.

facility

Facility refers to any real or personal property (such as a yacht, hunting lodge, swimming pool, apartment, or hotel suite in a resort area) that is owned, rented, or used by taxpayers for recreational, entertainment, or amusement activities. However, certain facilities, such as automobiles or airplanes, that are not necessarily recreational may not fall within the above limitation. Deductions for these items continue to be allowed for business trips. Generally deductions for depreciation and operating costs of facilities, such as yachts, lodges, and so forth, are a thing of the past. Those deductions otherwise allowable to individuals that are not predicated on a business connection (such as interest expense on mortgage debt, real estate taxes, and casualty losses) are still available to the taxpayer who owns a facility used for business entertaining.

Out-of-pocket expenses for entertaining at a facility, such as the cost of food and beverages, fall within the general entertainment rules. However, membership dues and fees for business, social, athletic, sporting, luncheon, airline and hotel clubs, and country clubs are no longer deductible, regardless of whether the taxpayer uses the club for business purposes. Professional, civic, and public service organizations are not considered clubs for this purpose, so membership fees paid to such organizations are not subject to the entertainment rules. They are deductible if they qualify as ordinary and necessary business expenses.[11]

Although fees and membership dues are nondeductible, out-of-pocket expenses incurred while entertaining at a club may be deductible as business expenses if the general requirements described in this chapter are met. Such expenses would, of course, be subject to the 50 percent limitation.

---

11. Treas. Reg. Sec. 1.274-2(e)(3)(ii).

Deductions for tickets to entertainment events that qualify as business expenses are limited to the face value of the tickets. The face value limitation will make the premium paid to a scalper, as well as the premium paid to a legitimate ticket agency, nondeductible. The deduction, of course, is then further reduced by the 50 percent limitation.

Business Gifts

The deduction for business gifts that are ordinary and necessary business expenses will be disallowed to the extent they exceed $25 per donee.[12] A husband and wife are considered one donor, and they are limited to $25 per donee.[13] Gifts to spouses of business associates are deemed to be gifts to the business associate, unless the spouse is also a bona fide business associate of the taxpayer.[14]

Gifts of admission tickets to business associates for such entertainment as the theater or sporting events are considered entertainment expenses if the taxpayer accompanies the associates to the event. Thus the taxpayer would have to meet the associated-with test to obtain a deduction. The directly related test could not be met because of the distractions of such places.

On the other hand, if the taxpayer does not accompany the associates to the place of entertainment, the taxpayer has the choice of treating the expense as either a gift ($25 deduction limit) or entertainment (meeting the associated-with test) in order for it to be deductible. The taxpayer will probably elect to treat the expense as associated-with business only when the cost of the admission ticket is in excess of $25 and the event either precedes or follows a business discussion.

Substantiation Requirement for Travel and Entertainment Expenses

Even if the taxpayer meets the previously discussed requirements and limitations, travel and entertainment expense deductions will be disallowed unless the taxpayer can adequately

---

12.   IRC Sec. 274(b). The $25 limitation relates to the donor's cost rather than to the value of the property at the time of the gift.
13.   Treas. Reg. Sec. 1.274-3(e)(2).
14.   Treas. Reg. Sec. 1.274-3(d). Under IRC Sec. 274(b)(1)(A) and (B) the following items are not regarded as constituting business gifts but would, of course, be otherwise deductible if incurred in connection with a taxpayer's trade or business: an item costing $4 or less on which the taxpayer's name is clearly and permanently imprinted, and which is one of a number of identical items generally distributed, such as pens, desk sets, plastic bags, calendars, and cases; signs, display racks, or other promotional material to be used on the business premises of the donee.

substantiate the deductible expenses.[15] This requires the taxpayer either to maintain an account book or diary in which the expenditures are recorded at or near the time of expenditure or to substantiate the deductions with other sufficient evidence. The use of an account book is the better way to meet the substantiation requirements, and it must include the following information:

- the amount of each expenditure
- the date of the entertainment
- the place of the travel or entertainment, including name and address
- the business purpose
- for entertainment expenses, the business relationship, meaning the name, title, or other description of the person entertained, sufficient to establish a business relationship to the taxpayer[16]

If entertainment is merely associated with the taxpayer's business, then the taxpayer must record the place and duration of the business discussion and must identify the persons entertained who participated in the discussion.[17]

Lodging expenses and other expenses of $75 or more require documentary evidence, such as a receipt, to support the deduction.[18] Incidental items, such as taxi fares or telephone calls, may be aggregated on a daily basis.[19]

The statutory substantiation requirements superseded the well-known Cohan case,[20] which held that if evidence indicated the taxpayer had incurred deductible travel or entertainment expenses, but these amounts could not be determined, then a court must make "as close an approximation as it can, rather than disallow the deduction entirely."

The substantiation requirements have been construed to require a detailed accounting.[21] For example, in one case the taxpayer offered a virtual blizzard of more than 1,700 chits, bills, and statements to support his deductions. The court denied the deduction, holding that his bills contained only monthly aggregates of time, place, or individual amount, and that almost all

---

15.   IRC Sec. 274(d).
16.   IRC Sec. 274(d); Treas. Reg. Sec. 1.274-5T(b).
17.   Treas. Reg. Sec. 1.274-5T(b)(4).
18.   Treas. Reg. Sec. 1.274-5(c)(2)(iii) .
19.   Treas. Reg. Sec. 1.274-5T(c)(6)(i)(b).
20.   *Cohan v. Comm'r*, 39 F.2d 540 (2d Cir. 1930).
21.   *Phillip Handelman v. Comm'r*, 509 F.2d 1067 (2d Cir. 1975).

the exhibits failed to contain a record of the business purpose or business relationship of the persons entertained.[22]

Reporting of Deductible Business Travel and Entertainment Expenses

Depending on the business situation of the taxpayer, travel and entertainment expenses may or may not be one of the items deducted from gross income in determining adjusted gross income.

If the taxpayer is a sole proprietor or partner, travel and entertainment expenses are considered deductible from gross income to determine adjusted gross income.[23] These taxpayers may deduct such expenses from gross income.[24]

If a partnership pays for or reimburses the travel and entertainment expenses of its partners, the expenses are part of the partnership's deductions from gross income.[25] The partner's share of the taxable income of the partnership after all deductions is added to the partner's individual gross income.[26] If a partner is not reimbursed for these expenses, the partner is allowed to deduct them from gross income to determine adjusted gross income on an individual return, provided that the partnership agreement specifically requires that the partner pay expenses of the partnership without reimbursement.[27]

On the other hand, all employees who have unreimbursed business expenses must itemize their deductions on Schedule A of Form 1040 to take advantage of these deductions.[28] For employees, these deductions are taken from adjusted gross income to determine taxable income and are generally subject to the 2 percent floor on miscellaneous itemized deductions.

Employees who adequately account to their employer for reimbursed expenses are entitled to net the reimbursements and deductions in lieu of the more cumbersome method of including the reimbursements as income and then taking the deductions.[29] If reimbursements exceed the deductible expenses, the employee must include this excess income.

---

22.   *Dowell v. U.S.*, 36 AFTR 75 6314 (5th Cir. 1975). Also see *Earle v. Comm'r*, 28 T.C.M. 138 (1969).
23.   IRC Sec. 62(a)(2).
24.   Sole proprietors report these deductions on Schedule C of the Form 1040.
25.   These expenses are reported by the partnership on IRS Form 1065.
26.   The partner must incorporate Form 1065 K-1 with his or her individual return.
27.   *Wallendal v. Comm'r*, 31 T.C. 1249 (1962).
28.   Employees must report such expenses under miscellaneous deductions on Schedule A of the Form 1040.
29.   Treas. Reg. Sec. 1.274-5T(e)(2).

If taxpayers are fully reimbursed for their expenses for which they adequately account to their employers, they will not be required to substantiate the expenses again to the Internal Revenue Service.[30] However, the employer and employee must be unrelated for this rule to apply. Employees will have to substantiate expenses if they deduct amounts in excess of their reimbursements.

LO 7.3   **Explain the requirements for deducting nonbusiness expenses paid for the production of income.**

EXPENSES FOR THE PRODUCTION OF INCOME

Basic Rules

production of income expenses

Production of income expenses are deductible by individual taxpayers. These are expenses that are paid in the course of an activity that is engaged in for profit but does not rise to the level of a business activity. Code Sec. 212 states that such deductible expenses must be "ordinary and necessary expenses paid or incurred during the taxable year." They must fall within one of the three following definitions:

- expenses made for the production or collection of income. An example of such an expense would be the costs of managing stock and bond investment and trading activities (but not the actual cost of an investment or an expense taken directly from the proceeds of a sale).

- expenses for the management, conservation, or maintenance of property held for the production of income. An example of this type of expense would be expenses for repair and maintenance of a rental property owned by the taxpayer.

- expenses made in connection with the determination, refund, or collection of any tax. An example of this type of expense would be the fee paid by an individual for the preparation of his or her income tax return or for representation at a tax return audit.

Such expenses are sometimes referred to as "nonbusiness" expenses or "investment" expenses.

---

30. Treas. Reg. Sec. 1.274-5T(e)(2)(ii).

Determining Whether a Particular Expense Is Deductible

There are certain guidelines that can be applied in determining whether a given expense is deductible as a nonbusiness expense. First, the expense 38. must not be purely personal in nature. It must be clearly related to an activity engaged in for profit. For example, consider the cost of renting a safe deposit box. If the box contains only documents relating to the ownership of stocks, bonds, and other securities held for investment, the cost of the box would be deductible as a nonbusiness expense. However, if the safe deposit box contained personal effects or even valuable property that is owned by the taxpayer primarily for personal reasons, the cost would be nondeductible. As another example, fees paid to an investment adviser are deductible nonbusiness expenses. However, fees for music lessons paid by an amateur musician would be nondeductible personal expenses. The cost of a taxpayer's hobby is neither a business expense nor a deductible nonbusiness expense.

Amounts paid for sophisticated estate planning documents are deductible only to the extent that the documents or other work produced relate to the collection (or legitimate avoidance) of taxes including income, estate, and gift taxes. If the estate planning involves both tax planning and the implementation of personal dispositive intent, an allocation can be made between the deductible and nondeductible portions of the fees. Fees for the drafting of a simple will are nondeductible because the expense is essentially personal. Legal fees paid in connection with litigation may or may not be deductible, depending generally on the nature of the litigation.

current expense

As in the case of a business expense, a nonbusiness expense must be a **current expense** and not a capital expenditure in order to be deductible. For example, it is settled that the costs of acquiring, perfecting, or defending a taxpayer's legal title to property are not deductible as nonbusiness expenses because such costs are included in the taxpayer's capital investment in the property. Such costs, however, may be recovered for tax purposes when the property is sold or depreciated for income tax purposes.

Another area where deductibility must be carefully considered is the cost of obtaining a divorce. Although a divorce proceeding will usually involve a property settlement that will have important financial consequences for both spouses, the legal fees and other costs associated with a divorce are generally nondeductible. This is so because of the origin of the nature of the claim and rights involved in a divorce. The marital relationship is not fundamentally an income-producing activity in the eyes of the law. Therefore the dissolution of that relationship is not considered to be an activity engaged in for the production of income. The same principle holds in the case of a taxpayer who is defending a tort action for a personal injury resulting from a personal auto accident. Although the taxpayer may lose a significant amount of money because of the action, the incident that gave rise to the claim is personal in nature, and therefore the cost of defending the claim is nondeductible. In determining the deductibility of costs incurred in legal actions, consider the fundamental nature of the right or claim that is being pursued or defended, not simply the monetary consequences of the action. Furthermore, it should be remembered that to the extent legal fees or other costs are directly attributable to tax planning or tax advice, a deduction will be allowed because Sec. 212 specifically provides for such a deduction. However, expenses paid or incurred in connection with the production of tax-exempt income are specifically nondeductible under Sec. 265.

Claiming Deductible Nonbusiness Expenses

Most nonbusiness expenses are deductible as below the line miscellaneous itemized deductions on Schedule A of Form 1040. They are generally subject to the "2 percent floor" as discussed later in this chapter. However, deductible expenses with respect to rental property owned by the taxpayer are claimed on Schedule E of Form 1040 as an above the line deduction taken in determining the taxpayer's adjusted gross income.

LO 7.4   **Explain the rules regarding the deductibility of expenses for home offices and vacation homes.**

DEDUCTIBILITY OF HOME-OFFICE EXPENSES

Basic Rules

Many businesses are operated partially or entirely out of the home. The Internal Revenue Code, under Sec. 280A, provides as a general rule that a taxpayer is not entitled to deductions for the business use of a home. Exceptions are made if the taxpayer qualifies under any one of certain tests.

Home-office deductions will be allowed if the residence or portion of the residence falls within any of the following categories of use:

- It is used exclusively and regularly as the principal place of business for any trade or business of the taxpayer.

- It is used exclusively and regularly by patients, clients, or customers in meeting or dealing with the taxpayer in the normal course of the taxpayer's trade or business.

- It is separate from the main home (an office, studio, garage, greenhouse, darkroom, or therapy room) and used exclusively and regularly in connection with the taxpayer's trade or business.

- (In the case of an employee) it is used for the convenience of the taxpayer's employer and if one of the above three requirements is met.

There are certain other home office deduction rules that apply to taxpayers who store inventory or product samples in their homes or who provide day-care services.

"Principal Place of Business" Test

In 1999, Congress provided a special avenue for taxpayers to qualify under the "principal place of business" test listed above for home office deductions. Under this provision, a taxpayer can pass the principal place of business test if the taxpayer uses the home office for "administrative or management activities," and there is no other fixed location where the taxpayer performs a substantial portion of such activities for the business conducted in the home office.

In the Soliman case, the U.S. Supreme Court had previously given its own interpretation of the principal place of business test. In short, Soliman held that there are two primary considerations in determining whether a home office is a principal place of business: the relative importance of the activities performed at each location of the business conducted in the home office, and the relative amount of time spent at each location. Some taxpayers could be considered to fail this test even if they have no fixed office outside the home office, especially taxpayers who spend most of their time at the business locations of their clients or customers. Soliman must still be considered under the principal place of business test. However, if the legislative "administrative or management activities" rule is met, the taxpayer will qualify for home office deductions under the principal place of business requirement even if the criteria of Soliman are not otherwise satisfied.

Limitation on Amount Deductible

Even if a taxpayer qualifies under one of these tests, the deduction permitted for business use is limited. Allowable home office deductions cannot exceed the gross income derived from the business conducted in the home office minus (1) deductions attributable to the business other than home office deductions and (2) the expense deductions that are allowable regardless of business use (such as mortgage interest and real estate taxes). The home office expense includes the pro rata share (generally based on square footage) of mortgage interest or rent, real estate taxes, insurance, utilities, maintenance, and depreciation. In computing the deduction, taxpayers must first subtract all business expenses not connected with the home office deduction. The mortgage interest and real estate tax component is deductible next, followed by the other home office expenses. Although the home office's mortgage interest and real estate tax allocation can create a loss, the other home office expenses cannot. Any amounts disallowed are deductible in succeeding years against income from the business conducted in the home office, subject to the same limits. In effect, a taxpayer cannot use home office expenses to create a net loss from a business activity.

Since 2013, a taxpayer can elect under Rev. Proc. 2013-13 to calculate the home office deduction to be an amount equaling the product of the IRS rate of $5 per square foot and the square footage not to exceed 300. This simplicity comes with a cost to the taxpayer as he or she cannot deduct any other actual expenses related to the qualified business use of the home.

Example

Patrick Riley uses a room in his house exclusively and regularly as an office. The gross income from the business this year is $50,000. The mortgage interest and real estate taxes allocable to that space are $3,500. Patrick also has $7,500 of home office expenses and $45,000 of business deductions that are not home office expenses. The amount of home office expenses that may be deducted is $5,000 ($50,000 income minus $45,000 of business expenses). Patrick can carryover the disallowed $6,000 of home office expenses to the following year.

Types of Expenses That May Be Deductible

Deductible home office expenses for a qualifying home office are as follows:

- depreciation on business furniture (studio furniture or equipment, office furniture, and so on)
- depreciation on the business premises. The portion of the acquisition costs and improvements allocable to the portion of the home used exclusively and on a regular basis for the conduct of a trade or business may be depreciated.
- rent. If the home is rented, rent for the portion of the home allocated to business use may be deducted.
- utilities. The cost of electricity, heating, and air conditioning for the portion of the home used for business is deductible.

Home Office Expenses
- The office must be used "exclusively and regularly" for business purposes.
- The office must be EITHER the principal place of business, a "meeting place," OR a separate structure.
- Non-mortgage interest and real estate tax expenses are not allowable to the extent they create or increase a net loss from the business activity.

DEDUCTIBILITY OF VACATION HOME EXPENSES

For taxpayers who own a second or "vacation" home and rent that home to others for a portion of the year, the income tax treatment of deductions related to the home is hair-pullingly complex. Several different restrictions and limitations contained in the Internal Revenue Code (such as Sec. 280A) converge on such taxpayers. Also, the mathematical calculation of how certain deductions are limited is a matter of judicial controversy with the IRS, which has not yet been settled by the Supreme Court. Taxpayers who own vacation homes that are used for both personal and rental purposes are in serious need of an unusually capable tax adviser. The following is a basic view of the three fundamental tax categories into which a vacation home may fall and how such property may be treated for income tax purposes.

Treatment of the Property as Having Minimal Rental Use

The simplest tax treatment of a vacation home results where the taxpayer actually rents the home for less than 15 days during the taxable year. In such cases, the rental income is excludible from the taxpayer's gross income, and no deductions attributable to rental use are allowed. Therefore a home can be rented for up to 2 weeks during the year with no tax consequences. As long as the taxpayer owns no more than two homes, the mortgage interest will be treated as qualified residence interest. The property taxes on the home will be deductible on Schedule A of Form 1040.

Treatment of the Property as Rental Property

The vacation home will be treated for tax purposes as a rental property if the number of days that the home is used as a residence during the year does not exceed the greater of

- 14 days or
- 10 percent of the number of days during the year that the property is rented at fair market value

For example, suppose a home is used as a residence for 21 days during the year and is rented for 240 days. The period of use as a residence (21 days) does not exceed 10 percent of the period of rental use (10 percent of 240 days, or 24 days). Therefore the home will be treated as a rental property for tax purposes, and deductions attributable to rental use may be allowed. There are, however, complex rules associated with rental property treatment. The two most significant complications are as follows:

- The rental property will be subject to the "passive loss" provisions. These provisions may significantly restrict deductible expenses for the property. If the taxpayer has less than $150,000 of adjusted gross income for the year, he or she may be able to utilize the "active participation" exception to the passive loss rules.

- The portion of mortgage interest paid on the property that is allocable to days of personal use will be nondeductible personal interest and not deductible qualified residence interest because the property is not treated as a residence. This may be a significant tax trap for many property owners. However, property taxes allocable to the days of personal use will be deductible as an itemized deduction on Schedule A of Form 1040.

Treatment of the Property as a Residence

If the property is used for personal purposes for more than the greater of 14 days or 10 percent of the days it is rented during the year (in other words, if the taxpayer does not meet the requirement discussed above to have the home treated as a rental property), the tax treatment of the property becomes even more complicated. Suppose the taxpayer uses the property for personal purposes for 21 days during the year and rents it for 150 days. The 21 days are more than 10 percent of 150 days. Therefore the property is treated as a **residence**, not as a rental property, and the so-called "vacation home" rules apply.

How do the vacation home rules work? The basic intent of these rules is that the taxpayer should not be permitted to claim a tax loss with respect to a property that is essentially a residence. In other words, deductions in excess of the income generated by the property are not permitted. To enforce this limitation, the gross income from the rental use is computed first. Next, that portion of mortgage interest and property taxes that is allocable to the days of rental use is subtracted from the rental income. Next, any expenses such as advertising and broker's fees that are attributable solely to rental use are subtracted from the remaining income. The resulting figure is the maximum amount of expenses paid for depreciation, repairs, maintenance, and utilities for the property that is deductible. At any point in the calculation at which the rental income is reduced to zero, no further deductions are permitted. Any amounts disallowed by this calculation can be carried forward to future tax years subject to the same limitations.

The "judicial controversy" mentioned previously in this discussion of vacation homes relates to the percentage of the taxpayer's mortgage interest and property taxes that is "allocable" to rental use for purposes of the vacation home deduction limitation. Is the allocable percentage calculated by dividing the rental days by the total number of days the property is actually used? Or is it calculated by dividing the rental days by 365 days? The second method will allocate less interest and taxes to rental use, leaving more rental income to be "sheltered" by other rental expenses. Subject to limitations, the mortgage interest and taxes not allocable to rental use are deductible on Schedule A of Form 1040 because the property is treated as a residence. There-fore the "365 days" allocation percentage is better for most taxpayers. This approach has been approved by courts but not accepted by the IRS.

Complexity in Vacation Home Provisions

The vacation home area is one in which several provisions of the Code interact and overlap, and this can paralyze taxpayers with mind-numbing complexity. In fact, one observer's opinion is that the tax treatment of **second homes** is enough to drive a person to own just one home and stay in a hotel for vacation.

LO 7.5   **Explain the 2 percent floor on miscellaneous itemized deductions.**

THE "2 PERCENT FLOOR" ON MISCELLANEOUS ITEMIZED DEDUCTIONS

Most miscellaneous itemized deductions can be deducted only to the extent that they exceed 2 percent of AGI for the taxable year. For example, if a taxpayer's adjusted gross income is $100,000, miscellaneous itemized deductions are allowable only to the extent the total of such deductions exceeds $2,000. Miscellaneous itemized deductions may be defined as itemized deductions other than medical expenses, interest, taxes, charitable contributions, and casualty and theft losses. Miscellaneous itemized deductions are covered here because the majority of these are either employee business expenses or expenses for the production of income that are discussed in this chapter. Miscellaneous itemized deductions are generally subject to the 2 percent floor, except for the following deductions:

- impairment-related work expenses of a handicapped taxpayer
- the deduction for estate tax related to income in respect of a decedent
- deductions related to personal property used in a short sale
- deduction for the restoration of the amount held under claim of right
- deduction for annuity payments ceasing before the taxpayer's recovery of investment in the contract
- amortizable bond premiums
- cooperative housing costs
- gambling losses to the extent of gambling winnings

Examples of the types of deductions that are subject to the 2 percent floor are as follows:

- unreimbursed employee transportation travel and entertainment expenses
- union dues and dues to professional organizations
- cost of an employee's subscriptions to business and professional journals
- most investment expenses such as fees for investment advice, deductible safety deposit box fees, payments for clerical help, and other expenses incurred in caring for investments
- tax advice, including tax-return preparation fees and attorney's fees paid in connection with a dispute with the IRS
- depreciation on business property purchased by an employee
- employment-agency fees
- deductible employment-related education expenses of employees
- malpractice insurance premiums of employees
- expenses for a qualified home office used regularly and exclusively for the convenience of the taxpayer's employer
- work clothes and uniforms required for employment

CHAPTER REVIEW

Key Terms and Concepts

ordinary expense
necessary expense
capital expenditures
reasonable compensation
temporary business locations
entertainment

directly related requirement
associated-with requirement
facility
production of income expenses
current expense

Review Questions

Review questions are based on the learning objectives in this chapter. Thus a [7.3] at the end of a question means that the question is based on learning objective 3. If there are multiple objectives, they are all listed.

1. What are the basic requirements for deductibility of trade or business expenses? [7.1]

2. Are illegal payments made in the course of a business activity deductible? Explain. [7.1]

3. List the business expenses of a political nature which are specifically nondeductible. [7.1]

4. An attorney engaged in estate analysis for a prospective client at the client's place of business receives a parking ticket. Explain why the cost of this ticket would or would not be deductible. [7.1]

5. What factors are taken into account to determine reasonableness of compensation? [7.1]

6. a. What is the rule of "excessive employee remuneration"?

   b. What is a "covered employee" under this rule? [7.1]

7. Don, a tax attorney, pays $500 for tuition to attend an income tax seminar. Is this a deductible business expense? Explain. [7.1]

8. What is the deductible percentage for health insurance premiums paid on behalf of self-employed individuals for purposes of calculating federal income tax ? [7.1]

9. Explain two different ways that a taxpayer may deduct expenses for the business use of a car. [7.1]

10. What test is used to determine whether a taxpayer, such as a salesperson who travels frequently, is away from home? [7.1]

11. George Collins is a self-employed computer consultant. Several times a year he drives to New York, where business requires that he stay for one week at a time. He stays in a suite at the Plaza Hotel. Which of the following expenses would be deductible?

    a. the suite at the Plaza

    b. driving to and from New York

    c. garaging his auto for a week and having the car serviced while there

    d. taxi fares while in New York for traveling alone to his favorite museum

    e. his business calls back to his office

    f. taxi fares between the hotel and his clients' offices [7.1]

12. What are the general requirements for deductibility of entertainment expenses? [7.2]

13. a. Explain what is meant by goodwill expenses that are associated with the conduct of business.

b.   When are these expenses deductible? [7.2]

14. Dwayne, an auto parts distributor, invites his supplier, Eddie, to a basketball game to continue their good working relationship. At no time before, during, or after the game was business discussed. Explain whether Dwayne's expenses for the game are deductible. [7.2]

15. Explain how the 50 percent limitation makes the after-tax cost of business meals and entertainment higher. [7.2]

16. Explain the rules for deductibility of expenses for entertainment facilities and tickets. [2]

17. What portion, if any, of Gwen's $1,000 annual membership fee at the Gotham Country Club is deductible if 60 percent of her use of the facility is directly related to her trade or business and the rest is purely personal? [7.2]

18. Frosty Forrest is a businessman in New York. He has a business meeting with a major client, and immediately after the meeting Frosty takes his client to the hit Broadway show "Bats" to increase goodwill. Frosty had to pay $200 for a pair of tickets. Their face value is $50 each. How much may Frosty deduct as a business entertainment expense? [7.2]

19. Nancy Sellers, owner of a restaurant, gave each of her employees a $40 gift at Christmas. How much of that amount will be deductible? [7.2]

20. What is the substantiation requirement for the allowance of entertainment deductions? [7.2]

21. Explain whether the directly related entertainment expenses actually incurred by John Curley, a beer distributor, will be deductible in the following circumstances:

a.   He has no records of his expenditures.

b.   He has a box full of receipts but does not maintain a diary.

c.   He reconstructs his records a year after he incurs his expenses. [7.2]

22. Identify the three types of expenses for the production of income that are always deductible. Give an example of each. [7.3]

23. Clarke invests heavily in stocks and bonds. He also owns several apartment houses and a sizable municipal bond portfolio. Each of these investments was made at the advice of Clarke's investment counselor who charged two separate fees for her advice. During the same year Clarke's attorney and other members of the estate planning team

helped Clarke to establish an estate plan. Which, if any, of the following fees would probably be deductible? Explain.

a. an investment counselor's fee for advice on stocks and bonds

b. an investment counselor's fee for advice on apartment house management

c. an attorney's fee for drafting a simple will

d. an attorney's fee solely for advice as to the tax consequences of contemplated income and estate tax planning [7.3]

24. Lord Skidrow owns an apartment building that he manages for investment purposes. An heir of the previous owner files suit against Skidrow, alleging that Skidrow does not have valid legal title to the property. Lord Skidrow incurs substantial legal fees in his successful defense against this action. Are his legal expenses currently deductible? Explain. [7.3]

25. An employee has an office at home that is regularly used to promote the employer's business. On those evenings when not used for business, the employee's family uses the office as a family room to relax, watch television, and entertain personal friends. Would the employee be entitled to claim a deduction for home-office expenses? [4]

26. Explain the "principal place of business" requirement under the home office deduction rules as it is applied under current law. [7.4]

27. Explain the limitation on the allowable amount of deductible home office expenses. [7.4]

28. Jim Real owns a vacation home as a second home. He rents it for 14 days for a rental of $1,000 in one particular year.

a. May Jim deduct the other rental expenses attributable to the 14 days?

b. How much of the rental income must Jim include in his income for the year? [7.4]

29. List the miscellaneous itemized deductions that are not subject to the 2 percent floor. [7.5]

Review Answers

1. Code Sec. 162 states that there shall be allowed as a deduction all the ordinary and necessary expenses paid or incurred during the taxable year in carrying on any trade or business. An expense is ordinary if it is a customary or usual expense made by many taxpayers involved in the same business activity. An expense is necessary if it is appropriate and helpful to the taxpayer's business, even if it is not necessary in the strictest sense. In most situations, an expense that is ordinary will also be considered necessary.

In addition, the expense must be business related. This means that the activity must be engaged in with the intent and expectation of making money and that there be an element of regularity and continuousness in the taxpayer's participation in the activity.

2. Although business expenses are generally deductible, the Code describes certain payments that are specifically nondeductible. Among these are payments in violation of any federal law or of any state law that is generally enforced and subjects the payer to either a criminal penalty or the loss of a license or privilege to engage in a business. Examples of nondeductible illegal payments are bribes to government officials or expenses paid in the conduct of an illegal business, such as drug trafficking.

3. Certain expenses of a political nature are nondeductible. These include

    •   expenses in connection with influencing legislation

    •   expenses for participation in a political campaign on behalf of or in opposition to a candidate for public office

    •   expenses for influencing public opinion on a political issue

    •   expenses for communication with certain executive branch officials to influence their official positions

    Note that expenses for influencing legislation at the local level are not subject to this rule and are therefore deductible. Also, if the taxpayer is a professional lobbyist who is paid to influence legislation, he or she may deduct expenses related to that activity as business expenses.

4. A fine or penalty paid to a government for the violation of any law is nondeductible. Such payments include fines paid for tickets received in connection with speeding or parking violations while conducting business.

5. "Reasonable" compensation may be loosely defined as that amount that would ordinarily be paid to an employee for similar services by similar companies operating in similar circumstances. Under the judicial decisions on this issue (of which there are many), several factors are taken into account in making the factual determination of reasonableness. These factors include (but are not limited to)

    •   the degree and nature of the employee's responsibility in his or her position (including responsibility for the production of profits)

    •   the amount the employee could have earned in similar employment for another company

    •   the salary paid in prior years for the same services

- the time the employee devotes to the performance of the services

- the nature of the services and any unique or peculiar abilities of the employee in rendering those services

- the amount of salaries paid to other employees providing similar services who are not shareholders

- general economic conditions in the region

The employee's total compensation is considered in determining reasonableness, including commissions, overrides, bonuses, and payments to pension, profit-sharing, or 401(k) plans.

6. a.   One special rule limiting deductions for compensation applies only to payments by publicly held corporations. The general definition of "excessive employee remuneration" is remuneration paid to a "covered employee" that is in excess of $1 million for the taxable year.

    b.   A "covered employee" is either one of the following people:

    - the chief executive officer of the corporation or an individual acting in such capacity at the close of the taxable year

    - one of the four most highly paid officers of the corporation for the taxable year (other than the chief executive officer)

Under this definition, the rule of excessive employee remuneration applies to no more than five employees of a company for any taxable year.

7. Treasury regulations deal with the question of whether expenses for education that is related to a business activity are deductible as business expenses. Such expenses are deductible if they meet either of the two following criteria:

    - The expenses are deductible if incurred primarily for the purpose of meeting the requirements of the taxpayer's employer or of local law as a condition for the taxpayer's retention of employment.

    - The expenses are deductible if incurred primarily for the purpose of maintaining or improving skills needed by the taxpayer in his or her current employment or business activity.

The $500 that Don paid for tuition to attend an income tax seminar is deductible under the second criterion listed above. Don is trying to maintain or improve his skills as a tax attorney. Also, it is possible that the state in which Don practices law has a continuing education (CE) requirement that he must meet in order to maintain his law license. If this is the case, then the $500 is also deductible under the first criterion listed above.

8. The deductible percentage is now 100 percent. (This is an "above-the-line" deduction in computing AGI.)

9. Car expenses may be deducted in one of two different ways. The taxpayer may claim a standard mileage allowance for business transportation. This allowance is deemed to include depreciation, fuel, insurance, repairs, and other normal operating expenses. The only actual expenses that are deductible in addition to the mileage allowance are those for highway tolls, parking charges, and interest payments with respect to the car that are otherwise deductible under the tax law. Taxpayers who lease their cars may generally use the mileage allowance, but it must be used for the entire lease period. The mileage allowance can be claimed only with respect to those miles actually driven for business purposes.

In lieu of claiming the standard mileage allowance, taxpayers may claim their actual expenses (including depreciation) in using a car for business. Any depreciation deductions will be limited by that percentage of the overall use of the car that represents business use. Cars used for business are also subject to special "luxury auto" limits on depreciation. Repairs made to the car will also be deductible only to the extent of the percentage of business use. The "actual expense" method requires significant record keeping to substantiate deductions. Many taxpayers find it easier to simply keep a log of business miles, and claim deductions under the standard mileage allowance.

Taxpayers who lease a car used for business are not permitted to claim depreciation for the car, since the required ownership does not exist. However, such taxpayers are permitted to deduct their lease payments to the extent the car is used for business if the standard mileage allowance is not used. This deduction is, however, subject to an "add-back" rule. Depending on the car's fair market value, a specified amount of the lease payment must be included in the taxpayer's gross income to offset part of the lease payment deduction. This rule corresponds to the "luxury auto" limitations that apply to taxpayers who claim depreciation for the business use of a car. These add-back amounts are relatively low and are published annually by the IRS to reflect adjustments for inflation.

10. A taxpayer is generally considered to be "away from home" on a trip if the taxpayer stays overnight or longer at a temporary business location.

11. a. Since George Collins's trip is primarily for business, his lodging cost at the Plaza is deductible.

    b. His travel expenses to New York and back are also deductible since the trip is primarily for business.

    c. The cost of garaging the car is deductible. The servicing expenses are also deductible as costs of maintaining and operating a car used in Collins's trade or business. However, Collins could elect to take the standard mileage rate approved by the IRS in lieu of his actual operation costs.

    d. These expenses are not deductible. They are not directly attributable to Collins's business, even though the trip is primarily for business.

    e. Business phone calls are deductible as an ordinary and necessary business expense.

    f. These expenses are deductible since the taxi fares are directly attributable to Collins's business.

12. In order for an entertainment expense to be deductible, it must be "ordinary and necessary," plus it must also be either "directly related to" or "associated with" the active conduct of the trade or business. Moreover, the taxpayer must be able to substantiate the entertainment expenditures with adequate records of the business-related event or with other sufficient corroborating evidence.

13. a. Goodwill expenses associated with the conduct of business are entertainment expenses to promote goodwill. Such goodwill entertainment expenses often are incurred in an effort to obtain new business or to encourage the continuation of existing business relationships.

    b. Goodwill entertainment expenses may be deductible if the expenses directly precede or follow a bona fide business discussion. "Directly preceding or following" has been interpreted in the regulations to mean that the entertainment occurs on the same day as the business discussions. However, entertainment expenses that occur on a day other than the day of business discussions may still qualify for deduction depending on the facts and circumstances.

14. The primary purpose of any combined business and entertainment activity must not be a social one, but one to further the taxpayer's business. In order for Dwayne's expenses for taking Eddie to the basketball game to be deductible, the entertainment activity (that is, attending the basketball game) must be directly related to or associated with the active conduct of the trade or business of being an auto parts distributor.

In the scenario presented in the question, Dwayne's expenditures fail the "directly related" requirement. Dwayne is not actively engaged in a business negotiation or discussion with Eddie and the expenditures are not made in a clear business setting. Moreover, since Dwayne did not discuss business with Eddie either before or after the game, the expenditures also fail the "associated with" requirement. Therefore Dwayne will not be able to deduct his expenses for the game as business entertainment expenses.

15. Deductions for all business meal and entertainment expenses are limited to 50 percent of the amount that is deductible after taking into account all other limitations and restrictions. Because of this limitation, the after-tax cost of business meals and entertainment is higher than it would be otherwise. For example, if the total cost of entertainment is $100 and the whole amount is deductible, the after-tax cost for a taxpayer in the 28 percent bracket would be $72 (.28 × $100 = $28; $100 − $28 = $72). However, with a 50 percent limitation on the amount that is deductible, the after-tax cost of entertainment will increase to $86 (.28 × $50 = $14; $50 − $14 = $36; $50 + $36 = $86).

16. Deductions for expenses paid or incurred in connection with the operation and maintenance of an entertainment facility are generally disallowed. No depreciation deductions may be taken even when a facility is primarily used for business entertainment. Out-of-pocket expenses for entertaining at a facility, such as the cost of food and beverages, fall within the general entertainment rules.

   Deductions for tickets to entertainment events that qualify as business expenses are limited to the face value of the tickets. The face value limitation will make the premium paid to a scalper, as well as the premium paid to a legitimate ticket agency, nondeductible. The deduction, of course, is then further reduced by the 50 percent limitation.

17. No portion of Gwen's membership fee to the country club is deductible. However, business entertainment expenses incurred while using the club may be deductible, subject to the 50 percent limitation.

18. Deductions for tickets to entertainment events that qualify as business expenses are limited to the face value of the tickets. Therefore the $100 premium paid by Frosty Forrest is nondeductible. Moreover, the $100 face value for the pair of tickets must be further reduced by the 50 percent limitation. Consequently, only $50 of the original $200 paid by Frosty for the tickets is deductible as a business entertainment expense.

19. The deduction for business gifts that are ordinary and necessary business expenses is limited to $25 per donee. Thus only $25 of each $40 gift given by Nancy Sellers to her employees is deductible.

20. Entertainment expense deductions will be disallowed unless the taxpayer can adequately substantiate the deductible expenses. This requires the taxpayer either to maintain an account book or diary in which the expenditures are recorded at or near the time of expenditure or to substantiate the deductions with other sufficient evidence. The use of an account book is the better way to meet the substantiation requirements, and it must include the information that follows:

    - the amount of each expenditure

    - the date of the entertainment and its duration

    - the place of the entertainment, including name and address

    - the business purpose

    - the business relationship, meaning the name, title, or other description of the person entertained, sufficient to establish a business relationship to the taxpayer

    If entertainment is merely "associated with" the taxpayer's business, then the taxpayer must record the place and duration of the business discussion and must identify the persons entertained who participated in the discussion.

    Lodging expenses and other expenses of $75 or more require documentary evidence, such as a receipt, to support the deduction. Incidental items, such as taxi fares or telephone calls, may be aggregated on a daily basis.

21. a. Although John Curley has incurred ordinary and necessary entertainment expenses directly related to his business, he cannot deduct these expenses unless he can substantiate the expenses by adequate records.

    b. A box full of receipts is not considered to be adequate record keeping. The taxpayer should maintain a diary where he records (at or near the time of the expenditure) the (1) amount of the expenditure, (2) date and operation, (3) place of entertainment, (4) business purpose, and (5) business relationship. If a diary is not kept, corroborating evidence will be required on audit.

    c. Records should be made at or near the time when expenditures are incurred.

22. "Production of income" expenses are deductible by individual taxpayers. These are expenses that are paid in the course of an activity that is engaged in for profit but does not rise to the level of a business activity. The Code states that such deductible expenses must be "ordinary and necessary expenses paid or incurred during the taxable year." They must fall within one of the three following categories:

- expenses made for the production or collection of income. An example of such an expense would be the costs of managing stock and bond investment and trading activities (but not the actual cost of an investment or an expense taken directly from the proceeds of a sale).

- expenses for the management, conservation, or maintenance of property held for the production of income. An example of this type of expense would be expenses for repair and maintenance of a rental property owned by the taxpayer.

- expenses made in connection with the determination, refund, or collection of any tax. An example of this type of expense would be the fee paid by an individual for the preparation of his or her income tax return or for representation at a tax return audit.

23. a. An investment counselor's fee for advice on stocks and bonds is a deductible nonbusiness expense. This type of expense is clearly related to an activity engaged in for profit and is an example of an expense for the production or collection of income.

    b. An investment counselor's fee for advice on apartment house management is a deductible nonbusiness expense. This type of expense is clearly related to an activity engaged in for profit and is an example of an expense for the management, conservation, or maintenance of property.

    c. An attorney's fee for drafting a simple will is a nondeductible expense because it is essentially personal in nature.

    d. An attorney's fee solely for advice as to the tax consequences of contemplated income and estate tax planning is a deductible nonbusiness expense. This type of expense is an example of an expense made in connection with the determination, refund, or collection of taxes.

24. Lord Skidrow's expenses in defending a lawsuit challenging his title to the apartment building are not deductible as nonbusiness expenses. The costs of acquiring, perfecting, or defending a taxpayer's legal title to property are part of the capital investment in the property and therefore do not qualify as current nonbusiness expenses. Such costs may be recovered for tax purposes when the property is sold or depreciated.

25. Even though the employee uses the office regularly to promote the employer's business, it is not used exclusively as an office. Therefore the employee would not be entitled to claim a deduction for home-office expenses.

26. There are two primary considerations in determining whether a home office is a "principal place of business." They are as follows:

    • the relative importance of the activities performed at each location of the business conducted in the home office

    • the relative amount of time spent at each location

    However, even if these two considerations are not otherwise satisfied, a taxpayer may still qualify for a home-office deduction under the principal place of business requirement if the newer "administrative or management activities" rule is met. The principal place of business test can be passed if the taxpayer uses the home office for "administrative or management activities," and there is no other fixed location where the taxpayer performs a substantial portion of such activities for the business conducted in the home office.

27. All deductions allocable to the business activity, including both deductions otherwise allowable as personal expenses (i.e., allocable mortgage interest expense and real estate taxes) and business deductions not attributable to the home office, must be subtracted from the gross income of the business conducted in the home office to determine the amount of home office deductions that will then be allowable. As a result, the remaining home office deductions (excluding mortgage interest expense and real estate taxes) can reduce the business activity's income to zero, but can not create a loss. Excess home office deductions can be carried over to future years and applied against business income under the same test.

28. a. No deductions attributable to rental use are allowed since Jim Real actually rented the home for less than 15 days during the taxable year.

    b. The $1,000 rental income is excludible from Jim's gross income because the home was rented for less than 15 days during the taxable year.

29. Miscellaneous itemized deductions that are not subject to the 2 percent floor are as follows:

    • impairment-related work expenses of a handicapped taxpayer

    • the deduction for estate tax related to income in respect of a decedent

    • deductions related to personal property used in a short sale

    • deduction for the restoration of the amount held under claim of right

    • deduction for annuity payments ceasing before the taxpayer's recovery of investment in the contract

- amortizable bond premiums
- cooperative housing costs
- gambling losses to the extent of gambling winnings

Chapter 8

Losses and Bad Debts

Learning Objectives

An understanding of the material in this chapter should enable you to

LO 8.1   **Explain the rules regarding the deductibility of losses.**

LO 8.2   **Explain the rules regarding the deductibility of bad debts.**

> When everybody has got money they cut taxes, and when they're broke them [politicians] raise 'em. That's statesmanship of the highest order.
>
> —Will Rogers

Loss deductions and bad debt deductions are different yet related topics. Each has its own rules and limitations depending on the type of loss or bad debt and the nature of the taxpayer's relationship to the loss or bad debt. An understanding of the fundamentals of these income tax rules can help the taxpayer and the adviser minimize the financial damage resulting from events or transactions that result in a loss of money or other property.

The deductibility of losses sustained by individuals and business entities, and the law applicable to the deductibility of bad debts are events or transactions causing economic damage to a taxpayer. Both types of deductions have restrictions as to their deductibility where damage does not arise in the course of the taxpayer's trade or business.

LO 8.1   **Explain the rules regarding the deductibility of losses.**

DEDUCTIONS FOR LOSSES

Sec. 165 of the Internal Revenue Code states as a general rule that "there shall be allowed as a deduction any loss sustained during the taxable year and not compensated for by insurance or otherwise." However simplistic this general rule may seem to be, there are many different categories of losses. Certain losses are exceptions to the general rule and are nondeductible.

Certain deductible losses may not be deductible in full by most taxpayers. There are several different categories of deductible losses subject to their own rules and limitations.

The rules applicable to a loss depend on the nature of the activity engaged in by the taxpayer that generated the loss, and also on the specific type of transaction that resulted in the loss.

An economic loss may result from the sale or exchange of property. A loss may also result from a fire, storm, accident, or other event that physically damages property. Other losses may be caused by theft, gambling, an event that results in property becoming worthless, or abandonment of property that has ceased to be useful. The loss may arise in the course of the taxpayer's trade or business, a transaction entered into for profit, or the taxpayer's personal affairs. There are, however, some general rules that apply to the deductibility of any of these categories of losses.

General Rules for Deductibility

Regardless of the activity or the specific transaction that gives rise to an economic loss, the following rules must be satisfied in order to claim a loss deduction:

- The loss must be suffered by the taxpayer who is claiming the deduction. One taxpayer cannot claim a deduction for a loss suffered by another taxpayer.

- The loss must result from an identifiable event. This means that the loss must be "realized" or "sustained" by the taxpayer from an economic standpoint. The identifiable event must be examined to reveal the nature and the extent of the loss. For example, a theft of property would be an identifiable event that results in an ascertainable and measurable loss. The same would be true of a fire, shipwreck, or a sale of a publicly traded security for an amount less than what the taxpayer paid for the security. However, a reduction in the value of such a security owned by a taxpayer, without a sale, exchange, or other disposition of the asset, is not an identifiable event for purposes of a loss deduction.

- The property that is the subject of the loss must have had a determinable monetary value. Mere personal or emotional value is not sufficient for damage or loss with respect to the property to produce a deductible loss.

- There must be economic substance to the loss, and not just the form of a transaction that appears to result in a loss. This rule involves the general principle of "substance over form" that can look through the facade or formal structure of a transaction to its actual economic effect to determine the income tax result. For example, a sale of property between closely related parties at a loss would generally not result in a deductible loss because there is no actual realization of economic detriment suffered by the selling taxpayer.

- A loss of an expected economic benefit or item of income is not a deductible loss. To be deductible, the loss must be attributable to an asset or property that was already in the taxpayer's hands. In other words, the loss must occur with respect to the taxpayer's existing capital. For example, if an individual taxpayer was promised a large salary increase from his or her employer, and as a result of market changes the increase never materialized, this loss of anticipated wages would not be a deductible loss.

Worthlessness or Abandonment of Property

A loss deduction is allowable for property that has become worthless. Remember, however, that the taxpayer must be able to show that there was an identifiable event that resulted in the worthlessness of the property. The deduction cannot be taken for property that merely decreases in value, as mentioned above. The property must become completely worthless in order for a change in value to result in a deductible loss without a sale or exchange. Any available deduction would generally be calculated by reference to the taxpayer's adjusted basis in the property.

Corporate Securities

Stocks, bonds, or other corporate securities are examples of assets that may become worthless and produce a loss deduction. If a corporation is dissolved pursuant to a bankruptcy proceeding and the shareholders receive nothing for their stock, the dissolution in bankruptcy would be an identifiable event that could fix the time at which the loss occurs.

However, a problem can arise regarding the time the corporate security becomes worthless. Code Sec. 165(g) states that the deduction is allowable for an asset that "becomes worthless during the taxable year . . ." Even if there is an identifiable event that proves the worthlessness of the asset, there may be a timing problem in claiming the deduction. The deduction must be claimed in the year that worthlessness occurs, which may have been prior to the actual bankruptcy in the example just discussed. For this reason, the law allows a 7-year period for the amendment of a return or the filing of a claim with respect to a deduction for worthlessness of a corporate security. This 7-year period also applies to bad debt deductions, which are discussed later in this chapter. The 7-year period generally runs from the due date for filing of the tax return for the year in which the worthlessness or bad debt actually occurred. The normal time limit for filing a claim for a refund or an amended return is 3 years from the date the return was filed.

For purposes of calculating a deduction, losses from worthless securities are generally treated as a loss from the sale or exchange of a capital asset that takes place on the last day of the taxable year.

An exception to this treatment applies under Sec. 1244. Losses from the sale or worthlessness of certain small business stock can be deducted as ordinary losses. Requirements for eligibility for ordinary loss treatment include a rule that the corporation's paid-in capital (amount paid to the corporation for its stock by shareholders) cannot exceed $1 million. The maximum amount deductible as an ordinary loss cannot exceed $50,000 in any tax year ($100,000 for a joint return). Any remaining loss for the year is a capital loss.

Abandonment

A loss deduction may also arise from the **abandonment of property**. If the owner of the asset acts affirmatively and with manifest intent to abandon the property, the amount of the taxpayer's adjusted basis in the property is generally deductible as an ordinary loss. However, a loss deduction is not permitted if the property is personal use property.

Losses Covered by Insurance

Sec. 165 specifies that a deduction is allowed for losses "not compensated for by insurance or otherwise." This means that deductions are allowed only to the extent that the loss is not otherwise compensated for. If there is no insurance, the loss is deductible if it otherwise meets the loss deduction requirements. If the loss is partially compensated for by insurance or through some other arrangement, the portion of the loss not compensated for is deductible.

What if the company that insures the loss contests the taxpayer's claim for reimbursement? In such cases, the loss is deductible if the insurance company firmly disputes the payment of the claim. However, if the taxpayer prevails in the dispute with the insurance company and later receives compensation, the compensation must be included in the taxpayer's income to the extent that a loss deduction generated a tax benefit for the taxpayer.

A special rule applies to individual taxpayers claiming casualty or theft losses. In addition to the requirement that any insurance recovery must offset the amount of the deductible loss, a loss will be deductible for property that is insured only if a timely insurance claim is filed with respect to the loss. This means that individuals who suffer casualty or theft losses and have insurance coverage must file an insurance claim in order for any part of the loss to be deductible. Casualty and theft losses of individuals will be discussed in detail below.

The Identity of the Taxpayer

Business Entities

For business entities such as corporations and partnerships, losses are generally deductible in the year incurred if the loss meets the overall requirements for deductibility. No special restrictions on losses generally apply to these entities. However, specific limitations apply to individuals regarding both the types of losses deductible and the extent to which they are deductible.

Individuals

casualty losses

The Internal Revenue Code specifically addresses loss limitations for individuals in Sec. 165(c). Individual taxpayers may claim loss deductions if the loss is incurred in the course of a trade or business or in the course of any transaction entered into for profit. If a loss does not fall into either of these categories, it is a personal loss for income tax purposes. Personal losses are deductible only if they are theft losses or **casualty losses** (losses arising from fire, storm, shipwreck, or another type of casualty).

In other words, an individual's losses that result from a business or profit-seeking activity are deductible subject to the same rules that apply to a business entity. Other losses are nondeductible except for theft and casualty losses. For example, a loss on the sale of a personal residence is not deductible by an individual unless and only to the extent the residence had been rented or otherwise actually used in a business or income-producing activity.

Theft and casualty losses are subject to special limitations on deductibility as discussed later in this chapter.

Wagering Losses

The Code specifically provides that losses from wagering are deductible only to the extent that wagering gains are reportable as income. Unless the taxpayer can show that he or she is a professional gambler, such losses must be deducted as a miscellaneous itemized deduction on Schedule A of Form 1040. Such losses are not subject to the 2 percent floor that applies to most miscellaneous itemized deductions.

Personal Casualty and Theft Losses of Individuals

An individual's losses that arise from a casualty or theft and that are not incurred in the course of a business or profit-seeking activity are itemized deductions claimed on Schedule A of Form 1040.

Casualty loss may be generally defined as damage, destruction, or loss occurring to a taxpayer's property as a result of a sudden, unusual, or unexpected cause. Common examples include damage from storms, fire, flood, vandalism, or traffic accidents. However, a "loss" of property that has been mislaid or misplaced is not a casualty loss. A theft loss is defined in the Treasury Regulations as a loss "deemed to include, but shall not necessarily be limited to larceny, embezzlement, and robbery." The IRS has held that blackmail, extortion, and kidnapping for ransom may also constitute a theft loss.

Rules for the Deductibility of Casualty and Theft Losses

The following basic rules apply to the deductibility of an individual's casualty and theft losses:

- Casualty losses must be deducted in the year the loss is incurred or sustained. For theft losses, the loss must be deducted in the year the theft is discovered.

- There must be a sudden event or sudden impact that results in the loss for a deduction to be allowed. This requirement of "suddenness" is discussed in more detail below.

- The amount of a casualty or theft loss eligible for a deduction is reduced by $100 for each loss suffered by the taxpayer. In other words, the first $100 of a personal casualty or theft loss is nondeductible.

- Personal casualty and theft losses of individuals are also subject to a "floor" of 10 percent of the taxpayer's adjusted gross income. This means that the total amount of the taxpayer's personal casualty and theft losses for the year (after the subtraction of $100 per loss) can only be deducted to the extent the total of such losses exceeds 10 percent of adjusted gross income.

- The amount of a casualty or theft loss is the difference (i.e., decline) in the fair market value of the property before and after the event that resulted in the casualty or theft (the fair market value of the property after a theft is deemed to be zero). However, if this amount is more than the taxpayer's adjusted basis in the property, the deductible amount is limited to the taxpayer's adjusted basis. This computation will be discussed in more detail below.

The Requirement of a Sudden Event

Fires, storms, shipwrecks, accidents, floods, freezes, and earthquakes are examples of sudden and unexpected events that result in casualty losses. Normal wear and tear of property, and even gradual damage to property resulting from undiscovered causes, are not events that result in deductible personal casualty losses.

Termite damage has frequently been an issue in litigation over the claiming of a casualty loss deduction. The Internal Revenue Service has adhered to the position that this type of damage is not a sudden event or impact because of the gradual nature of the damage. Other more sudden damage resulting from infestation has sometimes been allowed as a casualty loss. The issue of suddenness is a question of fact over which taxpayers and the IRS have frequently disagreed.

Another issue is whether damage to property is a deductible loss resulting from a casualty or simply damage or breakage resulting from routine household activity. The dropping of a valuable plate during dishwashing would not be an event resulting in a deductible loss. However, the falling and breaking of the same plate during an earthquake would be.

The willfulness of the act that results in the damage to the property may also be an issue. For example, auto accidents are presumed to be events that result in casualty losses. However, if it can be shown that the taxpayer intentionally caused an accident rather than causing it from mere negligence, the deduction can be disallowed. Damages incurred as a result of an accident in an automobile race have been held to be nondeductible since accidents often occur and are not unusual events in auto racing. Using the previous example, if, in a fit of anger, the taxpayer hurled the valuable plate against a wall, the loss would not be a deductible casualty loss.

Calculating the Deductible Loss

The mechanics of the casualty loss rules as discussed above may be best illustrated through a specific example of a deductible casualty.

Example

Nancy Fleet's home is damaged by flood. Her home is not insured for this loss because flood is specifically excluded under her homeowner's policy. Therefore she has no insurance reimbursement for her losses. The fair market value of her home and its contents before the flood was $135,000. After the flood, the value is $90,000. Her basis in her home and its contents is $100,000. The amount of her loss is $45,000 ($135,000 – $90,000). This loss amount is not in excess of her basis in the property. Nancy's adjusted gross income for the year is $95,000. She has suffered no other casualty losses during the year.

One hundred dollars must be subtracted from the amount of Nancy's loss. Thus her loss is now $44,900 for deduction purposes. She is permitted to deduct this loss only to the extent it exceeds 10 percent of her adjusted gross income of $95,000. Her deductible loss is therefore $35,400 ($44,900 − [$95,000 × .10]). In this example, there is no insurance recovery. Of course, if Nancy's loss was covered by insurance, she would not be able to deduct any of it unless she filed a timely claim for reimbursement. Then her loss would be deductible only to the extent the amount of the loss exceeded the reimbursement.

Steps in Calculating Casualty and Theft Losses
- The amount of loss is the difference between property's FMV before and after the event.
- The amount cannot be greater than the property's adjusted basis.
- The amount of each specific loss is reduced by $100.
- Total amount of all casualty and theft losses is subject to 10 percent of AGI floor.

Casualty Losses of Business and Income-Producing Property

Sometimes a sudden impact or event causes the complete destruction of a particular property. In the case of a personal loss, the deductible amount is computed the same way regardless of whether the loss is a complete or a partial one. The amount is the lesser of the difference between the fair market value of the property before and after the casualty or the taxpayer's adjusted basis in the property.

A somewhat different rule applies if the loss occurs with respect to business property or property held for the production of income. For such property that is completely lost or destroyed as a result of a casualty, the deductible amount is equal to the taxpayer's adjusted basis in the property. In other words, the amount of the taxpayer's adjusted basis may be claimed as a casualty loss in such cases if that amount is greater than the property's fair market value before the loss. Similarly, in the case of stolen business or income-producing property, the property is deemed to be completely destroyed, resulting in a deductible theft loss equal to the adjusted basis of the property stolen.

If business or income-producing property is partially damaged by a casualty, but not completely lost or destroyed, then the deduction is the lesser of the property's adjusted basis or the difference in fair market value before and after the casualty (same rule as for a personal casualty loss).

With regard to casualty losses of business or income-producing property, three other points should be mentioned. First, losses to such property are not subject to the $100 per loss reduction that applies to personal casualty and theft losses. Second, losses to business or income-producing property are not subject to the 10 percent "floor" of adjusted gross income that applies to personal casualty and theft losses. Third, if a deductible loss occurs to property eligible for depreciation or other cost recovery deductions, the amount of the loss is measured or limited by the property's "adjusted basis." Such adjusted basis reflects depreciation deductions previously claimed. Therefore, such depreciation deductions, depending on the particular case, may reduce the allowable amount of the casualty loss. These points also apply to theft losses of business or income-producing property.

Tax Reporting and Treatment of Loss Deductions

Losses that may be deductible by individual taxpayers include casualty and theft losses, losses from the sale or exchange of property, losses from abandonment or worthlessness of property, wagering losses, and certain other losses. The type of event or transaction that gives rise to the loss and the character of the property involved will generally determine the specific tax treatment applicable to the loss.

Personal casualty and theft losses are claimed as itemized deductions on Schedule A of Form 1040. These losses, to the extent allowable under the rules described in this chapter, are deductible against the taxpayer's ordinary income.

Wagering losses are deductible only to the extent of wagering gains. They must be deducted as a miscellaneous itemized deduction (not subject to the 2 percent of AGI limitation) on Schedule A unless the taxpayer is a professional gambler.

Losses from the sale or exchange of property are treated differently. If the property is a capital asset of the taxpayer, then the loss is deductible as a capital loss on Schedule D of Form 1040. Losses from the sale of assets described in Sec. 1231 may be deductible as ordinary losses arising from the sale of business property.

For individuals, the tax reporting of a deductible loss depends on the type of loss that occurs. The basic rule to remember is that if the taxpayer has a loss other than a casualty or theft loss, the loss must be sustained in the course of a business or an activity engaged in for profit in order for a deduction to be allowed. The loss will then be reported on the tax return in connection with the particular activity that produced it.

LO 8.2   **Explain the rules regarding the deductibility of bad debts.**

DEDUCTIONS FOR BAD DEBTS

bad debt

A **bad debt** deduction may arise when a debt becomes worthless, that is, when there is no longer a reasonable expectation that the debt will be repaid. The deduction is generally claimed by the primary creditor of the debt. However, under certain circumstances as discussed below, a guarantor of a debt may be eligible for the deduction. The deduction for bad debts is based on the unpaid principal amount of the debt.

Clearly, there must be a bona fide legal obligation of debt between the debtor and the creditor in order for a deduction to be available. For example, a gift of property that has merely been characterized as a debt obligation by the parties involved would not give rise to a bad debt deduction. The initial question is whether the taxpayer seeking the deduction (that is, the creditor) had obtained the unconditional obligation of the debtor to make repayment at the time the loan was made. Also, there must have been a reasonable expectation of repayment at that time. In common terms, a debt that was never "good" cannot become "bad" for purposes of an income tax deduction.

If the debt involves an item of income to the creditor, such as unpaid salary, unpaid rent, or an unpaid account receivable, the item cannot produce a bad debt deduction unless it was previously included in the gross income of the creditor. This requirement does not apply to a debtor's failure to repay the principal amount of a loan, because the loan principal itself is not an item of income to the creditor.

Once the existence of a bona fide debt is established, then the taxpayer must show that the debt became worthless during the taxable year. The debt must then be characterized as either a business or nonbusiness bad debt for tax purposes. These two categories of bad debts are treated differently.

The Nature and Timing of Worthlessness of a Debt

Code Sec. 166 specifies that a bad debt deduction is allowed for a "debt which becomes worthless within the taxable year." The debt must become worthless for a deduction to be allowable, and it must be claimed for the tax year in which worthlessness occurs.

The occurrence and the timing of the worthlessness of a debt is a question of fact. Generally, the taxpayer (creditor) claiming the deduction makes a reasonable determination of the time when worthlessness occurs. Examples of situations that result in the worthlessness of a debt might include the bankruptcy of the debtor, the obtaining of a claim reduced to judgment against the debtor that cannot be collected because the debtor has no funds, the debtor's going out of business, or the disappearance, imprisonment, or other significant event in the life or business existence of the debtor that results in the creditor no longer having a reasonable expectation of repayment. The rules in this area are not hard and fast. The governing principle is the somewhat abstract concept that the debt has become worthless. Generally, the IRS has been reasonable in evaluating factual situations involving this issue.

Business Bad Debts

A more generous tax deduction is allowed for business bad debts as compared with nonbusiness bad debts. Business bad debts are deductible in full from the taxpayer's ordinary income, while nonbusiness bad debts are specifically characterized by the Internal Revenue Code as short-term capital losses. Therefore nonbusiness bad debts are subject to the limitations on deductions for capital losses. In most cases, worthless debts owed to business entities will be characterized as business bad debts. Corporations do not have nonbusiness bad debts.

Generally, the amount of the deduction is the actual amount of the debt that became worthless during the year. Certain financial institutions are permitted to use a reserve method for calculating bad debt deductions.

How is a business bad debt defined and distinguished from a nonbusiness bad debt? Sec. 166(d) defines a business bad debt as either one of the following definitions:

- a debt that is created or acquired (as the case may be) in connection with the taxpayer's trade or business, or
- a debt in which the worthlessness of the debt is incurred in the taxpayer's trade or business

This definition is intended to include situations in which the loan was made by the creditor in the course of conducting his or her business, but becomes worthless at a time during which the creditor is no longer in the business for which the debt was created or acquired. In such cases the debt is still treated as a business bad debt. Likewise, in any situation in which the worthlessness of the debt (as distinguished from its origination) occurs at a time when the debt is part of the creditor's business activity, the debt will be a business bad debt.

The most common example of a business bad debt is where the creditor is engaged in the specific business of lending money and the debt becomes worthless. However, the creditor does not always have to be in the business of lending money in order to have a business bad debt. For example, if a taxpayer lends money to a client or customer for the express purpose of improving the business relationship with that customer, the debt could be a business bad debt if it becomes worthless. The characterization of a bad debt as a business or nonbusiness bad debt is determined by reference to the nature of the creditor's activity in lending the money and not by reference to the purpose for which the borrower used the funds. One good reason for this approach is that it is the creditor, not the debtor, who seeks a bad debt deduction for a worthless obligation.

Example

The Rentabuck Corporation is a private company in the business of lending money. Mr. Gamble has a loan of $50,000 outstanding from the company. He becomes insolvent during the year, files for bankruptcy, and then is arrested and imprisoned for writing false checks. Rentabuck no longer has a reasonable expectation of repayment of Gamble's debt and may claim a business bad debt deduction for the principal balance of the loan ($50,000) this year.

In some situations, taxpayers may seek to claim business bad debt deductions for worthless debts that the IRS views as nonbusiness bad debts. A common example is where a stockholder of a corporation loans money to the corporation and the debt becomes worthless. The IRS will generally take the position that this is a nonbusiness bad debt because the stockholder is seeking to protect his or her interest as an investor seeking to make a profit from ownership of the company rather than as a taxpayer engaged in a business activity. To claim a business bad debt deduction, it is not sufficient for the taxpayer to merely have a profit motive in making the debt. The debt must be created in the actual course of the taxpayer's business activities.

Partial Worthlessness of a Business Bad Debt

partial worthlessness

In the case of a business bad debt (but not a nonbusiness bad debt) a deduction may be claimed for **partial worthlessness** of the debt. Sec. 166 specifies that when a business debt is "recoverable only in part," a deduction may be allowed for the part of the debt that becomes worthless during the tax year.

Recovery of a Bad Debt Previously Deducted

As stated previously, the creditor must have no reasonable expectation of repayment in order to claim a bad debt deduction. However, in some cases the debt is later repaid unexpectedly, even though a bad debt deduction was legitimately claimed. When this occurs, the taxpayer who claimed the deduction must include the amount of the repaid debt in gross income to the extent that the previous deduction of the debt produced a tax benefit.

Investment Vehicles and the Bad Debt Deduction

Bank Accounts

If a taxpayer has a bank account in a financial institution that becomes insolvent or bankrupt and the funds are actually lost, two options are available. The taxpayer may elect to treat the loss as a casualty loss in the year it occurs with reasonable certainty. The loss is then subject to the rules and limitations applicable to personal casualty losses. This election cannot be made by either a taxpayer or relative who is an officer or 1 percent or greater stockholder of the financial institution. Alternatively, the taxpayer may elect to treat the loss as a transaction entered into for profit. However, this election is available only with respect to uninsured federal deposits, and is limited to $20,000 for married couples filing a joint return ($10,000 for married individuals filing separately). Further, the loss is reduced by any insurance proceeds anticipated under state law. Under this election, the loss is treated as an ordinary loss on Schedule A, but subject to the 2-percent-of-AGI limitation for miscellaneous itemized deductions. If neither option is elected, the taxpayer may treat the loss as a nonbusiness bad debt that is deductible as a short-term capital loss.

Corporate Debt Obligations

If an investment in a corporate debt security (such as a bond or debenture) becomes worthless, the loss is treated as a loss from a worthless security, as previously discussed in this chapter, and not as a bad debt. The security owner's deduction is calculated as if the owner had disposed of the worthless security on the last day of the taxable year. That is, it will be treated as a short-term or long-term capital loss depending upon the taxpayer's holding period for the security.

Tax Treatment of Nonbusiness Bad Debts

Any legitimate bad debt that does not meet the definition of a business bad debt is treated for tax purposes as a nonbusiness bad debt. The amount of the uncollectible debt is deductible as a short-term capital loss. An individual's net capital losses are deductible against ordinary income only to the extent of $3,000 per year. Business bad debts, on the other hand, are deductible in full against ordinary income. This is significantly more favorable tax treatment than that which applies to nonbusiness bad debts. Consequently, the issue of whether the creditor entered into the debt in the actual course of a business activity, or merely to make a profit or investment, can be very significant for the taxpayer seeking to claim a deduction.

Loan Guarantees and the Bad Debt Deduction

A bad debt deduction may be available to a guarantor of a loan who is required to make payment when the loan becomes uncollectible from the debtor. Essentially, the same principles that apply to the lender also apply to the guarantor when evaluating the availability of the deduction. The payment of the guarantee will result in a business bad debt deduction only if the guarantor entered into the loan arrangement in the course of a business activity. If there was a profit motive in making the guarantee, but the guarantee was not actually part of the guarantor's business, then the payment on the guarantee will result in a nonbusiness bad debt deduction and short-term capital loss treatment. Guarantors should be mindful of these rules before entering into such arrangements.

If a loan is made purely for personal reasons (such as a loan between family members), there may be no "debt" at all, and therefore no bad debt deduction for either the creditor or the guarantor. There must be a legally enforceable debt and a legitimate profit motive on the part of the guarantor in order for payment on a loan guarantee to result in any bad debt deduction.

Deductibility of Bad Debts

- Business bad debts are deductible against ordinary income.
- Nonbusiness bad debts are deductible only as short-term capital losses.
- Partial worthlessness of a business bad debt is deductible.
- Debt arising from items of income must have been previously included in income to be deductible.

CHAPTER REVIEW

Key Terms and Concepts

casualty losses
bad debt

partial worthlessness

Review Questions

Review questions are based on the learning objectives in this chapter. Thus a [8.3] at the end of a question means that the question is based on learning objective 3. If there are multiple objectives, they are all listed.

1. List the general rules that apply to the deductibility of losses. [8.1]

2.   Explain the deduction for worthlessness or abandonment of property. [8.1]

3.   Explain the tax rules that apply to losses that are partially or fully covered by insurance. [8.1]

4.   What types of losses are deductible by

   a.   business entities?

   b.   individuals? [8.1]

5.   Tony Morrison, president of Swinging Door Company, has had a difficult year. As luck would have it, Tony has no insurance coverage. Tony's adjusted gross income for this year is $250,000.

   This year Tony's office was burglarized. His new answering machine, purchased for $500, was stolen after one week. The next morning Tony missed several calls that he estimated cost him $5,000 in loss of business.

   For personal use Tony bought a new automobile during the summer for $50,000 and drove to Miami Beach for an American Legion convention. On the way to the convention Tony ran into a tree, partially wrecking his automobile. After the wreck the car was worth $20,000. Repairs cost $30,000. Tony has no collision coverage on the car.

   In December Tony sold his home for $300,000, although he had originally bought it for $500,000. At the settlement for his home on December 31, Tony read *The Wall Street Journal* while waiting for the purchasers to arrive. He noted that his 100 shares of Magic Barker stock had dropped $1,000 in value since he had purchased the stock.

   Is Tony allowed to take a deduction for each of the following incidents, and if so, how much?

   a.   theft of the answering machine

   b.   loss of business

   c.   auto collision

   d.   loss on the sale of his home

   e.   loss in value of Magic Barker stock [8.1]

6.   Kathy lives in a home she has owned and occupied for some time. Over the years local wind and weather conditions have steadily weakened the house. Would a casualty loss deduction be allowed? Explain. [8.1]

7.   Mr. T is involved in an accident with his van, which he uses in his business. Its adjusted basis was $10,000. Its value before the accident was $9,000. After the accident, it was worth $2,000. Determine the amount of Mr. T's deductible loss. [8.1]

8. Distinguish between a business bad debt and a nonbusiness bad debt. [8.2]

9. Marjorie lends her friend Tommy $10,000 to purchase a new machine for his manufacturing corporation. Marjorie is not in the business of lending money, and makes the loan as a personal favor. She receives interest at the rate of 12 percent per year, and she has a signed note from him both personally and as president of the closely held business. Tommy's business goes bankrupt when there is still $7,300 due on the balance of the obligation and Tommy has no assets with which to pay the debt.

   a. Would Marjorie treat this as a business or nonbusiness bad debt? Why?

   b. When can she deduct the amount?

   c. If the corporation had borrowed the money from a bank to finance the machinery and Tommy's accountant, Bill, had guaranteed the debt, what would the tax result of Bill's payment on the guarantee be? [8.2]

10. How is a partially worthless bad debt treated for tax purposes? [8.2]

11. How is the recovery of a bad debt in a later year treated for tax purposes when a deduction was taken in an earlier year? [8.2]

12. Describe how a loss from a nonbusiness bad debt is treated for tax purposes. [8.2]

13. Explain how a taxpayer treats a bad debt loss arising from the guarantee of a loan in the following circumstances:

   a. It arises directly from the guarantor's trade or business.

   b. The transaction was entered into by the lender for a nonbusiness-related investment.

   c. The loan was made for personal reasons and is not legally enforceable. [8.2]

Review Answers

1. The general rules that must be satisfied to claim a loss deduction are as follows:

   • The loss must be suffered by the taxpayer who is claiming the deduction.

   • The loss must result from an identifiable event.

   • The property that is the subject of the loss must have had a determinable monetary value.

   • There must be economic substance to the loss, and not just the form of a transaction that appears to result in a loss.

- A loss of an expected economic benefit or item of income is not a deductible loss.

2. A loss deduction is allowable for property that has become worthless. However, the taxpayer must be able to show that there was an identifiable event that resulted in the worthlessness of the property. The deduction cannot be taken for property that merely decreases in value. The property must become completely worthless in order for a change in value to result in a deductible loss without a sale or exchange. A loss deduction may also arise from the abandonment of property. If the owner of the asset acts affirmatively and with manifest intent to abandon the property, the amount of the taxpayer's adjusted basis in the property is generally deductible as a loss.

3. The Code specifies that a deduction is allowed for losses "not compensated for by insurance or otherwise." This means that deductions are allowed only to the extent that the loss is not otherwise compensated for. If there is no insurance, the loss is deductible if it otherwise meets the loss deduction requirements. If the loss is partially compensated for by insurance or through some other arrangement, the portion of the loss not compensated for is deductible.

4. a. For business entities, such as corporations and partnerships, losses are generally deductible in the year when they occur if the loss meets the overall requirements for deductibility. No special restrictions on losses generally apply to these entities.

   b. Individual taxpayers may claim loss deductions if the loss is incurred in the course of a trade or business or in the course of any transaction entered into for profit. If a loss does not fall into either of these categories, it is a personal loss for income tax purposes. Personal losses are deductible only if they are theft losses or casualty losses (losses arising from fire, storm, shipwreck, or another type of casualty). In other words, an individual's losses that result from a business or profit-seeking activity are deductible subject to the same rules that apply to a business entity. Other losses are nondeductible except for theft and casualty losses.

5. a. Tony is entitled to deduct the purchase price of his new machine, $500, as a business loss.

   b. The loss of an estimated $5,000 worth of business is not deductible. The Code requires that the loss be of capital, not just expected income. Tony's "loss" of business is not the loss of capital with an ascertainable value. It is merely his estimate of what might have occurred if the answering machine had been in operation.

   c. Although the automobile accident was Tony's fault, the loss may be deductible as a casualty loss since it was not intentional. The computation of the casualty loss is as follows:

Loss ($50,000 – $20,000)	$30,000
Minus $100 reduction	(100)
	29,900
Minus 10% of adjusted gross income	(25,000)
	$4,900

d. Although Tony realized a loss by selling his house for $200,000 less than he paid for it, he cannot deduct a loss for income tax purposes. Losses from the sale of private residences are nondeductible personal losses.

e. Tony saw in the newspaper that his stock had declined in value by $1,000, but unless he actually sells the stock—and realizes a loss—he is not entitled to any deduction. There has been no identifiable event.

6. The term casualty may be generally defined as damage, destruction, or loss occurring to a taxpayer's property as a result of a sudden, unusual, or unexpected cause.

Fires, storms, shipwrecks, accidents, floods, freezes, and earthquakes are examples of sudden and unexpected events that result in casualty losses. Normal wear and tear of property, and even gradual damage to property resulting from undiscovered causes, are not events that result in deductible personal casualty losses.

Since the damage to Kathy's house occurred over a period of time and therefore was not sudden, she is not eligible for a casualty loss deduction.

7. Mr. T's deductible loss would be the lesser of the van's adjusted basis or the difference in its fair market value before and after the loss. Therefore, the deductible loss would be $7,000, the difference in the van's value before and after the accident. The van was not completely destroyed, so Mr. T cannot deduct the full amount of his basis since that is larger than the difference in value.

8. A more generous tax deduction is allowed for business bad debts as compared with nonbusiness bad debts. Business bad debts are deductible in full from the taxpayer's ordinary income, while nonbusiness bad debts are specifically characterized by the Internal Revenue Code as short-term capital losses. Therefore nonbusiness bad debts are subject to the limitations on deductions for capital losses. In most cases, worthless debts owed to business entities will be characterized as business bad debts. Corporations do not have nonbusiness bad debts.

The characterization of a bad debt as a business or nonbusiness bad debt is determined by reference to the nature of the creditor's activity in lending the money and not by reference to the purpose for which the borrower used the funds.

9. a. A business bad debt must be one of the following:

    - a debt that is created or acquired (as the case may be) in connection with the taxpayer's trade or business

    - a debt in which the worthlessness of the debt is incurred in the taxpayer's trade or business

    Neither one of these situations characterizes the $10,000 loan by Marjorie to her friend Tommy. Since Marjorie is neither in the business of lending money nor is the money lent for the purpose of improving the business relationship with Tommy, the bad debt should be treated as a nonbusiness bad debt.

    b. The Code specifies that a bad debt deduction is allowed for a debt which becomes worthless within the taxable year. The debt must become worthless for a deduction to be allowable, and it must be claimed for the tax year in which worthlessness occurs.

    c. Bill's payment on the guarantee will result in his being able to take a nonbusiness bad debt deduction. The payment on a guarantee will result in a business bad debt deduction only if the guarantor had entered into the loan arrangement in the course of a business activity. Bill, as Tommy's accountant, is not in the business of guaranteeing loans and consequently is not eligible for a business bad debt deduction. However, even though Bill's guarantee was not actually part of his accounting business, there was nonetheless a profit motive in making the guarantee, and under these circumstances Bill's payment on the guarantee will result in a nonbusiness bad debt deduction and short-term capital loss treatment.

10. The Code specifies that when a business bad debt (but not a nonbusiness bad debt) is recoverable only in part, a deduction may be allowed for the part of the debt that becomes worthless during the tax year. In other words, a deduction may be claimed for partial worthlessness of a business debt.

11. When a bad debt for which a deduction was legitimately claimed in an earlier tax year is repaid unexpectedly, the taxpayer who claimed the deduction must include the amount of the repaid debt in gross income to the extent that the previous deduction of the debt produced a tax benefit.

12. The loss from a nonbusiness bad debt is deductible as a short-term capital loss. However, since an individual's net capital losses are only deductible against ordinary income up to $3,000 per year ($1,500 if married filing separately) while business bad debts are deductible in full against ordinary income, the tax treatment of nonbusiness bad debts is significantly less favorable than that which applies to business bad debts.

13. a. Under these circumstances, the payment on the guarantee will result in a business bad debt deduction.

   b. Under these circumstances, the payment on the guarantee will result in a nonbusiness bad debt deduction and short-term capital loss treatment.

   c. Under these circumstances, the payment on the guarantee will not result in a bad debt deduction. There must be a legally enforceable debt and a legitimate profit motive on the part of the guarantor in order for payment on a loan guarantee to result in any bad debt deduction.

Chapter 9

Itemized Deductions for Individuals

Learning Objectives

An understanding of the material in this chapter should enable you to

LO 9.1   **Explain the underlying principle regarding the deductibility of expenses, and describe the tax treatment of personal expenses.**

LO 9.2   **Explain the rules regarding the deductibility of medical and dental expenses, and describe what constitutes an eligible expense under these rules.**

LO 9.3   **Explain the tax treatment of long-term care expenses and insurance premiums.**

LO 9.4   **Explain the rules regarding the deductibility of tax payments.**

LO 9.5   **Explain the rules regarding the deductibility of interest payments.**

LO 9.6   **Explain the rules regarding the deductibility of charitable contributions.**

[A tax loophole is] something that benefits the other guy. If it benefits you, it is tax reform.

—Russell B. Long

Individual taxpayers may "itemize," or claim, various deductions on Schedule A of Form 1040. The categories of deductions claimed on Schedule A include medical and dental expenses, certain taxes, certain interest payments, charitable contributions, casualty and theft losses, and miscellaneous itemized deductions.

The first four categories listed on Schedule A are medical expenses, taxes, interest, and contributions, all of which apply to individual taxpayers. Business entities are entitled to claim many of the same types of items as deductions; however, for a business taxpayer most of these (except for charitable contributions) are treated as business expenses under the general principles of Internal Revenue Code Sec. 162. For individual taxpayers, these items are mostly expenses of a personal nature that Congress has decided should generate income tax benefits even though they are typically not associated with the production of income.

LO 9.1   **Explain the underlying principle regarding the deductibility of expenses, and describe the tax treatment of personal expenses.**

UNDERLYING PRINCIPLES GOVERNING DEDUCTIONS

Capital Expenditures versus Current Expenses

As a general principle of tax law, only items that are considered to be current expenses, as distinguished from capital expenditures, are deductible on a taxpayer's current income tax return. A capital expenditure is considered to be a new investment in property, while a current expense is more akin to a repair or a maintenance item that is necessary for the operation or well-being of a property or asset that the taxpayer already has. If a capital expenditure is made for an asset that is eligible for cost recovery deductions, the cost of the asset may be deducted over a number of tax years, but not, as a general rule, fully deducted in the year the expense is made. One important exception to this rule applies if the taxpayer acquires property that is eligible for the first-year expensing election under Sec. 179.

What, then, is the specific test that distinguishes a capital expenditure from a deductible current expense? One principle is that if the expense is for the acquisition of property that has a useful life of more than one year, the expense is a capital expenditure. Another principle is that if the expense is for an enhancement or improvement to an asset the taxpayer already owns, it will be treated as a capital expenditure if the expense either enhances the value of the taxpayer's property or results in an improvement to the property that has a useful life of more than one year.

Examples of expenses that will generally be treated as capital expenditures rather than currently deductible expenses are as follows:

- an individual's fees for obtaining a professional license, such as a license to practice law or medicine
- expenses (such as attorney's fees) for perfecting or defending a taxpayer's legal title to property or for acquiring an ownership interest in property
- business investigation or start-up costs
- the cost of purchasing a building or of replacing substantial parts of a building, or the cost of machinery, equipment, furniture, and fixtures

Examples of expenses that are treated as current expenses and not capital expenditures are as follows:

- routine repairs to property, such as painting, lawn maintenance, and repairs to equipment
- frequently recurring ordinary and necessary business expenses, such as expenses for advertising, marketing, and employee compensation
- rent paid on a taxpayer's business property (unless the rental payments are to be credited toward the purchase price of the property)

Tax Treatment of Personal Expenses

All items of income received by a taxpayer during the year are includible in gross income unless the Internal Revenue Code expressly states otherwise. A similar principle applies to deductions. No expense is deductible unless the Code expressly provides a deduction for that specific expense or type of expense. Essentially, the Code allows deductions for current expenses paid or incurred in the course of conducting a business or an income-producing activity. Deductions for personal expenses, on the other hand, are generally disallowed. However, certain personal expenses are expressly deductible under the income tax law in spite of the general rule of disallowance. The most significant of these are the deductible personal expenses that are claimed on Schedule A of Form 1040.

Among the personal expenses that are generally nondeductible under the rule of disallowance are as follows:

- payments for basic local telephone service for the first telephone line provided to any residence of a taxpayer
- homeowners insurance premiums including payments for fire and casualty insurance as well as additional premiums for specific personal property
- life insurance premiums paid for personally owned insurance contracts
- expenses for commuting to and from the taxpayer's place of employment
- attorney's fees for the drafting of a will or administration of an estate (except to the extent the legal services pertain to tax advice)
- expenses for groceries, utilities, and other normal expenses of maintaining a personal household
- expenses paid to obtain a divorce (except to the extent the expenses pertain to tax advice)

The following sections of this chapter will focus on those expenses that are deductible as itemized deductions on Schedule A. Most, but not all, of these expenses are personal expenses for which the Code allows deductions, subject to definitions, limitations, and restrictions.

LO 9.2 **Explain the rules regarding the deductibility of medical and dental expenses, and describe what constitutes an eligible expense under these rules.**

MEDICAL AND DENTAL EXPENSES

A deduction is allowed for expenses paid for the medical care of the taxpayer, the taxpayer's spouse, or the taxpayer's dependents (unless compensated for by insurance or otherwise) to the extent that the total of such expenses for the year exceeds 10 percent of adjusted gross income. Under Sec. 213, medical expenses include amounts paid for the diagnosis, cure, treatment, or prevention of disease, or for the purpose of affecting any structure or function of the body. Deductible expenses include expenses for dental care. Cosmetic surgery expenses, however, are deductible only under a narrow definition as set forth below. The deduction also encompasses premiums for medical expense insurance, expenses for qualified long-term care services, and premiums for qualified long-term care insurance contracts. Certain expenses incidental to medical care may also be deductible subject to limitations, including transportation and lodging expenses incurred in the course of receiving medical treatment.

Taxpayers who participate in tax-advantaged plans for funding medical expenses such as flexible spending accounts (FSAs) or health savings accounts (HSAs) can set aside limited sums of money to finance medical expenses on a pretax basis without being subject to the applicable percentage "floor" for deductibility. The details of such plans are beyond the scope of this text. This discussion will focus on medical expenses not paid from such plans.

The 10 Percent "Floor" Applicable to Medical Expense Deductions

For the majority of taxpayers, no medical expenses are actually deductible in most tax years because of the 10 percent "floor" that limits such deductions. As stated above, medical expenses can be deducted only to the extent that unreimbursed medical expenses exceed 10 percent of adjusted gross income for the year.

Example 1

The adjusted gross income of Mr. Delaney (age 50) for this year is $40,000. His total medical expenses for the year that were not compensated for by insurance equal $3,500. The floor applicable to his medical expense deduction is $4,000 ($40,0000 × .100). Since the floor amount of $4,000 is greater than his otherwise deductible expenses of $3,500, no medical expense deduction is actually allowable on Mr. Delaney's return.

Example 2

Assume the same facts as in the previous example, except that Mr. Delaney's adjusted gross income is $30,0000 rather than $40,000. His 10 percent floor amount is now $3,000 ($30,000 × .100). As a result, Mr. Delaney may deduct the excess of his expenses over the floor amount, or $500 ($3,500 – $3,000).

For purposes of computing the alternative minimum tax, the floor is 10 percent of adjusted gross income for all taxpayers for 2016 and future tax years.

Eligible Medical Expenses Under the Deduction Rules

Deductible medical expenses include such obvious expenses as doctor and hospital charges, expenses for nursing services, laboratory tests, and surgical procedures. Expenses for artificial limbs also qualify, as does the cost of prescription drugs and insulin. The cost of nonprescription drugs other than insulin is not a deductible medical expense. However, the cost of certain nonprescription items other than drugs, including equipment and supplies such as crutches, bandages, and blood sugar kits, is deductible.

Special restrictions apply to expenses for cosmetic surgery. Such expenses are deductible only if the surgery is done to correct a condition resulting from an accident, a congenital abnormality, or a disfiguring disease. Expenses for surgery performed to improve the appearance of an individual, such as a face-lift procedure or similar surgery, do not qualify for the deduction. The question in evaluating the deductibility of cosmetic surgery is whether the procedure either meaningfully promotes the proper function of the body or prevents or treats illness or disease.

If a taxpayer travels away from home primarily to receive essential medical care, a deduction for the taxpayer's lodging while away from home is allowable up to a limit of $50 per night. The $50 limitation on lodging applies to each individual. Therefore, if a patient is accompanied by a parent, the taxpayer may deduct an additional $50 per night for lodging. However, there must be no significant element of personal pleasure or recreation for the deduction to apply. Transportation expenses incurred in the course of receiving medical care are also deductible.

For automobile travel, a standard mileage rate of 17 cents per mile may be claimed in 2017 for travel necessary for medical care. Furthermore, parking fees and highway tolls may be deducted in addition to the mileage rate.

The following expenses have been accepted by the Internal Revenue Service as qualifying for the medical expense deduction:

- the cost of dentures and orthodontic treatment
- premiums for part B of Medicare (and also part A for taxpayers not covered by Social Security)
- the cost of guide animals, including hearing aid and seeing eye animals
- the cost of treatment for alcohol or drug addiction
- fees for psychiatric care
- the cost of legal abortions
- fees of chiropractors, osteopaths, and psychotherapists
- fees of Christian Science practitioners and for acupuncture for a specific medical treatment
- medical conference fees
- the cost of special schools specializing in learning disorders
- the cost of eyeglasses, contact lenses, and hearing aids

One principle that the IRS will generally follow in determining whether a given expense qualifies as a deductible medical expense is the question of whether the service, product, or activity paid for is simply for the general preservation of the individual's health or well-being or rather is for the alleviation or treatment of a specific disease or defect. If the expense is for something that only promotes the individual's overall general health, it will generally not be deductible. On the other hand, if a physician prescribes an activity or program of treatment to improve or correct a specific medical condition, the expense is more likely to be deductible. For example, a few years ago the IRS modified its stance on the deductibility of expenses for weight loss programs. Such expenses (not including substitute foods) are now generally deductible if incurred pursuant to a physician's diagnosis of obesity or hypertension. In effect, the IRS now regards obesity itself as a specific disease if it is so diagnosed.

In addition, the cost of smoking cessation programs and prescription drugs to assist in nicotine withdrawal are deductible as medical expenses. In the past, the IRS had disallowed deductions for expenses for quitting tobacco use unless the taxpayer had a specific smoking-related disease. However, the IRS does not permit a deduction for over-the-counter gums and patches.

Premiums paid for health insurance are deductible as medical expenses. Deductible premiums include those for both individually owned and group contracts. Premiums for supplemental policies are also generally deductible. However, premiums for a policy that provides a type of benefit that is associated with a disability policy, such as a benefit for the loss of a limb or a replacement of lost income while the covered individual is ill, are not deductible as medical expenses.

Medical Expenses That Are Capital Expenditures

As explained earlier in this chapter, capital expenditures are generally not deductible in the year in which they are made. A special rule applies to medical expenses that can also be categorized as capital expenditures. If an improvement is made to a taxpayer's property for medical reasons, and the improvement increases the value of the property, a medical expense deduction will be allowed only for the excess of the cost of the improvement over the increase in value to the property. Elevators, escalators, and swimming pools are examples of this type of expense.

Example

Jordan's physician recommends that he install a swimming pool in his home as a therapeutic device for his problems with the connective tissue in his joints. The cost of the pool is $15,000. The value of Jordan's home increases by $10,000 as a result of the pool installation. Jordan can claim $5,000 ($15,000 cost – $10,000 value increase) as a medical expense deduction subject to the applicable percentage floor.

Note that capital expenditures that qualify as medical expenses and do not increase the value of property are deductible in full. Specific examples of medical care improvements that are not deemed to increase the value of the home at all include expenditures incurred to remove structural barriers in the home of an individual who is physically handicapped, such as entrance ramps, widening of doorways and hallways, and railings. In addition, the entire cost of special equipment to assist an individual with a physical impairment is deductible. The specific rule that applies to expenses that are both medical expenses and capital expenditures is more liberal than the general rule previously described that applies to most capital expenditures.

LO 9.3   **Explain the tax treatment of long-term care expenses and insurance premiums.**

LONG-TERM CARE AND LONG-TERM CARE INSURANCE

Expenses for qualified long-term care services are generally deductible as medical expenses. Premiums for qualified long-term care insurance policies are also deductible as medical expenses, subject to dollar amount limitations based on the covered individual's age. Individual taxpayers and their financial advisers should be aware of the basic rules that apply to the deductibility of long-term care expenses. Although these expenses are generally subject to the applicable 10 percent floor that applies to all medical expense deductions, the fact that long-term care expenses are often high enough to exceed the floor makes an understanding of the basic rules more important. With regard to qualified long-term care insurance policies, there are limitations on deductibility of premiums and also limits on the income tax exclusion that applies to benefits paid from such policies. The design of a long-term care policy that will qualify for these tax benefits is the responsibility of the issuing insurance company. However, the basic attributes of qualified long-term care services and insurance contracts should be understood so that individuals know what tax benefits to expect.

Qualified Long-Term Care Services

Qualified long-term care services for purposes of tax deductibility is defined as the diagnostic, preventive, therapeutic, rehabilitative, and other services required by a chronically ill person under a plan prescribed by a licensed health care professional. The income tax definition of a chronically ill person is as follows: a person who is unable to perform at least two activities of daily living (ADLs) for at least 90 days. "Activities of daily living" for purposes of that definition include the following activities: eating, toileting, transferring, bathing, dressing, and continence.

There is a restriction on the deductibility of services provided by a spouse or relative of the individual for whom the services are performed. Expenses paid for care rendered by a relative will not be deductible as medical expenses unless the spouse or relative is a licensed health care professional. A "relative" for this purpose includes a parent, child, grandparent, grandchild, sibling, niece, nephew, or in-law of the individual receiving care.

An individual suffering from Alzheimer's disease or a related disorder involving severe cognitive impairment is considered a chronically ill person without regard to the requirement regarding ADLs.

Deductibility of Long-Term Care Insurance Premiums

Premiums paid for qualified long-term care insurance contracts are deductible as medical expenses. However, the deduction is limited to a maximum dollar amount per year that varies according to the age of the person covered under the policy. The dollar limits are indexed annually for inflation. For tax years beginning in 2017, the limits are as follows:

Age of Covered Person	Premium Deduction Limit
40 or under	$410
Above 40 but not above 50	$770
Above 50 but not above 60	$1,530
Above 60 but not above 70	$4,090
Above 70	$5,110

Example

Esther owns a qualified long-term care policy covering herself. At the end of 2017, she is 82 years old. She pays a premium of $5,860 for the policy in 2017. She may deduct $5,110 of the premium subject to the 10 percent medical expense deduction floor available to taxpayers. The remaining $750 of the premium is nondeductible.

Note that the limits apply per covered individual and not with respect to each tax return. This means, for example, that a married couple filing jointly who each own a long-term care policy covering themselves could deduct the premiums paid for each policy subject to the applicable limitation. Remember too that the applicable percentage of AGI floor is applied to all of the taxpayer's medical expenses taken together and not to each separate expense.

Qualified Long-Term Care Insurance Contracts

The medical expense deduction includes premiums paid for qualified long-term care contracts issued after 1996. However, under a grandfathering rule, most contracts in existence before 1997 are still eligible for tax benefits as long as the applicable state legal requirements were met with respect to the contract when it was issued. Furthermore, not all insurance contracts providing long-term care benefits are "qualified" for tax purposes. Individuals considering purchase of a long-term care policy should be fully informed regarding the income tax status of all contracts being considered.

The tax law requirements for a qualified long-term care insurance contract currently issued are as follows:

- It must not have a cash value.

- It must be guaranteed renewable.

- It must include a nonforfeiture provision.

Tax qualification of a long-term care contract is the responsibility of the insurance company that issues the contract. Not all contracts are designed to be qualified.

Deductible Long-Term Care Expenses
- **qualified expenses generally deductible as medical expenses**
- **restrictions on expenses for care provided by relatives of patient**
- **expenses for care of Alzheimer's patients deductible without ADL test**
- **premiums for qualified LTC policies deductible subject to limits based on age of covered person**

Exclusion for Benefits Paid from Long-Term Care Contracts

Benefits received from qualified long-term care contracts are generally excludible from gross income. It is not a part of the medical expense deduction as discussed in this chapter, which covers only deductions for medical expenses and not exclusions for benefits paid from insurance contracts. However, the exclusion is mentioned in this context again for the sake of clarity. The benefits are fully excludible to the extent they are actually used for long-term care expenses. If benefits paid exceed actual long-term care expenses, they are excludible up to a fixed daily dollar amount that is indexed annually for inflation. For 2017, the per diem limitation is $360.

Long-Term Care Insurance in Business Situations

Premiums for qualified contracts are eligible for the "above-the-line" deduction for health insurance premiums paid by self-employed taxpayers. For other individual taxpayers, however, the deduction must be claimed as an itemized deduction subject to the applicable percentage floor.

Long-term care coverage cannot be provided to employees on a tax-favored basis as part of a cafeteria plan. In addition, if an employer offers a flexible spending account as part of its employee benefits package, employees may not use the tax-favored flexible spending account to pay for long-term care insurance premiums. A detailed discussion of cafeteria plans and flexible spending accounts is beyond the scope of this text.

LO 9.4   Explain the rules regarding the deductibility of tax payments.

TAXES

Individuals may deduct expenses for certain taxes on Schedule A of Form 1040. These are taxes that constitute personal expenses of the taxpayer for which the Internal Revenue Code allows a deduction.

If taxes are incurred in a trade or business or a transaction entered into for profit, the expenditure is normally an "above the line" deduction. However, as with the other itemized deductions, personal taxes claimed on Schedule A are a "below the line" deduction. This distinction was covered in an earlier chapter. However, federal income taxes (other than self-employment taxes) and certain other taxes are not deductible regardless of the activity with which they are connected.

Taxes That Are Deductible on Schedule A

The following types of taxes not incurred in the course of a business or income-producing activity are deductible on Schedule A by individual taxpayers:

- state, local, and foreign real property taxes
- state and local personal property taxes
- state and local income taxes
- state and local general sales taxes in lieu of state and local income taxes
- the generation-skipping transfer tax imposed on income distributions
- the environmental tax imposed by IRC Sec. 59A

Certain other taxes are deductible, including foreign income, war profits, and excess profit taxes for taxpayers who do not claim a foreign tax credit for these taxes.

Categories of taxes that are not deductible include federal income, estate, and gift taxes and certain penalty taxes imposed by the Internal Revenue Code.

Taxes on real property are deductible including property taxes paid on the taxpayer's principal residence. State and local income taxes are deductible, whether paid through withholding by the taxpayer's employer, by estimated tax payments, or paid with the filing of a return. These two types of taxes are generally the most important deductible taxes for individuals. A deduction for state and local sales taxes is available in lieu of the deduction for state and local income taxes (see below).

Deduction for State and Local General Sales Taxes

The deduction must be taken in lieu of the deduction for state and local income taxes. In other words, taxpayers must choose between deducting general sales taxes or state and local income taxes on Schedule A. This provision may benefit taxpayers who live in states where no state income tax is imposed, such as Florida.

Note that state and local property taxes may still be deducted regardless of whether sales taxes or income taxes are claimed.

Specifics of the Deduction

The deduction may be calculated in one of two ways. Taxpayers can deduct general sales taxes by saving receipts showing the actual amount of sales tax paid during the year. Alternatively, most taxpayers are permitted to use tables created by the Treasury Department.

The tables are based on average consumption data. The deductible amounts under the government tables vary according to taxpayer-specific information, such as income level, number of exemptions claimed on Form 1040, and state of residence. The tables reflect adjusted gross income (with certain modifications) up to a specified amount. This means that sales tax table deductions do not increase further for taxpayers whose AGI is above the highest table amount. Note that general sales taxes paid for purchases of certain items, including motor vehicles, boats, aircraft, homes, and materials to build a home, may generally be added to the table amounts, subject to certain restrictions. Any sales taxes paid on motor vehicles or motor homes at a rate higher than the general sales tax rate are deductible only to the extent of the general sales tax rate.

State and local tax deductions are still not allowable for AMT purposes. It is possible therefore that deducting state and local taxes could cause a taxpayer to be subject to the AMT.

Nondeductible Assessments

Amounts that are assessed to pay for improvements or "betterments" to a taxpayer's property are not deductible as taxes because such amounts are really charges for capital improvements rather than actual taxes assessed with respect to property. For example, an assessment by a local municipality for improvements to the taxpayer's sidewalk or municipal waste disposal systems would not constitute a deductible tax.

Another type of expense that is not deductible as a tax is a charge for the use of a product or service provided by a municipality. For example, an annual sewer fee is not a deductible tax. Likewise, a taxpayer's bill for use of a municipal water supply is not deductible as a tax. Such nondeductible charges would also include highway tolls and municipal parking fees. In order to have a tax deduction, the assessment in question must be a tax rather than a fee or charge imposed by a government or municipality. Remember, however, that if a taxpayer incurs such charges with respect to a business or income-producing property, a deduction may be available on the portion of the taxpayer's return that reflects such activity.

Other Pertinent Rules

Generally, a deduction for taxes is allowed only to the taxpayer who is actually liable or responsible for the payment of the taxes. For example, if a mother paid her adult daughter's real estate taxes, she would not be permitted to deduct that payment. Would the daughter be entitled to a deduction on her return during the year her mother paid her real estate taxes? The Tax Court in *Judith F. Lang v. Commissioner*, TC Memo 2010-286 concluded the daughter was entitled to a deduction notwithstanding that she did not pay the tax directly. The Tax Court examined the entire "substance" of the transaction and concluded the mother's payments to the taxing authorities were a gift to the daughter who was treated as making the payments.

Taxpayers who own property jointly (or as tenants by the entirety) are typically each liable for the full amount of any tax assessed on that property. Therefore any joint owner or owners who actually pay the taxes may deduct the amount paid on their returns.

One exception to this principle applies in the case of real property taxes assessed to a property owner (such as a homeowner) who sells the property during the period covered by an existing assessment. In such cases the property taxes are subject to a rule of apportionment. For deduction purposes, the taxes are treated as assessed to the seller of the property for the time period up to but not including the date of sale. As of the sale date, the taxes are treated as having been assessed to the buyer for deduction purposes. The apportionment is calculated based on the number of days of the assessment period that each party owns the property. This treatment is consistent with the usual apportionment of tax payments that appears on a closing statement or settlement sheet upon the sale of a home.

Homeowners frequently have escrow accounts with a mortgage lender from which real property taxes are paid. The homeowner makes a monthly or bimonthly payment into the escrow account, and the lending institution pays or arranges to pay the property tax before the due date. A deduction is available to the homeowner only for tax payments actually made to the taxing authority, not for the periodic payments made to the escrow account.

Finally, under Sec. 266, taxpayers may elect to charge certain taxes and other expenses to a property's capital account rather than currently deduct those taxes. Such charges would then be added to the taxpayer's basis in the property for purposes of determining the gain or loss realized on a later sale. This election would typically be made in cases where the property does not produce income and the taxpayer will not obtain a tax benefit from claiming a current deduction.

LO 9.5   Explain the rules regarding the deductibility of interest payments.

DEDUCTIONS FOR INTEREST

interest

The term **interest** may be generally defined as payment by a borrower (or "debtor") for the use of money provided by a lender (or "creditor"). From an economic standpoint, there must be a bona fide debtor/creditor relationship between two or more parties in order to generate interest payments. Such a relationship is also required under the income tax law. For example, certain transactions between family members may not actually be bona fide loans for tax purposes, even though the parties characterize them as such.

Some interest payments are deductible for income tax purposes, and others are not. The distinctions between deductible and nondeductible interest will be explained below. The deductibility of interest is, for the most part, determined by how the interest payment is categorized for income tax purposes. However, no interest payment is deductible unless there is an enforceable obligation on the part of the debtor to pay a determinable sum to the creditor in exchange for the use of a determinable sum.

principal amount

The amount of money provided by the lender for the borrower's use may be called the **principal amount**. The amount the borrower is obligated to pay the lender will consist of both a repayment of the principal amount at or over some period of time, plus an additional amount (interest) as payment for the use of the funds. There are many different ways in which the interest portion of a loan repayment can be calculated. The most common form is as a percentage of the principal amount. There are also many different economic methods by which a loan can be repaid, such as a direct reduction loan, a balloon loan, or a revolving credit arrangement.

Questions may arise as to whether a certain payment to a lender constitutes interest and therefore whether it may qualify under one of the categories of deductible interest. For example, "points" paid as a premium to a lender at the inception of a mortgage loan might be considered to be either a payment for the use of money (a prepaid interest payment) or a payment for services rendered by the lending institution. Generally, a prepayment of interest by a taxpayer not using the accrual method of tax accounting is not currently deductible. However, as discussed below, the tax law provides specific rules for the deductibility of points paid in connection with the acquisition or improvement of a taxpayer's personal residence. A prepayment penalty on a loan is another type of payment that may be difficult to characterize. If the lender charges the borrower an extra amount in the event the borrower pays off the loan before full repayment is actually due, is such a payment an interest payment? Generally, for income tax purposes, if such a prepayment penalty is calculated as a percentage of the principal amount, the penalty will be treated as an interest payment.

In order for a payment of interest to qualify for a tax deduction, the taxpayer making the interest payment must have a legal obligation to repay the loan. For example, if a parent pays the interest on a loan incurred by the parent's adult child, the parent cannot claim a tax deduction for the payment. If there is a joint obligation on the part of two or more parties to repay a loan, the payment of part or all of the interest by any obligated party can be deducted if the payment otherwise qualifies for a deduction. The most significant exception to this principle is the fact that the IRS permits a purchaser of a home to deduct mortgage "points" that were actually paid by the seller of the home if the points would otherwise qualify for an interest deduction. This rule allows sellers to offer the incentive of paying points for the buyer without jeopardizing the buyer's income tax deduction. However, note that in this situation the points are not deductible by the party who pays them (the seller). Such points are, in turn, treated as a reduction of the property's purchase price.

Categorization of Interest Payments

To determine whether the interest paid on indebtedness is a deductible expense, the interest payment must be properly categorized. This is so because the Internal Revenue Code expressly defines, limits, and allows or disallows deductions for interest payments based essentially on what type of interest payment the taxpayer has made. There are many types of debt arrangements that a taxpayer might enter into; consequently, there are numerous types of interest payments on indebtedness. The Internal Revenue Code provides several categories of interest payments and imposes rules for the deductibility or nondeductibility of each category. The most significant basic categories of interest payments for purposes of this text are as follows:

- interest on indebtedness incurred in the course of a trade or business ("business interest")

- interest on indebtedness incurred in the course of an activity entered into for profit that is not a business activity ("investment interest")

- interest on indebtedness incurred in connection with a passive activity ("passive activity interest")

- certain interest on indebtedness secured by the taxpayer's residence ("qualified residence interest")

- personal interest

An interest payment is generally categorized by looking to the purposes for which the underlying loan was borrowed, that is, the specific activity for which the borrowed money was used. The Treasury regulations contain so-called "tracing" rules that generally help to determine which category a payment of interest should fall into. Each of these categories will be examined below.

Business Interest

The general rule for interest payments on indebtedness incurred in the course of a business activity is that the payments are deductible. If the payments are made by a regular or "C" corporation, they are deductible on the corporation's tax return. If the payments are made by an individual taxpayer or by a "pass-through" business entity such as a partnership or S corporation, they are ultimately deducted on the appropriate schedule of the business owner's individual tax return as an above-the-line deduction.

Even though business interest is generally deductible, there may be another set of rules that applies to the interest payment to limit or prevent its deductibility. For example, the interest payment, although incurred in the course of a business activity, may also be paid or incurred in connection with a passive activity. If so, it is subject to the limitations on passive activity losses. Or the interest may be paid with respect to a loan that is borrowed from or allocable to the values in a life insurance or annuity contract. If so, the interest is subject to additional limitations. Interest payments may be subject to multiple layers of complex rules. The first step is to determine the classification of the interest payment under one of the basic categories. Then, if the interest is deductible under that category, it must be determined whether there are other additional rules that may limit or prohibit a deduction.

Business interest, investment interest, qualified residence interest, and nondeductible personal interest are mutually exclusive categories. One interest payment cannot fall into more than one of these categories. However, the passive loss limitations might apply to interest that would otherwise be either business or investment interest. The limitations on interest deductions that are related to a life insurance or annuity contract can apply to any category of interest payment except qualified residence interest.

Investment Interest

Interest payments on a nonbusiness loan incurred in the course of an investment activity are referred to as investment interest. Deductions for investment interest expenses are allowed but are limited to the taxpayer's "net investment income" for the year.

To determine the applicable limitation on investment interest, the taxpayer's net investment income must be determined. The term "net investment income" means the excess of the taxpayer's investment income over the taxpayer's investment expenses. Investment income is the sum of gross income from property held for investment other than qualified dividends taxed at the preferential and reduced maximum rates, plus gain other than capital gain attributable to the disposition of property held for investment purposes. Note that the definition of investment income for this purpose does not include tax-exempt interest income. Investment expenses are generally all deductible expenses (other than interest expenses) that are connected with the production of the taxpayer's investment income.

Capital gains and qualified dividend income may, at the election of the taxpayer, be included in the calculation of investment income. Such inclusion will increase the taxpayer's investment income, thereby increasing the deductible amount of investment interest. The trade-off for such an election is that any capital gain so included in the calculation is not eligible for the lower maximum income tax rates on long-term capital gain of individual taxpayers. The same rule applies to dividend income. Any such income included in the calculation of investment income will not be eligible for the lower maximum tax rates on qualified dividends.

Example

Muriel wanted to purchase bonds of the Laramie Corporation, a publicly traded company that sells western-style fashions. She borrowed $250,000 from her bank last year and used all of the loan proceeds to fund the purchase. This year, Muriel paid $17,500 in interest on the loan. She also received $12,500 of interest income from the Laramie bonds. In addition, Muriel received $3,000 of interest income this year from a money market account. Muriel has no other investment income or investment expenses this year. Muriel's deduction for investment interest on this year's tax return would be limited to $15,500, the total of her net investment income ($12,500 + $3,000).

Any investment interest that is nondeductible because of the net investment income limitation may be carried forward to future tax years and deducted (subject to the same limitation in that year) until the carryover of excess investment interest is fully used up. Therefore, in the example above, Muriel could carry over her remaining $2,000 ($17,500 – $15,500) of investment interest to her future tax years. In no tax year, however, can either current or "carried over" investment interest be deducted in excess of the taxpayer's current net investment income.

Note that if an interest payment is made in connection with an activity that would be treated as an investment activity except that it meets the definition of a passive activity under the passive activity loss limitations, the interest is not treated as investment interest, but is instead included in the computation of passive activity income or loss under those rules.

Investment Interest Expenses
- Deductions for investment interest payments limited to taxpayer's "net investment income"
- "Net investment income" equals "investment income" minus "investment expenses"
- "Investment expenses" do not include interest expenses
- Special rules for capital gains and dividends in calculation of "investment income"

An individual's investment interest deductions are generally claimed on Schedule A of Form 1040 as an itemized deduction.

Qualified Residence Interest

qualified residence interest

The term **qualified residence interest** means interest paid on a loan secured by the taxpayer's personal residence that is deductible for federal income tax purposes. For interest payments to be qualified residence interest, the loan must be secured by a "qualified residence." A qualified residence includes the taxpayer's principal residence plus one other residence (such as a vacation home) that the taxpayer selects to be treated as a qualified residence. Such other residence need not be a house but could include vehicles and water vessels that have sleeping and eating accommodations. If such other residence is rented by the taxpayer for part of the year, it must not qualify under the "rental use" test of the vacation home deduction limitations. If it does qualify under that test, it cannot also be a "qualified residence" for purposes of deducting qualified residence interest.

For qualified residences, there are two types of qualified residence interest: interest paid on "acquisition indebtedness" and interest paid on "home equity indebtedness."

Acquisition Indebtedness

The term "acquisition indebtedness" means any indebtedness that is incurred in acquiring, constructing, or substantially improving a qualified residence, and that is secured by such residence. The term also includes the refinancing of such indebtedness, but only to the extent the principal amount of the refinancing does not exceed the amount of the refinanced indebtedness. Amounts refinanced in excess of the existing principal balance may qualify as home equity indebtedness as discussed below.

The maximum amount of acquisition indebtedness for any one taxpayer (including a married couple filing jointly) is $1 million. For married taxpayers filing separately, the limit is $500,000. Indebtedness in excess of these amounts will not be treated as acquisition indebtedness and will not give rise to deductible interest unless the debt qualifies as home equity indebtedness.

Example

Ryan Lyon wins the lottery this year and purchases a home in the city and a vacation home at the beach. His mortgage on the city home is $500,000, and his mortgage on the beach home is $300,000. Both homes will be qualified residences. Since his total acquisition indebtedness is less than $1 million, the interest on both his mortgages will be deductible as qualified residence interest.

The $1 million limit applies to mortgages and refinancings beginning on or after October 14, 1987. If a mortgage loan was originally taken before that date, however, it may be refinanced in an amount not greater than the existing principal balance at the time of refinancing, and the $1 million limit will not apply to limit deductibility of the refinanced indebtedness.

For payments made or accrued before 2017, a deduction is available as a special category under the acquisition indebtedness rules for premiums paid for certain qualified mortgage insurance. The deduction is phased out for taxpayers with adjusted gross income in excess of $100,000 and is unavailable for taxpayers with AGI exceeding $109,000. A more detailed discussion of this deduction, which requires Congressional reauthorization for 2017 and future tax years, is beyond the scope of this text.

Home Equity Indebtedness

home equity indebtedness

The term **home equity indebtedness** means indebtedness other than acquisition indebtedness secured by a qualified residence to the extent of the following:

- The total amount of acquisition and home equity indebtedness does not exceed the fair market value of the residence.

- The aggregate amount of the taxpayer's home equity indebtedness does not exceed $100,000 ($50,000 for married taxpayers filing separately).

Note that the $100,000 limit (as well as the $1 million limit on acquisition indebtedness) is a per-taxpayer, and not a per-residence, limitation. Also, the total of acquisition indebtedness and home equity indebtedness may exceed the taxpayer's cost for the home but may not exceed the fair market value of the home. Finally, home equity indebtedness does not have to be used for any specific purpose in order to generate qualified residence interest. Such loans can generally be used for any purpose desired by the taxpayer.

Example

Bubby purchased a home three years ago for $400,000. His acquisition indebtedness on the home was $350,000. This year the fair market value of the residence is $450,000. Bubby takes a home equity loan of $75,000 secured by the residence and uses the money to buy a racing car for his use as an amateur racer. The interest payments on both the original mortgage and the home equity loan are deductible because each of the loan principal amounts are less than the applicable dollar amount limitations, are secured by the residence, and when added together ($425,000) do not exceed the fair market value of the residence ($450,000) even though they do exceed its cost.

Qualified residence interest is deductible by individual taxpayers as an itemized deduction on Schedule A of Form 1040.

Prepaid Interest and Mortgage "Points"

Sometimes a debtor will prepay interest on a loan. Prepaid interest is generally an amount paid on a loan that represents a charge for the use of borrowed funds that is allocable to a future tax year or accounting period. For taxpayers on the cash basis method of tax accounting (including almost all individual taxpayers), the general rule for prepaid interest payments is that such payments are not deductible in the year paid but rather must be allocated to the tax year or years with respect to which the interest payments actually represent a payment or charge for the use of the borrowed funds. In other words, prepaid interest is generally not deductible in the year it is paid, but rather amortized over the life of the loan. However, there are special rules that apply to so-called mortgage "points" paid to a mortgage lender in the year when a loan secured by the taxpayer's principal residence is obtained.

points

Points can be described as a charge imposed by mortgage lenders at the inception of a loan. They are calculated as a percentage of the principal amount of the loan and are not fees for a mortgage application or other services provided by the lender. Points paid in connection with certain loans secured by a principal residence are deductible in the year paid rather than being subject to the general rule just described for prepaid interest.

In order for taxpayers to be assured that points paid upon the origination of a loan will be currently deductible, the following requirements must be met:

- The loan must be incurred in connection with the acquisition of the taxpayer's principal residence.
- The loan must be secured by the taxpayer's principal residence.
- The points must be calculated as a percentage of the principal amount of the loan.
- The points must be paid to the lender directly by the taxpayer rather than added to or derived from the principal amount of the loan.
- The lender's charging of the points must be consistent with an established business practice in the area in which the loan is made and must not exceed the amount generally charged for points in such area.
- The settlement statement describing the acquisition of the home must designate the payments as points by using a term such as "points," "discount points," "loan origination fees," or similar terminology.

The above "safe harbor" rules provided by the IRS for the deductibility of points do not include points paid for a loan used for the improvement, rather than acquisition, of a principal residence. However, the Code expressly provides that such points may also be deductible. If the loan is used to make improvements to the taxpayer's residence, and all the requirements other than the first and last requirements listed above are met, the points will in all probability be currently deductible. However, points paid in connection with a simple refinancing of the taxpayer's mortgage on a residence are generally not currently deductible in full.

Personal Interest: Interest Expense from Qualified Education Loans

Under current law no interest on loans borrowed for personal use is deductible unless the interest is either qualified residence interest or interest on "qualified education loans." However, there is a deduction for "qualified education loans."

Deductible interest on qualified education loans, also referred to as the "student loan interest deduction," includes interest payments of up to $2,500 per year per taxpayer for certain loans borrowed for the funding of higher education. The deduction is currently phased out completely for married taxpayers filing jointly with adjusted gross income (subject to certain modifications) in excess of $165,000 and for other taxpayers with AGI in excess of $80,000. There are additional restrictions and limitations on the student loan interest deduction that are beyond the scope of this text. If available, the deduction is claimed not as an itemized deduction on Schedule A of Form 1040 but as an above-the-line deduction taken in determining the taxpayer's adjusted gross income.

Virtually all other interest on loans borrowed for personal use is nondeductible. Such interest would include interest on an individual's credit card purchases, car loans not secured by the taxpayer's home, and interest on most loans arranged between friends or family members.

Expenses and Interest Relating to Tax-Exempt Income

As a general rule of tax law, an otherwise allowable deduction for an interest payment or any other expense will be disallowed if the interest expense or other expense is incurred in the course of producing income that is exempt from income tax. The most common example of this general rule would probably be where a taxpayer borrows money to purchase tax-exempt bonds. Interest on such a loan would not be deductible, even though the interest would qualify as investment interest if the bonds generated taxable rather than excludible interest payments. If other expenses, such as fees for financial advice, were incurred in the course of purchasing tax-exempt bonds and directly connected to that purchase, then the fees would also be nondeductible.

Uncertainty may arise in interpreting this disallowance of deductions because there is not always conclusive proof of a connection between the interest or other expense and the production of tax-exempt income. For example, the proceeds of a loan do not necessarily have to be directly traceable to the purchase of a tax-exempt investment for the disallowance to apply to a given taxpayer. In this regard, the Internal Revenue Service has provided guidelines under which it will infer or conclude that a portion of a taxpayer's interest payments or other expenses should be allocated to those activities of the taxpayer that produce tax-exempt income.

The disallowance of deductions relating to tax-exempt income applies in addition to all other limits and restrictions on interest deductions imposed by the tax law.

LO 9.6   **Explain the rules regarding the deductibility of charitable contributions.**

CHARITABLE CONTRIBUTION DEDUCTIONS

People make gifts to charity. Whether motivated by a combination of social, moral, or economic reasons, individuals have traditionally contributed large amounts to public charities. The vastness of both these sums and the possible tax savings to individuals make it imperative for the financial adviser to have a working knowledge of the charitable contribution deduction rules.

Charitable contributions have tax value. They result in current income tax savings, they may reduce federal estate taxes, and they can be made gift tax free. From the charity's point of view, charitable contributions are also tax favored. The charity itself pays no tax upon the receipt of either a lifetime gift or a bequest, and generally no income tax is paid by the qualified charity on income earned by donated property.

A charitable contribution deduction is allowed for contributions to certain charitable, religious, scientific, educational, and other specified organizations. Deductions may be taken by either individuals or corporations. The deduction by individual taxpayers is allowed only from adjusted gross income. Therefore it may be wise from a tax standpoint for individuals to make charitable contributions only in years in which they have itemized deductions in excess of the standard deduction amount.

Four Requirements for Deductibility of Charitable Contributions

The first requirement for deductible charitable contributions is that they must be made to organizations that are qualified. Qualified organizations include nonprofit schools and hospitals, churches and synagogues, organizations formed to help the poor and homeless, charitable health and disaster relief organizations, and similar entities.[1]

A donee cannot be considered a qualified charity unless it meets three conditions. First, it must be an organization operated exclusively for religious, charitable, scientific, literary, or

---

1.   A list of qualified organizations is contained in IRS publication no. 78 entitled, "Cumulative List, Organizations Described in Section 170(c) of the Internal Revenue Code of 1986," published by the Superintendent of Documents, U.S. Government Printing Office in Washington, D.C. A taxpayer is not entitled to rely on the statements of an organization as to whether contributions to it are tax deductible.

educational purposes, or for the prevention of cruelty to children or animals. Second, no part of the organization's earnings can benefit any private shareholder or similar individual. Third, no substantial part of such an organization's work can consist of propaganda or legislation-influencing activities.

qualified public charity

Technically there are two types of qualified charities: (1) the public charity and (2) the private charity. Gifts to **qualified public charities** are subject to higher deductible limits than gifts to private charities. Public charities (also called 50 percent charities because individuals can take a deduction of up to 50 percent of their contribution base for gifts to these charities) include such charities as the American Red Cross, the United Way, and most nonproprietary schools and churches. All qualified charities that are not public (50 percent) charities are considered private (20 or 30 percent) charities. (See the Table 9-1 later in this chapter.) Included under the category of private charities would be most private foundations. It is important to recognize that an organization is not automatically a qualified charity merely because it is tax exempt.

For example, civic associations, social clubs, chambers of commerce, and other business leagues are generally exempt from tax. However, they are not considered qualified organizations. Therefore gifts to these organizations are not deductible as charitable contributions, but they may be deductible as ordinary and necessary business expenses. Even direct contributions of cash or other property to a needy family are generally nondeductible because of the rule that contributions must be made to a qualified charity to be deductible.

A second requirement necessary for a charitable contribution deduction is that property must be the subject of the gift. The value of a taxpayer's time or services, even if contributed to a qualified charity, is not deductible.

For example, if Whipsaw, a carpenter, spent 10 hours building a podium for his church, he could not deduct his normal hourly rate as a charitable contribution. However, if he built the podium at home and gifted it to the church, he could deduct the cost of the materials used in producing the finished product (not including the value of his working time) as a charitable contribution.

If Marlon Brandi—the famous streetcar conductor turned actor—entertained at a charity ball, he could not deduct the value of his personal services, mainly because he has not been charged with income as the result of rendering such services. However, he could deduct any out-of-pocket expenses incurred in rendering such services. For example, if he had to fly into New York from Chicago solely to appear at the charitable event, his transportation expenses incurred in rendering services for the charity in question would be deductible. If a car is used to render charitable services, a deduction of 14 cents per mile is generally permitted for 2017.

A third requirement for a charitable contribution deduction is that there must in fact be a contribution to the charity in excess of the value received. In some cases, donors will receive a benefit in conjunction with their charitable gifts. Such contributions are deductible only to the extent that the value of the contributed property exceeds any consideration or benefit to the donor. For example, if Pam purchases bonds issued by a nonprofit hospital to finance a new building, the purchase price of the bond would not be deductible as a contribution. However, if Pam later donated the bonds to the hospital, she would then become entitled to a deduction. A similar question often arises in the case of dues, fees, or assessments paid to qualified organizations. These items are deductible as contributions only to the extent that they exceed the monetary value of benefits received by the donor. Charitable organizations are now required to inform donors of the extent to which the contribution exceeds the value of benefits received in return if the contribution is more than $75. Dues, fees, or assessments paid to country clubs, veterans and fraternal organizations, or lodges are specifically nondeductible as charitable contributions.

If the local church or synagogue was to sponsor a bingo night, amounts paid to play (or for raffle tickets or other games of chance) would not be considered contributions. They would be treated as wagering losses. Likewise, if a qualified charitable organization sponsors a picnic (or a night at the theater, a charity ball, a sporting event, or a show), only the difference between the fair market value of the picnic lunch purchased and the amount actually paid is considered a charitable contribution. The balance is treated as a nondeductible personal expenditure. For example, if you paid $20 for a box lunch at a church picnic and the lunch plus entertainment was worth $3, only the difference—$17—would be a charitable contribution assuming the entire net proceeds of the picnic went to the church. The $3 balance is considered a personal outlay that is specifically nondeductible.

It is often difficult to distinguish between a tax-deductible contribution to charity and a nondeductible personal expense. A commonly litigated example is the cost of tuition paid by taxpayers to a parochial school for their children. Even where the tuition payment was not legally required by the church (only expected), no deduction was allowed because the outlay was considered essentially an expense in payment of personal educational services received rather than a charitable contribution.

A fourth requirement that must be met for a deduction to be allowed is that the contribution must actually be paid in cash or other property before the close of the tax year in question. This rule applies regardless of the accounting method used by the taxpayer. In other words, even an accrual-basis taxpayer must actually pay cash or contribute other property before the close of the tax year. A contribution made by credit card is equivalent to payment in cash when the transaction is made. Taxpayers are entitled to charitable deductions in the year they charge the contributions to their bank credit cards and not in the year they actually make payment to the bank.

Often a donor will give a charitable organization a promissory note. The issuance and even the delivery of the note are not enough to meet the requirement that the contribution be paid within the tax year. However, the donor will be allowed a deduction when payments on the note are actually made.

Strict substantiation requirements now apply to charitable contributions. As of 2007, any monetary charitable contribution made in cash or by check cannot be deducted unless the donor maintains either a bank record of the contribution (such as a canceled check or equivalent) or a written communication from the donee substantiating the contribution. Additional substantiation requirements apply to deductible contributions of property other than cash if such contributions exceed specified amounts. There are also special restrictions on the deductibility of contributions of clothing or household items. Also, if a taxpayer donates a motor vehicle, boat, or aircraft, and the donee charity sells such property, the donor's deduction is generally limited to the amount of the sale proceeds.

Deductible Amounts

Taxpayers are entitled to a deduction for contributions to qualified charities; that is, governmental bodies, public or private corporations, trusts, and foundations organized as well as operated predominantly for charitable, religious, scientific, literary, or educational purposes. However, the taxpayer's deduction is limited.

The amount of a charitable contribution deduction depends on the following five factors, which will be discussed in detail:

1. the type of property given away. This chapter will consider the following items under the heading of property: (1) rent-free occupancy, (2) cash, (3) capital-gain property, (4) ordinary-income property, (5) tangible personal property where the use of that property by the donee is related to the exempt functions of the donee, (6) tangible personal property where the use of that property is unrelated to the exempt purposes of the donee, and (7) future interests in property.

2. the identity of the donee. Generally contributions to publicly supported domestic organizations—so-called "public charities"—are more favorably treated than contributions to foreign organizations or most private foundations. The deduction for an individual's contributions to nonpublic (private) charities, regardless of the type of property given away, is limited to the lesser of (1) 20 or 30 percent (see the preceding chart) of the taxpayer's contribution base, which is basically AGI, or (2) 50 percent of

the taxpayer's contribution base minus the amount of charitable contribution deductions allowed for contributions to the public-type charities. For example, if Richblood donates property worth 40 percent of his contribution base (AGI) to a public charity, such as the Boy Scouts, his additional contributions to 20 or 30 percent charities (private charities) are deductible only up to 10 percent of his contribution base. Donations to individuals are not deductible.

3. the identity of the contributor. Individuals are limited to specified percentages of adjusted gross income, while a corporation is limited to a deduction based on a percentage of its taxable income.

4. the amount of property given away. Generally there is a carryover of excess contributions—contributions above their deductible limit—for up to 5 years. (See the preceding chart.)

5. the place where the charity is organized. Gifts made to foreign charities are not deductible (except where allowed by treaty).

Table 9-1: Charitable Contribution Deduction Limitations Chart

| | | Percentage Limitation | | Excess Carryover* | | |
Type of Property (1)	Donee (2)	Individual (Adjusted Gross Income) (3)	Corporation (Taxable Income) (4)	Individual (5)	Corporation (6)	Amount Deductible (7)
(A) Rent-free occupancy						No deduction No deduction
(B) Cash	Public Private	50% 30%	10% 10%	5 yrs. 5 yrs.	5 yrs. 5 yrs.	Full deduction Full deduction
(C) Capital-gain property						
(1) Real estate and intangible personal property	Public	30% or	10%	5 yrs.	5 yrs.	Full deduction for fair market value (FMV)
		50% on election (see column 7)	No corp. election	5 yrs.		FMV minus 100% of appreciation (donor's cost basis)†
	Private	20%	10%	5 yrs.	5 yrs.	Full deduction for FMV‡
(2) Tangible personal property Use related	Public	30% or	10%	5 yrs.	5 yrs.	Full deduction for FMV
		50% on election		5 yrs.		Donor's cost basis
	Private	20%	10%	5 yrs.	5 yrs.	Donor's cost basis
Use unrelated	Public	50%	10%	5 yrs.	5 yrs.	Donor's cost basis
	Private	20%	10%	5 yrs.	5 yrs.	Donor's cost basis
(D) Ordinary-income property	Public Private	50% 30%	10% 10%	5 yrs. 5 yrs.	5 yrs. 5 yrs.	Donor's cost basis Donor's cost basis

*No carryback.
†Example: Basis is $3,000. FMV is $5,000; 100 percent of appreciation is $2,000. Therefore deduction is limited to $3,000 ($5,000 – $2,000).
‡Applicable only to qualified appreciated stock that is limited to 10 percent of the outstanding stock of a corporation for which market quotations are available.

As mentioned above, the actual amount of a charitable contribution deduction depends on a number of factors. The primary questions to ask in each case are the following: (1) What type of property was gifted? (2) Was the donee a private organization or publicly supported? (3) Was the donor an individual or a corporation? (4) How much property was given? In order to illustrate the effect of these factors on the amount of a charitable contribution deduction that will be allowed in a given case, review Table 9-1 as well as the accompanying text.

Deductible Contributions

Right to Use Property and Partial Interests

Contributions consisting of a mere right to use property (such as a rent-free lease to the Boy Scouts) are not deductible. To be deductible, contributions must be made in cash or other property. The mere right to use property is considered neither cash nor other property. The IRS considers a contribution of the right to use property as a contribution of less than the donor's entire interest in the property.

Generally a charitable contribution of less than a donor's entire interest in property is nondeductible. Gifts of a partial interest in property are deductible in the following three narrowly defined situations:

1.   The first is a gift of an undivided portion of the donor's entire interest. For example, if Xavier gave his original Ramlo sculpture to the Philadelphia Museum of Art but agreed with the museum that he could keep it as long as he or his wife lived, no current deduction would be allowed. However, if Xavier gave an undivided one-half interest in the sculpture (that is, if he gave the museum an immediate, absolute, and complete right of ownership for display purposes or otherwise) for one-half of each year, he would likely be successful in obtaining a current deduction.

2.   The second situation involves a gift of a remainder interest in a personal residence or farm. If Tammy gives a qualified organization her home or farm with the stipulation that she may live there for life, Tammy may take a current income tax deduction for the present value of the future gift. This assumes, of course, that the gift is irrevocable.

3.   Finally, a gift of a partial interest would be deductible if transferred in trust. This exception allows a charitable deduction for outright transfers of property, even if less than the taxpayer's entire interest is transferred. Gifts in trust will be discussed in detail later in this chapter.

Cash

Depending on who is the donee, cash contributions are fully deductible subject to a maximum that is a percentage of adjusted gross income. If the donee is a publicly supported charity, the deduction ceiling is 50 percent of the individual taxpayer's adjusted gross income. The deduction ceiling for private charities is 30 percent of adjusted gross income. A corporation's deduction is limited to 10 percent of its taxable income (with certain adjustments). Regardless of the type of property gifted, a corporation can always take a current deduction of 10 percent of its taxable income (column 4 of the Table 9-1). Likewise, regardless of the identity of the donee, a corporation may carry over excess contributions for up to 5 years (column 6 of Table 9-1).

Individuals who make contributions to public organizations in excess of the deductible limit for the taxable year may carry over their excess deductions (column 5 of Table 9-1) for a period of up to 5 years. In other words, excess contributions are not wasted and can be used as itemized deductions in future years. For example, if Goldberg contributed $20,000 in cash to a synagogue this year, but his adjusted gross income was only $36,000, he could currently deduct only 50 percent of his adjusted gross income, which is $18,000. However, he could carry over the $2,000 excess ($20,000 contribution–$18,000) to next year. Individuals who make excess cash contributions to private charities may deduct the excess contributions in subsequent years.

A full deduction, up to the percentage limitation of 50 percent of adjusted gross income for individuals (or 10 percent of taxable income for corporations), is allowed for gifts of cash to a public charity (column 7 of the Table 9-1).

If a taxpayer makes a contribution to a college or university and receives the right to purchase tickets for an athletic event in one of the institution's athletic stadiums as a result of the contribution, only 80 percent of the amount contributed will be deductible by the taxpayer. This provision applies to contributions made, for example, by an alumnus of a university that requires the alumnus to make the contribution in order to be eligible to purchase season tickets for the university's basketball team.

Capital-Gain Property

intangible personal property

real property

Capital-gain property, for purposes of the charitable contribution deduction, is property that the taxpayer has held for more than 12 months as of the date the property is contributed. Capital-gain property can be divided into two types. The first type would consist of **intangible personal property** and all **real property**. A gift of publicly traded stock purchased 10 years ago at $100 a share, now worth $400 a share, would be considered intangible, personal, capital-gain property. Appreciated land that is held for the requisite holding period would be an example of real property properly classified as capital-gain property. Generally, gifts of such real property and intangible personal property are deductible in an amount equal to the property's fair market value, subject to the limitations discussed below. The second type of capital-gain property is tangible personal property, such as a car, a painting, a sculpture, an antique, or jewelry.

Contributions of patents and most other intellectual property are now deductible only to the extent of the lesser of the property's adjusted basis or fair market value. The deductibility of such contributions therefore is now treated in generally the same way as contributions of ordinary income property as discussed in the following section. However, the donor of the property is entitled to deduct a portion of the income subsequently generated by such property, subject to restrictions and limitations.

Where intangible personal property or real property is given to a public donee (column 2 of Table 9-1), an individual's deduction generally may not exceed 30 percent of adjusted gross income (column 3 of Table 9-1). If the gift exceeds this percentage limitation, the taxpayer may carry over the deduction for up to 5 future years (column 5 of Table 9-1). The full fair market value of the gift is deductible (column 7 of Table 9-1).

Example

Phil Anthropist donates stock worth $25,000 to the Gotham Library. The stock cost Phil $13,000 when he purchased it 4 years ago. Phil's adjusted gross income is $30,000. His maximum contribution deduction would be $9,000 (30 percent of $30,000). He would be able to carry over the $16,000 balance of the contribution ($25,000 – $9,000) and apply that as a deduction against future income for up to 5 years.

There is an election that taxpayers may want to make in situations similar to the example above. The 30 percent limit can be increased to 50 percent of adjusted gross income if donors are willing to reduce the value of their gifts by 100 percent of their potential gain. In other words, Phil, in the example above, could elect to exclude 100 percent of his potential gain, $12,000, thus decreasing the deductible value to $13,000 ($25,000–$12,000). By doing so, he is currently able to deduct the entire $13,000. This is because the election allows him to currently deduct up to 50 percent of his adjusted gross income of $30,000.

The election can be important for a taxpayer whose income fluctuates widely from year to year. It is of particular value when the amount of appreciation is small. For example, capital-gain property with a basis of $980 and a fair market value of $1,000 would be reduced by only $20. In this way taxpayers could qualify for the higher 50 percent limitation at the expense of losing only a very small portion of their deductions. However, note that the amount representing 100 percent of the potential gain may not be carried over and deducted in a later year if the election is made. Note that by reducing the deductible amount by 100 percent of the potential gain, the deduction is, in effect, limited to the donor's basis in the property.

Ordinary-Income Property

ordinary-income property

Ordinary-income property is an asset that would have resulted in ordinary income (rather than capital gain) on the date of contribution had it been sold at its fair market value rather than contributed. Ordinary-income property includes (1) capital assets held 12 months or less at the time contributed, (2) works of art, books, letters, and similar creative property, but only if given by the person who created or prepared them or for whom they were prepared, and (3) a business person's stock in trade and inventory (which would result in ordinary income if sold).

Other than certain exceptions for specific types of property, taxpayers' deductions are generally limited to their basis (cost) for ordinary-income property (column 7 of Table 9-1). For example, if Papa Chezman, the famous painter, donated a genuine Chezman painting worth $25,000 to an art museum, his deduction would be limited to his cost for producing the painting. This means that only the cost for canvas, paint, and so forth, would be deductible. Here is another situation: Gary Gibbs has owned his Specific Motors stock for 5 months. A sale would result in short-term capital gain. He purchased the stock at a cost of $12,000. It is now worth $20,000 and he donates it to the Red Cross. Since the property is considered ordinary-income property, Gary is limited to a charitable deduction of $12,000 even though the property has a current fair market value of $20,000. The fair market value of the ordinary-income property is deductible only if it is lower than the taxpayer's basis.

However, exceptions exist for corporations that donate inventory to certain public charities. For example, as an incentive to corporations to make charitable contributions of scientific equipment to colleges or universities, a deduction is allowed in an amount equal to the cost of the property plus one-half of the unrealized appreciation limited to a maximum deduction of twice the basis of the property. The property that qualifies for this increased deduction must be either new inventory-type scientific equipment or an apparatus manufactured by the donor corporation. This rule applies only to contributions of scientific equipment to colleges, universities, and certain research organizations to be used for research purposes, including research training. Other corporate incentives include contributions of inventory used solely for the care of the ill, needy, or infants, and contributions of computer technology and equipment donated to public libraries and elementary and secondary schools. In all cases, the charitable deduction cannot exceed twice the cost of the property regardless of the amount of the unrealized appreciation.

Ordinary-income property gifted to a public charity is subject to the 50 percent of AGI limitation. Consequently, in the previous example, Phil Anthropist would need an AGI of at least

$26,000 to deduct his $13,000 basis for his gift to the Boy Scouts if the property given had been ordinary-income property (rather than long-term capital-gain property).

Lifetime gifts of ordinary-income property should be avoided where the estate will be subject to federal estate taxes. Ordinary-income property left by will to charity can be more beneficial, since a federal estate tax deduction for the full value of the property can be taken. However, where it appears that the estate will not be subject to federal estate tax, a lifetime gift of ordinary-income property will permit a current income tax deduction, although it will be somewhat limited as described previously.

Tangible Personal Property

tangible personal property

Tangible personal property (which would have produced capital gain if sold) includes cars, jewelry, sculptures, artworks, books, and so forth, but only if created or produced by persons other than the donor. With respect to this type of property, a distinction must be made between (1) gifts that will be used by the donee-charity in such a manner that the use of the gift is related to the exempt purposes of the donee, and (2) gifts that will not be used by the charity in a manner related to the exempt purposes of the donee.

For example, a gift of a painting (not by the artist) could be use related if the painting was donated to a museum that planned to exhibit the painting in its public galleries. The same gift would be use unrelated if given to the Red Cross or to the Campfire Girls. There are rules that help to ensure that the donee organization makes proper use of property that is claimed to be use related.

Another example might be the contribution of a stamp collection to an educational institution. If the stamp collection is placed in the donee-organization's library for display and study by students, the use of the donated property is related to the educational purposes constituting the basis of the charitable organization's tax exemption. But if the stamps are sold, the use of the property is an unrelated one, even if the proceeds are used by the organization for educational purposes.

This distinction is important because where appreciated tangible personal property is considered use related, the entire fair market value at the date of the gift is generally deductible. In other words, a use-related gift of tangible personal property held for the requisite period is generally treated in the same way as any other long-term capital-gain property. Thus the donor is subject to the 30 percent of AGI limitation or may elect to reduce the value of the gift by 100 percent of the potential gain realized if the gift was sold rather than contributed. By doing this, the percentage limitation on the donor's adjusted gross income ceiling would be increased to 50 percent. In some cases this would result in a larger, immediate deduction.

Example

Denise Donor has an adjusted gross income of $10,000. She contributes a collection of whaling harpoons for display purposes to the Cape May County Historical Museum (a public charity). The collection cost Denise $6,000, but it was worth $10,000 on the date of contribution. The type of property contributed is tangible personal property. The donee is a public charity, and the gift is use related to the exempt purposes of the museum. Therefore Denise can deduct up to 30 percent of her contribution base (AGI), $10,000, or $3,000. She gets credit for the full $10,000 contribution, enabling her to carry over the excess contribution, $7,000, for up to 5 years (subject to the 30 percent rule each year). Alternatively, Denise may elect to reduce the value of her gift by 100 percent of the potential gain, or $4,000 ($10,000–$6,000). Under the election Denise would have a current deduction of $5,000 (50 percent of adjusted gross income), and the remaining $1,000 ($6,000–$5,000) could be deducted in a later year.

If the gift is use unrelated (that is, made to a donee whose direct use of the asset is unrelated to the charitable function of the donee), the fair market value of the gift must be reduced by 100 percent of the potential gain. If that were true in the above example, the gift by Denise Donor would be deductible only to the extent of $6,000 (her basis in the property). However, it would be deductible up to 50 percent of her contribution base.

Future Interests in Property

A future interest is any interest or right that will begin at some time in the future. The term future interest includes situations where donors purport to give tangible personal property to a charitable organization but have made a written or oral agreement with the organization reserving to themselves or members of their immediate families the right to use, possess, or enjoy the property. For example, suppose Fulton Flushbucks donates a genuine Meccariello photograph to an art museum but arranges with the museum to keep the photograph in his home for as long as he lives. The museum has only a future interest in the photograph.

Some of the basic rules governing charitable contribution deductions are that contributions must (1) actually be paid, (2) be paid in cash or other property, and (3) be paid before the close of the tax year. Furthermore, no deductions are allowed for a contribution of less than the donor's entire interest in property. Three narrow exceptions are as follows: (1) an undivided portion of the donor's entire interest, (2) remainder interest in personal residences or farms, or (3) partial interest that would be deductible if transferred in trust. A charitable contribution (not made by a transfer in trust) of a partial interest in property may not be deducted.

Since the benefit to the museum—and consequently to the public—was deferred in the Flush-bucks gift of the Meccariello photograph above, no current tax deduction would be allowed. The implication is that a deduction will not be allowed until the charity receives actual possession or enjoyment of the artwork. The gift of tangible personal property must be complete in the sense that all interests and rights to the possession and enjoyment of the property must vest in the charity. This means that a transfer of a future interest in property to a charity is not deductible until all intervening interests in and rights to possession held by the donor or certain related persons or organizations have expired (or unless the gift is in the form of a future interest in trust that meets the requirements discussed below).

Remainder interests are a form of future interest in which an income interest is given by the donor to someone other than the donor, and at the death of that income beneficiary, the principal goes to a designated charity. An example would be a gift to Sue for life and at the death of Sue (the income beneficiary) the remainder (the principal at Sue's death) goes to charity (the remainder beneficiary). A gift "to Sue for life, remainder to The American College" would be considered a gift of a future interest to The American College.

Gifts in Trust

Gifts of a remainder interest either in real property or in trust are deductible only if made in one of three ways: (1) an annuity trust, (2) a unitrust, or (3) a pooled-income fund. These three permissible trust forms are a result of congressional concern over potential abuses of gifts of a remainder interest in trust to charity. For example, suppose Mr. and Mrs. Weltodo were a financially secure but childless couple. Mr. Weltodo might leave his property to his wife in trust. Mrs. Weltodo, according to the terms of the trust, would receive the income for life if she survived her husband. At her death, the principal in the trust would pass to a designated charity. Mr. Weltodo would take a current charitable contribution deduction for the present value of the gift that the charity would receive at the death of the income beneficiary. In order to counteract inflation and provide for contingencies, a clause might be inserted in the trust agreement authorizing an invasion of principal for Mrs. Weltodo's benefit.

The potential for abuse was that the trust principal was often invested in securities that produced an extremely high income but at the cost of a correspondingly high risk. This situation naturally worked to the detriment of the charitable remainderman. In addition, the trustee's ability to make substantial invasions into the trust principal further increased the likelihood that little, if any, of the original contribution would be received by the charity. The result was a decrease in the value of the charity's remainder interest.

For these reasons, rules were designed to prevent a taxpayer from receiving a current charitable contribution deduction for a gift to charity of a remainder interest in trust that is substantially in excess of the amount the charity may ultimately receive. (This is so because the assumptions used in calculating the value of the remainder interest had little relation to the actual investment policies of the trust.)

Pursuant to these rules, deductions are basically limited to situations where the trust specifies (1) a fixed annual amount that is to be paid to the noncharitable income beneficiary (an annuity trust); or (2) the amount the income beneficiary will receive in terms of a fixed percentage of the value of the trust assets ascertained each year (a unitrust); or (3) that property contributed by a number of donors is commingled with property transferred by other donors, and each beneficiary of an income interest will receive income determined by the rate of return earned by the trust for such year (a pooled-income fund).

Annuity Trust

charitable remainder annuity trust

More specifically, a **charitable remainder annuity trust** is a trust designed to permit payment of a fixed amount annually to a noncharitable (income) beneficiary with the remainder going to charity. In order to qualify for income tax (and estate or gift tax) deductions, the trust must meet a number of tests. The primary requirements are as follows:

- A fixed amount or fixed percentage of the initial value of the trust must be payable to the noncharitable beneficiary.

- This annuity must not be less than an amount equal to 5 percent nor more than 50 percent of the initial net fair market value of all the property transferred in trust. The charitable remainder interest must be at least 10 percent of the initial net fair market value of all property placed in trust.

- The specified amount must be paid at least annually to the beneficiary out of income and/or principal.

- The trust must be irrevocable and not subject to a power by either the donor, the trustee, or the beneficiary to invade, alter, or amend the trust.

- The trust must be for the benefit of a named individual or individuals who must be living at the time the property is transferred to the trust. An amount can be paid to a person for life or for a term of years not greater than 20 years. The remainder must go to charity (charities) and cannot be split between charitable and noncharitable beneficiaries.

If all the necessary tests are met, the donor of a charitable remainder annuity trust will be entitled to an income tax deduction limited to the present value of the remainder interest.

Unitrust

A charitable remainder unitrust, like a charitable remainder annuity trust, is basically designed to permit payment of a periodic sum to a noncharitable beneficiary with a remainder to charity. In addition to allowing additional contributions beyond the initial contribution, the key distinction is in how the periodic sum is computed. In order to qualify for income, estate, and gift tax deductions, a charitable remainder unitrust must meet a number of tests, the most important of which are the following:

- A fixed percentage of the net fair market value of the principal, as revalued annually, must be payable to the noncharitable beneficiary. Therefore the amount payable to the income beneficiary may fluctuate from year to year.

- The percentage payable must not be less than 5 percent nor more than 50 percent of the annual value.

- The charitable remainder interest must be at least 10 percent with respect to the net fair market value of each contribution to the unitrust.

- The unitrust may provide that the noncharitable beneficiary can receive the lesser of (1) the specified fixed percentage or (2) the trust income for the year, plus any excess trust income to the extent of any deficiency in the prior years by reason of the limitation to the amount of trust income in such years. For this test, trust income excludes capital gains.

- The noncharitable income beneficiaries must be living at the time of transfer in trust, and their interests must be for a term not exceeding 20 years or for their respective lives.

- The entire remainder must go to charity (or charities).

The tax deductions allowed are the same as in the case of a charitable remainder annuity trust.

Pooled-Income Fund

pooled-income fund

A **pooled-income fund** is a trust created and maintained by a public charity rather than a private donor. The basic requirements are as follows:

- The donor must contribute an irrevocable, vested remainder interest to the charitable organization that maintains it.

- The property transferred by each donor must be commingled with the property transferred by other donors.

- The fund cannot invest in tax-exempt securities.

- No donor or income beneficiary can be a trustee.

- The donor must retain a life income interest for himself or herself or one or more named income beneficiaries.

- Each income beneficiary must be entitled to and receive a pro rata share of the income (annually) based on the rate of return earned by the fund.

If these tests are met, the donor will be entitled to income and gift tax deductions. The economic advantage to the donor of making this transfer is that the donor is obtaining diversification for the income beneficiary without incurring the capital-gains tax that would ordinarily be imposed if the donor exchanged securities for other securities.

Advantages of Charitable Gifts of Life Insurance

Life insurance, like any other property, can be and often is the subject of a gift. In fact, life insurance is a favored means of making charitable contributions for a number of reasons.

First, the death benefit going to charity is guaranteed as long as premiums are paid. This means that the charity will receive an amount that is fixed in value and not subject to the potential downside risks of securities.

Second, life insurance provides an amplified gift that can be purchased on the installment plan. Through a relatively small annual cost (premium), a large benefit can be provided for the charity. A large gift can be made without impairing or diluting the control of a family business interest or other investments. Assets earmarked for the donor-insured's family can be kept intact.

Third, life insurance is a self-completing gift. If the donor lives, cash values (which can be currently used by the charity) grow constantly from year to year. If the donor becomes disabled, the policy will remain in full force through the waiver-of-premium feature, guaranteeing both the ultimate death benefit to the charity as well as the same cash values and dividend buildup that would have been earned had the insured not become disabled. Even if death occurs after only one deposit, the charity is assured of its full gift.

Fourth, the death proceeds can be received by the designated charity free of federal income and estate taxes, probate and administrative costs and delays, brokerage fees, or other transfer costs. Thus the charity in fact receives 100-cent dollars. This prompt cash payment should be compared with the payment of a gift to the selected charity under the terms of an individual's will. In that case, probate delays of up to several years are not uncommon.

Fifth, because of the contractual nature of the life insurance contract, large gifts to charity are not subject to attack by disgruntled heirs. Life insurance proceeds also do not violate the so-called mortmain statutes that prohibit or limit gifts made within a short time of death.

Finally, a substantial gift may be made with no attending publicity. Since the life insurance proceeds paid to charity can be arranged so they will not be part of the decedent's probate estate, the proceeds can be paid confidentially. Of course, publicity may be given if desired.

Taxation of Charitable Gifts of Life Insurance

To the surprise of most tax commentators, Rev. Rul. 2009–13 determined that a life insurance policy is a capital asset. If a life insurance policy is surrendered at a gain, its composition will be a combination of ordinary income and capital gain. It will be ordinary income to the extent of the inside buildup of the policy. It will be capital gain only if the gain is greater than the inside buildup of the policy.

Assuming at the time of contribution the value of the policy (interpolated terminal reserve plus unearned premium on the date of the gift) exceeds the policyowner's net premium payments, the deduction for a gift of a policy is equal to the policyowner's basis (cost), that is, the net premium payments paid by the policyowner. The applicable limitation should be 30 percent of AGI.

Example

Mary McClu assigns a policy on her life to The American College. Her charitable contribution deduction is limited to her basis; that is, her cost for the contract (or the value of the policy if lower). If Mary paid net premiums of $15,000, even if the policy had a value of $18,000, her charitable contribution deduction would be limited to $15,000. On the other hand, if the value of the policy in this case was $15,000 and the net premium payments were $18,000, the amount of the charitable deduction would still be $15,000.

The income tax value of a paid-up policy depends on the replacement cost of the policy. The replacement cost of a single-premium or paid-up policy is the single premium the same insurer would charge for a policy of the same amount at the insured's attained age (increased by the value of any dividend credits and reduced by the amount of any loans outstanding). The insurance company in question will generally calculate the exact value on IRS Form 712 upon request. Remember that the charitable deduction is limited to the policyowner's basis if that is less than the policy's value.

The charitable deduction for a newly issued policy is the gross premium paid by the policyowner.

Premium Payments as Contributions

Premium payments are considered gifts of cash and therefore are fully and currently deductible as charitable contributions if the charity owns the policy outright.

Occasionally, a donor might attempt to split dollar the charitable gift; that is, name the donor's personal beneficiary as the recipient of the policy's death benefit (the amount at risk) but make the charity the owner of the cash value. The IRS has maintained that this is a gift of a "partial interest" in property and denies a deduction for the premium payment. The same principle applies where the donor retains an interest in the policy cash value but makes the charity the beneficiary of the policy's death benefit. Therefore the donor should make an absolute assignment of the ownership of the policy to the charity in order to qualify for the desired tax benefits. If the charity initially applies for and owns a life insurance policy, and the insured pays the premiums, the charity must have an insurable interest in the insured under local law in order for the insured to obtain the desired tax benefits. In general, it may be preferable to transfer ownership of an existing policy.

The donor should send a check directly to the charity and have it pay the premium to the life insurance company in order to ensure the most favorable tax results. The canceled check will serve as proof (1) of the fact that a gift was made to the charity, (2) of the date the gift was made, and (3) of the amount of the gift. It will also ensure a full deduction of up to 50 percent of the donor's adjusted gross income.

There should be no adverse gift or estate tax implications. Gifts to charity are deductible in full for federal gift tax purposes. There is no percentage limitation on the amount of the gift tax deduction. Likewise, the death proceeds of a life insurance policy payable to a charity do not generate any federal estate tax.

Focus On Ethics: Claiming Charitable Contributions and Other Deductions

In recent years, the substantiation requirements for claiming deductions for charitable contributions have been significantly tightened. Substantiation requirements also apply to many types of business deductions, including travel and entertainment expense deductions. Substantiation requirements in the tax law discourage taxpayers from claiming deduction amounts that are in excess of the amounts actually paid or incurred. Placing specific substantiation requirements in the tax law makes it more costly and dangerous for taxpayers to overstate deductions. However, taxpayers are legally and ethically required to claim deductions in accurate amounts regardless of whether the tax law contains a specific substantiation requirement for the deduction claimed.

In preparing tax returns, taxpayers and paid preparers should limit the amount of deductions claimed to amounts that equal the taxpayer's actual corresponding expenses. It can be a temptation, for example, to claim charitable deductions in amounts greater than the actual value of charitable gifts, particularly if the taxpayer's actual contributions are less than the average amounts claimed for other taxpayers in the same income range. Some taxpayers may also claim amounts that are substantially equal from year to year, regardless of actual amounts paid. Some individuals tout or promote the idea that only a small percentage of tax returns actually become involved in a tax audit, and therefore it may be to the taxpayer's advantage to play "audit roulette" in light of what is perceived to be a low risk of getting caught.

From both a legal and an ethical standpoint, taxpayers are well advised to submit honest income tax returns which can be authenticated upon request by the IRS. From a pragmatic standpoint, the cost and the aggravation generated by a tax audit or other dispute with the IRS is simply not worth the few dollars in illegal tax "savings" generated by the overstatement of deductions.

CHAPTER REVIEW

Key Terms and Concepts

interest
principal amount
qualified residence interest
home equity indebtedness
points
qualified public charity

intangible personal property
real property
ordinary-income property
tangible personal property
charitable remainder annuity trust
pooled-income fund

Review Questions

Review questions are based on the learning objectives in this chapter. Thus a [9.3] at the end of a question means that the question is based on learning objective 3. If there are multiple objectives, they are all listed.

1. a. What is the general rule for tax treatment of capital expenditures?

    b. What are two factors generally examined to determine if an outlay is a capital expenditure or a current expense? [9.1]

2. What is the general rule for deductibility of personal expenses? [9.1]

3. Explain the general tax treatment of the following expenses incurred by Larry Lotus this year:

    a. homeowners' insurance premiums

    b. personal life insurance premiums]

    c. commuting expenses for traveling to and from the office

    d. expenses for groceries and utilities [9.1]

4. This year a taxpayer aged 67 spends $300 for prescription drugs and an additional $569 for doctors' and hospital bills. Medical care insurance costs $3,000. Assuming adjusted gross income is $30,000, calculate the total medical expense deduction for the year. [9.2]

5. What are the rules regarding cosmetic surgery and the medical expense deduction? [9.2]

6. Explain how the IRS determines whether or not a medical expense is deductible. [9.2]

7. How are long-term care expenses generally treated for income tax purposes? [9.3]

8. How are the deductions for payment of long-term care insurance premiums limited? [9.3]

9. Does the "above-the-line" deduction for health insurance costs of a self-employed taxpayer apply to long-term care insurance? Explain. [9.3]

10. What types of taxes are specifically deductible by individuals? [9.4]

11. Cecil owns a building in Philadelphia. The city makes an assessment to rework the water and sewage pipes as well as to widen the sidewalks in front of his building. He deducts the amount of the assessment. Is the IRS likely to challenge this deduction? Explain. [9.4]

12. What is the exception to the general rule that the deduction for real property taxes is only available to the taxpayer who is liable for the tax? [9.4]

13. Identify five basic categories of interest payments. [9.5]

14. Explain deductibility of business interest payments. [9.5]

15. a. What is the general limitation on the deduction for investment interest?

    b. How does a taxpayer compute "net investment income"? Explain. [9.5]

16. a.   What is "qualified residence interest"?

    b.   Explain the rules for the deductibility of "acquisition indebtedness."

    c.   Explain the rules for the deductibility of "home equity indebtedness." [9.5]

17. Explain the requirements for deducting "points" upon origination of a mortgage loan. [9.5]

18. What is the general rule for deductibility of personal interest? [9.5]

19. What is the general rule for deductibility of interest and expenses relating to tax-exempt income? [9.5]

20. Mrs. Temponi recently purchased municipal bonds by borrowing $100,000 from the bank. May she deduct the following expenses?

    a.   her interest payments on the loan

    b.   the $500 paid to First Investment Corporation, a municipal bond adviser, as a retainer fee [9.5]

21. What are the basic requirements for the deductibility of charitable contributions? [9.6]

22. Explain the tax consequences of giving a partial interest in property to a qualified charity. [9.6]

23. Robert Rhineday had an adjusted gross income this year of $100,000. He made 10,000 square feet of office space available to the Heart Fund free of charge for the entire year. He could have rented this space for $79,000. How much may he deduct on this year's income tax? Explain. Ignore any unreimbursed out-of-pocket expenses. [9.6]

24. Egbert donates $60,000 in cash to a public charity. During the year of the contribution, his adjusted gross income was $100,000. How much of a deduction, if any, would Egbert be allowed to take in the current year? Explain. [9.6]

25. As the end of this year approaches, Gladstone will consider the following donations. State whether each item would be deductible and, if so, the amount of each deduction. Assume that Gladstone's adjusted gross income for this year is $200,000. For purposes of this question, ignore the overall limitation on itemized deductions under IRC Sec. 68 discussed in Chapter 4.

    a. $3,000 in cash to Hughie and Louie, two needy neighbors

    b. $2,000 to the Valley Stream Chamber of Commerce

    c.   use of San Lamente, Gladstone's mansion, for an American Red Cross regional conference. Gladstone volunteers about 60 hours a year in his position as head of the Red Cross Speakers Bureau.

    d. $5,000 in cash to the Salvation Army

    e.   stock he purchased several years ago for $15,000, now worth $20,000, to the United Way

    f.   various famous papers and letters written by Gladstone many years ago, valued today at $25,000, to Donald University. Gladstone expended $100 for the production of these papers and letters.

    g. $5,000 to Oxford University in England

    h. $200,000 to a trust that will provide income to Gladstone's mother for her life. At her death, the assets in the trust are to be paid to Slippery Rock University. The bank, as trustee, has power to invade the trust principal to provide for Gladstone's mother's health or welfare.

    i.   a $10,000 paid-up life insurance policy on Gladstone's life to the Clear Springs Charity, Inc., whose literature states that all contributions to the organization are tax deductible. Would your answer be the same if Gladstone merely names Clear Springs as revocable beneficiary? Explain.

    j.   a life insurance policy with a cash surrender value of $8,500 to Daisy Hospital. The net premiums paid for the policy have amounted to $6,800. [9.6]

26. Larry Churnkey, a successful businessman, has season tickets to see the Wayne University Leopards, his alma mater's basketball team. This year Larry is required to make a $1,000 donation to the university in order to keep his season tickets. He must pay for the tickets in addition. How much of this donation is Larry permitted to deduct? Explain. [9.6]

27. a.   There are limitations on deductions for gifts of capital-gain property by individual donors to qualified public charities. Explain these limitations when the gift property is either in the form of intangible personal property or real property.

    b.   Explain the special election that individual donors may make to increase the current deductible limit for contributions of capital-gain property that is either intangible personal property or real property. [9.6]

28. a.   Define ordinary-income property under the charitable contribution rules.

    b.   Explain the limitations on the deductibility of gifts of ordinary-income property. [9.6]

29. What is the maximum deduction allowed an individual taxpayer for charitable gifts of tangible personal property that are

    a. use-related?

    b. use-unrelated? [9.6]

30. Explain the deductibility for charitable gifts of future interests in tangible personal property. [9.6]

31. Describe the requirements that each of the following kinds of trusts must meet in order for a remainder interest in donated property to be deductible.

    a. annuity trusts

    b. unitrusts

    c. pooled-income fund [9.6]

32. For what reasons is a gift of a life insurance policy considered a favorable choice for a charitable gift? [9.6]

33. a. How is a gift of a life insurance policy valued when the value of the policy exceeds net premium payments?

    b. How is a gift of a life insurance policy valued when the net premium payments exceed the value of the life insurance policy?

    c. What is the maximum charitable deduction allowed for a paid-up or a single-premium policy?

    d. What is the maximum charitable deduction allowed for a newly issued policy? [9.6]

34. Sidney Supersales, CLU, contributes a life insurance policy on his life to his alma mater, Mississippi University. Explain the limitations on his current deduction for the gift:

    a. assuming he could surrender the policy at a gain

    b. assuming net premiums exceed the value of the paid-up policy he contributed [9.6]

Review Answers

1. a. If a capital expenditure is made for an asset that is eligible for cost recovery, the cost of the asset may be deducted over a number of tax years, but not, as a general rule, fully deducted in the year the expense is made. One important exception to

this rule applies if the taxpayer acquires property that is eligible for the first-year expense election under Code Sec. 179.

b. First, if the outlay is for the acquisition of property that has a useful life of more than one year, the outlay will be considered a capital expenditure. Second, if the outlay is for the enhancement or improvement of an asset the taxpayer already owns, it will be treated as a capital expenditure, provided it either enhances the value of the property or results in an improvement with a useful life of more than one year. In other words, a capital expenditure is considered to be a new investment in property, while a current expense is more akin to a repair or a maintenance item that is necessary for the operation or well-being of a property or asset that the taxpayer already has. Current expenses are deductible on a taxpayer's current income tax return; capital expenditures typically are deductible over a number of tax years.

2. The general rule regarding the deductibility of personal expenses is that they are disallowed. Nonetheless, certain personal expenses are expressly deductible under the Code in spite of the general rule of disallowance.

3. a. Homeowners insurance premiums are nondeductible personal expenses.

b. Personal life insurance premiums are nondeductible personal expenses.

c. Commuting expenses for traveling to and from the office are nondeductible personal expenses.

d. Expenses for groceries and utilities are nondeductible personal expenses.

4. Nonreimbursed medical expenses (including amounts paid for medical insurance as well as prescription drugs and insulin) incurred primarily for the prevention or treatment of physical or mental defects or illness are deductible in the year paid to the extent they exceed 10 percent of adjusted gross income for taxpayers who are 65 at the close of the tax year. The taxpayer may add all his or her medical care expenses and calculate the total deductible amount as follows:

Drugs	$300
Nonreimbursed doctor and hospital expenses	569
Insurance premium	3,000
Total nonreimbursed medical expenses	$3,869
Minus 10% floor	(3,000)
Amount deductible	$869

5. Special restrictions apply to expenses for cosmetic surgery. Such expenses are deductible only if the surgery is done to correct a condition resulting from an accident, a congenital abnormality, or a disfiguring disease. Expenses for surgery performed to improve the appearance of an individual, such as a face lift procedure or similar surgery, do not qualify for the deduction. The question in evaluating the deductibility of cosmetic surgery is whether the procedure either meaningfully promotes the proper function of the body or prevents or treats illness or disease.

6. One principle that the IRS will generally follow in determining whether a given expense qualifies as a deductible medical expense is the question of whether the service, product, or activity paid for is simply for the general preservation of the individual's health or well-being or rather is for the alleviation or treatment of a specific disease or defect. If the expense is for something that only promotes the individual's overall general health, it will generally not be deductible. On the other hand, if a physician prescribes an activity or program of treatment to improve or correct a specific medical condition, the expense is more likely to be deductible.

7. Qualified long-term care expenses are generally treated as medical expenses for income tax purposes, and qualified long-term care insurance premiums are also generally deductible subject to limitations.

8. The deduction for long-term care insurance premiums is limited to a maximum dollar amount per year that varies according to the age of the person covered under the policy. The dollar limits are indexed annually for inflation and apply per covered individual rather than to each tax return.

9. Yes, premiums for qualified long-term care insurance contracts are eligible for the above-the-line deduction for health insurance premiums paid by self-employed taxpayers.

10. Taxes not incurred in the course of a business or income-producing activity that are deductible on Schedule A by individual taxpayers are as follows:

    •   state, local, and foreign real property taxes

    •   state and local personal property taxes

    •   state and local income taxes

    •   state and local general sales taxes in lieu of the deduction for state and local income taxes

    •   the generation-skipping transfer tax imposed on income distributions

- the environmental tax imposed by IRC Sec. 59A

Certain other taxes are deductible, including foreign income, war profits, and excess profit taxes for taxpayers who do not claim a foreign tax credit for these taxes.

11. Yes, the IRS would challenge this deduction if Cecil were audited. Assessments for improvements are not deductible taxes.

12. The exception applies to a property owner who sells the property during the period covered by an existing assessment. In such cases, the property taxes are subject to a rule of apportionment. For deduction purposes, the taxes are treated as assessed to the seller of the property for the time period up to but not including the date of sale. As of the sale date, the taxes are treated as having been assessed to the buyer for deduction purposes. The apportionment is calculated based on the number of days of the assessment period that each party owns the property. This treatment is consistent with the usual apportionment of tax payments that appears on a closing statement or settlement sheet upon the sale of a home.

13. Five basic categories of interest payments are as follows:

- interest on indebtedness incurred in the course of a trade or business ("business interest")

- interest on indebtedness incurred in the course of an activity entered into for profit that is not a business activity ("investment interest")

- interest on indebtedness incurred in connection with a passive activity ("passive activity interest")

- certain interest on indebtedness secured by the taxpayer's residence ("qualified residence interest")

- personal interest

14. The general rule for interest payments on indebtedness incurred in the course of a business activity is that the payments are deductible. However, notwithstanding the general rule of deductibility for business interest, there may be another set of rules that applies to the interest payment that could limit or prevent its deductibility.

15. a. Deductions for investment interest expenses are limited to the taxpayer's "net investment income" for the year.

b. "Net investment income" is the excess of the taxpayer's investment income over the taxpayer's investment expenses. Investment income is the sum of gross income from property held for investment other than qualified dividends taxed at the special reduced maximum rates, plus gain other than long-term capital gain attributable to the disposition of property held for investment. Investment expenses are generally all deductible expenses (other than interest expenses) that are connected with the production of investment income.

16. a. "Qualified residence interest" is interest paid on a loan secured by the taxpayer's personal residence that is deductible for federal income tax purposes.

For interest payments to be qualified residence interest, the loan must be secured by a "qualified residence." A qualified residence includes the taxpayer's principal residence plus one other residence (such as a vacation home) that the taxpayer selects to be treated as a qualified residence. Such other residence need not be a house but could include vehicles and water vessels that have sleeping and eating accommodations. If such other residence is rented by the taxpayer for part of the year, it must not qualify under the "rental use" test of the vacation home deduction limitations. If it does qualify under that test, it cannot also be a "qualified residence" for purposes of deducting qualified residence interest.

For qualified residences, there are two types of qualified residence interest: interest paid on "acquisition indebtedness" and interest paid on "home equity indebtedness."

b. "Acquisition indebtedness" is any indebtedness that is incurred in acquiring, constructing, or substantially improving a qualified residence and that is secured by such residence. It also includes the refinancing of such indebtedness, but only to the extent the principal amount of the refinancing does not exceed the amount of the refinanced indebtedness. Amounts refinanced in excess of the existing principal balance may qualify as home equity indebtedness.

The maximum amount of acquisition indebtedness for any one taxpayer (including a married couple filing jointly) is $1 million. For married taxpayers filing separately, the limit is $500,000. Indebtedness in excess of these amounts will not be treated as acquisition indebtedness and will not give rise to deductible interest unless the debt qualifies as home equity indebtedness.

c. "Home equity indebtedness" is indebtedness other than acquisition indebtedness secured by a qualified residence to the extent that

- the total amount of acquisition and home equity indebtedness does not exceed the fair market value of the residence

- the aggregate amount of the taxpayer's home equity indebtedness does not exceed $100,000 ($50,000 for married taxpayers filing separately)

Note that the $100,000 limit (as well as the $1 million limit on acquisition indebtedness) is a per-taxpayer, and not a per-residence, limitation. Also, the total of acquisition indebtedness and home equity indebtedness may exceed the taxpayer's cost for the home but may not exceed the fair market value of the home. Finally, home equity indebtedness does not have to be used for any specific purpose in order to generate qualified residence interest. Such loans can generally be used for any purpose desired by the taxpayer.

17. In order for taxpayers to be assured that points paid upon the origination of a loan will be currently deductible, the following requirements must be met:

    • The loan must be incurred in connection with the acquisition of the taxpayer's principal residence.

    • The loan must be secured by the taxpayer's principal residence.

    • The points must be calculated as a percentage of the principal amount of the loan.

    • The points must be paid to the lender directly by the taxpayer rather than added to or derived from the principal amount of the loan.

    • The lender's charging of the points must be consistent with an established business practice in the area in which the loan is made and must not exceed the amount generally charged for points in such area.

    • The settlement statement describing the acquisition of the home must designate the payments as points (using terms such as points, discount points, loan origination fees, or similar terminology).

18. The general rule is that personal interest is not deductible unless it is qualified residence interest or certain interest paid in connection with a loan for higher education.

19. As a general rule of tax law, an otherwise allowable deduction for an interest payment or any other expense will be disallowed if the interest expense or other expense is incurred in the course of producing income that is exempt from income tax.

20. The Code specifically prohibits the deduction of expenses incurred in connection with the purchase of tax-exempt obligations. Thus Mrs. Temponi's

    a. interest payments on the $100,000 loan incurred to purchase the bonds would not be deductible, and the

    b. payment of $500 to First Investment Corporation as a fee for advice about purchasing the bonds would likewise not be deductible

21. Contributions are generally subject to a limit of 50 percent of AGI as well as an overall limitation on itemized deductions. In addition to these limits, charitable contributions must meet four other requirements to be deductible. These requirements are as follows:

    • The donee organization must be qualified.

    • Property, not services, must be the subject of the gift.

    • The contribution must be in excess of value received.

    • The contribution must be paid in cash or other property before the close of the tax year in question.

22. Generally a charitable contribution of less than a donor's entire interest in property is nondeductible. However, gifts of a partial interest in property are deductible in the following three narrowly defined situations:

    a. a gift of an undivided portion of the donor's entire interest

    b. a gift of a remainder interest in a personal residence or farm

    c. a gift of a partial interest if transferred in trust

23. Robert can deduct nothing. A contribution of rent-free use of property is nondeductible. A contribution of services to a charity is also nondeductible. The contribution must be of the property itself.

24. Egbert may currently deduct $50,000 (50 percent of his $100,000 adjusted gross income). The remaining $10,000 can be carried over as an excess contribution.

25. a. The $3,000 contribution to the needy neighbors would not be deductible, since one of the requirements for deductibility is that the charity be a qualified organization and not an individual.

    b. The $2,000 contribution to the Chamber of Commerce would not be deductible. While a Chamber of Commerce is a tax-exempt organization, it is not considered a qualified charitable organization even though it pays no income tax. Qualified charitable organizations are those that are operated exclusively for charitable, religious, scientific, literary, or educational purposes.

    c. Gladstone cannot claim a deduction for allowing a charitable organization the rent-free occupancy of his mansion. Likewise, he cannot claim a deduction for volunteering services because he has not contributed any property to a charity. However, any out-of-pocket expenses that Gladstone incurs for the conference, such as rental of chairs or heating and lighting the mansion, are tax deductible.

d. Gladstone would obtain a $5,000 deduction for his cash contribution to the Salvation Army. His maximum deductible cash contribution to all public qualified charities can be $100,000, which is 50 percent of his $200,000 adjusted gross income. Excess contributions above $100,000 can be carried over to the 5 following tax years. Gladstone must also comply with the substantiation requirements that apply to deductible contributions of $250 or more for each such contribution. (Any monetary contributions made in cash or by check require the donor to maintain either a bank record of the contribution or written communication from the donee substantiating the contribution. Additional substantiation requirements exist if the amount of a single contribution exceeds $250.)

e. Gladstone may deduct the full value of the stock contributed to the United Way. He will avoid taxation of the potential gain on his stock. The maximum charitable deduction for property that will give rise to long-term capital gain (such as stock) in any year is 30 percent of adjusted gross income. Gladstone's donation is less than 30 percent of his AGI of $200,000 ($60,000). Hence he may deduct the entire $20,000.

f. Gladstone may only deduct his cost of producing the papers and letters, which in this case is $100. A taxpayer's deduction is limited to his cost for property that would result in ordinary income if sold. If Gladstone sold his papers, he would have ordinary income.

g. Contributions to charitable organizations in foreign countries are not deductible (unless there is a reciprocal agreement with a foreign government in a tax treaty).

h. Gladstone would not be able to deduct the present value of the remainder interest, since the trust does not qualify as a charitable remainder unitrust or charitable remainder annuity trust. A trustee's discretionary power to invade trust principal for the benefit of the noncharitable beneficiary will disqualify such a trust.

i. Assuming that Clear Springs is a qualified public charity, Gladstone is entitled to deduct the lesser of the replacement cost of a paid-up policy (that is, the single-premium cost of a comparable contract at the donor's attained age), or the amount of his basis in the policy. No income tax deduction would be allowed if Gladstone retains ownership of the policy and merely names the charity as revocable beneficiary.

j. The charitable contribution deducted for this policy is limited to the lesser of the cash surrender value (interpolated terminal reserve plus unearned premium) or the net premium cost. Here Gladstone's deduction is limited to $6,800.

26. Larry Churnkey will be able to deduct 80 percent of the $1,000 donation to the university, which amounts to $800. This 80 percent provision applies to contributions made by an alumnus of a university that requires the alumnus to make the contribution in order to be eligible to purchase season tickets for the university's athletic teams.

27. a. When intangible personal property or real property is given to a qualified public charity, the individual donor's deduction generally may not exceed 30 percent of his or her AGI. If the gift exceeds this percentage limitation, the donor taxpayer may carry over the deduction for up to 5 future years. The full fair market value of the gift property is generally deductible.

    b. There is a special election that an individual donor may use to increase the 30 percent limit to 50 percent of his or her AGI. To increase the 30 percent limit to 50 percent, the donor taxpayer must be willing to reduce the value of the gift property by 100 percent of the potential gain.

    The election can be important for a donor taxpayer whose income fluctuates widely from year to year. It is of particular value when the amount of appreciation is small. Note, however, that the amount representing 100 percent of the potential gain may not be carried over and deducted in a later year if the election is made. Consequently, the deduction under the special election is limited to the donor taxpayer's basis in the property, which if not completely deducted in the current year can be carried over and deducted in a later year.

28. a. Ordinary-income property is an asset that would have resulted in ordinary income (rather than capital gain) on the date of contribution had it been sold at its fair market value rather than contributed. Ordinary-income property includes (1) capital assets held 12 months or less at the time contributed, (2) works of art, books, letters, and similar property, but only if given by the person who created or prepared them or for whom they were prepared, and (3) a business person's stock in trade and inventory (which would result in ordinary income if sold).

    b. Taxpayers' deductions are generally limited to their basis (cost) for ordinary-income property. For example, if a famous painter donated one of his paintings worth $25,000 to an art museum, the deductions would be limited to the cost for canvas, paint, and so forth. No deduction would be allowed for the value of the painter's efforts or reputation nor would a deduction be allowed for the fair market value of the painting. In other words, only the cost of the materials that go into producing the painting are deductible.

    One exception to this rule provides for an increased incentive to corporations to make charitable contributions of scientific equipment to colleges or universities.

In this situation, the deduction is allowed in an amount equal to the cost of the property plus one-half of the unrealized appreciation limited to a maximum deduction of twice the basis of the property. There are other similar exceptions.

29. a. Where appreciated tangible personal property is use related, the entire fair market value at the date of the gift is deductible. In other words, a use-related gift of tangible personal property held for the requisite period is treated exactly the same as any other long-term capital-gain property. Thus the donor is subject to the 30-percent-of-AGI limitation or may elect to reduce the value of the gift by 100 percent of the potential gain realized if the gift was sold rather than contributed. By doing this, the percentage limitation on the donor's adjusted gross income ceiling would be increased to 50 percent. In some cases this would result in a larger, immediate deduction.

    b. Where appreciated tangible personal property is use unrelated, the fair market value of the gift must be reduced by 100 percent of the potential gain. By doing this, the percentage limitation on the donor's AGI ceiling is increased to 50 percent.

30. The gift of tangible personal property must be complete in the sense that all interests and rights to the possession and enjoyment of the property must vest in the charity. This means that a transfer of a future interest in property to a charity is not deductible until all intervening interests in and rights to possession held by the donor or certain related persons or organizations have expired (or unless the gift is in the form of a future interest in trust that meets certain specified requirements).

31. a. To qualify for a charitable tax deduction, a charitable remainder annuity trust must meet all the following requirements:

    • A fixed amount or fixed percentage of the initial value of the trust must be payable to the noncharitable beneficiary.

    • This annuity must not be less than an amount equal to 5 percent nor more than 50 percent of the initial fair market value of all the property transferred in trust. Further, the charitable remainder interest must be at least 10 percent of the initial net fair market value of all property placed in trust.

    • The specified amount must be paid at least annually to the beneficiary out of income and/or principal.

    • The trust must be irrevocable and not subject to a power by either the donor, the trustee, or the beneficiary to invade, alter, or amend the trust.

- The trust must be for the benefit of a named individual or individuals who must be living at the time the property is transferred to the trust. An amount can be paid to a person for life or for a term of years not greater than 20 years. The remainder must go to charity (charities) and cannot be split between charitable and noncharitable beneficiaries.

If these requirements are met, the donor will be entitled to an income tax deduction limited to the present value of the remainder interest.

b. To qualify for a charitable tax deduction, a charitable remainder unitrust must meet all the following requirements:

- A fixed percentage of the net fair market value of the principal, as revalued annually, must be payable to the noncharitable beneficiary. Therefore the amount payable to the income beneficiary may fluctuate from year to year.

- The percentage payable must not be less than 5 percent nor more than 50 percent of the annual value. For most transfers in trust, the value of the charitable remainder interest must be at least 10 percent with respect to the net fair market value of each contribution.

- The unitrust may provide that the noncharitable beneficiary can receive the lesser of (1) the specified fixed percentage or (2) the trust income for the year, plus any excess trust income to the extent of any deficiency in the prior years by reason of the limitation to the amount of trust income in such years.

- The noncharitable income beneficiaries must be living at the time of transfer in trust, and their interests must be for a term not exceeding 20 years or for their respective lives.

- The entire remainder must go to charity (or charities).

If these requirements are met, the donor will be entitled to an income tax deduction limited to the present value of the remainder interest.

c. To qualify for a charitable tax deduction, a pooled-income fund must meet all the following requirements:

- The donor must contribute an irrevocable, vested remainder interest to the charitable organization that maintains it.

- The property transferred by each donor must be commingled with the property transferred by other donors.

- The fund cannot invest in tax-exempt securities.

- No donor or income beneficiary can be a trustee.

- The donor must retain a life income interest for himself or herself or one or more named income beneficiaries.

- Each income beneficiary must be entitled to and receive a pro rata share of the income (annually) based on the rate of return earned by the fund. If these requirements are met, the donor will be entitled to income and gift tax deductions. The economic advantage to the donor of making this transfer is that the donor is obtaining diversification for the income beneficiary without incurring the capital-gains tax that would ordinarily be imposed if the donor exchanged securities for other securities.

32. Life insurance is a favored means of making charitable contributions for several reasons:

    - The death benefit going to charity is guaranteed as long as premiums are paid.

    - Life insurance provides an amplified gift that can be purchased on the installment plan.

    - Life insurance is a self-completing gift.

    - The death proceeds can be received by the designated charity free of federal income and estate taxes, probate and administrative costs and delays, brokerage fees, or other transfer costs.

    - Because of the contractual nature of the life insurance contract, large gifts to charity are not subject to attack by disgruntled heirs.

    - A substantial gift may be made with no attending publicity.

33. a. When the value of the policy (interpolated terminal reserve plus unearned premium on the date of the gift) exceeds the policyowner's net premium payments, the deduction for a gift of the policy is equal to the policyowner's basis (cost), that is, the net premium payments paid by the policyowner.

    b. When the policyowner's net premium payments exceed the value of the policy, the deduction for a gift of the policy is equal to the policy's value.

    c. The charitable deduction allowed for a paid-up or a single-premium policy is the lesser of the policy's replacement cost or the policyowner's basis. The replacement cost of a single-premium or paid-up policy is the single premium the same insurer would charge for a policy of the same amount at the insured's attained age (increased by any dividend credits and reduced by any loans).

    d. The maximum charitable deduction allowed for a newly issued policy is the gross premium paid by the policyowner.

34. a. Rev. Rul. 2009–13 determined that a life insurance policy is a capital-gain asset. If a life insurance policy is surrendered at a gain, the gain is taxed as ordinary income to the extent of the inside buildup of the policy and capital gain to the extent of the excess (if any) over the inside buildup. The amount of the charitable deduction for Sidney's gift will be the fair market value of the policy reduced by the ordinary income element (the inside buildup) had the policy been sold. Capital-gain property gifted to a public charity is subject to the 30 percent-of-AGI limitation.

    b. Even though the amount of net premiums paid by Sidney exceeds the policy's paid-up value, his charitable contribution for the policy gift is limited to the policy's replacement cost.

Chapter 10

Individual Income Tax Credits

Learning Objectives

An understanding of the material in this chapter should enable you to

LO 10.1   **Describe the difference between tax credits and deductions, and explain the tax credit for children.**

LO 10.2   **Explain the tax credit for adoption expenses.**

LO 10.3   **Explain the tax credit for dependent-care expenses.**

LO 10.4   **Explain the "American" opportunity credit and the "Lifetime" learning credit.**

> The Eiffel Tower is the Empire State Building after taxes.
>
> —Anonymous

LO 10.1   **Describe the difference between tax credits and deductions, and explain the tax credit for children.**

Tax credits are highly beneficial to taxpayers because they constitute dollar-for-dollar reductions of the actual tax owed to the government. A tax deduction, on the other hand, only reduces the amount of the taxpayer's income that is subject to taxation. It produces a net tax benefit equal to the taxpayer's marginal tax rate multiplied by each dollar deducted. For example, a taxpayer whose top marginal rate is 39.6 percent would receive a benefit equal to 39.6 cents for each deductible dollar. Although deductions are certainly beneficial, credits are more beneficial because they are applied directly to the tax liability.

Although numerous credits surface and become available annually, this chapter examines four important tax credits that are available to individual taxpayers: the tax credit for children, the adoption credit, the dependent-care credit, and the credits for higher education expenses. The higher education credits are actually two different credits: the "American" opportunity credit and the "Lifetime" learning credit. The American Opportunity Tax Credit has expanded and replaced the Hope scholarship credit.

All of these credits reflect the concern of Congress with providing tax incentives for socially beneficial or economically necessary activities of individual taxpayers. Each credit has its own set of rules for eligibility, availability based on the taxpayer's income level, and credit amounts. Knowledge of how these credits operate is essential to a fundamental understanding of the income tax law.

TAX CREDIT FOR CHILDREN

The tax law provides an annual tax credit that may be claimed against an individual's tax liability for each qualifying child of the taxpayer. The amount of the credit (without regard to the phase-out provision explained below) is $1,000 for each qualifying child.

The credit amount applies per qualifying child. Therefore taxpayers with more than one child receive the credit amount for each child.

Qualifying Child

A "qualifying child" under the credit rules is one who meets the definition of a qualifying child for purposes of claiming a dependency exemption under Sec. 151. In addition, the child must be under the age of 17 at the close of the tax year. Under new Sec. 24(a), the child tax credit now requires that each qualifying child be younger than the person claiming the credit for the child, be unmarried, and be a dependent of the taxpayer. A child's parents should now be the only taxpayers eligible to claim the credit. Finally, the child must be a citizen, national, or resident of the United States.

The taxpayer must include the name and Social Security number of the child on the tax return in order to claim the credit. Through 2017 all or a portion of the credit may be refundable for certain lower-income taxpayers if the amount of the credit exceeds the tax liability shown on the taxpayer's return.

Phaseout of Credit

The credit is phased out for upper-income taxpayers. The phaseout occurs based on the taxpayer's adjusted gross income (AGI) with certain minor modifications ("modified adjusted gross income"). The phaseout begins at the following levels of modified AGI:

Married filing joint return	$110,000
Married filing separately	$55,000
Unmarried taxpayers	$75,000

The otherwise allowable credit is phased out by $50 for each $1,000 (or fraction thereof) by which modified AGI exceeds the threshold amount. For example, a married couple filing jointly with one child this year would have no child credit if their modified AGI was more than $129,000. This is because their AGI exceeds $110,000 by $19,000 plus a fraction of $1,000. Therefore the credit is phased out by $20 \times \$50$, or $1,000, the total amount of the credit.

Under the language of the statute, the credit is phased out sequentially (rather than simultaneously) per child for taxpayers with more than one child. Therefore taxpayers with more than one child will have a larger "phaseout range" for the credits. This is different from the phaseout of dependency exemptions for upper-income taxpayers. Such exemptions phase out simultaneously regardless of the number of exemptions claimed.

Relationship to Dependency Exemption

Remember that the taxpayer who claims the dependency exemption for the child is the taxpayer who is entitled to the credit. This rule is important in cases involving divorced, separated, or unmarried parents.

LO 10.2   Explain the tax credit for adoption expenses.

TAX CREDIT FOR ADOPTION EXPENSES

Amount of Credit

Adoption Tax Credit

For 2017, there was an **adoption tax credit** of up to $13,570 per eligible child available for qualified expenses paid in the course of adopting a child. This figure is subject to annual inflation adjustments. The limit on the credit is a cumulative limit per child. In other words, no more than the maximum amount may be claimed for any one child regardless of the number of years for which the credit is claimed for that child. However, an additional credit or credits may be claimed for the adoption of more than one child. The credit applies to adoptions of children with special needs in a different and more beneficial way as explained below. The adoption credit is phased out for upper-income taxpayers as also explained below. Since 2012, the tax credit was made nonrefundable.

Definitions

eligible child

child with special needs

An **eligible child** is a person who is either under the age of 18 or is physically or mentally incapable of self-care. A **child with special needs** is defined as a citizen or resident of the United States who is determined by state authorities to be unable to be returned to the parents' home and probably will not be placed for adoption without adoption assistance. Requirements for such a determination by state authorities include findings that the child should not be returned to his or her biological parents, and that there is a specific factor or condition that makes the child unable to be placed without adoption assistance.

Qualified Adoption Expenses

It is important for clients considering adoption or in the process of adoption to understand what expenses qualify for the credit. Qualified adoption expenses include legal fees, court costs, attorney fees, and other related fees and costs that have the principal purpose of a tax-payer's legal adoption of an eligible child or a child with special needs.

Costs associated with the adoption of a child of the taxpayer's spouse or costs for surrogate parenting arrangements are not qualified expenses for purposes of the credit.

Special Rule for Adoption of Children with Special Needs

The full amount of the adoption credit is now allowed to taxpayers who adopt a special needs child regardless of the amount of qualified adoption expenses paid by the taxpayer. This means that taxpayers will be eligible for the maximum credit even if they have little or even no actual adoption expenses. Special needs adoptions are typically less expensive than other adoptions. Congress enacted this provision to help taxpayers who have decided to adopt special needs children and to encourage these adoptions. The credit will not be available, however, until the year in which the adoption becomes final.

For adoption of children other than special needs children, the amount of the credit will continue to depend on the amount of qualified expenses.

When Credit Is Claimed

For tax years in which an adoption becomes final, the taxpayer is allowed to claim the credit for expenses paid during that year. For years in which qualified expenses are paid but in which the adoption does not become final, the taxpayer must claim the credit for those expenses for the tax year following the year in which the expenses are paid, even if the adoption never becomes final. If expenses are paid in a year following the year the adoption becomes final, the expenses may be claimed for the year in which they are made.

Foreign adoptions or adoptions of children with special needs qualify for the credit only if the adoption becomes final and must be claimed in that year even if paid in a prior year.

There is a 5-year carryover period available for taxpayers whose allowable adoption credit exceeds their tax liability for the year the credit is first allowable.

Phaseout of Credit

The adoption credit is phased out for taxpayers whose adjusted gross income for the year 2017 exceeded $203,540. The credit is completely phased out at $40,000 above the threshold. Adjusted gross income for this purpose is determined with certain minor modifications similar to those used for the tax credit for children.

To calculate the amount of the credit that is phased out, divide the amount of the taxpayer's adjusted gross income in excess of $203,540 by $40,000. Then multiply the resulting percentage by the otherwise allowable amount of the credit.

Example

Jim and Denise Oliver pay $20,000 in legal fees and other costs this year to adopt Michael, a 2-year-old U.S. citizen who is not a special needs child. The adoption is completed this year in 2017. The Olivers' adjusted gross income this year is $221,540. The maximum allowable credit for their expenses is $13,570. This amount must be reduced by a percentage equal to $18,000 (the amount of AGI in excess of $203,540) divided by $40,000, or 45 percent. Therefore the amount of the allowable credit that is "phased out" is $6,106 ($13,570 × .45). The allowable credit is $7,464 ($13,570 − $6,106). It may be claimed this year since the adoption is completed in this year.

Related Income Tax Exclusion

In planning for the adoption credit, it is important to know that there is also an income tax exclusion available for amounts paid by a taxpayer's employer for qualified adoption expenses on behalf of the taxpayer/employee. Such amounts must be furnished under a nondiscriminatory adoption assistance program. The rules defining and limiting this exclusion for adoption assistance payments are similar to the rules just described for application of the adoption credit. For example, the dollar amounts of the available exclusion are the same as the dollar amounts of the credit. Any amounts excluded from gross income under such a program are not eligible to be treated as qualified adoption expenses for purposes of the adoption credit.

Planning Considerations

The adoption credit is one of the largest of any allowable tax credits for an expense of a personal nature in the history of the income tax law. For that reason alone, it is significant. In addition, the credit reflects a congressional awareness of family values in a context that has not been so strongly recognized in the past.

Planners should remember that the adoption credit is a per child, not a per year, credit. This means that the credit can be claimed up to the maximum amount only once for each child. If expenses are paid in different years for the adoption of the same child, the maximum aggregate expenses that may be taken into account in computing the credit for that child cannot exceed one maximum credit amount for all taxable years. However, the maximum credit can be claimed again for the adoption of another child.

As previously noted, the full amount of the credit is allowable for adoption of a special needs child regardless of the amount of actual expenses. However, the credit's phase-out rules apply to adoptions of children with special needs as well as to other eligible children.

LO 10.3   Explain the tax credit for dependent-care expenses.

THE DEPENDENT CARE CREDIT

Expenses Eligible for the Dependent Care Credit

Dependent Care Credit

As previously stated, the expenses must be made in order to allow the taxpayer to be gainfully employed for the credit to be available. The expenses must be paid by a taxpayer who has a household in which one or more "qualifying individuals" resides for more than half of the taxable year. Expenses must be paid either for household services or specifically for the care of a qualifying individual. A qualifying individual must fall within one of the following definitions:

  •   the taxpayer's "qualifying child" (as defined under Sec. 152) who is under the age of 13

  •   an individual who is physically or mentally incapable of caring for himself or herself and is also the taxpayer's dependent for tax purposes

  •   the taxpayer's spouse who is physically or mentally incapable of caring for himself or herself

Generally the expenses must be paid for services rendered inside the taxpayer's home, unless the services are for the care of either the taxpayer's dependent child who is under the age of 13 (that is, day care services), or for the care of another qualifying individual who regularly spends at least 8 hours per day in the taxpayer's household. Furthermore, employment-related expenses do not include expenses paid for an overnight camp. However, qualifying child care expenses include amounts incurred for nursery school or kindergarten, but not expenses incurred for first grade.

There is a rule that disallows expenses paid to certain individuals who are related to the taxpayer. Eligible expenses do not include payments for care provided by a child of the taxpayer who is under the age of 19 (such as a sister or brother of the qualifying individual), even if the child is not the taxpayer's dependent. Also, eligible expenses do not include those paid for services rendered by any individual who is a dependent of the taxpayer for dependency exemption purposes. The purpose of this rule is to prevent child care payments made to certain family members from generating a tax credit.

There is a limit on the amount of expenses that can be counted in calculating the allowable credit. For taxpayers caring for one qualifying individual, the maximum amount is $3,000 per year. If there are two or more qualifying individuals, the maximum amount is $6,000. Qualifying expenses may not exceed the amount of the taxpayer's earned income for the year.

Calculation of the Dependent Care Credit

The allowable credit currently ranges from 20 to 35 percent of eligible expenses. The allowable percentage is reduced by 1 percent for each $2,000 (or fraction thereof) of adjusted gross income in excess of $15,000. The credit is fully reduced to 20 percent once the taxpayer's AGI exceeds $43,000.

Example

Sue Broadstring is a single taxpayer with two children aged 8 and 10. The children attend a day care facility to allow Sue to be gainfully employed. Sue's adjusted gross income is $50,000 this year and she pays $10,000 this year to the facility for her children's care. Sue has $6,000 in eligible expenses (the maximum amount) and is permitted to claim a 20 percent credit for those expenses since her income exceeds $43,000. Therefore Sue's allowable credit is $1,200 ($6,000 × .20).

Other Rules and Restrictions

Coordination with Dependent-Care Assistance Programs

The same eligible expenses cannot be used for both the dependent care credit and the income tax exclusion for amounts received from an employer-provided dependent care assistance program. In addition, if a taxpayer is a participant in such a program, the maximum amount of qualifying expenses for credit purposes is reduced by one dollar for each dollar paid from the employer program and excluded from the taxpayer's gross income. Therefore taxpayers are often forced to choose between the income tax exclusion for such plans and the dependent care credit. Generally speaking, if a married taxpayer or head of household is in a marginal tax bracket of 25 percent or higher, the exclusion provides a more efficient method of funding dependent care expenses than the otherwise available credit amount.

Additional Rules for Married Couples

Certain special rules apply to married couples claiming the dependent care credit. These rules are as follows:

- Married couples must generally file a joint return to be eligible for the credit. However, if the spouses live apart for the last 6 months of the taxable year, the credit may be available even if separate returns are filed.

- Eligible expenses are limited to the earned income of the spouse with the lesser earned income. Therefore, generally speaking, both spouses must be working to claim the credit, although there is no requirement of full-time employment.

- A significant exception to the rule just described involves spouses who are either full-time students for at least 5 calendar months during the year or who are incapable of self-care during the year. Such spouses are currently deemed to have a monthly earned income of $250 for each month during which they are students or incapable of self-care. If there are two or more qualifying individuals in the household, then such spouses are currently deemed to have $500 per month of earned income.

LO 10.4   **Explain the "American" opportunity credit and the "Lifetime" learning credit.**

THE "AMERICAN" AND "LIFETIME" EDUCATION TAX CREDITS

Individual taxpayers are permitted to claim tax credits for certain expenses for higher education. There are two credits for higher education: the "American" opportunity credit and the "Lifetime" learning credit.

Relationship of One Credit to the Other

Before describing the specific rules for these credits, it is important to know how they interact. First, the credits cannot be claimed together with respect to the education expenses of the same student. The American Opportunity Credit applies on a per-student basis, while the Lifetime Learning Credit applies on a per-taxpayer basis. This means that the American Opportunity Credit applies separately with respect to each student for whom the taxpayer pays education expenses, while the Lifetime Learning Credit applies on an overall basis to all qualifying expenses (for one or more students for whom the American Opportunity Credit is not claimed) paid by a given taxpayer.

The taxpayer elects the credits with respect to qualifying expenses. The elections must be separate. For example, if a taxpayer elects the American Opportunity Credit for the college expenses of one child, he or she may still elect the Lifetime Learning Credit for the qualifying education expenses of another child or children. Alternatively, the American Opportunity Credit can be elected separately for each child in college. As previously stated, the Lifetime Learning Credit cannot be elected with respect to expenses that have been treated under the American Opportunity Credit.

Expenses Qualifying for the Credits

Both credits are available with respect to "qualified tuition and related expenses," which includes tuition and fees required for enrollment and course materials such as textbooks. Such expenses include those paid for the attendance by the taxpayer, the taxpayer's spouse, or the taxpayer's dependents at a postsecondary educational institution offering credit toward a degree or other recognized postsecondary educational credential. Qualified expenses do not include expenses for courses involving sports, games, or hobbies unless the course is part of the student's degree program. Room and board, transportation, and living expenses are also not qualified expenses for these credits.

Special Rules for the American Opportunity Credit Expenses

American Opportunity Credit

The **American Opportunity Credit** is allowed for qualifying expenses incurred for a maximum period of 4 years of the student's postsecondary education. The first 4 years of postsecondary education are measured as of the beginning of the taxable year. If the first 4 years have not been completed by the beginning of the taxable year, the student remains eligible for the credit in the current year. The 4-year period is determined by whether the academic institution awards the student 4 years of academic credit. The student also must be at least a "half-time" student; that is, he or she must carry at least one-half the normal full-time workload for the course of study being pursued. The American Opportunity Credit will not be allowed if the student has been convicted of a felony drug offense during the year.

Lifetime Credit Expenses

Lifetime Learning Credit

Unlike the American Opportunity Credit, the **Lifetime Learning Credit** may be claimed for all postsecondary years of education expenses including graduate and professional school expenses. The Lifetime Learning Credit is also available with respect to expenses of a student who is taking courses to acquire or improve job skills, even if that student is not a half-time student as required under the American Opportunity Credit rules.

Interaction with Dependency Exemption

If the student is a dependent of another taxpayer, he or she may not claim the education credits on his or her own return. The taxpayer who claims the student as a dependent is the taxpayer who may claim the credits. Under Treasury regulations, it is permissible for the parent who is eligible to claim the student as a dependent to choose not to claim the dependency exemption to allow the student to claim an education credit on the student's own return. This may be advisable in cases where the student has tax liability that can be absorbed by the credit, and the parent is subject to phaseout of the credit because of the income limitations discussed below.

Rules for Calculating the American Opportunity Credit

The American Opportunity Credit can currently be claimed in amounts up to $2,500 per student for 2017. It is calculated based on 100 percent of the first $2,000 of qualifying expenses and 25 percent of the next $2,000 of expenses. Therefore the maximum credit is $2,500 for the first $4,000 of expenses.

Phaseout of the American Opportunity Credit

The allowable credit is phased out proportionately for taxpayers with modified adjusted gross income (AGI with certain minor modifications) in excess of certain levels. For married taxpayers filing jointly, the phaseout range for 2017 is between $160,000 and $180,000 (a $20,000 phaseout range). For single taxpayers, the phaseout range for 2017 is between $80,000 and $90,000 (a $10,000 phaseout range). Married taxpayers filing separately cannot claim the credit.

Example

Paul and Margie have a dependent son, John, who is attending his first year of college as a full-time student. The couple's adjusted gross income this year is $170,000. Their

> tuition payment eligible for the American Opportunity Credit this year is $10,000. Their maximum allowable American Opportunity Credit of $2,500 is reduced by the ratio of the amount of their modified AGI in excess of $160,000 to the $20,000 phaseout range. This ratio is $10,000/$20,000 or ½. Therefore $1,250 of their maximum $2,500 American Opportunity Credit is phased out ($2,500 × ½).

The ranges of income to which the phaseouts apply have historically been subject to annual indexing adjustments for inflation. Under current law through 2017, up to 40 percent of the allowable American Opportunity Credit is refundable.

Rules for Calculating the Lifetime Credit

The Lifetime Learning Credit is currently equal to 20 percent of up to the first $10,000 of qualifying expenses paid by the taxpayer. Therefore the maximum annual Lifetime Learning Credit is $2,000.

Phaseout of the Lifetime Credit

The Lifetime Learning Credit is phased out proportionately in the same way as the American Opportunity Credit. However, the phaseout range for 2017 was between $112,000 and $132,000 (a $20,000 phaseout range) for married taxpayers filing jointly, and between $56,000 and $66,000 (a $10,000 phaseout range) for all other taxpayers. Eligibility is similar to the American Opportunity Credit; that is, married taxpayers filing separately cannot claim the credit.

Coordination with Other Income Tax Provisions

These credits are not applicable with respect to distributions from a Coverdell education savings account under Sec. 530 that are excludible from the taxpayer's gross income. Expenses covered by a scholarship that are excludible from gross income under Sec. 117 also do not qualify for the credits. Expenses that are claimed for the credits will also reduce the amount of the exclusion available under Sec. 135 for certain U.S. savings bond interest used to pay expenses for higher education. Furthermore, expenses excluded from gross income under an employer-provided educational assistance program (Sec. 127) do not qualify for the credits. Finally, the education credits may not be claimed with respect to any student whose expenses have been deducted as qualified higher education expenses in the same tax year.

The purpose of these coordinating provisions is to prevent taxpayers from receiving multiple tax benefits for the same expenses.

CHAPTER REVIEW

Key Terms and Concepts

Adoption Tax Credit
eligible child
child with special needs

Dependent Care Credit
American Opportunity Credit
Lifetime Learning Credit

Review Questions

Review questions are based on the learning objectives in this chapter. Thus a [10.3] at the end of a question means that the question is based on learning objective 3. If there are multiple objectives, they are all listed.

1. State the amount of the current tax credit for children. [10.1]

2. Describe how the tax credit for children is phased out for certain upper-income taxpayers. [10.1]

3. Describe the allowable credit for adoption expenses for

    a. an eligible child who is not a special needs child

    b. a child with special needs [10.2]

4. Explain how the allowable amount of the adoption credit is phased out for certain upper-income taxpayers. [10.2]

5. a. Who is a "qualifying individual" for purposes of the dependent-care credit?

    b. What is the maximum amount of qualifying expenses available to a working tax-payer who is responsible for one qualifying individual? [10.3]

6. Explain the interaction of the American Opportunity Credit with the Lifetime Learning Credit in terms of how they are applied to a taxpayer's expenses for higher education. [10.4]

7. a. What expenses qualify for the American opportunity and Lifetime Learning Credits?

    b. What special rules apply to the American opportunity and Lifetime Learning Credit expenses? [10.4]

8. Explain how the American opportunity and Lifetime Learning Credits are phased out for upper-income taxpayers. [10.4]

Review Answers

1. The current amount of the credit is $1,000 per qualifying child.

2. The otherwise allowable credit is phased out by $50 for each $1,000 (or fraction thereof) by which modified AGI exceeds the threshold amount. The phaseout begins at the following levels of modified AGI:

Married filing joint return	$110,000
Married filing separately	$55,000
Unmarried taxpayers	$75,000

3. a. For adoptions of children without special needs, the amount of the credit depends on the amount of qualified expenses. The maximum amount of the credit per eligible child was $13,570 for 2017. No more than the maximum amount may be claimed for any one child regardless of the number of years for which the credit is claimed for that child. In other words, the limit on the credit is a cumulative limit per child.

    b. The full adoption credit is now allowed to taxpayers who adopt a special needs child regardless of the amount of qualified adoption expenses paid by the taxpayer. This means that taxpayers will be eligible for the maximum allowable credit even if they have little or even no actual adoption expenses.

4. The adoption credit is phased out for taxpayers whose AGI for the year 2017 exceeded $203,540. To calculate the amount of the credit that is phased out, divide the amount of the taxpayer's AGI in excess of $203,540 by $40,000. Then multiply the resulting percentage by the otherwise allowable amount of the credit. The credit is completely phased out when AGI reaches $243,540.

5. a. A qualifying individual must fall within one of the following definitions:

    - the taxpayer's "qualifying child" who is under the age of 13

    - an individual who is physically or mentally incapable of caring for himself or herself and is also the taxpayer's dependent for tax purposes

    - the taxpayer's spouse who is physically or mentally incapable of caring for himself or herself

b.   There is a limit on the amount of expenses that can be counted in calculating the allowable credit. For taxpayers caring for one qualifying individual, the maximum amount is $3,000 per year.

6.   It is important to know how the American Opportunity Tax Credit (formerly the Hope scholarship credit) and the Lifetime Learning Credit interact with one another.

First, the credits cannot be claimed together with respect to the education expenses of the same student. Similar to the Hope scholarship credit, the American Opportunity Tax Credit applies on a per-student basis, while the Lifetime Learning Credit applies on a per-taxpayer basis. This means that the American Opportunity Tax Credit applies separately with respect to each student for whom the taxpayer pays education expenses, while the Lifetime Learning Credit applies on an overall basis to all qualifying expenses (for one or more students for whom the Hope or American credit is not claimed) paid by a given taxpayer. If a taxpayer elects the American Opportunity Tax Credit for the college expenses of one child, he or she may still elect the Lifetime Learning Credit for the qualifying education expenses of another child or children. Alternatively, the American Opportunity Tax Credit can be elected separately for each child in college. As previously indicated, however, the Lifetime Learning Credit cannot be elected with respect to expenses that have been claimed under either the American Opportunity Tax Credit or former Hope scholarship credit.

7.   a.   Both credits are available with respect to qualified tuition and related expenses. Such expenses include those paid for attendance at a postsecondary educational institution offering credit toward a degree or other recognized credential. They do not include expenses for courses involving sports, games, or hobbies unless the course is part of the degree program. Room and board, transportation, and living expenses are also not qualified expenses for these credits.

b.   The Hope scholarship credit is allowed only for expenses incurred during the first two years of the student's postsecondary education and can be elected for only 2 taxable years for any one student. The student must carry at least one-half the normal full-time workload for the course of study being pursued. It is calculated based on 100 percent of the first $2,000 of qualifying expenses and 25 percent of the next $2,000 of expenses. The expense limits are indexed for inflation. The American Opportunity Credit is available for all four years of postsecondary education and adds course materials to "qualifying expenditures." In addition, the credit is 100 percent of the first $2,000 of qualifying expenses, and 25 percent of the next $2,000 in qualifying expenses.

Unlike the Hope scholarship credit and current American Opportunity Tax Credit, the Lifetime Learning Credit may be claimed for all postsecondary years of education expenses, including graduate and professional school expenses. It is also available with respect to expenses of a student who is taking courses to acquire or improve job skills, even if that student is not a half-time student as required under both the Hope credit and American opportunity rules. It is equal to 20 percent of the first $10,000 of qualifying expenses paid by the taxpayer for the year.

8. The allowable American opportunity/Hope scholarship and Lifetime Learning Credits are phased out proportionately for taxpayers with modified AGIs in excess of certain levels, which are adjusted annually for inflation. To calculate the amount of the credit that is phased out, divide the amount of the taxpayer's modified AGI within the phaseout range by the amount of the phaseout range. Then multiply the resulting fraction by the allowable credit. The credit is completely phased out when the fraction reaches 1. However, the American Opportunity Tax Credit phases out at significantly higher levels of AGI than both the Hope scholarship and Lifetime Learning Credits.

Chapter 11

Cost Recovery
Deductions

Learning Objectives

An understanding of the material in this chapter should enable you to

LO 11.1   Explain what is meant by cost recovery, recovery method, and recovery period, and identify four basic conditions for the allowance of cost recovery deductions.

LO 11.2   Describe several methods used to compute depreciation deductions for pre-ACRS assets, and distinguish depreciation from obsolescence.

LO 11.3   Explain how accelerated cost recovery systems (ACRS and MACRS) allow the recovery of investment capital for income tax purposes.

LO 11.4   Explain what is meant by depreciation recapture, and describe the election to expense certain depreciable business assets.

LO 11.5   Describe the cost recovery limitations on certain depreciable assets collectively known as listed property, and explain the concept of amortizing certain intangible assets.

I have something my tax doctor calls "narcotaxis." Within 20 seconds of hearing someone launch into an explanation of tax laws, my eyes become glassy, my body loses all feeling, and I go into a shallow coma.

—Russell Baker

depreciation

The most common type of cost recovery deduction is referred to as **depreciation**. Cost recovery is an important concept in the tax law because it reflects the intent of Congress to provide income tax benefits for capital investment.

The concept of cost recovery in the income tax law allows taxpayers who invest capital in business and income-producing property to recoup their investment through tax deductions for the cost of the capital investment. Generally, the taxpayer's cost is "recovered" for tax purposes over a specified number of years. This type of cost recovery generally takes the form of depreciation deductions. However, the cost of certain assets may be recovered immediately or "expensed" in the year the asset is placed in service by the taxpayer, up to a specific dollar limit per year.

Of course, allowing deductions for the cost of assets does not completely reimburse the taxpayer for a capital investment. It only makes that cost deductible for income tax purposes over a period of time. Still, cost recovery is a powerful concept for taxpayers, since the total cost being recovered may often be leveraged. In addition, deductions for depreciation—the most common type of cost recovery deduction—are most often claimed in tax years in which there is no actual cash expense corresponding to the deduction during the year the deduction is claimed. As a result, tax benefits generated by depreciation are often referred to as "paper" deductions or losses.

A special type of cost recovery deduction called obsolescence is sometimes allowable with respect to an asset that has become useless due to economic, technological, or other changes or advances.

Certain intangible assets (such as goodwill of a business) are eligible for cost recovery through amortization deductions. Amortization is a concept that corresponds to depreciation except that it applies to intangible assets.

The law also imposes special limitations on the cost recovery of certain assets such as automobiles and computers.

LO 11.1 **Explain what is meant by cost recovery, recovery method, and recovery period, and identify four basic conditions for the allowance of cost recovery deductions.**

RECOVERY METHODS AND RECOVERY PERIODS

Depreciation and other cost recovery deductions are calculated under a number of different formulas. The amount of the deduction in a given year is basically a function of the following two elements:

- the rate at which the asset's cost is recovered (the "recovery method")
- the period of time over which the cost is recovered (the "recovery period")

The recovery method is typically a mathematical formula that determines how much of an asset's cost can be deducted in a given year. This amount does not represent a loss in the actual economic value of the asset. In fact, many assets eligible for cost recovery may actually be appreciating in economic value during the time their cost is being recovered for tax purposes.

The recovery period is generally a fixed number of years over which the cost is recovered. The recovery period may or may not be based on the actual economic useful life of the asset. The only true economic assumption made in connection with cost recovery deductions is that during the time such deductions are being claimed, the asset is somehow being used in connection with the production, or the attempt to produce, income.

The tax law provides recovery periods and recovery methods for each kind of asset that is eligible for cost recovery. These periods and methods may vary for a particular type of asset depending on the year that the asset was placed in service.

The year that an asset eligible for cost recovery is originally placed in service by a particular taxpayer generally determines which cost recovery period and method will be applied to that asset in calculating depreciation or amortization. Depreciable property is categorized by "class" depending on the type of property and the date it is placed in service.

One set of rules applied to assets placed in service before 1981. Those rules provided for the more traditional types of cost recovery calculations. A second set of rules generally applies to assets placed in service between 1981 and 1986. These rules are referred to as the "accelerated cost recovery system" (ACRS). A third set of rules applies to assets placed in service after 1986. This cost recovery system is called the "modified accelerated cost recovery system" (MACRS). The basics of each of these will be examined. First, however, some fundamental requirements for the allowance of cost recovery deductions should be explained.

BASIC CONDITIONS FOR THE ALLOWANCE OF COST RECOVERY DEDUCTIONS

The most basic condition for the allowance of cost recovery deductions is that the asset must be either used in the taxpayer's business activity or held for the production of income. Because of this requirement, assets held for the taxpayer's personal use or enjoyment are not eligible for cost recovery deductions. Such assets would include the taxpayer's personal residence, home furnishings, jewelry, automobiles, and so forth. However, if any personal assets are used for business or for an income-producing activity, all or a part of their cost may become eligible for recovery, based on the percentage of business or investment use for which the asset is placed in service. An example of such a conversion of use would be where a taxpayer owns a car that was previously used only for personal purposes, and places the car in service in her business as a sales representative. In such a case, if the car is used less than 100 percent for business, the cost that is depreciable is correspondingly reduced.

A second condition for the allowance of cost recovery deductions is that the taxpayer must generally have an ownership interest in the asset. For example, if depreciable property is subject to a mortgage, and the mortgagee (lender) has a secured interest in the property, the mortgagor (borrower) is considered to be the equitable owner of the property for the purpose of claiming cost recovery deductions. Also, lessees of property generally may not claim cost recovery deductions with respect to leased property. However, if the lessee makes an improvement to the property, cost recovery may be allowable as discussed later in this chapter.

A third condition for the allowance of cost recovery deductions is that the taxpayer must have a depreciable basis in the property. Without an income tax basis in the property, no cost recovery can be deducted. If a taxpayer buys the property in a taxable sale, the basis is generally equal to the taxpayer's cost, plus the cost of any capital improvements to the property, minus any losses that are properly chargeable to the capital account. As cost recovery deductions are claimed, the taxpayer's basis in the property is correspondingly reduced. Once the taxpayer's basis is reduced to zero, no further cost recovery may be claimed for tax purposes.

A fourth condition for the allowance of cost recovery deductions is that the asset must be considered to have a limited useful life. Buildings, machinery and equipment, vehicles, and intangible assets such as patents, copyrights, and even the goodwill of a business are considered to have a useful life that is limited. On the other hand, the cost of land may not be depreciated since land is not an asset that is considered to be used up or "worn out" over time. This means that when real estate is depreciated, the basis of the property must be properly allocated between the land and building(s) to determine the portion of the basis eligible for cost recovery. One very limited exception to this rule involves deductions for depletion available to industries that extract natural resources from the ground.

LO 11.2   **Describe several methods used to compute depreciation deductions for pre-ACRS assets, and distinguish depreciation from obsolescence.**

HISTORICAL PERSPECTIVE ON DEPRECIATION DEDUCTIONS

Sec. 167 of the Internal Revenue Code generally applies to determine the amount of depreciation deductions for tangible assets placed in service by the taxpayer before January 1, 1981, when ACRS went into effect. Most of such assets are either no longer in service or have been sold and placed in service by a different taxpayer after 1980. However, in order to understand the fundamentals of cost recovery deductions, traditional methods of depreciation must be examined.

With respect to pre-ACRS assets, four established methods were used to compute depreciation. These four methods are

- the straight-line method

- the declining-balance method (which is applied using varying rates of recovery, as explained below)

- the "sum-of-the-years-digits" method

- any other consistent method that during the first two-thirds of the depreciable asset's recovery period does not result in cost recovery greater than that obtainable under the declining-balance method. Such methods, including the unit of production method, were employed less frequently than the first three methods listed above.

With respect to certain assets placed in service before 1981, a "salvage value" was subtracted from the property's basis in determining annual depreciation. This was an amount that was presumed to be the asset's economic value at the end of the recovery period. The salvage value concept does not apply with respect to assets placed in service in 1981 or later.

Straight-Line Method

straight-line method

The first method, the **straight-line method**, is the easiest method to apply. It is still used for real estate currently placed in service and for certain other property. Under this method, the taxpayer simply divides the depreciable basis in the property by the number of years of the property's applicable recovery period to arrive at an annual deduction that remains the same over the course of the recovery period. The deduction may be somewhat different in the first and last year of the recovery period if the property is placed in service for depreciation purposes under a "convention" that allows only partial depreciation for the first and last years of the recovery period.

Example

Assume that Dominic places property in service in early January of this year under the straight-line method of depreciation with a 25-year recovery period. Assume there is no special convention for determining depreciation in the year the property is placed in service. The basis of the property is $100,000. Dominic can claim $4,000 per year ($100,000 ÷ 25) in depreciation deductions for the property.

Declining-Balance Method

declining-balance method

The second method, the **declining-balance method**, uses a somewhat more complex calculation. This method is also used as a recovery method for ACRS and MACRS property placed in service after 1980. Under the declining-balance method, a fixed percentage of the taxpayer's original basis in the depreciable property is allowed in the first year. The following year the same percentage is applied to the basis of the property as adjusted to that point. Unlike the straight-line method that applies a fixed percentage to the initial basis of the property and then allows the same dollar amount of depreciation each year, the declining-balance method applies the same percentage to the property's current adjusted basis each year.

The declining-balance method is typically an accelerated method of depreciation because a percentage higher than that used under the straight-line method is allowable. That percentage cannot be more than twice the percentage used in applying the straight-line method to the original basis of property in the year it is placed in service. For example, assume that property having a recovery period of 10 years is depreciated under the straight-line method. Depreciation equal to 10 percent of the property's initial basis would be allowable each year. Under the declining-balance method, up to 20 percent of the basis would be allowable each year (this would be the "double-declining-balance" method). Twenty percent would then be applied to the property's basis each year as adjusted for previous depreciation.

"Sum-of-the-Years-Digits" Method

sum-of-the-years-digits method

The **sum-of-the-years-digits method** is more esoteric since it is not a standard method used under ACRS or MACRS with respect to property currently being placed in service. Under this method, a changing percentage, not a fixed percentage, is applied to the basis of the property to calculate allowable depreciation. The fraction is determined as follows:

- The numerator of the fraction is the number of years remaining in the cost recovery period as of the year the depreciation is being claimed.

- The denominator of the fraction is the sequential sum of the numbers representing each year in the total recovery period of the property.

In each successive year of the recovery period, the numerator of the fraction will change but the denominator will not. For example, suppose the recovery period for the property being depreciated under the sum-of-the-years-digits method is 5 years. The denominator of the fraction will be equal to 1+2+3+4+5, or 15. In the first year, the numerator of the fraction will be 5. Therefore for tax purposes in the first year the property will be depreciated by multiplying its basis by $\frac{5}{15}$ or $\frac{1}{3}$. In the second year, the fraction will be $\frac{4}{15}$. Note that the fraction is applied to the original basis of the property under this method (the basis on the date the property was placed in service) and not to the basis as already adjusted for depreciation, as under the declining-balance method.

Other Methods

Other methods that were allowable for pre-ACRS property included the so-called "unit-of-pro-duction" and "machine-hours" methods, along with other unusual depreciation methods. Generally these methods could not be used if they resulted in a more accelerated depreciation schedule than that available under the double-declining-balance method.

The foregoing explanation of basic methods of depreciation is presented to make the basic concepts of depreciation more understandable. For purposes of this text, specific cost recovery periods and methods used for various assets will be discussed below only in connection with property placed in service after December 31, 1980, under ACRS or MACRS.

The Concept of "Useful Life"

Under ACRS and MACRS, there are fixed recovery periods for each category of depreciable assets. These recovery periods cannot be changed except in certain situations where the tax-payer elects an alternative depreciation system. Under the law in effect before 1981, however, it was sometimes allowable to calculate an asset's recovery period by making an estimate of the actual economic useful life of the property. Depreciation deductions would then be allowed under the applicable depreciation method for the period estimated to be the asset's useful life. Under ACRS and MACRS, the fixed recovery periods may or may not correspond closely to the actual economic life of the asset, and they cannot be altered to more accurately reflect its actual "life span." Therefore the concept of useful life has for the most part been supplanted by the application of fixed recovery periods to specifically defined categories of assets. However, the overall concept of claiming deductions for depreciation is still generally based on the con-cept that taxpayers should be able to deduct, or "recover" for tax purposes, the amount of an investment in an income-producing asset over the period of time that the asset is useful for its intended purpose.

One rule that still applies and is related to the useful life concept is the rule that the basis of depreciable property must be reduced by the amount of depreciation allowable for a given year, even if the depreciation was not actually deducted on the taxpayer's return. This means that if the taxpayer omits a depreciation deduction for an asset from a tax return in a given year, the basis of the asset will still be adjusted over the term of its recovery period in a systematic way.

On the other hand, the depreciation rules do not require that the asset actually be used to the same extent for each year of the recovery period. The asset must be placed in service initially for an income-producing purpose. However, even if the asset is used sparingly (or even not at all) in a given year for economic or business reasons, depreciation is still allowable so long as the asset is available for the purpose for which it was placed in service.

DEDUCTIONS FOR OBSOLESCENCE

obsolescence

Obsolescence occurs when an asset becomes economically useless to the taxpayer who owns it. It may occur as a result of technological or scientific advances in a given business or industry, through changes in applicable laws that essentially prohibit the use of the asset, or simply because of changes in economic conditions that remove profitability from the use of the asset. Another form of obsolescence is where the asset's actual condition deteriorates much more rapidly than was expected so that the asset can no longer be used for the purpose for which it was placed in service. Obsolescence involves a loss of usefulness resulting from abnormal conditions rather than from normal wear and tear on the property.

In such cases, a deduction is available for the underpreciated basis the taxpayer has left in the obsolete asset. The deduction becomes available at the point in time when the taxpayer can determine with reasonable certainty that the asset has or will become obsolete. At that time, the taxpayer's remaining basis in the asset may be deducted ratably between the time when obsolescence becomes reasonably certain and the time of actual obsolescence. These two situations may happen at the same time or at different times. Obsolescence is still available under ACRS and MACRS, unlike the salvage value calculation, which no longer applies.

LO 11.3   Explain how accelerated cost recovery systems (ACRS and MACRS) allow the recovery of investment capital for income tax purposes.

ACRS AND MACRS

The advent of the accelerated cost recovery system (ACRS) in 1981 significantly modified the way in which the tax law allows the recovery of investment capital for income tax purposes. Since ACRS, the term "depreciation" has been somewhat supplanted in tax parlance by the term "cost recovery." Although the difference in terminology does not indicate a radical departure from traditional concepts of depreciation, there are significant theoretical differences between the older system of depreciation and ACRS (along with its current counterpart, the modified accelerated cost recovery system or MACRS). For example, fixed recovery periods are assigned to assets eligible for cost recovery, rather than allowing an evaluation and estimate of the asset's actual economic life to be made to determine the applicable period of cost recovery.

These fixed periods are generally shorter than what taxpayers would typically estimate to be the asset's actual span of "useful life." Most assets (but not real property) are eligible for "accelerated" methods of cost recovery (that is, depreciation). The term "accelerated" in this context means any method of cost recovery that provides a higher deduction in the earlier years of the asset's recovery period than that which would be provided by a straight-line recovery method.

ACRS applied to depreciable assets placed in service between January 1, 1981, and December 31, 1986. MACRS generally applies to assets placed in service after December 31, 1986. Therefore the date that property is "placed in service" for an income-producing purpose that qualifies it for cost recovery will dictate which system applies to it and consequently what the asset's applicable recovery method and applicable recovery period will be. ACRS and its progeny MACRS are substantially different with respect to both the recovery periods and the recovery methods assigned to specific types of assets. Both systems generally classify assets in groups according to their applicable recovery periods; hence the terms "5-year property class," "15-year property class," and so on. ACRS and MACRS are described under Sec. 168 of the Internal Revenue Code.

First, the property classes and recovery methods for property placed in service after December 31, 1986, under the MACRS system will be examined. The rules for the original ACRS system applicable to assets placed in service between 1981 and 1986 will then be briefly summarized.

THE MODIFIED ACCELERATED COST RECOVERY SYSTEM (MACRS)

modified accelerated cost recovery system (MACRS)

The **modified accelerated cost recovery system (MACRS)** currently applies to most depreciable property placed in service after 1986. Certain property is not depreciated under the MACRS system including most public utility property, motion pictures, sound recordings, intangible property, and property for which a depreciation method not determined by an annual recovery period (such as the unit of production method that is available for certain property) has been elected by the taxpayer. However, most depreciable property placed in service after 1986 is governed by MACRS.

MACRS Recovery Periods

recovery periods

The property "classes" or applicable **recovery periods** for MACRS are as follows. (The components of this list are not all-inclusive.)

- 3-year property. This property class includes most racehorses, tractors, breeding hogs, certain manufacturing tools, qualified rent-to-own property, and certain computer software that is readily available to the public.
- 5-year property. This class includes cars, most trucks, computers, copiers, typewriters, qualified technological equipment, solar and wind energy equipment, breeding and dairy cattle, and semiconductor manufacturing equipment.
- 7-year property. This class includes office furniture and fixtures, most machinery and industrial equipment, and railroad equipment.
- 10-year property. This class includes property used in petroleum refining, fruit-bearing trees and vines, and barges, tugboats, and other water transportation vessels.
- 15-year property. This class includes telephone distribution plants, service station buildings, pipelines, billboards, and such land improvements as roads, sidewalks, and bridges.
- 20-year class. This class includes certain farm buildings and municipal sewers.
- 27½-year class. This important class of property includes residential real estate.
- 39-year class. This class includes nonresidential rental property, such as office buildings, factories, and warehouses. If the property was placed in service before May 13, 1993, the recovery period is 31½ years.

Typical "Recovery Periods"
- Automobiles: 5 years
- Computers: 5 years
- Office furniture: 7 years
- Most heavy machinery: 7 years
- Residential real estate: 27.5 years
- Nonresidential real estate: 39 years

MACRS Recovery Methods

recovery methods

The cost **recovery methods** used for MACRS property are assigned by property class. Assets in the 3-, 5-, 7-, and 10-year classes are generally depreciated under the double- (or "200 percent") declining-balance method with a switch to the straight-line method at the point where the straight-line method produces a higher deduction. However, computer software subject to a 3-year recovery period is depreciated using the straight-line method. Property in the 15- and 20-year classes is depreciated under the 150 percent declining-balance method with a similar switch to the straight-line method. Property included under the 27½-year, 31½-year, or 39-year classes is depreciated under the straight-line method. This includes all real estate, both residential and nonresidential. Therefore, as it applies to real estate, the modified accelerated cost recovery system is really not "accelerated" at all.

The following tables illustrate MACRS depreciation schedules in the form of depreciation percentages over the property's useful life.

If the recovery year is	If the recovery period is					
	200 percent				150 percent	
	3 years	5 years	7 years	10 years	15 years	20 years
1	33.33	20.00	14.29	10.00	5.00	3.750
2	44.45	32.00	24.49	18.00	9.50	7.219
3	14.81	19.20	17.49	14.40	8.55	6.677
4	7.41	11.52	12.49	11.52	7.70	6.177
5		11.52	8.93	9.22	6.93	5.713
6		5.76	8.92	7.37	6.23	5.285
7			8.93	6.55	5.90	4.888
8			4.46	6.55	5.90	4.522
9				6.56	5.91	4.462
10				6.55	5.90	4.461
11				3.28	5.91	4.462
12					5.90	4.461
13					5.91	4.462
14					5.90	4.461
15					5.91	4.462
16					2.95	4.461
17						4.462
18						4.461
19						4.462
20						4.461
21						2.231

Table 11-1: MACRS Depreciation System—Personal Property (Bonus Depreciation Not Included)
Method: 200 percent or 150 percent declining-balance switching to straight-line
Convention: Half-year

Table 11-2: MACRS Depreciation—Real Estate
Method: Straight-line
Convention: Mid-month Recovery period: 27.5 years

Residential Rental Property

The month in the first recovery year the property is placed in service:					
1	**2**	**3**	**4**	**5**	**6**
First Year 3.485%	3.182%	2.879%	2.576%	2.273%	1.970%
Years 2–27 3.636%	3.636%	3.636%	3.636%	3.636%	3.636%

7	**8**	**9**	**10**	**11**	**12**
First Year 1.667%	1.364%	1.061%	0.758%	0.455%	0.152%
Years 2–27 3.636%	3.636%	3.636%	3.636%	3.636%	3.636%

Table 11-3: MACRS Depreciation—Real Estate
Method: Straight-line
Convention: Mid-month Recovery period: 31.5 years

Nonresidential Real Property
(Placed in service prior to May 13, 1993)

The month in the first recovery year the property is placed in service:					
1	**2**	**3**	**4**	**5**	**6**
First Year 3.042%	2.778%	2.513%	2.249%	1.984%	1.720%
Years 2–31 3.175%	3.175%	3.175%	3.175%	3.175%	3.175%

7	**8**	**9**	**10**	**11**	**12**
First Year 1.455%	1.190%	0.926%	0.661%	0.397%	0.132%
Years 2–31 3.175%	3.175%	3.175%	3.175%	3.175%	3.175%

Table 11-4: MACRS Depreciation—Real Estate Method: Straight-line Convention: Mid-month Recovery period: 39 years					
Nonresidential Real Property (Placed in service on or after May 13, 1993)					
The month in the first recovery year the property is placed in service:					
	1	2	3	4	5	6
First Year	2.461%	2.247%	2.033%	1.819%	1.605%	1.391%
Years 2–39	2.564%	2.564%	2.564%	2.564%	2.564%	2.564%

	7	8	9	10	11	12
First Year	1.177%	0.963%	0.749%	0.535%	0.321%	0.107%
Years 2–39	2.564%	2.564%	2.564%	2.564%	2.564%	2.564%

Example 1

Jimmy places office furniture costing $10,000 in service this year. The recovery period for the property is 7 years. Jimmy's first-year depreciation deduction (assuming he does not use the expensing election discussed later in this chapter) is $1,429 ($10,000 × .1429).

Example 2

Caroline places nonresidential real property in service for cost recovery purposes in April of this year. The portion of her basis in the property allocable to the building on the property is $150,000. Her first-year deduction for cost recovery will be $2,728.50 ($150,000 × .01819).

Cost Recovery Conventions

Certain "conventions" are required to determine how much cost recovery will be allowed for the year the asset is placed in service and the year when it is disposed of or otherwise retired from cost recovery. Assets in property classes of 20 or fewer years are subject to a "half-year" convention for cost recovery. This means that the equivalent of 6 months of depreciation is allowed for the asset in the year it is placed in service. The same convention applies in the year the asset is disposed of or in the last year of its recovery period. Since there is a half-year's depreciation in the first year of the recovery period and a half-year's depreciation in the last year, assets are actually depreciated over a period of taxable years that is one year longer than the statutory recovery period.

A special convention applies if more than 40 percent of all property placed in service that year and otherwise subject to the half-year convention is placed in service during the last 3 months of the taxable year. In such cases, a "mid-quarter" convention will be applied to all property otherwise eligible for the half-year convention. The property will be depreciated for the first year as if it had been placed in service in the middle of the quarter in which it was actually placed in service. The purpose of this rule is to prevent the taxpayer from claiming 6 months of depreciation for assets placed in service toward the end of the year.

For real estate, a "mid-month" convention applies. Depreciable real estate placed in service or disposed of during any month of the taxable year is treated as being placed in service or disposed of in the middle of that month in calculating allowable depreciation.

Alternatives Under MACRS

There are elective alternatives available with respect to MACRS property. First, taxpayers may elect the straight-line method of depreciation for classes of property that are eligible for the declining-balance method. The straight-line method is then used over the property's MACRS recovery period.

There is a second type of elective treatment under an alternative depreciation system (ADS). ADS allows taxpayers to elect the 150 percent declining-balance method for certain property otherwise eligible for the 200 percent declining-balance method, or to elect the straight-line method for property otherwise eligible for the 150 percent declining-balance method. Under this election, such property is generally depreciated over a recovery period longer than its MACRS recovery period.

However, the longer ADS recovery periods do not apply to most tangible personal property placed in service after December 31, 1998, if the taxpayer elects the 150 percent declining-balance method in lieu of the 200 percent declining-balance method. In such cases, the regular MACRS recovery period is used with the election of the 150 percent declining-balance method and not a longer recovery period. The same calculation is used for such property in computing depreciation for purposes of the alternative minimum tax (AMT). The purpose of this election is to provide equivalent treatment for such property for both AMT and regular tax purposes by making the 150 percent declining-balance method available under the regular tax calculation.

As previously mentioned, straight-line depreciation may be elected for MACRS property over either its regular recovery period or over ADS recovery periods that are generally longer than the regular MACRS period (except for certain assets such as automobiles and qualified technological equipment). For real estate, which in any circumstance is subject to straight-line depreciation under MACRS, the ADS election is available to depreciate the property over a 40-year period.

Alternative depreciation may be elected on a property-by-property basis for real estate. For other property, it is elected on a property class basis.

Certain property is required to be depreciated under ADS. Therefore, for such property, ADS is not an elective treatment.

Improvements to Leased Property

If a lessee or lessor makes an addition or improvement to real property subject to a lease, the lessee or lessor may deduct the cost of the addition or improvement under MACRS. The pre-scribed recovery period is used regardless of the term or remaining term of the lease. If a lessee does not retain the improvement at the end of the lease, the lessee generally may deduct the amount of the remaining basis in the improvement at the time the lease is terminated.

If the property is "qualified leasehold improvement property," the improvement can be depre-ciated over a 15-year period using the straight-line method. Qualified leasehold improvement property is generally an improvement to the interior portion of a nonresidential building, subject to certain limitations. The 15-year recovery period is available to the lessor or the lessee, depending upon which party makes the improvement. This rule requires straight-line deprecia-tion with the half-year or mid-quarter convention, whichever is applicable.

Improvements other than qualified leasehold improvement property are depreciated over the recovery period applicable to the class of the improved property beginning in the month the improvement is placed in service.

DEPRECIATION OF PROPERTY PLACED IN SERVICE BETWEEN 1981 AND 1986 (ACRS)

accelerated cost recovery system (ACRS)

The original **accelerated cost recovery system (ACRS)** generally provided faster cost recovery than does the current MACRS system. At this time only certain real property originally placed in service under the original ACRS would still be in service for tax purposes. Some of the major differences between the original system and the current MACRS are as follows:

- Automobiles. Autos were depreciated over a 3-year period using a recovery rate similar to the 175 percent declining-balance method. Under MACRS, autos are in the 5-year class of property.

- Office furniture, fixtures, equipment, and heavy machinery. These assets were depreciated over a 5-year period using a 175 percent declining-balance method. Under MACRS, these assets are depreciated over 7 years, although the 200 percent declining-balance method applies.

- Real property. Under ACRS, depreciable real estate was recovered over a 15-, 18-, or 19-year recovery period depending on the date the property was placed in service. Real estate was also eligible for an accelerated method of depreciation corresponding to the 175 percent declining-balance method. Under the current MACRS, real property is depreciated using the straight-line method over a recovery period of 27½ years (residential) or 39 years (nonresidential). Clearly, MACRS cut back substantially on the cost recovery benefits associated with real estate investments.

There were also elective alternatives under the original ACRS. The alternative to the ACRS recovery methods and periods was the straight-line method of depreciation with recovery periods significantly longer than the regular prescribed ACRS periods.

LO 11.4   Explain what is meant by depreciation recapture, and describe the election to expense certain depreciable business assets.

RECAPTURE OF DEPRECIATION DEDUCTIONS

When an asset that has been depreciated for tax purposes is later sold or exchanged in a taxable transaction, all or a portion of prior depreciation deductions claimed with respect to the asset may be "recaptured." The term "recapture" in this context means the taxation of certain gain from the sale of the asset as ordinary income rather than as capital gain.

Section 1245 Property

With respect to depreciable tangible personal property (as distinguished from depreciable real property) and certain intangible assets under Sec. 1245, all depreciation (and amortization) claimed is generally subject to recapture upon the sale of the property regardless of the depreciation method used. This means that gain from the sale of the property will be taxable as ordinary income to the extent of the cumulative depreciation deductions claimed for the property. However, the gain recaptured as ordinary income cannot exceed the amount of the gain realized upon sale of the property. As a result, the amount taxed as ordinary income is the lesser of the accumulated depreciation or gain realized upon sale. In addition, this provision does not apply to losses.

Example

Sophie sells a piece of machinery that was used in her business as an architect. Her original cost for the property was $6,600 and the adjusted basis in the machine at the time of the sale is $3,600. The machine is sold for $6,800. Sophie has claimed a total of $3,000 of depreciation deductions for the machine. Her realized gain from the sale is $3,200 ($6,800 sale price – $3,600 adjusted basis). Of that $3,200 in gain, $3,000 is taxable as ordinary income because of depreciation recapture. The balance of Sophie's gain ($200) is taxable as capital gain. It should be noted that the real gain (that is, the excess of selling price over original cost) is taxed as a capital gain.

Section 1250 Property

The recapture rules for depreciable real estate are different from those that apply to personal property. Whether there is recapture on real property depends on the method of depreciation used for the property and the date the property was placed in service.

Only real estate that has been depreciated under an accelerated method (that is, a more rapid recovery method than the straight-line method) will generally be subject to depreciation recapture under Sec. 1250. Therefore real property placed in service after 1986 under MACRS is not subject to recapture since it is depreciated under the straight-line method. Property placed in service between 1981 and 1986 under ACRS may be subject to recapture. The amount of depreciation recaptured depends on whether the property is residential or nonresidential real property. For residential property, only that amount of depreciation claimed that is in excess of the amount allowable under the straight-line method is recaptured. For nonresidential property, there is generally recapture of the full amount of depreciation unless the straight-line method is elected for the property. Interestingly, nonresidential property placed in service between 1981 and 1986 is Sec. 1245 property unless the straight-line method was elected. If the straight-line method was elected, it is Sec. 1250 property.

For real property placed in service before 1981, somewhat different recapture rules apply that are beyond the scope of this text.

However, for real property placed in service after 1986 (MACRS), it is important to know that a special long-term maximum capital-gains tax rate of 25 percent applies to the portion of capital gain that is attributable to depreciation upon the sale of real property by an individual taxpayer. This 25 percent rate, or "unrecaptured Sec. 1250 gain rate" is higher than the regular maximum capital-gains rate of 20 percent that currently applies to individual taxpayers.

Unrecaptured Sec. 1250 gain is defined as the amount of long-term capital gain which would be taxed as ordinary income if Sec. 1250 provided for the recapture of all depreciation and not just the excess depreciation. As a result, any long-term capital gain due to depreciation other than excess depreciation is unrecaptured Sec. 1250 gain and taxed at a maximum rate of 25 percent. This rule is separate from the depreciation recapture rules and may be applied in addition to those rules. The recapture rules, as previously stated, may tax a portion of the capital gain as ordinary income.

ELECTION TO EXPENSE CERTAIN DEPRECIABLE BUSINESS ASSETS

Under Sec. 179, taxpayers other than trusts, estates, or certain noncorporate lessors may elect to deduct or "expense" the full cost of certain depreciable property in the year such property is placed in service. This election generally applies only to depreciable tangible personal property that is acquired by purchase for active use in the taxpayer's trade or business. Under this definition, real estate does not qualify for the "expensing election." However, certain off-the-shelf computer software used in a business currently qualifies for expensing. In addition, depreciable property that is held for the production of income but not used in a trade or business (that is, investment property) does not qualify.

There is a dollar amount limit on the amount of property that may be expensed under this rule. This limit has been adjusted several times in recent years. Under current law the maximum amount that a business can expense is $510,000. However, a reduced Sec. 179 allowance of $25,000 applies to taxpayers acquiring sport utility vehicles (SUVs) weighing between 6,000 and 14,000 for their businesses (placed in service after October 22, 2004).

There is an additional rule that may further limit the first year expensing election for Sec. 179 property. The applicable dollar amount limitation is reduced by one dollar for each dollar of the cost of qualifying property in excess of a specified amount that the taxpayer places in service during the taxable year. The $510,000 maximum amount must be reduced dollar for dollar for assets acquired in excess of $2,030,000.

Example

In 2017, Bear Foot places $2,180,000 of Sec. 179 property in service. Mr. Foot must reduce his expensing allowance by $150,000 ($2,180,000 – $2,030,000). Therefore he may elect to expense an amount up to only $360,000 ($510,000 – $150,000) of the cost of the property placed in service. To avoid the threshold amount, Mr. Foot may have been better off tax-wise if he had placed some of the property in service in the following taxable year.

The amount of the expensing allowance for any year cannot exceed the amount of taxable income derived from all of the taxpayer's businesses for the year (including wages). The limitation is determined without regard to the expensing election. Any amount disallowed under this limitation may be carried forward indefinitely and applied to future tax years.

Any amount claimed under the expensing election reduces the tax basis of the asset. Therefore the amount of depreciation deductions allowable for the expensed property will be reduced, perhaps to zero, by the election to expense the property's cost.

Also, to the extent that the cost of property is "expensed" in its first year, gain on the subsequent sale of the property will be taxable as ordinary income rather than as capital gain under the recapture rules.

The expensing election is a substantial incentive for capital investment by business taxpayers. For tax purposes it essentially treats property that would otherwise have to be depreciated over a cost recovery schedule as a current expense that is immediately deductible.

In addition to the Sec. 179 expensing allowance, Congress permits "bonus depreciation." Bonus depreciation allows taxpayers to expense 50 percent of the cost of qualifying property having a MACRS recovery period of less than 20 years (generally non-real estate). Qualified property includes tangible property that has a recovery period of under 20 years, purchased computer software, water utility property, and qualified leasehold improvement property. Bonus depreciation is also allowable for the alternative minimum tax (AMT), with no additional adjustments required for the AMT. However, similar to Sec. 179, bonus depreciation is subject to the recapture rules. Furthermore, property requiring the MACRS alternative depreciation system (ADS) is not eligible for bonus depreciation.

Taxpayers may claim both the expensing election and bonus depreciation if the property qualifies under both provisions. In addition, if there is any excess basis, regular depreciation can also be calculated. In determining the total deduction, Sec. 179's expensing election is claimed first for the property. Next, the bonus depreciation is applied to the remaining basis of the property, followed by the regular MACRS depreciation calculation. The combination of these tax benefits can result in taxpayers recovering a significant portion of the asset's cost in the initial year an asset is placed in service.

LO 11.5   **Describe the cost recovery limitations on certain depreciable assets collectively known as listed property, and explain the concept of amortizing certain intangible assets.**

COST RECOVERY LIMITATIONS ON AUTOMOBILES AND OTHER "LISTED" PROPERTY

"Listed" Property

Certain depreciable assets are subject to special limitations on cost recovery deductions. These assets include passenger vehicles having unloaded gross vehicle weight of 6,000 pounds or less, computers and peripheral equipment, and any property of a type generally used for entertainment, recreation, or amusement.

If such property is not used more than 50 percent for business purposes, depreciation of the property must be computed under the MACRS alternative depreciation system (ADS). This means that straight-line depreciation must be used over the applicable ADS recovery period. For automobiles, the ADS recovery period is 5 years, the same as the regular MACRS period. For computers, the recovery period is also 5 years.

The amount eligible for cost recovery of any asset is limited to the percentage of the cost of the asset that corresponds to the percentage of its business use. If such business use is not more than 50 percent, expensing of such assets under Sec. 179 (and bonus depreciation) is effectively prohibited because of the requirement that ADS depreciation be used.

If an employee uses personally owned listed property in the course of his or her employment, no depreciation is permitted unless the use of the listed property is for the employer's convenience and is required as a condition of employment.

With respect to computers, the term "listed property" does not include computers used exclusively at a regular business establishment that are owned or leased by the person operating that establishment. An office in a home is treated as a business establishment for this purpose only if it is a qualified home office under the home office deduction rules. For such computers, the percentage of business use does not have to be monitored in order to claim full cost recovery.

"Luxury" Automobiles

There are also annual dollar amount limitations on total annual cost recovery deductions for so-called **"luxury automobiles."** The limitations apply to both depreciation deductions and the first-year expensing election. Therefore the first-year expensing election described previously in this chapter cannot be used to circumvent the limitations. First year bonus depreciation is $8,000 for property placed into service before January 1, 2018. This increased limitation of $11,160 applies to all cost recovery claimed for the auto, whether attributable to first-year expensing, bonus depreciation, or regular depreciation. The dollar amount limits are indexed annually for inflation (excluding bonus depreciation).

For automobiles placed in service during 2017, the limitations are as follows:

Year of Recovery Period	Cost Recovery Limit
First	$3,160 (bonus depreciation of $8,000 available for property placed into service before January 1, 2018)
Second	$5,100
Third	$3,050
Fourth and subsequent years	$1,875

Example

Susie purchased a new car in 2017 that she uses 100 percent for business. The cost of the car was $40,000. Her maximum cost recovery deductions are limited to $3,160 in 2017 (or $11,160 if bonus depreciation is elected) regardless of whether she claims the expensing election for the car or just uses her available depreciation deduction.

For property placed into service during 2018 the bonus depreciation is $6,400. For property placed into service during 2019 the bonus depreciation is $4,800.

If the dollar limitations result in the taxpayer having unrecovered basis in the vehicle after the normal 5-year recovery period, the maximum amount for the fourth year can be claimed in succeeding taxable years until the vehicle is fully depreciated. Note that these amounts are maximum amounts. If the depreciation deduction under the normal MACRS calculation is less than the maximum amount, then the MACRS calculation applies.

If the vehicle is not used 100 percent for business, taxpayers must compute the regular MACRS depreciation amount, identify the ceiling amount (above "Cost Recovery Limits"), and then reduce each by the percentage of personal use. The allowable depreciation deduction is the lesser of the two calculations. This ensures that vehicles used partially for personal purposes will not be eligible for 100 percent of the dollar amount limitations.

The limitations apply to passenger vehicles that are treated as "listed property." Increased limitations apply to trucks, vans, and certain clean-fuel passenger automobiles. Not included in the definition of "listed property" are trucks or vans having gross vehicle weight of over 6,000 pounds, ambulances, hearses, and certain vehicles used directly in the business of transporting people or property for hire or specially modified for business use.

As previously indicated, sport utility vehicles (SUVs) weighing over 6,000 pounds but not over 14,000 pounds are subject to a special $25,000 per-vehicle limitation on the first-year expensing election. In addition, such vehicles are not subject to the dollar amount limits described above for passenger or "luxury" automobiles.

DEDUCTIONS FOR AMORTIZATION OF INTANGIBLE ASSETS

amortization

Certain intangible assets may be "amortized" for income tax purposes as a means of allowing taxpayers to recover their cost. The concept of **amortization** is similar to that of depreciation, although from a conceptual standpoint it is unrelated to the idea of physical wear and tear over the period of an asset's "useful life." The cost of intangibles eligible for amortization is recovered ratably over a 180-month period under Sec. 197. Since the recovery period is based on months rather than taxable years, no cost recovery timing "conventions" are applied to the asset when it is placed in service or when it is disposed of. The cost of the asset is recovered proportionately over the 180-month period. The amortization calculation is similar conceptually to the calculation under the straight-line method of depreciation.

Assets that are eligible for the 180-month amortization deduction include

- the goodwill of a business
- the "going concern" value of a business
- a company's "workforce in place," including its composition and terms and conditions of its employment
- business books and records, information bases, and operating systems (but not computer software available for public purchase and subject to a nonexclusive license)
- patents and copyrights acquired in a transaction involving an acquisition of an interest in a business
- formulas, processes, designs, know-how, and similar property

- licenses, permits, or other rights granted by a governmental unit

- franchises, trademarks, and trade names

- a covenant not to compete entered into in connection with an acquisition of an interest or a substantial portion of an interest in a trade or business

To qualify for amortization, the asset must be used in a trade or business or held for the production of income. If it is business property, it is also treated as being "depreciable" property specifically for purposes of special favorable tax treatment under Sec. 1231. In addition, gain on disposition of an intangible asset is subject to the recapture rules. Furthermore, the property eligible for amortization may not be depreciated.

There are special limitations regarding the income tax recognition of losses realized upon the disposition of amortizable intangible assets. Basically, if a taxpayer acquires a group of such assets in the same transaction (or in a related transaction), no loss upon disposition can be recognized until the taxpayer disposes of all the intangibles so acquired.

These rules generally apply to intangible assets acquired after August 10, 1993.

CHAPTER REVIEW

Key Terms and Concepts

depreciation
straight-line method
declining-balance method
sum-of-the-years-digits method
obsolescence
modified accelerated cost recovery
  system (MACRS)

recovery periods
recovery methods
accelerated cost recovery system
  (ACRS)
amortization

Review Questions

Review questions are based on the learning objectives in this chapter. Thus an [11.3] at the end of a question means that the question is based on learning objective 3. If there are multiple objectives, they are all listed.

1. What basic conditions are necessary for the allowance of a cost recovery deduction? [11.1]

2. Describe several methods for computing a depreciation deduction for property placed in service before 1981. [11.2]

3. Explain the rule requiring that depreciation must be deducted during the asset's useful life. [11.2]

4. a. When may a deduction for obsolescence be taken?

   b. Is the deduction always related to the physical condition of the property? Explain. [11.2]

5. Explain the distinction between ACRS and MACRS. [11.3]

6. What are the MACRS recovery periods and type of property covered by each period? [11.3]

7. What are the depreciation methods for each of the following types of post-1986 property?

   a. 3-, 5-, 7-, and 10-year recovery property

   b. real property [11.3]

8. This year Handy Andy—a repair business owned by Andy and his wife, Mandy—acquires new office furniture, which costs $7,000. Andy also buys an automobile for $20,000.

   a. Under what class of property will the furniture be included?

   b. What will be the depreciation method applicable to the furniture?

   c. Under what class of property will the auto be included?

   d. What will be the depreciation method applicable to the auto? [11.3]

9. What convention will be used in determining first-year and last-year depreciation for real estate? [11.3]

10. Explain how taxpayers may elect to treat MACRS property for cost recovery purposes. [11.3]

11. Describe three major differences between the original ACRS and the current MACRS. [11.3]

12. Describe the basic rules for recapture of depreciation for

   a. personal property

    b.   real property [11.4]

13. a.   Explain the rules for expensing certain depreciable property.

    b.   Explain how the applicable maximum amount eligible for expensing may be reduced for certain taxpayers. [11.4]

14. A taxpayer may elect to expense rather than depreciate the cost of certain assets, subject to limitations. What effect, if any, does the election to expense have on the depreciation deduction? [11.4]

15. What special rules apply to depreciation deductions taken for "listed" property, such as computers? [11.5]

16. Describe the limitations on cost recovery deductions that apply to so-called "luxury automobiles" used for business. [11.5]

17. What types of intangible assets are eligible for cost recovery through amortization? [11.5]

18. Over what period of time may qualifying intangible assets be amortized? [11.5]

Review Answers

1.   Four basic conditions are necessary for the allowance of cost recovery deductions:

- The asset must be either used in the taxpayer's business activity or held for the production of income.

- The taxpayer must have an ownership interest in the asset.

- The taxpayer must have a depreciable basis in the property.

- The asset must be considered to have a limited useful life.

2.   Methods used for computing a depreciation deduction for property placed in service before 1981 are as follows:

- the straight-line method, under which the taxpayer simply divides the depreciable basis in the property by the number of years of the property's applicable recovery period to arrive at an annual deduction that remains the same over the course of the recovery period

- the declining-balance method, under which a fixed percentage of the taxpayer's original basis in the depreciable property is allowed in the first year. In the following year, the same percentage is applied to the basis of the property as adjusted to that point. In other words, this method applies the same percentage to the property's basis each year as adjusted for previous depreciation claimed. The percentage used cannot be more than twice the percentage used in applying the straight-line method to the original basis of property in the year it is placed in service.

- the sum-of-the-years-digits method, under which a changing percentage is applied to the basis of the property to calculate allowable depreciation. This percentage is determined by using a fraction, the numerator of which is the number of years remaining in the cost recovery period as of the year the depreciation is being claimed. The denominator of the fraction is the sequential sum of the numbers representing each year in the total recovery period of the property. In each successive year of the recovery period, the numerator of the fraction will change but the denominator will not. The fraction for each year is applied to the original basis of the property and not to the basis as adjusted for depreciation.

- any other consistent method under which the first two-thirds of the depreciable asset's recovery period does not result in cost recovery greater than that obtainable under the declining-balance method. Other such methods include the "unit-of-production" and "machine hours" methods.

3. The concept of claiming deductions for depreciation is based on the premise that taxpayers should be able to deduct, or recover for tax purposes, the amount of an investment in an income-producing asset over the period of time that the asset is useful for its intended purpose. A rule related to the useful life concept requires that the basis of depreciable property be reduced by the amount of depreciation allowable for a given year. This means that if the taxpayer omits a depreciation deduction for a certain asset from a tax return in a given year, the basis of the asset will still be adjusted over the term of its recovery period in a systematic way that corresponds to a systematic use of the asset.

4. a. A deduction for obsolescence becomes available at the point in time when the taxpayer can determine with reasonable certainty that the asset has or will become obsolete. At that time, the taxpayer's remaining basis in the asset may be deducted ratably between the time when obsolescence becomes reasonably certain and the time of actual obsolescence.

    b. Obsolescence is not always related to the physical condition of the asset. It occurs when an asset becomes economically useless to the taxpayer who owns it. This could be the result of technological or scientific advances in a given business or industry, through changes in applicable laws that essentially prohibit the use of the asset, or simply because of changes in economic conditions that remove profitability from the use of the asset.

5. ACRS applied to depreciable assets placed in service between January 1, 1981, and December 31, 1986. MACRS generally applies to assets placed in service after December 31, 1986. In addition, ACRS and MACRS are substantially different with respect to both the recovery periods and the recovery methods assigned to specific types of assets. ACRS generally provides for faster cost recovery than does the current MACRS system.

6. The property "classes" or applicable recovery periods for MACRS are as follows:

   • 3-year property. This property class includes most racehorses, tractors, breeding hogs, certain manufacturing tools, qualified rent-to-own property, and certain computer software that is readily available to the public.

   • 5-year property. This class includes cars, most trucks, computers, copiers, typewriters, solar and wind energy equipment, breeding and dairy cattle, and semiconductor manufacturing equipment.

   • 7-year property. This class includes office furniture and fixtures, most machinery and industrial equipment, and railroad equipment.

   • 10-year property. This class includes property used in petroleum refining, fruit-bearing trees and vines, and barges, tugboats, and other water transportation vessels.

   • 15-year property. This class includes telephone distribution plants, service station buildings, pipelines, billboards, and such land improvements as roads, sidewalks, and bridges.

   • 20-year class. This class includes certain farm buildings and municipal sewers.

   • 27½-year class. This important class of property includes residential real estate.

   • 39-year class. This class includes nonresidential rental property, such as office buildings, factories, and warehouses. If the property was placed in service before May 13, 1993, the recovery period is 31½ years.

7. a. Assets in the 3-, 5-, 7-, and 10-year recovery classes are generally depreciated under the double- (or 200 percent) declining-balance method with a switch to the straight-line method at the point where the straight-line method produces a higher deduction.

  b. Property in the 27½-year, 31½-year, or 39-year recovery classes is depreciated under the straight-line method. This includes all real estate, both residential and nonresidential.

8. Answers:

  a. 7-year class

  b. double-declining-balance method, with a later switch to straight line (MACRS Table)

  c. 5-year class

  d. double-declining-balance method, with a later switch to straight line (MACRS Table)

9. A mid-month convention is used for real estate. Depreciable real estate placed in service (or disposed of) during any month of the taxable year is treated as being placed in service (or disposed of) in the middle of that month in calculating allowable depreciation.

10. Elective alternatives available under MACRS are as follows:

- Taxpayers may elect the straight-line method of depreciation for classes of property that are eligible for the declining-balance method. The straight-line method is then used over the property's MACRS recovery period.

- An alternative depreciation system (ADS) allows taxpayers to elect the 150 percent declining-balance method for certain property otherwise eligible for the 200 percent declining-balance method, or to elect the straight-line method for property otherwise eligible for the 150 percent declining-balance method. Under this ADS election, such property is generally depreciated over a recovery period longer than its MACRS recovery period.

11. Major differences between ACRS and MACRS involve the following types of property:

- automobiles. Under ACRS, autos were depreciated over a 3-year period using a recovery rate similar to the 175 percent declining-balance method. Under MACRS, autos are in the 5-year class of property.

- office furniture, fixtures, equipment, and heavy machinery. Under ACRS, these assets were depreciated over a 5-year period using a 175 percent declining-balance method. Under MACRS, these assets are depreciated over 7 years, although the 200 percent declining-balance method applies.

- real property. Under ACRS, depreciable real estate was recovered over a 15-, 18-, or 19-year recovery period depending on the date the property was placed in service. Real estate was also eligible for an accelerated method of depreciation corresponding to the 175 percent declining-balance method. Under the current MACRS, real property is depreciated using the straight-line method over a recovery period of 27.5 years (residential) or 39 years (nonresidential).

12. a. All depreciation claimed for tangible personal property is generally subject to recapture on the sale of the property regardless of the depreciation method used. This means that gain from the sale of the property will be taxable as ordinary income to the extent of the cumulative depreciation deductions claimed for the property.

b. Only real estate that has been depreciated under an accelerated method will be subject to depreciation recapture. The amount of depreciation recaptured depends on whether the property is residential or nonresidential real property. For residential property, only that amount of depreciation claimed that is in excess of the amount allowable under the straight-line method is recaptured. For nonresidential property, there is generally recapture of the full amount of depreciation unless the straight-line method is elected for the property. For real estate acquired and placed in service after December 31, 1986, only the straight-line method of depreciation is allowed. However, although recapture does not technically exist, a special 25-percent capital gain rate applies to "unrecaptured Sec. 1250 gain" or "unrecaptured depreciation," meaning all of the depreciation allowed or allowable may be subject to a tax rate of no higher than 25 percent (and not the preferential long-term capital gain rate of 20 percent).

13. a. Taxpayers other than trusts, estates, or certain noncorporate lessors may elect to deduct or "expense" the full cost of certain depreciable property in the year such property is placed in service. This election generally applies only to depreciable tangible personal property that is acquired by purchase for active use in the taxpayer's trade or business. Real estate does not qualify for the "expensing election." Also, other depreciable property not used in a trade or business (that is, investment property) does not qualify.

b. The maximum dollar amount eligible for expensing is reduced by one dollar for each dollar of the cost of qualifying property in excess of a specified amount as adjusted for inflation (or legislation) that the taxpayer places in service during the taxable year.

    In addition, the amount of the expensing allowance for any year is also limited by the taxpayer's taxable income derived from the business for the year (determined without regard to the expensing election). Any amount disallowed under this limitation may be carried forward to future tax years.

14. Any amount claimed under the expensing election must be subtracted from the taxpayer's depreciable basis; that is, a taxpayer cannot claim both expensing and depreciation with respect to the same dollars of capital investment.

15. If such property is not used more than 50 percent for business purposes, depreciation of the property must be computed under the MACRS alternative depreciation system (ADS). This means that straight-line depreciation must be used over the applicable ADS recovery period. For computers, the ADS recovery period is 5 years.

    The amount eligible for cost recovery of any asset is limited to the percentage of the cost of the asset that corresponds to the percentage of its business use. If such business use is not more than 50 percent, expensing of such assets under IRC Sec. 179 is effectively prohibited because of the requirement that ADS depreciation be used.

16. The dollar amount limitations on cost recovery for luxury autos apply to both depreciation deductions and the first-year expensing election. The limits are indexed annually for inflation. If the dollar limitations result in the taxpayer having unrecovered basis in the vehicles after the normal 5-year recovery period is over, the maximum amount for the fourth year can be claimed in succeeding taxable years until the vehicle is fully depreciated. Note that these amounts are maximum amounts. If the vehicle is not used 100 percent for business (and for the production of income), the dollar amount limitations are applied before the percentage reduction in allowable depreciation that reflects the percentage of personal use is applied. This ensures that vehicles used partially for personal purposes will not be eligible for 100 percent of the dollar amount limitations. Different rules apply to certain vehicles, including those with gross vehicle weight of over 6,000 pounds.

17. The following intangible assets are eligible for cost recovery through amortization:
    * the goodwill of a business
    * the "going concern" value of a business
    * a company's "workforce in place," including its composition and terms and conditions of its employment

- business books and records, information bases, and operating systems (but not computer software available for public purchase and subject to a nonexclusive license)

- patents and copyrights acquired in a transaction involving an acquisition of an interest in a business

- formulas, processes, designs, know-how, and similar property

- licenses, permits, or other rights granted by a governmental unit

- franchises, trademarks, and trade names

- a covenant not to compete entered into in connection with an acquisition of an interest or a substantial portion of an interest in a trade or business

18. Qualifying intangible assets may be recovered ratably over a 180-month period. The amortization calculation is similar conceptually to the calculation under the straight-line method of depreciation.

Chapter 12

Limitations on "Passive Activity" Losses and Credits

Learning Objective

An understanding of the material in this chapter should enable you to

LO 12.1   Explain the limitations on passive activity losses and credits.

> [American tax laws] are constantly changing as our elected representatives seek
> new ways to ensure that whatever tax advice we receive is incorrect.
>
> —Dave Barry

Sec. 469 of the Internal Revenue Code deals with the limitations on tax benefits associated with "passive activities." This section was enacted because Congress was concerned with the availability of substantial tax "losses" (deductions in excess of income) claimed by taxpayers with respect to business activities in which the taxpayer owns an interest but does not substantially participate in on a regular and continuous basis. The most common examples of such activities include rental activities (particularly rental real estate) and the ownership of limited partnership interests and similar types of business ownership. The rules were designed to reduce losses of tax revenues resulting from so-called "tax shelters."

LO 12.1   Explain the limitations on passive activity losses and credits.

LIMITS ON DEDUCTIBILITY OF LOSSES

Basically, the rules limit deductions for excess passive activity losses. Excess passive activity losses are the excess of otherwise allowable deductions from the taxpayer's passive activities over the amount of income from the taxpayer's passive activities. In other words, deductions for net losses from the taxpayer's passive activities are not allowed.

Example

John has $50,000 of income from passive activities and $65,000 of deductions from passive activities. The amount of John's deductions in excess of his passive income ($15,000) may not be deducted on his current tax return.

In general, the taxpayer's passive losses and passive income are aggregated for purposes of the limitation, so that losses from one passive activity may offset income from another passive activity. There are restrictions on such aggregation of passive activities for purposes of the overall limitations that are beyond the scope of this text.

Excess passive activity losses are disallowed on the taxpayer's current tax return. However, for tax purposes, such excess losses are not lost forever but are deferred. These "suspended losses" are allowable in subsequent tax years in which the taxpayer has excess passive income. The suspended losses are then allowed to the extent of the taxpayer's excess passive income. Furthermore, any remaining suspended losses are fully allowed in the year in which the taxpayer disposes of his or her entire interest in the passive activity in a taxable transaction. If the taxpayer sells the passive activity to a related party, the suspended losses cannot be deducted until the related party disposes of the passive activity in a taxable transaction to a nonrelated party.

PASSIVE ACTIVITY CREDITS

Similar limitations apply to excess passive activity credits, except that suspended credits are not allowed upon disposition of the passive activity. Passive activity credits may be used to offset the tax attributable to net passive income, computed as the difference between the tax on all income and on taxable income other than net passive income. Unused credits may be carried over to subsequent taxable years subject to the same limitation

APPLICATION OF PASSIVE ACTIVITY LIMITATIONS

passive activity

A **passive activity** may be generally defined as a trade or business in which the taxpayer does not "materially participate." (The term "material participation" will be defined below.)

However, rental activities of the taxpayer are subject to the passive activity limitations, regardless of whether the taxpayer materially participates in the activity or not. There is also a special, and more favorable, rule that applies to extractive industries. Under this rule, any direct ownership of a working interest in a gas or oil venture is not treated as a passive activity, regardless of whether the taxpayer materially participates in the activity, so long as the taxpayer is not a limited partner in the activity. A limited partnership interest in a business activity is a prime example of the type of ownership that the passive activity limitations were designed to cover.

The passive activity limitations do not apply to all taxpayers. The limitations apply to individual taxpayers, estates, trusts, certain personal service corporations, any "closely held" corporation, and certain publicly traded partnerships. The limitations also effectively apply to partnerships and "S" corporations because they are "pass-through" entities in which the reporting of income and losses flows through to the individual owners. If the owners have an insufficient degree of participation in the business of the entity, then the passive loss limitations will be applied on their returns.

A corporation is a "closely held" corporation for purposes of the passive loss limitations if more than 50 percent of the value of its outstanding stock is owned by five or fewer individuals at any time during the last half of the corporation's taxable year. Although the passive loss limitations apply to such corporations, the rules are more lenient as explained below. The rules apply fully to personal service corporations, which for passive loss purposes are defined as corporations "whose principal activity is the performance of personal services that are substantially performed by employee-owners." The passive loss limitations do not apply to C corporations that are neither closely held corporations nor personal service corporations.

DETERMINATION OF "PASSIVE" INCOME AND LOSSES

Categories of Income

The passive activity rules require that taxpayers classify their income into three general categories:

- portfolio income
- active income
- passive income

portfolio income

Portfolio income includes dividends, interest, royalties, income from annuities, and the gain or loss realized from the disposition of property that generates portfolio income for the taxpayer. It would also include gain or loss realized from the disposition of property held for investment, even if the property was not income producing. Portfolio income does not include any income generated in the conduct of a business.

After a taxpayer's portfolio income has been segregated, then the remaining income of the taxpayer is characterized as either active or passive income. This characterization essentially depends on whether or not the taxpayer has material participation in the activity generating the income. Wages and other compensation are treated as active income because they are generated by the efforts of the taxpayer. The characterization of income from a pass-through business entity such as a partnership or S corporation depends on whether or not the taxpayer materially participates in the activity of the entity.

After income has been characterized, the passive loss limitations are applied. If a taxpayer has a net loss from passive activities (that is, total expenses and other deductions from passive activities exceed the income from passive activities), the loss cannot be used to offset active income or portfolio income. In the case of a closely held corporation (but not a personal service corporation), excess passive losses can be used to offset active income but cannot be used to offset portfolio income.

Material Participation

material participation

A taxpayer will be treated as having **material participation** in an activity only if the taxpayer is involved in the operations of the activity on a regular, continuous, and substantial basis. Generally, no limited partner in a limited partnership is treated as materially participating in the partnership's activity. There are special rules for closely held corporations and professional service corporations regarding material participation. These rules involve the nature of the corporation's activity and the extent to which the owners materially participate in that activity.

Rental Activities

The general rule for rental activity is that such activity is treated as a passive one regardless of the taxpayer's participation. However, there is an exception for taxpayers who essentially work full-time in the real property trade or business. If the taxpayer performs more than 750 hours of service during the taxable year in a real property trade or business, and that participation represents more than one-half of the total hours of service provided by the taxpayer for active businesses during the year, then the rental activities for that taxpayer are not automatically treated as passive activities. Services performed as an employee do not count toward the 750-hour requirement (unless the employee owns at least 5 percent of the employer). If the taxpayer qualifies for this exception to the rental activity rules, the taxpayer must still meet the requirements of material participation in the real estate activity to have income and deductions from the activity classified as active.

The "Active Participation" Exception

Even though rental activities are generally classified as passive, there is an important exception for rental real estate activities known as the "active participation" exception. This exception applies to individual taxpayers only. It provides a significant opportunity for individuals who own rental real estate to avoid the passive loss limitations. To qualify, the taxpayer must have "active participation" in the real estate activity. This definition is completely separate and different from the definition of "material participation" that generally applies to a taxpayer's activities to determine whether they are active or passive.

To meet the standard of active participation, a taxpayer must own at least a 10 percent interest in the rental real estate (determined by reference to the value of the property) and must also actively participate in the rental activity. However, the strict standard of material participation need not be met in order to qualify under the active participation standard.

Qualifying taxpayers may deduct up to $25,000 per year of net losses from the real estate activity against their active or portfolio income if the active participation standard is met. If the taxpayer's adjusted gross income (AGI) with certain modifications exceeds $100,000, the $25,000 allowance is reduced by 50 percent of the amount by which AGI exceeds $100,000. Any losses in excess of the active participation allowance may be carried forward to succeeding tax years, subject to the same limitations.

Example

Buddy owns and manages a residential rental property. This year his net loss generated by the property for tax purposes is $21,000. Buddy's adjusted gross income this year is $120,000. Therefore his $25,000 allowance is reduced by $10,000 ([$120,000 – $100,000] × .5). His maximum allowance under the active participation exception is $15,000 ($25,000 – $10,000). As a result, only $15,000 of his $21,000 of losses can be deducted this year. Buddy can carry forward a $6,000 suspended passive activity loss, subject to the same limitations next year.

PASSIVE ACTIVITY LIMITATIONS

This is a simplified summary of the passive activity limitations. Treasury regulations cover many complex issues regarding the definition of various activities, as well as the aggregation rules for multiple activities and many other related topics. Since many passive activities involve assets eligible for cost recovery deductions, those deductions as well as deductions for loan interest and other expenses may be restricted by the passive activity limitations where the total deductions attributable to a taxpayer's passive activity exceed the income generated by it.

CHAPTER REVIEW

Key Terms and Concepts

passive activity
portfolio income

material participation

Review Questions

Review questions are based on the learning objectives in this chapter. Thus a [12.1] at the end of a question means that the question is based on learning objective 1. If there are multiple objectives, they are all listed.

1. Describe the types of activities that are subject to limitations on tax deductions under the passive activity rules. [12.1]

2. Describe the following types of income under the passive activity rules:

    a. portfolio income

    b. active income

    c. passive income [12.1]

3. Describe the "active participation" exception to the passive loss limitations. [12.1]

Review Answers

1. The passive activity rules of Sec. 469 were enacted because Congress was concerned with the availability of substantial tax "losses" (deductions in excess of income) claimed by taxpayers with respect to business activities in which the taxpayer owns an interest but does not substantially participate in on a regular and continuous basis. The most common examples of such activities include rental activities (particularly rental real estate) and the ownership of limited partnership interests and similar types of business ownership. The rules were designed to reduce losses of tax revenues resulting from so-called "tax shelters."

2. a. "Portfolio income" includes dividends, interest, royalties, income from annuities, and the gain or loss realized from the disposition of property that generates portfolio income for the taxpayer. It would also include gain or loss realized from the disposition of property held for investment, even if the property was not income

producing. Portfolio income does not include any income generated in the conduct of a business.

b.   "Active income" includes wages and other compensation generated by the efforts of the taxpayer. It essentially depends on whether the taxpayer has materially participated in the activity generating the income.

c.   "Passive income" is the income remaining after a taxpayer's portfolio income and then active income has been segregated. Income from a business entity in which the taxpayer does not materially participate in the activity of the entity would be characterized as passive income.

3.   An individual taxpayer who actively participates in a rental real estate activity may deduct up to $25,000 of losses from the activity against nonpassive income. The $25,000 amount is phased out by 50 percent of the amount by which the taxpayer's adjusted gross (with certain modifications) income exceeds $100,000. "Active" participation under this exception requires less participation than the general rule of "material" participation.

Chapter 13

Sales and Exchanges of Property

Learning Objectives

An understanding of the material in this chapter should enable you to

LO 13.1 **Explain how gain or loss on the sale or exchange of property is ascertained for federal income tax purposes.**

LO 13.2 **Describe the rules for determining basis when property is acquired by purchase, exchange, gift, or inheritance.**

LO 13.3 **Explain the rules with respect to like-kind exchanges of business or investment property.**

LO 13.4 **Explain the rules with respect to nontaxable exchanges of insurance or annuity contracts.**

LO 13.5 **Explain the rules for exclusion of gain when a principal residence is sold.**

LO 13.6 **Describe the wash sale rules.**

Another difference between death and taxes is that death is frequently painless.

—Anonymous

Death and taxes and childbirth. There's never any convenient time for any of them.

—Margaret Mitchell

The federal income tax law applies to the sale or exchange of property by generally requiring that the sale or exchange be treated as a taxable event. A taxable event can be roughly defined as a transaction that results in the recognition of income or loss for federal income tax purposes. There are many types of taxable events other than the sale or exchange of property (such as the receipt of wages or other compensation for services rendered, or the receipt of income from property held for investment). In any event, property sales are an important element in the collection of tax revenues, and these transactions involve some of their own basic principles of taxation.

LO 13.1   **Explain how gain or loss on the sale or exchange of property is ascertained for federal income tax purposes.**

REALIZATION AND RECOGNITION OF GAIN OR LOSS

In order to determine the taxable amount resulting from the sale of property, the amount of gain or loss realized from the sale must be ascertained. Specifically, Sec. 1001 states, "the gain from the sale or other disposition of property shall be the excess of the amount realized therefrom over the adjusted basis provided in Section 1011 for determining gain, and the loss shall be the excess of the adjusted basis provided in such Section for determining loss over the amount realized." Therefore, in order to calculate realized gain or loss, two elements of the transaction must be determined: the amount realized from the sale or exchange, and the taxpayer's basis in the asset transferred.

amount realized

According to Sec. 1001, the **amount realized** is simply the value of all property received in exchange for the asset transferred. This would be the amount of any money received for the property, plus the fair market value of any other property received as consideration for the property transferred.

basis

adjusted basis

The taxpayer's **basis** in the property transferred (or **adjusted basis** as referred to in Sec. 1001) is generally the taxpayer's cost for the property, subject to certain adjustments. These adjustments may include reductions in basis for previously claimed depreciation deductions, or increases in basis for additions or improvements that the taxpayer made to the property. The rules for basis adjustments will be discussed later in this chapter. If the taxpayer previously acquired the property in a taxable exchange, the cost for the property would be equal to the fair market value of the property given up at the time of that exchange. The cost basis rule generally applies to determine the taxpayer's initial basis in the property when it is acquired, unless the property is acquired in a nontaxable transaction, as explained below. The taxpayer's basis in an asset must be known to calculate the amount of realized gain or loss upon the sale of the asset, as well as the amount of any depreciation or other cost recovery deductions available with respect to that asset.

Once the amount realized and the taxpayer's adjusted basis in the property have been deter-mined, realized gain or loss is calculated by subtracting the adjusted basis from the amount realized in the sale or exchange.

Example

Alexandra pays $7,500 for a violin and later sells it for $10,000. There have been no adjustments to the violin's tax basis. Alexandra's realized gain from the sale is $2,500 ($10,000 – $7,500).

As so calculated, realized gain may be described as the economic gain that a taxpayer obtains from the sale or exchange of property. As a general rule, any gain *realized* on the sale or exchange of property must also be *recognized* for federal income tax purposes; that is, it must be included in the taxpayer's gross income for the year it is realized.

Any income a taxpayer realizes is includible in gross income unless some provision of the Internal Revenue Code specifically states otherwise. The Internal Revenue Code does con-tain several provisions that define sales or exchanges of property in which realized gain does not have to be recognized for tax purposes. These exchanges of property, such as like-kind exchanges or qualifying exchanges of insurance contracts (discussed later in this chapter), do not result in current recognition of gain. Still, in such transactions realized gain is not altogether eliminated but merely deferred to a later date when the taxpayer disposes of the property received in the tax-deferred exchange. This deferral (but not elimination) of realized gain is accomplished largely through the mechanism of a "substituted" or "carryover" basis, as explained below.

In a tax-deferred exchange, the taxpayer generally substitutes his or her basis in the old prop-erty for tax purposes to the newly acquired property rather than obtaining cost or fair market value basis in the new property. In this way, any untaxed gain in the old property is carried over to the new property and preserved until the new property is sold in a taxable transaction.

In certain other situations, the Code provides that a sale of property will not be taxed at all. This is accomplished by providing that the gain realized from such a sale will be excludible from the selling taxpayer's gross income. In such transactions, no carryover of basis applies to any newly acquired property because the realized gain is not merely being deferred, it is being eliminated. This makes an exclusion a significantly more beneficial provision than one that merely defers tax on realized gain. The most common example of a sale of property that produces gain exclu-dible from gross income is the sale of a taxpayer's principal residence.

If property is sold or exchanged at a loss (that is, the amount realized is less than the basis of the asset sold or exchanged), the loss is generally not deductible unless the transaction was in connection with a trade or business or an activity entered into for profit.

LO 13.2 **Describe the rules for determining basis when property is acquired by purchase, exchange, gift, or inheritance.**

CONSIDERATIONS REGARDING A TAXPAYER'S BASIS IN PROPERTY

Nontaxable Exchanges

As previously stated, a taxpayer's basis in property is generally the cost of the property subject to certain adjustments. However, in a nontaxable exchange the basis of property acquired is determined by reference to the same taxpayer's basis in the property transferred or given up in the exchange. Such a basis is typically referred to as a substituted basis. This is different from the cost basis rule that applies to assets acquired in taxable transactions. A more detailed discussion of how basis is determined in a nontaxable exchange of property is presented later in this chapter.

Gifts

In the case of a gift, the taxpayer receiving the gift (the donee) generally has a basis equal to that of the same property in the hands of the taxpayer making the gift (the donor). This type of basis calculation is somewhat different from the calculation used in a nontaxable exchange. This is because the taxpayer's basis in the property is determined by reference to another taxpayer's basis in the same property rather than by reference to the same taxpayer's basis in a different property previously owned. This basis rule may be referred to as a carryover basis.

Example

Conner receives stock in Specific Motors as a gift from his father. The father's basis in the stock is $5,000. Its fair market value is $20,000. Conner's basis in the stock will be $5,000, the same as his father's basis.

Variations in the Application of Cost Basis Rules

Regarding the general rule of cost basis, certain variations in how the rule is applied should be examined. The following circumstances illustrate how the cost basis rule is applied in certain specific types of situations:

- The taxpayer may have received the property as compensation for services rendered. In such a case, the taxpayer receiving the property will have a basis equal to the fair market value of the property at the time it was received. This amount would also generally be the amount of income that would be taxable as a result of the payment of compensation in the form of property.

- If the taxpayer purchases property and takes a mortgage (or assumes a mortgage) on the property to finance its purchase, the taxpayer's basis is equal to the entire cost of the property including the amount subject to the mortgage.

- Certain difficulties may arise in determining basis when a taxpayer wishes to sell publicly traded securities such as stocks or bonds. If the taxpayer has bought the same stocks or bonds at different times and has a different basis in the units or shares depending on when they were purchased, one of two rules will be used to determine cost basis. If the taxpayer can adequately identify the actual shares or units being sold, then the basis of those specific shares or units can be used as his or her basis in calculating realized gain or loss. If the taxpayer cannot specifically identify the shares sold, basis will be calculated using a "first-in, first-out" (FIFO) method of identification whereby the shares the taxpayer first purchased are deemed to be sold first. However, when a taxpayer sells or redeems shares in a mutual fund, the taxpayer is permitted to use the average cost of all the mutual fund shares he or she owns in determining the basis of the shares sold or redeemed. The average cost method may be used for mutual fund redemptions in place of either the FIFO method or the actual identification method.

PROPERTY ACQUIRED FROM A DECEDENT

"Step-Up" in Basis at Death

basis step-up

A special basis rule generally applies when the taxpayer acquires property through a decedent's estate. If the property is includible in the gross estate of the decedent for federal estate tax purposes, the taxpayer receiving the property takes a basis in the property equal to its fair market value as of the date of the decedent's death. If the fiduciary of the decedent's estate elects the so-called "alternate valuation date" (6 months from the date of death) for the valuation of property for federal estate tax purposes, then the taxpayer takes a basis equal to the fair market value of the property at that time. However, if property is distributed by the estate to the heirs or sold prior to the alternate valuation date, basis is equal to the fair market value as of the date of distribution or disposal. The basis adjustment at death is a significant tax advantage in cases where the property received from the estate has substantial untaxed appreciation. That appreciation will escape income taxation because of the **basis step-up** in to the property's current fair market value resulting from its passing through the decedent's estate.

Example

Buck owns a personal residence with a basis of $75,000. Buck dies this year. His executor does not elect the alternate valuation date for estate tax purposes. The fair market value of Buck's residence is $300,000 on the date of his death. Therefore the income tax basis of the property in the hands of his estate (and of his heir) is $300,000.

The step-up in basis to its current market value applies to most property includible in the decedent's estate for federal estate tax purposes and not just to probate property passing under the terms of the decedent's will. Certain property does not qualify for this special basis rule.

The basis step-up applies to property that was held jointly by the decedent with another individual or individuals. The portion of the jointly owned property that is includible in the decedent's gross estate will be eligible for a fair market value basis adjustment. In the case of property held by married couples in a tenancy by the entirety or in joint ownership, federal estate tax law requires that one-half of the property's value be included in a decedent spouse's estate. Therefore the surviving spouse in such cases receives a basis step-up (or step-down if the property has experienced a reduction in value) to fair market value with respect to one-half of the property. Different rules apply to property that is community property under applicable state law.

If the decedent acquired property in his or her estate as a gift within one year of death, and if the donor of the gift to the decedent is the same person (or that person's spouse) to whom the property passes from the decedent's estate, the basis step-up will not be available. This rule exists to prevent taxpayers from artificially acquiring a basis step-up in property by giving property to a donee in anticipation of the donee's death where the donee's will makes a bequest or devise of the property back to the donor. However, the disallowance of the basis step-up does not apply if the donee-decedent lives for more than one year after the date of the gift.

There are certain other transfers of property that do not qualify for a basis step-up. These include benefits that death beneficiaries receive under most nonqualified deferred annuity contracts. Also any money or other property that constitutes income in respect of a decedent ("IRD") under Sec. 691 of the Internal Revenue Code does not qualify for the special basis rule for property acquired from a decedent. A detailed discussion of the concept of IRD is beyond the scope of this text.

Comparison with Basis of Property Acquired by Gift

In contrast to the basis step-up rule, if a taxpayer receives property by means of a gift made during the donor's lifetime, a **carryover basis rule** applies. With respect to gifted property, the donee's basis is computed by reference to the property's adjusted basis in the hands of the donor. An additional basis rule applies to gifted property. If the donor paid gift taxes in connection with the donative transfer, an adjustment to the carryover basis is made as discussed below.

The basis rule for property acquired from a decedent's estate is much more beneficial to the taxpayer receiving the property than the basis rules that apply to a gift, unless the property's value has decreased significantly. This benefit is of particular significance with respect to depreciable property where the property's adjusted basis in the hands of the decedent was adjusted substantially downward to reflect depreciation deductions. Because of the basis step-up at death, the beneficiary of such property will never have to pay taxes on the gain that would have resulted from depreciation adjustments if the decedent had sold the property during his or her lifetime. This advantage will not be obtained by a donee if the property is given away before the donor's death.

SPECIAL BASIS RULES FOR GIFTED PROPERTY

Adjustment for Gift Taxes Paid

As previously mentioned, the basis of gifted property in the hands of the taxpayer who received the gift is the same as the property's basis in the hands of the taxpayer who made the gift. In other words, a carryover basis rule applies to gifted property. If the property had appreciated in value during the donor's ownership, and a gift tax was paid with respect to the gift of the property, a basis increase is allowable to the donee. That increase is equal to the percentage of the value of the gifted property that is attributable to the appreciation of the property in the donor's hands, multiplied by the amount of the gift tax paid with respect to the property

Example

John owns a rare coin with a basis of $10,000. The coin has a fair market value of $25,000 when gifted to his son. John pays a gift tax of $5,000 on the transfer of the coin. As a result of gifting an appreciated asset to his son, an adjustment for gift taxes paid will apply. The son's basis in the gifted property is $13,000 ($15,000 in appreciation divided by the coin's fair market value of $25,000, or 60 percent). Therefore 60 percent of the gift tax paid by John will serve as a basis adjustment for his son.

Sales of Gifted Property

As a result of the carryover basis rule for gifted property, the gain realized upon a subsequent sale of the property by the donee will be equal to the amount realized on the sale minus the donee's carryover basis in the property (as adjusted for any gift tax attributable to appreciation at the time of the gift).

However, another special basis rule applies if, at the time of the sale, the fair market value of the gifted property is less than the donor's adjusted basis. As a result, the donee may have to use one basis (carryover basis) if the property is subsequently sold at a gain and another (fair market value) if sold at a loss. In calculating a realized loss resulting from such a sale, the donee's basis will be the lower of the carryover basis received by the donee, as adjusted by any gift taxes, or the property's fair market value at the time of the gift (not at the time of the sale). This rule discourages taxpayers from giving property that has experienced a significant reduction in value to other taxpayers who can use a realized loss from the sale of the property more efficiently for income tax purposes than the donor taxpayer can. If a donor makes a gift of such property that has declined in economic value, the loss of value during the donor's period of ownership will not produce a deductible loss for either the donor or the donee taxpayer. However, please keep in mind that these rules may result in neither a gain nor a loss being realized by the donee on the subsequent sale of the gifted property. This occurs when the selling price is less than the basis used for determining a gain but is more than the basis used for determining a loss.

Example

John owns stock in the Siavash Corporation, a privately owned company. He gives his stock in Siavash to his friend, Oliver. John's basis in the stock at the time of the gift was $100,000, and the value of the stock was $10,000. Oliver sells the stock a year later for $8,000. Oliver's realized loss from the sale for tax purposes is $2,000 ($10,000 – $8,000), because the stock's value at the time of the gift ($10,000) was less than John's basis at that time ($100,000). Oliver cannot use John's basis of $100,000 to calculate a deductible loss on the sale of the property. Alternatively, if Oliver sold the stock for $110,000, his realized gain from the sale is $10,000 ($110,000 − $100,000). However, if Oliver sold the stock for $80,000, Oliver would realize neither a gain nor a loss on the sale (the selling price falls between the gain basis of $100,000 and the loss basis of $10,000).

SIGNIFICANT CATEGORIES OF BASIS ADJUSTMENTS

There are certain items for which an adjustment must be made to the basis of a taxpayer's assets. These adjustments will generally occur regardless of whether the asset was acquired in a transaction that resulted in a carryover basis in the taxpayer's hands or in a transaction in which the cost basis rule was originally applied. Basis adjustments that may be required for various types of property include, but are not limited to, the types that follow:

- Adjustments for cost recovery and related types of deductions claimed with respect to the property. These include adjustments for depreciation, bonus depreciation, first-year expensing for tangible personal property used in a trade or business, and deductions for amortization, obsolescence, and depletion.

- Adjustments for permanent improvements to property made after the taxpayer acquires the property. In this connection, any expenditures made for the property that are allocable to the property's capital account (as distinguished from items allocable to the income account) will generally result in a basis adjustment. Expenditures for normal maintenance or repairs to an asset that do not either increase the value of the asset or add to its useful life will generally not result in basis adjustments.

- Various adjustments that are made to the basis of a taxpayer's ownership interest in a business as a result of distributions, proportionate shares of the business entity's income or loss, and other items. These adjustments occur with respect to the ownership of a partnership interest, stock in an "S" corporation, and also stock in a "C" corporation. Each type of business entity is subject to its own rules for these adjustments, which will be discussed in later chapters of this text.

As stated above, one significant adjustment that a taxpayer makes to the initial cost basis in property is an adjustment to reflect deductions for depreciation or other cost recovery deductions. The amount of such deductions is subtracted from the taxpayer's cost basis in calculating the taxpayer's adjusted cost basis at the time of a property sale.

It is important to note that the paying down of a mortgage and the corresponding increase in the owner's equity in property does not result in any basis adjustment. Similarly, a refinancing of the property or the taking of an additional mortgage to increase the amount of debt on the property during the period of the taxpayer's ownership does not result in an adjustment to basis. However, if a property is sold subject to a mortgage and the buyer takes over the existing loan, any loan amount assumed is treated as part of the amount realized by the selling taxpayer on the sale, which may result in realized gain.

There are many other required adjustments to the basis of property listed under Sec. 1016. The adjustments mentioned above represent the more common and more significant types of basis adjustments to property.

NONTAXABLE SALES AND EXCHANGES OF PROPERTY

Certain sales or other dispositions of property do not give rise to a taxable event for federal income tax purposes. This means that even though an economic gain or loss may be realized as a result of the sale or exchange, that gain or loss is not recognized for income tax purposes. This concept of nonrecognition of realized gain takes one of two forms under the income tax law. It may be a "tax-deferred" event in which gain or loss is not completely eliminated but rather deferred through the application of a carryover (i.e., substituted) basis rule for potential taxation at a later date. Alternatively, it may be truly a "tax-free" event in which the gain or loss is permanently eliminated from gross income without any basis rule or other provision that will expose the untaxed gain or loss to recognition at some future date. This latter type of tax rule is an exclusion from gross income.

Whether the transaction is treated as a tax-deferred exchange of property or a tax-free disposition of property, there must be a specific provision in the Internal Revenue Code authorizing such treatment. This is so because all items of economic income the taxpayer receives during the year are subject to income tax, unless the Code expressly provides otherwise. This non-recognition treatment under the Code may be justified in part by the fact that taxpayers may lack the wherewithal to pay the tax despite the existence of a realized gain on the sale or other disposition.

Four general categories of nontaxable sales and exchanges will be discussed in this chapter. First, the rules under Sec. 1031 for "like-kind" exchanges of property will be examined. Next, the rules for nontaxable exchanges of insurance contracts under Sec. 1035 will be explained. Third, the tax rules for the exclusion of gain under Sec. 121 from the sale of a personal residence will be set forth. Finally, an overview of the "wash sale" rules will follow. The first two areas fall within the category of tax-deferred exchanges where untaxed gain is preserved for potential taxation to a future date. The third topic, the sale of a personal residence, is an exclusion from gross income specifying that the taxpayer's gain, subject to definitions and limitations, is "eliminated" and will never be taxed. The final topic, wash sales, is a provision under Sec. 1091 of the Internal Revenue Code that specifically disallows the recognition of tax losses resulting from certain sales of stock or other securities.

LO 13.3   **Explain the rules with respect to like-kind exchanges of business or investment property.**

LIKE-KIND EXCHANGES OF INCOME-PRODUCING PROPERTY

Under Sec. 1031, no gain or loss will be recognized on the exchange of certain properties held either for an investment or for productive use in a trade or business. This provision allows tax-deferred exchanges of many types of business or investment property, but excludes personal use property. These exchanges are referred to as "like-kind" exchanges. Sec. 1031 is not an elective provision. The general concept of the like-kind exchange rules is this: Where a taxpayer uses an exchange to continue an investment in a specific type of income-producing property but needs a different piece of such property from that which was needed before, the continuation of what is essentially the same investment in the same type of property should not give rise to a taxable event.

The like-kind exchange provisions have the effect of deferring, but not completely eliminating, unrecognized gain or loss because a substituted basis rule applies to the properties involved in the exchange, as explained below. In addition, the exchange can be a direct exchange, three-party exchange, or a non-simultaneous exchange. A non-simultaneous exchange is treated as a like-kind exchange if the property to be received in the exchange can be identified within 45 days of the transfer of the property relinquished in the exchange. The replacement property must be received within the earlier of 180 days or the due date of the return (including extensions) for the tax year in which the relinquished property was transferred. However, a sale of property and subsequent purchase of like-kind property does not qualify as a tax deferred transaction under the like-kind exchange rules.

Qualifying Property

Property eligible for the like-kind exchange provisions includes domestic real estate, machinery, equipment, vehicles, office furniture, computers, and most other real and personal property that would typically be used for income-producing purposes. It must be understood that one type of qualifying property cannot be exchanged for another type of qualifying property under Sec. 1031. Rather, the qualifying properties must be of generally the same type;

that is, they must be of "like kind." For example, a vehicle used for business may be exchanged for another vehicle used for business without recognition of gain or loss. One piece of income-producing real estate may be exchanged for another. However, a computer could not be exchanged for a vehicle and receive tax-deferred treatment under Sec. 1031. Treasury regulations under Sec. 1031 provide guidance as to which types of qualifying property are of like kind and which are not, and specify that the words "like kind" refer to the nature or character of the property and not to its grade or quality. In most cases, common sense will guide taxpayers to the correct conclusion.

Qualification of property depends essentially on the nature of the property rather than the purpose for which the taxpayer uses it. For example, a residential apartment building could be exchanged for a commercial office building even though the properties being exchanged have not been used for the same purpose.

Nonqualifying Property

Certain types of property do not qualify under the like-kind exchange rules.

Property that is specifically *ineligible* for like-kind exchanges includes

- inventory (or stock in trade) of a business taxpayer
- corporate securities (including stocks, bonds, or any debt or equity securities) or ownership of interests in an unincorporated business (i.e., partnerships)
- real and personal property held or used outside the United States that is exchanged for property held within the United States

Characterization of Property

In a manner similar to situations under the capital-gain rules and other provisions in the tax law, a factual issue may arise as to whether a certain property is inventory of the taxpayer (held for sale to customers) or whether the property is held for use in the taxpayer's business or other income-producing activity. The issue frequently arises in situations involving real estate. Is the taxpayer a dealer in real estate who holds the properties primarily for resale? Or is the taxpayer holding the properties for rental or other investment purposes, hoping for wealth accumulation through the properties' income stream or long-term appreciation? In the former case, an exchange of the property will not be treated as a like-kind exchange because inventory is not a property held for investment or for productive use in a business. In the latter case, however, the exchange will qualify.

Exchanges Between Related Persons

A special limitation applies if an exchange that otherwise qualifies as a like-kind exchange is between taxpayers who are related persons. The definition of "related persons" for this purpose includes immediate family members, ancestors, descendants, and certain business entities that are owned or controlled by other business entities.

If the taxpayers taking part in an exchange are related persons, generally each taxpayer must keep the property for 2 years after the date of the exchange. If one of the parties to the exchange sells the property received in the exchange before the 2-year period is up, both the selling party and the other party to the exchange will have a taxable event. The party who received the property that is later sold will be taxed, and the party who transferred the property to the related person will also be taxed. The party who transferred the property sold by the transferee will be taxed as if the property was sold in a taxable transaction at the time it was exchanged, except that the recognition occurs at the time of the sale, not as of the date of the exchange. The party to the exchange who sells the property within 2 years of the exchange will also have a taxable event. The gain or loss recognized by the transferor (the party from whom the selling party received the property) is taken into account in determining the gain or loss to be recognized by the selling party.

Example

Lonnie and Clem are brothers. One year ago Clem received a parcel of land from Lonnie in a like-kind exchange. Lonnie's basis in the land transferred to Clem was $50,000. The value of the land at the time of the exchange was $70,000. Clem now sells the land for $80,000. As a result of this sale, Lonnie will recognize $20,000 ($70,000 – $50,000), the amount of his gain that was deferred in the exchange. Clem will recognize $10,000 of gain ($80,000 – $70,000) when he sells the land. His gain is only $10,000 because the amount of gain recognized by Lonnie is "taken into account" (that is, added to Clem's basis) in calculating Clem's gain from the sale.

Like-Kind Exchanges Involving "Boot" Property

Partially Taxable Exchanges

like-kind property

boot property

In a like-kind exchange, often cash or other property will be involved in the exchange along with the **like-kind property** to equalize the value of property surrendered to that of the value of property received. In such an exchange, the cash or other property that is not property of like kind is referred to as **boot property**.

The inclusion of boot in a like-kind exchange does not disqualify the exchange from tax-deferred treatment. However, it does result in the exchange being treated as partially taxable. Note that the taxpayer who pays the boot property will not have to recognize gain or loss on an otherwise qualifying exchange. However, the taxpayer who receives the boot property must recognize any realized gain but only to the extent of the value of the boot received. In essence, realized gain serves as the ceiling with regard to recognition of gain. For example, if a taxpayer exchanges a business computer plus $1,000 in cash for another business computer, that taxpayer does not recognize gain or loss on the exchange. However, the other taxpayer receiving the $1,000 pursuant to the exchange must recognize any realized gain up to the amount of the cash received. If the exchange resulted in $3,000 of realized gain to the taxpayer receiving the cash, that taxpayer would have to recognize $1,000 of the $3,000 of realized gain. If however, the realized gain were $500, only $500 would be recognized on the exchange. Note, however, that no loss will be recognized by the taxpayer (only gain) as a result of the receipt of boot in a Sec. 1031 exchange.

Assumption of Liabilities

A common type of like-kind exchange involves real estate. There are certain cases where the properties being exchanged are subject to liabilities (that is, they are mortgaged). Under this scenario, the parties to the exchange take the properties subject to the liabilities by taking over the loans owed on the properties and relieving the other party from liability on the property being surrendered. In such cases, assumption of liability is treated as payment of boot. In other words, a party who has been relieved of a debt pursuant to an exchange is basically treated for tax purposes as having received an amount of money equal to the principal amount of the debt. However, if both properties in the exchange are subject to liabilities that are transferred, only the net amount of debt relief received by a taxpayer is treated as boot received.

Example

Laura and Woody are exchanging rental apartment buildings. Laura's property is worth $1 million and is subject to a mortgage with a principal balance of $500,000. Woody's property is worth $900,000 and is subject to a mortgage with a principal balance of $400,000. In each property there is equity of $500,000, so the equities are balanced in the exchange. However, Laura will be treated as having received $100,000 of "boot" because the amount of the mortgage she is relieved of ($500,000) is $100,000 more than the amount of the mortgage she is assuming ($400,000). Laura's potential tax liability as a result of this relief from liability may be a factor in negotiating the terms of the exchange.

"Like-Kind" Exchanges
- Qualification of "like-kind" property depends more on the NATURE of property than the PURPOSE for which it is used.
- Business ownership interests and inventory do NOT qualify.
- Exchanges between related parties are restricted.
- "Boot" creates partially taxable exchange.

Determination of Basis in Like-Kind Exchanges

Basis of Property Received in an Exchange

A specific type of basis rule is applied in calculating the basis of a taxpayer's property received in a like-kind exchange. This rule may be referred to as a "substituted" basis. It provides that the basis of the property received in the exchange will be the same as the adjusted basis the taxpayer had in the property surrendered in the exchange. Note that the taxpayer's basis in the property received is not determined by reference to the other party's basis in the same property now owned by the taxpayer (as would be the case in a donative transaction). Rather, it is determined by the same taxpayer's basis in a different property: the property surrendered in the exchange.

Example

Charlotte and Wilbur exchange farm properties in a transaction that qualifies as a like-kind exchange. Wilbur's basis in the property he transfers to Charlotte is $200,000, and its fair market value is $300,000. Charlotte's basis in the property she transfers to Wilbur is $250,000, and its fair market value is also $300,000. Wilbur's basis in the property he receives from Charlotte will be $200,000, the same as his basis in the property he transferred. Charlotte's basis in her new property will be $250,000.

Basis Rules for Exchanges Involving Boot Property

There are basis adjustments that must be made to the substituted basis of the taxpayer's property in cases where the exchange does not solely involve property of like kind. The required basis adjustments fall within two general categories under Sec. 1031:
- The taxpayer's basis in the like-kind property received must be decreased by the amount of any money and/or the value of any other "boot" property received in the

exchange, or increased by the amount of any money or other "boot" property paid in the exchange.

- The taxpayer's basis must be increased by the amount of any gain that was recognized on the exchange or decreased by the amount of any loss recognized on the exchange. The Code provides for a basis decrease for any loss recognized on an exchange even though a realized loss is not permitted to be recognized as a result of the receipt of boot in a partially taxable exchange.

Remember that a transfer of a liability such as a mortgage that relieves the taxpayer from an obligation to pay a debt is treated as boot received in an exchange, and therefore triggers the requirement for a basis adjustment. Note also that if the realized gain in a partially taxable exchange is greater than the amount of cash or other boot received, then gain will be recognized to the full amount of the boot. In such cases, there will be a negative adjustment (or decrease in basis) for boot received followed by a positive adjustment (or increase in basis) of the same amount for recognized gain, resulting in a "wash" for purposes of the basis calculation.

Example

Assume the same facts as in the previous example except that the property transferred by Charlotte has a fair market value of $315,000 and is subject to a mortgage of $175,000, and the property transferred by Wilbur has a fair market value of $300,000 and is subject to a mortgage of $160,000. Each party to the exchange is to assume the mortgage on the transferred properties. Charlotte has a net "debt relief" of $15,000 ($175,000 – $160,000). Therefore Charlotte will recognize $15,000 of her realized gain. Her basis in the property received from Wilbur will remain at $250,000 after corresponding adjustments for boot received ($15,000) and gain recognized ($15,000). The adjustments are equivalent, thereby resulting in a "wash."

LO 13.4   **Explain the rules with respect to nontaxable exchanges of insurance or annuity contracts.**

NONTAXABLE EXCHANGES OF INSURANCE CONTRACTS

Sec. 1035 of the Internal Revenue Code provides that no gain or loss will be recognized for income tax purposes upon the exchange of one life insurance, endowment, or annuity contract for another life insurance, endowment, or annuity contract if certain requirements are met. This Code section, generally similar to the like-kind exchange provisions just discussed, allows nonrecognition of gain with a corresponding basis rule to preserve untaxed gain in the new contract until a later taxable disposition or other transaction. It is—like Sec. 1031, which describes like-kind exchanges—a provision for deferral of taxation rather than permanent exclusion of gain.

No loss will be recognized in a Sec. 1035 exchange. However, a loss is generally not allowable for the surrender of a life insurance policy anyway since the purchase was not in connection with the taxpayer's trade or business nor made with the intention of earning a profit. The deductibility of a loss upon the surrender of an annuity contract is more of an open question as some tax commentators argue the purchase of an annuity qualifies as a transaction entered into for profit within the meaning of Sec. 165.

The purpose of Sec. 1035 is to allow taxpayers to continue what is essentially the same investment in an insurance or annuity contract by replacing a contract that no longer serves the taxpayer's best interests with a contract that is better suited to his or her needs. This may occur, for example, where the investment risk attributes of the old policy no longer suit the needs or preferences of the policyowner, or where a more modern and economically efficient policy has become available.

Rules for Qualifying Exchanges

A life insurance contract may be exchanged under Sec. 1035 for another life insurance contract, an endowment contract, or an annuity contract. An endowment contract may generally be exchanged for another endowment contract or for an annuity contract. An annuity contract may be exchanged without recognition of gain only for another annuity contract and not for a life insurance or endowment contract. For example, an exchange of a life insurance contract for an annuity would be a permissible exchange under Sec. 1035, while an exchange of an annuity contract for a life insurance contract would not be permissible.

The United States Tax Court held that in an exchange involving annuities, it is not necessary to surrender the old annuity contract for a new contract to qualify under Sec. 1035.[1] The Court decided that a withdrawal of some of the funds from an existing annuity followed by a purchase of a new contract with those funds is sufficient to qualify as a tax-deferred exchange of annuity contracts. The IRS has acquiesced in this decision. Rev. Proc. 2008-24 outlines the requirements for a partial exchange of an annuity contract to receive non recognition of gain treatment under Section 1035. If the taxpayer can avoid withdrawing or surrendering any amount during the 12 month period beginning with the date of transfer, Section 1035 exchange treatment will be available. If any amount was withdrawn during this 12-month period, the taxpayer may still qualify for Section 1035 treatment if he can qualify for an

---

1.   *Conway v. Comm'r.*, 111 T.C. 350 (1998)

exception such as attainment of age 59½, disability, or death, as well as others listed under Code Section 72 (q).

For transactions completed after October 24, 2011, Rev. Proc. 2011-38 liberalizes the treatment afforded by Rev. Proc. 2008-24. The 12-month period is reduced to 180 days. Additionally the requirement of satisfying one of the conditions or life events such as death, disability or other events under code section 72(q) has been eliminated. Lastly, the limits on amounts received or withdrawn from an annuity contract involved in a partial exchange do not apply to amounts received as annuity for either (a) a period of 10 years or more or (b) during one or more lives. If the taxpayer does not automatically qualify under Rev. Proc. 2011-38, the taxpayer can argue general principles of tax law justifying the qualifying exchange treatment.

same-insured requirement

There is a **same-insured requirement** under Sec. 1035. Specifically, the insured under a life insurance contract must be the same person in both the old and the new contracts when a life insurance policy is exchanged for another life policy. Where an annuity contract is exchanged for another annuity, the same insured requirement is satisfied by having the primary annuitant under the new contract be the same person as under the old contract. Presumably, in a life policy to annuity exchange, the insured under the life insurance contract must be the same person as the primary annuitant under the annuity contract.

The IRS has taken the position that two life insurance contracts separately insuring the lives of a married couple cannot be exchanged for one joint life policy insuring both their lives.[2] Their rationale is not that two policies cannot be exchanged for one policy (this is generally permissible), but rather that all the contracts involved in the exchange do not cover the life or lives of the same insured. The logic involved in this position would appear to be somewhat specious.

Sec. 1035 does not apply to any exchange involving a foreign person, that is, a person other than a United States person.

The policyowner may not receive cash from an old policy and then decide to invest it at a later time in a new policy and treat that series of transactions as a 1035 exchange. Rather, the surrender or use of funds from the old policy and the acquisition of a new one must be done as an integrated transaction in which the policyowner does not obtain unfettered control over cash.

---

2.   PLR 9542037.

Income Tax Mechanics of Sec. 1035 Exchanges

A substituted basis rule applies under Sec. 1035 in basically the same way as in a like-kind exchange under Sec. 1031, as previously explained. Essentially, the policyowner takes the same basis in the new contract as he or she had in the old contract. If the policyowner makes an additional premium payment for the new contract (which is permissible), the basis will then be increased. Note that if the policy being surrendered carries an economic loss (that is, the cash value is less than the basis in the policy), the substituted basis rule will actually result in a higher basis in the new policy than if the policyowner had surrendered the old contract and then purchased a new one in a separate transaction.

The like-kind exchange rules regarding "boot" also apply to an exchange of insurance contracts under Sec. 1035. If the policyowner receives cash or other property pursuant to an exchange that otherwise qualifies under Sec. 1035, the policyowner will have to recognize gain in the old policy to the extent of the "boot" received in the exchange. The payment of cash by a policyowner in an exchange does not constitute the receipt of boot.

Example

Horace owns a life insurance policy covering his own life. He has paid a total of $100,000 for the policy, and the policy has paid dividends as a nontaxable return of capital to the extent of $15,000. Therefore the tax basis of the policy to Horace is currently $85,000 ($100,000 – $15,000). The current cash surrender value of the policy is $125,000. Horace exchanges the policy for a new policy issued by a different life insurance company. The cash value of the old policy is used to fund the purchase of the new policy. The exchange qualifies under Sec. 1035. Horace has $40,000 of realized gain on the exchange ($125,000 – $85,000), but the realized gain will not be recognized for income tax purposes. The basis in the new policy will be $85,000, the same as the basis in the old policy at the time of the exchange. If Horace makes additional premium payments into the new policy, his basis will then be increased.

Note that if the old policy had an outstanding policy loan against it, and the loan is simply extinguished pursuant to the exchange, the principal amount of the outstanding loan will be treated as boot. This corresponds to the rules governing like-kind exchanges.

LO 13.5   **Explain the rules for exclusion of gain when a principal residence is sold.**

EXCLUSION FOR GAIN REALIZED UPON THE SALE OF A PRINCIPAL RESIDENCE

Under current law, Sec. 121 provides a relief provision in the form of an exclusion from gross income for gain realized from the sale of a taxpayer's home. However, there has traditionally been tax relief available for the sale of a principal residence. Under prior law, there were two provisions:

- a rollover of gain provision that was similar to a tax-deferred exchange rule because it required the taxpayer to purchase another residence within 2 years
- a once-in-a-lifetime exclusion of gain provision that was available to taxpayers age 55 and over

Both of those provisions were repealed and replaced by the current law that grants an exclusion from gross income for the sale of a taxpayer's home, without any requirement for a replacement residence, any age requirement, or any fixed limit on the number of times the exclusion can be used in a taxpayer's lifetime.

Ownership and Use Requirements

To claim the exclusion, the taxpayer must have owned and used the home as a principal residence for an aggregate time period of 2 years out of the 5-year period immediately preceding the home's date of sale.

Taxpayers who are incapable of self-care and who reside in nursing homes or other similar facilities may treat such periods of residence as "use" of their principal residence for a total of up to one year of the 2-year use requirement for the exclusion. This wrinkle in the use requirement obviously helps such taxpayers qualify for the exclusion.

An unmarried taxpayer whose spouse has died before the date of the home sale can "tack on" any period of ownership and use by the deceased spouse prior to the taxpayer's ownership and use of the home.

If a taxpayer receives a home in a transfer incident to a divorce proceeding or settlement, the taxpayer may "tack on" the transferor's period of ownership under the ownership test. Similarly, if the taxpayer owns the property and his or her spouse or former spouse was granted use of the property under a divorce or separation agreement, the taxpayer can treat such occupancy as his or her use of the property for purposes of the use requirement for the exclusion.

A provision effective for sales of homes occurring after October 22, 2004 prohibits taxpayers from acquiring property in a like-kind exchange and then, within a 5-year period beginning on the date of the exchange, converting the property to a personal residence and claiming the exclusion of gain from a sale. This provision does not change the 2-year requirement for use of the home as a personal residence. It does, however, extend the ownership requirement to a full 5 years for properties acquired in a like-kind exchange.

Finally, if the taxpayer used the "rollover of gain" provision under prior law in the process of acquiring the home being sold (that is, the home was the replacement residence under that provision), the period of ownership and use of the taxpayer's prior residence sold pursuant to the rollover rules is counted as ownership and use of the replacement residence.

Amount of the Exclusion

For married taxpayers filing jointly, the maximum amount of realized gain that may be excluded from gross income is $500,000. The $500,000 limit applies if both spouses meet the ownership and use requirements, but also if only one spouse meets the ownership requirement as long as both spouses meet the use requirement. This law allows spouses to choose the ownership arrangement for a home without directly affecting the amount of the available exclusion. However, if only one spouse meets the use requirement, the maximum amount of the exclusion is $250,000. For other taxpayers, the maximum exclusion is $250,000. Taxpayers who have realized gain in excess of the applicable amount will have to pay tax on the amount of the excess as a capital gain.

Example

Terry and Carol Outman sell their home this year for $950,000 (net of expenses of the sale). Their basis in the home is $400,000. Carol has owned the home for 20 years and the couple have lived together in the home for the entire period. The Outmans' realized gain is $550,000 ($950,000 – $400,000), and the maximum exclusion is $500,000. Therefore the couple will have a recognized gain of $50,000 ($550,000 realized gain – $500,000 maximum exclusion) taxed as a long-term capital gain.

Other Significant Rules

Under Sec. 121, a taxpayer can claim the exclusion only once every 2 years. If a single taxpayer marries a person who has used the exclusion within the past 2 years, then the maximum exclusion available is $250,000 rather than $500,000 until such time as 2 years have passed since the exclusion was used by either spouse.

Under certain circumstances the maximum amount of the available exclusion is reduced. If the taxpayer fails to fully meet the ownership and use rules or the "once every 2 years" rule, and the sale of the home is due to a change of the taxpayer's place of employment, a change of health, or other "unforeseen" circumstances, the $250,000 or $500,000 maximum amount (whatever amount would otherwise be available if the taxpayer fully met the requirements) is reduced. The maximum exclusion is multiplied by the ratio of the amount of time that the taxpayer's qualifying period of ownership and use (this numerator may be expressed in days or months) bears to 2 years. The resulting figure is the maximum amount of gain that the taxpayer is permitted to exclude from gross income.

Unlike the former "rollover of gain" provision, there is no requirement that the taxpayer purchase a replacement residence. Also the taxpayer does not have to make an election to have the exclusion apply. The exclusion will apply automatically unless the taxpayer elects out of it. There is no apparent reason for him or her to do so.

If the taxpayer has used a portion of the home for business or rental purposes and claimed depreciation deductions, the amount of depreciation the taxpayer claimed with respect to the home after May 6, 1997, will reduce the amount of his or her realized gain that is eligible for the exclusion. This means that the exclusion does not apply to gain that is realized as a direct result of basis adjustments for depreciation claimed on the residence. In addition, for sales of a principal residence after December 31, 2008, a realized gain will not be excluded for periods that the residence was not used as a principal residence. This "nonqualifying use," whether as a vacation home, second home, or a rental property, will determine the amount of gain subject to taxation. The gain on sale is allocated to periods of nonqualified use based on a ratio which bears the nonqualified use to the total time that the property was owned by the taxpayer. It is important to note that nonqualifying use before January 1, 2009 is disregarded for this test.

Example

Tommy and Connie Outlier acquire a vacation home on June 1, 2015 for $250,000 and convert the home to their principal residence on June 1, 2018. On June 1, 2020, the Outliers sell their home for $750,000, realizing a gain of $500,000. The Outliers have owned the property for 5 years and have used it as their principal residence for 2 years. Based on their period of use and ownership, 40 percent of the gain (2 years/5 years or 24 months/60 months) is eligible for the $500,000 exclusion. However, the remainder of the gain (60 percent or ⅗ minus nonqualifying use divided by total use) will be taxed at applicable capital gains tax rates in the year of sale. Although the total realized gain is

$500,000, $300,000 ($500,000 × .60) will be treated as a capital gain, with only $200,000 escaping taxation.

Sale of Personal Residence

- The exclusion generally applies if taxpayer owned AND used the home as a principal residence for at least 2 years of the 5-year period ending on the date of sale.
- The maximum exclusion is $500,000 for joint filers; $250,000 for other filers.
- For married couples, only one spouse must meet the OWNERSHIP requirement to obtain $500,000 amount.

LO 13.6   Describe the wash sale rules.

WASH SALES

Taxpayers are not permitted to recognize a realized loss from the sale of corporate stock or other securities if the same stock or security is repurchased by the taxpayer within a 30-day period beginning before or ending after the sale in which the loss was realized. The purpose of this provision is to prevent a tax-avoidance technique in which a taxpayer could (in the absence of the wash sale rule) sell stock, claim a tax loss from the sale, then quickly repurchase the same stock so that the taxpayer's economic position regarding the stock is essentially unchanged, but a tax savings is generated.

wash sale rules

The 30-day period imposed under the **wash sale rules** for repurchase of the same stock or security helps to ensure that if the taxpayer does repurchase the stock sold at a loss and wishes to claim a tax loss for the sale, he or she will be subject to market fluctuations affecting the stock price during the 30-day period before or after the sale. Therefore the taxpayer cannot be assured the repurchase price will be substantially identical to the sale price.

For purposes of the wash sale rules, options to buy or sell a stock or security will generally be treated as a purchase or sale of the stock or security.

The wash sale rules do not apply to transactions made by the dealer in stock or securities in the ordinary course of the dealer's business.

Finally, note that the wash sale rules operate only to disallow the recognition of certain realized losses from the sale of securities. The rules do not apply to exclude or defer gain realized from a stock sale.

CHAPTER REVIEW

Key Terms and Concepts

amount realized	like-kind property
basis	boot property
adjusted basis	same-insured requirement
basis step-up	wash sale rules

Review Questions

Review questions are based on the learning objectives in this chapter. Thus a [13.3] at the end of a question means that the question is based on learning objective 3. If there are multiple objectives, they are all listed.

1. Describe how realized gain or loss on the sale or other disposition of an asset is determined. [13.1]

2. a. Distinguish between realized gain and recognized gain.

    b. Explain how a "substituted" basis preserves a realized gain which has not yet been recognized. [13.1]

3. Janet Jantzen purchased 500 shares of American Oil Reserves at $50 per share. Two years later the price per share doubled, and she sold the stock.

    a. What is her basis for the 500 shares?

    b. What is the total amount realized on the sale?

    c. What is the total gain realized? [13.1]

4. Rocksalt exchanges land (his cost was $10,000) for Apex stock owned by Tickertaper. The stock is worth $15,000 at the time of this taxable exchange.

    a. What is Rocksalt's basis for the stock he receives?

    b. Calculate Rocksalt's gain on the exchange. [13.2]

5. What is the rule for determining basis when property is acquired by gift? [13.2]

6. How is the basis of property determined when it is acquired as compensation for services? [13.2]

7. When property is acquired subject to a mortgage, how is the basis of the property determined? [13.2]

8. Assuming each share is readily identifiable, what method may a taxpayer use to determine the basis of shares in a company that were purchased at different times and at different prices when the shares are being sold on the stock exchange? [13.2]

9. Arnold is an executive with the Air Arrow Corporation. His annual compensation is $60,000. This year, in addition to his normal salary, he is given a bonus in the form of an airplane worth $9,000. Explain the tax implications to Arnold of each of the ones that follow:

    a. Arnold receives the airplane as a bonus.

    b. Arnold later sells the airplane for $12,000. [13.2]

10. a. How is the basis of property inherited from a decedent determined?

    b. What is the effect of the executor's election to use the alternate valuation date for federal estate tax purposes? [13.2]

11. How is the basis of jointly held property affected by the death of one of the joint tenants? [13.2]

12. Under what circumstances will the stepped-up basis be denied for certain property included in a decedent's gross estate that the decedent received as a gift? [13.2]

13. What is the general rule for determining the basis of property acquired by gift? [13.2]

14. a. When property received by gift is sold at a gain, how is the basis of that property determined?

    b. How would your answer differ if the property was sold at a loss? [13.2]

15. Lynne purchased land for $1,000. She gave the land to her brother, Jim, at a time when the property was worth $2,000. Jim later sold the property for $3,000. Calculate Jim's taxable gain on the sale. [13.2]

16. Mary purchased land 2 years ago for $10,000 in cash. Its value dropped to $5,000 this year when she gave the land to her brother, Bob. Bob waited for 2 months and sold the property for $4,500. Calculate Bob's deductible loss on the sale. [13.2]

17. List three types of adjustments that increase or decrease the original cost basis of property. [13.2]

18. a.   What is the general concept behind the like-kind exchange rules? Explain.

　　b.   What types of property are eligible for like-kind exchange treatment?

　　c.   Are there special rules if the exchange is between related persons? Explain. [13.3]

19. a.   What is meant by the term "boot"?

　　b.   What is the rule for determination and recognition of gain or loss when boot is received in a like-kind exchange along with like-kind property? [13.3]

20. What adjustment to basis must be made when an exchange is not solely in kind (that is, involves boot)? [13.3]

21. Sam Sellmore, a successful salesman, owns an apartment building worth $75,000 with an adjusted basis of $80,000. Recently, he received an offer from Carol Rosenboom to exchange ownership of apartment buildings. Ms. Rosenboom's building is also valued at $75,000 with an adjusted basis of $50,000.

　　a.   Does either party have any gain or loss to recognize if they exchange buildings?

　　b.   Would your answer be the same if they were both dealers and traders of many apartment buildings?

　　c.   Does either party recognize gain or loss if

　　　　(1)   Sam Sellmore receives $2,000 in cash in the deal?

　　　　(2)   Ms. Rosenboom, instead of Sam, receives $2,000 in cash in the deal?

　　d.   Calculate the following problems:

　　　　(1)   Sam's basis in the property received if he receives $2,000 in cash in the deal

　　　　(2)   Carol's basis in the property received if she receives $2,000 in cash in the deal [13.3]

22. What is the general rule for exchanges of insurance policies, endowment contracts, and annuity contracts? [13.4]

23. Marty is interested in rearranging his life insurance policies. Explain whether he can enter into the following transactions without paying any income taxes on potential gains:

　　a.   the exchange of his life insurance contract for an annuity contract

　　b.   the exchange of his endowment contract for an ordinary life insurance contract

　　c.   the exchange of his policy on his wife's life for a policy on his life [13.4]

24. What effect will the exchange of one life insurance policy for another have

    a. on the policyowner's basis for the policy received in the exchange?

    b. on any cash received by the policyowner? [13.4]

25. Describe the ownership and use requirements for the exclusion of gain from the sale of a principal residence. [13.5]

26. What is the maximum amount of gain from the sale of a principal residence that may be excludible from gross income by

    a. married taxpayers filing jointly?

    b. other taxpayers? [13.5]

27. Describe how taxpayers who do not fully meet the requirements for the exclusion of gain from the sale of a principal residence may be eligible for a reduced exclusion. [13.5]

28. a. What is the purpose of the wash sale rules?

    b. When will the repurchase of the same stock or security that a taxpayer sells at a loss result in a disallowance of the loss for tax purposes? [13.6]

Review Answers

1. To determine realized gain or loss on the sale or other disposition of an asset, it is first necessary to ascertain the amount realized from the sale or exchange as well as the taxpayer's basis in the transferred asset.

    The "amount realized" is simply the value of all property received in exchange for the asset transferred. This would be the amount of any money received for the property, plus the fair market value of any other property received as consideration for the property transferred.

    The taxpayer's "basis" in the property transferred (or "adjusted basis" as referred to in IRC Sec. 1001) is generally the taxpayer's cost for the property, subject to certain adjustments. These adjustments may include reductions in basis for previously claimed depreciation deductions, or increases in basis for additions or improvements that the taxpayer made to the property.

    The taxpayer's basis in an asset must be known to calculate the amount of realized gain or loss upon the sale of the asset as well as the amount of any depreciation or other cost recovery deductions available with respect to that asset. Once the amount realized and the taxpayer's adjusted basis in the property have been determined, realized gain or loss is calculated by subtracting the adjusted basis from the amount realized in the sale or exchange.

2. a. Realized gain may be described as the economic gain that a taxpayer obtains from the sale or exchange of property. As a general rule, any gain realized on the sale or exchange of property must also be recognized for federal income tax purposes; that is, it must be included in the taxpayer's gross income for the year it is realized. Any income a taxpayer realizes is includible in gross income unless some provision of the Code specifically states otherwise. The Code does contain several provisions that define exchanges of property in which realized gain does not have to be recognized for tax purposes.

    b. When an exchange of property does not result in current recognition of gain, the gain realized is not altogether eliminated but merely deferred until the taxpayer disposes of the property received in the exchange. This deferral of realized gain is accomplished largely through the mechanism of a "substituted" basis, under which the taxpayer transfers his or her basis in the old property over to the newly acquired property rather than obtain a cost or fair market value basis in the new property. In this way, any untaxed gain in the old property is preserved in the new property and will be recognized when the new property is sold in a taxable transaction.

3. a. Janet's basis in the shares is $25,000 ($50 × 500).

    b. The total amount realized by Janet on the sale of the shares is $50,000 ($25,000 × 2).

    c. The total gain realized by Janet is $25,000 ($50,000 – $25,000).

4. a. Rocksalt's basis for the Apex stock he receives in the exchange is $15,000.

    b. Rocksalt's gain on the exchange is $5,000 ($15,000 – $10,000).

5. The taxpayer receiving the gift (the donee) generally has a basis equal to that of the same property in the hands of the taxpayer making the gift (the donor). This basis rule may be referred to as a carryover basis.

6. A taxpayer receiving property as compensation for services will have a basis in the property equal to its fair market value at the time it was received.

7. If a taxpayer purchases property and takes (or assumes) a mortgage on the property to finance its purchase, the taxpayer's basis in the property is equal to its entire cost, including the amount subject to the mortgage.

8. If the taxpayer can adequately identify the actual shares being sold, then the basis of those specific shares can be used as his or her basis in calculating realized gain or loss.

9. a. The $9,000 airplane is taxable income received as compensation.

    b. The sale of the airplane generates a $3,000 gain ($12,000 – $9,000).

10. a. If the property is includible in the gross estate of the decedent for federal estate tax purposes, the taxpayer receiving the property takes a basis in the property equal to its fair market value as of the date of the decedent's death.

    b. If the fiduciary of the decedent's estate elects the so-called "alternate valuation date" (6 months from the date of death) for the valuation of property for federal estate tax purposes, then the taxpayer takes a basis equal to the fair market value of the property at that time.

11. The portion of jointly owned property that is includible in a decedent's gross estate is eligible for a fair market value adjustment. Therefore the surviving joint tenants receive a basis step-up (or step-down if the property has experienced a reduction in value) to fair market value for the portion of the property that was includible in the decedent's gross estate.

12. If the decedent acquired property in his or her estate as a gift within one year of death, and if the donor of the gift to the decedent is the same person (or that person's spouse) to whom the property passes from the decedent's estate, the basis step-up will not be available.

13. If a taxpayer receives property by means of a gift made during the donor's lifetime, a carryover basis rule applies. With respect to gifted property, the donee's basis is computed by reference to the property's adjusted basis in the hands of the donor. An additional basis rule applies to gifted property—if the donor paid gift taxes in connection with the donative transfer, an adjustment to the carryover basis is made.

14. a. As a result of the carryover basis rule for gifted property, the gain realized upon a subsequent sale of the property by the donee will be equal to the amount realized on the sale minus the donee's carryover basis in the property (as adjusted for any gift tax attributable to appreciation at the time of the gift).

b. A special basis rule applies in order for a donee's sale of property received by gift to result in a realized loss for income tax purposes. In calculating a realized loss resulting from such a sale, the donee's basis will be the lower of the carryover basis received by the donee, as adjusted, or the property's fair market value at the time of the gift (not at the time of the sale).

15. The general rule is that property acquired by gift in the hands of the donee has the same basis as it had in the hands of the donor. In this case Lynne's basis was $1,000, and that is the basis Jim takes; so his gain on the sale is $2,000 ($3,000 – $1,000).

16. For purposes of determining loss, the basis of the property in the hands of the donee is (1) the donor's basis or (2) the fair market value of the property at the time of the gift, whichever is lower. The fair market value at the time of the gift is $5,000, which is lower than the donor's basis. Therefore Bob has a $500 loss ($5,000 – $4,500).

17. Basis adjustments that may be required for various types of property are as follows:

- adjustments for cost recovery and related types of deductions claimed with respect to the property

- adjustments for permanent improvements to property made after the taxpayer acquires the property

- various adjustments that are made to the basis of a taxpayer's ownership interest in a business as a result of distributions, proportionate shares of the business entity's income or loss, and other items

18. a. The general concept behind the like-kind exchange rules is that where a taxpayer uses an exchange to continue an investment in a specific type of income-producing property but needs a different piece of such property from that which was needed before, the continuation of what is essentially the same investment in the same type of property should not give rise to a taxable event.

b. Property eligible for the like-kind exchange provisions includes domestic real estate, machinery, equipment, vehicles, office furniture, computers, and most other real and personal property that would typically be used for income-producing purposes. It must be understood that one type of qualifying property cannot be exchanged for another type of qualifying property. The qualifying properties must be of generally the same type; that is, they must be of "like kind."

c. If the taxpayers taking part in an exchange are related persons, generally each taxpayer must keep the property for 2 years after the date of the exchange. If one of the parties to the exchange sells the property received in the exchange before the 2-year period is up, both the selling party and the other party to the exchange will have a taxable event.

19. a.   In a like-kind exchange, often cash or other property will be involved in the exchange along with the like-kind property to make the total of the value of property surrendered in the exchange equivalent to the total of the value of property received. In such an exchange, the cash or other property that is not property of like-kind is referred to as "boot."

     b.   The inclusion of boot in a like-kind exchange does not disqualify the exchange from tax-deferred treatment. However, it does result in the exchange being treated as partially taxable. Note that the taxpayer who pays the boot property will not have to recognize gain or loss on an otherwise qualifying exchange. However, the taxpayer who receives the boot property must recognize any realized gain but only to the extent of the value of the boot received. Also note that no loss will be recognized by the taxpayer (only gain) as a result of the receipt of boot in the exchange.

20. There are basis adjustments that must be made to the substituted basis of the taxpayer in cases where the exchange does not solely involve property of like-kind. The required basis adjustments fall within two general categories:

     •   The taxpayer's basis must be decreased by the amount of any money and/or the value of any other "boot" property received in the exchange, or increased by the amount of any such property paid in the exchange.

     •   The taxpayer's basis must be increased by the amount of any gain that was recognized on the exchange or decreased by the amount of any loss recognized on the exchange. The Code provides for a basis decrease for any loss recognized on an exchange even though a realized loss is not permitted to be recognized as a result of the receipt of boot in a partially taxable exchange.

21. a.   Neither party has any gain or loss to recognize upon the exchange of the buildings, since their exchange is of a like-kind investment property. The basis in the new building for each party is the basis in their old building. This is known as a substituted basis.

     b.   If both were dealers and traders of buildings, the nonrecognition provisions would not apply. Both Sam's business loss and Carol's gain would be recognized.

     c.   If Sam or Carol receives cash in the deal, then the exchange is not solely in kind-it is a boot transaction.

(1) If Sam receives cash, he is taking a loss on the deal. He realizes $77,000 in the exchange, but his basis is $80,000. No loss is recognized in like-kind exchanges where boot is received.

(2) On the other hand, if Carol receives cash, she has a gain of $27,000 ($77,000 − $50,000) but recognizes it only to the extent of boot received. Hence, Carol would recognize $2,000.

d.

(1) Sam's basis in the new building is the basis of his old property ($80,000) decreased by the amount of money received ($2,000), or $78,000.

(2) Carol's basis in the new property is the basis of her old property ($50,000) decreased by the amount of money received ($2,000) and increased by the amount of gain recognized in the exchange ($2,000), or $50,000.

22. The Code provides that no gain or loss will be recognized for income tax purposes upon the exchange of one life insurance, endowment, or annuity contract for another life insurance, endowment, or annuity contract.

What this means is that a life insurance contract may be exchanged for another life insurance contract, an endowment contract, or an annuity contract. An endowment contract may generally be exchanged for another endowment contract or for an annuity contract, but not for a life insurance contract. An annuity contract may be exchanged without recognition of gain only for another annuity contract and not for a life insurance or endowment contract.

23. a. Yes, no gains will be recognized from this exchange.

b. No, any gains will be recognized from this exchange.

c. No, the insurance contracts must be on the life of the same insured.

24. a. The policyowner takes the same basis in the new contract as he or she had in the old contract. If the policyowner makes an additional premium payment for the new contract (which is permissible), the basis will then be increased.

b. If the policyowner receives cash or other property pursuant to an exchange that otherwise qualifies under Sec. 1035, the policyowner will have to recognize gain in the old policy to the extent of the "boot" received in the exchange. The payment of cash by a policyowner in an exchange does not constitute the receipt of boot.

25. In general, to claim the exclusion, the taxpayer must have owned and used the home as a principal residence for an aggregate time period of 2 years out of the 5-year period immediately preceding the home's date of sale.

26. a. $500,000 is the maximum amount of the exclusion.

    b. $250,000 is the maximum amount of the exclusion.

27. If the taxpayer fails to fully meet the ownership and use rules or the "once every 2 years" rule for claiming the exclusion, and the sale of the home is due to a change of the taxpayer's place of employment, a change of health, or other "unforeseen" circumstances, the $250,000 or $500,000 maximum amount (whatever amount would otherwise be available if the taxpayer fully met the requirements) is reduced. The maximum exclusion is multiplied by the ratio of the amount of time that the taxpayer's qualifying period of ownership and use bears to 2 years. The resulting figure is the maximum amount of gain that the taxpayer is permitted to exclude from gross income.

28. a.   The purpose of this provision is to prevent a tax-avoidance technique in which a taxpayer could (in the absence of the wash sale rule) sell stock, claim a tax loss from the sale, then quickly repurchase the same stock so that the taxpayer's economic position regarding the stock is essentially unchanged, but a tax savings is generated.

    b.   Taxpayers are not permitted to recognize a realized loss from the sale of corporate stock or other securities if the same stock or security is repurchased by the taxpayer within a 30-day period beginning before or ending after the sale in which the loss was realized.

Chapter 14

The Taxation of Capital Gains and Losses

Learning Objectives

An understanding of the material in this chapter should enable you to

LO 14.1   **Explain what a capital asset is, and identify items that are not treated as capital assets.**

LO 14.2   **Explain how the capital gain and loss rules apply to the sale or exchange of a capital asset.**

LO 14.3   **Describe the special rule for taxation on the sale or exchange of depreciable or real property used in a trade or business.**

LO 14.4   **Summarize the relationship between an asset's classification and its tax treatment for a sale or exchange.**

LO 14.5   **Describe the applicability and calculation of the tax on net investment income; identify strategies minimizing exposure to it.**

> Any reasonable system of taxation would be based on the slogan "Soak the Rich."
>
> —Heywood Broun

> Don't soak the rich, soak the poor. There's more of them.
>
> —Eric Wright

There are special, and generally more favorable, rules that apply to the taxation of capital gains and losses as distinguished from the taxation of ordinary income. The income tax rules for capital gains and losses apply to the proceeds realized upon the taxable sale or exchange of property that fits the Internal Revenue Code's definition of a capital asset.

The tax treatment of capital gains and losses has long been a social, political, and economic issue in the United States. Some observers believe that capital gains should not be taxed at all on the grounds that such gains are often attributable only to inflation, or on the grounds that appreciation of a capital asset held for investment is an accretion of wealth that should not be intruded on by the government. Other observers believe that capital gains and losses are merely one type of economic income, that there is nothing unique or special about such gains and losses, and that they should be taxed under the same rules as ordinary income, such as wages and salaries. For the most part, however, Congress has taken a path somewhere in the middle ground of these two opposite poles, taxing capital gains but providing more lenient treatment for such gains than that which is applicable to ordinary income.

There is generally a maximum tax rate of 20 percent applicable to most long-term capital gains of individual taxpayers. Under certain circumstances the maximum rate may be higher or lower depending on the type of asset involved and the income level of the taxpayer. Corporate taxpayers do not receive any special rate differential for capital gains as compared with other corporate income. There are special rules for the deductibility of capital losses, and these provisions also differ depending on whether the taxpayer is an individual or a corporation.

The specific rules for taxation of capital gains and losses will be discussed below. First, however, when considering the taxation of a specific transaction, the following questions should generally be asked:

- Is the asset giving rise to the gain or loss a capital asset under the Internal Revenue Code?

- Was there a taxable sale or exchange of the asset?

- In the case of an individual taxpayer, was the gain or loss a long-term or short-term gain or loss?

In addition to the rules applicable to specific transactions, there are procedures for combining or "netting" all of a taxpayer's capital gains and losses for the year. There are also provisions defining and limiting under what circumstances capital losses can be deductible. Finally, there is a special category of assets called "Sec. 1231" assets that combine the tax features of capital assets with those that give rise to ordinary income or loss. Those assets will also be discussed.

LO 14.1   Explain what a capital asset is, and identify items that are not treated as capital assets.

THE DEFINITION OF A CAPITAL ASSET

capital asset

Under Sec. 1221 of the Internal Revenue Code, a **capital asset** is defined as any property the taxpayer owns (connected with a business activity or not) except for the following types of property that are specifically excluded from the definition:

- "stock in trade" (that is, inventory) of the taxpayer or other property held by the taxpayer primarily for sale to customers in the ordinary course of the taxpayer's business

- depreciable or real property used in the taxpayer's trade or business

- a copyright; a literary or artistic composition; a letter or memorandum; or similar property held either by the creator of the property, or by a taxpayer whose basis in the property is determined in whole or in part by reference to its basis in the hands of the creator of the property, or by (in the case of a letter or memorandum) the taxpayer for whom the property was prepared or produced

- accounts or notes receivable acquired in the ordinary course of business for services rendered or for the sale of inventory or inventory-type property

- supplies of a type regularly used or consumed in the ordinary course of a trade or business

- publications of the United States government that are held by a taxpayer who did not purchase the publication or by a nonpurchasing transferee (i.e., a gift) of such a taxpayer

The types of assets listed above are those that are *not* treated as capital assets. Any other property held by a taxpayer is defined as a capital asset for income tax purposes. Consequently, most assets owned by taxpayers are treated as capital assets. Capital assets are typically personal use and investment property.

As of 2007, a musical composition or copyright in a musical work that is held by the creator(s) of the work or by a taxpayer whose basis in the work is determined by reference to its basis in the hands of the creator(s) can be treated as a capital asset at the election of the taxpayer. For sales and exchanges prior to 2007, such an asset was not treated as a capital asset. Do note that a painter or an author is not eligible for this election.

LO 14.2   **Explain how the capital gain and loss rules apply to the sale or exchange of a capital asset.**

THE REQUIREMENT OF A SALE OR EXCHANGE

Generally, there must be either a sale or an exchange of a capital asset in order for the capital gain and loss rules to apply. For example, the mere holding of investment property over a period of time does not give rise to a capital gain or loss, even though the property may have substantially appreciated. There must be a realization of gain or loss for a taxable event to occur. In the case of capital assets, realization of gain or loss generally occurs through a sale or a taxable exchange of the asset.

Example

Hannah owns stock in General Motors with a current value of $10,000. Her basis in the stock is $7,500. If Hannah sells the stock, she will realize a gain of $2,500, which is taxable. However, if she keeps the stock, no taxable event has occurred.

If some specific rule of the Internal Revenue Code provides that a particular asset can be sold without recognition of gain (such as the sale of a principal residence, subject to limitations), the sale of such an asset is not a taxable event. Also there are tax rules that limit the deductibility of various types of losses incurred by an individual taxpayer. Basically, losses of individual taxpayers are deductible only if they are incurred in a business activity or in a transaction entered into for profit, or if they are casualty or theft losses. The sale or exchange of the asset must give rise to a taxable gain or deductible loss under other requirements of the Internal Revenue Code before the specific rules determining the treatment of capital gain and loss are applied.

LO 14.3　　**Describe the special rule for taxation on the sale or exchange of depreciable or real property used in a trade or business.**

LONG-TERM VERSUS SHORT-TERM GAINS AND LOSSES

With regard to individual taxpayers, different rules and tax rates apply depending on whether the capital gain or loss is long-term or short-term. This discussion will be restricted to the rules in effect as of the date of printing of this text. The rules in this area have frequently been changed.

Holding Periods

holding period

Whether a sale or exchange of an asset results in long-term or short-term gain or loss for tax purposes depends on the period of time the asset was held by the taxpayer (the **holding period**). Sales of capital assets held by the taxpayer for "more than" 12 months result in long-term gains and/or losses. Sales of capital assets held by the taxpayer for 12 months or less result in short-term gains and/or losses. Note that the long-term holding period is not exactly 12 months but "more than" 12 months. It is important to note that the holding period is counted by months, and not by days. For example, publicly traded stock the taxpayer held as an investment would give rise to long-term gain or loss if sold one year and one day after it was purchased but not if it were sold exactly one year later. In cases of sales of property by a decedent's estate or other taxpayer who acquired property by bequest, devise, or inheritance, the applicable holding period is generally deemed to be more than 12 months regardless of the period of time actually held by the decedent and/or party inheriting the property.

Carryover of Holding Period

In certain situations, the holding period of one taxpayer who previously owned an asset carries over to the holding period of another taxpayer who currently owns it. This typically occurs in donative transactions where one person gives property to another. In such a case, the property's basis in the hands of the taxpayer who currently owns it is determined by reference to its basis in the hands of the previous owner, so the holding period will "carry over." Similarly, if property has a basis in the hands of the taxpayer that is determined by reference to other property previously held by the taxpayer, the holding period will also carry over from the ownership of the other asset. This typically occurs where a taxpayer surrenders one property in exchange for another in a like-kind or nontaxable exchange transaction under the Internal Revenue Code (i.e., Sections 1031 and 1035).

> **Example**
>
> Gail owns an antique ring that she gives to her daughter, Daria. Gail's cost for the ring was $1,000, and she had owned it for 5 years. Its value is now $2,000. Daria's basis in the ring for purposes of computing taxable gain is $1,000, and her holding period is 5 years.

Corporations

For corporations, there is no tax significance regarding the holding period of a capital asset. This is so because no special tax rates apply to corporate capital gains and losses; such gains and losses are simply netted against one another. If there is a net capital gain for the year, the corporation pays tax on the net gain at ordinary income tax rates. If there is a net loss, the corporation cannot deduct the net capital loss against its other income but can carry it over to offset past or future capital gain. For individual taxpayers, the rate system and the netting procedures applicable to capital gains and losses are more complicated.

TAX RATES APPLICABLE TO CAPITAL GAINS OF INDIVIDUALS

Sales of capital assets held by an individual for more than 12 months are generally eligible for a maximum long-term capital gains rate of 20 percent. Sales of capital assets held for 12 months or less are treated as short-term capital gains and are subject to ordinary income tax rates, unless the short-term gains are offset by capital losses under the netting procedures discussed later in this chapter. Therefore there is a significant maximum rate differential between long-term and short-term capital gains. The maximum statutory tax rate on ordinary income is currently 39.6 percent.

collectible capital assets

Not all long-term capital gains of individuals are eligible for the maximum rate of 20 percent. First, the portion of long-term gain from the sale of depreciable real property that is attributable to unrecaptured depreciation (unrecaptured Sec. 1250 gain) claimed on the property is taxed at a rate of no higher than 25 percent. Second, long-term gain from the sale of **collectible capital assets** is taxed at a rate of no higher than 28 percent rather than 20 percent. "Collectible" assets include works of art, rugs, antiques, certain stamps, coins, precious stones and metals, and alcoholic beverages. Third, to the extent that the 10 or 15 percent marginal tax rate on ordinary income would otherwise apply to the capital gain, the maximum rate on most long-term gain is reduced from 20 percent to zero percent. This means that individuals in the 10 or 15 percent tax bracket do not pay tax on most long-term capital gains up to the point where their total taxable income, including such gains, exceeds the maximum amount subject to the 15 percent bracket. Any additional gains will be subject to the 20 percent maximum rate. Individuals in the 25, 28, 33 and 35 percent bracket pay a maximum rate of 15 percent. The highest capital gains tax rate of 20 percent is paid by taxpayers who are in the marginal tax bracket of 39.6 percent.

> **Maximum Tax Rates for Long-Term Capital Gains**
> - 28 percent: "collectibles" gain
> - 25 percent: gain attributable to unrecaptured depreciation on real estate
> - 20 percent: maximum long-term gains
> - 15 percent rate (25, 28, 33, 35 ordinary income rate bracket taxpayers) and zero percent rate (10 and 15 ordinary income rate bracket taxpayers)

LO 14.4   **Summarize the relationship between an asset's classification and its tax treatment for a sale or exchange.**

TAX TREATMENT OF CAPITAL LOSSES

For corporations, capital losses are deductible only against capital gains. If capital losses exceed capital gains for the year, the corporation will have a capital loss carryover as previously mentioned. Corporate taxpayers may carry capital losses back to each of the three preceding years (earliest year first) and forward to the next five years to offset capital gains in such years.

Corporate carryback or carryover losses are deemed short-term capital losses for netting purposes.

For individuals, there are more involved rules for the treatment of capital losses. First, capital losses are fully deductible against capital gains for the year. If a taxpayer has both short-term and long-term capital gains and/or losses, there are specific procedures for the "netting" of those gains and losses that will be discussed below. If the taxpayer has only capital losses and no capital gains, or if, under the netting procedures, the taxpayer's capital losses exceed capital gains for the year, the capital losses may be deducted from the taxpayer's ordinary income in an amount up to $3,000 per year. If such net capital losses exceed $3,000, the excess may be carried forward to future tax years by individual taxpayers until the excess losses are used up. For married taxpayers filing separately, the $3,000 capital loss limitation is reduced to $1,500. Losses retain their original character as carried forward, with a short-term capital loss carryover applied before a long-term capital loss carryover. Capital losses may never be carried backward to a prior tax year. Additionally, any unused carry forward capital losses expire at the death of the taxpayer.

HOW CAPITAL GAINS AND LOSSES ARE NETTED FOR INDIVIDUAL TAXPAYERS

netting baskets

Because there are different tax rates applicable to different categories of capital gains, and because capital gains and losses may be either long-term or short-term, the taxpayer needs to organize these gains and losses and take specific steps to determine whether he or she will have a net capital gain or loss and what type of net gain or loss it will be. To accomplish this result, gains and losses are first separated into various groups (commonly referred to as **netting baskets**) and netted separately against each other. Next, the net gains and/or losses from the various groups or baskets are once again netted against each other to calculate the amount and the character of a net gain or loss. The steps in this netting process may be summarized in the following way:

- Any short-term capital gains and losses are netted together to determine the amount of the taxpayer's net short-term capital gain or loss.

- Any long-term gains and losses from the sale of "collectibles" (the gain from which would be taxed at a maximum rate of 28 percent) are netted together to determine the taxpayer's net "collectibles" gain or loss.

- The portion of any long-term gains from the sale of real estate attributable to unre-captured depreciation (the gain from which would be taxed at a maximum rate of 25 percent) are added together to determine the taxpayer's total gain in this category.

- Long-term gains and losses from the sale of capital assets (the gain from which would generally be subject to the 20 percent maximum tax rate) are netted together to determine the taxpayer's net long-term capital gain or loss in this category.

Example

Natalie has $10,000 in long-term gains from the sale of assets eligible for the 20 percent maximum capital-gains rate this year. She also has $4,000 of losses from sales of the same type of assets. Her net gain in the 20 percent rate basket is $6,000 ($10,000 – $4,000).

After the gains and losses have been separated into these various baskets and netted against each other, there are additional netting procedures if one or more of the baskets contains a net capital loss. However, if there are only capital gains in the separate baskets there is no additional netting, and each category of capital gains is taxed at its applicable rate. For example, net short-term gains would be taxed at the rates applicable to the taxpayer's ordinary income. Net "collectibles" gain would be taxed at a maximum rate of 28 percent. Net long-term gains eligible for the 20 percent maximum rate would be taxed at that rate. But remember some taxpayers will have their capital gains taxed at rates of zero or 15 percent. The zero percent applies if the taxpayer's marginal rate on order income is 15 percent or less. It is 15 percent if the taxpayer's marginal rate on ordinary income is 25, 28, 33 or 35 percent.

If the taxpayer has net capital loss in any of the original netting baskets, the following additional netting steps apply:

- Any net short-term capital loss is first netted against net gains subject to the maximum rate of 28 percent ("collectibles" gain), then to gains subject to the maximum rate of 25 percent, then to gains subject to the maximum rate of 20 percent (or a lower rate, if applicable). In other words, net short-term capital losses are netted against the capital gains subject to the highest rates first.

- Any net long-term loss from collectibles is netted against any net 25 percent gain first, then against any net 20 percent gain. If the collectibles loss still has not been fully utilized, the balance may be netted against the taxpayer's net short-term capital gain for the year. Any remaining loss would be deductible against ordinary income subject to the $3,000 limitation.

- A net long-term capital loss from the sale of assets that would result in 20 percent gain if sold at a gain is handled in basically the same way: the excess loss is netted first against any net 28 percent gain, then against any net 25 percent gain, then against any net short-term capital gain. Any remaining loss would be deductible against ordinary income subject to the $3,000 limitation.

Example

Assume the same facts as in the previous example except that Natalie also has a net long-term loss from the sale of collectibles of $5,000 this year. Natalie may offset $5,000 of her $6,000 of net capital gain subject to the 20 percent maximum rate with the $5,000 of losses from her collectibles. She will then have $1,000 of long-term capital gain subject to the maximum rate of 20 percent.

Although this netting process seems quite complicated, it is actually rather logical and arises from a simple concept. The long-term loss netting "baskets" (those containing 28 percent, 25 percent, or 20 percent net losses) are first netted against the long-term gain baskets that have gain subject to the highest maximum rate first, then the next highest, and so forth. Net long-term losses are netted against net short-term capital gains only after all the long-term gain baskets have been "netted out." Similarly, net losses in the short-term baskets are netted against net gains in the long-term baskets subject to the highest maximum rates first. In this way, net long-term capital gains subject to higher rates are netted out before the baskets subject to the lower rates. This is a reasonably fair netting system for taxpayers, although the structure of the overall tax system for capital gains and losses still looks more complicated than it really should.

SEC. 1231 GAINS AND LOSSES: THE "BEST OF BOTH WORLDS"

In the foregoing discussion of the taxation of capital gains and losses, it was noted that the Internal Revenue Code defines a capital asset as property owned by the taxpayer except for certain specifically enumerated types of property that are excluded from the definition of a capital asset. One of the exceptions to the definition of a capital asset is "depreciable or real property used in the taxpayer's trade or business."

Generally, property that is excluded from the definition of a capital asset will produce ordinary income or loss if sold rather than capital gain or loss. However, depreciable or real property used in the taxpayer's trade or business is a special type of property for tax purposes that is treated under Sec. 1231. This section of the Internal Revenue Code requires that in order to receive the special tax treatment provided to Sec. 1231 assets, the property must have been held by the taxpayer for more than one year. In other words, depreciable and real property used in the taxpayer's trade or business will be treated as a Sec. 1231 asset if held by the taxpayer for more than one year. If such property is held for a year or less, it will be treated as ordinary income property in a manner similar to property that falls within any of the other exceptions to the definition of a capital asset (such as inventory or stock in trade).

The Taxation of Sec. 1231 Assets

Simply stated, upon the sale or taxable exchange of property that meets the definition of a Sec. 1231 asset, gain will be treated as long-term capital gain and loss will be treated as ordinary loss. This means that gain from the sale of such property will be eligible for the lower maximum tax rates on long-term capital gain, while loss from the sale of such property will be deductible from the taxpayer's ordinary income without regard to the capital loss limitations.

> **Example**
>
> Michael owns a pickup truck that he acquired for $22,000 and uses exclusively in his business. His adjusted basis in the truck is $19,000 (after deducting depreciation of $3,000). He sells the truck for $12,000 and does not acquire another vehicle at the time of the sale. His $7,000 loss on the sale of the truck is treated as an ordinary loss. If he had sold the truck for $25,000, his $6,000 of gain would be treated as a capital gain of $3,000 and ordinary income of $3,000 (The ordinary income of $3,000 represents that portion of his gain subject to recapture of depreciation).

If a taxpayer has more than one sale or taxable exchange of Sec. 1231 assets during one year, all gains and losses from such sales are grouped or "netted" together to calculate the net gain or loss from the disposition of Sec. 1231 assets. If the result is a net gain, the gain is taxed as long-term capital gain. If the result is a net loss, the loss is treated as an ordinary loss deductible in full from the taxpayer's ordinary income. This is a unique type of treatment under the federal income tax law, and it really does give the taxpayer the "best of both worlds": long-term capital-gain treatment and ordinary loss treatment with respect to the same type of asset.

As illustrated in the above example, if an asset is sold that is subject to depreciation recapture, capital-gain treatment under Sec. 1231 will apply only to that portion of the gain that is not subject to depreciation recapture (i.e., only the real gain, the excess of selling price over original cost, receives long-term capital gain treatment).

Special "Recapture" of Sec. 1231 Losses

There is a "catch" to this best of both worlds treatment. To the extent that a taxpayer in the prior 5 taxable years has deducted net Sec. 1231 losses from ordinary income, any net gains from Sec. 1231 property otherwise taxable as capital gain will be taxed as ordinary income. This rule in effect creates a 5-year window for looking back to previously deducted Sec. 1231 losses to determine whether Sec. 1231 net gains for the current year must be converted from long-term capital gains to ordinary income. If there have been net losses from Sec. 1231 assets during the previous 5 years, the best of both worlds treatment does not apply until an amount of net Sec. 1231 gains equal to the amount of such previously deducted losses has been reported by the taxpayer as ordinary income. In essence, the previously deducted Sec. 1231 losses are recaptured as ordinary income.

Example

Jake sells real property used in his business this year at a gain of $50,000. Two years ago, Jake sold other real property used in his business at a loss of $35,000 and deducted the loss as an ordinary loss. Therefore $35,000 of Jake's gain in the current year will be treated as ordinary income, and only $15,000 of the current gain will be eligible for capital-gains tax rates.

LO 14.4   **Summarize the relationship between an asset's classification and its tax treatment for a sale or exchange.**

SUMMARY OF PROPERTY CLASSIFICATIONS

To determine the proper tax treatment for the sale or exchange of an asset as described in this chapter, the asset must be properly classified by the taxpayer. Generally assets can be thought of as falling into one of three categories:

- capital assets
- Sec. 1231 assets
- assets that are neither capital assets nor Sec. 1231 assets

Capital assets will be subject to the rules applicable to capital gains and losses. Sec. 1231 assets will receive long-term capital-gains treatment for net gains (subject to the recapture rule just discussed) and ordinary loss treatment for net losses. All other assets will result in ordinary income or ordinary loss if sold. Remember, however, that the tax law allows loss deductions to individual taxpayers only for sales of assets that are used in a business, or assets that are used in an activity engaged in for profit, or for casualty and theft losses. Specific rules for each of these types of losses limit and define how the losses can be deducted. Remember also that not all sales and exchanges that result in a realized gain will result in a taxable event. If the sale or exchange qualifies under a provision in the Code that provides nonrecognition of realized gain, the gain from the sale of the asset may not be recognized for income tax purposes even though it is realized from an economic standpoint.

For business taxpayers, perhaps the most common type of ordinary income asset (one that is neither a capital asset nor a Sec. 1231 asset) is the taxpayer's inventory or property held primarily for sale to customers in the ordinary course of business. The sale of inventory will give rise to ordinary income or loss. For investors, a common type of property sold would be publicly traded stocks and bonds. Such property falls within the definition of a capital asset because it does not meet any of the exceptions to the definition (for example, it is not inventory and it is not depreciable property used in a business). The sale of such property will fall squarely into the tax rules for capital gains and losses. On the other hand, property eligible for depreciation deductions that is used in the taxpayer's business (such as machinery and equipment) is Sec. 1231 property that would receive the unique tax treatment available under that section after considering the impact of depreciation recapture. Before the tax consequences of a sale or exchange of property can be determined, the property must be correctly classified for income tax purposes.

Tax Uncertainty in Property Classifications

There may be uncertainty as to how a particular piece of property should be classified for income tax purposes. For example, some sales of real estate may raise the issue of whether the real estate was held as an investment or held for sale in the ordinary course of the taxpayer's business. If the former classification applies, gain will be taxed as capital gain. If the latter classification applies, the gain will be taxed as ordinary income. The answer to such a question may depend on whether the taxpayer was primarily engaged in renting properties as a profit-making activity (which would make the property a Sec. 1231 asset) or in buying properties for the purpose of reselling them (which would make the property the taxpayer's inventory).

These and other issues are factual questions that a court will examine if a dispute with the IRS results in litigation. Among the factors a court may consider are how often the taxpayer bought and sold properties, how long the taxpayer typically owned such properties, and the purposes the property served during the time held by the taxpayer. Similar questions may also arise with regard to sales of tangible and intangible personal property.

Rights to Receive Income

It should be noted that a right to receive income is generally not treated as "property" for purposes of the capital asset or Sec. 1231 definitions. Such a right is not even tested to determine what type of property it is under those definitions because, for tax purposes, it is not considered to be "property" at all. It is merely an anticipatory right to receive income. Therefore, if such a right is assigned for a price, the amount received for the right is treated as a receipt of the income generated by that right, and it is taxable as ordinary income. Examples of such rights to receive income include royalty and licensing rights, and income rights from extractive industries, such as oil and gas drilling.

NET INVESTMENT INCOME TAX

LO 14.5   **Describe the applicability and calculation of the tax on net investment income; identify strategies minimizing exposure to it.**

Applicability of Tax to Selected Individuals

For tax years beginning after December 31, 2012, certain high income taxpayers will be subject to a tax on net investment income. This tax is sometimes referred to as the "unearned income Medicare contribution tax." The tax equals 3.8 percent of the lesser of (1) net investment income or (2) the excess, if any, of modified adjusted gross income (MAGI) over the applicable threshold amount.

Net investment income includes investment income less deductions permitted against such income. Investment income includes interest, dividends, annuities, royalties and capital gains other than those held in a trade or business.

MAGI is derived by increasing adjusted income by the amount of any foreign earned income excluded less deductions taken regarding such foreign earned income. For most taxpayers, MAGI will be adjusted gross income.

The applicable threshold amount depends on the filing status of the taxpayer. If married filing jointly or a surviving spouse, it is $250,000. If married filing separately, it is $125,000. In all other cases, it is $200,000.

Calculation of the Net Investment Income Tax

It is possible for two taxpayers with identical MAGIs to pay different levels of net income tax. Remember the tax is imposed on the lesser of (1) net investment income or (2) the excess of MAGI over the applicable amount. Let's consider the income of Harry and Sally to illustrate this point.

Example

A single taxpayer, Harry, has $250,000 in wages and net investment income of $50,000 for a MAGI of $300,000. Harry would owe net investment income of 3.8 percent on the lesser of (1) net investment income of $50,000 or (2) $300,000 less $200,000 or $100,000. The tax would be 3.8% of $50,000 or $1,900. Contrast the tax result for Sally who has identical MAGI of $300,000 consisting of net investment income of $70,000 and wages of $230,000. Her net investment income tax would be 3.8 percent of $70,000 or $2,660.

Strategies to Minimize Application of the Tax

A taxpayer with MAGI less than the applicable amount avoids taxation of his net investment income. Taxpayers will seek to derive income from distributions from qualified plans or IRAs as well as interest from tax-exempt bonds, all of which are exempt from the tax. Additionally income from a trade or business as well as self-employment income are also exempt from the tax.

CHAPTER REVIEW

Key Terms and Concepts

capital asset
holding period

collectible capital assets
netting baskets

Review Questions

Review questions are based on the learning objectives in this chapter. Thus a [14.3] at the end of a question means that the question is based on learning objective 3. If there are multiple objectives, they are all listed.

1. Describe the policy behind capital-gains taxation and the issues involved in the development of that policy. [14.1]

2. What is the maximum tax rate that generally applies to long-term capital gains of individual taxpayers from sales of capital assets? [14.1]

3. a. How is the term "capital asset" defined in the Internal Revenue Code?
   b. What assets are specifically excluded by the Code from the definition of a capital asset? [14.1]

4. Explain the requirement that a sale or exchange of a capital asset must take place before determining how the asset is taxed. [14.2]

5. Explain the taxation of capital gains of individual taxpayers. [14.2]

6. How are capital losses treated for income tax purposes? [14.2]

7. Explain how an individual's capital gains and losses are "netted" for a given year. [14.2]

8. There are special rules pertaining to the gain or loss on the sale of depreciable or real property used in a trade or business. How are gains and losses of this type of property treated? [14.3]

9. Billy Bob owns a building used in his business. He has owned the building for 5 years. For various business reasons, Billy decides to sell the building at a loss. Explain how Billy's loss will be deductible, assuming that this is Billy's only sale or exchange of property during the year. [14.3]

10. Explain how taxpayers must carefully classify different types of property in order to properly determine the tax treatment of a sale of property. [14.4]

11. Describe the applicability and operation of the net investment income tax. [14.5]

Review Answers

1. The tax treatment of capital gains has long been a social, political, and economic issue in the United States. Some observers believe that capital gains should not be taxed at all on the grounds that such gains are often attributable only to inflation, or on the grounds that appreciation of a capital asset held for investment is an accretion of wealth that should not be intruded on by the government. Other observers believe that capital gains are merely one type of economic income, that there is nothing unique or special about such gains, and that they should be taxed under the same rules as ordinary income, such as wages and salaries. For the most part, however, Congress has taken a path somewhere in the middle ground of these two opposites poles, taxing capital gains but providing more lenient treatment for such gains than that which is applicable to ordinary income.

2. There is generally a maximum tax rate of 20 percent applicable to most long-term capital gains of individual taxpayers. This maximum rate may be higher or lower depending on the type of asset involved and the income level of the taxpayer.

3. a. Under Sec. 1221 of the Internal Revenue Code, a capital asset is defined as any property the taxpayer owns (connected with a business activity or not) except for certain types of property specifically excluded from the definition.

    b. The following types of property are specifically excluded by the Code from the definition of a capital asset are as follows:

    - "stock in trade" (that is, inventory) of the taxpayer or other property held by the taxpayer primarily for sale to customers in the ordinary course of the taxpayer's business

    - depreciable or real property used in the taxpayer's trade or business

    - a copyright; a literary or artistic composition; a letter or memorandum; or similar property held either by the creator of the property, or by a taxpayer whose basis in the property is determined in whole or in part by the creator of the property, or by (in the case of a letter or memorandum) the taxpayer for whom the property was prepared or produced.

    - accounts or notes receivable acquired in the ordinary course of business for services rendered or the sale of inventory or inventory-type property and supplies of a type regularly used or consumed in the ordinary course of a trade or business.

    - publications of the United States government that are held by a taxpayer who did not purchase the publication or by a nonpurchasing transferee (i.e., a gift) of such a taxpayer

    Note that musical compositions or copyrights in musical works held by the creator(s) of the work or by a taxpayer whose basis in the work is determined by reference to its basis in the hands of the creator(s) can now be treated as a capital asset.

4. In order for gain with respect to an asset to be taxed, there must be a realization of gain. In the case of a capital asset, realization of gain generally occurs through a sale or a taxable exchange of the asset.

5. Sales of capital assets held by an individual for more than 12 months are generally eligible for the maximum rate of 20 percent on long-term capital gains. Sales of capital assets held for 12 months or less are treated as short-term capital gains and are subject to ordinary income tax rates, unless the short-term gains are offset by capital losses. For lower bracketed taxpayers, the rate of taxation on long term capital gains is either 15 or zero percent. These two lower rates apply to taxpayers whose incomes fall below

$470,700 for joint filers and surviving spouses, $444,550 for heads of household, and $418,400 for single filers.

6.   For corporations, capital losses are deductible only against capital gains. If capital losses exceed capital gains for the year, the corporation will have a capital loss carryover.

For individuals, capital losses are fully deductible against capital gains for the year. If the individual has both short-term and long-term capital gains and/or losses, there are specific procedures for the netting of those gains and losses. If the individual has only capital losses and no capital gains, or if, under the netting procedures, the individual's capital losses exceed capital gains for the year, the capital losses may be deducted from the individual's ordinary income in an amount up to $3,000 per year. If such net capital losses exceed $3,000, the excess may be carried forward to future tax years by individual taxpayers until the excess losses are used up. For married taxpayers filing separately, the $3,000 capital loss limitation is reduced to $1,500.

7.   The steps in the netting process are as follows:

- Any short-term capital gains and losses are netted together to determine the amount of the taxpayer's net short-term capital gain or loss.

- Any long-term gains and losses from the sale of "collectibles" (the gain from which would be taxed at a maximum rate of 28 percent) are netted together to determine the taxpayer's net "collectibles" gain or loss.

- The portion of any long-term gains from the sale of real estate attributable to unrecaptured depreciation (the gain from which would be taxed at a maximum rate of 25 percent) are added together to determine the taxpayer's total gain in this category.

- Long-term gains and losses from the sale of capital assets (the gain from which would generally be subject to the 20 percent maximum tax rate) are netted together to determine the taxpayer's net long-term capital gain or loss in this category.

After the gains and losses have been separated into these various baskets and netted against each other, there are additional netting procedures if one or more of the baskets contains a net capital loss. However, if there are only capital gains in the separate baskets there is no additional netting, and each category of capital gains is taxed at its applicable rate.

If the taxpayer has net capital loss in any of the original netting baskets, the following additional netting steps apply:

- Any net long-term loss from collectibles is netted against any net 25 percent gain first, then against any net 20 percent gain. If the collectibles loss still has not been fully utilized, the balance may be netted against the taxpayer's net short-term capital gain for the year. Any remaining loss would be deductible against ordinary income subject to the $3,000 limitation.

- A net long-term capital loss from the sale of assets that would result in 20 percent gain if sold at a gain is handled in basically the same way: the excess loss is netted first against any net 28 percent gain, then against any net 25 percent gain, then against any net short-term capital gain. Any remaining loss would be deductible against ordinary income subject to the $3,000 limitation.

- Any net short-term capital loss is first netted against gains subject to the maximum rate of 28 percent ("collectibles" gain), then to gains subject to the maximum rate of 25 percent, then to gains subject to the maximum rate of 20 percent (zero or 15 percent rate, if applicable). In other words, net short-term capital losses are netted against the capital gains subject to the highest rates first.

8. Depreciable or real property used in the taxpayer's trade or business is a special type of property for tax purposes that is treated under the rules of Code Sec. 1231. On the sale or exchange of such property, gain will be treated as long-term capital gain and loss will be treated as ordinary loss.

9. The building owned by Billy Bob is a Sec. 1231 asset. If Billy sells the building this year at a loss and it is Billy's only sale or exchange of property during the year, the loss will be deductible from Billy's ordinary income without regard to the capital loss limitations.

10. To determine the proper tax treatment for the sale or exchange of an asset, the asset must be properly classified by the taxpayer. Generally assets fall into one of three categories. Capital assets, the first category, will be subject to the rules applicable to capital gains and losses. Sec. 1231 assets, the second category, will receive long-term capital-gains treatment for net gains (subject to the recapture rule) and ordinary loss treatment for net losses. The third category is all other assets, and they will result in ordinary income or ordinary loss if sold. Since the tax treatment for the sale or exchange of an asset differs between the categories, it is necessary that an asset be correctly classified before the tax consequences of its sale or exchange can be determined.

11. Under current law, a 3.8 percent "net investment income" tax applies to taxpayers whose MAGI exceeds the threshold amounts. The tax is imposed on the lesser of (1) net investment income or (2) the excess of MAGI over the applicable amount.

Chapter 15

The Alternative Minimum Tax

Learning Objectives

An understanding of the material in this chapter should enable you to

LO 15.1   Explain how the alternative minimum tax (AMT) is applied.

LO 15.2   Describe the special AMT rules that apply to corporations.

> The art of taxation consists in so plucking the goose as to obtain the largest possible
> amount of feathers with the least possible amount of hissing.
>
> —Jean Baptiste Colbert (attributed)

alternative minimum tax (AMT)

The **alternative minimum tax (AMT)** is a separate method of calculating income tax liability. It is often referred to as a "parallel" system of income taxation. It applies in cases where the calculation of the AMT results in a higher tax liability than the calculation of the regular income tax. The purpose of the AMT is to prevent the taxpayer from reducing his or her tax liability below reasonable levels through the use of certain tax benefits targeted by the AMT rules. Therefore, in calculating the AMT, certain tax benefits available under the regular tax rules are limited or prohibited under the AMT calculation. Consequently when the AMT is calculated using different rules for these tax benefits, certain taxpayers will have a higher tax liability under the AMT calculation. Such tax benefits that are restricted under the AMT system may be loosely referred to as "tax-preference" items. Our current AMT system applies to individuals, corporations, estates, and trusts.

alternative minimum taxable income (AMTI)

The AMT is calculated by first determining the taxpayer's **alternative minimum taxable income (AMTI)**. The calculation of AMTI uses the taxpayer's regular taxable income as a starting point and then makes adjustments to reflect the impact of tax-preference items, including the elimination or reduction of certain deductions and/or credits and the addition of certain items of income that are excludible for regular tax purposes. The AMTI is reduced by an exemption, if applicable, to arrive at the AMT base. The AMT base is multiplied by special rates to compute the tax, which is called the tentative minimum tax (TMT). Taxpayers are required to pay the greater of the TMT or their regular income tax.

Taxpayers who are subject to the AMT in one or more years may be able to claim a credit against the regular income tax in later tax years when they are not subject to the AMT.

LO 15.1   Explain how the alternative minimum tax (AMT) is applied.

ITEMS OF TAX PREFERENCE

Some of the more significant tax-preference (and adjustment) items that are handled differently in computing AMTI as compared with taxable income for regular tax purposes are as follows:

Some itemized deductions allowable on Schedule A of Form 1040 for regular tax purposes cannot be claimed for AMT purposes; that is, they are tax-preference items.

Deductions for state and local taxes or sales taxes, real estate taxes, and miscellaneous itemized deductions are examples of itemized deductions not allowable for AMT purposes.

However, certain itemized deductions of individuals *are* permitted to be claimed as deductions in calculating AMTI. These are as follows:

- charitable contributions
- casualty and theft losses
- interest on indebtedness used to acquire or improve a qualified residence of the taxpayer
- investment interest not in excess of qualified net investment income
- the deduction for estate taxes attributable to income in respect of a decedent
- medical expenses deductible for regular tax purposes and exceeding 10 percent of AGI.

The overall limitation on itemized deductions does *not* apply in calculating AMTI.

There are deductions or exclusions taken for regular tax purposes which are added to regular taxable income as part of calculating AMTI. The most notable are as follows:

- The standard deduction is not allowable in computing AMTI. If an individual taxpayer uses the standard deduction for regular tax purposes, the amount of the standard deduction is added back to taxable income in calculating AMTI.
- Personal and dependency exemptions are not allowable in computing AMTI. Like the standard deduction, any exemption amounts claimed for regular tax purposes must be added to the taxpayer's regular taxable income in calculating AMTI .

- When the actual value of an incentive stock option at the time the option holder's rights become nonforfeitable exceeds the price paid for the option, the excess must be included in calculating AMTI.

- A portion of certain deductions for depreciation allowable for regular tax purposes is not allowable for AMT purposes. For example, in claiming deductions for depreciation on real property, only straight-line depreciation using a 40-year recovery period is allowable in calculating AMTI. Any excess of that amount claimed for regular tax purposes is disallowed. Also, with respect to depreciable personal property placed in service after 1998, the 150 percent declining-balance method (switching to straight-line depreciation) must be substituted for property that qualifies for the 200 percent declining-balance method for regular tax purposes. Certain different adjustments were made to depreciation deductions for personal property placed in service before 1999. These adjustments apply to both individuals and corporations. However, "bonus" depreciation is allowed in full for purposes of the AMT

- Interest on nongovernmental purpose bonds (i.e., private activity bonds) issued after August 7, 1986, that is excludible from gross income for regular tax purposes, must be included in the calculation of AMTI by both individuals and corporations.

Other deductions allowable for regular tax purposes are disallowed or otherwise partially restricted for AMT purposes for both individuals and corporations. These preference items include

- amortization of pollution control facilities

- mining exploration costs

- certain intangible drilling costs incurred by businesses engaged in extractive industries

Corporations are subject to an AMT adjustment for "adjusted current earnings." This preference will be discussed in more detail later in this chapter.

THE AMTI EXEMPTION

After AMTI is calculated, it may be reduced by an exemption amount. The applicable exemption amount is determined by the taxpayer's filing status and is phased out for upper-income taxpayers. The phaseout of the AMTI exemption is determined by calculating the amount of the taxpayer's AMTI that is in excess of a specified threshold amount and then multiplying that excess by 25 percent. The resulting figure is the amount of the AMTI exemption that is disallowed. If the amount disallowed is more than the AMTI exemption, then the exemption is zero.

For the tax year 2017, the exemption amounts and the threshold amounts for phasing out the exemption are shown in the following table:

Filing Status	Exemption Amount	Phaseout Threshold Range
Married filing jointly	$84,500	$160,900
Single and head of household	54,300	120,700
Married filing separately	42,250	80,450
Estate or trust	24,100	80,450
Corporations	40,000	150,000

Example

In 2017 Anthony, a single taxpayer has AMTI of $104,300. Their AMT exemption amount ($54,300) is reduced by $12,500 (25% × $50,000 [$104,300 − $54,300]).
So, their AMT exemption amount for 2017 is $41,800 ($54,300 − $12,500).

The AMT exemption amounts have, in recent years, been adjusted on a short-term basis by Congress. The AMT exemptions are substantially and permanently increased minimizing the likelihood of upper middle-income taxpayers owing AMT. However, the Congress may always change the exemptions as it sees fit.

AMT TAX RATES

Once the taxpayer's AMTI has been reduced by the applicable exemption amount, the amount of the remaining AMTI, or tentative minimum taxable income (AMT base) is multiplied by the applicable alternative minimum tax rate to arrive at the tentative minimum tax (TMT). The applicable rates are shown in the following table:

Taxpayer	AMT Tax Rate
Individuals other than married filing separately	26 percent of the first $187,800
	28 percent of the excess over $187,800
Married filing separately	26 percent of the first $93,900
	28 percent of the excess over $93,900
Corporations	20 percent

Individuals who have net long-term capital gains or qualified dividends for regular tax purposes receive the benefit of a lower maximum tax rate on such gains and dividend income. Those lower maximum rates also apply to those categories of income for AMT purposes. Therefore, if a taxpayer has long-term capital gains or qualified dividend income, the AMT will not result in a higher tax rate on those items. *Note: The inclusion of net long-term capital gains and qualifying dividend income in the AMTI calculation can result in loss of the AMT exemption by increasing AMTI.*

Example

Mary, a single taxpayer, has AMTI of $234,500 this year after the application of her AMTI exemption. She has no dividend income or long-term capital gains. Her alternative minimum tax liability is the sum of $48,828 (.26 x $187,800) plus $13,076 {($234,500 − $187,800) x .28)} or $61,904.

OTHER FACTORS IN THE CALCULATION OF THE AMT

Net Operating Loss

Generally, if a taxpayer has a net operating loss (NOL) from a business activity, the NOL may currently be used to eliminate up to 90 percent of the taxpayer's AMTI. The NOL allowable for AMT purposes may be different from that calculated under the regular tax rules since it is adjusted for any preference items that were used in determining the regular NOL.

Tax Credits

The tax credit for children and the adoption credit may be used to offset AMT liability as well as liability for the regular tax. Also, any foreign tax credit allowable in computing the regular tax may be used to offset AMT liability. However, the overall credits cannot exceed the sum of both the regular tax liability (less the foreign tax credit) and the excess of the TMT over the regular tax (the AMT). Certain business energy credits may also be claimed for AMT purposes.

Other nonrefundable individual tax credits are also generally allowable against AMT liability under current law.

LO 15.2   **Describe the special AMT rules that apply to corporations.**

APPLICATION OF THE AMT TO CORPORATIONS

S Corporations

The AMT does not apply to S corporations because they are pass-through entities that are not subject to income tax at the entity level. However, shareholders in S corporations may be subject to the AMT on their individual returns.

C Corporations and the "Small Corporation" Exemption

C corporations are generally subject to the AMT. However, certain C corporations are exempt from the application of the AMT. For tax years beginning after 1997, the AMT does not apply to C corporations that fit a specific definition of a "small corporation." To meet this exception, the corporation must meet an average annual gross receipts test. This test is applied as follows:

- For new corporations, average annual gross receipts must not exceed $5 million for the corporation's first 3 taxable years. The corporation's first year is counted under the 3-year test, but the corporation will not be subject to the AMT for its first year. The initial year's gross receipts are annualized under the test. After the initial test is passed, the corporation must not have 3-year average annual gross receipts in excess of $7.5 million or its exemption will be lost.

- For corporations in existence before 1997, a $5 million average annual gross receipts test is applied to the 3 taxable years beginning with the first taxable year ending after December 31, 1993. If the corporation was not in existence for 3 years when this test is applied, it is then applied on an average basis to the period of the corporation's existence. Note that all corporations in existence in 1997 must have passed the test for the 1997 tax year and qualified for the exemption or else the exemption was permanently lost. Once the gross receipts test is passed, the corporation must not have 3-year average annual gross receipts in excess of $7.5 million or the exemption will be lost.

The ACE Adjustment for Corporations

adjusted current earnings (ACE) adjustment

book income

One tax-preference item that applies only to corporations subject to the AMT and not to individual taxpayers is the **adjusted current earnings (ACE) adjustment**. Essentially, this adjustment takes into account certain items that are not treated as taxable income for regular tax purposes but are treated as so-called "book" income for accounting purposes. **Book income** may be loosely defined as a calculation of income for accounting purposes that is computed somewhat differently than the calculation of income for tax purposes.

An important element included in the ACE adjustment is book income attributable to life insurance owned by a corporation. Such income for purposes of calculating adjusted current earnings includes both death benefits that are received tax free for regular tax purposes and increases in a life insurance policy's cash value that are not subject to the regular income tax. The ACE adjustment is calculated by adding to AMTI 75 percent of the amount by which the corporation's adjusted current earnings exceeds its AMTI. To avoid a circular calculation, the excess of adjusted current earnings over AMTI is computed using AMTI without regard to the adjustment. Seventy-five percent of the excess is then added to the corporation's AMTI base.

This adjustment can potentially result in up to 75 percent of a corporation's life insurance proceeds being subject to the AMT. Using a 20 percent AMT tax rate, an effective tax rate of up to 15 percent on life insurance proceeds could result (that is, the amount of proceeds $\times$ .75 $\times$ .20 tax rate).

Note that premiums paid on a life insurance contract reduce the ACE adjustment. Therefore premiums paid can reduce the amount of the corporation's income subject to the AMT. Correspondingly, increases in cash value of insurance contracts (as well as the receipt of death benefits) raise the adjustment.

It is also important to understand that the effective AMT rate of 15 percent on life insurance proceeds is the most severe tax result possible under the ACE adjustment. The actual result of the adjustment in many cases will be considerably less than the 15 percent effective rate. This is so because the AMT is only payable to the extent that the TMT exceeds the regular income tax. Corporations with few tax-preference items other than the ACE adjustment may not have AMT liability substantially in excess of regular tax liability. Consider also that the highest corporate tax rates under the regular tax are much higher than the 20 percent AMT rate. Even though 75 percent of adjusted current earnings may be includible in AMTI, this does not necessarily mean that there will ultimately be a 15 percent additional tax on life insurance benefits and cash values because the TMT liability may not be significantly higher (or higher at all) than regular tax liability. In cases where the corporation's regular tax exceeds its TMT, there will be no additional tax resulting from the ACE adjustment.

The term "adjusted current earnings" corresponds somewhat closely to the calculation of a corporation's earnings and profits. Earnings and profits is a calculation used as a measure to determine the taxability of distributions to corporate shareholders. It is related to, but not the same as, a corporation's taxable income. Similarly, the ACE adjustment includes items not included in the regular taxable income computation.

There are items other than life insurance values and benefits included in the ACE adjustment for AMT purposes. However, discussion of other specific items is beyond the scope of this text.

CHAPTER REVIEW

Key Terms and Concepts

alternative minimum tax (AMT)
alternative minimum taxable income
    (AMTI)

adjusted current earnings (ACE)
    adjustment
book income

Review Questions

Review questions are based on the learning objectives in this chapter. Thus a [15.2] at the end of a question means that the question is based on learning objective 2. If there are multiple objectives, they are all listed.

1. What is the alternative minimum tax (AMT)? [15.1]

2. Explain the meaning of the following concepts pertaining to the AMT:

    a. alternative minimum taxable income (AMTI)

    b. tax-preference items

    c. the AMTI exemption [15.1]

3. What itemized deductions are allowable to individuals in computing AMTI? [15.1]

4. How is the standard deduction treated for AMT purposes? [15.1]

5. How is personal property placed in service after 1998 and depreciated under the 200 percent declining balance method for regular tax purposes treated as a tax-preference item under the AMT? [15.1]

6. Explain how the benefit of the AMT exemption amount is phased out for taxpayers who have AMTI in excess of certain levels. [15.1]

7. a. What is the tax rate if an individual taxpayer is subject to the AMT?

    b. What is the tax rate if a corporation is subject to the AMT? [15.2]

8. Under the "small corporation" exemption from the AMT, what is the maximum amount of 3-year average annual gross receipts that applies when

    a. the corporation is initially being tested for the small corporation exemption?

    b. the corporation is already exempt from the AMT and is being tested for retaining its exemption? [15.2]

9. Explain the adjusted current earnings (ACE) adjustment that affects the calculation of the corporate AMT. [15.2]

10. How can the ACE adjustment affect the income tax treatment of life insurance proceeds? [15.2]

Review Answers

1. The alternative minimum tax, or AMT, is a separate method of calculating income tax liability. It is often referred to as a "parallel" system of income taxation. It applies in cases where the calculation of the AMT results in a higher tax liability than the calculation of the regular income tax. The purpose of the AMT is to prevent the taxpayer from reducing his or her tax liability below reasonable levels through the use of certain tax benefits targeted by the AMT rules. Therefore, in calculating the AMT, certain tax benefits available under the regular tax rules are limited or prohibited under the AMT calculation.

2. a. The AMT is calculated by first determining the taxpayer's alternative minimum taxable income (AMTI). The calculation of AMTI uses the taxpayer's regular taxable income as a starting point, then makes adjustments to reflect the impact of tax-preference items including the elimination or reduction of certain deductions and/or credits and the addition of certain items of income that are excludible for regular tax purposes.

b. In calculating the AMT, certain tax benefits available under the regular tax rules are limited or prohibited under the AMT calculation. Consequently when the AMT is calculated using different rules for these tax benefits, certain taxpayers will have a higher tax liability under the AMT calculation. Such tax benefits that are restricted under the AMT system may be loosely referred to as "tax-preference" items.

c. After AMTI is calculated, it may be reduced by an exemption amount. The applicable exemption amount is determined by the taxpayer's filing status and is phased out for upper-income taxpayers.

3. Certain itemized deductions of individuals are permitted to be claimed as deductions in calculating AMTI. These are as follows:

- charitable contributions
- casualty and theft losses
- interest on indebtedness used to acquire or improve a qualified residence of the taxpayer
- investment interest not in excess of qualified net investment income
- the deduction for estate taxes attributable to income in respect of a decedent
- medical expenses deductible by taxpayer(s) of any age to the extent of exceeding 10 percent of AGI.

The overall limitation on itemized deductions does not apply in calculating AMTI.

4. Taxpayers who have used the standard deduction for regular tax purposes must add back the amount of the standard deduction in computing AMTI.

5. With respect to depreciable personal property placed in service after 1998, the 150 percent declining-balance method (switching to straight-line depreciation) must be substituted for property that qualifies for the 200 percent declining-balance method for regular tax purposes.

6. The phaseout of the AMTI exemption is determined by calculating the amount of the taxpayer's AMTI that is in excess of a specified threshold amount and then multiplying that excess by 25 percent. The resulting figure is the amount of the AMTI exemption that is disallowed. If the amount disallowed is more than the AMTI exemption, then the exemption is zero.

7. a. For individuals, the tax rate is 26 percent on the first $187,800 of income subject to the AMT, or Tentative Minimum Taxable Income (other than long-term capital gains and qualified dividends) and 28 percent on amounts in excess of $187,800.

    b.   For corporations, the tax rate is 20 percent.

8. a.   For new corporations, average annual gross receipts must not exceed $5 million.

    b.   For corporations that passed the initial test, average annual gross receipts must not exceed $7.5 million.

9. The ACE adjustment takes into account certain items that are not treated as taxable income for regular tax purposes but are treated as so-called book income for accounting purposes. The ACE adjustment is calculated by adding to AMTI 75 percent of the amount by which the corporation's adjusted current earnings exceeds its AMTI. To avoid a circular calculation, the excess of adjusted current earnings over AMTI is computed using AMTI without regard to the adjustment. Seventy-five percent of the excess is then added to the corporation's AMTI base.

10. The ACE adjustment can potentially result in up to 75 percent of a corporation's life insurance proceeds being subject to the AMT. Using a 20 percent AMT tax rate, an effective tax rate of up to 15 percent on life insurance proceeds could result (that is, the amount of proceeds x .75 x .20 tax rate).

Note that premiums paid on a life insurance contract reduce the ACE adjustment. Therefore premiums paid can reduce the amount of the corporation's income subject to the AMT. Correspondingly, increases in cash value of insurance contracts (as well as the receipt of death benefits) raise the adjustment.

Chapter 16

Income Taxation
of Life Insurance

Learning Objectives

An understanding of the material in this chapter should enable you to

LO 16.1   **Describe the extent to which life insurance death benefits may be excluded from gross income, and explain how life insurance living benefits are treated for income tax purposes.**

LO 16.2   **Explain the income tax treatment of disability income payments, benefits payable from medical expense coverages, and premiums paid for both personal and business life and health insurance.**

LO 16.3   **Explain the tax consequences of life insurance with respect to transfers for value, lack of insurable interest, corporate distributions, charitable contributions, separation and divorce, additional compensation, and split-dollar arrangements.**

LO 16.4   **Explain the income tax restrictions on certain amounts paid in connection with insurance contracts.**

I'm proud to be paying taxes in the United States. The only thing is—I could be just as proud for half the money.

—Arthur Godfrey

Life insurance has received favorable tax treatment since 1916 when the federal income tax law first exempted life insurance death benefits from taxation. Although the laws concerning taxation of life insurance have changed since then, Congress has continued to recognize both the social value and utility of sheltering life insurance from the erosion imposed by the federal income tax.

Although death proceeds of life insurance enjoy shelter from the impact of federal income tax in the vast majority of instances, the very nature of life insurance as valuable property as well as its flexibility in solving human problems has led to its imaginative use in business and personal situations where careful planning is required to avoid income tax pitfalls. Thus all proposed transfers of life insurance should be closely examined to avoid transfer for- value problems; the requirement of insurable interest should be taken into account as a tax-oriented dimension of concern; the proper arrangement of policy ownership and beneficiary designation should be given thorough consideration where premiums are paid with business dollars; and the disposition or use of life insurance in separation and divorce cases should be accomplished with specialized guidance to avoid unfavorable tax results. It should also be understood that there are now strict limitations on deductibility of policy loan interest.

The questions of life insurance premium deductibility and taxation are of special concern in charitable giving and in planning life insurance fringe benefits for selected employees. Again, in these complicated yet common transactions, the desired tax results can best be accomplished through an awareness of the tax principles involved.

LO 16.1   **Describe the extent to which life insurance death benefits may be excluded from gross income, and explain how life insurance living benefits are treated for income tax purposes.**

GENERAL RULES

Life Insurance Death Benefits

Lump-Sum Payments

Generally, life insurance death benefits payable by reason of death of the insured are excluded from the gross income of the beneficiary,[1] regardless of whether the beneficiary is an individual or an entity. In addition to death benefits payable under individual life insurance policies, the term death benefit payments, for purposes of exclusion from income tax, includes death benefits payable under accident and health insurance contracts as well as workers' compensation insurance,[2] but does not include death benefits payable under an annuity contract. Death gratuity payments made by the United States government to families of deceased military personnel are tax exempt, even though not paid under a life insurance policy.

Death Benefits from Currently Issued Employer-Owned Policies

With respect to employer-owned policies issued after August 17, 2006, there are special rules and limitations on the income tax exclusion for death benefits. These rules are generally in conformity with currently accepted practices in the insurance industry. In general, to preserve the full benefit of the income tax exclusion for death proceeds, an insured employee under an employer-owned policy must have been an employee of the policyowner at any time during the 12-month period before the insured's death, or must have been a director, a highly

---

1.   IRC Sec. 101(a)(1).
2.   Treas. Reg. Sec. 1.101-1.

compensated employee, or a highly compensated individual with respect to the policyowner at the time the insurance policy was issued. The terms "highly compensated employee" and "highly compensated individual" are defined in generally the same way (with certain modifications) as those terms are defined for purposes of the tax laws governing qualified retirement plans and self-insured medical reimbursement plans, respectively.

The death proceeds will be excludible from income tax without regard to these limitations if the proceeds are paid to a member of the insured's family, to the insured's designated beneficiary, or to the insured's estate or a trust established for a family member or designated beneficiary. The rules are generally intended to restrict the use of employer-owned life insurance where the death proceeds are payable to the employer.

There are also recordkeeping requirements in the form of employer notice and employee consent provisions that must be followed for employer-owned contracts issued after August 17, 2006.

These rules are covered here for the purpose of providing a general awareness of these so-called "best practices" rules that apply to currently issued employer-owned policies. A more detailed explanation of the rules is beyond the scope of this text.

Interest Option

When death proceeds are held by the insurer for future withdrawal or distribution and only interest on the proceeds is paid to the beneficiary, the full amount of the interest payment is taxable.[3]

Installment Options

For policies maturing by death, that portion of each payment made under the fixed-period, fixed-amount, or life income installment options representing the principal of death proceeds is received tax free, but that portion representing interest is taxable. To calculate the taxable portion, the lump-sum death benefit that could have been received tax free is prorated over the payment period of the option, and the portion of each payment representing principal is tax free. The remainder representing interest is reportable as ordinary income.[4] In this calculation, the payment period of the option must be determined. Where the fixed-period option is in operation, the payment period is the number of guaranteed annual installments; where the fixed-amount option is in operation, it is the number of annual installments of a specified

---

3.   IRC Sec. 101(c).
4.   IRC Sec. 101(d)(1).

amount produced under the guaranteed interest rate in the policy; and, under the life income option, the payment period is the life expectancy of the beneficiary. (If the life income option has a refund or period-certain feature, the present value of such feature must be subtracted from the lump-sum death proceeds before proration.) Life expectancy and valuation of refund features are determined on the basis of mortality tables prescribed by the secretary of the Treasury in the regulations.

Amounts paid as a survivor annuity on account of the death of a public safety officer killed in the line of duty are generally excludible from gross income and not subject to the rules just described.

Interest Exclusion

With respect to deaths of insureds that occurred before October 23, 1986, a surviving spouse-beneficiary may still exclude from income up to $1,000 of interest payable under a settlement option, but only where the option is installment in nature—that is, if the payments are a true combination of both interest and principal. This special interest exclusion was repealed with respect to deaths of insureds occurring after October 22, 1986.[5]

Accelerated Death Benefits Paid to Terminally or Chronically Ill Insureds

Amounts received under a life insurance contract covering the life of an insured who is terminally or chronically ill are now excludible from gross income as amounts payable by reason of the death of the insured if certain requirements are met. The amounts received qualify for the exclusion if paid by the insurance company or by a licensed viatical settlement provider. The exclusion does not apply if the amounts are paid to a taxpayer other than the insured if the insured is a director, officer, or employee of the taxpayer or has a financial interest in a business conducted by the taxpayer.

terminally ill insured

A **terminally ill insured** is one who has been certified by a physician as having an illness or condition that can be expected to result in death within 24 months of the date the certification is given.

There are additional requirements for the exclusion to apply if the insured is "chronically ill" rather than "terminally ill." Basically, the exclusion for accelerated benefits paid to a chronically ill insured applies only if the benefit is paid under a rider or provision of the life insurance

---

5.   P.L. 99-514, Tax Reform Act of 1986, Sec. 1001(a).

contract that is treated as a qualified long-term care insurance contract within the meaning of IRC. Sec. 7702B. Therefore a life insurance contract without such a provision or rider can pay excludible accelerated benefits only to a terminally ill insured. A "chronically ill" insured has the same meaning as it has for purposes of the income tax rules applicable to long-term care insurance contracts. The tax rules applicable to benefits paid from such contracts also generally apply for purposes of the accelerated benefits exclusion.[6]

Life Insurance Living Benefits

Policy in Force

Many types of permanent life insurance policies permit withdrawals without policy termination. However, tax-deferred buildup of internal policy values is still allowed for policies that permit withdrawals, and the doctrine of constructive receipt will not apply if such an insurance policy meets certain actuarial tests. If these tests are not met, then the policy will be treated as a combination of term life insurance and a currently taxable fund.

Life insurance policy dividends are generally not taxable income but are treated as a return of a portion of the premium, whether they are received in cash, used to either reduce or purchase additional coverage, or left with the company.[7] However, if aggregate dividends received or credited exceed the taxpayer's cost basis in the contract, such excess is taxable as ordinary income.[8] Interest earned on dividend accumulations is taxable in the year the taxpayer has the right to withdraw the interest. The taxpayer has constructive receipt of such interest income whether or not it is withdrawn.

Withdrawals of cash value from a life policy are generally taxed on a first-in first-out (FIFO) basis; that is, withdrawals are treated as a nontaxable return of capital to the extent of premiums paid. Withdrawals in excess of premiums paid are taxable.

However, it is critically important to understand that withdrawals will be taxed as income first (a last-in first-out [LIFO] treatment) if the policy is classified as a modified endowment contract (MEC).

In addition, withdrawals from a life insurance policy that are made during the first 15 policy years and are associated with a reduction in the policy's death benefit will also be subject to LIFO tax treatment, even if the policy is not a MEC.

---

6.   IRC Sec. 101(g).
7.   IRC Sec. 72(e)(1)(B); Treas. Reg. Sec. 1.72-11(b)(1).
8.   Ibid.

Withdrawal features are typically associated with universal life policies. Taxable withdrawals during the first 5 policy years will have a higher taxable portion than withdrawals made during policy years 6 through 15. The maximum portion of any such withdrawal subject to income tax is that amount by which the policy cash value exceeds aggregate premiums paid on the policy.

There is a ceiling on the amount of taxable income associated with such withdrawals, however. The ceiling is based on the policy year during which the taxable withdrawal is made and the applicable test for life insurance used to satisfy the definition of life insurance after the withdrawal. The applicable test could be either the cash value accumulation test or the guideline premium test.

Lump-Sum Payments

Where the owner of a life insurance contract receives the lifetime maturity proceeds or cash surrender value of the policy in one lump-sum payment from the insurance company, the amount received in excess of the owner's cost basis is taxed as ordinary income.[9] Cost basis may be defined as the investment in the contract, which is the sum of premiums paid, minus nontaxable policy dividends and other nontaxable distributions actually received, minus extra premiums paid for certain supplementary benefits, such as waiver of premium and accidental death protection.[10]

Outstanding loans on a life insurance policies at the time of surrender or termination require additional planning to inform clients of a very real risk of being deemed to have received taxable income in an amount much greater than the actual cash received. To the extent the amount of the outstanding loan exceeds the policy holder's basis in the contract, there will be gain taxed as ordinary income. In *Kenneth F. Reinert v. Commissioner*, TC Summ. Op. 2008-163, the taxpayer had paid $8,685.60 in premiums while borrowing a total of $28,664.21. At the time of termination, the policy had cash value of $29, 933.78. The Tax Court held the taxpayer liable in the amount of $21,248.18 representing the sum of the outstanding debt of $28,664.21 and the net cash received of $1,269.57 or $29,933.78 less the aforementioned premium payments of $8,685.60.[11]

Gain realized upon surrender or maturity of United States Government Life Insurance (WWI) or National Service Life Insurance (WWII) is exempt from tax.[12]

---

9.   IRC Sec. 72(e).

10.   Rev. Rul. 55-349, 1955-1 C.B. 232.

11.   *John Morgan Sanders v. Commissioner* (termination of a policy), T.C. Memo. 2010-279, and *Reid Chambers et al. v. Commissioner (termination of a policy)*, T.C. Summ. Op. 2009-63 reached similar results.

12.   38 USC Sec. 3101(a).

No loss is recognized where, upon maturity or surrender, the amount received is less than the policyowner's basis. The difference often represents the cost of pure insurance protection— a nondeductible expense.

When the owner of a life insurance contract sells the policy to a third party, such a transaction has not been considered a sale or exchange of a capital asset for income tax purposes by the IRS.[13] Possibly in response to the growing secondary market for the sale of life insurance policies, the IRS has provided some guidance on the tax consequences to the seller of a life insurance contract (Rev. Rul. 2009-13) and the purchaser (Rev. Rul. 2009-14).

Rev. Rul. 2009-13 covered three different situations producing different characterizations of the income. Situation 1 dealt with an owner-insured who surrendered a policy to the insurer for a cash surrender value of $78,000, $10,000 of which reflected a cost-of-insurance charge. The taxpayer had paid $64,000 in premiums. The taxpayer was found to have ordinary income of $14,000 reflecting the difference between the cash surrender value and premiums paid.

Situation 2, incorporating the facts of Situation 1, dealt with the same owner-insured who sold the policy in its eighth year for $80,000 to an unrelated investor who lacked an insurable interest. Recognizing both "investment" and "insurance" characteristics of life insurance contracts, the IRS concluded part of the gain was taxable as ordinary income and part as capital gain. The gain element was calculated by subtracting from the $80,000 the $64,000 in premium payments reduced by the $10,000 in cost-of-insurance charges. The gain of $26,000 was deemed to be ordinary income of $14,000 to reflect the inside build-up and $12,000 in capital gain ($26,000 gain less $14,000 of inside build-up).

Situation 3 dealt with the sale of a term life policy with no cash surrender value. The owner-insured sold for $20,000 to an unrelated individual after paying $45,000 in premiums. While the entire amount of the proceeds was treated as capital gain, the Service calculated the basis in the policy by reducing the premiums paid by $44,750, the cost of insurance protection. Thus the taxpayer had capital gain of $20,000 less basis of $250 or $19,750.

Rev. Rul. 2009-14 covered the tax consequences to the purchasers of term life insurance. In Situation 1, the purchaser acquired for $20,000 a fifteen year term policy from the owner- insured. The purchaser had no insurable interest in the insured and his sole goal was profit. At the death of the insured 18 months later, the purchaser had made additional premium payments of $9,000. The purchaser received $100,000 as a death benefit. Citing the transfer for value rule of Section 101(a) of the Internal Revenue Code, the Service ruled the purchaser had ordinary

---

13. *Commissioner v. Phillips,* 275 F.2d 33 (CA 4, 1960). *Barr,* TC Memo 2009–250; *Eckersley et ux. v. Commissioner,* TC Memo 2007–282.

income in the amount of $71,000 [the difference between the death benefit ($100,000) and the basis ($20,000 purchase price plus $9,000 in premium payments].

Situation 2, incorporating the facts of Situation 1, addressed the tax consequences at the time of sale to another investor while the insured remained alive. The original purchaser received $30,000 from the second investor. His gain was treated as $1,000 of long term capital gain deeming the life insurance contract a capital gain asset since it did not qualify as an exclusion as a capital asset under Section 1221(a)(1) through 1221 (a)(8). The gain represented the difference between the proceeds ($30,000) and adjusted basis of $29,000 (The sum of the original purchase price of $20,000 and $9,000 in additional premium payments).

Interest Option

Where the policyowner leaves maturity or cash surrender values with the insurance company under the interest-only option, the interest earned will be taxable as ordinary income when received or credited to the payee.[14] In addition, at the time of maturity or surrender, if the values available to the policyowner exceed the cost basis, the gain will be taxed as ordinary income even though the lifetime proceeds are left with the insurance company, provided the policyowner also reserves the right to withdraw the proceeds at any time.[15] This right of withdrawal places the policyowner in constructive receipt of the gain. To avoid constructive receipt and thereby postpone the tax on any gain, the policyowner must elect the interest option before maturity or surrender and give up the right to withdraw the proceeds.[16] In such a case, the person who ultimately receives the proceeds will bear the tax liability for the gain.

Installment Options

When the policyowner places maturity or cash surrender values under any of the installment options, the annuity provisions of the Internal Revenue Code apply.[17] Part of each installment payment is considered a return of principal and is not subject to tax. The percentage of each installment received tax free is found by dividing the investment in the contract by the expected total return.[18] The Code provides a "60-day rule"[19] that affects the definition of "investment in the contract." The rule has significance when, at the time of maturity or surrender, the lifetime proceeds exceed the owner's cost basis. The rule enables the policyowner to avoid

---

14. IRC Sec. 72(j).
15. Treas. Reg. Sec. 1.451-2; *Blum v. Higgins,* 150 F.2d 471 (CA 6, 1945).
16. *Constance C. Frackelton,* 46 B.T.A. 883, acq. C.B. 1944, p. 10.
17. IRC Sec. 72(a).
18. IRC Sec. 72(b).
19. IRC Sec. 72(h)(2).

immediate tax on the gain, but as a result a larger percentage of the installment payments will be subject to tax. The rule works this way: If the policyowner elects the installment option no later than 60 days following the date of maturity or surrender of the policy, there will be no tax on the unrealized gain until installments begin, and investment in the contract will be the aggregate of premiums paid minus dividends, loans, and premiums for certain supplementary benefits.[20] If, on the other hand, the owner delays electing the installment option until beyond the 60-day period, the owner will be taxed on the total unrealized gain as of the time of maturity or surrender. Correspondingly, the investment in the contract will then be increased to the total maturity or surrender value to reflect this taxable event, thus enlarging the tax-free portion of future installments. This will be accomplished, however, at the expense of exposing the total gain on the contract to taxation in one year.

Where the option selected is the life income option, the investment in the contract is reduced by the actuarial value of any refund or period-certain feature.[21] The expected total return under the fixed-period option is determined by multiplying the fixed number of years or months by the amount of the guaranteed payment provided in the contract for such period.[22] Under the fixed-amount option, the expected total return is determined by multiplying the fixed-installment amount by the number of guaranteed installments.[23] Under the life income option, the expected return is determined by multiplying the periodic payment by the payee's life expectancy as determined by government tables.[24]

Contingent Beneficiaries

contingent beneficiary

Where the primary payee dies before receiving all installments under the fixed-period or fixed-amount options, the **contingent beneficiary** will be taxed in the same manner as was the primary payee. That is, the contingent beneficiary will exclude the same portion of each installment from income and include the same portion of each installment in income.[25] However, where the primary payee is receiving a life income settlement and dies during a period of guaranteed payments, the contingent beneficiary will have no taxable income until the total amount received, when added to the amount that was received tax free by the primary payee,

---

20.   Treas. Reg. Sec. 1.72-12.
21.   IRC Sec. 72(c).
22.   Treas. Reg. Sec. 1.72-5(c).
23.   Treas. Reg. Sec. 1.72-5(d).
24.   Treas. Reg. Sec. 1.72-5(a).
25.   Treas. Reg. Sec. 1.72-11(c)(1)(2), Example 4.

exceeds the investment in the contract.[26] Thereafter the full amount of each payment will be taxed as ordinary income.

LO 16.2 **Explain the income tax treatment of disability income payments, benefits payable from medical expense coverages, and premiums paid for both personal and business life and health insurance.**

Health Insurance Benefits

Disability Income Payments

Disability income insurance can be provided as a rider to a life insurance policy or through a separate contract. In either event, income payments on policies owned and paid for by the insured are received by the insured tax free.[27] When payments are made to a policyowner other than the insured—for example, to a corporation that has purchased the disability income insurance as key person insurance—the benefits paid by the insurance company continue to be tax free.[28]

A different situation arises, however, where disability income insurance is paid for by an employer to fund a wage continuation plan for employees, and the benefits are paid by the insurance company directly to the individual employees. Upon receipt of disability income from such a policy, an employee must include amounts received under the policy in income.

Medical Reimbursement

Benefits payable from hospital and surgical policies, major medical policies, and other insured medical expense coverages, whether from an individual or group policy, are exempt from income tax.[29] This rule also applies to qualified long-term care contracts, subject to certain limitations.

However, any benefits received must be used to reduce the amount of related medical expenses otherwise deductible for the year. In addition, to the extent that reimbursement is received for medical expenses taken as a tax deduction in a prior year, it will be taxable in the current year.

---

26. Treas. Reg. Sec. 1.72-11(c)(1)(2), Example 1.
27. IRC Sec. 104(a)(3).
28. *Castner Garage, Ltd.,* 43 B.T.A. 1, acq. (1935).
29. IRC Sec. 105(b).

Income Tax Treatment of Premiums

Personal Life Insurance

The general rule with respect to the income tax treatment of life insurance premiums is that they are a personal expense and as such are not deductible.[30] The rule applies whether the premium is paid by the insured, the beneficiary, or the policyowner. Exceptions to the general rule exist in certain situations based upon the use to which the life insurance is put. Examples include premiums paid for life insurance owned by a qualified charitable organization, premiums paid for life insurance by an ex-spouse as part of an alimony decree, and premiums paid by a business for life insurance used to fund certain employee compensation plans.

Business Life Insurance

Generally premiums paid on business life insurance are not deductible. The Internal Revenue Code is explicit: "No deduction shall be allowed for . . . premiums on any life insurance policy, or endowment or annuity contract, if the taxpayer is directly or indirectly a beneficiary under the policy or contract."[31] Moreover, premiums on business life insurance have been characterized by the Internal Revenue Service as a capital investment and not a business expense, even though the policy is term insurance.[32] However, in certain situations where an employer is not a policy beneficiary, premiums paid on a policy covering the life of an employee may be deductible.

Personal Health Insurance

The Internal Revenue Code provides that premiums paid for personal disability income insurance are not deductible.[33] Included in the definition of disability income insurance are policies that pay a weekly income payment to the insured while hospitalized.[34]

Premiums paid for medical reimbursement insurance are considered a medical care expense under the Code[35] and are deductible to the extent that they, along with other itemized medical expenses, exceed 10 percent of adjusted gross income. Different rules apply to self-employed taxpayers.

---

30.   Treas. Reg. Sec. 1.262-1(b)(1); IRC Sec. 264(a)(1).
31.   IRC Sec. 264(a)(1).
32.   OD 699 C.B. 3, 1261.
33.   IRC Sec. 213(d)(1).
34.   Rev. Rul. 68-451, 1968-2, C.B. 111.
35.   IRC Sec. 213(d)(1)(C).

Business Health Insurance

Where an employer pays premiums on a disability income policy on the life of an employee and benefits are payable to the employer, no premium deduction is allowable,[36] but benefits are received tax free. This tax treatment is similar to key person life insurance owned by a business on a key employee.

However, where the employer pays premiums on disability income insurance with benefits paid directly to the employees under a wage continuation plan, such premiums are deductible by the employer and are not taxable to the covered employee,[37] provided such premium payments, when added to all other compensation paid to the covered employees, do not exceed a reasonable allowance for personal services rendered.[38]

Premiums paid by an employer on a policy providing medical reimbursement to the employee are deductible to the employer and are not taxable to the employee,[39] if they meet the test of reasonableness and are part of an employee benefit plan.[40]

LO 16.3   **Explain the tax consequences of life insurance with respect to transfers for value, lack of insurable interest, corporate distributions, charitable contributions, separation and divorce, additional compensation, and split-dollar arrangements.**

LIFE INSURANCE ARRANGEMENTS GIVING RISE TO TAX CONSEQUENCES

Transfer for Value

transfer-for-value rule

Perhaps the most prominent exception to the general rule that life insurance death proceeds are tax exempt is the **transfer-for-value rule**.[41] Where a policy transferred by assignment or otherwise for a valuable consideration matures by reason of death, the transferee will be liable for income tax on the amount of death proceeds in excess of the actual value of the

---

36.   Rev. Rul. 66-262, 1966-2 C.B. 105.
37.   IRC Sec. 106.
38.   IRC Sec. 162(a)(1).
39.   IRC Sec. 106.
40.   Treas. Reg. Sec. 1.162-10(a).
41.   IRC Sec. 101(a)(2).

consideration paid for the contract plus the total of net premiums and other amounts subsequently paid by the transferee.[42] This rule, which seems to be deeply grounded in public policy, is designed to prevent a tax-free windfall that might come about from speculation in life insurance policies. Life insurance enjoys an income tax-favored position because of its unique economic function of protecting families and business interests that would profit more by the insured's continued life than by death. Therefore one who buys life insurance policies for speculation with the hope of realizing a substantial monetary profit on the death of the insured will not enjoy a tax exemption.

However, certain transfers of life insurance for consideration are not motivated by a desire for profit but for valid personal or business reasons. Therefore Congress included five exceptions in the Code to the transfer-for-value rule.[43] When any one of these exceptions applies, the full death proceeds will be income tax free in the hands of the beneficiary even though the policy was transferred for a valuable consideration.

The five specified exceptions are (1) transfers to the insured, (2) transfers to a partner of the insured, (3) transfers to a partnership in which the insured is a partner, (4) transfers to a corporation in which the insured is a shareholder or an officer, and (5) transfers in which the transferee's basis in the transferred policy is determined in whole or in part by reference to the transferor's basis. This latter exception (occasionally referred to as the carryover-basis exception) would apply in a tax-free exchange, where, for example, one corporation transfers a corporate-owned key person policy to another corporation in a tax-free reorganization. The carryover-basis exception may also apply where a policy is transferred in a part-sale/part-gift transaction.[44] In part-sale/part-gift transfers the basis of the property transferred in the hands of the transferee is determined by reference to the transferor's basis where the amount paid by the transferee for the property is less than the transferor's adjusted basis in the property.[45] This exception also applies to transfers of policies between spouses incident to a divorce, since such transfers are nontaxable.[46]

It is worthwhile to reflect on other transfer situations that are not covered by these exceptions and yet may be motivated by personal or business reasons that are equally as valid as those

42.   Treas. Reg. Sec. 1.101-1(b).
43.   IRC Sec. 101(a)(2)(A)(B).
44.   Rev. Rul. 69-187, 1969-16 I.R.B. 8.
45.   "Where a transfer of property is in part a sale and in part a gift, the unadjusted basis of the property in the hands of the transferee is the sum of—(1) Whichever of the following is the greater: (i) the amount paid by the transferee for the property, or (ii) the transferor's adjusted basis for the property at the time of the transfer . . . ." Treas. Reg. Sec. 1.1015-4(a).
46.   IRC Sec. 1041.

surrounding the exceptions enumerated in the Code. One can think of many family transfers that would not involve speculation but would be made for sound estate planning reasons. One significant omission is the transfer of a policy from an insured who is a shareholder in a closely held corporation to a fellow shareholder. As in the transfer of a policy from a partner-insured to a fellow partner, there may be sound business reasons for such a transfer, yet the rule excepts the latter but not the former. Conscientious planners need to be especially mindful of these nonexceptions.

The tax results of a transfer-for-value problem can be onerous. Because of the aleatory nature of a life insurance contract, the amount exposed to ordinary income in one year can be substantial. Thus careful attention must be paid to every transfer of a life insurance policy in order to avoid the tax pitfall of the transfer-for-value rule. Examples of transfers that are not uncommon but that violate the rule include the ones that follow:

- A policyowner sells a policy on his or her life to a corporation in which he or she is an employee and/or member of the board of directors. (The insured must be a shareholder or officer.)

- Alice and Bruce own all the stock of a corporation and enter into a buy-sell agreement on a cross-purchase basis. Instead of buying new life insurance on each other's lives to fund the agreement, Alice and Bruce each transfer to the other an existing policy on their lives. (Coshareholders are not exempt transferees.)

- The Alice-Bruce Corporation has a stock redemption agreement with Alice and Bruce funded with corporate-owned insurance on Alice and Bruce. The parties wish to change the stock retirement arrangement to a cross-purchase plan. The corporation transfers Alice's policy to Bruce and Bruce's policy to Alice.

The above transactions are clearly transfers for value subject to tax at the death of the insured. Planning techniques may be available to achieve the desired results without falling into the transfer-for-value "trap." Other more subtle situations may bring the rule into play. In some instances the parties may be unaware that a transfer is being made or of the consideration involved.

For example, assume that corporate owners, Alice and Bruce, enter into a cross-purchase buy-sell arrangement and elect to fund it with group life insurance—a procedure not normally recommended. Alice, on her group certificate, names Bruce as beneficiary; and Bruce, on his certificate, names Alice as beneficiary. Alice and Bruce may not be consciously aware that they are transferring anything to each other, but the broad definition of "transfer for a valuable consideration" given in the regulations seems to suggest that Alice and Bruce are transferees for value:

> . . . a "transfer for a valuable consideration" is any absolute transfer for value of the right to receive all or a part of the proceeds of a life insurance policy. Thus the creation, for value, of an enforceable contractual right to receive all or a part of the proceeds of a policy may constitute a transfer for a valuable consideration of the policy or an interest therein.[47]

Thus it might be argued that Alice and Bruce have transferred for consideration an interest in their group life insurance to each other. The consideration seems to consist of reciprocal promises to fund their business agreement with cross-beneficiary designations.

A policy that has been transferred for value can be cleansed of the taint by a subsequent transfer of the policy, for value or otherwise, to an exempt transferee—for example, the insured.[48] However, the transfer-for-value taint is not removed by a subsequent gift of the policy to a nonexempt transferee. Thus where Robert, the insured, sells his $10,000 policy to Stanley, his son, for $3,000 and Stanley then gives the policy to his sister, Dawn, the policy is still subject to the transfer-for-value rule. At the insured's death, the proceeds in excess of $3,000, plus premiums paid subsequent to the transfer to Stanley, will be subject to income tax.[49]

Lack of Insurable Interest

insurable interest

The concept of **insurable interest** has had an influence on the taxation of life insurance proceeds. Lacking the requisite insurable interest, life insurance has been viewed as a mere wagering contract entered into for profit. This was the view of the court in a case[50] where a corporation paid the premium on accidental death insurance on its truck drivers, with the corporation named as beneficiary of the death proceeds. When a driver was killed, the proceeds collected by the corporation were held to be profits subject to income tax. It was the view of the court that the truck driver was not a key person and that the corporation did not at any time have an insurable interest in the truck driver's life. The question of insurable interest in a business insurance situation is one that continues to merit careful attention.

In an earlier case[51] the Tax Court went so far as to tax the proceeds of a key person policy where an insurable interest existed at the inception of the contract but presumably not when the

---

47.   Treas. Reg. Sec. 1.101-1(b)(4).
48.   Treas. Reg. Sec. 1.101-1(b)(3).
49.   See citation in footnote 46, *supra*.
50.   *Atlantic Oil v. Patterson,* 331 F.2d 516 (CA 5, 1964).
51.   *Francis H. W. Ducros,* 272 F.2d 49 (CA 6, 1959).

policy matured as a death claim. On appeal, however, the U.S. Court of Appeals for the Sixth Circuit reversed and held that the proceeds were not taxable for lack of an insurable interest. The court pointed out that local law required an insurable interest only at the time of inception of the contract. As a general rule, the requirement of insurable interest applies only at the time of policy inception.

It is possible for a business to have an insurable interest in a key person who is not an employee. In one Tax Court decision,[52] the IRS argued that key person life insurance proceeds received by a corporation on the life of an independent contractor were taxable as ordinary income. But the Tax Court disagreed, holding that the insured's services as a real estate developer were essential to the success of the corporation and that the corporation had a valid insurable interest in the real estate developer's life. As a result, the tax-free nature of the death proceeds was preserved. The question of insurable interest at policy inception continues to be important.

Proceeds as Corporate Distributions

If business life insurance is arranged so that proceeds of policies that are owned and paid for by a corporation are paid to beneficiaries other than the corporation, complex tax problems will arise. For example, when the beneficiaries are shareholders of the corporation, they may think the proceeds paid directly to them by the life insurance company retain their tax-free character. The IRS has refused to accept this point of view, maintaining instead that such insurance proceeds are taxable as dividends because the result is the same as if the proceeds had been received tax free as life insurance proceeds by the corporation and then distributed to the shareholder as a dividend.[53] The IRS's position has the logical advantage, and this was acknowledged in at least one case.[54] Therefore in situations where a corporation owns and pays for life

---

52. *M. Lucille Harrison,* 59 T.C. No. 57 (1973).
53. Rev. Rul. 61-134, I.R.B. 1961–2.
54. *Golden v. Commissioner,* 113 F.2d 590 (CA 3, 1940); Rev. Rul. 71–79, I.R.B. 1971–7, 17. But see *Estate of J. E. Horne,* 63 T.C. No. 98 (1975), acq. in result, 1980–1 C.B. 1, where proceeds payable to a shareholder on a corporate-owned policy were held not to be dividends where the proceeds could also be included in the gross estate of the deceased for federal estate tax purposes by Treas. Reg. Sec. 20.2042-1(c)(6). The Horne case is perhaps an aberration. Its result was a unique attempt by the court to achieve a degree of equity between conflicting ownership concepts. Although in fact the corporation owned the life insurance policy, the Treasury's own estate tax regulations attributed ownership to the insured. In a 1981 Technical Advice Memorandum (LTR 8144001), the IRS took the position that when the death proceeds of a corporate-owned life insurance policy on a majority shareholder were paid to the deceased shareholder's spouse, the proceeds were excludible under IRC Sec. 101(a) because the beneficiary spouse was not a shareholder.

insurance to fund a buy-sell arrangement or to protect the corporation against the loss of a key employee, the corporation, and not the shareholders, should be the beneficiary.[55]

A collateral issue raised by unorthodox business insurance arrangements is taxability of the premiums. If a corporation pays premiums on business life insurance where shareholders are beneficiaries, or where shareholders are beneficiaries as well as owners of the life insurance, the premiums are taxable to the shareholders as dividends unless the premiums are taxable as compensation.[56]

It is key to remember that three types of losses are deductible to an individual: (1) losses incurred in a trade or business, (2) losses incurred in a transaction entered into for profit, and (3) casualty or theft losses. Section 165 of the Code generally allows deductions for such losses provided they are "not compensated by insurance or otherwise." The quoted language has been interpreted by the Tax Court in the Johnson case to include the death proceeds of life insurance. Therefore where a taxpayer purchased life insurance on the life of a partner to protect the investment in the partnership, and in fact such a loss was incurred on the partner's death, a loss deduction under Section 165 was disallowed because, according to the Tax Court, the life insurance proceeds compensated for the loss.[57]

The result in the Johnson case normally should not present a tax problem for businesses obtaining key person life insurance protection to provide funds to find a replacement or to fund a 303 stock redemption, a salary continuation arrangement, or a stock purchase or partnership purchase plan. The Johnson case will hopefully be applied as a precedent only in similar cases, namely, when the key person life insurance is specifically obtained to protect the surviving partner's investment in the partnership. There is a clear and direct link between an anticipated Section 165 loss and the acquisition of life insurance to compensate that loss—a link that is not normally associated with the acquisition of key person life insurance.

---

55. Where the insured is a controlling shareholder of a corporation, life insurance on the insured's life owned by the corporation but payable other than for the benefit of the corporation will be includible in its entirety in the insured's estate for federal estate tax purposes. Treas. Reg. Sec. 20.2042-1(c)(6).

56. Rev. Rul. 59-184, 1959-1 C.B. 65.

57. *A. N. Johnson,* 66 T.C. 897, (1976), aff'd. 78-1 USTC (CA-4, 1978). When the insured partner died, the surviving partner claimed a capital loss on liquidation of the partnership. It was this loss that the court held as compensated for by life insurance. The surviving partner argued unsuccessfully that (1) the life insurance compensated him for the loss of his partner's life, not for the loss of his investment in the partnership; (2) IRC Sec. 165 does not apply to life insurance; (3) unlike casualty insurance, the payment of life insurance death proceeds is not dependent on an investment loss; and (4) the disallowance of his loss deduction had the effect of taxing the life insurance death proceeds in contravention of IRC Sec. 101(a).

Charitable Contribution

Premiums paid on life insurance owned by a qualified charitable organization are deductible to the donor as a charitable contribution, subject to the charitable contributions limitations.[58] It is important that the charity be the owner of the policy and have the exclusive right to cash in the policy, borrow on it, or change the beneficiary.

One technique for achieving deductibility of life insurance premiums that is occasionally suggested is simply to name the charity as irrevocable beneficiary of the policy proceeds. This technique should be avoided because the desired tax benefits will not be obtained. The irrevocable beneficiary is given some ownership interest in the policy, but the exact result is frequently clouded, especially in the area of charitable giving. More importantly, the Internal Revenue Code denies a charitable deduction for gifts to charities where less than the taxpayer's entire interest in the property is contributed.[59] The Code specifically prohibits a charitable deduction under a charitable reverse split dollar arrangement.[60]

Separation and Divorce

Income tax consequences need to be considered carefully where life insurance is involved in separation agreements and divorce decrees.

Life Insurance in the Property Settlement

The transfer of property between two spouses incident to a divorce is generally nontaxable. The spouse who receives the property has a carryover basis and pays income tax on appreciation if the property is sold. This means that there is no taxable event with respect to cash values when life insurance is transferred as a result of a divorce.

Premium Payments

Premium payments by one spouse or former spouse for life insurance owned by and benefiting the other spouse are deductible as alimony by the payer-spouse under Section 215 of the Code and taxable to the payee-spouse under Section 71 of the Code if the following occurs:

---

58.   IRC Sec. 170; *Eppa Hunton IV*, 1 T.C. 821.

59.   IRC Sec. 170(f)(3).

60.   See IRC Sec 170 (f) (10) and Notice 99–36. The IRS, in two Revenue Rulings, anticipated this view. Rev. Rul. 76-1, I.R.B. 1976-1, 8 denied a charitable deduction for premiums paid on "split-life" insurance and in Rev. Rul. 76-143, I.R.B. 1976-16, 9 deductibility was denied for split-dollar plan premiums. In each instance the charity had a partial ownership interest in the plan.

- Payments are made in cash and terminate at the death of the payee-spouse.

- Payments are made under a divorce decree or separation agreement.

- The parties are not members of the same household and do not file joint tax returns.

- Payments are not for child support.

- Payments must be made for at least 3 years unless either spouse dies or the payee-spouse remarries.

Death Proceeds

Life insurance proceeds on the life of one spouse payable to the other spouse to discharge legal obligations imposed by a divorce decree, separation agreement, or support decree are exempt from income tax.

Additional Compensation

Where the employee is the policyowner and the employer has no beneficial interest in the policy, premium payments by an employer on an individual policy insuring the life of an employee may be deductible by the employer.

An employer might select certain favored employees for such a nonqualified fringe benefit. The employee applies for the policy and possesses all incidents of ownership. The employee names his or her own personal beneficiary for the death benefit, and the employer pays the annual premium. Such payment, if considered reasonable additional compensation to the employee for services rendered, will be deductible under Section 162 of the Code as an ordinary and necessary business expense.[61] It is important that the total amount of compensation realized by the employee, including the premium payment, meet the test of reasonableness. Also, the employer must not be a beneficiary of the policy, either directly or indirectly.[62]

Such premium payments by the employer are taxable to the employee when paid. The questions are often asked, Why arrange such a plan? Wouldn't it be equally effective if the employer simply increased the employee's salary by the amount of the premium and let the employee buy the life insurance with the increase in salary? It is true that the same tax result would follow, but whether the effect would be equal is the question to ponder. The employer has an opportunity to place himself or herself in a psychologically advantageous position by selecting one or

---

61.   *Twin City Tile and Marble Co.,* 32 F.2d 229 (CA 8, 1929); *Hubert Transfer and Storage,* 7 T.C.M. 171; Treas. Reg. Sec. 1.61-2(d)(2)(ii)(a).

62.   IRC Sec. 264(a); Rev. Rul. 70-148, I.R.B. 1970-14, 9; 1970-1 C.B. 60.

more key employees for the benefit plan. The package of benefits embodied in a life insurance contract such as a substantial death benefit, disability features, and lifetime guaranteed retirement income may be more appreciated by an employee (and especially by the family) than a nominal salary increase to cover the premium payment.

Split-Dollar Life Insurance

A well-known fringe benefit for selected employees is the split-dollar life insurance plan. Under such an arrangement, an employee and employer share or split the premium payments. In the most basic form of split-dollar, cash-value-type policies are used and the employer's share of the annual premium is measured by each year's increase in cash value. Correspondingly, the employee's share of each premium payment is the difference between each year's cash value increase and the amount of net premium due. The employer can be named beneficiary to the extent of the cash value. The employee can have the right to name his or her own beneficiary for the difference between the total death proceeds payable and the cash value.

Under such a plan, an employee receives a substantial amount of life insurance at a relatively low cost. The employer pays the major share of each premium (at some point in the life of the policy, the employer may be paying *all* the premium) and thus bestows an economic benefit on the employee. The employee is generally required to include in gross income each year the value of the economic benefit received.

The amount included in gross income can be determined under one of several different methods, depending upon the design of the plan and the date the plan was established. IRS guidance determines what method or methods of calculating the economic benefit are acceptable. Such methods are based upon the covered employee's age and the amount of insurance coverage. Any portion of the premium paid by the employee is subtracted from the amount otherwise taxable to the employee. If the employee's benefit under the plan consists only of current life insurance protection, the taxation of the arrangement can be relatively simple.

If the covered employee is provided with an interest in the policy's cash value as well as life insurance protection (a so-called "equity" split-dollar plan), the income tax consequences become more complex. Such arrangements can be taxed under economic benefit principles or under loan principles, depending upon the configuration of the plan. The tax consequences of these plans can be far more complicated than split-dollar in its simplest form. The IRS has issued regulations that govern the tax consequences of these plans.[63]

---

63.   See Regs 1.61–22 and 1.7872–15. See also Notice 2002–8.

No deduction is available to the employer for contributions to a split-dollar plan because the employer is also a beneficiary under such a policy within the meaning of Section 264(a) (1) of the Code.

LO 16.4   **Explain the income tax restrictions on certain amounts paid in connection with insurance contracts.**

Income Tax Restrictions on Certain Amounts Paid in Connection with Insurance Contracts

IRC Sec. 264 imposes severe restrictions on the deductibility of two types of payments typically incurred in connection with insurance contracts: premium payments and interest payments on policy loans.

Nondeductibility of Premiums

Premium payments on life insurance contracts are generally nondeductible, regardless of whether the policy is held as a personal asset or for business purposes. The only exceptions to this general rule arise when the taxpayer paying the premiums is not directly or indirectly a beneficiary under the policy, and the premiums qualify for a deduction under some specific rule of tax law. Such situations include certain premium payments deductible as charitable contributions, or as alimony payments, or as compensation paid to an employee. It must be emphasized that a deduction for premium payments may not be claimed in any case in which the taxpayer is a policy beneficiary.

This restriction applies to life insurance, endowment, and annuity contracts. The taxpayer need not be the named beneficiary of the policy for the disallowance of a premium deduction to apply. Basically any beneficial interest in the policy (such as the right to name or change the beneficiary) will prevent any deduction for premium payments.

Nondeductibility of Interest Payments

The current income tax law restrictions on the deductibility of interest paid or incurred in connection with insurance contracts are complex and severe. There are multiple layers of restrictions, one or more of which may apply depending on the context in which the policy is held, the policy's date of issue, and the specific nature of the circumstances surrounding the financial transaction involving the policy.

The general rule is that no interest deduction is allowable with respect to indebtedness incurred in connection with a life insurance, endowment, or annuity contract issued after June

8, 1997. Exceptions to this general rule provide for limited interest deductions for loans in connection with certain business-owned contracts, as discussed below. There are complex and overlapping sets of rules regarding interest deductions for policy loans with respect to policies issued on or before June 8, 1997. Those rules will be briefly discussed.

key person rule

key person

The "Key Person" Rule. This provision is the most significant exception to the general rule that interest deductions on policy loans are disallowed. The **key person rule** provides that interest on loan amounts not in excess of $50,000 per insured person is deductible if the insured or other covered person under the contract is a key person. The definition of a **key person** is an officer or 20 percent owner of the taxpayer. Clearly, this definition restricts the application of the key person rule to contracts owned by business taxpayers. Such taxpayers include both incorporated and unincorporated business entities.

There are further restrictions on the definition of a key person. The total number of key persons per business taxpayer may not exceed the GREATER of

- five individuals or
- the LESSER of
  - 5 percent of the total number of officers and employees of the business taxpayer, or
  - 20 individuals

This restriction means that in order for a business taxpayer to have more than five key persons for purposes of the tax rules for interest deductions on policy loans, the taxpayer has to have more than 100 employees. In addition, in order to have the maximum number of 20 key persons, the business taxpayer claiming the interest deductions would have to have at least 400 employees.

If the taxpayer is a corporation, the ownership rule of 20 percent is applied based on stock ownership. For unincorporated entities, the ownership test is based on ownership of a capital or profits interest in the business.

There are also limitations on the interest rate that may be used in calculating allowable interest deductions under the key person rule. The applicable interest rate for purposes of calculating deductions is the lesser of the interest rate specified in the contract or the rate of interest described as "Moody's Corporate Bond Yield Average—Monthly Average Corporates" as published by Moody's Investors Service, Inc., for the month in which the interest is paid or accrued.

The key person rules generally apply to policy loan interest paid or accrued after October 13, 1995. Different limitations applied to certain interest payments under so-called "transitional" rules pursuant to 1996 tax legislation. These transitional rules do not apply to any interest paid or accrued after 1998, so they will not be discussed here.

"Grandfather" Rule and Effective Dates. If an insurance contract was entered into before June 21, 1986, the key person rules and the $50,000 of indebtedness limitation do not apply. Interest on loans connected with such contracts may be deductible, subject to other layers of rules imposed by IRC Sec. 264. However, the monthly "Moody's" rate applies to current payments to limit the interest rate that may be used in calculating allowable deductions.

Contracts entered into between June 21, 1986, and June 8, 1997, that are owned by business entities are generally subject to the key person rules and $50,000 of indebtedness limitations with respect to interest paid or accrued after October 13, 1995. Under certain circumstances loans from policies owned by taxpayers other than business entities may be deductible if the contract was entered into on or before June 8, 1997. Contracts issued after June 8, 1997, can be eligible for interest deductions for policy loans only under the key person rules (which require business ownership of the contract), subject to the $50,000 of indebtedness limitation and other restrictions discussed below.

Interest on Loans from Nonbusiness Policies. As already stated, contracts issued after June 8, 1997, can generate interest deductions on policy loans only under the key person rules. This means that no personally owned policy issued after that date can generate interest deductions. What about contracts issued on or before June 8, 1997? If all the other requirements of IRC Section 264 are met, interest on such personally owned policies may be deductible as investment interest if the taxpayer can demonstrate that the loan was used for investment purposes according to the loan "tracing" rules pursuant to IRC Sec. 163. This is probably the only avenue for individual taxpayers to claim interest deductions with respect to loans from personally owned policies.

Additional Restrictions on Interest Deductions for Policy Loans. If the indebtedness is incurred or continued to purchase or carry a single-premium life insurance contract, no interest deduction for policy loans is allowable even if the interest qualifies under any of the other rules just described. For this purpose, a "single-premium contract" is one in which substantially all the premiums are paid within a 4-year period from the date of purchase, or a contract for which an amount is deposited with the insurer for payment of a substantial number of future premiums on the contract.

Also no interest deduction will be allowed if the interest is paid pursuant to a plan of purchase that contemplates the systematic borrowing of part or all of the increases in cash value of the contract. This rule applies to contracts purchased after August 6, 1963. However, there are four exceptions to the disallowance rule for contracts involving a "systematic borrowing" plan:

- *the 7-year or "four-out-of-seven" exception.* The systematic borrowing rule will not apply if at least four of the first seven annual premiums under the contract are paid without using borrowed funds.

- *the $100-a-year exception.* The systematic borrowing rule will not apply if the taxpayer's total interest paid for the year that would be subject to the rule does not exceed $100.

- *the unforeseen event exception.* If the indebtedness was incurred because of an unforeseen substantial loss of income or unforeseen substantial increase in the taxpayer's financial obligations, the systematic borrowing rule will not apply.

- *the trade or business exception.* The systematic borrowing rule will not apply if the indebtedness was incurred in connection with the taxpayer's trade or business. Note that borrowing to finance split-dollar or key person life insurance plans is not treated as indebtedness incurred in connection with a business. There must be a business purpose apart from the insurance coverage itself.

Note that the exceptions to the systematic borrowing rule do not apply to single-premium contracts. The single-premium contract rule is separate from the systematic borrowing rule.

Coordination of Rules Limiting Interest Deductions on Policy Loans. The restrictions under IRC Sec. 264 generally apply separately and cumulatively. This means, for example, that interest payments qualifying under the key person rules must also satisfy the rules for single-premium contracts and systematic borrowing plans. In addition, the limitations of Sec. 264 apply after all other tax rules that limit or prohibit interest deductions have been applied. This means that the general rules regarding interest deductions must first be applied to policy loan interest before the additional rules under Sec. 264 are considered.

Interest on Policy Loans
- Interest is deductible only if the business-owned policy insures "key person".
- Key person must be either an officer or 20 percent owner of taxpayer/business.
- No business can have more than 20 "key persons".
- Interest is deductible only to extent of $50,000 of loan principal.
- Moody's rates must be used.

Allocation of Interest Expenses to Policy Cash Values

This rule is a different type of restriction that also applies to life insurance, annuity, and endowment contracts issued after June 8, 1997. Under an allocation formula that takes into account both a taxpayer's policy cash values and the tax basis of any other assets owned by the taxpayer, deductions for interest on *any* loan payable by the taxpayer may be disallowed to the extent that the allocation formula determines that the interest payment is allocable to the taxpayer's unborrowed policy cash values. The taxpayer's entire asset portfolio is counted in determining what portion of an interest payment is allocable to the taxpayer's unborrowed policy values, and therefore is treated as nondeductible interest.

The rule has two important exceptions that limit its applicability to certain types of taxpayers. First, it does not apply to contracts owned by natural persons (human beings). Second, it does not apply to contracts insuring or covering 20 percent owners, officers, directors, or employees of a business taxpayer. The second exception means that interest qualifying under the key person rules described above will not be disallowed by this allocation rule. The original legislative intent of the allocation rule was to limit interest deductions of financial institutions that own life insurance contracts on the lives of their debtors and that borrow money from sources other than insurance contracts.

FOCUS ON ETHICS: The Promotion of Tax Benefits Over Economic Substance

In promoting the benefits of financial products or services, financial advisors should take care not to emphasize the tax benefits of investment and/or insurance products to the point where the fundamental economic purpose of the product or vehicle is obscured or even forgotten. In the case of life insurance, a policy's fundamental purpose is to provide a death benefit to the policy beneficiary upon the death of the insured. The need for a death benefit is the cornerstone of evaluating a client's need for life insurance. Permanent life insurance policies do provide significant opportunities for accumulation of funds in a tax-advantaged vehicle. However, they should not be sold as tax shelters.

There are reasons for prudence in marketing life insurance other than the ethical importance of remembering the basic economic function of a life policy. Unwarranted or overly aggressive marketing based on a policy's tax attributes can result and has resulted in Congress and/or the Treasury Department paying special attention to marketing claims and then closing perceived tax loopholes in insurance products.

The advent of numerous restrictions on the tax benefits available to corporate-owned life insurance (COLI) and split-dollar insurance applications are prime examples of how both Congress and the Treasury Department have responded to real and/or perceived income tax abuses involving life insurance. In the past, loans taken from the cash value of COLI were used extensively to generate interest deductions and to create financial arbitrage before Congress stepped in and restricted the deductibility of policy loan interest. A number of courts also disallowed tax benefits generated from COLI plans on the grounds of lack of economic substance as well as on other grounds. Single-premium policies provide another example of how the marketing of tax advantages played a significant role in motivating Congress to eliminate some of the advantages that such policies were previously able to provide.

Of course, the marketing of products is not the only reason why Congress or the Treasury Department closes perceived loopholes. Revenue enhancement is always a primary factor. But the impression created by inappropriate marketing upon lawmakers and other government officials and employees who influence the creation and interpretation of tax laws can tip the scales regarding which benefits are eliminated through changes in the Internal Revenue Code, Treasury regulations, or court decisions.

For ethical reasons as well as to avoid negative attention, life insurance should be marketed appropriately. There is nothing wrong with informing and advising clients of the tax benefits that insurance products provide. However, sound judgment should be used to determine when sales strategies place too much emphasis on tax benefits and not enough on the basic policy economics. These principles apply to any financial product or vehicle, and not exclusively to insurance products.

CHAPTER REVIEW

Key Terms and Concepts

terminally ill insured	insurable interest
contingent beneficiary	key person rule
transfer-for-value rule	key person

Review Questions

Review questions are based on the learning objectives in this chapter. Thus a [16.3] at the end of a question means that the question is based on learning objective 3. If there are multiple objectives, they are all listed.

1. What is the general rule for income taxation of life insurance death benefits received in each of the following ways?

    a.   in a lump sum

    b.   under the interest option

    c.   under one of the installment options [16.1]

2. Sue Guru died on August 20, 1986. Two hundred thousand dollars is credited to her widower by the XYZ Life Insurance Company, which pays him a settlement option of an annual level payment of $11,200, consisting of $10,000 principal (proceeds) and $1,200 interest. Describe the income taxation of

    a. the portion representing the $200,000 principal amount

    b. the interest portion of the payment [16.1]

3. Assume the same facts as question 2 except that Sue died on December 1 of last year. Explain how the annual payments to her surviving spouse will be taxed. [16.1]

4. Describe the tax treatment of accelerated death benefits paid under a life insurance policy where the insured is a terminally ill individual. [16.1]

5. Jan purchases a $100,000 whole life policy. Dividends are used to purchase paid-up additional insurance. Twenty years later, Jan surrenders the policy for $53,000, which includes the cash value of the paid-up additions. Her total annual premium has been $2,300 including $40 a year for waiver of premiums and $20 a year for accidental death benefits. Compute her taxable gain. [16.1]

6. Bones purchased a 20-year level-premium endowment life insurance policy 20 years ago. He paid a total of $48,000 in net premiums. The policy matures this year with a cash value of $70,000. Explain when Bones would be taxed on his monetary gain if he

    a. received payment in a lump sum

    b. received payment in installments over a 20-year period pursuant to a settlement option he signed 5 weeks after the maturity date of the policy

    c. received payment in installments over a 20-year period pursuant to a settlement option he signed 10 weeks after the maturity date of the policy

    d. received payments of interest under an interest-only option signed 5 weeks after the maturity date of the policy [16.1]

7. Explain the income taxation of payments to a contingent beneficiary upon the death of the primary payee who was receiving guaranteed payments under a life income settlement option. [16.1]

8. Explain the income tax treatment of premiums for

    a. personal life insurance

    b. business life insurance [16.2]

9. The Glimmer Corporation is the owner of a policy on the life of Richards, its president. The corporation pays premiums and is named as beneficiary. Are these premiums deductible by the Glimmer Corporation? Explain. [16.2]

10. Explain the general rule for taxation of life insurance proceeds when a transfer for value has occurred during the insured's lifetime. [16.3]

11. Explain the income tax consequences of transferring the life insurance policy or policies in each of the following situations:

    a. Ralph takes out a policy on his own life. He later assigns the policy to the Bull Corporation for which he works as an account executive. He receives the cash value of the policy as consideration.

    b. Leonard is a partner in the L&M partnership. The partnership owns a policy on Leonard's life that it no longer needs. It sells the policy to Leonard for its current value.

    c. Sharon gives a policy on her life to her son, who later sells it to Sharon's friend Bonnie. Sharon's business provides a market for almost 100 percent of the products of Bonnie's company, and Bonnie fears a financial setback at Sharon's death.

    d. Quint and Clint own 100 percent of the stock of the QC Corporation. The corporation currently owns a policy on each of their lives. For personal reasons, Quint and Clint purchase the policies on their own lives from the corporation and enter into a buy-sell agreement on a cross-purchase basis. Quint and Clint trade policies so that each shareholder holds a policy on the other's life in order to fund the buy-sell agreement. [16.3]

12. What are the exceptions to the transfer-for-value rule? [16.3]

13. a. Explain the concept of insurable interest.

    b. What effect does a lack of insurable interest at the time a policy is issued have on the taxation of proceeds?

    c. What effect does a lack of insurable interest at the time a policy matures have on the taxation of proceeds? [16.3]

14. How will the death proceeds be taxed when a corporation owns a life insurance policy on the life of an employee and the proceeds are paid to shareholders of the corporation to fund a buy-sell agreement? [16.3]

15. If a corporation's shareholders are not employees, how will the payment of premiums on a life insurance policy by the corporation be treated for income tax purposes if

    a.   the shareholders are beneficiaries?

    b.   the shareholders are both beneficiaries and owners of the policy? [16.3]

16. a.   What is the general rule for deductibility of premiums paid on life insurance owned by a qualified charitable organization?

     b.   What problems may occur if the charity is named irrevocable beneficiary of the proceeds but the taxpayer continues to own the policy? [16.3]

17. What are the requirements that must exist for premium payments by one spouse or former spouse for life insurance owned by and benefiting the other spouse to be deductible as alimony by the payer-spouse and taxable to the payee-spouse? Explain. [16.3]

18. Where an employer makes premium payments on an individual policy insuring the life of an employee and the employee is the policyowner, explain the tax implications:

    a.   to the employer

    b.   to the employee [16.3]

19. How is the taxable economic benefit under a basic split-dollar plan calculated? [16.3]

20. Explain the following aspects of the deductibility of interest on loans from business-owned life insurance policies:

    a.   the key person rule

    b.   the "grandfather" rule [16.4]

21. Five years ago, the Husky Corporation bought a policy on the life of its president, Teddy. Husky does not have insurance policies or annuities covering the lives of any other officers or stockholders. Husky borrows $50,000 from the policy on Teddy's life. Will Husky be permitted to deduct interest payments on this loan? [16.4]

22. What is the rule regarding deductibility of interest on loans from single-premium life insurance policies? [16.4]

Review Answers

1. a.   Generally, life insurance death benefits payable in a lump sum by reason of the death of the insured are excluded from the gross income of the beneficiary, regardless of whether the beneficiary is an individual or an entity.

b. When death proceeds are held by the insurer for future withdrawal or distribution and only interest on the proceeds is paid to the beneficiary, the full interest payment is taxable. When the death proceeds being held by the insurer are finally distributed, they are paid tax free.

c. For policies maturing by death, that portion of each payment made under the fixed-period, fixed-amount, or life income installment options representing the principal of death proceeds is received tax free, but that portion representing interest is taxable.

2. a. The portion of the payments representing death proceeds is received income tax free.

   b. Since Sue died before the date of enactment of the Tax Reform Act of 1986 (October 22, 1986), her widower is entitled to exclude up to $1,000 of the interest portion annually. The settlement option is not an interest-only option. The $200 of interest in excess of $1,000 per year is taxable.

3. Sue's widower is not eligible for the surviving spouse's interest exclusion because Sue died after October 22, 1986. Therefore the $1,200 of interest is included in his income annually. The portion representing death proceeds is still received tax free.

4. Amounts received under a life insurance contract covering the life of an insured who is terminally ill are excludible from gross income as amounts payable by reason of the death of the insured if certain requirements are met. The amounts received qualify for the exclusion if paid by the insurance company or by a licensed viatical settlement provider. The exclusion does not apply if the amounts are paid to a taxpayer other than the insured if the insured is a director, officer, or employee of the taxpayer or has a financial interest in a business conducted by the taxpayer.

5. Jan's gain is computed as follows:

Amount realized	$53,000
Minus basis ([$2,300 - $40 - $20] x 20)	(44,800)
Gain (ordinary income)	$ 8,200

6. a. Bones would be taxed this year on the entire gain of $22,000 ($70,000 - $48,000).

   b. Bones would be taxed on the payments under the annuity exclusion ratio, which was discussed in Chapter 5, since he elected the installment option within 60 days of the maturity date.

    c.   Bones would be taxed this year on the entire $22,000 gain since he allowed the 60-day period after maturity to lapse without electing the installment option.

    d.   Bones would be taxed this year on the entire $22,000 gain since the interest-only option must be signed before the maturity date in order to defer taxation on the gain.

7.   Where the primary payee is receiving a life income settlement and dies during a period of guaranteed payments, the contingent beneficiary will have no taxable income until the total amount received, when added to the amount that was received tax free by the primary payee, exceeds the investment in the contract. Thereafter the full amount of each payment will be taxed as ordinary income.

8.   a.   The general rule with respect to the income tax treatment of life insurance premiums is that they are a personal expense and as such are not deductible. The rule applies whether the premium is paid by the insured, the beneficiary, or the policyowner.

    b.   Premiums paid on business life insurance generally are not deductible.

9.   No, the premiums are not deductible by the Glimmer Corporation because it is the beneficiary and owner of the policy on the life of Richards, its president. In this regard, the Code states that no deduction shall be allowed for premiums on any life insurance policy if the taxpayer is directly or indirectly a beneficiary under the policy or contract.

10.   Where a policy transferred by assignment or otherwise for a valuable consideration matures by reason of death, the transferee will be liable for income tax on the amount of death proceeds in excess of the actual value of the consideration paid for the contract plus the total of net premiums and other amounts subsequently paid by the transferee.

11.   a.   Bull Corporation will be liable for income tax on the amount of death proceeds in excess of the consideration (cash value) paid for the policy plus the total of net premiums (and other amounts) subsequently paid by Bull Corporation. The fact that Ralph works for Bull Corporation as an account executive has no bearing since it is not one of the exceptions to the transfer-for-value rule.

    b.   This policy transfer falls under one of the exceptions to the transfer-for-value rule. Therefore, the full death proceeds will be income tax free to Leonard's designated beneficiary even though the policy was transferred for a valuable consideration.

    c.   Bonnie will be liable for income tax on the amount of death proceeds in excess of the consideration paid for the policy plus the total of net premiums subsequently paid by Bonnie. The fact that Bonnie has an insurable interest in Sharon has no bearing on Bonnie's liability for income taxes.

    d.   Both Quint and Clint will be liable for income tax on the amount of death proceeds in excess of the consideration paid for the policy plus the total of net premiums subsequently paid by each. The transfer of a policy from an insured who is a shareholder in a closely held corporation to a fellow shareholder is not one of the exceptions to the transfer-for-value rule.

12. The five specified exceptions to the transfer-for-value rule are

- transfers to the insured

- transfers to a partner of the insured

- transfers to a partnership in which the insured is a partner

- transfers to a corporation in which the insured is a shareholder or an officer

- transfers in which the transferee's basis in the transferred policy is determined in whole or in part by reference to the transferor's basis

13. a.   The concept of insurable interest specifies that in order to obtain insurance on the life of another, there must be a reasonable expectation of benefit or advantage to the applicant from continuation of the life to be insured or an expectation of loss or detriment from the cessation of that life. Lacking the requisite of insurable interest, life insurance is viewed as a mere wagering contract entered into for profit.

    b.   A life insurance policy that lacks the requisite insurable interest at the time of policy inception is a wagering contract and hence illegal. However, if the parties decide to observe the promises made under the contract, the death proceeds will be viewed as profits subject to income taxation.

    c.   The requirement of insurable interest generally applies only at the time of policy inception. Therefore, assuming insurable interest exists when a policy is issued, the fact that it does not exist when the policy matures as a death claim will not subject the proceeds to income taxation. The tax-free nature of the death proceeds will be preserved under these circumstances.

14. When the death proceeds of a life insurance policy owned by a corporation to fund a buysell agreement are paid directly to shareholders as beneficiaries, the proceeds are taxable as dividends (because the result is the same as if the proceeds had been received tax free as life insurance proceeds by the corporation and then distributed to the shareholders as dividends).

15. a. If the corporation pays premiums on a life insurance policy where the shareholders are beneficiaries, the premiums will be taxable to the shareholders as dividends and nondeductible to the corporation.

    b. If the corporation pays premiums on a life insurance policy where the shareholders are beneficiaries as well as owners of the policy, the premiums will still be taxable to the shareholders as dividends and nondeductible to the corporation.

16. a. Premiums paid on life insurance owned by a qualified charitable organization are deductible to the donor as a charitable contribution, subject to the charitable contributions limitations.

    b. The Code denies a charitable deduction for gifts to charities where less than the taxpayer's entire interest in the property is contributed.

17. The requirements for premium payments to be deductible as alimony by the payer-spouse and taxable to the payee-spouse are that

    - the payments be made in cash and terminate at the death of the payee-spouse

    - the payments be made under a divorce decree or separation agreement

    - the parties not be members of the same household and do not file joint tax returns

    - the payments not be for child support

    - the payments be made for at least 3 years unless either spouse dies or the payee-spouse remarries

18. a. Where an employee is the policyowner and the employer has no beneficial interest in the policy, premium payments by the employer on an individual policy insuring the life of the employee may be deductible by the employer as an ordinary and necessary business expense if they are considered reasonable additional compensation to the employee for services rendered.

    b. The premium payments by the employer are taxable compensation to the employee when paid.

19. The employee must generally include in gross income each year the value of the economic benefit received, which is measured by one of several different methods prescribed by IRS Regs 1.61–22 and 1.7872–15. These methods calculate the taxable benefit based upon the employee's age and the amount of insurance protection.

20. a. This provision is the most significant exception to the general rule that interest deductions on policy loans are disallowed. The key person rule provides that

interest on loan amounts not in excess of $50,000 per insured person is deductible if the insured is a "key person." The total number of key persons per business taxpayer may not exceed the GREATER of

- five individuals or

- the LESSER of

    – 5 percent of the total number of officers and employees of the business taxpayer, or

    – 20 individuals

This restriction means that in order for a business taxpayer to have more than five key persons for purposes of the tax rules for interest deductions on policy loans, the taxpayer has to have more than 100 employees. In addition, in order to have the maximum number of 20 key persons, the business taxpayer claiming the interest deductions would have to have at least 400 employees.

b. If an insurance contract was entered into before June 21, 1986, the key person rules and the $50,000 of indebtedness limitation do not apply. Interest on loans connected with such contracts may be deductible, subject to other layers of rules imposed by IRC Sec. 264.

21. Husky will be able to deduct interest payments because the loan qualifies under the "key person" rule. However, the amount of interest deductible may be limited by the Moody's rate, depending upon the rate of interest specified in the policy.

22. If the indebtedness is incurred or continued to purchase or carry a single premium life insurance contract, no interest deduction for policy loans is allowable even if the interest qualifies under any other rules. A "single premium contract" is one in which substantially all the premiums are paid within a 4-year period from the date of purchase, or a contract for which an amount is deposited with the insurer for payment of a substantial number of future premiums on the contract.

Chapter 17

Tax Treatment of Modified Endowment Contracts

Learning Objectives

An understanding of the material in this chapter should enable you to

LO 17.1   **Explain what determines whether a life insurance policy is classi-fied as a modified endowment contract (MEC).**

LO 17.2   **Describe the concept of material change in a life insurance policy, and explain how a material change can convert a policy into a MEC.**

Internal Revenue Service: The world's most successful mail-order business.

—Bob Goddard

HISTORICAL PERSPECTIVE ON SINGLE-PREMIUM POLICIES

Single-premium life insurance policies experienced an 800 percent increase in sales volume between 1984 and 1988. This was mainly due to the Tax Reform Act of 1986, which eliminated many of the tax advantages of what had been popular tax-sheltered investments. After that legislation was enacted, many investors purchased single-premium life insurance policies. In many cases the income tax deferral was the primary motivation for the purchase. Some stock brokerages were promoting and selling single-premium life insurance policies as tax shelters. These policies were often described as the last remaining tax shelter under our tax law.

Single-premium life insurance policies and other limited pay policies enjoyed the same tax treatment as other life insurance policies (that is, cash value buildup is generally income tax free until the policy is terminated). The policyowner was able to borrow against the policy in the form of policy loans and gain possession and management of the purchase price of the policy without being taxed.

LO 17.1   **Explain what determines whether a life insurance policy is classified as a modified endowment contract (MEC).**

TAXATION OF MODIFIED ENDOWMENT CONTRACTS

modified endowment contract (MEC)

During the 1980s, members of Congress were disturbed by the marketing of single-premium life insurance. In 1988, Congress changed the income tax treatment of any policy entered into on or after June 21, 1988, that fails a test titled the 7-pay test and consequently is classified as a **modified endowment contract (MEC)**.

Policies entered into before June 21, 1988, were grandfathered and are not affected by this law unless they undergo a "material change." The material changes that can jeopardize the grandfather protection will be explained below.

The objective of the changes in tax treatment for insurance policies classified as modified endowment contracts was to discourage the use of high-premium life insurance policies as short-term investments. This treatment makes the use of high-premium life insurance policies as short-term investments more costly and thereby decreases the return to the policyowner who takes possession of the cash value through loans, withdrawals, or terminations. However, the rules in no way decrease the return to policyowners who leave the funds with the insurer and look to the death benefit as the primary benefit of the contract.

The 7-Pay Test

7-pay test

The modified endowment contract rules affect the tax treatment of any policy entered into on or after June 21, 1988, in which the aggregate premiums paid at any time during the first 7 years of the contract exceed the sum of the "net level premiums" that would have been paid by that time if the contract provided for paid-up benefits after the payment of seven level annual premiums. This is called the **7-pay test**.

Policies that fail the 7-pay test because too much has been paid within the first 7 years are considered modified endowment contracts (MECs). For example, if the annual net level premium for a $100,000 7-pay policy is $4,500, then any $100,000 policy for the same insured will be considered a modified endowment contract if the aggregate premiums *exceed*

- $4,500 during the first policy year

- $9,000 during the first 2 policy years

- $13,500 during the first 3 policy years

- $18,000 during the first 4 policy years

- $22,500 during the first 5 policy years

- $27,000 during the first 6 policy years

- $31,500 during the first 7 policy years

If the aggregate premiums paid during the first 7 years are *equal to or less than* the aggregate premiums that would have been paid on a level-annual-premium basis using the net level premium amount ($4,500 a year in this example) for a 7-pay policy (for the same insured), the policy will *not* be a modified endowment contract and will receive the same tax treatment previously applicable to all policies.

net level premium

The definition of a net level premium under these rules is based on the net single-premium concept under IRC Sec. 7702, which provides the definition of a life insurance contract. The net level premium is *not* the same as the actual premium payable under the contract. It is also not the same as what many life insurance professionals refer to as a net premium. **Net level premium** is a technical term of art created and defined by the tax law. Stated simply, however, net level premium is an artificially constructed amount based on reasonable mortality charges, an assumed interest rate, and (in some cases) reasonable insurance company expense charges. Therefore it is possible that in some cases policies that require 7 annual premiums will not pass the 7-pay test because the net level premium may be less than the actual premium. Conversely, in some cases policies that require fewer than 7 annual premiums will pass the 7-pay test if the aggregate net level premiums after each year are more than the actual aggregate premiums paid.

Those policies entered into on or after June 21, 1988, that are classified as modified endowment contracts may be subject to income taxes and penalty taxes not applicable to other life insurance policies. Policy loans and partial withdrawals of funds from such modified endowment contracts are subject to last-in first-out (LIFO) treatment to determine the applicable taxes. This means that any income earned on the contract fund is taxed as if it was withdrawn *before* the policyowner's cost basis in the contract. In addition to the regular income tax, a 10 percent penalty tax is generally applicable to taxable gains withdrawn from a modified endowment contract before the policyowner reaches age 59 ½. However, the 10 percent penalty does not apply to payments attributable to disability or to annuitized payments.

Example

Penelope purchased a life insurance contract 5 years ago. Her basis in the policy is $100,000, and the contract has a cash value of $140,000. The policy is a MEC. She borrows $50,000 from the policy's cash value on her 50th birthday. Penelope's taxable gain from the loan is $40,000 ($140,000 cash value – $100,000 basis in the policy). If Penelope is in the 35 percent tax bracket, she must pay an income tax of $14,000 ($40,000 × .35). She must also pay a 10 percent penalty on the taxable amount. The penalty will be $4,000 ($40,000 × .10). Therefore Penelope's total tax bill on the loan from the policy is $18,000 ($14,000 + $4,000).

Note that all amounts included in Penelope's gross income as a result of taking a loan from the policy are added to her basis in the policy for purposes of determining future taxable amounts. Therefore Penelope's basis in the policy after taking the loan will be $140,000 ($100,000 original basis plus $40,000 taxable portion of loan). The $10,000 nontaxable portion does not affect Penelope's basis in the contract because the transaction is a loan and not a withdrawal.

These rules are similar to those applicable to deferred-annuity contracts issued after August 13, 1982. Income earned within such contracts is deemed to be withdrawn (and therefore taxable) before the cost basis of the contract is recovered when withdrawals are made before the annuity's starting date. However, life insurance policies that are not classified as modified endowment contracts, as well as so-called "pre-TEFRA" annuity contracts (those funded before August 14, 1982), are still subject to a more favorable first-in first-out (FIFO) tax treatment on withdrawals.

Contracts with Death Benefits of $10,000 or Less

There is a variation on the application of the net level premium amount in the 7-pay test that applies to policies of $10,000 or less in face amount. The law provides an annual allowance of $75 to be added to the 7-pay test premium. The $75 additional allowance permits some small 7-pay policies to pass the 7-pay test when they otherwise might not. The smaller the policy is, the more likely it is that the actual premium will be less than the net level premium plus $75. The full $75 can be used for any amount of coverage between $1,000 and $10,000, resulting in a maximum allowable additional expense loading of $7.50 per $1,000 of coverage.

Congress anticipated the added attractiveness of this small policy expense allowance and its potential abuses. Therefore the law requires that all policies issued by the same insurer to the same policyowner be treated as one policy for purposes of determining that the face amount does not exceed $10,000. This prevents policyowners from purchasing a large number of small policies to take advantage of the allowable expense loading. Note that the statute does not require that policies from *different* insurers be aggregated for this purpose. This may present a planning opportunity for taxpayers purchasing several small policies from different insurance companies.

Grandfathered Policies

Policies entered into prior to June 21, 1988 (as well as policies entered into on or after that date that pass the 7-pay test), are generally treated the same as when they were issued. There is no income tax applicable to withdrawals until after the cost basis has been recovered tax free. This is the first-in first-out (FIFO) treatment long associated with life insurance policy taxation. Generally no penalty tax is applicable to taxable gains from life insurance policies unless the policy is reclassified as a MEC.

It is important to remember that withdrawals from life insurance policies that are associated with a reduction in policy benefits during the first 15 policy years may be subject to a limited LIFO-type federal income taxation. The MEC rules apply separately and in addition to these rules. Also, the MEC rules apply to loans as well as to withdrawals.

Subsequent Exchanges of a MEC

Once a policy is classified as a MEC, it will automatically make any policy subsequently received in exchange for it also a MEC. Even if the new policy received in the exchange passes the 7-pay test, it will be classified as a MEC.

Example

Merlin purchased a single-premium policy 3 years ago. The policy failed the 7-pay test and is treated as a MEC. This year, Merlin exchanges his single-premium policy for a level premium whole life policy that clearly passes the 7-pay test. However, the new policy will be treated as a MEC because it was received in exchange for a MEC.

At first glance this appears to be a harsh result. However, Congress was apparently concerned about the potential for using untaxed internal policy gains to purchase additional life insurance coverage. In the absence of this provision a tax benefit similar to a deduction for premium payments would have existed.

LO 17.2   Describe the concept of material change in a life insurance policy, and explain how a material change can convert a policy into a MEC.

MATERIAL CHANGE RULES

A policy that at first passes the 7-pay test when it is issued can later become a MEC if there is a "material change" in the policy. In addition, a single-premium policy entered into before June 21, 1988, is not a MEC but could become one if the policy is materially changed anytime after June 20, 1988, and fails the 7-pay test after the change.

What constitutes a material change under the MEC rules? An increase in future benefits under the contract will generally be considered a material change. However, the following will *not* be treated as material changes:

- cost-of-living increases in death benefits that are based on a broad-based index (such as the consumer price index)

- death-benefit increases inherent in the policy design because of the crediting of interest or other earnings. (This appears to exempt the increasing death benefits of a type II universal life policy from classification as a material change.)

- increases in death benefits because of the premiums paid for the policy to support the level of benefits for the first 7 contract years. (This appears to exempt from material change classification any increase in death benefits necessary to keep the required relationship between the death benefit and the policy guideline cash value or guideline premiums as specified in Sec. 7702.)

A policy that was previously not classified as a MEC will be subject to the 7-pay test after a material change. If the policy then fails the test, it will be a MEC and therefore subject to LIFO taxation of policy loans, withdrawals, and terminations. The change in taxation will be applicable only for the year of the material change and subsequent years. There will not be retroactive taxation of loans or distributions in years prior to the application of the 7-pay test unless the distributions were made in anticipation of the failure or made within 2 years before such failure. In such cases the distribution will be taxed in the year it was made.

Special Rule for Death Benefit Increases to Grandfathered Contracts

A policy entered into prior to June 21, 1988, that experiences an increase of death benefits in excess of $150,000 on or after October 20, 1988, will be subject to the material change provisions. This means that such a policy could lose its grandfathered status if it does not pass the 7-pay test. The policy will be subject to the 7-pay test at each increase unless the death benefit increases were due to cost-of-living adjustments, to interest or earnings increases, or attributable to premiums needed to fund the lowest level of benefits during the first 7 policy years.

What increase in death benefits would be attributable to premiums needed to fund the lowest level of benefits during the first 7 policy years? If the increase in the cash value of the contract forces an increase in the death benefit in order to satisfy the definition of a life insurance contract under IRC Sec. 7702, such an increase in the death benefit is attributable to those premiums. Therefore such an increase will not cause the policy to be reclassified as a MEC.

However, the loss of grandfather status applies only to policies that require fewer than seven level annual premiums. If a policy required at least seven level annual premiums as of June 21, 1988, and the policyowner actually makes seven level annual premium payments, the $150,000 death benefit increase provision will not apply, and the policy will retain its grandfathered status.

Benefit Increases without Additional Evidence of Insurability

As previously explained, if the death benefit of a grandfathered policy increases by more than $150,000, the policy may be subjected to the material change rules and be reclassified as a MEC if it fails the 7-pay test. In addition, Congress anticipated other potential abuses with respect to grandfathered policies.

One potential abuse would be the granting of benefit increases on policies that originally did not contractually provide for such increases without additional evidence of insurability. If the insurance company provides a benefit increase on a policy that would have required additional evidence of insurability for such an increase before June 21, 1988, the policy will be treated as if it were entered into on or after June 21, 1988. This means that the policy will be subject to the 7-pay test based on the benefit increases, regardless of whether the benefit has increased by more than $150,000. However, if the policy originally provided for benefit increases for events such as birth or marriage without additional evidence of insurability, the policy will retain its grandfathered status until the aggregate of all such benefit increases exceeds $150,000, as previously discussed.

Conversion Rights

Term insurance policies entered into before June 21, 1988, that are converted to cash value policies after June 20, 1988, will be treated as if originally entered into on the date of conversion. This means that they will have to satisfy the 7-pay test at the time of conversion.

Example

Angelica purchased a term life insurance policy in 1987. On January 1 of this year, she converts her term policy to a whole life policy. Angelica's new policy is subject to the 7-pay test.

Reduction in Benefits

If there is a reduction of policy death benefits during the first 7 policy years, the 7-pay test will be applicable to the policy after the reduction. The test will be applied as if the contract had originally been issued at the reduced benefit level.

The law does allow a 90-day grace period for policy reinstatement that will prevent the conversion of the policy to MEC status if there is a reduction of benefits during the first 7 policy years because of nonpayment of premiums. In other words, a policy that lapses during the first 7 years but is reinstated within 90 days will not be reclassified as a MEC because of the temporary reduction of benefits prior to the reinstatement.

Example

Bret purchased a $100,000 universal life policy in January 2017. In the fifth policy year, on January 31, 2021, he negotiates a reduction in the death benefit to $70,000. Bret must now pass the 7-pay test for a $70,000 policy entered into in January 2017. If the policy does not pass the test, the policy will be treated as a MEC beginning on the date the benefits were reduced, January 31, 2021.

With respect to policies entered into or materially changed on or after September 14, 1989, that insure more than one life (so-called survivorship policies), a reduction in death benefits after the first 7 contract years will also cause the policy to be subject to the 7-pay test as if the policy had originally been issued at the reduced benefit level. This provision was designed to plug a technical loophole in the MEC statute, which seemed to permit survivorship policies with fewer than seven annual premiums to pass the 7-pay test by taking advantage of benefit reductions after 7 years and the low probability of the death of both insureds during the first 7 policy years.

Treatment of Premiums Returned

There is a 60-day grace period for returned premiums to keep the premiums paid under the 7-pay net level premium amount. The insurer can return excess premiums within 60 days after the end of the contract year. The returned amount will reduce the sum of premiums paid under the contract during such contract year. If any part of such payment from the insurance company is interest, it will be includible in the gross income of the recipient.

Aggregation Rules

Congress foresaw potential abuses in withdrawing funds from MECs by splitting up funds between many policies and withdrawing funds from one policy. In that manner the gain on that one policy could be withdrawn and the remainder of the withdrawals would be a nontaxable return of the policyowner's basis in the contract. To prevent this the law requires that all MECs issued by the same insurer to a policyowner during any calendar year be treated as one MEC. This forces recognition of all gain from all such policies before the policyowner is able to withdraw the investment in the contract.

Revenue Ruling 2007-38 further clarifies MEC aggregation rules. This ruling holds that if a taxpayer owning multiple MECs issued by the same insurance company in the same calendar year exchanges some of those MECs for new MECs issued by a second insurance company, the new contracts are not aggregated with the remaining contracts.

Example

Four years ago Arnie purchased ten single-premium life insurance policies. He paid $100,000 for each one. This year, the policies have a cash value of $117,000 each. Arnie is now 57 years old and has held all of the contracts at the original insurer. He withdraws $50,000 of cash value from one of his policies. The aggregate untaxed gain on all of Arnie's policies is $170,000 ($17,000 x 10). Therefore the entire $50,000 withdrawal is subject to both federal income tax and the 10 percent penalty, even though the gain in the policy from which the funds were withdrawn is only $17,000.

If Arnie were to have 1035 exchanged half of the contracts to a new insurer, the new contracts would still be considered MECs. However, the new contracts would not be aggregated with the original five contracts for the purpose of determining a gain or loss from aggregated old policies.

Burial Contracts

Another provision in the law exempts assignments or pledges of MECs with face amounts of less than $25,000 from current taxation if the assignment or pledge is for funeral services or prearranged funerals. It is important to remember that all other pledges or assignments of MECs are treated as loans from the policy. Therefore the pledge or assignment will result in both the federal income tax and the 10 percent penalty.

Material Change Checklist

The following are checklists for policies that originally were not classified as MECs. They involve changes that could result in the application of a new 7-pay test.

Can a grandfathered life insurance policy become a MEC if	Yes	No
it remains in force with no policy changes		X
it has a death-benefit increase of more than $150,000 after October 20, 1988	X	
it has an increase in benefits for which there is no policy guarantee or provision waiving evidence of insurability requirements, and such increase would normally require additional evidence of insurability	X	
it is terminated		X
it is a single life policy and is kept in force, but the death benefit is reduced after the 7th policy year		X
it is a survivorship policy and is kept in force, but the death benefit is reduced after the 7th policy year	X	
it experiences death-benefit increases due to interest or earnings internal to the policy		X
it has death-benefit increases in order to satisfy the definition of life insurance, and the premium has not increased above the level during the first 7 policy years		X
it has death-benefit increases due to a cost-of-living provision linked to the consumer price index (CPI)		X
it experiences death-benefit increases from exercising the guaranteed purchase provisions in the policy		X
it experiences death-benefit increases as a result of purchase options exercised when the insured has a newborn		X

Can a policy entered into after June 20, 1988, that initially passes the 7-pay test be subjected to the test again if	Yes	No
the death benefit is decreased during the first 7 policy years (or thereafter in the case of a survivorship policy)	X	
the death benefit increases due to premium increases after the first 7 policy years	X	
the death benefit increases due to paid-up additions from premium amounts greater than required to fund the benefit levels provided during the first 7 policy years	X	
the death benefit increases due to cost-of-living adjustments tied to the CPI or some other widely accepted index		X

Can a policy entered into after June 20, 1988, that initially passes the 7-pay test be subjected to the test again if	Yes	No
the death benefit must be increased to satisfy the definition of life insurance, but the premiums paid are not in excess of those required to fund the level of benefits maintained in the first 7 policy years		X
the death benefit must be increased to satisfy the definition of life insurance because of excess interest or earnings credited inside the policy, but premiums are not in excess of those required to fund the level of benefits maintained in the first 7 policy years		X

PLANNING CONSIDERATIONS

In summary, funds received from a MEC policy (including policy loans or other loans secured by the modified endowment contract and dividends paid out by the policy) will be considered taxable income first. Amounts in excess of the gain in the policy will be considered tax-free recovery of cost basis. This is similar to the treatment of withdrawals of funds during the accumulation phase under a deferred annuity.

Taxpayers still owning single-premium or limited pay policies that were entered into before June 21, 1988, should be aware of the grandfathering they enjoy and that their policy loans will not be subject to LIFO-based income taxes. However, policyowners must be cautioned that their grandfathered status can be lost if the policy is exchanged for a new policy that requires additional premiums or if the death benefit on the existing policy is increased in such a way that it is treated as a material change.

Owners of non-MEC contracts should be reminded that the income tax law also imposes LIFO taxation on withdrawals from non-MEC policies that are made during the first 15 policy years and are associated with a reduction in policy benefits. This is most likely to occur under certain universal life policies.

Policyowners who purchase policies that fail the 7-pay test should be aware that they are subject to the MEC rules. They should carefully consider their options before initiating a financial transaction involving the policy. At first these policies will probably have relatively small gains subject to taxation and penalty, but they may face significant surrender charges. The surrender charges will decrease with policy duration, but the taxable gains will increase with duration. Each individual policy has its own pattern and trade-offs; therefore individual evaluations are required to determine the optimal treatment of these policies. In some cases the policyowner may be justified in terminating early and limiting taxation even though it means paying surrender charges. Some may choose to keep the policy in force but not take possession of policy cash values. All policyowners should be able to find less-costly sources of funds than policy loans from a MEC.

By congressional design, single-premium policies are no longer useful as a strictly investment-oriented tax-deferral vehicle. However, it is important to realize and emphasize that single-premium policies can still be viable and desirable. They provide a way to pass assets to others without subjecting them to the costs, delays, and uncertainties of probate; attacks on or elections against the insured's will; or the claims of creditors. These policies also provide a way to fully prefund future debts or pledges with discounted tax-advantaged dollars. At death they are still income tax free and can be arranged to be both estate and inheritance tax free.

CHAPTER REVIEW

Key Terms and Concepts

modified endowment contract (MEC)
7-pay test

net level premium

Review Questions

Review questions are based on the learning objectives in this chapter. Thus a [17.2] at the end of a question means that the question is based on learning objective 2. If there are multiple objectives, they are all listed.

1. Explain how withdrawals and loans from insurance policies that are classified as modified endowment contracts (MECs) are taxed. [17.1]

2. State whether each of the following life insurance policies will be treated as a MEC:

   a. a single-premium policy entered into on June 20, 1988

   b. a whole-life policy received this year in exchange for a single-premium policy entered into on January 1, 1998

   c. a level premium whole life policy entered into on June 1, 1988, that experiences a death benefit increase of $125,000

   d. an old term policy that is converted to a new cash-value policy on January 1 of this year and fails the 7-pay test

   e. a universal life policy insuring one life that experiences a reduction in death benefits during the 10th policy year [17.1]

3. What is the result when there is a "material change" to a life insurance policy? [17.2]

4. a. Explain how a reduction in policy benefits affects the application of the 7-pay test to a life insurance policy.

   b. Is a policy covering more than one insured subject to any special rules? Explain. [17.2]

Review Answers

1. Policy loans and partial withdrawals of funds from modified endowment contracts (MECs) are subject to last-in first-out (LIFO) treatment to determine the applicable taxes. This means that any income earned on the contract fund is taxed as if it was withdrawn before the policyowner's cost basis in the contract. In addition to the regular income tax, a 10 percent penalty tax is generally applicable to taxable gains withdrawn from a MEC before the policyowner reaches age 59 ½. However, the 10 percent penalty does not apply to payments attributable to disability or to annuitized payments.

2. a. no

   b. yes

   c. no

   d. yes

   e. no

3. A "material change" results in the application of the 7-pay test to a policy as of the date of the material change. If the policy fails the 7-pay test, it will then be treated as a MEC.

Note that a material change does not automatically cause the policy to be treated as a MEC. A policy that experiences a change will not be a MEC if it then passes the 7-pay test.

4. a. If there is a reduction of policy death benefits during the first 7 policy years, the 7-pay test will be applicable to the policy after the reduction. The test will be applied as if the contract had originally been issued at the reduced benefit level.

    b. With respect to policies entered into or materially changed on or after September 14, 1989, that insure more than one life (so-called survivorship policies), a reduction in death benefits after the first 7 contract years will also cause the policy to be subject to the 7-pay test as if the policy had originally been issued at the reduced benefit level.

Chapter 18

Taxation of Corporations and Shareholders

Learning Objectives

An understanding of the material in this chapter should enable you to

LO 18.1   **Describe the characteristics of the corporate form of business, and explain its advantages and disadvantages.**

LO 18.2   **Explain the requirements for the formation of an S corporation, and describe the advantages and disadvantages of being taxed as an S corporation.**

LO 18.3   **Describe the requirements for incorporating a business under the nonrecognition provisions of the Code, and explain the respective roles of debt and equity in the corporate structure.**

LO 18.4   **Describe how a corporation determines taxable income or loss, and explain the issues associated with deductions for salaries, charitable deductions, deductions for dividends received, and other deductions.**

LO 18.5   **Describe the purposes of the accumulated-earnings tax and the personal-holding-company tax, and explain corporate policy with respect to dividend distributions.**

If Patrick Henry thought that taxation without representation was bad, he should see how bad it is with representation.

—*The Old Farmer's Almanac*

There can be no taxation without misrepresentation.

—J.B. Handelsman

Cheesman, Reebel, and Baily are engineers. They have developed a relatively inexpensive process for manufacturing an aircraft safety component that is in great demand for new jet airliners.

Cheesman is a sole proprietor currently engaged in producing aircraft parts. Reebel, a young man who has a postgraduate degree in business administration and an undergraduate degree in engineering, has worked for Cheesman for a number of years. He first started as an engineer and almost by accident moved into the firm's sales division. Reebel's sales efforts have been so successful that Cheesman would like to offer him an interest in a new business venture. Baily is slightly older than

Cheesman and Reebel. He is a well-known and highly-respected authority in the area of aircraft safety parts. He does quite a bit of consulting work for both government and private enterprise. He met Cheesman and Reebel on such a consulting project, and the three men have become good friends. Baily is quite wealthy, and he is interested in keeping both his money and his mind at work.

The three engineers have decided to form a business and have invited Bob Kress, a CPA attorney who is an expert in tax planning, to help them decide on a course of action. Kress has suggested that the best vehicle for their new business venture might be a corporation. They have asked Kress to discuss the taxation of a corporation on a detailed basis so that they could get an idea of what advantages and disadvantages corporate status entails, as well as some of the tax implications of doing business in corporate form.

LO 18.1   **Describe the characteristics of the corporate form of business, and explain its advantages and disadvantages.**

LEGAL ASPECTS OF A CORPORATION

corporation

Kress: A **corporation** is essentially a legal entity created under state law for the purpose of conducting a business or philanthropic activity. Under traditional principles of state corporation law, there are four legal characteristics that distinguish a corporation from other forms of business operation. These four corporate characteristics are as follows:

- limited liability
- transferability of interest
- centralized management
- continuity of life

Cheesman: Bob, would you go into more detail on exactly what you mean by those phrases?

limited liability

Kress: Yes. An organization possesses **limited liability** if the organization's creditors cannot proceed against its individual owners personally in satisfaction of a corporate debt. This is one of the best-known reasons for choosing the corporate form.

If the formalities of corporate procedure are followed, then for legal purposes the corporation is really operating as a business and financial unit entirely separate from its shareholders. Shareholders will not be personally liable for the corporation's debts or other liabilities. As a practical matter, principal shareholders of small corporations will often be required to cosign a note or give a personal guarantee for the corporation and therefore become personally liable for loans to the corporation from banks or other lending institutions. Generally, however, the most a shareholder can lose is his or her investment in the business.

transferability of interest

Transferability of interest generally means that a shareholder of a corporation can transfer interest in the profits, assets, and control of the business freely and without restraint. If each shareholder, without the consent of the other shareholders of the organization, can transfer interest to a person who is not a shareholder, there is free transferability of interest. It is permissible, however, to impose reasonable restrictions on shareholders to preserve the nature of close corporate membership. These restrictions are often contained in buy-sell agreements and facilitate family estate planning with respect to a business interest.

centralized management

Centralized management exists if the operating authority is concentrated in one person or a relatively small class within the group as opposed to the sharing of management decisions commonly found in partnerships. If any person or group of persons (which does not include all of the members) has continuing, exclusive authority to make the decisions necessary to the management and daily operation of the business, there will be centralized management.

The group in which that authority is legally vested is called the board of directors. The board of directors uses its best judgment and independent discretion to determine and execute corporate policies. Although these individuals are in fact elected by the shareholders and are removable by them for cause (and possibly without cause), the directors are not agents of the shareholders. They are fiduciaries whose duties primarily run to the corporation itself, and indirectly to the shareholders.

It is the board of directors, not the shareholders, who make policy decisions with respect to the products, services, prices, and wages of the company. Likewise, even in the smallest corporation, legally speaking it is the board of directors that has the right to select, supervise, and remove officers and other personnel. For example, the board of directors, and not the shareholders, fixes compensation and decides on the installation and benefit levels of pension and profit-sharing plans, as well as other employee benefits. In short, the supervision and vigilance for the welfare of the entire corporate enterprise is vested in the hands of a very select group.

continuity of life

Continuity of life means that death, disability, incapacity, addition of a new shareholder, or withdrawal of an old shareholder will not cause legal dissolution of the business. If the effect of the death of a shareholder is the automatic death of the business, a vital element of corporate status would be lacking. A corporation is a form of business enterprise that—theoretically at least—has the advantage of perpetual existence. For example, even the death of a 100 percent shareholder would not automatically cause the legal termination of the business. Practically speaking, however, without successor management, such a corporation will die as quickly as a sole proprietorship.

Under modern business law, business entities other than corporations, such as limited partnerships and limited liability companies, may also exhibit one or more corporate characteristics.

CLASSIFICATION UNDER FEDERAL INCOME TAX LAW

If an organization is classified as a corporation for federal tax purposes, it will be treated as a separate taxable entity, distinct and apart from the owners of its stock. A corporation therefore has a tax existence separate from its shareholders. The result is that a corporation must compute its own income and deductions, file its own return, and pay its own tax at the applicable corporate rates.[1]

In the past, the courts and the Internal Revenue Service applied the traditional concepts of corporate law to determine whether a business organization should be taxed as a corporation or as a partnership. If an organization was found to possess three out of those four characteristics, it would be taxable as a corporation under federal law, regardless of how it was formed under applicable state law.

Under the check-the-box regulations, the IRS has simplified its approach in determining the federal tax classification of business organizations. Generally, an organization that is incorporated under state law will be taxed as a corporation under federal law.[2] Organizations that are unincorporated under state law (such as partnerships and limited liability companies) can generally elect whether to be treated as partnerships or corporations for federal tax purposes.

---

1. IRC Secs. 11 and 6012.
2. Reg. Sec. 301.7701-1, 2.

TYPES OF CORPORATIONS

There are many different types of corporations. For example, there is the ecclesiastical corporation that is organized to hold property in connection with the advancement of a particular religious faith. An eleemosynary corporation is created to hold property for the benefit of a charity or benevolent society. The type of corporation you are contemplating is a subsection of a third general type, the civil corporation. The civil corporation encompasses all corporations other than ecclesiastical or eleemosynary. The civil corporation can be political, quasi-public, or private.

Reebel: Would we be considered private?

Kress: Yes, political corporations are created by governments to manage public affairs. The Post Office Corporation is a good illustration. Sometimes companies are privately owned but exist to serve the public. Where the state maintains close control and supervision over the conduct of a corporation's business, it is considered quasi-public. An example would be a gas or electric company.

The organization you are considering would be organized for the benefit of its members, the three of you. Such a private corporation, operated for a profit, is called a "stock" company. This means that the capital of the business is divided into transferable portions known as shares that are evidenced by stock certificates. These certificates will entitle holders to participate in a distribution of profits. As you know, a certificate represents a stockholder's proportionate interest in the profits, the net assets, and the control of the corporation.

close corporation

closely held corporation

Initially your organization will probably be a private stock corporation classified as a "close" rather than a publicly traded corporation. A **close corporation** or **closely held corporation** is one that has no shares of its stock available for purchase by or in the hands of the general public.

Someday you may want to expand the business and finance the growth with money from outside investors. In a sense, you would be "opening" such a close or private corporation by offering to issue shares of stock through a listing of the stock on a public stock exchange.

As long as a corporation remains close, however, there will likely be only a few shareholders. These same people will probably also serve as directors and working officers. Therefore ownership, management, and key employees in your organization will be identical in fact—although separate for legal and tax purposes.

Disadvantages of Corporate Status

Baily: Are there reasons why we wouldn't want to operate as a corporation?

Kress: There are several disadvantages to the corporate form. Let's look at the non-tax-oriented disadvantages first. The corporate form lends itself to control of the minority by the majority. In the absence of appropriate control devices, the holder of a minority interest cannot readily cause the venture to be dissolved or force payment of dividends. For example, in the event of a shareholder's death—absent agreement on the subject—there is no easy way for the decedent's family to force a distribution of its share of corporate profits.

Another nontax disadvantage is that a corporation has to strictly observe corporate form. This entails charter documents, bylaws, and board of directors' as well as shareholders' meetings—all a bit complicated in comparison with a sole proprietorship or partnership. Incorporating may also entail legal and accounting costs, as well as state filing fees and franchise taxes over and above those of a partnership.

Now let's consider the tax disadvantages. The basic tax disadvantage is the potential of double taxation of earnings. Since the corporation is a separate tax entity, earnings will be taxed to the corporation as earned, and then again to the shareholders (although at special reduced rates) if a corporate distribution to them is classified as a dividend.

Advantages of Corporate Status

However, once corporate status is attained, you'll obtain a number of benefits that may substantially outweigh the costs.

I'll discuss the nontax advantages first. Primary among non-tax-oriented advantages is the ability to freely transfer ownership. It is relatively easy when using the corporate form to provide for a new owner's entrance and an old owner's exit. Second, the corporate form affords a limited liability to its shareholders. The corporation, and not its shareholders, is responsible for corporate obligations.

Now let's examine some of the tax-oriented advantages of corporate status. Since the three of you would be employees of the corporation, you would become entitled to a number of benefits that would be tax free to you and tax deductible by the corporation. For example, as an employee you would be permitted to borrow from the corporation's pension or profit-sharing plan. The corporation—as your employer—could establish a sizable group life insurance plan to cover you and your family, again at little or no tax cost to you. Since this would be considered an "ordinary and necessary" business expense, premium payments could be deducted by the corporation. A third benefit is that premiums on the disability income policies you each personally own and pay for with after-tax dollars could be taken over by your company. Such payments would then be tax free to you and tax deductible to the business.[3]

Reebel: I understand that by incorporating we would be eligible for loans from qualified deferred-compensation plans and certain other tax-favored fringe benefit arrangements.

Kress: That is correct. The Code permits the corporation to offer you—as an employee—a number of fringe benefits. Keep in mind that these benefits must be reasonable in amount and in return for services you have rendered.[4]

There are other tax-oriented factors you may find advantageous. For instance, assuming your corporation does not have to pay out substantial dividends, the overall tax result may be lower federal income taxes. It might be easiest to illustrate this point by comparing partnership with corporate tax treatment. If you formed a partnership, the three of you would be taxed on all the income you earned as partners—even if you didn't actually withdraw all your partnership earnings from the firm. However, as stockholder-employees, you would be taxed only on your salaries (assuming no dividend is paid). Lower total federal income tax under the corporate form may result because a new taxpaying entity, the corporation, has been created. The total tax payable depends upon how much taxable income is left inside the corporation. Let's look at the current tax rate structure for corporations.[5]

Certain corporations engaged in the business of rendering personal services are taxed at a flat rate of 35 percent. We'll discuss this further when we talk about the taxation of a corporation as a separate entity.

A corporation can generally control the salaries paid (as long as payments are reasonable) so as to avoid bunching income in those years when your personal income is highest. On the other hand, if you established your business in the partnership form, you'd have little control over the receipt and taxation of income. This ability to time income is important, since you may be able to reduce your ultimate tax liability by allowing some income to remain in the corporation and be taxed at a 15, 25, or even 34 percent all of which are lower than the two top marginal rates on income of individuals (35 and 39.6 percent).

---

3.   IRC Secs. 402, 403, 79, 105, and 106.
4.   IRC Sec. 162(a).
5.   The effect of state corporate taxes should not be overlooked. In addition, both payroll and local taxes (i.e., business privilege taxes) need to be considered.

Table 18-1: Corporate Tax Rates	
Taxable Income	**Tax Rate**
$0–$50,000	15%
$50,001–$75,000	25
$75,001–$100,000	34
$100,001–$335,000	39
$335,001–$10,000,000	34
$10,000,001–$15,000,000	35
$15,000,001–$18,333,333	38
Over $18,333,333	35

Cheesman: Is there a way to have our cake and eat it too? That is, can we get the loss flow-through so that we can deduct any corporate losses against our personal income but still get many of the benefits you just mentioned?

LO 18.2 **Explain the requirements for the formation of an S corporation, and describe the advantages and disadvantages of being taxed as an S corporation.**

S CORPORATIONS

S corporation

C corporation

Kress: What you are referring to sounds like an **S corporation.** The Internal Revenue Code allows a closely held corporation to elect not to be taxed as a regular corporation, or **C corporation**, if it meets certain requirements. Basically the result is that the corporation is not taxed as a separate entity.[6]

In other words, the corporation itself does not (with certain exceptions) pay tax.[7] Instead, corporate net income is taxed directly to its shareholders. This enables shareholders of a small, closely held corporation to obtain some of the tax and nontax advantages of corporate form

---

6.   IRC Secs. 1361-1363; IRC Secs. 1366-1368.
7.   IRC Sec. 1374 (tax imposed on certain built-in gains).

without its disadvantages. The S corporation election avoids double taxation of corporate income resulting from dividend payments (even with lower dividend tax rates). It also avoids the tax penalty on accumulated earnings as well as the personal-holding-company tax. Corporate income and losses will be immediately passed through to the shareholders.

However, some of the tax-advantaged fringe benefits that are available to employees of a regular corporation do not apply to more than 2 percent shareholders of an S corporation. These shareholders are taxed on their fringe benefits including Sec. 79 group term life insurance and Sec. 106 employer-provided health insurance.

All these characteristics are consistent with the underlying purpose of an S corporation, which is to promote tax neutrality when choosing the form in which to do business (for example, a sole proprietorship, partnership, or corporation). Congress felt that, to the extent tax treatment influenced the choice of business form, the result was a potential distortion of normal business practices. Therefore provisions were made in the Code to allow for S corporation treatment.

To qualify for S corporation status, the following requirements must be met:

- An S corporation can have only one class of stock.
- An S corporation must have no more than 100 shareholders. Members of the same family are treated as one shareholder. For this purpose, "members of the family" include a common ancestor and all lineal descendants of the common ancestor (including spouses and former spouses of such descendants). However, the common ancestor cannot be more than six generations removed from the youngest generation of shareholders at the time the election is made. Different rules applied to S elections made before 2005.
- An S corporation can have no shareholder other than an individual, an estate, or certain types of trusts (except for qualified Subchapter S subsidiary corporations).
- An S corporation must be a domestic corporation—that is, incorporated in the United States.
- An S corporation may not have nonresident alien shareholders.

Types of trusts that are permitted to be S corporation shareholders include the following ones:[8]

- voting trusts
- grantor trusts
- trusts treated as owned by an individual other than the grantor under IRC Sec. 678
- qualified subchapter S trusts (QSSTs)

---

8.   IRC Sec. 1361(c), (d), and (e).

- electing small business trusts (ESBTs)

Any such trust that owns S corporation stock or trusts that receive the stock under the terms of a will may hold the stock for a 2-year period after the death of the grantor of the trust or previous owner of the stock. A QSST is a trust that, among other requirements, must distribute all of its income currently to one individual. In general, an ESBT is a trust whose beneficiaries are all individuals or estates. Charitable organizations may, however, hold a contingent remainder interest in an electing small business trust. No interest in an electing small business trust may be acquired by purchase.

An S corporation does not pay corporate tax on its income. The result is that the shareholders are taxed on the taxable (i.e., ordinary) income of the corporation in proportion to their stock ownership. If the corporation has a loss, it can be deducted directly by the shareholders. As I have already noted, using this type of election, the corporation and its shareholders are taxed in most (but not all) respects in a manner similar to the way they would be taxed if they were operating as a partnership.

The S corporation election is used in a number of situations. For example, if you expected high initial losses in your first year or two of business operations, you would want to pass through the corporation's losses since you are all in high individual income tax brackets, so that you could use them against your own income tax liability.[9]

An S corporation election might also be indicated where business owners want to take advantage of limited liability but do not want to incur a double taxation when income earned and taxed by the corporation is later distributed to its shareholders.

An S corporation election may also be indicated when shareholders intend to withdraw substantially all corporate earnings and (1) not all stockholders are employees who could justify their shares as salary payments, (2) the amount of earnings is so great that any attempt to pay them out as salaries would result in unreasonably high salaries, or (3) the corporation has taxable income that would be taxed at a corporate rate higher than the shareholders' individual marginal rates without an S election. The S corporation election also avoids the double tax that still occurs to both a corporation and its shareholders when an actual or constructive dividend is paid out of earnings.

By an irrevocable and unqualified gift of shares of stock, a taxpayer can arrange to split income with another family member. Thus it is possible to transfer income to lower-bracket donees. By getting stock into the hands of various family members, it is possible to shift income to other

9. IRC Sec. 1366(a) and (d).

taxpayers even though the income may be used to satisfy support or other family obligations that the donor would otherwise have to pay with after-tax dollars.

In fact, you could even use the S corporation election to allow the corporation to continue income payments to you at retirement (or to your widow should you predecease her) without double tax consequences. You know that the IRS may question high salaries to older stockholder-employees, claiming that part of the pay is really a nondeductible, yet still taxable dividend. The election generally avoids this question since payments to shareholders are not taxed as dividends. Thus where a shareholder is inactive, less able to contribute services, or in need of retirement income, but does not want to create a double tax, the S corporation may be the answer, depending on the circumstances.

Baily: How long is the S corporation election effective?

Kress: Once made, an S election is effective indefinitely. However, the election can be terminated in any of the following ways:

First, the corporation can elect to revoke the election with the consent of the shareholders who own more than 50 percent of the stock.

Second, the election terminates if the corporation no longer qualifies as a "small business corporation"—that is, if it has more than 100 shareholders, or a nonresident alien acquires stock, or if an entity other than permitted shareholders acquires stock. Also the issuance of a second class of stock would terminate the election.

Third, if more than 25 percent of the S corporation's gross receipts for 3 successive tax years is from certain types of passive income and the corporation has accumulated earnings and profits from its days prior to the S election, the election will be terminated.[10] Certain banks, bank holding companies, and financial holding companies are exempted from this rule.

The revocation can be elected on or before the 15th day of the third month of the present taxable year and will be effective for that entire taxable year, unless the revocation specifically requests a revocation date in the future. If so, the revocation will be effective on the date selected. If no future date of revocation is specified but the revocation election is filed after the permissible period, the revocation is effective at the beginning of the following taxable year. Voluntary revocations generally result in an inability to reelect the S status for 5 years without obtaining IRS consent to the reelection. The IRS can, in appropriate circumstances, waive the 5-year waiting period and permit the corporation to make a new election effective for the

---

10.　　IRC Sec. 1362(d).

following taxable year. Also, if an S corporation election is invalid or late, the IRS may grant relief if the proper remedial action is taken by the corporation.

Let's get back to our discussion of regular corporations. We'll begin with a discussion of some tax issues that arise when a corporation is formed.

FORMATION OF A CORPORATION

Kress: All three of you have something to contribute to the corporation. In return you will want to participate in the control and profits of the business while it is running or in a distribution of the assets of your business if the corporation's life ends. In other words, you will expect shares of the corporation. For discussion purposes, let's assume Cheesman will contribute his business (his sole proprietorship). Baily will contribute cash or securities. Reebel wants to contribute his services and a small amount of cash in return for his stock.

Assuming this is the case, here is what might happen: if Baily decides that his contribution to the capital of the corporation will be cash, the stock he receives will normally have a value at the time of the exchange equal to the cash. For example, if he transfers $10,000 of cash to the corporation, he will ordinarily receive back stock with a fair market value of $10,000. Since the value of the stock he receives is no more or less than the value of the cash he transfers to the corporation, he realizes neither a gain nor a loss. If he later sells his stock, the cash he paid will determine the basis of his stock. If he realizes $21,000 on the sale of the stock, his gain would be $11,000, the difference between his basis for the stock ($10,000) and the amount he realizes on the sale ($21,000).[11]

Reebel: Is it correct to assume that, as long as the value of the cash and/or property we transfer to the corporation is equal to the value of the stock we get, we will have neither gain nor loss?

Kress: Not exactly. The general rule is that when property is exchanged for stock in a corporation, there is a sale or exchange. In the absence of any other provisions in the Code, you would have a recognized gain or loss. The amount of gain or loss would be measured by the difference between the amount you realize in the transaction (the value of stock you get) and the adjusted basis (the cost) of the property transferred to the corporation. Therefore, if you transferred mutual funds that had a present fair market value of $100,000 in exchange for $100,000

---

11. Reebel, who is transferring cash in exchange for stock, will also receive stock in exchange for services he is to render to the corporation. The stock he receives will be counted in determining whether the transferors of *property* have control of the corporation. However, the fair market value of the stock he receives for the future performance of services will be currently taxable to him as compensation.

of the newly formed corporation's stock, you might still have a taxable gain. For example, if you had paid only $10,000 for the mutual funds (now worth $100,000) and you exchanged the mutual funds for stock, there would be a taxable gain of $90,000. This same general principle applies if Cheesman was to exchange his appreciated business for cash—he would have a gain. The same result could occur when you transferred appreciated property to the corporation in exchange for its stock.[12]

Reebel: I guess that rules out Cheesman putting in his sole proprietorship and also Baily transferring his appreciated securities into a new corporation.

Kress: Not really—what we have just discussed is the general rule. But, like most provisions of the Code, there is an exception to the general rule. The exception was designed to encourage the formation of new corporations. It enables a taxpayer to transfer appreciated property or even a going business into a new corporation without the transferor recognizing income on the appreciation at the very time when his or her other expenses—the expenses involved in the organization and operation of the corporation—are the highest. The exception provides that even if the transferor realizes a gain when appreciated property is transferred to his or her new corporation, gain does not have to be recognized for tax purposes.[13]

NONRECOGNITION PROVISION FOR TRANSFER TO A CORPORATION CONTROLLED BY TRANSFEROR(S)

This nonrecognition provision must meet certain basic requirements. Where a person or persons transfer property to a corporation solely in exchange for the corporation's own stock (other than certain "nonqualified" preferred stock), and the transferor(s) control the corporation immediately after the transfer, no gain will be recognized on the appreciated property or securities contributed to the new corporation.

The philosophy here is similar to that of a tax deferred like-kind exchange. The transferor who receives stock in exchange for property has really maintained interest in the original property. It has merely changed form. The new form continues his or her interest in the original property, though it now has the physical identity of stock. This continuity-of-interest concept is the key to nonrecognition of the gain on the appreciated property transferred.

---

12.   IRC Sec. 1001.
13.   IRC Sec. 351.

For example, suppose Cheesman, who is now operating as a sole proprietor, decides to transfer his going business to the new corporation. If his basis for the sole proprietorship is $10,000 and the fair market value of his business is $50,000 at the time he transfers it to the new corporation, he would probably receive $50,000 worth of stock. Under the general rule for taxing sales and exchanges, he would recognize a $40,000 gain. However, the nonrecognition provision provides that since he got back only stock and through that stock controlled the corporation (just as he previously controlled his sole proprietorship), what has happened is really only the substitution of stock certificates for his former physical possession of the property. In other words, he now owns stock that is evidence of ownership in the same property owned before. His interest has changed merely in form, not in substance.

This rule is logical, since to recognize gain there must be a taxable event that usually occurs in the form of a sale, or exchange, or other disposition of property. Although technically there may be a sale (a transfer of property in return for money or a promise to pay money) or exchange (a transfer of property in return for other property or services), there has been no exchange in substance. Cheesman, in our example, hasn't disposed of his property. He has merely received certificates that evidence that he changed the form (and not substance) of his ownership in the original property. This would apply no matter how many people transfer property to the corporation. As long as it was done collectively, if the taxpayers transferring property to the corporation still have both (1) control and (2) interest in the property they originally owned, they would not have to recognize any gain on receipt of the new corporation's stock. Thus Cheesman would not have to recognize the $40,000 gain until and unless he later sells his stock.

LO 18.3   **Describe the requirements for incorporating a business under the nonrecognition provisions of the Code, and explain the respective roles of debt and equity in the corporate structure.**

Requirements for Nonrecognition

There are three formal requirements that must be satisfied to obtain an exception to the general rule so that there will be no recognition of a gain. Perhaps the chart below—Nonrecognition Provision—will help.

First, there must be one or more persons transferring property (which may include cash) to the newly formed corporation. The example we have just discussed meets the transfer-of-property requirement, since we assumed Cheesman transferred his business to the corporation.

Second, the transfer must be solely in exchange for stock in such a corporation. Since all Cheesman received from the corporation was the stock of the new corporation, the example above meets this requirement. If, however, Cheesman had received stock plus other property (such as cash or corporate notes) his transfer would not have met this requirement. If he had received stock (which does qualify) plus that other property to boot (other property or cash which does not qualify), he would have had to recognize part of his gain. Generally to the extent of this boot received, or to the extent of the gain on his transaction (whichever is less), the transferor of appreciated property will have to recognize income. For example, in the situation above, if Cheesman had received $30,000 worth of stock plus $20,000 of cash, he would have received $20,000 worth of boot. He would have to recognize income to the extent of the cash he received ($20,000), since the figure is the lower of (a) $20,000 boot or (b) the $40,000 gain realized ($50,000 amount realized minus $10,000 basis for the sole proprietorship transferred).[14]

Table 18-2: Nonrecognition Provision

If the transfer of property is

1. solely in exchange for the corporation's own stock and
2. transferor(s) control the corporation immediately after the transfer, then no gain (or loss) is recognized.

Money or Other Property Received to Boot

Receives			
Stock	$30,000		
Cash	$20,000		$50,000
Transfers			
Property (Basis)			$10,000
Gain			$40,000
Reportable			$20,000

Gain ($40,000) is recognized to extent of boot ($20,000).

The third requirement for nonrecognition is that the transferor(s) (the person or persons transferring cash and/or property to the corporation in return for stock of the corporation) must be in control immediately after the exchange. This requirement also makes sense. For nonrecognition to follow, the incorporation must be merely a change in the physical form of ownership—that is, an exchange of cash and/or property in return for stock.

If the original transferors no longer own their original property (where there has been a drastic shift in the proportion of ownership interest and control), the transaction takes on the effect of a sale or exchange and, as such, will be taxable. Control is defined as ownership of stock possessing at least 80 percent of the combined voting power, plus at least 80 percent of the total

14. IRC Sec. 351(b).

number of shares of the new corporation. This 80 percent test of control must be met for tax purposes even though, from a legal standpoint, a shareholder could actually control a corporation with as little as a 51 percent interest.

If the three tests are met (that is, if any one of you or even all three of you transfer property to a corporation, if the transfer is solely in exchange for the stock of the new corporation, and if you as transferors are in control immediately after the exchange), the following will result.

First, no gain will have to be recognized on the exchange either by the transferor(s) or by the corporation. Second, the corporation takes the transferor's basis for the property contributed. If Cheesman's basis for the property he transfers to the corporation was $10,000 and the corporation later sells that same property, its basis for tax purposes would be $10,000. Thus, if it sold the property for $30,000, its gain would be the difference, or $20,000. Third, the stockholder who receives stock from the corporation takes a substituted basis—that is, for tax purposes his or her basis for the stock acquired from the corporation is typically the same as the stockholder's basis for the property he or she transferred.

If a stockholder receives boot, he or she must (1) decrease the stock's basis to the extent of the fair market value of any boot property as well as any cash received, but (2) his or her basis can be increased by the amount of any gain that must be recognized. If Cheesman, for example, received $40,000 worth of stock plus $20,000 in cash boot, he would report the $20,000 of cash as income. Therefore Cheesman must (1) decrease the basis of his stock by $20,000 since this is the amount of the boot he received; then (2) he may increase his basis by the amount of any gain that he must recognize. Since he recognizes $20,000 of income in this particular situation, the net result of the boot transaction is a $10,000 basis. Basis is first decreased by the amount of boot received but then increased by the amount of boot that was taxable. In this case it resulted in a washout so that Cheesman's basis remains at $10,000.

The basis to the corporation of the property received would be the transferor's basis ($10,000), plus the amount of gain the transferor had to recognize because of the boot he or she received ($20,000). Suppose the corporation later sold the property it received. If the amount the corporation realized on the sale of the property was $40,000, its gain would be only $10,000 ($40,000 amount realized minus $30,000 adjusted basis [$10,000 original basis, plus $20,000 increase in basis because of the recognition of income by the transferor]). No gain or loss is recognized by a corporation for the receipt of cash or property in exchange for stock of the corporation.

ORGANIZATIONAL EXPENDITURES

Baily: Are the expenses of forming a corporation currently deductible in determining corporate taxable income?

Kress: The costs of creating a corporation ordinarily constitute capital expenditures, since in a sense they create an asset that will be exhausted over the lifetime of the corporation.

There are a number of such expenses incurred in the organization of the corporation. For example, there are state filing fees and legal expenses in obtaining the charter, costs for accounting services incident to the organization, and fees paid for drafting the corporation charter and bylaws as well as for the terms of the original stock certificates.

A corporation can recover the cost of these organizational expenditures through amortization deductions. In other words, the corporation can deduct these costs in even amounts over a period of 180 months beginning with the month in which the corporation begins business. In most cases this would be after the corporation is legally formed.[15]

However, corporations may deduct up to $5,000 of such organizational expenses in the tax year in which business begins. This rule applies so long as the total organizational expenses do not exceed $50,000. The $5,000 deductible amount is reduced (but not below zero) by the amount of any excess of the total organizational expenses over $50,000. The remaining expenses are amortized over the 180-month period.

Different rules applied to expenses made before October 23, 2004. Those were generally amortized over a 5-year period.

OTHER METHODS OF FINANCING

One of the key advantages of business in the corporate form is that many different avenues for raising capital can be created. We have just discussed the general definition of stock. This includes common stock, preferred stock, convertible securities, warrants, and options. The interests of any particular investor can be met by creating a security that fits his or her special needs and desires. This factor facilitates the acquisition of capital. Suppose the corporation issued bonds to acquire working capital as well as capital for long-term planning. As you know,

---

15.   IRC Secs. 195 and 248. (For purposes of determining the *earnings and profits* of a corporation for dividend payments, organizational expenses are to be capitalized and written off as part of the basis of the corporate asset[s] to which the expenditure applies.)

a bond is a written obligation to repay a definite sum of money on a definite date, usually at least 10 and often 20 or more years, from the date the bond was issued.

Bonds may be a favored means of raising corporate capital. One reason for this is that a corporation will obtain a deduction for the interest paid on the indebtedness. By contrast, no deduction is allowed for dividends paid on either preferred or common stock. As long as a corporation can earn money at a higher rate (with the cash raised by issuing the bond) than it costs the corporation (in interest necessary to service the debt), it usually makes sense for the corporation to borrow money. This is known as "leverage."

Of course, issuance of the bonds themselves would create no tax liability to either the corporation or the bondholder. This is because the corporation has merely borrowed money and agreed to return it. Conversely, the bondholders have merely loaned money. When the bond matures, the principal becomes payable and the bondholders are entitled to a tax-free return of their capital investment. In contrast, when a corporation makes payments to its shareholders with respect to their stock, the general rule is that the payment will be taxed as a dividend.

Any money bondholders receive in the form of interest will be taxable as ordinary income, while any money they receive at the maturity of their bonds in excess of their capital investment may be taxed as capital gain. This occurs when bonds are purchased at a discount but are paid off at face value. (When bonds are issued at a discount by the issuing corporation, a bondholder generally must include a ratable portion of the discount in income each year as the bond matures. For example, if a bond with a par value of $1,000 was issued for $800 and is payable in 10 years, the $200 discount would be included in the taxpayer's income at the rate of $20 a year.)

Another reason bonds are favored over stock is that the accumulation of earnings and profits within the corporation to pay debt obligations can be justified more readily than accumulating earnings to redeem stock. This helps avoid an additional tax on an unreasonable accumulation of earnings.

Reebel: Is there any reason stockholders couldn't lend money to the corporation in return for bonds?

Kress: No, it is quite common for a shareholder to forgo an equity (stock) interest with regard to some of his or her contribution in return for the greater security of a loan. As you know, the bond promises to pay a specified sum of money by a specified date. This date is usually at least 10 years from the date of issue. Of course, bonds generally pay a fixed rate of interest each year until that specified date. Typically, in the event the corporation fails financially, bondholders have preferred rights to corporate assets. Since the interest paid on corporate indebtedness is deductible, the after-tax cost of raising capital through long-term corporate debt is substantially reduced.

However, some shareholders attempt to overdo it—they contribute almost no equity investment and characterize the major portion of their contribution as debt owed to them by the corporation. This is known as "thin capitalization," since the equity investment is thin in relation to the debt, but the debt is really disguised stock.

Reebel: What is the effect of thin capitalization?

Kress: Once the form of the debt is disregarded by the IRS and the substance is treated appropriately, corporate deductions for interest payments to shareholders are disallowed. Second, receipt of interest payments by shareholder-creditors are reclassified and treated as dividends. Third, when the corporation pays off its debt to the shareholders, that payment is taxed as a dividend. This means that instead of treating the amount received as a tax-free repayment of a debt, the shareholder-creditor must report the payment as a dividend, taxable at the applicable dividend rate. Finally, money that the corporation purportedly was accumulating to pay off the debt is now potentially subject to the accumulated-earnings tax, which we'll discuss in a few moments. Also a debt that is reclassified as stock could cause a termination of an S election since an S corporation is allowed to have only one class of stock.

Baily: How do the courts distinguish between debt and equity?

equity

Kress: The courts usually examine a number of factors such as the ones that follow: Was there an intention by shareholders to enforce payment of the debt? Was there collateral for the debt? Was there a debt instrument (note), and did it give the shareholders management or voting rights (like stock)? What was the ratio of debt to equity? One rule of thumb is that if the amount of debt exceeds shareholders' equity by more than four to one, the corporation is thinly capitalized. Basically the court would examine all the factors relevant to determine if a "loan" by shareholders was in reality more like **equity** (ownership interest) than a debtor-creditor relationship.[16]

Keep in mind that while bonds might be a tax-favored means of obtaining corporate funds, frequently a corporation does not want to become obligated to make fixed payments for interest and debt amortization. To avoid a cash-flow problem therefore corporations often finance

---

16.   IRC Sec. 385; see also *Kraft Foods Co. v. Comm'r* , 232 F.2d 118 (Ratio of Debt to Equity); *J. S. Biritz Construction Company v. Comm'r* , 387 F.2d 454 (Initial Working Capital Requirements); *McSorley's Inc. v. U.S.* , 323 F.2d 900 (Loans Proportionate or Disproportionate to Shareholdings); *Nassau Lens Co. v. Comm'r* , 308 F.2d 39 (Terms of Loan).

long-term operations or investments with common stock, which entails no obligation to pay dividends, or preferred stock, on which dividend payments can frequently be avoided. Furthermore, stocks are used in preference to bonds because, unlike bonds, stocks never mature— there is no requirement that a corporation pay off either preferred or common stock.

Cheesman: Assuming we've properly capitalized the corporation, how is its income actually taxed?

TAXATION AS A SEPARATE ENTITY

Kress: A corporation is taxed as an entity separate from its shareholders. The rates are 15 percent of the first $50,000 of taxable income, 25 percent of the next $25,000, 34 percent on amounts of taxable income between $75,001 and $100,000, 39 percent on amounts between $100,001 and $335,000, 34 percent on amounts between $335,001 and $10 million, 35 percent on amounts from $10 million to $15 million, 38 percent on amounts from $15 million to $18,333,333, and 35 percent on amounts over $18,333,333. Thus if your corporation (let's call it the Bradwell Corporation) has $60,000 of taxable income, its tax will be $10,000 (15 percent of $50,000, plus 25 percent of the $10,000 excess above $50,000).

Figure 18-1
The Corporate Tax Funnel

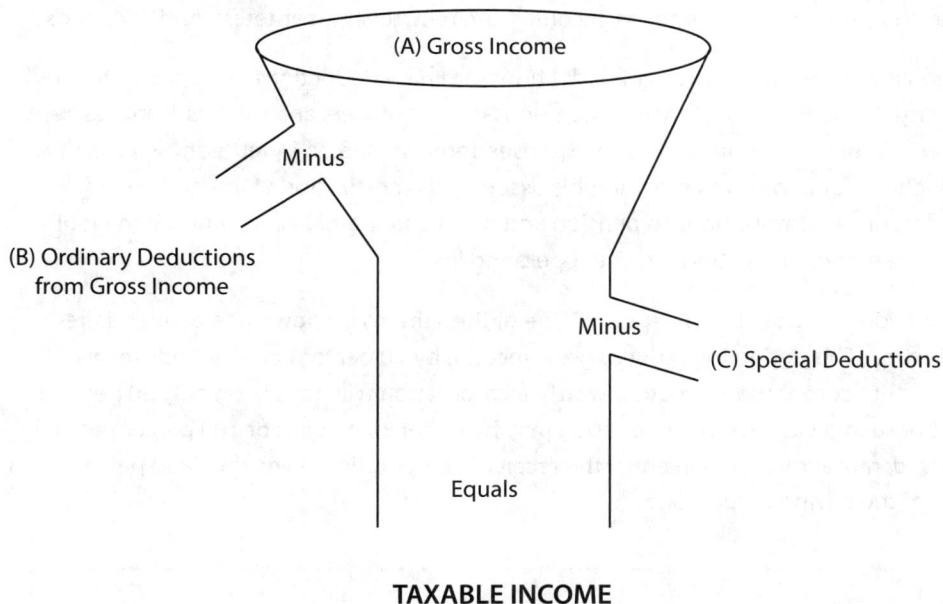

(A) Gross Income

Minus

(B) Ordinary Deductions
from Gross Income

Minus

(C) Special Deductions

Equals

TAXABLE INCOME

However, under current law the taxable income of a "qualified personal service corporation" is taxed at a flat rate of 35 percent. Under Sec. 448(d), a qualified personal service corporation for this purpose is one in which (1) substantially all the activities involve the performance of services in the fields of health, law, engineering, architecture, accounting, actuarial science, performing arts, or consulting, and (2) substantially all the stock (95 percent or more) is held by employees or retired employees or by their estates.

Since the Bradwell Corporation will be engaged in a manufacturing business, the flat rate of 35 percent will not apply. However, should the Bradwell Corporation become a consulting business in the future, the flat tax rate would apply since all three shareholders will be working for the business. This, of course, is only the federal income tax. Corporations, like individuals, are liable for a number of other state and local taxes as well. Bradwell Corporation would report its federal income tax on IRS Form 1120.

Graphically, Bradwell Corporation's return might look like the illustration above.

LO 18.4   Describe how a corporation determines taxable income or loss, and explain the issues associated with deductions for salaries, charitable deductions, deductions for dividends received, and other deductions.

Computation of Taxable Income

Gross income would include such items as profit from sales and receipts from services. It would also include gains on sales or exchanges, income from rent, royalties, interest, and dividends.

A corporation is entitled to two types of deductions: ordinary deductions and special deductions. Ordinary deductions would include compensation of officers and salaries, bonuses, rent payments, charitable contributions, repair expenses, interest paid on indebtedness, casualty losses, deductions for depreciation of tangible assets and amortization of intangibles, advertising, and corporate contributions to pension and profit-sharing plans. A corporation would also receive a carryover deduction for a net operating loss.

Several deductions are classified as "special." One of these items is known as a dividends-received deduction. This deduction reduces gross income by 70 percent of dividends received from certain other corporations. In other words, a corporation will pay tax on only 30 percent of the amount of such dividends. The deduction may be either 80 percent or 100 percent of dividends received, rather than 70 percent, if the receiving corporation owns specified percentages of the stock of the paying corporation.[17]

---

17.   IRC Sec. 243.

Taxable income is what is left after taking ordinary and special deductions. It is the amount to which the corporate income tax rates are applied. Certain credits are then directly applied against this tax, such as corporate overpayments of tax in previous years, payments for estimated taxes (paid on a quarterly basis), credit on certain foreign taxes paid, and investment credit.

Kress: Let me go into more detail on some of those items.

Deductions for Salaries

The first item we discussed under the category of "ordinary deductions" was salaries. Bradwell Corporation would be entitled to a deduction for salaries or any other compensation for personal services, but only if the services were actually rendered and the amount paid as compensation for those services was considered reasonable. "Reasonable" means only the amount that would ordinarily be paid for similar services by corporations like Bradwell under similar circumstances.

This reasonableness test is imposed most frequently on closely held corporations because of the large degree of coincidence of executive and shareholder interest. It is designed to prevent the shareholders of Bradwell from draining out corporate profits in the disguise of tax-deductible salaries. Corporate profits are usually paid out in the form of dividends that are taxable to the shareholders but are nondeductible by the corporation. The portion of the salary considered unreasonable is usually classified as a disguised dividend, and to that extent the corporation's deduction is disallowed. However, even though that amount may not be deducted by the corporation, it is still taxable as ordinary income to the shareholder-recipient.[18]

Reasonableness is a question of determining the amount that would ordinarily be paid for like services by like enterprises under like circumstances. Generally, where an executive employee does not own or have options to purchase stock, arm's-length bargaining as to the amount of salary is assumed. One element that could be considered in determining reasonableness is the fact that a given individual was not adequately compensated in prior years. Thus if high compensation in the current year can be attributed to services rendered in prior years, the total current salary might be considered reasonable.

However, the amount of cash compensation is not the only relevant factor. Corporate contributions to pension and profit-sharing plans are considered business expenses and are allowed as deductions as long as the total amount of all forms of compensation paid on behalf of an

---

18. IRC Sec. 162; see also *Chesapeake Mfg. Co., Inc.*, T.C. Memo 1964-214, aff'd. 347 F.2d 507; *R. J. Reynolds Tobacco Co.*, 260 F.2d 9, aff'g. T.C. Memo 1956-161; Treas. Reg. Sec. 1.162-7(b).

individual does not exceed a reasonable total. Some of the other indirect forms of compensation may be premiums for life insurance, hospitalization, medical care, and salary continuation plans.

Costs of these plans, although deductible by the corporation, often do not result in taxable income to the individual. Since the corporation is a separate and distinct tax entity, and since the three of you would be considered salaried employees, you would be eligible for these forms of indirect compensation. This is true even though you would be not only employees, but also officers, directors, and shareholders of the corporation.

excess golden parachute payments

With respect to reasonable payments to executives or key employees, you should be aware of a concept called **excess golden parachute payments.** These are payments to executives or key employees (1) that are contingent upon a change or threatened change of ownership or control of a corporation and (2) that have a present value equal to or in excess of three times the individual's average annual compensation for the 5 preceding years. These payments are not deductible by the corporation, and they subject the individual to an excise tax of 20 percent of the excess payment in addition to the regular income tax.

In addition, if compensation paid to an executive fits the definition of "excessive employee remuneration," the compensation will not be deductible by the employer.

Cheesman: What is "excessive employee remuneration"?

Kress: First, the compensation must be paid by a publicly held corporation to fall within the rule. Second, the definition applies generally to compensation of over $1 million per year paid to one employee.

performance-based compensation

Compensation for purposes of this definition does not include commissions, contributions to qualified plans, and tax-free fringe benefits. It also does not include any **performance-based compensation**. In order to be treated as performance based, the compensation must be payable solely on account of the attainment of one or more performance goals determined by a compensation committee of the corporation's board of directors. Such a committee must be comprised solely of two or more outside directors. Also, in order to be treated as performance based, the compensation must be both disclosed to the corporation's shareholders and approved by a shareholder vote.

The $1 million limitation applies only to the chief executive officer of the company and its four most highly compensated officers for the taxable year. Therefore it will apply only to a maximum of five employees in any given corporation. If the corporation has made so-called excess golden parachute payments that are nondeductible under Sec. 280(G), such payments will reduce the $1 million annual cap.

Deduction for Qualified Production Activities Income

A deduction designed specifically for businesses engaged in manufacturing activities took effect for tax years beginning after 2004. The deduction is equal to a specified percentage of the taxpayer's "qualified production activities income." Qualified production activities income is generally equal to the taxpayer's "domestic production gross receipts," minus the cost of goods sold allocable to those receipts, and reduced by certain other directly allocable and ratable (i.e., not directly allocable) deductions, expenses, and losses described in the law.

Domestic production gross receipts are essentially funds received for the sale or rental of property produced in a "qualified production activity." Therefore the key question in understanding this deduction is, "What is a qualified production activity?" In very general terms, the answer is that it is a manufacturing activity. The deduction is designed to benefit taxpayers engaged in the business of manufacturing (such as Bradwell).

The manufacture or development (in whole or significant part) in the United States of the following types of property is generally treated as a qualified production activity: tangible personal property; most computer or video game software; certain film productions; production of electricity, natural gas, or water; and construction or substantial renovation of real property. The performance of engineering or architectural services also generally qualifies. Only one taxpayer is entitled to the deduction with respect to the manufacturing of tangible personal property. Food and beverages prepared at a retail establishment do not qualify. Also, the business of transmission of electricity, gas, or water does not qualify.

It is significant to note that this is an unusual type of deduction because the deductible amount represents an item of income, not an item of expense. Even though the provision is technically a deduction under the Code, its net effect is to reduce the effective rate of tax applicable to income from a qualified production activity.

C corporations, pass-through entities (S corporations and partnerships), and individual taxpayers are all eligible for the deduction if they meet the rules. For pass-through entities, the deduction is applied at the shareholder or partner level.

Another key question is, "What is the amount of the deduction?" Presently, it is 9 percent of the taxpayer's qualified production activities income. There are limitations, however, on the amount allowable. The deduction generally cannot exceed the taxpayer's taxable income (determined without regard to the deduction itself). For individuals, the deduction cannot exceed the individual taxpayer's adjusted gross income, as determined with certain modifications. Also, the deduction currently cannot exceed 50 percent of the wages allocable to domestic production gross receipts that are paid by the taxpayer to employees and reported on Form W-2. For example, if the taxpayer has no employees, the deduction cannot be claimed.

The deduction is allowable for purposes of both the regular tax and the alternative minimum tax (AMT).

There is considerable detail and complexity in these rules. This discussion is intended to be only an overview of the basics of the deduction for qualified production activities income. However, Bradwell's manufacturing activity should qualify, based upon current interpretation of this provision.

Charitable Deduction

It is generally felt that corporations owe some type of obligation to the communities in which they exist. Consequently the corporate statutes of most states permit corporations to make charitable contributions. The Internal Revenue Code permits a charitable deduction for contributions by a corporation. However, the deduction is limited to a maximum of 10 percent of the corporation's taxable income. (Certain adjustments are made to taxable income before the 10 percent maximum deduction is computed. For example, taxable income for this purpose is computed without regard to the deduction for charitable contributions in order to avoid a circular calculation.) If the corporation should make a contribution in excess of 10 percent of its adjusted taxable income, it can carry the deduction forward for up to 5 years and use that carryforward to reduce its future taxable income. For example, if taxable income was $100,000, and the corporation made a charitable deduction of $100,000, it would get a $10,000 ordinary deduction it could use in the current year. The balance could be carried over and applied against future years' income.[19]

Net Operating Loss

net operating loss

Suppose Bradwell Corporation didn't do as well as originally planned. In fact, suppose the expenses of operating the business exceeded the corporation's income. Because a corporation is treated as a separate tax entity, losses will not be allowed to pass through to Bradwell's shareholders. Unlike the case in a partnership or S corporation, a regular corporation's shareholders

---

19.   IRC. Secs. 170 and 162(b).

will not be able to use a loss to offset personal income. The loss may only be used by the corporation itself. Bradwell could use this **net operating loss** to reduce income in certain other tax years. In other words, if the corporation has more operating expenses than it has income, it could carry the loss as a deduction to certain other tax years. The loss would then reduce tax liability for the year to which it is carried. Unlike charitable deductions where the corporation is only allowed to carry a deduction forward, in the case of a net operating loss, the corporation can carry back the loss and then also carry it forward.

The corporation can generally carry the loss back 2 years and carry it forward 20 years. The effect of this provision is to enable a corporation to average operating income or loss over a continuous 23-year period. The process works like this: First, the corporation carries back its loss just as if that loss had been incurred 2 years before the year in which the loss was actually sustained. Appropriate adjustments are made on that year's tax return. Then any unused loss is carried back to the first year preceding the actual year when the loss is sustained. If there is any excess loss not applied to the previous 2 years, the remaining net operating loss is carried forward over the next 20 years.

A corporation may elect not to utilize the carryback period, even though this does not extend the carryforward period. A corporate taxpayer may waive the carryback period when it was in an unusually low bracket or when it was already shielded by tax credits that could not be carried to later years.

The purpose of the carryback or carryforward of operating losses is to enable the corporate taxpayer to stabilize business income. If there were no provisions for carrying operating losses backward or forward, the entire gain from successful years would be taxed, but in loss years only a portion of the loss could be utilized. A loss in a given year that exceeded earnings for that year would be useless.

Capital Gains and Losses

Often a corporation will sell or exchange capital assets. If Bradwell sells a capital asset at a loss, then, unlike an individual, it may not apply any portion of that loss against ordinary income. A corporation can use capital losses (treated as short-term capital losses) only as an offset against capital gains. Corporations are permitted to carry an unused net capital loss back 3 years and then, if further loss still remains, carry the excess over to the 5 succeeding years. Note that the loss still cannot be used to reduce ordinary income. Corporate capital losses must be utilized only to offset capital gains. Such losses must first be applied to the earliest of the years involved (3 back through 5 forward), then to the next year, and so on until the losses are exhausted.[20]

---

20. IRC Sec. 1211(a), 1212.

Cheesman: What if the sale resulted in a gain?

Kress: A corporation must include its full capital gain in income. However, there is an alternative method of taxation that may apply to a corporation's net capital gains in some cases. The alternative method provides for a flat rate of 35 percent instead of the regular corporate tax rates. The alternative tax applies only if the applicable regular tax rate is higher than 35 percent (excluding the additional phase-out rates). If the corporation's taxable income (including the capital gain) does not exceed $100,000, the regular rates must be used for capital gains. As a result, the alternative tax rate of 35 percent is applied to the lesser of the net capital gain or the corporation's taxable income. The following chart is a comparison assuming that the corporation has $75,000 of taxable income this year, which includes $5,000 of net long-term capital gain. As indicated, the alternative tax rate only apples when a corporation's ordinary income tax rate exceeds 35 percent. Since the top corporate tax rate is currently 35 percent, this rule generally does not apply under our current corporate rate structure.

Table 18-3: Corporation Has $75,000 of Taxable Income (Ordinary Income of $70K including $5,000 of LTCG)			
Regular Tax Computation		**Alternative Tax Computation**	
(1) 15% of $50,000 of taxable income	$7,500	(1) Taxable income	$75,000
		(2) Less—$5,000 net long-term capital gain	$5,000 $70,000
(2) 25% of taxable $ 5,000 income between $50,001 and $75,000	$6,250		
		(3) Tax on $70,000 at regular rates	$12,500
		(4) 35% of $5,000 capital gain	$1,750
Regular tax	$13,750	Alternative tax	$14,250
Note: The alternative method of taxation would not be used in this example because it is more than the regular tax.			

Deduction for Dividends Received from Certain Corporations

I mentioned before that a corporation may be entitled to certain special deductions. The most common of the special deductions is the deduction for dividends received from certain corporations. For example, Bradwell Corporation might purchase stock in other corporations, such as AT&T or General Motors, as an investment. Perhaps Baily will transfer stock of other corporations to Bradwell Corporation as part of his original contribution of capital in return for Bradwell's stock. Bradwell would be allowed a special deduction for a percentage of dividends received during its tax year from stock it holds in certain other corporations. Specifically, it may deduct (subject to certain limitations) 70 percent of the dividends it receives.

dividends

These **dividends** must be distributions from the earnings and profits of taxable domestic corporations. Since dividends on deposit or withdrawal accounts in domestic building and loan associations or mutual savings banks are not really dividends at all, they are treated as interest and do not qualify for this deduction.

Likewise, Bradwell cannot deduct 70 percent of the dividends received from many tax-exempt corporations, because the deduction for dividends received is intended to prevent triple taxation of corporate income. Since tax-exempt corporations and many foreign corporations are either not taxed at all or not taxed at full corporate rates, to allow a dividends-received deduction for dividends received from these corporations would be to favor them rather than to treat them equitably.[21]

The amount of the dividends-received deduction can vary depending on how much stock in the paying corporation is owned by the receiving corporation. The dividends-received deduction is 70 percent if the receiving corporation owns less than 20 percent of the paying corporation. If the receiving corporation owns 20 percent or more but less than 80 percent of the paying corporation, the dividends-received deduction is 80 percent. Different rules apply if the corporation receiving the dividends owns 80 percent or more of the corporation paying the dividends. If certain conditions are met, the dividends-received deduction is 100 percent.

There is a reduction in the dividends-received deduction when the corporation owns a portfolio of stock acquired by incurring debt. The theory is that the benefit of the dividends-received deduction should be neutralized, since the corporation obtained the added benefit of a deduction for interest on the debt incurred to purchase stock.

The dividends-received deduction is not available to S corporations.

LO 18.5   **Describe the purposes of the accumulated-earnings tax and the personal-holding-company tax, and explain corporate policy with respect to dividend distributions.**

THE ACCUMULATED-EARNINGS TAX

Assuming that Bradwell Corporation is as successful as the three of you have been individually, in a few years the corporation will reach its maturity stage. As the corporation begins to be profitable, it will need money to grow and expand, just as it needed capital at its formation.

---

21.   IRC Sec. 246.

One of the easiest ways of financing growth is by accumulating earnings and plowing them back into the corporation to purchase new machinery, buildings, and other necessary capital assets. These plow-back earnings and profits begin to add up very quickly. You may want to use your business as a vehicle for accumulating money. You can do that merely by having the corporation retain earnings rather than make distributions to shareholders in the form of non-deductible dividends. If Bradwell Corporation allows earnings to accumulate in order to fund current or anticipated needs or projects that the corporation has planned, there is no problem. However, once earnings are allowed to accumulate beyond the reasonable needs of the business, those earnings may be subject to an additional tax.[22]

accumulated-earnings tax

The **accumulated-earnings tax** is a tax imposed on every corporation that is formed or used for the purpose of avoiding personal income tax with respect to its shareholders by permitting earnings and profits to accumulate instead of being distributed. The purpose of the tax is to discourage the use of a corporation as an accumulation vehicle to shelter its individual stockholders from taxation resulting from dividend distributions. Without such a tax on improper accumulations, stockholders could arrange to have dividends paid in years when their incomes were low, or they could indefinitely accumulate earnings and profits inside the corporation until the corporation was liquidated. Accumulations of $250,000 or less will automatically be considered to be for the reasonable needs of the business. Accumulations of $150,000 or less will be considered to be for the reasonable needs of the business in the case of professional service corporations.[23] However, if Bradwell is profitable and begins to accumulate amounts in excess of $250,000, it should be prepared to show a bona fide business reason for not distributing these earnings in the form of dividends.

As I mentioned, the purpose of this tax is to discourage the corporation from retaining profits in the absence of legitimate business motives. If earnings could remain in the corporation indefinitely, then its stockholders might never have to pay personal income tax on corporate earnings and profits. As a regulatory device, the accumulated-earnings tax was designed to force the distribution of retained earnings at the point where they no longer serve a legitimate business purpose.

The accumulated-earnings tax is designed to tax only earnings retained beyond the reasonable needs of the business. The question then becomes, "What reasonable needs would Bradwell Corporation have for accumulating profits?" Treasury regulations state that working capital needs and capital for building expansion or for the replacement of plant or equipment are

---

22.   IRC Secs. 531 and 532.
23.   IRC Sec. 535(c)(2).

among the needs that would allow Bradwell to properly accumulate earnings. In addition to these needs, a sinking fund to retire corporate bonds at maturity has often been found to be a reasonable need to accumulate cash. In other cases, funds set aside to acquire minority interests or quarreling stockholders' interests were also deemed to be retained for reasonable business needs.[24]

Baily: Our financial advisor suggested we purchase cash value key person insurance. Would accumulated earnings in the form of cash values be a reasonable business need?

Kress: That depends on whether or not the insurance answers a valid corporate business need. There must also be a close correlation between the type of policy and amount of death benefit and the alleged corporate need. Generally, hedging against the loss of a key employee's service because of unexpected death is considered to be a reasonable business need.

Key person life insurance is insurance owned by the corporation insuring the life of a key employee. The purpose of such a policy is to provide a fund at the employee's death that will compensate the corporation for the financial loss resulting from the unavailability of the employee to render services to the corporation. Often key person insurance death proceeds are also used to help in finding and compensating a suitable replacement. Therefore the purchase of life insurance as well as the earnings used to pay policy premiums should not be, per se, subject to the penalty tax.[25]

In one case enough insurance to generate $1.5 million worth of life insurance proceeds was considered reasonable. The point is that it is not the amount but the purpose of the accumulation that is important.

The same question may arise as to the effect of a split-dollar plan. If a corporation attempts to prevent taxation of income to shareholders by accumulating its earnings rather than distributing them, the existence or nonexistence of a split-dollar policy will not, by itself, deter the imposition of the tax penalty provided by the law. Conversely, the existence of a split-dollar policy will not, per se, incur the accumulations tax penalty if the corporation is not, in fact, accumulating earnings beyond the reasonable needs of the business. It is important to remember that this section of the Code exists to deter tax evasion and not to prevent a business from operating in a normal businesslike manner. The same principle applies in cases where the corporation has obligated itself to make preretirement death benefits to a key executive under

24. IRC Sec. 537; Treas. Reg. Sec. 1.537-1(b)(1) and (2); Treas. Reg. Sec. 1.537-1(a); *Hardin's Bakeries, Inc.* v. *Martin, Jr.*, D. C. Miss., 1/10/67; Rev. Rul. 67-64, 1967-1 C.B. 150.

25. *General Smelting Co.*, 4 T.C. 313; *Reynard Corp.*, B.T.A. 552; *Harry A. Koch Co. v. Vinal* (Dist. Ct., Neb.) 228 F. Supp. 782; *Vuono-Lione, Inc.*, T.C. Memo 1965-96; *Emeloid Co. v. Comm'r*, 189 F.2d 230; *Bradford-Robinson Printing Co.* (Dist. Ct., Colo., 1958) 1 AFTR 2d 1278.

a deferred-compensation agreement. An accumulation of corporate earnings to meet obligations under such an agreement is generally considered a reasonable business need (just as the funds accumulated to retire an outstanding corporate bond would be considered reasonable).[26]

This question also often arises when accumulated earnings are used to provide surplus cash for the redemption of stock. In this case, if the redemption is to be utilized to shift partial or complete control to the remaining shareholders without depleting their personal funds (for example, if by shareholder agreement the corporation will retire shares on the death of a shareholder), it is doubtful that accumulations to reach this result would be found to be a reasonable need. However, if a business purpose can be found, such as an accumulation to purchase the shares of the dissenting minority, then the accumulation will be found to be reasonable. The primary purpose must be a corporate, rather than an individual, benefit from the stock redemption.[27]

Reebel: What is the maximum we could reasonably accumulate?

Kress: The critical factor is not the size of the accumulated earnings and profits but rather the reasonableness and nature of that surplus. For this reason, part of the surplus may be justifiably earmarked in the form of reserves for specific business needs.

Keep in mind that for the tax to be imposed it is not necessary that tax avoidance be the primary reason for the accumulation. As long as it is even one of the purposes for retention of earnings, the tax could be levied.

Most corporations will have little trouble in proving a reasonable business need for most of the earnings they retain. However, a corporation must be prepared to create and preserve adequate records to show that it had a specific plan to use the assets accumulated.

Among the evidence that could be used to support the corporation's case might be the fact that the business in question needs large amounts of cash for operating purposes at certain times during the year because of the nature of the business. It might show the actual use of the profits of past years as well as documented plans for future use of accumulated dollars. Corporations that rarely pay dividends are generally suspect, but if the corporation has a strong history of paying dividends, this would be another evidential factor that the current accumulation was not for the prohibited purpose of avoiding personal income tax.

26. *John P. Scripps Newspapers*, 44 T.C. 453; *Okla. Press Pub. Co. v. U.S.*, 437 F.2d 275; Treas. Reg. Sec. 1.537-2(b)(3).
27. *Mountain State Steel Foundries, Inc. v. Comm'r*, 284 F.2d 737; *Oman Construction Co.*, T.C. Memo 1965-325; *Dill Mfg. Co.*, 39 B.T.A. 1032; *Gazette Publishing Co. v. Self*, 103 F. Supp. 779. See also *Prunier v. Comm'r*, 248 F.2d 818; *Sanders v. Fox*, 253 F.2d 855; *Hedberg-Freidheim Contracting Co.*, T.C. Memo 1956-275, aff'd 25 F.2d 839.

The Internal Revenue Service will give weight to a pattern of expenditures or loans to or on behalf of shareholders to show that the corporation had the financial capacity to distribute retained earnings as dividends but has chosen instead to avoid payment of such funds as dividends in order to prevent personal income taxes at the shareholder level. For the same reason, the Service might question the purpose of corporate funds placed in passive investments, such as the stock of unrelated corporations.

Cheesman: What is the penalty for retaining earnings that are not for the business's needs?

Kress: The penalty for accumulating earnings "beyond the reasonable needs of the business" is as follows: Improper accumulations are currently taxed at a flat rate of 20 percent.[28] It is important to note that the tax, if applicable, is imposed only on accumulated taxable income, an amount derived from the taxable income of the corporation for the particular year in question. Thus the tax does not apply to all the accumulated earnings and profits of the corporation but only to the accumulated taxable income of the year or years in which the tax is assessed.

This tax on a corporation's accumulated taxable income is payable in addition to the regular tax payable by the firm. "Accumulated taxable income" basically means the corporation's taxable income for the year in question with certain adjustments (such as a reduction for federal income taxes paid) minus the sum of

- distributions from current earnings and profits that the shareholders have reported as ordinary income (dividends paid), plus
- amounts from earnings and profits that the shareholders have reported as dividends even though no actual distribution was made (disguised dividends), plus
- the accumulated-earnings credit[29]

Keep in mind that in determining whether or not this year's accumulated taxable income has been retained for the reasonable needs of the business, you must also consider the availability of prior years' accumulated earnings. If past years' accumulations are sufficient to meet current needs (that is, this year's business needs) you would have no justification for accumulating this year's earnings.

I just mentioned an accumulated-earnings credit. In Bradwell's case, this is a $250,000 minimum credit, but it is important to note that it includes earnings from prior years. For example, if prior years' accumulated earnings were in excess of $250,000, there would be no credit. Every dollar of this year's accumulated taxable income would be subject to tax, unless it could be proven

---

28. IRC Sec. 531.
29. IRC Sec. 535.

that the income was for the reasonable needs of the business. Let me go into more detail about this credit.

The minimum credit "shall in no case be less than the amount by which $250,000 exceeds the accumulated earnings and profits of the corporation at the close of the preceding taxable year."[30] Thus if the accumulated earnings and profits on December 31 of last year were $20,000, the minimum credit for this year would be $230,000. If no earnings or profits were accumulated in the past, a surplus of at least $250,000 can be accumulated this year without incurring an accumulated-earnings tax. This means that corporations can accumulate up to $250,000 of their earnings and profits without any possibility of being subject to the tax, even though they have no reason for the retention of those earnings. However, that is merely the minimum credit. The maximum credit equals the greater of (1) the minimum credit or (2) the earnings and profits retained for the reasonable needs of the business.

PERSONAL-HOLDING-COMPANY TAX

personal holding company

Reebel: Is a personal holding company a tax-avoidance device similar to the unreasonable accumulation of corporate earnings?

Kress: Yes. A **personal holding company** is a device stockholders have used to place income with a corporation to prevent themselves from being taxed on a personal level. The formulation of a personal holding company generally has taken two forms—the "incorporated-talent" form and the "incorporated-wallet" form. The incorporated-talent or personal-service form of a personal holding company is set up as a result of this type of situation. A highly compensated individual, such as a movie star or athlete, normally receives a very high fee in return for services. This earned income may be subject to the highest individual income tax rates.

Under the incorporated-talents scheme, the financial superstar chose not to receive his or her fee directly, and so formed a corporation and contracted to work for it at a modest, fixed salary. The corporation then contracted the superstar's talents out at the going rate, and it received the normally high fee his or her unusual talent brought. Because of the separate entity concept, income attributable to the superstar's services was taxed, not to the individual, but to the corporation at corporate tax rates which were significantly lower than individual rates when this provision was enacted. For example, a baseball player would form a corporation and contract to render services to it for, perhaps, $50,000 a year. The corporation would then contract out the

---

30.   IRC Sec. 535(c).

player's services for a great deal more, say $120,000 a year. The $70,000 balance would be held and accumulated by the corporation, subject to the lower corporate tax. The corporation could later be liquidated and the individual would pay only a relatively low capital-gain tax on the liquidation.

A second scheme was known as the incorporated-wallet personal holding company. Its purpose was to form a corporation to hold passive investments. Property would be transferred to such a personal holding company so that dividends and interest earned by that property would be taxed at corporate rather than individual rates. The corporate wallet would merely hold the assets; collect the dividends, interest, or rental income; and pay tax at the relatively lower corporate rates in effect under prior law.

In response, Congress enacted a penalty tax on the undistributed income on corporations that operate as incorporated-talent or incorporated-wallet corporations. In the event that certain mechanical standards of receipt of passive income, personal-service income, and stock ownership found in the Internal Revenue Code are met, such corporations known as personal holding companies will be subject to taxation in addition to both the regular corporate tax and corporate alternative minimum tax (where applicable).[31] The additional tax is currently imposed at a flat rate of 20 percent. It applies to "undistributed personal-holding-company income," which is basically taxable income minus taxes paid and dividends distributed.[32]

Baily: When will a corporation be considered a personal holding company?

Kress: To be classified as a personal holding company, two conditions must be present: first, most of the corporation's income (at least 60 percent of adjusted ordinary gross income) must come from personal-holding-company income. Second, more than 50 percent of the value of the stock must be held by five or fewer individuals (this test is broad because ownership attribution rules apply).

Assume Harry Hughes, a billionaire, forms and is the sole shareholder of the Harry Corporation, which holds only his large corporate bond portfolio. It will be the policy of the corporation never to distribute dividends. When the Harry Corporation receives interest payments on the

---

31. To be considered personal-service (incorporated-talents) income, the following two tests must be met: (1) the person with whom the corporation has contracted for the services of its "star" has the right to designate that the "star" is the one who must perform the services contracted for, and (2) the individual who must or did perform the services owns 25 percent or more of the stock in the corporation. In Rev. Rul. 75-67, 1975-9, I.R.B.-7, a doctor, a specialist, incorporated his practice. The Internal Revenue Service ruled that this one-man corporation would not be considered a personal holding company as long as the doctor was not designated orally or in writing to personally perform services, and the services would not be so unique as to preclude substitution.
32. IRC Sec. 541.

bonds, the corporation is taxed. However, such a corporation would be found to be a personal holding company under the passive income and stock ownership standards, and Harry Corporation would incur, in addition to the corporate tax, a personal-holding-company penalty tax.

Cheesman: Can the personal-holding-company tax be avoided?

Kress: Yes. The principal way to avoid such a penalty tax is to cause the corporation to distribute dividends. If liability for personal-holding-company tax is found, the Code allows a corporation to mitigate this tax liability by paying a retroactive deficiency dividend.[33] However, liabilities for interest and penalties will not be eliminated. Of course, the distribution of dividends defeats the attempt by taxpayers to have income taxed only once at the corporate level. Several types of corporations are specifically exempted from the personal-holding-company tax. Among these are life insurance companies, banks, and other financial institutions that are required by law to maintain certain asset reserves.[34]

Reebel: What happens when distributions to shareholders are finally made?

Kress: The taxation of shareholders in this case is the same as under any corporate distribution to shareholders.

With the highest statutory rates for individuals at 39.6 percent, the significance of the personal holding company as a tax avoidance tool has increased. The personal-holding-company tax still remains an effective tax-avoidance deterrent when wealthy individual investors are in a higher marginal tax bracket than controlled corporations with effective tax rates below 35 percent. In addition, Congress's continual tinkering with the Internal Revenue Code always creates the opportunity that there will again be an even greater tax rate difference between individuals and their controlled corporations.

DIVIDEND DISTRIBUTIONS BY THE CORPORATION

Although close corporations are not usually inclined to distribute dividends, a corporation that is already paying the highest reasonable salaries possible may want to distribute some or all of its profits in the form of dividends. The general rule is that any distribution made by a corporation to its shareholders will be considered a dividend for federal income tax purposes. Qualified dividends are currently taxed to individuals at a maximum rate of 20 percent.[35]

---

33. IRC Sec. 547.
34. IRC Sec. 542(c) and (d).
35. IRC Secs. 301 and 316. Dividends of certain high-income taxpayers will also be subject to the net investment income tax described in Chapter 14.

There is a limitation on the general rule as well as three basic exceptions. The limitation to the general rule is that a distribution is a taxable dividend only to the extent that it is paid out of either accumulated earnings and profits or current earnings and profits. The three basic exceptions to the general rule are that (1) certain stock dividends are tax free, (2) certain redemptions of stock qualify for capital-gains treatment, and (3) the proceeds of certain liquidations qualify for capital-gains treatment.

Cheesman: Would you discuss these principles in more detail?

Kress: Certainly.

First, it might be helpful to discuss exactly how the Code and regulations define the term "dividends." As I have already mentioned, we start with the general rule that all distributions are dividends. However, there is an earnings and profits test. This test provides the tax limit—it tells us how much of any given distribution will be taxable as a dividend and also what portion of that distribution will be considered a tax-free return of capital.[36]

You might think of a corporation as if it were a money machine. We put money into the machine hoping to get a lot more out. Part of the money coming out could be considered earnings and profits, while the balance could be considered part or all that was originally put in. If we think of a corporation this way, then some method has to be devised to determine what portion of a given corporate distribution is taxable as a dividend and what portion of each distribution is nontaxable as a return of capital. This is exactly what the tax law gives us— an arbitrary method for distinguishing between (1) what we put in (capital) and (2) what we get out (capital and/or dividend income and/or capital gains). Therefore some distributions are considered dividends in part, return of capital in part, or even a capital gain in part. Perhaps an example would be helpful.

If current and accumulated earnings and profits are $20,000, and the stockholder's basis for his or her stock is $10,000, a $50,000 distribution would have the following effect:

- To the extent of earnings and profits ($20,000), the distribution is treated as a dividend for income tax purposes.

- Any remaining portion of the distribution has the effect of returning the shareholder's cost. In this case $10,000 of the distribution would be applied against and reduce the shareholder's basis and would therefore be recovered tax free.

- If any portion of the distribution remains, the balance is considered to be a gain from the sale or exchange of property. If the stock was a capital asset in the shareholder's

36. IRC Secs. 301 and 316(a); Treas. Reg. Sec. 1.316-1(a) and (c).

hands and was held for the requisite holding period, long-term capital gain will result. In this example there would be a capital gain of $20,000. (From the $50,000 distribution, $20,000 was applied against earnings and profits and is therefore taxed as a dividend; the next $10,000 was considered a recovery of cost and is therefore tax free; and the remainder, $20,000, is considered gain and will be taxed as a capital gain.)

Baily: What is the effect if the shareholder in this example sells his or her stock after the distribution?

Kress: If the stock is subsequently sold, the stockholder's basis for determining gain or loss on the sale will be zero. Let me point out another important thought on the subject of dividend distributions. When a distribution is made to all shareholders in proportion to the number of shares owned by each shareholder, the distribution will be typically considered a dividend. I want to emphasize that a dividend can be found even in the absence of a formal pro rata distribution. Without any other explanation, the word dividend implies any corporate distribution in any form to shareholders from the surplus of the corporation. Therefore dividends can be paid as cash, notes, or stock of other corporations, or in various other forms.

Note that even though dividends are taxable to the recipient-shareholder, the distributing corporation receives no deduction for the distribution. However, the maximum tax rate of 20 percent is favorable as compared to the regular maximum rates on ordinary income.

When the distribution consists of cash, the amount of cash determines how much dividend income must be reported by the shareholder-recipient. If the dividend is in the form of property, the fair market value of the property determines what is reportable. If the property distributed by the corporation is subject to a liability, the taxable amount is reduced by the amount of the liability assumed by the shareholder (but not below zero).

Baily: Will the corporation itself have a gain if it uses appreciated property for corporate distributions?

Kress: The rule is that when appreciated property is distributed in any type of distribution, gain (but not loss) is recognized. This rule is applicable to distributions of dividends and in redemption of stock. The amount realized would be equal to the gain that would have been realized if the property had been sold at the time of the distribution.

Reebel: What effect does a dividend distribution have on the accumulated earnings and profits?

Kress: The accumulated earnings and profits of the corporation will be reduced by the amount of the dividend. When cash is distributed, corporate earnings and profits will be reduced by the amount of that cash. When property other than cash is distributed, earnings and profits are generally reduced by the adjusted basis of that property to the corporation. If appreciated property is distributed by the corporation, then earnings and profits are increased by the gain recognized and decreased by the property's fair market value. If the distributed property (i.e., fair market value or adjusted basis) is subject to a liability or the shareholder assumes the liability, then the reduction to earnings and profits is reduced by the amount of the liability.

CHAPTER REVIEW

Key Terms and Concepts

corporation	equity
limited liability	excess golden parachute payments
transferability of interest	performance-based compensation
centralized management	net operating loss
continuity of life	dividends
close corporation	accumulated-earnings tax
closely held corporation	personal holding company
S corporation	
C corporation	

Review Questions

Review questions are based on the learning objectives in this chapter. Thus an [18.3] at the end of a question means that the question is based on learning objective 3. If there are multiple objectives, they are all listed.

1. What are the four characteristics that have traditionally distinguished a corporation from other business entities? [18.1]

2. How will an organization that is organized as a corporation under state law be taxed under federal law? [18.1]

3. What are the tax and nontax disadvantages of corporate status? [18.1]

4. What are the tax and nontax advantages of corporate status? [18.1]

5. For what reasons might a corporation elect to be taxed as an S corporation? [18.2]

6. Jones operates a gold mining company as a sole proprietorship. He is thinking of incorporating the business in order to obtain limited liability and wants to know whether he will be able to utilize corporate losses on his own individual tax return. Explain. [18.2]

7. What are the requirements for qualification as an S corporation? [18.2]

8. a. How does a corporation terminate its S corporation status?

   b. What are the consequences of an S termination? [18.2]

9. What is the general rule for transfer of appreciated property to a corporation? [18.3]

10. What are the requirements for nonrecognition of gain when property is transferred to a newly formed corporation? [18.3]

11. Jules forms the Crestwood Corporation and transfers the assets of his successful sole proprietorship to the corporation. The assets are worth $100,000 but have a basis of only $30,000. Jules receives $80,000 worth of stock and $20,000 in cash. Will Jules have to recognize any gain? Explain. [18.3]

12. This year A, B, C (a C corporation), D, and E organize the X Corporation. They transfer to the X Corporation properties with the following fair market values (FMV) and adjusted bases (AB) in exchange for the corporation's stock or a combination of stock and cash:

Transfers to X	AB ($)	FMV ($)	Shares	Cash Received from Corporation ($)
A - Cash	50	50	50	
B - Land and building	50	100	100	
C - Inventory	10	20	20	
D - Machinery	10	30	20	10
E - Trucks	30	20	10	10

   a. Will A, B, C, D, or E recognize any gain or loss? What basis does each have in the X stock received?

   b. What gain, if any, must X recognize at the time of the transfer?

   c. X Corporation eligible to elect S corporation status? [18.3]

13. How are organizational expenses of forming a new corporation treated for tax purposes? [18.3]

14. Other than contributions of property and cash in exchange for stock, what methods exist for financing a new corporation? [18.3]

15. Suppose that the IRS claims that the Rollo Corporation is "thinly capitalized." The IRS characterizes the payments on the corporation's bonds as dividend payments. Then the Rollo Corporation takes the case to court since this characterization is unfavorable.

    a. What are some of the factors the court would examine before disregarding the debt classification?

    b. What is one rule of thumb applied by the courts with regard to debt-equity ratio? [18.3]

16. a. What are the income tax rates imposed on corporations other than S corporations?

    b. How is a corporation that is classified as a "qualified personal service corporation" taxed? [18.4]

17. What are the steps in computing corporate taxable income? [18.4]

18. a. Explain the "reasonableness" standard for determining whether a salary paid by a corporation is deductible.

    b. Explain the rule disallowing a deduction for "excessive employee remuneration." [18.4]

19. What types of business activities qualify for the deduction for "qualified production activities income"? [18.4]

20. a. What is the maximum amount a corporation may deduct as a charitable contribution in a given taxable year?

    b. How is the excess treated for tax purposes? [18.4]

21. The Secane Corporation has a net operating loss of $4,000 this year. In what years can Secane take advantage of the loss? Explain. [18.4]

22. Can a corporation offset its capital losses against ordinary income? Explain. [18.4]

23. Arnold Allwin, the president of Daffy Defense Corporation, arranged a government contract that results in gross income to the corporation of $3 million. Explain whether the corporation is entitled to deductions for the following items:

    a. $1 million salary to Arnold

    b. $50,000 capital loss (the corporation has no capital gains for the year)

    c. $10,000 charitable contribution to the American Red Cross [18.4]

24. Explain how the deduction for dividends received applies to corporations that own stock in other corporations. [18.4]

25. Explain the purpose of the accumulated-earnings tax, when it is imposed, and the rate at which it is imposed. [18.5]

26. Last year Zoom Corporation had net earnings in excess of the accumulated-earnings credit. It does not distribute any dividends to its shareholders. Zoom's board of directors has no plans to use its undistributed earnings.

    a. Will Zoom be subject to the accumulated-earnings tax?

    b. Would your answer be different if Zoom Corporation accumulated this sum in the form of cash value key person insurance on its key executives and officers? Explain. [18.5]

27. It has been suggested by a financial adviser that Price Corporation purchase $500,000 of key person cash value life insurance on the life of Preston Yukon, the firm's skilled operational vice president. For many years, earnings of the corporation have been substantial, but no dividends have ever been declared or paid. The corporation now has substantial cash it does not need for current operations or anticipated growth and the firm's CPA is fearful of an accumulated-earnings tax problem. Will the proposed purchase of cash value life insurance by Price Corporation aggravate its potential problem? Explain. [18.5]

28. a. Describe the penalty tax imposed on undistributed income of personal holding companies.

    b. Explain how this tax may be avoided. [18.5]

29. What are the tax consequences to a corporation on the distribution of appreciated property to its shareholders? [18.5]

Review Answers

1. There are four legal characteristics that traditionally distinguish a corporation from other forms of business operation. These characteristics are as follows:

    *   limited liability

    *   transferability of interest

    *   centralized management

    *   continuity of life

2. An organization formed as a corporation under state law will generally be taxed as a corporation under federal law.

3. The basic tax disadvantage is the potential of double taxation of earnings. The non-tax disadvantages include the fact that the corporate form lends itself to control of the minority by the majority and that corporate form has to be strictly observed; this entails charter documents, bylaws, and board of directors' as well as shareholders' meetings.

4. The non-tax advantages of corporate status are the ability to freely transfer ownership and the limited liability of the owners. One of the tax advantages of corporate status is that the overall tax result may be lower federal income taxes if the corporation does not pay out substantial dividends. Although dividends remain preferentially taxed, they are still nondeductible by the corporation. The ability to time the receipt and taxation of income enables the owners to reduce their ultimate tax liability by allowing some income to remain in the corporation and be taxed at lower rates. In addition, employees of the corporation are entitled to receive a number of tax-free benefits that are tax deductible to the corporation, the major requirement being that these benefits must be reasonable in amount and provided in return for services rendered.

5. In an S corporation, the firm's net income (i.e., ordinary income) is taxed directly to its shareholders. This enables shareholders of a small, closely held corporation to obtain the tax and non-tax advantages of corporate form without its disadvantages. The S corporation election avoids double taxation of corporate income upon the payment of dividends. This still exists even with lower dividend tax rates. It also avoids the problems of a penalty on accumulated earnings as well as the personal holding company tax. Depreciation as well as corporate income and losses will be immediately passed through to the shareholders.

An S corporation election may also be indicated when shareholders intend to withdraw substantially all corporate earnings and (1) not all stockholders are employees who could justify their shares as salary payments, (2) the amount of earnings is so great that any attempt to pay them out as salaries would result in unreasonably high salaries, or (3) the corporation has taxable income that would be taxed at a corporate rate higher than the shareholders' individual marginal rates without an S election. The S election avoids the double tax that occurs to both a corporation and its shareholders when a dividend is paid out of earnings. Circumstances will dictate whether an S election will help in this regard.

By an irrevocable and unqualified gift of shares of stock, a taxpayer can arrange to split income with another family member. Thus it is possible to transfer income to lower-bracket donees. By getting stock into the hands of various family members, it is possible to shift income to other taxpayers despite the fact that the income may be used to satisfy support or other family obligations that the donor would otherwise have to pay with after-tax dollars.

In fact, a taxpayer could even use the S corporation election to allow the corporation to continue income payments to the taxpayer at retirement (or to the taxpayer's spouse should the taxpayer predecease him or her) without double tax consequences.

6. Jones will be able to deduct the corporation's losses on his individual return if the corporation elects to be taxed as an S corporation.

7. To qualify for S corporation status, the following requirements must be met:

   - An S corporation can have only one class of stock.

   - An S corporation must have no more than 100 shareholders. Members of the same family are treated as one shareholder.

   - An S corporation can have no shareholder other than an individual, an estate, or certain types of trusts (except for qualified Subchapter S subsidiary corporations).

   - An S corporation must be a domestic corporation—that is, incorporated in the United States.

   - An S corporation may not have nonresident alien shareholders.

8. a. S corporation status can be terminated in any of the following ways:

   First, the corporation can elect to revoke the election with the consent of the shareholders who own more than 50 percent of the stock.

   Second, the election terminates if the corporation no longer qualifies as a "small business corporation"—that is, if it has more than 100 shareholders, or a nonresident alien acquires stock, or if an entity other than permitted shareholders acquires stock. Also the issuance of a second class of stock would terminate the election.

   Third, if more than 25 percent of the S corporation's gross receipts for 3 successive tax years is from certain types of passive income and the corporation has accumulated earnings and profits from its days prior to the S election, the election will be terminated. Certain banks and other companies are exempted from this rule.

b. Voluntary revocations generally result in an inability to reelect the S status for 5 years without obtaining IRS consent to the reelection. The IRS can, in appropriate circumstances, waive the 5-year waiting period and permit the corporation to make a new election effective for the following taxable year. Also, if an S corporation election is invalid or late, the IRS may grant relief if the proper remedial action is taken by the corporation.

9. The general rule is that when property is exchanged for stock in a corporation, there is a sale or exchange. In the absence of any other provisions in the Code, there would be a recognized gain or loss. The amount of gain or loss is measured by the difference between the amount realized in the transaction (the value of stock received) and the adjusted basis (the cost) of the property transferred to the corporation.

10. There are three formal requirements that must be satisfied in order to avoid recognition of gain when property is transferred to a newly formed corporation.

First, there must be one or more persons transferring property (which may include cash) to the newly formed corporation.

Second, the transfer must be solely in exchange for stock in such a corporation.

Third, the transferors (the person or persons transferring cash and/or property to the corporation in return for stock of the corporation) must be in control immediately after the exchange.

11. A transferor of appreciated property who receives stock in a corporation in exchange for the property and realizes a gain on the transfer generally does not recognize the gain if he or she is in control of the corporation immediately after the transfer. However, since Jules received cash (boot) in addition to stock, gain is recognized to the extent of the lesser of the cash received ($20,000) or the gain realized ($70,000). In this case, the gain recognized would be $20,000.

12. a. Upon the formation of a corporation, no gain or loss is generally recognized as long as the transfer of property to the corporation is solely in exchange for the corporation's own stock and the transferors are in control of the corporation (under IRC Sec. 351) immediately after the transfer. In the event that money or other property is received, gain will be recognized but losses will not. A stockholder's basis in the stock received from the corporation will be the same as the basis in the property contributed, but it will be decreased by any money the stockholder receives in the exchange and then increased by the amount of any gain

the stockholder must recognize. When applying these general rules to the five stockholders, the following will result:

A has no realized gain, so there could not be any recognized gain. His basis in the X stock is his basis in the cash $50.

B has a realized gain of $50, but has no recognized gain since her transfer qualifies under the general rule of nonrecognition. Her basis in the X stock is the same as her basis in the contributed property $50.

C has a realized gain of $10, but it has no recognized gain since its transfer qualifies under the general rule of nonrecognition. Its basis in the X stock is its basis in the contributed property $10.

D has a realized gain of $20 and a recognized gain of $10 since he received boot. His basis in the X stock is his basis in the property contributed ($10), decreased by cash received ($10), and increased by gain recognized ($10). Therefore his basis is $10.

E has a realized loss of $10, but it is not a recognized loss. His basis in the X stock is the basis of his contributed property ($30) minus the amount of money received ($10) for a basis of $20. It would be more advantageous to E to sell the property to the X Corporation, recognize his loss, and then invest $20 in cash in the corporation.

b. X Corporation has no gain or loss upon the receipt of cash or property in exchange for its stock. Therefore X Corporation has no gain to recognize.

c. X is not entitled to elect S corporation status because the election is limited to corporations whose shareholders are individuals, estates, and certain types of grantor or voting trusts. C, one of the shareholders of X Corporation, is a corporation itself.

13. The costs of creating a corporation ordinarily constitute capital expenditures. However, most of those costs may be amortized (that is, deducted by the corporation) in even amounts over a period of 180 months beginning with the month the corporation begins business. Subject to restrictions, $5,000 of such costs can be deducted in the corporation's first year of business.

14. Bonds are a favored means of raising corporate capital. One reason for this is that a corporation will obtain a deduction for the interest paid on the indebtedness. By contrast, no deduction is allowed for dividends paid on either preferred or common stock. As long as a corporation can earn money at a higher rate (with the cash raised by issuing the bond) than it costs the corporation (in interest necessary to service the

debt), it usually makes sense for the corporation to borrow money. This is known as "leverage."

Another reason bonds are favored over stock is that the accumulation of earnings and profits within the corporation to pay debt obligations can be justified more readily than accumulating earnings to redeem stock. This helps avoid an additional tax on an unreasonable accumulation of earnings.

15. a. Questions asked by the court to ascertain whether or not Rollo Corporation is thinly capitalized would include the following questions:

- Was there an intention by shareholders to enforce payment of the debt?

- Was there collateral for the debt?

- Was there a debt instrument (note), and did it give the shareholders management or voting rights (like stock)?

- What was the ratio of debt to equity?

Basically, the court would examine all the factors relevant to determine if a "loan" by shareholders was in reality more like an ownership interest (stock) than a debtor-creditor relationship.

b. If the amount of debt exceeds shareholders' equity by more than four to one, the corporation may be thinly capitalized.

16. a. The rates are 15 percent of the first $50,000 of taxable income, 25 percent of the next $25,000, 34 percent on amounts of taxable income between $75,001 and $100,000, 39 percent on amounts between $100,001 and $335,000, 34 percent on amounts between $335,001 and $10 million, 35 percent on amounts over $10 million up to $15 million, 38 percent on amounts over $15 million up to $18,333,333, and 35 percent on amounts over $18,333,333.

b. The taxable income of a "qualified personal service corporation" is taxed at a flat rate of 35 percent.

17. The steps in computing corporate taxable income are

Gross Income

– Ordinary Deductions

–   Special Deductions

Taxable Income

Corporate gross income includes such items as profit from sales and receipts from services. Subtracted from gross income are ordinary deductions and special deductions. Ordinary deductions include such items as compensation of officers and salary, charitable contributions, repair expenses, interest paid on indebtedness, deductions for depreciation, advertising, and corporate contributions to pension and profit-sharing plans. In addition, a corporation would also receive a carryover deduction for a net operating loss. Special deductions include such items as the dividends-received deduction. Taxable income is what is left after taking ordinary and special deductions. It is also the amount to which the corporate income tax rates are applied.

18. a. Reasonableness is a question of determining the amount that would ordinarily be paid for similar services by corporations under similar circumstances.

b. Only compensation paid by a publicly held corporation can be classified as "excessive employee remuneration." If the compensation paid to the executive is over $1 million per year, it typically would be considered "excessive" and not deductible by the corporation. Compensation for purposes of the definition of "excessive employee remuneration" does not include commissions, contributions to qualified plans, and tax-free fringe benefits. It also does not include any compensation that is "performance based." The $1 million limitation applies only to the CEO of the company and its four most highly compensated officers. Therefore it will apply only to a maximum of five employees in any given corporation.

19. Qualified production activities include the manufacture or development of tangible personal property; most computer or video game software; certain film productions; electricity, water, and natural gas production; and construction or substantial renovation of real property. The performance of engineering or architectural services also generally qualifies.

20. a. The maximum amount a corporation may deduct as a charitable contribution in a given taxable year is 10 percent of its taxable income. This requires that certain adjustments be made to taxable income before the maximum deduction is computed.

b. If a corporation should make a contribution in excess of 10 percent of its adjusted taxable income, it can carry the excess forward for up to 5 years and apply it as a deduction to reduce its future taxable income.

21. Secane is able to carry back its net operating loss to the 2 previous years and carry it forward for 20 subsequent years. Secane may elect to utilize only the carryforward period.

22. A corporation cannot offset capital losses against ordinary income. It may only use capital losses as an offset against capital gains. In doing so, a corporation is permitted to carry an unused net capital loss back 3 years and then, if further loss still remains, carry the excess over to the 5 succeeding years.

23. a. Daffy Defense Corporation is entitled to deduct amounts paid for salaries as long as they are reasonable. What is reasonable is determined by the facts in each case. An amount that would ordinarily be paid for like services by like business firms under similar circumstances would be reasonable.

    b. Daffy Defense Corporation cannot deduct its capital loss currently because a corporation can only deduct its capital losses to the extent of its capital gains. Daffy Defense has no capital gains this year. However, the capital loss can be carried back for 3 years and then, if not used up, forward for 5 years.

    c. Daffy Defense Corporation can deduct the full amount of its charitable contribution this year since it will almost certainly be less than 10 percent of its taxable income.

24. A corporation is allowed a special deduction for a percentage of dividends received during its tax year from stock it holds in certain other corporations. To be eligible for the deduction, these dividends must be distributions from the earnings and profits of taxable domestic corporations.

    The amount of the dividends-received deduction can vary depending on how much stock in the paying corporation is owned by the receiving corporation. The dividends-received deduction is 70 percent if the receiving corporation owns less than 20 percent of the paying corporation. If the receiving corporation owns 20 percent or more but less than 80 percent of the paying corporation, the dividends-received deduction is 80 percent. Different rules apply if the corporation receiving the dividends owns 80 percent or more of the corporation paying the dividends. If certain conditions are met, the dividends-received deduction is 100 percent.

25. The accumulated-earnings tax is a tax imposed on every corporation that is formed or used for the purpose of avoiding personal income tax with respect to its shareholders by permitting earnings and profits to accumulate instead of being distributed. The purpose of the tax is to discourage the use of a corporation as an accumulation vehicle to shelter its individual stockholders from taxation resulting from dividend distributions. Accumulations of $250,000 or less will automatically be considered to be for the reasonable needs of the business. Accumulations of $150,000 or less will be

considered to be for the reasonable needs of the business in the case of professional service corporations.

The penalty for accumulating earnings beyond the reasonable needs of the business is taxation at a rate of 20 percent. This penalty tax is payable in addition to the regular tax payable by the firm. If applicable, the tax is imposed only on accumulated taxable income, an amount derived from the taxable income of the corporation for the particular year in question. Thus the tax does not apply to all the accumulated earnings and profits of the corporation but only to the accumulated taxable income of the year or years in which the tax is asserted.

26. The accumulated-earnings tax is imposed if earnings and profits accumulate beyond the reasonable needs of the business. What constitutes the reasonable needs of the business is a factual determination in each case.

    a. Here, where Zoom Corporation accumulates earnings and profits so that its shareholders can avoid taxation at higher rates, the prohibitive purpose is present. Therefore the accumulated-earnings tax would be imposed on all accumulated taxable income in excess of the accumulated-earnings credit.

    b. On the other hand, an accumulation in the form of cash values on key person policies is a reasonable need as long as the policies were purchased for a valid business purpose of the corporation.

27. The purchase of $500,000 of key person life insurance by the Price Corporation as well as the earnings used to pay policy premiums will not, per se, subject the corporation to the accumulated-earnings penalty tax if it is not accumulating earnings beyond the reasonable needs of the business. Generally, hedging against the loss of a key employee's service because of unexpected death is considered to be a reasonable business need.

Most corporations will have little trouble in proving a reasonable business need for most of the earnings they retain. However, corporations that never pay dividends, like the Price Corporation, are generally suspect and must be prepared to prove with appropriate records that they have specific plans to use the accumulated earnings.

In determining whether or not Price Corporation's accumulated taxable income for the current year is being retained for the reasonable needs of the business, the availability of prior years' accumulated earnings must also be considered. Since Price Corporation's past years' accumulations are more than sufficient to meet current needs or anticipated growth, it would have no justification for accumulating this year's earnings whether to purchase key person life insurance or for use to cover some other business need. Therefore, to avoid aggravating Price Corporation's potential accumulated-earning tax problem, it should allocate some of the prior years' accumulated earning to purchase key person cash value life insurance while also instituting a dividend program. The purchase of key person cash value life insurance with prior years' accumulated earnings will help to alleviate Price Corporation's potential problem, even though it can accumulate a surplus of up to $250,000 of earnings and profits without any possibility of being subject to the tax.

28. a. Personal holding companies are subject to taxation in addition to the regular corporate taxes. The additional tax is currently imposed at a rate of 20 percent. It applies to undistributed personal holding company income, which is basically taxable income minus taxes paid and dividends distributed.

    b. The principal way to avoid the penalty tax is to cause the corporation to distribute dividends. If liability for personal-holding-company tax is found, the Code allows a corporation to mitigate this tax liability by paying a retroactive deficiency dividend.

29. The rule is that when appreciated property is distributed in any type of distribution by a corporation, it must recognize gain (but not loss). This rule is applicable to distributions of dividends and in redemption of stock. The amount realized would be equal to the gain that would have been realized if the property had been sold at the time of the distribution. Gain is measured by the extent to which the property's fair market value exceeds its adjusted basis.

Chapter 19

Taxation of Distributions to a Corporation's Shareholders

Learning Objectives

An understanding of the material in this chapter should enable you to

LO 19.1   **Explain the tax implications of corporate distributions to stockholders.**

LO 19.2   **Explain the various requirements for treating stock redemptions as capital transactions.**

LO 19.3   **Explain the attribution rules that apply to corporate stock redemptions.**

LO 19.4   **Explain the requirements for Section 303 stock redemptions.**

> In my own case the words of such an act as the Income Tax, for example, merely dance before my eyes in a meaningless procession; cross-reference to cross-reference, exception upon exception—couched in abstract terms that offer no handle to seize hold of—leave in my mind only a confused sense of some vitally important, but successfully concealed, purport, which it is my duty to extract, but which is within my power, if at all, only after the most inordinate expenditure of time.
>
> —Learned Hand

Many problems in financial and estate planning for shareholders in closely held corporations can be solved through redemptions of some or all of their stock. The Internal Revenue Code under Sec. 317 defines a redemption of stock as an acquisition by a corporation of its own stock from a shareholder "in exchange for property, whether or not stock so acquired is canceled, retired, or held as Treasury stock."

In many states local law provides that a corporation cannot purchase its own stock without adequate surplus funds. For this reason the planner should be aware of local corporation law, including how it determines the amount of a corporation's surplus, whenever a redemption of stock is considered.

CURRENT TAX RATE ENVIRONMENT

For tax planning purposes the primary objective in arranging a stock redemption has tradition-ally been to achieve capital-gain treatment as opposed to dividend treatment on the exchange of stock for money or other property. For many years dividend income was taxed to individual taxpayers at the marginal rates applicable to ordinary income. Those ordinary income tax rates can currently be as high as 39.6 percent. Now qualified dividends and most long-term capital gains are currently taxable to individual taxpayers at a maximum rate of 20 percent. They may also be subject to the 3.8% surtax on net investment income received by taxpayers with high Modified Adjusted Gross Income. Taxpayers whose ordinary income would be taxed at either 10 or 15 percent will enjoy a zero rate of taxation on qualified dividends and capital gains. Taxpayers whose ordinary income would be taxed at either 25, 28, 33, or 35 percent will pay a 15 percent rate. For 2017 the top rate of 20 percent will apply to those with taxable income over the applicable threshold ($470,700 for married filing jointly; $444,550 for head of house-hold; $418,400 for single filers; and $235,350 for married filing separately). The availability of a zero percent rate for such taxpayers can create significant tax savings on dividends and capital gains.

The zero percent rate that applies only to qualified dividends and most long-term capital gains of lower-bracket taxpayers is not the same as an exclusion of those dividends and capital gains from gross income, and does not necessarily produce the same tax result as an exclusion would. This is because the income taxed at a rate of zero percent is still included in the taxpay-er's gross income, even though the applicable tax rate on such income may be zero percent. Therefore the income will be included in the calculation of both the taxpayer's adjusted gross income (AGI) and taxable income. Consequently, income subject to the zero percent rate may, for example, affect the taxpayer's eligibility for certain tax deductions, credits, or exclusions that are calculated or phased out based on the amount of the taxpayer's AGI. Therefore it should be remembered that a taxpayer's "zero-bracket" income may still produce collateral tax con-sequences for the taxpayer even though such income itself is taxed at a marginal rate of zero percent.

The concepts presented in this chapter have more significant practical application during times when the tax rates on dividends exceed the tax rates on long-term capital gains. These concepts, however, are still important. First, the tax rates applicable to dividends as compared to capital gains can be changed by Congress at any time. Traditionally, dividends have not been bestowed with the same favorable tax treatment typically associated with capital gains. Second, as explained below, the differences in the tax treatment of a stock redemption when it is characterized as a capital transaction rather than as a dividend distribution extend beyond the comparison of the tax rates applicable to dividends versus capital gain.

"Qualified" dividends for purposes of the 20 percent (or lower) maximum tax rate include dividends from most domestic corporations, whether or not publicly traded. Dividends from certain foreign corporations also qualify, including those paid by companies traded publicly on an established U.S. exchange. Qualified dividends may include dividends paid directly to the taxpayer by individual corporations as well as those passed through by mutual funds. Certain dividends are not qualified dividends, including those paid by credit unions or mutual insurance companies, and any dividend paid on stock purchased with borrowed funds if the dividend was included in net investment income for purposes of claiming an investment interest expense deduction. Certain preferred stock may be treated as debt by the issuing corporation for tax purposes, and dividends paid on such stock are not qualified dividends for purposes of the 20 percent maximum rate. Other exceptions also apply. In order to qualify for the reduced maximum rates, a shareholder must own the stock with respect to which the dividend is paid for more than 60 days during the 121-day period beginning on the date which is 60 days before the stock's "ex-dividend" date.

Even with the tax rate equivalency under current law, capital transactions are subject to tax treatment that is more favorable than the treatment that applies to dividends. First, an individual's capital losses are deductible in full against capital gains for any given year. On the other hand, net capital losses are deductible against ordinary income only to the extent of $3,000 per year ($1,500 for taxpayers married filing separately). Capital losses therefore can "shelter" capital gains fully, but they cannot be fully applied against dividend income. Second, in a capital transaction a taxpayer receives back his or her basis as a tax-free return of capital when property is sold. This can be very important, for example, if a shareholder's basis in redeemed stock is high. Of course, return of basis is much less significant if the redeemed shareholder's basis in the shares is very low.

It is important to note in this context that an estate receives a stepped-up basis in a decedent's stock that is generally equal to the value of the stock at the date of the decedent's death. Therefore the qualification of a redemption from an estate as a capital transaction is especially important. Stock redemptions from estates that qualify as capital transactions will usually provide little or no income tax liability because the redemption price will be approximately equal to the estate's basis in the decedent's stock.

On the other hand, if a stock redemption from a decedent's estate is treated as a dividend, the estate's stepped-up basis in the stock is ignored, and the full amount of the redemption proceeds will be taxed as a dividend to the extent of the corporation's earnings and profits.

This chapter will examine the technical requirements for qualifying a redemption as a capital transaction. Certain planning opportunities that the tax law presents in this area will then be explored.

LO 19.1 **Explain the tax implications of corporate distributions to stockholders.**

GENERAL RULES FOR TAXATION OF CORPORATE DISTRIBUTIONS

Unless the Internal Revenue Code provides otherwise, a distribution of property from a corporation to a shareholder is taxed as a dividend to the extent of the corporation's current and accumulated earnings and profits. "Earnings and profits" are computed according to tax accounting principles. It may be said that the earnings and profits of a corporation for a given taxable year are determined by reference to the corporation's taxable income. Taxable income is the starting point in calculating earnings and profits. However, several significant positive and negative adjustments to taxable income are made to determine the amount of earnings and profits for tax purposes. The specific adjustments are beyond the scope of this chapter.

If a distribution that would otherwise be taxable as a dividend is in excess of the corporation's earnings and profits, the amount distributed by the corporation in excess of its earnings and profits is treated as a capital transaction. That is, the amount in excess is treated as a return of capital to the extent of the shareholder's basis in the stock. The balance, if any, will be treated as capital gain.

Stated another way, a three-part tax treatment generally applies to a corporate distribution to a shareholder:

- The portion of the distribution not in excess of the corporation's current and accumulated earnings and profits is taxed as a dividend.

- The portion of the distribution in excess of the corporation's current and accumulated earnings and profits is then treated as a nontaxable return of capital to the extent of the shareholder's basis in his or her stock.

- The portion of the distribution not treated as a dividend that exceeds the shareholder's basis in his or her stock is taxed as a capital gain.

Example

Linda is the sole shareholder in the Allston Corporation, which has $40,000 in current and accumulated earnings and profits. Linda's basis in her Allston stock is $6,000. The corporation distributes to Linda $50,000, which is not compensation for her services. Of this amount Linda must treat $40,000 as a dividend for income tax purposes. The next $6,000 of the distribution is treated as a return of Linda's capital investment in the

Allston stock. Her basis in the stock is thereby reduced to zero. The remaining $4,000 of the distribution will be treated as capital gain.

These rules apply in basically the same way regardless of whether the distribution to the shareholder is made pursuant to a redemption of stock or simply paid with respect to the shareholder's ownership of stock, as in the above example.

THE PROBLEM OF CONSTRUCTIVE DIVIDENDS

Certain transactions may be taxed to shareholders of a corporation as dividends even though they are not cast in the structure of a dividend by formal resolution of the corporation's board of directors. Such transactions are not intended by the corporation to be treated as dividends for tax purposes or any other purpose. However, if the economic effect of such a transaction is the same as a dividend distribution, the IRS may recharacterize the transaction for income tax purposes as a taxable dividend. In general, and particularly in this context, it should be understood that dividends to shareholders do not necessarily have to be paid in the form of cash. Dividends can be paid in the form of property other than money. Such property might be real estate or personal property such as vehicles or equipment. The taxation of such dividends is generally measured by the fair market value of the property distributed. Transactions that could be treated as so-called "constructive dividends" include the following:

- where a debtor of the corporation makes payments directly to the corporation's shareholders rather than to the corporation itself

- where a corporation relieves a shareholder of liability for a debt the shareholder owes the corporation

- where a corporation receives life insurance proceeds and then later pays the amount of the proceeds to its shareholders on a pro rata basis

- where a corporation pays premiums on a life insurance policy that is owned by and insures its principal shareholder, and the corporation is not the beneficiary of the policy

- where a corporation sells property to its shareholders for less than the property's fair market value (a "bargain sale")

- where a shareholder-employee of a corporation is paid a salary that is more than the value of the services furnished to the corporation

- where a shareholder enjoys personal use of property owned by the corporation, such as a residence or a vehicle

The IRS will examine the actual economic effect of such transactions in determining whether dividend tax treatment should be applied. In many of these transactions, there may be a question as to whether the economic benefit was incurred in exchange for services rendered to the corporation, or simply as a constructive dividend payment. The above list is not all inclusive; there are many other transactions that may have the economic effect of a dividend distribution to a corporation's shareholders. A "substance over form" analysis would generally be applied by the IRS to such a situation in determining whether dividend treatment should be imposed.

There may be a valuation issue in such situations. For example, in the case of a bargain sale, the amount taxable as a dividend would be the fair market value of the property sold to the shareholders minus the amount of consideration paid by the shareholders for the property. In a case involving unreasonable compensation, the dividend amount would be the amount of compensation paid minus the value of the services provided to the corporation by the shareholder-employee. A transaction may be characterized as a dividend for tax purposes even if the dividend is not provided pro rata to all the shareholders of the same class. Under state corporate law, dividends are required to be paid pro rata with respect to shares of stock of the same class.

These are some of the basic tax principles that apply to corporate distributions to shareholders. The remainder of this chapter will focus on the specific rules applicable to stock redemptions. Redemptions generally involve distributions to shareholders, which may or may not be taxable as dividends.

LO 19.2   **Explain the various requirements for treating stock redemptions as capital transactions.**

REDEMPTIONS THAT ARE TAXED AS CAPITAL TRANSACTIONS

As already stated, the general rule provides that dividend treatment is applied to distributions to shareholders, including the proceeds of a redemption, to the extent of the corporation's current and accumulated earnings and profits. However, the tax law provides exceptions to the general rule. These exceptions apply to certain types of redemptions in which the redeemed shareholder's percentage of ownership of the corporation is materially affected by the redemption. These types of redemptions are treated as capital transactions rather than as dividend distributions.

One type of redemption treated under the general rule is a pro rata redemption. A redemption that is pro rata among shareholders does not change the percentages of ownership, so the redeemed shareholder's percentage of ownership is not affected.

Example

Two shareholders each own a 50 percent interest in a corporation, and the corporation redeems half of each shareholder's stock. After the redemption both shareholders still have the same proportionate interest in the corporation that they had before the redemption. The ownership of the corporation has not been materially affected by the transaction. Therefore the proceeds will be treated as a dividend distribution to the extent of current and accumulated earnings and profits.

The Internal Revenue Code contains specific provisions describing certain types of redemptions that materially affect a shareholder's percentage of ownership. If a given redemption qualifies under one of these provisions, the transaction will be treated as a capital transaction for tax purposes. Sec. 302 allows such treatment for the following four types of redemptions:

- a redemption that is "not essentially equivalent to a dividend"
- a "substantially disproportionate" redemption
- a "complete" redemption
- a distribution to a noncorporate shareholder in "partial liquidation" of the distributing corporation

Redemptions Not Essentially Equivalent to a Dividend

This first category involves questions of fact. Each redemption for which a taxpayer seeks treatment under this provision must be evaluated according to its particular facts if the IRS challenges capital-gain treatment claimed by the redeemed shareholder. There are several revenue rulings in which the IRS has conceded that certain redemptions resulted in a "meaningful reduction" in a shareholder's interest in a corporation. A meaningful reduction is required for a redemption to be considered not essentially equivalent to a dividend. This is not a mathematical test, but a subjective one.

Substantially Disproportionate Redemptions

substantially disproportionate redemption

The second category under Sec. 302 is that of a **substantially disproportionate redemption.** Sec. 302 provides for automatic qualification of a substantially disproportionate redemption as a capital transaction if a mathematical safe-harbor test is met. The test defines a substantially disproportionate redemption as follows:

- After the redemption the shareholder must own less than 50 percent of the total voting power of the corporation.

- The shareholder's percentage ownership of *voting* stock of the corporation after the redemption must be less than 80 percent of his or her percentage ownership of voting stock before the redemption.

- The shareholder's percentage ownership of *common* stock of the corporation after the redemption must also be less than 80 percent of his or her percentage ownership of common stock before the redemption.

Example

Sobel and Sherman (unrelated individuals) each own 400 of the 800 outstanding voting common shares of Thor Industries, Inc. Thor has no other classes of stock outstanding. A proposal is made to redeem 300 of Sobel's shares. Under the test for substantially disproportionate redemptions the following results occur:

- After the redemption Sobel will own 100 of the 500 outstanding Thor shares. This is less than 50 percent, so the first test is met.
- Before the redemption Sobel's interest was 50 percent of Thor. 80 percent of 50 percent is 40 percent of Thor. After the redemption Sobel's interest will be 20 percent of Thor (100 of the 500 outstanding voting common shares). Since this is less than 40 percent, the 80 percent test is met for both voting and common stock, since only one class of stock is outstanding.

The redemption will qualify as substantially disproportionate.

It is important to note that for purposes of the 80 percent test, the shareholder's proportionate percentage of ownership is the ratio of his or her shares owned to the total shares outstanding. Therefore both parts of the ratio will change after the redemption. The postredemption ratio must reflect the reduction in the total number of shares outstanding. The planner should multiply the preredemption ratio of ownership by 80 percent. Any postredemption ratio that is less than 80 percent of the preredemption ratio is an acceptable reduction of percentage ownership under the 80 percent test.

Complete Redemptions

A complete termination of the shareholder's interest in the redeeming corporation is the third category under Sec. 302. To qualify for capital treatment under this category, the corporation must redeem all of the stock the shareholder owns. If the redemption is a complete redemption, it will be treated in its entirety as a capital transaction.

Partial Liquidations

The fourth category under Sec. 302 is that of a distribution in which there is **partial liquidation** of the distributing corporation. In determining whether a redemption qualifies under this category, the nature of the distribution must be examined at the corporate level, rather than from the point of view of the shareholder receiving proceeds. Distributions in partial liquidation are beyond the scope of this chapter.

LO 19.3   Explain the attribution rules that apply to corporate stock redemptions.

ATTRIBUTION OF STOCK OWNERSHIP

attribution of stock ownership

Attribution of stock ownership means that stock owned by one individual or entity is considered to be owned by another individual or entity for the purpose of determining how a particular transaction is taxed.

constructive ownership

In evaluating a redemption under each of the first three categories described above, the rules for attribution of stock ownership must be considered. Attribution may adversely affect the tax treatment of a redemption. Also referred to as **constructive ownership**, attribution can cause a redemption that would otherwise be taxable as a capital transaction to be treated as a dividend distribution to the extent of the corporation's current and accumulated earnings and profits, because attribution changes a shareholder's percentage of ownership for purposes of determining the tax effects of a redemption.

The rationale for attribution of ownership is that a shareholder may effectively control the operation of a corporation through shares owned by related individuals and entities as well as through shares he or she actually owns. Although this may not in fact be true in many instances, redemptions should always be structured to comply with the attribution rules when these rules are applicable.

Any redemption involving stock of a corporation owned by related parties should be evaluated with these rules in mind.

Family Attribution

Stock owned by an individual shareholder's parents, spouse, children, and grandchildren will be attributed to the shareholder for purposes of determining the tax treatment of a redemption. Stock owned by the shareholder's grandparents or siblings will not be attributed. There is a rationale for these distinctions. In most instances dealings between siblings are more likely to be at arm's length than are dealings between parent and child or between spouses. In addition, it is a more natural situation for stock of a grandparent to pass to a grandchild and remain effectively controlled by the grandparent than for a grandchild to attempt to effectively exercise rights of ownership in stock owned by a grandparent.

Attribution from an Entity

In general, ownership of stock is attributed to a shareholder from an entity in proportion to the shareholder's interest in the entity. However, partnerships, estates, trusts, and corporations are all treated somewhat differently in the application of this general rule.

Attribution from Partnerships

If a partnership owns stock in a corporation, a partner is deemed to own that amount of stock that is in proportion to the partner's interest in the partnership.

Example

The Hamilton partnership owns 100 shares in Commonwealth Realty Corporation. Harold is a 50 percent partner in Hamilton and owns 100 shares in Commonwealth Realty, which redeems 25 of Harold's shares. For purposes of determining the tax treatment of Harold's redemption, he is also deemed to own 50 of the 100 shares in Commonwealth Realty owned by the Hamilton partnership.

Attribution from Estates

The general rule that ownership of stock is attributed to a shareholder from an entity in proportion to the shareholder's interest in the entity applies to attribution from an estate to a beneficiary of the estate. However, the beneficiary must have a direct present interest in the estate for attribution to occur. An individual holding a remainder interest in an estate would not have ownership of stock attributed from the estate. Also after an estate has completed its distribution of property to a beneficiary, any stock still owned by the estate will generally no longer be attributed to the beneficiary.

Attribution from Trusts

To determine whether stock owned by a trust is attributable to a trust beneficiary, another variation of the general rule is applied. An actuarial computation of a beneficiary's interest in a trust is made to determine the percentage of stock owned by the trust that will be attributed to the beneficiary. Therefore a beneficiary having only a remainder interest in a trust is subject to attribution of ownership from the trust, even though a remainder interest in an estate would not result in attribution to the beneficiary from the estate.

Attribution from Corporations

The general rule also applies in attributing ownership of stock from a corporation to a shareholder of the corporation, with one important modification. Stock ownership will be attributed from a corporation to a shareholder only if the shareholder is a 50-percent-or-greater owner of the value of all the outstanding stock of the corporation that owns the stock to be attributed.

Example

Suppose Kevin is a 60 percent owner of the Building Corporation and also owns stock in the Hammer and Nail Corporation. The Building Corporation is also a shareholder in the Hammer and Nail Corporation. When the Hammer and Nail Corporation redeems a portion of Kevin's shares, 60 percent of the stock in Hammer and Nail owned by the Building Corporation will be attributed to Kevin for purposes of determining the tax treatment of Kevin's redemption. However, if Kevin were only a 49 percent owner of the Building Corporation, the stock in Hammer and Nail owned by Building would not be attributed to Kevin when Hammer and Nail redeems a portion of Kevin's shares.

Special Rule for S Corporations

It is important to note that the stock attribution rules treat an S corporation as if it were a partnership. Therefore to determine the attribution of stock ownership both to an S corporation and from an S corporation, the rules that apply to partnerships must be used.

Attribution to an Entity

When a corporation redeems shares owned by a partnership, estate, trust, or another corporation, the attribution rules must be examined to determine the tax treatment of the entity receiving proceeds of the redemption.

In general, all the stock owned by a partner, a beneficiary of an estate or trust, or a controlling shareholder in a corporation will be attributed to the partnership, estate, trust, or corporation.

Example

The Horseshoe Corporation redeems stock owned by the Trail partnership. Louis, a partner in Trail, also owns stock in the Horseshoe Corporation. For purposes of determining the tax treatment of the redemption of Trail's stock in Horseshoe, Trail is deemed to own the stock in Horseshoe owned by Louis.

There are modifications to this general rule that apply to trusts and to corporations. Stock owned by a contingent beneficiary of a trust will not be attributed to a trust if, considering the trustee's discretionary powers under the trust instrument, the beneficiary's largest potential interest in the value of the trust property, determined actuarially, is 5 percent or less of the value of the trust property.

Stock in one corporation owned by a shareholder who also owns stock in a second corporation will not be attributed to the second corporation unless the shareholder owns 50 percent or more of the value of the second corporation that is receiving proceeds of a redemption by the first corporation.

Example 1

Paul is a 40 percent owner of Landscape Corporation. Both Paul and Landscape Corporation own stock in the Tractor Corporation. Tractor redeems the Tractor stock owned by Landscape. To determine the tax treatment to Landscape in this transaction, stock in Tractor owned by Paul is not considered to be owned by Landscape since Paul owns less than 50 percent of Landscape.

Example 2

Suppose Paul in the above example is a 50 percent owner of Landscape Corporation. Paul and Landscape each own 100 shares of the Tractor Corporation. If Tractor redeems Landscape's stock in Tractor, Landscape will be considered to own all 100 shares in Tractor owned by Paul. However, if Tractor redeems Paul's stock in Tractor, Paul will be considered to own only 50 of the shares in Tractor owned by Landscape.

Note how attribution to a corporation is different from attribution *from* a corporation. A corporation is deemed to own *all* the stock in another corporation owned by one of its shareholders if attribution applies. However, attribution of stock from a corporation to a shareholder receiving proceeds of a redemption by another corporation applies only to the extent of the shareholder's percentage interest in the corporation from which ownership is attributed.

Reattribution

reattribution

The term **reattribution** refers to situations in which constructive ownership rules are combined to attribute ownership from one shareholder to another shareholder not directly related under the rules.

Example 1

A father will be considered to own the stock owned by a trust of which his son is the sole beneficiary.

Example 2

A corporation will be considered to own 50 percent of the stock owned by a partnership in which the corporation's sole shareholder is a 50 percent partner.

There are certain situations in which the Internal Revenue Code prohibits reattribution. For instance, family ownership rules cannot be applied two times in succession.

Example

A father will be considered to own stock owned by his son. Likewise, a daughter will be considered to own stock owned by her father. However, family attribution rules cannot be applied twice in succession to attribute ownership of the son's stock to the daughter. If this type of constructive ownership applied, it would result in sibling attribution.

Waiver of Family Attribution in Complete Redemptions

If a corporation redeems all of the stock a shareholder owns, it is possible for the shareholder to avoid the application of the family attribution rules. In order to qualify for a waiver of family attribution in a complete redemption, a shareholder must comply with a number of requirements imposed by the Internal Revenue Code. These include the following:

- The redeemed shareholder may retain no interest in the corporation after the redemption. For these purposes "interest" includes the status of officer, director, or employee of the corporation. It is permissible for the redeemed shareholder to remain a creditor of the corporation.
- The redeemed shareholder must not acquire any prohibited interest in the corporation for a period of 10 years beginning on the date of the distribution of the redemption

proceeds. However, if the redeemed shareholder receives stock in the corporation by bequest or inheritance, this provision is not violated.

- The redeemed shareholder must file an agreement with the IRS to notify it if any acquisition of a prohibited interest takes place within the 10-year period. The redeemed shareholder must retain the necessary records to comply with this requirement.

- The redeemed shareholder must not have acquired any portion of the stock redeemed during a 10-year period prior to the date of the redemption from a person whose stock would be attributable to the redeemed shareholder.

- The redeemed shareholder must not have transferred any stock in the redeeming corporation to any person whose stock would be attributed to the redeemed shareholder within a 10-year period before the date of distribution of the redemption proceeds. This requirement will not apply if the corporation also redeems such stock of the person to whom it was transferred by the redeemed shareholder.

The last two requirements may not apply if the redeemed shareholder can show that the transfer or acquisition in question did not have the avoidance of federal income tax as one of its principal purposes. The waiver of attribution is available only in the case of a complete redemption and generally only for the family attribution rules (not entity attribution).

However, an entity (estate, partnership, trust, or corporation) can also make use of the waiver of family attribution provisions, as long as all individuals whose stock would be attributable to the entity comply with the conditions for waiver of family attribution. Note, however, that waiver by an estate has limited application because in most cases stock in a family corporation will be owned by family members or left to family members under the decedent's will, so that beneficiaries of the estate will also be stockholders. Still, in certain situations an estate may be able to effectively claim the waiver.

Example

The Connecticut Corporation plans to redeem its stock owned by Biff's estate. Biff's estate is a 50 percent shareholder in Connecticut. The other 50 percent of Connecticut is owned by Bunny, Biff's wife. Biff and Bunny's son and daughter, Rollo and Muffy, are the sole beneficiaries of Biff's estate. Biff's estate can achieve capital-gain treatment on the redemption of Connecticut stock through the waiver of family attribution rules as long as Rollo and Muffy agree not to acquire any interest in the corporation that is prohibited by those rules during the time period prescribed by the rules. In effect, the waiver of family attribution rules in this situation operate as if the beneficiaries of the estate were the parties whose stock was redeemed.

LO 19.4   Explain the requirements for Section 303 stock redemptions.

SEC. 303 REDEMPTIONS

The Internal Revenue Code contains a relief provision that applies to estates in which stock of a closely held corporation constitutes a substantial portion of total estate assets. The purpose of this section is to provide liquidity for such estates in order to avoid forced sales of the closely held stock to meet tax obligations and administration expenses.

Sec. 303 redemption

This relief provision, Sec. 303 of the Code, allows distributions in redemption of such stock to be treated as made in exchange for a capital asset and therefore eligible for capital-gains treatment, subject to certain requirements and limitations. Sec. 303 is totally independent of the other Code provisions describing the tax treatment of redemptions of stock. Therefore neither the rules under Sec. 302 nor the constructive ownership rules need to be considered in determining whether capital-gains treatment is available under Sec. 303. Sec. 303 operates independently, and as long as its own requirements are met, capital-gains treatment can be achieved.

What Estates May Qualify Under Sec. 303?

In order for an estate to be eligible for a Sec. 303 redemption, the value of the stock in the redeeming corporation that is includible in the gross estate for federal estate tax purposes must be more than 35 percent of the value of the adjusted gross estate. The adjusted gross estate is defined for this purpose as the gross estate minus deductions for funeral and administration expenses, debts, and deductible losses of the estate. To determine whether the corporate stock meets the percentage test, all classes of stock in the corporation owned by the estate are counted; that is, preferred is counted as well as common.

For estates that own stock in two or more corporations, there is a variation of the 35 percent test. If the stock in the two or more corporations owned by the estate represents 20 percent or more of the outstanding value of all the stock in each corporation, the stock in the two or more corporations may be combined and treated as stock in one corporation for purposes of the 35 percent test. If the test is met by combining stock in two or more corporations, a Sec. 303 redemption may be made with shares of any of the two or more corporations.

Example

Spike's estate needs liquidity to meet its tax obligations and administration expenses. The estate owns 100 shares in the Jersey Video Corporation. These shares represent 25 percent of the value of Spike's adjusted gross estate and 33 percent of the value of Jersey Video, Inc. The estate also owns 100 shares in Philly Stereo, Inc. These shares represent 15 percent of the value of Spike's adjusted gross estate and 25 percent of the value of Philly Stereo, Inc. Because the stock in each corporation owned by the estate represents 20 percent or more of the value of the stock in each corporation, and because the stock in the two corporations has a total value in excess of 35 percent of Spike's adjusted gross estate, the estate will qualify for a Sec. 303 redemption.

There is one more wrinkle that applies *only* to the special rule for stock in two or more corporations. For purposes of the 20 percent requirement, 100 percent of the value of stock the decedent held with his or her surviving spouse as community property or in joint tenancy, tenants by the entirety, or tenancy in common is treated as having been included in the decedent's gross estate. This wrinkle applies only when the rule for stock in two or more corporations is applied and not to the 35 percent test in general.

How Much Stock May Be Redeemed Under Sec. 303?

There is a limitation on the dollar amount of proceeds received for redeemed stock that will qualify for favorable treatment under Sec. 303. Redemption proceeds eligible for favorable tax treatment may not exceed the sum of the estate, inheritance, legacy, and succession taxes for which the estate is liable (including interest, if any) and the amount of funeral and administration expenses allowable as deductions to the estate under the Internal Revenue Code.

The amount of proceeds qualifying for treatment under Sec. 303 will be further limited if the redeemed shareholder (usually the estate) is not legally liable for the full amount of the taxes and expenses. Only that portion of the taxes and expenses that the redeemed shareholder is legally obligated to pay is considered in determining the maximum amount of proceeds allowable under Sec. 303.

Example

A trust owns stock in the Texas Corporation that is included in Alvin's gross estate. The trust instrument does not require the trust to pay a portion of the taxes or administration expenses of Alvin's estate. However, Fergus, the trustee, uses proceeds of a redemption of the trust's stock in Texas to pay a portion of Alvin's estate taxes. In this situation the trust may not treat the redemption under Sec. 303.

Who May Receive Favorable Tax Treatment Under Sec. 303?

If the requirements of Sec. 303 are met, any shareholder owning stock included in determining a decedent's gross estate is eligible for a Sec. 303 redemption. Generally the eligible shareholder will be either the decedent's estate itself or a beneficiary of the estate. However, in this context it is important to remember that unless a beneficiary of the estate has an obligation to pay death taxes or administration expenses, the beneficiary will not be eligible for Sec. 303 treatment.

When Must a Sec. 303 Redemption Be Made?

Sec. 303 treatment is available for distributions in redemption of stock made after the decedent's death and within 3 years and 90 days after the filing of the estate's federal estate tax return. If the estate has filed a petition in the Tax Court concerning an estate tax dispute, the time limitation is extended until 60 days after the decision of the Tax Court becomes final. Furthermore, if the estate has elected to pay its estate tax in installments under Sec. 6166 of the Internal Revenue Code, redemption distributions may receive the benefit of Sec. 303 if they are made within the time period of the installment payments.

Under any of these rules if redemption proceeds are paid more than 4 years after the decedent's death, the amount of distributions eligible to be treated under Sec. 303 cannot exceed the lesser of the amount of taxes and administration expenses remaining unpaid or the amount of such expenses that are paid within one year after the redemption.

Planning Considerations Under Sec. 303

Minimal Taxable Gain

Because of its fiduciary duties to its other shareholders, a corporation will generally redeem the stock of a decedent shareholder at a price equal to the stock's current fair market value. For income tax purposes an estate or its beneficiary currently receives a "stepped-up" basis in a decedent's assets that is generally equal to the value of the assets as of the date of the decedent's death. Therefore if a redemption is made under Sec. 303 within a short time after the decedent's death, the redemption price should be equal to or very close to the basis in the stock held by the estate or the beneficiary. In a capital transaction, the basis of the stock is recovered without taxation. Since proceeds in a Sec. 303 redemption are treated as received in the sale or exchange of a capital asset, and not as a dividend, the redeemed shareholder will generally realize little or no taxable gain. If the stock has increased in value between the time of the decedent's death and the time of the redemption, any amount in excess of the estate's or beneficiary's basis in the stock will be taxed as long-term capital gain. Therefore unless there has been a significant change in the corporation's fortunes during that time, the amount of taxable gain will probably not be significant. This possibility of minimal gain produces a significant benefit for treatment of the redemption as a capital transaction, even if the tax rates applicable to dividends and capital gains are equivalent.

Accumulated-Earnings Tax

One problem that may arise in planning for the corporation to fund a Sec. 303 redemption is the accumulated-earnings tax. The Internal Revenue Code states specifically that corporate accumulations may be made to fund a Sec. 303 redemption without being subject to the accumulated-earnings tax. However, such accumulations are specifically exempt only when made in the corporation's taxable year in which the decedent died or any taxable year thereafter. Therefore accumulations prior to the year of the decedent's death to meet an anticipated funding need for a redemption may present the corporation with an accumulated-earnings tax problem. This problem is amplified by the requirement mentioned earlier that in some states a redemption may be effected only if the corporation has adequate surplus to fund the redemption.

If the IRS can show that the funding objective was not for a corporate purpose, but only for the benefit of the shareholder or the shareholder's estate, the accumulated-earnings tax may become a problem. It may be difficult to convince the IRS that a Sec. 303 redemption serves a business purpose of the corporation. Therefore, as a practical matter, the use of life insurance owned by the corporation may be the most appropriate method of funding a Sec. 303 redemption. Even though the accumulation of earnings to meet premium obligations for such insurance may be subject to the accumulated-earnings tax, the dollar amount needed for premiums will be substantially less than the dollar amount needed for cash funding. As a result, any possible exposure to the accumulated-earnings tax is minimized. The proper life insurance funding will also provide any surplus required to effect the redemption.

CHAPTER REVIEW

Key Terms and Concepts

substantially disproportionate redemption

attribution of stock ownership

constructive ownership

reattribution

Sec. 303 redemption

Review Questions

Review questions are based on the learning objectives in this chapter. Thus a [19.3] at the end of a question means that the question is based on learning objective 3. If there are multiple objectives, they are all listed.

1. What is the current maximum tax rate applicable to qualified dividends received by individual taxpayers? [19.1]

2. What is the general rule for taxation of a corporation's distribution to its shareholders with respect to its own stock? [19.1]

3. The Jimbo Corporation distributed $200,000 this year to its shareholders. Although Jimbo Corporation has no earnings and profits this year, it had accumulated $400,000 of earnings and profits from prior years. Will this $200,000 distribution be taxed to the shareholders as a dividend? [19.1]

4. Explain how the shareholders in question 3 would have been taxed if there had been neither current nor accumulated earnings and profits. [19.1]

5. The Darling Corporation has $100,000 of current and accumulated earnings and profits. This year its sole shareholder, Zsa Zsa, receives a $150,000 distribution. Her basis for the stock she owns is $30,000.

    a. How will Zsa Zsa be taxed on the first $100,000 of her distribution?

    b. Explain the tax treatment of the next $30,000 of the distribution.

    c. How will Zsa Zsa be taxed on the balance of the $150,000 distribution ($20,000)? [19.1]

6. Describe some situations in which distributions by a corporation may be taxed as constructive or indirect dividends. [19.1]

7. a. What is the general rule for taxation of distributions by a corporation in redemption of its stock?

    b. Identify the types of redemptions that will not be treated under the general rule. [19.2]

8. Frank owns all 100 outstanding shares of Hotdog Corporation. Assume the Hotdog Corporation redeemed 50 shares of stock from Frank.

    a. Explain the effect on Frank's:

       (1) control of the Hotdog Corporation

       (2) rights to the Hotdog Corporation's profits

       (3) proportionate share of and claim on the assets of the Hotdog Corporation upon liquidation of the corporation

    b. Would your answers change if Frank had sold the 50 shares to a friend? Explain. [19.2]

9. What is required for a stock redemption to be considered "not essentially equivalent to a dividend"? [19.2]

10. Describe the requirements that must be met for a stock redemption to be treated as substantially disproportionate. [19.2]

11. Abigail and Burton (unrelated individuals) own 50 shares each of the No Exit Corporation. There are no other outstanding shares. If Abigail redeems 25 shares, will the redemption qualify as a substantially disproportionate redemption? Explain. [19.2]

12. State whether each of the following transactions would qualify as substantially disproportionate redemptions or as complete termination redemptions. Each transaction involves a "cash-for-stock" transaction. The shareholders are individuals and unrelated unless otherwise stated.

    a. Anna and Boyd each own 50 shares of common stock of the Movie Corporation. Anna purchases 15 shares from Boyd.

    b. There are 100 shares issued and outstanding in the Movie Corporation. Anna and Boyd each own 50 percent of the common stock. The corporation acquires 10 shares from Anna. [19.2]

13. Explain the rationale of the rules for attribution of stock ownership. [19.3]

14. Nancy owns stock in the Jordano Corporation. She plans to have some of her stock redeemed by the corporation. In determining the tax treatment of her redemption, state whether she will be considered to own stock in Jordano owned by each of the following persons:

    a. her mother

    b. her sister

    c. her grandmother

    d. her son [19.3]

15. What is the general rule regarding attribution of stock ownership to a redeemed share-holder from an entity in which the shareholder has an interest? [19.3]

16. What is the general rule regarding attribution of stock ownership to an entity whose stock is redeemed from an individual who owns an interest in the entity? [19.3]

17. Describe the requirements for waiving the family attribution rules in the case of a complete redemption. [19.3]

18. State the purpose of and the requirements for a Sec. 303 redemption of stock. [19.4]

19. Claude, a 50 percent shareholder in the Longet Corporation, dies. The remaining stock in the corporation is owned by Claude's son, the sole beneficiary of Claude's estate. More than one-half of the value of his adjusted gross estate consists of stock in the Longet Corporation. The attribution rules would cause Claude's estate to have taxable dividend income in the event stock was redeemed to raise cash for payment of estate tax. Explain how Code Sec. 303 mitigates this situation. [19.4]

20. Explain why there is generally little or no gain subject to income taxation when stock is redeemed in a transaction that qualifies under Sec. 303. [19.4]

21. Explain how the accumulated-earnings tax may apply to corporate money set aside to fund a Sec. 303 redemption. [19.4]

Review Answers

1. The maximum tax rate currently applicable to qualified dividends is 20 percent. These rates are equivalent to the rates currently applicable to most long-term capital gains of individuals. For lower-bracketed taxpayers, the rate of taxation on qualified dividends is either 15 or zero percent. These two lower rates apply to taxpayers whose incomes fall below $470,700 for joint filers and surviving spouses, $444,550 for heads of household and $418,400 for single filers.

2. The general rule for taxing distributions of property from a corporation to its share-holders is that it will be taxed as a dividend to the extent of the corporation's current and accumulated earnings and profits.

3. Yes, the $200,000 distribution by Jimbo Corporation to its shareholders will be taxed to the shareholders as a dividend. Although Jimbo Corporation has no current earnings and profits, it had accumulated $400,000 of earnings and profits from prior years. Any portion of a distribution from that source will be treated as a dividend.

4. If there were neither current nor accumulated earnings and profits, the $200,000 distribution by Jimbo Corporation to its shareholders would not be treated as a dividend. The distribution would be treated as a nontaxable return of capital to the extent of the shareholders' basis in the stock. If any portion of the distribution exceeded the shareholders' basis in the stock, it would be taxed as a capital gain.

5. Answers:

   a. The first $100,000 will be taxed to Zsa Zsa as a dividend since there are accumulated earnings and profits.

   b. The next $30,000 reduces the basis of Zsa Zsa's interest in her stock to zero.

   c. The remaining $20,000 will be taxed to Zsa Zsa as capital gain.

6. Transactions that could be treated as so-called "constructive dividends" include the following:

   - where a debtor of the corporation makes payments directly to the corporation's shareholders rather than to the corporation itself

   - where a corporation relieves a shareholder of liability for a debt the shareholder owes the corporation

   - where a corporation receives life insurance proceeds and then later pays the amount of the proceeds to its shareholders on a pro rata basis

   - where a corporation pays premiums on a life insurance policy that is owned by and insures its principal shareholder, and the corporation is not the beneficiary of the policy

   - where a corporation sells property to its shareholders for less than the property's fair market value (a "bargain sale")

   - where a shareholder-employee of a corporation is paid a salary that is more than the value of the services furnished to the corporation

   - where a shareholder enjoys personal use of property owned by the corporation, such as a residence or a vehicle

   The IRS will examine the actual economic effect of such transactions in determining whether dividend tax treatment should be applied.

7. a. The general rule provides that dividend treatment is applied to distributions to shareholders, including the proceeds of a redemption, to the extent of the corporation's current and accumulated earnings and profits.

    b.   Exceptions to the general rule apply to certain types of redemptions in which the redeemed shareholder's percentage of ownership in the corporation is materially affected by the redemption. If a given redemption qualifies under one of these exceptions, the transaction will be treated as a capital transaction for tax purposes. Sec. 302 allows such treatment for the following four types of redemptions:

- a redemption that is "not essentially equivalent to a dividend"

- a "substantially disproportionate" redemption

- a "complete" redemption

- a distribution to a noncorporate shareholder in "partial liquidation" of the distributing corporation

8.   a.   (1) After the redemption, Frank still controls 100 percent of Hotdog Corporation.

        (2)   After the redemption, Frank has the same rights to Hotdog Corporation's profits as before the redemption.

        (3)   After the redemption, Frank's proportionate share of and claim on the assets of the Hotdog Corporation upon liquidation are the same as before the redemption.

    b.   Yes. In all three instances Frank has gone from 100 percent to 50 percent. In other words, if Frank sold 50 shares to a friend, Frank's control of Hotdog, his rights to Hotdog's profits, and his proportionate share of and claim on Hotdog's assets would all now be 50 percent instead of 100 percent.

9.   In order for a stock redemption to be considered "not essentially equivalent to a dividend," there must be a meaningful reduction in the shareholder's interest in the corporation. This is not a mathematical test, but a subjective one. Each redemption that a shareholder claims is "not essentially equivalent to a dividend" must be evaluated according to its particular facts.

10.   In order for a redemption to be considered substantially disproportionate, it must meet the following requirements:

- After the redemption, the shareholder must own less than 50 percent of the total voting power of the corporation.

- The shareholder's percentage ownership of voting stock of the corporation after the redemption must be less than 80 percent of his or her percentage ownership of voting stock before the redemption.

- The shareholder's percentage ownership of common stock of the corporation after the redemption must also be less than 80 percent of his or her percentage ownership of common stock before the redemption.

11. The redemption qualifies as a substantially disproportionate redemption. Before the redemption Abigail owns $^{50}/_{100}$, or 50 percent of the stock. After the redemption Abigail owns $^{25}/_{75}$, or 33 percent of the stock. Note that Abigail meets the two qualifications— (1) her postredemption ownership ratio of 33 percent is less than 80 percent of her preredemption ratio, since 50 percent × 80 percent is 40 percent, and (2) after the redemption Abigail owns less than 50 percent of the voting and common shares.

12. a. This transaction is not a redemption. Anna is purchasing shares directly from Boyd. A redemption involves a corporation's purchase of its own stock.

    b. This transaction cannot qualify as a complete termination because Anna still owns stock after the redemption. It will also not qualify as a substantially disproportionate redemption. Before the redemption Anna owns $^{50}/_{100}$, or 50 percent of the stock of the corporation. Afterward she owns $^{40}/_{90}$, or 44 percent. Note that her postredemption percentage interest of 44 percent is not less than 80 percent of her preredemption percentage interest since 50 percent × 80 percent is 40 percent. The other test—that Anna must own less than 50 percent of the voting and common shares after the redemption—is met.

13. The rationale for attribution of ownership is that a shareholder may effectively control the operation of a corporation through shares owned by related individuals and entities as well as through shares he or she actually owns.

14. a. Nancy will be considered to own stock in Jordano that is owned by her mother.

    b. Nancy will not be considered to own stock in Jordano that is owned by her sister.

    c. Nancy will not be considered to own stock in Jordano that is owned by her grandmother.

    d. Nancy will be considered to own stock in Jordano that is owned by her son.

15. In the case of attribution to a shareholder from an entity, the general rule is that the shareholder will be considered to own stock owned by the entity in proportion to the shareholder's interest in the entity. Some situations involve modifications to this general rule.

16. In the case of attribution from an individual to an entity, the general rule is that the entity will be considered to own all the stock owned by the individual having an

interest in the entity. There are modifications to this general rule that apply to trusts and to corporations.

17. To qualify for a waiver of family attribution in a complete redemption, a shareholder must comply with the following requirements:

- The redeemed shareholder may retain no interest in the corporation after the redemption. For these purposes "interest" includes the status of officer, director, or employee of the corporation. It is permissible for the redeemed shareholder to remain a creditor of the corporation.

- The redeemed shareholder must not acquire any prohibited interest in the corporation for a period of 10 years beginning on the date of the distribution of the redemption proceeds. However, if the redeemed shareholder receives stock in the corporation by bequest or inheritance, this provision is not violated.

- The redeemed shareholder must file an agreement with the IRS to notify it if any acquisition of a prohibited interest takes place within the 10-year period.

- The redeemed shareholder must not have acquired any portion of the stock redeemed during a 10-year period prior to the date of the redemption from a person whose stock would be attributable to the redeemed shareholder.

- The redeemed shareholder must not have transferred any stock in the redeeming corporation to any person whose stock would be attributed to the redeemed shareholder within a 10-year period before the date of distribution of the redemption proceeds. This requirement will not apply if the corporation also redeems such stock of the person to whom it was transferred by the redeemed shareholder.

18. Sec. 303 of the Code is a relief provision that applies to estates in which stock of a closely held corporation constitutes a substantial portion of total estate assets. The purpose of Sec. 303 is to provide liquidity for such estates in order to avoid forced sales of the closely held stock to meet tax obligations and administrative expenses. It allows distributions in redemption of such stock to be treated as made in exchange for a capital asset and therefore eligible for capital-gains treatment.

To be eligible for a Sec. 303 redemption, the value of the stock in the redeeming corporation that is includible in the gross estate for federal estate tax purposes must be more than 35 percent of the value of the adjusted gross estate. The redemption proceeds eligible for favorable tax treatment are limited to the sum of the estate, inheritance, legacy, and succession taxes for which the estate is liable and the amount of funeral and administration expenses allowable as deductions to the estate. Only that portion of taxes and expenses that the redeemed shareholder is legally obligated to pay is considered in determining the amount of proceeds allowable.

19. Sec. 303 guarantees sale or exchange treatment to the extent of death taxes, funeral costs, and administrative costs if (a) the stock of the redeeming corporation is includible in the decedent's gross estate and (b) the value of the stock is more than 35 percent of the decedent's adjusted gross estate and the distribution occurs within the same time period as the time for payment of estate tax, including any extensions. If the conditions of Sec. 303 are met, it overrides those sections of the Code otherwise applicable, including the attribution rules.

20. A corporation will generally redeem the stock of a decedent shareholder at a price equal to the stock's current fair market value. For income tax purposes an estate or its beneficiary receives a "stepped-up" basis in a decedent's assets that is generally equal to the value of the assets as of the date of the decedent's death. Therefore if a redemption is made under Sec. 303 within a short time after the decedent's death, the redemption price should be equal to or very close to the basis in the stock held by the estate or the beneficiary.

21. The Code states specifically that corporate accumulations may be made to fund a Sec. 303 redemption without being subject to the accumulated-earnings tax. However, such accumulations are specifically exempt only when made in the corporation's taxable year in which the decedent died or any taxable year thereafter. Therefore accumulations prior to the year of the decedent's death to meet an anticipated funding need for a redemption may present the corporation with an accumulated-earnings tax problem.

If the IRS can show that the funding objective was not for a corporate purpose, but only for the benefit of the shareholder or the shareholder's estate, the accumulated-earnings tax may become a problem. It may be difficult to convince the IRS that a Sec. 303 redemption serves a business purpose of the corporation.

Chapter 20

Taxation of Partners and Partnerships

Learning Objectives

An understanding of the material in this chapter should enable you to

LO 20.1　**Describe the significance of being classified as an unincorporated business entity for tax law purposes, and explain both the aggregate and entity theories for taxation of partnerships and partners.**

LO 20.2　**Describe the tax ramifications of forming a partnership, and explain how each partner is taxed.**

LO 20.3　**Explain the tax effects to the partnership and the partners upon the retirement or death of a partner.**

LO 20.4　**Describe the tax treatment of both limited partnerships and family partnerships.**

Two years ago it was impossible to get through on the phone to the IRS. Now it's just hard to get through. That's progress.

— Charles O. Rossotti

Note

In order to highlight some of the more essential areas of partnership taxation, the following case study is written as a narrative between a CLU (Steve), an attorney (Mike), and a CPA (Jim). Because of the complexity of partnership taxation, the following subject matter covered should be considered merely an introductory overview to this topic.

LO 20.1　**Describe the significance of being classified as an unincorporated business entity for tax law purposes, and explain both the aggregate and entity theories for taxation of partnerships and partners.**

TAX LAW CLASSIFICATION OF UNINCORPORATED BUSINESS ENTITIES

Steve: Mike, how do we know whether a business organization will be treated as a partnership or a corporation under federal tax law?

Mike: In the past, the tax classification of any business organization having more than one owner depended upon the presence or absence of a certain number of traditional legal corporate characteristics in the structure of the particular organization. If an organization exhibited a preponderance of corporate characteristics, it would be taxed as a corporation. If not, it would be taxed as a partnership.

However, the process of classifying a business organization for tax purposes has recently been greatly simplified. In general, an organization formed as a corporation under state law will be taxed as a corporation under federal law. Organizations that are not incorporated under state law, including partnerships and limited liability companies, will generally be permitted to choose whether to be taxed as corporations or partnerships.[1] In most cases, they will choose to be taxed as partnerships.

Steve: I'm a little confused by this. You're saying that most business organizations (other than sole proprietorships) will be taxed as either corporations or partnerships. Yet there are other types of business entities under state law, such as limited liability companies.

Mike: That's true. Under state law, business organizations may be formed as corporations, general partnerships, limited partnerships, limited liability partnerships, limited liability companies, or as variations of these business forms. However, all of these various types of entities are classified as either partnerships or corporations for federal tax purposes. Limited partnerships, for example, will generally be treated as partnerships for tax purposes. Although some special tax rules apply to limited partnerships, they are still taxed in generally the same manner as other partnerships. A limited liability company that elects to be taxed as a partnership is also taxed in generally the same manner as a state law partnership. Although there are many varieties of business entities under state law, federal tax law has just two general categories under which business organizations are classified. Note, however, that there are some variations within those two categories. For example, a corporation might elect to be treated as an "S" corporation under federal tax law. This would make the corporation taxable in a manner similar to a partnership, even though the entity is still basically a corporation under both state law and federal tax law.

Steve: You mentioned that unincorporated business entities are now permitted to choose whether to be treated as partnerships or corporations for federal tax purposes. How did this come about?

Mike: State business law has developed to the point where there are popular business entities, such as limited liability companies, that may exhibit some characteristics of a partnership and some of a corporation. From a legal standpoint, a limited liability company in its most basic form is really a partnership with the corporate characteristic of limited liability. Other

---

1.   Reg. Sec. 301.7701-1, 2, 3.

unincorporated entities, such as limited partnerships and limited liability partnerships, may also exhibit certain corporate characteristics. With the development of these "hybrid" business entities, it became administratively difficult for the IRS to classify them for tax purposes based upon the presence or absence of a preponderance of corporate characteristics. As a result, a more flexible system of classification (often referred to as "check the box") was developed. This is the means by which these entities select their federal income tax status.

Importance of Classification as a Partnership

Steve: Why is it important that we know how a given organization will be classified?

Jim: It is important to everyone concerned that a particular organization be taxed as the parties involved intended. There are important distinctions between a corporation and a partnership.

When the organization is taxed as a corporation, the organization and its members are treated as two separate and distinct taxable entities.[2] When profits are earned by a corporation, they are taxed once to the business and then taxed again to the shareholders if they are paid out in the form of dividends. This potential double taxation is avoided in a partnership. If the organization is treated as a partnership, these same profits earned by the same recipients will be taxed only once—on the recipients' individual returns. Also, if a business is classified as a corporation, losses may be claimed only by the corporation and are not available to offset the shareholder's other income. However, in the event that the partnership has a net loss, the partners may deduct their share of the loss on their individual returns.

THE AGGREGATE AND ENTITY THEORIES

Steve: Am I correct in thinking that there is no difference between partners and their partnership—so that for tax purposes a partnership is equivalent to the sum of its individual members?

Mike: This statement is only partially correct. Woven into the relevant sections of the Internal Revenue Code are two general theories used in developing the tax law relating to partnerships and their partners. These are called the aggregate theory and the entity theory.

aggregate theory

According to the **aggregate theory,** a partnership is considered as an aggregate of individual co-owners who have bound themselves together with the intention of sharing gains and

---

2.   S corporations are an exception to this rule.

losses. The key point here is that under the aggregate theory, the partnership itself has no existence separate and apart from its members. As the word "aggregate" implies, to the extent this theory influences tax law, a partnership is nothing more than the sum of its individual members.

The Code recognizes this theory by requiring that each partner include on his or her personal income tax return his or her share of certain partnership gains, losses, deductions, and credits. This means that it is not the partnership that is taxable. Rather, it is the partners who are subject to the income tax as an aggregate of individuals. In other words, the individual partners are the taxpayers, not the partnership.

entity theory

At the same time, however, the Code provides that for certain other purposes, the partnership is a separate entity that is distinct from its members. According to this **entity theory**, the partnership must file an income tax return for information purposes only—Form 1065—and show gross income, business deductions, and ordinary business income (or loss).

Three other indicia of the entity theory are that a partnership has a taxable year, its own accounting method, and the right to exercise various income tax elections.

Steve: Would you explain the aggregate and entity theories in more detail?

Mike: Let me start with the aggregate theory. According to the aggregate theory, since a partnership is not a separate entity, no tax is imposed on the partnership itself. The liability is instead passed through directly to each partner who pays tax on his or her share of the profits just as though he or she realized the share of income as an individual. Capital gains, Sec. 1231 gains, dividends, and other taxable items are also passed directly through to the partners, who add them to like items on their 1040s (i.e., individual tax returns).

In keeping with this conduit concept, these items retain their character. For example, as capital gains flow through the partnership conduit to the taxpaying partners, the aggregate theory keeps the nature of the gain the same—capital gain.

However, even while the aggregate theory makes the partnership a conduit for some purposes, the entity theory treats the partnership as separate from its individual partners. The entity theory requires the partnership itself to file a return. The return provides a way to inform both the IRS and the individual partners how the profits and losses are allocated.

For example, the partnership return breaks down the partnership's ordinary business income or loss, its net capital gain or loss, its Sec. 1231 gains or losses, its charitable contributions, and its receipt of dividends. Then each partner can readily see from his or her separate Schedule K-1 on Form 1065 his or her share of the partnership's income, credits, deductions, and so forth.

Another good example of the entity theory is the way partners who deal with their own partnership are treated. Generally a partner who engages in a transaction with his or her partnership is treated taxwise like a stranger. This rule does not apply to certain sales or exchanges of property between partners and partnerships. This means that when a partner is not acting in his or her capacity as a partner, a transaction between that partner and the partnership is treated as if it was conducted between the partnership and an unrelated third person.

For example, Debra and Lillian form a partnership with equal capital and income interests. The partnership agrees to pay Debra, the working member, $10,000 a year as a guaranteed payment (similar to a salary). If the income (after deductions for expenses other than guaranteed payments) of the partnership is $10,000 and that entire amount is paid to Debra as a guaranteed payment, she has taxable income of $10,000. The partnership itself has no ordinary business income. But if that same partnership had income after deductions (other than the guaranteed payment deduction) of $25,000, Debra would be taxable on $17,500. That $17,500 would be composed of the $10,000 guaranteed payment and Debra's distributive share of the partnership's ordinary business income. Her distributive share is one-half of $15,000, that is, one-half of the $25,000 of partnership income (after deductions other than her guaranteed payment), minus the business expense deduction of $10,000 for the guaranteed payment paid to Debra.

Other instances occur where a partner dealing with the partnership is treated as if he or she was not a partner when the partner lends money or property to the partnership or purchases property from the partnership.[3]

3.   An attempt to prevent a "disguised sale" by the partner to the partnership was the objective of the amendment of IRC Sec. 707(a) by the Tax Reform Act of 1984. If a transaction is characterized as a sale, then the partner would be acting as a nonpartner for this one transaction and, of course, would be required to recognize a gain or loss on the transaction.

LO 20.2   **Describe the tax ramifications of forming a partnership, and explain how each partner is taxed.**

TAX RAMIFICATIONS IN THE FORMATION OF A PARTNERSHIP

Steve: I know that it is possible to form a corporation without incurring a tax even if the members contribute appreciated property. Can you explain the tax ramifications of forming a partnership?

Jim: Say you and I are both engaged in the same type of work. We agree it would be mutually beneficial to pool our talents, money, and other property. We might just shake hands, or we might draw up a formal agreement that allocates partnership income, deductions, gain, loss, and credits. Any fees paid in connection with the organization, such as legal fees, are considered capital expenditures. Under Sec. 709, the partnership can elect to deduct the first $5,000 of these formational expenditures in the tax year business is first conducted. This rule applies if the cumulative organizational expenses do not exceed $50,000. The $5,000 deductible amount is reduced on a dollar for dollar basis to the extent that organizational expenses exceed $50,000 (but not below zero). The remaining expenses are amortized and deducted over a 180-month period beginning with the month the partnership commences business. Prior to October 23, 2004, organizational expenditures were generally amortized over a 5-year period.

We agree to form an equal partnership. You contribute $24,000 in cash—I'll contribute a building with a fair market value of $24,000. Generally speaking, no gain or loss is recognized on the exchange of property or money for an interest in a partnership.[4]

Assume my building, valued at $24,000, has a basis depreciated to $10,000. I've realized a $14,000 gain on the trade of my title to the building for a partnership interest. But I don't have to recognize that gain for tax purposes.

Instead, the basis for my partnership interest remains the same as the basis I had in the property I contributed, or $10,000.[5] If I should immediately sell my partnership interest for $18,000, I'd have an $8,000 gain. So the general rule is this: The basis a contributing partner had for property he or she contributes to the partnership becomes his or her initial basis for his or her partnership interest. Stated more precisely, the amount of cash contributed plus the adjusted

---

4.   IRC Sec. 721.

5.   IRC Sec. 722.

basis an individual had in the contributed property becomes the original basis for his or her new partnership interest.

When contributed property is subject to indebtedness, the original basis of the contributor's partnership interest must be lowered by the portion of the indebtedness taken over by the other partners.[6] So if the $10,000 property I contribute is subject to a $6,000 lien, and the partnership assumes this liability, the basis for my partnership interest will be reduced to the extent that you assume part of this $6,000 liability. In this example, being an equal partner, you'd assume half of the liability, so my basis would drop from $10,000 to $7,000. If you contributed $7,000 in cash, your basis would be the $7,000 you contributed plus the $3,000 share of the liability you assumed, for a total basis of $10,000. Note that if the property contributed to the partnership is subject to a liability in excess of its basis in the hands of the contributing partner, more complex tax problems arise and the contributing partner may realize taxable gain.

The partnership's basis in contributed property is generally the same as the contributing partner's basis in the asset. Therefore in the previous example, the partnership would have a $10,000 basis in the property I contributed. If the partnership later sells the property for $20,000, the partnership has a taxable gain of $10,000. However, if the contributed property has a fair market value substantially below the contributing partner's basis in the property, special basis rules apply to prevent the duplication of tax losses by the partnership. Note that there is a distinction between a partner's basis in his or her partnership interest and the partnership's basis in assets contributed by its partners.

Now I might not have cash to contribute—but I do have unique talents I can bring into the business. If I contributed property in return for my partnership interest, I would not have to recognize either gain or loss. But if I contribute either past services or the promise of future services, this general rule doesn't apply.

The receipt of an interest in partnership capital in return for services is regarded by the tax law as compensation for services rendered (or to be rendered).[7] So I may have to pay a current tax on the fair market value of the interest in partnership capital I receive in return for my services.

Sometimes an interest in partnership capital will be transferred to an individual subject to the condition that he or she must complete specified services at a future date. For example, you and I could form a partnership. You provide cash and I provide talent. You transfer an interest in the partnership capital to me conditioned on my completion of 5 years of service. I will realize

---

6.   IRC Sec. 752(b).

7.   Treas. Reg. Sec. 1.721-1(b)(1). (A capital interest in a partnership means an interest in its assets that is distributable to the owner of the capital interest upon the owner's withdrawal from or the liquidation of the partnership. The mere right to share in the earnings and profits is not a capital interest in the partnership.)

income as soon as there are no longer any substantial restrictions or conditions on my right to receive my interest in the partnership capital.

The Partnership in Operation

Steve: OK. Suppose we get a partnership in operation. Since the partners will pay the income tax on partnership income, is the partnership required to file a federal return?

Mike: Yes, the partnership must file a return—IRS Form 1065—but it is for informational purposes only. A civil penalty is now imposed on any partnership that fails to file a complete partnership information return, unless reasonable cause is shown. For 2017, the penalty consists of $200 times the number of partners for each month that the failure continues, up to 12 months. For partnership returns required to be filed after December 31, 2014, the penalty amount is indexed for inflation. This penalty is in addition to criminal penalties for willful failure to file a return, supply information, or pay tax.[8] The form is due 2½ months after the partnership fiscal year ends. Under Sec. 706, the partnership tax year must be the same as one or more majority partners who have an aggregate interest in partnership profits and capital exceeding 50 percent. If the tax year of the partner(s) owning a majority interest can not be used or does not apply, the partnership must use the tax year of the principal partners' (partners owning 5 percent of more of capital or profit interests), unless a business purpose for a different tax year can be established. Since most individuals are calendar-year taxpayers, most partnerships also will have a calendar-year reporting period and file their informational return on March 15 each year.

Steve: Let's discuss how the partner is taxed.

Jim: Each partner must include in his or her return for each taxable year his or her distributive share of the partnership income or loss items. Each partner's share of partnership income and loss is computed with regard to what was realized in the taxable year of the partnership.

Steve: Could you be more specific as to which items would be includible as distributive shares?

Jim: The partners must include in their individual tax returns their shares of the partnership income or loss. They must also take into account (and report on their 1040s) a number of separate partnership items,[9] including

- capital gains and losses
- Sec. 1231 gains and losses

---

8. IRC Sec. 6698(a) and (b).
9. IRC Sec. 702(a).

- charitable contributions
- dividends received by the partnership from stock holdings

The partners would then add their share of each of the above items to their individual income and deductions. For example, one partner's share of partnership capital gains and losses would be added to his or her personal capital gains and losses. In the same way, a partner's distributive share of the firm's charitable contributions is added to his or her individual contributions, and the individual charitable contribution deduction limitations are applied to the total.

Steve: How do the partners determine who gets what, that is, how are the distributive shares of each item determined?

Mike: Generally speaking, the distributive shares of each item are to be determined in accordance with the partnership agreement. If the partnership doesn't cover a particular item, the partner's distributive share of that item is the same percentage as his or her percentage share of partnership income or loss.[10] If the partner would normally receive one-third of all profits and losses, he or she would receive one-third of all capital gains.

Sometimes partners, through the partnership agreement, attempt to shift an item to the taxpayer in whose hands the item will be most beneficial. This allocation of one type of item to the partner who can obtain the greatest tax benefit (such as an allocation of all depreciation deductions to the highest tax bracket partner) may be ignored by the IRS. If such a provision does not have "substantial economic effect,"[11] the partners' shares of that item will be readjusted by the IRS just as if the partnership agreement contained no provision as to the item; that is, each partner's distributive share of that item is determined in accordance with his or her share of partnership income or loss.

It's difficult to determine the distinction between an acceptable and unacceptable allocation. Generally the dollar amounts of income received by the partners must be substantially affected by any special allocations independent of tax consequences.

If the economic after-tax consequences to one partner are enhanced by an allocation, the economic after-tax consequences to some other partner or partners should be diminished if the allocation is to be treated as having substantial economic effect. Using present-value concepts, this principle is applied for calculating economic consequences over the course of a number of years. Treasury regulations state the application of these principles in detail. Those regulations

---

10.   IRC Sec. 704(b).
11.   IRC Sec. 704(b)(2).

need to be studied to determine the effects of any special allocations that the partnership may be considering.

If special allocations do not satisfy the requirement of substantial economic effect, they will usually be allocated in accordance with the general provisions in the partnership agreement for sharing income and loss.[12]

With respect to contributed property by the partner to the partnership, the partnership will generally be required, rather than permitted, to allocate *built-in* gain or loss on contributed property to the contributing partner, and not in accordance with each partner's interest in the property.

Steve: Suppose that one partner feels his or her distributive share of partnership income is inadequate as compensation for the efforts provided. Can that partner obtain some type of salary from the partnership?

guaranteed payment

Jim: Yes, a partner can obtain a salary or, as previously illustrated, a **guaranteed payment**. A guaranteed payment is a sum paid to a partner, regardless of whether the partnership has income. This payment is deductible by the partnership.

Guaranteed payments are ordinary income to the recipient partner. Perhaps an additional illustration of the treatment of guaranteed payments would be helpful. Ethan, a partner in the Ethan Ward partnership, is to receive a payment of $10,000 for services, plus 40 percent of the ordinary business income or loss of the partnership. Assume that after deducting payment of the $10,000 salary to Ethan, the partnership has a loss of $8,000. Of this amount, $3,200 (40 percent of the loss) would be Ethan's distributive share of partnership loss. In addition, Ethan must report as ordinary income the guaranteed payment of $10,000 made to him by the partnership. This guaranteed payment would be reportable by Ethan in the taxable year of the partnership in which it deducted the payment and that ended with or within Ethan's own taxable year.

Steve: Suppose a partner wants to sell his or her partnership interest 2 or 3 years after the partnership is in operation. The amount received on the sale minus his or her basis in the partnership will be taxed. Is that partner's basis in the partnership interest the same as his or her original basis?

Jim: No, the partner's basis will not be the same.

A partner's basis is increased by the following three factors:

---

12. Treas. Reg. 1.704-1(b).

1. his or her capital contributions

2. his or her distributive share of partnership income

3. his or her share of liabilities assumed

A partner's basis is also reduced by the following three factors:

1. his or her share of losses

2. his or her distributions or draws

3. his or her share of liabilities relieved

Steve: Let's see if I understand. When a partnership is formed, the basis of a contributing partner's partnership interest is (1) the amount of money contributed plus (2) the adjusted basis of the property he or she contributes to the partnership.

This same rule applies to a new partner who contributes money or property. The initial basis of a partner who receives an interest as an inheritance is basically determined by valuing the interest at the date of the decedent's death. If an individual acquires a partnership interest by gift, the new partner's basis would be the same as the old donor-partner's basis plus any adjustment for gift tax paid on the transfer.

If a partner loans money to the partnership, that partner's basis is increased by his or her share of the partnership's liability to him or her as an outsider.

If only services are contributed, and the contributing partner receives an interest in partnership capital (i.e., an interest in the property contributed by his or her copartners), then the contributing partner realizes current ordinary income as long as there are no substantial restrictions on that partner's right to withdraw or dispose of his or her interest in partnership capital. When such income is realized, that income will be added to the partner's basis.

Abe and Benny open a delicatessen. Abe owned luncheonette equipment with an adjusted basis of $4,000 and a fair market value of $5,000. He entered into an agreement with Benny in which Abe would contribute his equipment to the partnership and Benny would contribute $5,000 in cash. By mutual agreement, each man will own a 50 percent interest.

Since the adjusted basis of Abe's property was $4,000, the basis for Abe's 50 percent interest is $4,000. On the other hand, Benny's basis is equal to the cash he contributed, which is $5,000.

Of course, the original basis is only a starting point. If we had to determine the basis of a partner's partnership interest one year after the formation of the partnership, we would have to adjust the original basis to reflect changes that have occurred.

We'd start with the original basis, increase that figure by any subsequent capital contributions, and also increase it by the sum of the partner's share of the partnership's ordinary income (both business and separately stated items of income, such as capital gains) as well as its tax-exempt receipts. So, for example, if the partnership received life insurance death proceeds, this cash would serve to increase each partner's basis.

Since an increase in a partner's share of liabilities is treated as if cash had been contributed, a partner's basis increases to the extent of his or her share of increased partnership obligations, such as accounts or notes payable and mortgages assumed.

Next, we'd reduce basis (but not below zero) by the amount of a partner's share of partnership losses (including separately stated items of loss, such as capital losses), distributions by the partnership to the partner, and the amount that the partner's share of liabilities was decreased.

Suppose the two of you formed a partnership. This year the firm lost $10,000. Jim's distributive share of the loss was $5,000. If the adjusted basis of his partnership interest, before considering his share of the partnership loss, was $2,000, he could claim only $2,000 of the loss this year. The adjusted basis of his interest would be reduced to zero. An individual partner's loss deduction cannot exceed his basis for his partnership interest at the end of the year for which the loss occurred. However, the partner is entitled to an unlimited carryover of nondeductible partnership losses.

If your partnership realized an $8,000 profit next year, Jim's $4,000 share of that profit would increase the adjusted basis of his interest to $4,000 (if we don't take into account the $3,000 excess loss he could not deduct last year). Next year's return should show his distributive share of partnership income to be $1,000 ($4,000 distributive share minus the $3,000 loss he was not allowed to take this year). The adjusted basis of his partnership interest at the end of next year would be $1,000.[13]

What's the purpose for those increases and reductions in basis?

Mike: When we increase a partner's basis, what we're doing in effect is shielding those amounts from a subsequent tax. For example, when you sell your partnership interest, you should not have to pay tax on income you've already paid tax on. By the same token, your share of the tax-exempt income (such as life insurance proceeds) received by the partnership should be considered an additional capital investment by you—so if you sell your partnership interest,

---

13. Where a partner cannot determine the adjusted basis in the partnership interest, the adjusted basis of his or her interest may be determined by reference to the partner's proportionate share of the adjusted basis of partnership property, as long as it is reasonable that the result produced will not vary substantially from the above basis rules. IRC Sec. 705(b); Treas. Reg. Sec. 1.705-1(b).

you should not be taxed on that item, either. Likewise, if you assume a portion of the partnership's liabilities, it's the same as if you contributed a like amount of cash. You should be able to recover that amount of cash tax free.

Reductions in basis serve just the opposite purpose. By reducing basis, you account for recoveries of basis on capital invested in the partnership resulting from losses deducted against other income, distributions of property or money from the partnership to you, and decreases in your share of partnership liabilities.

Partnership basis is important in determining the amount of loss that can be recognized. It also affects taxation upon the disposition of a partnership interest on a partner's retirement or death.

LO 20.3   Explain the tax effects to the partnership and the partners upon the retirement or death of a partner.

Tax Effects upon Retirement or Death of a Partner

Steve: Let's examine the tax effects when a partner retires or dies.

Mike: I think it's best to do this in two stages. Let's first talk about a sale by the retiring or deceased partner to his or her former partners or to an outsider. Later, we will discuss payments from the partnership itself to the retiring or deceased partner's estate or other successor in interest.

When a partner's interest in a partnership is sold, his or her gain (that is, the amount received minus that partner's basis in the partnership interest) is taxed. Such gain will be treated as all capital gain, unless a partnership has inventory items or unrealized receivables.

unrealized receivables

Unrealized receivables are essentially uncollected fees and other rights to income. The term includes the right to payment for (1) goods delivered (that were not capital assets or would not be treated as capital assets on a sale), or (2) services, to the extent that these rights are not currently includible in income under the partnership's method of accounting.[14]

In the event that a partnership has inventory or unrealized receivables, the selling partner must fragment his or her gain into both a capital-gain portion and an ordinary-income portion. The selling partner's share of the potential gain on inventory, if sold, plus the partner's share

14.   IRC Sec. 751(c).

of unrealized receivables, is taxed as ordinary income.[15] As previously mentioned, the balance is capital gain, including payments for goodwill. The remaining partners have the option to increase the basis of partnership assets in proportion to the gain recognized to the retiring partner.

Upon the sale of a deceased partner's partnership interest, the basis to his or her estate or successor in interest will be the value of the partnership interest (other than the value of unrealized receivables) on the date of that partner's death.[16] Any unrealized receivables will be taxed as income in respect of a decedent.[17] The partnership can make a special election under another section of the Code that allows adjustments to the bases of certain items held by the partnership.[18] If the partnership holds property with a substantial built-in loss (value substantially less than basis), special basis adjustment rules may apply to prevent duplication of tax losses when the partnership distributes such property or a partner's interest is transferred or liquidated.

Frequently partners will enter into a buy-sell agreement stating that on the death of a partner, the surviving partner or partners will purchase the deceased partner's interest. To fund this cross-purchase type agreement, often each partner acquires, pays for, and is the beneficiary of a policy on each other partner's life. The premiums each partner pays are not deductible. The insurance proceeds, however, will be income tax exempt.

Steve: Is there some way that the partnership can buy a partnership interest? I'm thinking of something similar to a stock redemption in the corporate area.

Mike: Yes, the partners may agree that the partnership will buy, or as it is sometimes termed, "liquidate," a partner's interest. Generally the partners enter into a buy-sell agreement, which states that upon the death or retirement of a partner, the partnership will purchase the former partner's interest. To fund this type of agreement, partnerships purchase life insurance on the lives of their individual partners. Premiums paid by the partnership are not tax deductible, and the insurance proceeds, when received, will be income tax free.

Steve: How is the retiring or deceased partner taxed when payment is received from the partnership for his or her interest?

Mike: If the partnership purchases a retiring partner's interest, the purchase price and the partner's share of the partnership basis in assets must be broken down into several parts. The

15. IRC Sec. 736.
16. IRC Sec. 1014.
17. IRC Sec. 691.
18. IRC Sec. 754.

purchase price and basis of the partnership in its assets must be segregated into amounts attributable to

- partnership property
- inventory
- unrealized receivables
- goodwill

There are now two different ways in which the payments are taxed. In a partnership in which capital is not a material income-producing factor (a service partnership), the liquidation of a general partner's interest is taxed in four layers.

First, that portion of the purchase price attributable to partnership property, exclusive of inventory, unrealized receivables, and goodwill, must be determined. If the retiring partner receives an amount for his or her interest in partnership property that exceeds that partner's share of the partnership basis in such assets, he or she will have a capital gain. The remaining partners have the option of increasing the basis of partnership assets in proportion to the gain recognized to the retiring partner.

Second, the retiring partner's share of the potential gain on inventory will be treated as ordinary income to the recipient. The partnership generally increases its basis for these inventory items in the amount that ordinary income is recognized.

Third, the portion of the purchase price attributable to unrealized receivables of the partnership, such as accounts receivable that were not previously taxed as partnership income, is taxed as ordinary income to the recipient but is deductible by the partnership.

goodwill

Fourth, the portion attributable to **goodwill** can be treated in one of two ways: If the partnership agreement states that payment will be made for goodwill, the recipients will report any gain as capital gain, but the payment is not deductible by the partnership. Of course, the amount paid for goodwill must be reasonable. If the agreement is silent as to goodwill, the payment is taxable to the recipient as ordinary income and is deductible by the partnership. In the case of such agreements, the Code treats any other amounts paid as "additional payments."[19] Additional payments are treated as ordinary income to the retiring partner. They are characterized as part of the retiring partner's distributive share or as a guaranteed payment to the retiring partner. Of course, amounts that are treated as part of the retiring partner's

---

19.   IRC Sec. 736(b)(2).

distributive share or as a guaranteed payment are not taxed to the remaining partners. Another way to look at this is that the partnership obtains a deduction for the amounts paid to the retiring partner. In this type of situation, the retiring partner prefers the partnership agreement to state that payment will be made for goodwill to ensure that capital-gains treatment will be obtained. The remaining partners prefer the partnership agreement to be silent as to goodwill, so the partners can obtain a deduction for the payment of additional payments. This issue must be negotiated by the partners. Often the retiring partner is willing to receive ordinary income rather than capital gain and allow the other partners a deduction, if a greater amount is received for his or her interest. Note that, in general, a partnership has no basis in its goodwill for tax purposes unless it purchased the goodwill in a taxable acquisition. In such cases, the partnership can amortize its cost for the goodwill over a 15-year period, thereby reducing its basis in the goodwill.

In the event of a liquidation of a deceased partner's interest, the partner's basis in his or her partnership interest will be increased to its date-of-death value under the rules for inherited property as discussed previously.

In the case of a liquidation of a partnership interest other than that of a general partner in a service partnership, both unrealized receivables and goodwill are automatically treated as partnership property. As a result, the partnership in such cases receives no deduction for payments for such property. This is a different rule from that which applies to a service partnership. There is also no deduction to the partnership with respect to payments for inventory, although a basis adjustment is made corresponding to such payments as in the case of a service partnership.

To the extent the partner receives more for his or her interest in the partnership's cash and other property than the partner's share of basis in those assets, he or she will have a capital gain. The remaining partners generally have the option of increasing the basis in partnership assets for the gain so recognized by the partner. However, any portion of the payments received for unrealized receivables and inventory that exceeds the partner's share of partnership basis in such assets is treated as ordinary income. The retiring partner must segregate the cash and other property from the inventory and unrealized receivables.

Table 20-1: Cartland Partnership Example		Adjusted Basis	Fair Market Value
Cash		$9,000	$9,000
Real estate		30,000	36,000
Accounts receivable		0	30,000
Goodwill		0	45,000
Total		$39,000	$120,000
Liabilities		0	0
Capital accounts			
	A = $40,000		
	B = 40,000		
	C = 40,000		
	Total $120,000		

Steve: Could you give me an example of how these rules operate?

Jim: Assume that Catherine wishes to retire from the Cartland partnership, a service partnership that utilizes the cash-basis method. Assume that Catherine's basis in her partnership interest is $13,000. Assume that the balance sheet of that firm on the date of retirement may be stated as in Table 20-1.

Assume that Catherine is willing to sell her interest for $40,000 cash. If her other partners purchase her interest, her taxable gain is $27,000. Catherine's gain is treated as a capital gain except for amounts attributable to her share of unrealized receivables and inventory.

Assume that this firm has no inventory items, and that its only unrealized receivables are its accounts receivable. Catherine's share of the unrealized receivables is $10,000 ($\frac{1}{3} \times$ $30,000), and since the partnership basis in the unrealized receivables is zero, $10,000 of her $27,000 gain must be treated as ordinary income. The balance is capital gain. The remaining partners have the option to increase the basis of partnership assets in proportion to the gain recognized to the retiring partner.

Table 20-2: Taxation of Payments to a Retiring Partner or Deceased Partner's Estate			
Nature of Partnership Asset	Type of Buy-Sell Agreement	Estate of Deceased or Withdrawing Partner	Partnership, Remaining, or Surviving Partner
Capital assets (cash, building, equipment, furniture, etc.)	Entity and cross purchase	Capital gain/loss	No deduction
Unrealized receivables (service partnership)	Entity and cross purchase	Ordinary income	Deduction
Unrealized receivables (nonservice partnership)	Entity and cross purchase	Ordinary income	No deduction
Inventory	Entity and cross purchase	Ordinary income	No deduction
Goodwill	Cross purchase	Capital gain/loss	No deduction
Specified goodwill (service partnership)	Entity	Capital gain/loss	No deduction
Unspecified goodwill (service partnership)	Entity	Ordinary income	Deduction
Goodwill (nonservice partnership)	Entity	Capital gain/loss	No deduction

Mike: If the partnership decides to liquidate Catherine's interest for $40,000, Catherine still has a $27,000 gain. However, her amount received must be fragmented into $15,000 for partnership property (⅓ × [$9,000 cash + $36,000 real estate]); $10,000 for unrealized receivables (⅓ × $30,000 of accounts receivable); and $15,000 for goodwill (⅓ × $45,000).

There is no inventory. The payments for (1) partnership property, (2) unrealized receivables, and (3) goodwill are taxed as follows:

- *Partnership Property:* Catherine receives $15,000 for her share. Her basis in her partnership interest that is allocable to those assets is $13,000. She has a $2,000 capital gain. The remaining partners have the option to increase the basis of partnership assets in proportion to the gain recognized to the retiring partner.

- *Unrealized Receivables:* Catherine receives $10,000 for her share. Since the partnership has no basis in this asset (cash-basis taxpayers have a zero basis in accounts receivable), neither does Catherine. The $10,000 would be ordinary income to Catherine and the partnership would have a $10,000 deduction.

- *Goodwill:* She receives $15,000 for her share. Since the partnership has no basis in this asset, neither does Catherine. If the partnership agreement states that payment shall be made for goodwill, then Catherine may treat the $15,000 as capital gain. If the partnership is silent as to goodwill, Catherine will treat the $15,000 as ordinary income. If Catherine does have ordinary income, then the partnership may treat the $15,000 as part of Catherine's distributive share or a guaranteed payment to her.

If instead Cartland is not a service partnership, the cash and other property consists of one-third of $9,000 cash, $36,000 real estate, and $45,000 goodwill, or $30,000. Catherine has one-third of $30,000 unrealized receivables, or $10,000. As she has no basis in the unrealized receivables, she recognizes $10,000 ordinary income. The partnership has no deduction. Catherine recognizes a $17,000 capital gain on the excess of the $30,000 attributable to cash or other property over her $13,000 basis.

LO 20.4   **Describe the tax treatment of both limited partnerships and family partnerships.**

Taxation of Limited Partnerships and Their Partners

Steve: Can we discuss the taxation of a limited partnership?

Jim: Basically, limited partnerships and their partners are taxed the same as general partnerships and their partners. As you know, a limited partnership is an arrangement in which the liability of some of the partners is limited to what they have contributed to the partnership. This is a useful device when a number of individuals are investing in an enterprise, but only one or a few individuals will be the managing and active members. Generally the limited partners are limited in authority as well as liability. The taxation of a limited partnership follows the same general rules we have already discussed.

Taxation of Family Partnerships and Their Partners

Steve: Can you explain how the taxation of family partnerships differs from the taxation of other types of partnerships?

family partnership

Jim: A **family partnership** is one whose members are closely related through blood, adoption, or marriage. The family, for this purpose, includes only husband or wife, ancestors, and lineal descendants, and any trusts for the primary benefit of such persons. Brothers and sisters are not included.

A family partnership is not essentially different from other partnerships. However, because family partnerships are sometimes formed solely to shift income within a family unit in order to minimize taxes, such partnerships receive special scrutiny both as to initial formation and actual operation.[20]

If there is economic (non-tax-motivated) reality to the arrangement, the partnership allocations of income will be accepted for income tax purposes. If the arrangement lacks economic reality, the Internal Revenue Service may ignore the entire partnership arrangement and reallocate income to properly reflect the interests of the partners.

There are certain guidelines designed to test the reality of the partnership arrangement. For example, in the determination of whether income can be shifted from the original sole proprietor to a new partner, a family member will be recognized as a partner only if his or her capital interest was acquired in a bona fide transfer (even if by gift or purchase from another family member), where capital is a material income-producing factor. To be treated as a partner for tax purposes, the family member must actually own the partnership interest and be vested with dominion and control over it.

Capital is considered a material income-producing factor if a substantial portion of the gross income of the business results from the use of capital (as when substantial inventories or investments in plant, machinery, or equipment are required).

If a family member acquires a capital interest by gift in a family partnership in which capital is a material income-producing factor, there are limitations on the amount that may be allocated as his or her distributive share of partnership income.

First, the donor of the interest must be allocated an amount that represents reasonable compensation for services rendered to the partnership. The remaining income generally may be divided among the partners according to their agreement for sharing partnership profits and losses. However, that portion of the remaining income allocated to the donee may not be proportionately greater than that allocated to the donor on the basis of their respective capital interests.

An interest purchased by one member of the family from another member of the family is considered to be created by gift for this purpose. Let me give you an example. A partnership in which the father sold (considered a gift) a 50 percent interest to his son had a profit of $60,000 for the year. Capital was a material income-producing factor. The father performed services worth $24,000 as reasonable compensation, and the son performed no services. The $24,000 must be allocated to the father as compensation. With respect to the $36,000 of income

---

20.   IRC Sec. 704(e).

attributable to capital, at least 50 percent, or $18,000, must be allocated to the father since he owns a 50 percent capital interest. The son's share of partnership income cannot exceed $18,000.

Steve: What happens when capital is not a material income-producing factor?

Mike: An individual can still be treated as a partner for tax purposes even if capital is not a material income-producing factor. However, in such cases the individual must contribute substantial or vital services.

Capital is not a material income-producing factor if the income of the business consists principally of fees, commissions, or other compensation for personal services performed by members or employees of the partnership. A law or accounting practice would be a good illustration. For a son to be recognized as a partner in his father's accounting firm for tax purposes, he'd have to contribute substantial services to the business. Otherwise, his share of partnership income would be reallocated by the IRS to the other partners.

Steve: In this brief review of the income tax treatment of partnerships, it's apparent to me that the area is quite complex, and that each situation merits thorough as well as thoughtful consideration and planning.

Mike: That's correct, but with proper structuring, the partnership is often the best means of conducting a profit-motivated undertaking when more than one individual has an interest. The benefits, however, may not be available if the partnership exists merely on a handshake, with no analysis, planning, or formalization of the understanding of the parties. For income tax purposes, a partnership may exist in such a situation, but it is likely that problems will arise in the future without carefully thought-out and formalized arrangements.

CHAPTER REVIEW

Key Terms and Concepts

aggregate theory   goodwill
entity theory   family partnership
guaranteed payment
unrealized receivables

Review Questions

Review questions are based on the learning objectives in this chapter. Thus a [20.3] at the end of a question means that the question is based on learning objective 3. If there are multiple objectives, they are all listed.

1. Describe the classification system for the federal taxation of unincorporated businesses. [20.1]

2. Give two examples of business organizations that are unincorporated under state law but may exhibit one or more corporate characteristics. [20.1]

3. For what reasons may it be important to characterize an organization as a partnership? [20.1]

4. Explain the aggregate and entity theories of partnership law and taxation. [20.1]

5. Explain the tax consequences to the contributing partners upon formation of a partnership. [20.2]

6. Bert and Ernie are auto mechanics. They decide to work together under the name Bedford Falls Auto Repairs, sharing profits and losses equally. Each contributes the following assets and liabilities to the business:

		Adjusted Basis	Fair Market Value	Mortgage
Bert:	Cash	$33,000	$33,000	$ 0
Ernie:	Equipment	2,000	5,000	2,000
	Building	20,000	40,000	10,000

   a. What is the form of the business for tax purposes? Does the form of the business have an effect on Bert and Ernie's tax liability?

   b. Assuming that Bedford Falls is a partnership, do Bert and Ernie recognize any gain on their transfer of assets to the partnership?

   c. What is Bert's basis in his partnership interest? What is Ernie's basis? [20.2]

7. What are the consequences to the partnership and the partners when contributed property is subject to indebtedness? [20.2]

8. What obligations does a partnership have with respect to filing a federal income tax return? [20.2]

9. Explain how the individual partners of a partnership are taxed. [20.2]

10. Explain the tax effects to a partner when he or she receives an interest in partnership capital in return for services. [20.2]

11. The Jomar partnership, owned equally by Joe and Marty, suffers a $50,000 loss this year. How will this loss be reported for tax purposes by

    a. the partnership?

    b. the partners? [20.2]

12. What effect does the partnership agreement have on the determination and allocation of items of a partner's distributive share? [20.2]

13. How will the IRS treat special allocations of income or loss among partners if the allocations do not have substantial economic effect? [20.2]

14. Wonder Burgers, a cash-basis partnership, opened its doors for business early last year. By the end of the year Wonder Burgers had received $10,000 in ordinary business income.

    a. What is Wonder Burgers' tax year, and when must it file a return?

    b. Does Wonder Burgers have any tax to pay on the amounts earned? Do the partners have any tax to pay on the amounts earned? [20.2]

15. Jessica and Beatrice form a partnership and plan to share profits and losses on a 60/40 basis. Their partnership agreement contains no specific provision that governs how distributive shares of each particular income item will be determined. Explain how Jessica will compute her distributive share. [20.2]

16. a. What factors will increase a partner's basis in his or her partnership interest?

    b. What factors will cause a reduction in a partner's basis?

    c. What are the reasons for the increases and reductions to a partner's basis? [20.2]

17. Explain the limitations on the deductibility of partnership losses by a partner. [20.2]

18. Why is it important for a partner to maintain records concerning his or her basis in his or her partnership interest? [20.2]

19. John contributed $10,000 to form the J&B partnership with Bobby as an equal partner. The partnership suffers a $30,000 loss this year.

    a. What is John's distributive share of the loss?

b. Compute the amount of loss John may currently deduct on his personal tax return, assuming John and Bobby are equal partners. [20.2]

20. Explain the tax effects of using life insurance to fully fund a buy-sell agreement among partners when

a. each partner acquires, pays for, and is the beneficiary of a policy on each other partner's life

b. the partnership acquires, pays for, and is the beneficiary of a policy on each partner's life [20.3]

21. John decides to retire from the J&B partnership, a retail drug store with inventory. If John sells his interest to Bobby at a gain, how will his gain on the sale be taxed? [20.3]

22. After 20 years in business Don wishes to retire. Jim, his partner, is willing to buy Don's partnership interest for $125,000. The partnership is a service business. At Don's retirement the balance sheet for the business is as follows:

	Adjusted Basis	Fair Market Value
Cash	$115,000	$115,000
Accounts receivable	0	30,000
Furniture and fixtures	5,000	5,000
Goodwill	0	100,000
Liabilities	0	
Capital accounts:		
Don	$125,000	
Jim	125,000	
Total	$250,000	

a. How is each partner's basis in the partnership computed?

b. If Jim buys Don's partnership interest for $125,000, is Don's gain of $65,000 treated solely as capital gain? Assume Don's basis is $60,000.

c. If the partnership liquidates Don's interest for $125,000, how will Don be taxed on the following portions of the purchase price? Again assume Don's basis is $60,000.

(1) $60,000 for partnership property

(2) $15,000 attributable to unrealized accounts receivable

(3) $50,000 attributable to goodwill. The partnership agreement states that payment will be made for goodwill. The partnership has a zero basis in its goodwill for tax purposes. [20.3]

23. Assume that the ABC partnership agreement requires that the partnership liquidate the interest of any deceased or retiring partner. ABC is a service partnership. Describe the income tax consequences to the retiring partner and to the remaining partners of

    a.   payments of the purchase price to the retiring partner for his or her interest in partnership property

    b.   additional payments that are part of the retiring partner's distributive share [20.3]

24. Explain the rules that apply to a liquidation of a partnership interest other than that of a general partner in a service partnership. [20.3]

25. Explain how limited partnerships and their partners are taxed. [20.4]

26. How are family partnerships and their partners taxed when

    a.   the arrangement has economic reality?

    b.   the arrangement lacks economic reality? [20.4]

27. What guidelines are used to test the reality of a partnership arrangement involving acquisition of a partnership interest by one family member from another when

    a.   capital is a material income-producing factor?

    b.   capital is not a material income-producing factor? [20.4]

Review Answers

1. Under state law, business organizations may be formed as corporations, general partnerships, limited partnerships, limited liability partnerships, limited liability companies, or as variations of these business forms. However, all of these various types of entities are classified as either partnerships or corporations for federal tax purposes.

    With the development of these "hybrid" business entities, it became administratively difficult for the IRS to classify them for tax purposes based upon the presence or absence of a preponderance of corporate characteristics. As a result, a more flexible system of classification (often referred to as "check the box") was developed.

    Under this approach, organizations that are not incorporated under state law will generally be permitted to choose whether to be taxed as corporations or partnerships. In most cases, they will choose to be taxed as partnerships.

2. Both limited liability companies and limited liability partnerships are unincorporated under state law but exhibit at least one corporate characteristic—limited liability.

3. It is important that a particular organization be taxed as the parties involved intended because of the tax distinctions between a corporation and a partnership. When an organization is treated for tax purposes as a partnership, the profits earned by the partners will be taxed only once on their individual returns. When profits are earned by a corporation, they are taxed once to the business and then taxed again to the shareholders if they are paid out in the form of dividends. Also, if a business is classified as a partnership, the partners may deduct their share of any net losses on their individual returns. If the business is a corporation, losses may be claimed only by the corporation and are not available to offset the shareholder's other income. Therefore it may be important to characterize an organization as a partnership if certain potential tax pitfalls are to be avoided.

4. According to the aggregate theory, a partnership is considered as an aggregate of individual co-owners who have bound themselves together with the intention of sharing gains and losses. The partnership itself has no existence separate and apart from its members. To the extent this theory influences tax law, a partnership is nothing more than the sum of its individual members. Tax liability passes through the partnership directly to each partner, who pays tax on his or her share of the profits just as though he or she realized the share of income as an individual.

   While the aggregate theory makes the partnership a conduit for some purposes, the entity theory recognizes that for certain other purposes the partnership is a separate entity that is distinct from its members. Accordingly, the partnership must file an income tax return for information-purposes only. The return provides a way to inform both the IRS and the individual partners how the profits and losses are allocated. Three other indicia of the entity theory are that a partnership has a taxable year, its own accounting method, and the right to exercise various income tax elections. Also in support of the entity theory is the fact that partners who engage in transactions with their own partnerships are typically treated taxwise like a stranger. In other words, when a partner is not acting in his or her capacity as a partner, a transaction between that partner and the partnership is treated as if it was conducted between the partnership and an unrelated third person.

5. The general rule is that the basis a contributing partner has in property he or she contributes to the partnership becomes his or her initial basis for his or her partnership interest. Stated more precisely, the amount of cash an individual contributes plus the adjusted basis in property the individual contributes becomes the original basis in the individual's new partnership interest.

6. a. The form of business for tax purposes of Bedford Falls Auto Repairs is a partnership. Bert and Ernie have the objective of carrying on a business and sharing profits and losses equally. There is no limited liability as long as Bert and Ernie do not incorporate. There is no centralization of management because each partner may act on behalf of the partnership in his capacity as a partner.

    The form of the business has a strong effect on the tax liability of Bert and Ernie. If Bedford Falls Auto Repairs is taxed as a corporation, then Bert and Ernie are only taxed on their compensation and dividends from the business. The corporation must pay tax on its own taxable income. If Bedford Falls is taxed as a partnership, then each partner pays tax on his share of the partnership's income. The partnership itself pays no income tax.

    b. Bert and Ernie have no gain to recognize upon the formation of the partnership due to the nonrecognition provisions in the Code.

    c. A partner's basis in his or her partnership interest is the basis in the property he or she contributed to the partnership, reduced by liabilities assumed by the partnership and increased by liabilities assumed by the partner. Applying this general rule, Bert's basis is $33,000 plus $6,000 in liabilities assumed (½ of $12,000), for a total basis of $39,000. Ernie's basis is $22,000 reduced by $6,000 for liabilities relieved, or a total basis of $16,000. Note that the basis is not the same as the amount of capital contribution. Each partner has contributed equity of $33,000.

7. When contributed property is subject to indebtedness, the original basis of the contributor's partnership interest must be lowered by the portion of the indebtedness taken over by the other partners.

8. A partnership must file a federal income tax return (IRS Form 1065) that is for informational purposes only. A civil penalty is now imposed on any partnership that fails to file a complete partnership information return, unless reasonable cause is shown. This penalty is in addition to criminal penalties for willful failure to file a return, supply information, or pay tax.

9. The partners must include in their individual tax returns their distributive shares of the partnership income or loss. They must also take into account (and report on their 1040s) a number of separate partnership items, such as the following ones:

    •   capital gains and losses

    •   Sec. 1231 gains and losses

    •   charitable contributions

- dividends received by the partnership from stockholdings

The partners would then add their share of each of the above items to their individual income and deductions.

In addition, a partner can obtain a salary or guaranteed payment. A guaranteed payment is a sum paid to a partner, regardless of whether the partnership has income. Such a payment is ordinary income to the recipient partner.

10. If only services are contributed, and the contributing partner receives an interest in partnership capital (that is, an interest in the property contributed by his or her copartners), then the contributing partner realizes current ordinary income as long as there are no substantial restrictions on that partner's right to withdraw or dispose of his or her interest in partnership capital. When such income is realized, that income will be added to the partner's basis.

11. a. The partnership will report the loss on the partnership informational return (Form 1065).

    b. Each partner reports his distributive share (in this case, 50 percent) of the losses on his individual income tax return to the extent that his basis in his partnership interest exceeds zero. Losses in excess of his basis may be carried over to future years when the partner's basis is greater than zero.

12. Generally speaking, the distributive shares of each item are to be determined in accordance with the partnership agreement. If the partnership does not cover a particular item, the partner's distributive share of that item is the same percentage as his or her percentage share of partnership income or loss.

13. Sometimes partners, through the partnership agreement, attempt to shift an item to the taxpayer in whose hands the item will be most beneficial. This allocation of one type of item to the partner who can obtain the greatest tax benefit (such as an allocation of all depreciation deductions to the highest tax bracket partner) may be ignored by the IRS. If such a provision does not have "substantial economic effect," the partners' shares of that item will be readjusted by the IRS just as if the partnership agreement contained no provision as to the item; that is, each partner's distributive share of that item is determined in accordance with his or her share of partnership income or loss.

14. a. The partnership must utilize the same tax year as that of its majority partner or principal partners unless there is a business purpose (such as a natural business cycle) for use of a fiscal year. In most cases this will be a calendar year. Therefore Wonder Burgers must file its informational return on March 15 of each year.

    b.   Wonder Burgers has no tax to pay on amounts earned. The partners must include their proportionate share of the partnership's income in their individual gross income for the year.

15. Jessica's distributive share will be deemed the same as her share of profits and losses.

16. a.   A partner's basis is increased by the following three factors:

      (1) his or her capital contributions

      (2) his or her distributive share of partnership income

      (3) his or her share of liabilities assumed

    b.   A partner's basis is reduced by the following three factors:

      (1) his or her share of losses

      (2) his or her distributions or draws

      (3) his or her share of liabilities relieved

    c.   Reasons for increases and reductions to a partner's basis are as follows:

      • By increasing basis, the partner is being protected from having to pay tax on the additional capital invested in the partnership upon a subsequent disposition of his or her partnership interest.

      • By reducing basis, the partner recognizes recoveries of capital invested in the partnership resulting from losses deducted against other income, distributions of property or money from the partnership to the partner, and decreases in the partner's share of partnership liabilities.

17. An individual partner's loss deduction cannot exceed his or her basis for the partnership interest at the end of the year for which the loss occurred. However, the partner is entitled to an unlimited carryover of nondeductible partnership losses.

18. A partner needs to know what his or her basis in his or her partnership interest is because basis is important in determining the amount of loss that can be recognized and deducted in any one tax year. It also affects taxation upon the disposition of a partnership interest on the partner's retirement or death.

19. a.   John's distributive share of the loss is $15,000 since he and Bobby are equal partners (Bobby's share would also be $15,000).

    b.   John may deduct $10,000 currently. His deduction is limited to his basis in the partnership. The remaining $5,000 loss may be carried over to future years.

20. a.   The premiums paid by each partner are not tax deductible. However, on the death of a partner, the insurance proceeds received by each surviving partner are income tax free.

    b.   The premiums paid by the partnership are not tax deductible. However, on the death of a partner, the insurance proceeds received by the partnership are income tax free.

21.   John's gain will be taxed as capital gain with the exception of amounts attributable to unrealized receivables and inventory. These items will be treated as ordinary income.

22. a.   Each partner's basis is determined each year by adding his capital contributions, his share of the partnership's income, and his share of any additional liabilities. His current basis is reduced by his share of losses, his distributions or draws, and his share of liabilities relieved.

    b.   If Jim buys Don's partnership interest, Don's gain is treated as capital gain with the exception of amounts attributable to unrealized receivables and inventory, which will be treated as ordinary income. This partnership has unrealized receivables in the form of accounts receivable but has no inventory. Therefore Don's gain will be $50,000 of capital gain and $15,000 of ordinary income.

    c.   (1)   The $60,000 received for partnership property will not be taxed because Don's share of the partnership property, exclusive of unrealized receivables, is $60,000. If Don had received more than $60,000 for his partnership property, he would have a capital gain.

        (2)   The amount received for unrealized receivables is treated as ordinary income. In this case Don has $15,000 of ordinary income.

        (3)   The amount attributable to goodwill ($50,000) is treated as a capital gain to Don, since the partnership agreement states that payment will be made for goodwill. If the partnership agreement is silent as to goodwill, then any other payments made by a service partnership are treated as additional payments and are taxed as ordinary income to the retiring partner. If the retiring partner has ordinary income, the partnership has a deduction for the same amount.

23.   If a retiring partner's interest in a service partnership is liquidated, the following tax consequences result:

    a.   Payments for partnership property (exclusive of unrealized receivables, inventory, and unspecified goodwill) that result in a gain to the taxpayer are treated as capital gain. Payments for unrealized receivables, inventory, and unspecified goodwill result in ordinary income.

The remaining partners generally have the option to increase the basis of partnership assets in properties by the amount of gain recognized to the retiring partner. If the retiring partner receives ordinary income for inventory items, the partnership basis in those assets will also be increased. If the retiring partner receives ordinary income for unrealized receivables or unspecified goodwill, the remaining partners have a corresponding deduction from partnership income. If ABC were not a service partnership, it would not be entitled to a deduction for the unrealized receivables or unspecified goodwill.

b. The retiring partner has ordinary income for amounts treated as additional payments that are part of his or her distributive share and not attributable to partnership property. Note that payment for goodwill can be treated as an additional payment (ordinary income) or partnership property (capital gain) depending upon whether the partnership agreement states that payment will be made for goodwill. If ABC were not a service partnership, any payment for goodwill would be taxed as capital gain.

The partnership will obtain a deduction for additional payments taxed as ordinary income to the retiring partner.

24. In the case of a liquidation of a partnership interest other than that of a general partner in a service partnership, both unrealized receivables and goodwill are automatically treated as partnership property. As a result, the partnership in such cases receives no deduction for payments for such property. There is also no deduction to the partnership with respect to payments for inventory, although a basis adjustment is generally made corresponding to such payments.

To the extent the partner receives more for his or her interest in the partnership's cash and other property than the partner's share of basis in those assets, he or she will have a capital gain. The remaining partners have the option of increasing the basis in partnership assets for the gain so recognized by the partner. However, any portion of the payments received for unrealized receivables and inventory that exceeds the partner's share of partnership basis in such assets is treated as ordinary income. The retiring partner must segregate the cash and other property from the inventory and unrealized receivables.

25. Basically, limited partnerships and their partners are taxed the same as general partnerships and their partners.

26. a. If there is economic (non-tax-motivated) reality to the arrangement, the partnership allocations of income will be accepted for income tax purposes.

b. If the arrangement lacks economic reality, the IRS may ignore the entire partnership arrangement and reallocate income to properly reflect the interests of the partners.

27. a. If a family member acquires a capital interest in a family partnership in which capital is a material income-producing factor, there are limitations on the amount that may be allocated as his or her distributive share of partnership income.

First, the donor of the interest must be allocated an amount that represents reasonable compensation for services rendered to the partnership. The remaining income generally may be divided among the partners according to their agreement for sharing partnership profits and losses. However, that portion of the remaining income allocated to the donee may not be proportionately greater than that allocated to the donor on the basis of their respective capital interests.

An interest purchased by one member of the family from another member of the family is considered to be created by gift for this purpose.

b. If a family member acquires an interest in a family partnership in which capital is not a material income-producing factor, the individual family member must contribute substantial or vital services; otherwise, his or her share of partnership income would be reallocated by the IRS to the other partners. Capital is not considered a material income-producing factor if the income of the business consists principally of fees, commissions, or other compensation for personal services performed by members or employees of the partnership.

Index

Symbols

A

B

C